Education of the

Intellectually Gifted

MERRILL'S
INTERNATIONAL EDUCATION SERIES

Under the Editorship of

KIMBALL WILES

Dean of the College of Education
University of Florida

Education of the

Intellectually Gifted

Milton J. Gold

Hunter College
The City University of New York

CHARLES E. MERRILL BOOKS, INC.
COLUMBUS, OHIO

To Esther, Bonnie, Debbie, and Janice

Preface

Two major social concerns of recent years have placed in sharp focus the quality of school efforts to identify and develop the high potential of gifted students. One of these is the sharpened sense of challenge from the Soviet Union, arising primarily from its scientific success in atomic and space technology. The other is an awakened national conscience disturbed by the failure of an affluent society to root out poverty and ignorance. With respect to scientific competition with Russia, schools are asked whether they are discovering all students of intellectual promise and whether they are stimulating them to adequate performance. As regards underprivileged segments of the population, schools must answer whether they are identifying talent that is hidden by the effects of poverty, and whether schools are compensating through their programs for these effects.

The tasks of developing talent and providing opportunity for the disadvantaged are not new assignments for the schools. The urgency of present needs places new emphasis on these long-established functions. As never before, schools must look about them to define new requirements, to formulate new plans, and to set in motion new programs.

Since 1950, a wealth of reports has accumulated in areas such as creativity, motivation and achievement, guidance of the gifted, the potential of underprivileged groups, characteristics of the gifted, application of new teaching methods, and employment of new curricula in the schools. Much of this research is still fragmentary and suggestive rather than conclusive, or on too small a scale to warrant definitive conclusions. However, so much has been reported that it is time to try to relate theoretical research and demonstration of practices in actual situations to problems in education of the gifted. New problems are not solved by applying old formulae which were discarded because they did not work in the past. An enhanced education of the gifted depends upon fresh perspectives tested in a crucible of objective research.

A large number of studies have been called upon in preparation of this volume. Space does not permit full discussion of many of these projects, but the writer hopes that brief descriptions will, in many cases, whet the reader's appetite for fascinating encounters with much of the primary source material. Acknowledgment is due here to the many authors whose work is cited throughout this book.

Special acknowledgment is also due to many of the author's colleagues in the past and in the present who have helped him cultivate a view of educational excellence—Harry N. Rivlin, first as a teacher and now as Dean of Teacher Education, City University of New York; Pearl A. Wanamaker, formerly Superintendent of Public Instruction of the State of Washington; Morris Meister, formerly Principal, Bronx High School of Science, and now President, Bronx Community College; Joseph Gallant, deceased, formerly Chairman, English Department, Bronx High School of Science; Frank T. Wilson, formerly Coordinator of Campus Schools, Hunter College; Florence N. Brumbaugh, formerly Principal, Hunter College Elementary School; Herbert Schueler, Director of Teacher Education, Hunter College; and the members of the Metropolitan Association for Study of the Gifted.

M. J. G.

May, 1965

Contents

Chapter 1

The Release of Human Potential

THE THEME IS INDIVIDUALIZATION

All the children of all the people march each year into America's public and private schools. They cover the full range of the ability spectrum.
Together they represent an awesome reservoir of human potential. The
unpredictable outcomes of creative endeavor are somewhere hidden in
their bones and personalities. In the course of time their dreams will
take shape as aspirations for future accomplishment. Eventually the
most able and the least able alike will play out the heroic tragedy of
human existence—that no man achieves all that he aspires to be.

The goals of education for human fulfillment can be no less heroic:
the birth and growth of aspiration, the development of potential, the
nurture of creative pursuits. These goals might well serve as motifs in
the education of all young people—bright children, handicapped children, boys and girls in elementary school, adolescents in secondary
schools, and young adults in colleges and graduate schools. In educating the gifted student, schools face the greatest challenge and heaviest
responsibility since the potential for achievement is brightest.

Education of the gifted, however, must be seen in its proper perspective as simply an extension of the doctrine of individual differences.
Ultimately, it is not the gifted group but each gifted individual within
the group who must seek to find himself and express his potential. The
theme of self-realization epitomizes education in a democracy because

1

of the value placed on the individual human being. To the extent that school programs are truly adapted to individual differences, they contribute to the self-realization of each student. And only as they contribute to the release of each learner's potential are they truly individualized.

AMERICAN SCHOOLS AS A UNITARY INSTITUTION

Education for the gifted began in the American Colonies with the establishment of the Boston Latin Grammar School in 1635, of Harvard College in 1636, and has been going on ever since. Education for the broad mass of American children began in 1642 with the passage of the Old Deluder Satan Act in Massachusetts. The path to universal education has been neither smooth nor continuous, but it is currently forging its way through elementary and secondary schools and has made its entry into higher education. The Latin grammar schools in the first two hundred years of the settlement of the American continent served the gifted and prepared students primarily for study in college and subsequent professions in the ministry, law and teaching. The village church and dame schools provided a broader public with the rudiments of education until the introduction of universal public school systems in the nineteenth century.

If the United States had continued the pattern of separation which continues to characterize European education, there might be less of the sound and fury which surrounds education of the gifted today. There might also have been no national pre-eminence to maintain and no democracy, depending on an educated citizenry, to defend. The convention of providing one education for the elite and another education for the general population was fought by Horace Mann, Henry Barnard, and others in the last century. Their success in establishing the public elementary school decided the issue toward the end of the century. The gradual substitution of the public high school for the Latin grammar school and the private academy laid the ghost of separateness at the secondary level. Although the struggle would seem to have ended with current enrollments of 80 to 85 per cent of American youth in high schools, battles continue to flare up.

Despite periodic attacks, however, the principle of a single school for all children has apparently been established. American interpretations of equality, brotherhood, and free opportunity are represented in this achievement. By and large the common schools have made good their promise to build a sense of unity among the extremely diverse elements that comprise the American population. They have not separated at an early age students who might later have the privilege of going to college from those who would be forever denied this opportunity. Except where prevented by local or regional custom, they have minimized differences in native intellectual ability and economic, social, and ethnic backgrounds.

INDIVIDUALIZATION WITHIN A MASS SYSTEM

Unfortunately, however, the very rapid extension of the elementary and secondary systems could not be accomplished without raising certain problems. For one thing, no comparable effort had been made elsewhere in modern times, particularly at the secondary level, and new trails had to be blazed. A new program of studies had to be forged. The demand for teachers far exceeded the capacity of teacher-preparation facilities. New materials of instruction had to be developed.

Perhaps the greatest problem in rapid extension of public education was the provision of a program that would be meaningful for the full range of abilities that the new schools enrolled. It was not strange that mass learning situations should have developed and that procedures were devised to deal with large groups of learners. The *old* programs had failed to consider needs for individualizing instruction because of their commitment to a prescribed curriculum for all—a kind of Procrustean Bed for which the individuals were stretched or shortened—rather than a structure which could be adjusted to fit the individual. The *new* programs often failed because of the need to handle large numbers of children and the procedure that was established of teaching to the assumed norm of the group rather than to individuals in it. In the old program the gifted who were able to adapt to the situation did not fare badly and could secure individual encouragement. In the new program the gifted might be overlooked. A result has been the recurrent blazing anew of the old battle for separateness. Normally this has been expressed in demands for special programs for the gifted rather than in separate schools as in the past. But, at the same time, some critics raise a sharp and disturbing question. They believe that our public schools sacrifice quality for quantity, and that a program which could challenge the gifted is being diluted in order to meet the needs of only the mediocre and less able. Can the schools provide a stimulating program for the intellectual elite, they ask, unless they can disburden themselves of the academically slower students?

This question is widely interpreted as presenting the country with an "either-or" choice—either schools for the masses or schools for the elite but not a single school that can do both. The choice of a single school has been established historically, and most authoritative statements from responsible groups have held fast to this concept even in times of greatest criticism of the public schools. James Conant, for example, in his study of the American high school (1959), avows his support of the single comprehensive high school. The Special Studies Project on America at Mid-Century sponsored by the Rockefeller Fund states simply that there is no problem of choice, that the country has no alternative but to provide education for all *and* for the few—and that it has the resources to do so (Rockefeller, 1958).

> Every democracy must encourage high individual performance. If it does not, it closes itself off from the mainsprings of its dynamism and talent and imagination, and the traditional democratic invitation to the individual to realize his fullest potentialities becomes meaningless. (*Ibid.*, p. 16)

To the writers of the report the contradiction is a false one:

> Behind such arguments (that education cannot at the same time be available to all and still maintain quality) is the assumption that a society can choose to educate a few people exceedingly well *or* to educate a great number of people somewhat less well, but that it cannot do both. But a modern society such as ours cannot choose to do one *or* the other. It has to chose to do both. Our kind of society calls for the maximum development of individual potentialities *at all levels*.
>
> Fortunately, the demand to educate everyone to the level of his ability and the demand for excellence in education are not incompatible. We must honor both goals. We must seek excellence in a context of concern for all. (*Ibid.*, p. 22) *

Actually, statements of the problem in terms of false dichotomies has served to engender more heat than light because of a false premise that has been assumed. Separate schools, separate programs, and homogeneous grouping are too often related to an assumption that youngsters can be typed and then be treated as a type. The old Lancaster monitorial system was based on the idea that hundreds of children might economically be taught the same matter simultaneously by one teacher and many student assistants. The very large numbers and the monitors have disappeared from the scene, but the belief lingers on that a class of youngsters can be treated simultaneously and in precisely the same way.

The real issue in education of the gifted, as in education of children

* From *The Pursuit of Excellence: Education and the Future of America*, Rockefeller Brothers Fund, Inc. Copyright © 1958 by Rockefeller Brothers Fund, Inc. (As it appears in *Prospect for America*, Copyright © 1961). Reprinted by permission of Doubleday & Company, Inc.

with moderate and low intellectual ability, is individualization in content, materials, and method. Other issues are secondary and have to be decided according to the criterion of individualization. Class size, special opportunities, homogeneous grouping, and acceleration must all be considered in the light of their contribution to treatment of the student as an individual.

OBSTACLES IN THE PATH OF INDIVIDUALIZATION

While individualization of the program has long been a stated goal in education, the objective has often been obscured. One of the reasons is the monolithic view of education which characterizes the thinking of many people. Education represents in this view a distillation of the best that has been thought, said, and written, comprising a fixed content to be presented in the same way to all men. The question in this case is not, "Is the program adapted to the individual so that his full potential may be realized?" but, "Does the individual measure up to the established program?" This position negates the ideal of individual self-realization as a basic goal of education.

A second reason for failure to observe the objective of individualization can be found in the nature of schools as institutions. School instruction takes place in a group situation which is found desirable and necessary for reasons of learning efficiency and administrative convenience. The teacher is tempted to treat all pupils alike, to propose a single curriculum, and to employ uniform teaching methods. The temptation is increased when we place children of the same age in a particular room since the illusion of sameness is reinforced. The temptation becomes almost overpowering when we further extend the illusion of sameness by grouping together children with similar school achievement or intelligence test scores.

The rapid development of a universal public school system in the United States has intensified the tendency to operate institutionally rather than individually. Large groups have become the unit for instruction and schools have adopted standardized techniques such as the employment of a single textbook for the whole class and the administration of uniform tests. Against this backdrop of an "average" program for all, it is not surprising that insistent pressures have developed for special programs for retarded children, for slow learners, for bright-average, and for intellectually gifted students. If the goal is the individual's self-realization, the monolithic program is doomed to failure since it is little likely to release the potential of any child. We should recognize that the failure is just as real for the child "in the middle" as it is for the mentally retarded child lost in the crowd or the highly gifted child whose potential is ignored and lost.

The key to education is to be found in our basic commitment to the principle of the individual's worth and dignity. At least two alternatives are available. We can set up small classes and prepare teachers to enhance the uniqueness of each learner's individuality. Or we can organize larger classes and hope that individuality is accommodated by grouping together students who seem quite similar.

Education of the gifted is no less an aspect of the individualization process than the education of other children. The aim is the release of the individual's potential. The only difference lies in the greater probable loss if the gifted individual does not fulfill his richer promise. The school's responsibility is to recognize the nature of individual requirements, to utilize the strength of group teaching for what it contributes to the individual, and to employ institutional resources for individual growth. As a consequence the school needs to be less obsessed with standard programs and standard needs and should be more concerned with the child as an individual. The bright child is not to be lost sight of as an indistinguishable member of the gifted group, all of whom follow a uniform program.

A MATTER OF DEFINITION

Granted the need to individualize programs if the most able are to reach their fullest potential, how are we to define giftedness? Part of our problem lies in the fact that sometimes we refer to aptitude or ability *in* a person and sometimes to talented performance *by* a person. Genius, like intelligence, is never seen directly; it is seen only in its results— superior performance of some kind. The problem in education is to define what is meant by talent so that schools may focus on its development. Part of the problem is recognizing such capacity in its inchoate, tentative, budding state, when performance is only foreshadowed and not yet realized.

What are the kinds of gifts that merit recognition? Witty suggests "consistently remarkable performance in any worth-while line of endeavor." This definition includes the commonly accepted gift of intellectual superiority, but it also encompasses promise in music, art, dance, creative writing, mechanical skills, and social leadership (AAGC, 1951, pp. 19-20). Schools, as they typically operate, can contribute more to the development of some of these skills than to others, and they can contribute more directly to some than to others.

The twenty thousand different job titles in the United States *Dictionary of Occupational Titles* indicate the variety of gifts necessary for operation of our economy alone. Many skills and competences are obviously needed in our world, and one would assume that superior skill and competence should make for a better world. To regard all such superiority as "giftedness" broadens the definition to unworkable proportions. For the educator it is perhaps more useful to adopt a definition with greater relevance to his own sphere of operation. A major concern of schools is academic growth; we are therefore concerned with intellectual ability as a major factor in academic achievement. Schools are concerned with citizenship education; we are accordingly interested in those types of social leadership which contribute to civic improvement. Many schools encourage young people to develop superior competence in music, the arts, and a number of skilled trades. In these fields schools generally work toward establishment of certain minimum levels of performance rather than a high degree of virtuosity. Discussion in this volume of these fields is accordingly limited in keeping with the school's normal function.

Because of the need for clear goals, school programs for the gifted most commonly focus upon the intellectually gifted child. This is not meant to deny the exceptionality of the violin prodigy, the adolescent painter, the All-American tackle, the prom queen, or the 4-H winner of cattle-judging prizes. The school has an obligation to stimulate and recognize the fulfillment of promise of every individual enrolled, but there is a need to distinguish between primary and secondary tasks. If the school is truly interested in individual development, it will help each student seek out his special talents and it will then help him reach for fulfillment. Moreover, in a democracy the school has an urgent responsibility to help young people understand that successful enterprise in any constructive occupation is worth-while socially and is desirable from the point of view of the individual. To the extent that the school recognizes intellectual ability only, the school neglects this responsibility. To the extent that schools fail to put primary focus on intellectual growth, however, they reject or weaken the function which society has assigned to them.

HOW GIFTED IS "GIFTED"?

The variety of talents to be encompassed represents one problem in a school definition of giftedness; the *degree* of exceptionality that should be considered represents a second. At one time the United States Office of Education used the top one-half of 1 per cent of the intelligence distribution as the group to be regarded as the exceptionally able. This represents exceptionality of more than three standard deviations from the mean on typical intelligence scales. A second definition, more widely used, includes 2 or 3 per cent, i.e., two standard deviations from the mean. Still another definition would take the top half of a school population, in some cases going down the intelligence scale to below one hundred. The cut-off point is significant because it may defeat its own purpose if set too high or too low. If set too high, it may eliminate youngsters of high ability who for one reason or another do not test well. If set too low it may include so wide a range that highly advanced, challenging, or difficult programs become impossible because they would result in frustration for a portion of the selected group.

Related to our definition are issues that involve selection of students. Should emphasis be placed on selection or on development of any student who is strongly motivated? Should selection stress aptitude or achievement? How can selection fathom the seas of apathy, low motivation, and impoverished cultural environment that hide unsuspected talents so well?

Both Bray (1954) and McClelland (1958) stress the inadequacy of identification instruments now available. Bray reasons by analogy to estimate the existence of a far higher reservoir of talent than we now suspect. McClelland points to present ignorance of the personal and environmental factors which make for success. These writers independently argue accordingly for focus on programs that include the maximum number of interested candidates so that no talent is lost as a result of poor identification measures. This issue is considered in detail in later chapters on Intelligence Testing and Identification.

RECURRING QUESTIONS ABOUT GIFTEDNESS

Greatness in human existence, aspiration, and achievement form a theme which has been treated since prehistoric times in literature and art and more recently through scholarly analysis and research. Certain questions recur from time to time. Does genius represent a difference from the generality in kind or only in degree? Does exceptional performance have its source in heredity, in environment, or in personality that is the result of both nature and nurture? Does giftedness represent so great a difference from the norm that it entails eccentricity bordering on insanity?

KIND OR DEGREE?

The sources of genius present a fascinating mystery. A Shakespeare, a Beethoven, an Einstein, even a Babe Ruth or a Red Grange seem not to follow normal curves of distribution, not merely to be on the extreme end of a continuous curve. They seem to bear out Hirsch's words:

> Genius differs in *kind* from the species, man. Genius can be defined only in terms of its own unique mental and temperamental processes, traits, qualities, and products. Genius is another psychological species differing as much from man, in his mental and temperamental processes, as man differs from the ape. (Quoted in Hollingworth, 1942, p. 298)

Basically the hypothesis is that genius is of only one degree; anything less differs not only in degree but in kind. The opposing point of view claims that genius *is* a matter of degree. Persons taking this position will often argue in addition that everyone has genius, or gifts, to some degree.

Wechsler has assembled impressive statistics in his volume *The Range of Human Capacities* indicating a general variability in physical functions such that the greatest is approximately two and one-half times the least. Conceding that comparatively few mental abilities have as yet been measured because there are only "a few simple mental abilities or rather types of performances which do lend themselves to such quantitative comparisons," Wechsler expresses the belief that "human beings differ from each other not so much with respect to the kind of abilities and traits which they possess, as regards the degree to which they possess them." The matter of degree, he feels, extends to the genius category as well. He quotes Baldwin's definition that "genius is superiority of ability in an unusual degree," that a person of genius is one "whose mental, moral or artistic capacity or achievement is of extraordinarily high quality or value." Wechsler remarks that writers in their description of genius fall back on intangible, subjective criteria such as "complete objectivity," "directed intuition," and "creative intelligence." When measurable yardsticks such as memory, general intelligence, and physical endurance are used, "men of genius may differ but little from the average individual." If other intangible traits may be accepted, "it does not follow that these qualities, whatever they may be, are necessarily entirely absent in ordinary mortals." Such qualities, insists Wechsler, will be found "in some degree, however small" in all men, and no evidence can be found to support Hirsch's claim that genius is a different psychological species. Wechsler tempers his attack on genius as difference in kind, however, by conceding that "qualitative changes may result from purely quantitative variations." This last observation might help to account for the apparent uniqueness of the individual of exceptional ability (Wechsler, 1952, pp. 15-18).

Kreuter (1962) has traced the gradual disappearance of the concept of genius in an article on Terman's approach to the problem. She attributes to Galton a definition of genius as early as 1859 which distinguishes the virtuoso from his fellow man in quantitative terms only but remarks that Galton subsequently doubted the accuracy of his own definition.

Terman implied a point of view in the title he selected at the outset for his work—*Genetic Studies of Genius*. His early writings are laced with the term "genius" and also with the conviction that heredity tells most of the story of genius. His major stress is on race and ethnic factors and the argument for eugenics. Apparently Terman found the experience of his own studies a sobering one. The word "genius" gradually dropped from his terminology when he realized that high intelligence meant nothing unless coupled with "social adaptability and moral stamina"; with the recognition that personal factors might outweigh the influence of heredity; with the finding that there was tremendous divergence within his group in educational achievement and vocational success; with a growing awareness (in Kreuter's words, 1962, p. 15) that "the *Zeitgeist* [is] a more reliable determinant of accomplishment than intelligence tests."

The assumption that giftedness represents a different type of human existence rather than a difference in degree may be followed with a set of educational proposals quite distinct from those warranted by the difference-in-degree hypothesis. Difference in kind argues for segregated programs, for highly limited groupings, and for hard-and-fast selection processes. Difference in degree argues for broadening the base of the program, for blurring the distinctions between above-average, very superior, and exceptionally gifted, and for regarding selection processes as highly tentative and not definitive in nature. The latter would seem to be more in keeping with the democratic ethos that human worth resides in each individual and that each individual has a potential contribution to make to the culture.

John Hersey has expressed this point of view eloquently in his pamphlet, *Intelligence, Choice, and Consent*:

> There are no rigid standards, no fixed norms, no definite categories among our young. Every human being is unique and constantly changing. Every child can be said to have potential talent of some degree and kind. The value of each individual to a democratic society lies precisely in his uniqueness, and in the extent to which he chooses to use, and is helped to use, his special talent, great or small, for the common good. It is the task of educators in a democracy to discover, release, and foster in each individual those traits and abilities that make him unique, and to give him the desire to put them to work in his own special way for the good of all. (Hersey, 1959, pp. 12-13) *

---

* From *Intelligence, Choice and Consent*, by John Hersey. Copyright 1959 by The Woodrow Wilson Foundation. Reprinted by permission of The Woodrow Wilson Foundation.

Public schools operating in a democracy would seem obliged to adopt the assumption that giftedness represents the upper extreme in a continuum of ability which encompasses and relates every citizen.

HEREDITY OR ENVIRONMENT?

The biographical studies of the nineteenth century indicated that high achievement tends to run in families. Without measures of ability available to them, the scholars could not distinguish in their research between the effects of heredity and favorable environment in these families. Terman's study on the West Coast (1925; 1947), Lewis' reports of a Midwestern population (1943), and Hollingworth's studies in the East (1926) tended to support high incidence of mental superiority and overall achievement in the families of children selected for their high intelligence scores. One important reservation, however, needs be noted. The presence of cultural (environmental) factors is generally recognized in the content of intelligence tests. Davis and Eells believe this content is so pervasive as to make the tests highly deceptive, particularly when administered to culturally deprived groups (Eells, 1951).

In more recent years there has been a tendency to question the influence of heredity alone. Murphy suggests quite practically, "The son of a composer is more likely to be a successful composer than the son of a mathematician or a bricklayer, but considered historically in terms of sheer numbers, more composers are the sons of artisans than of composers" (1958, pp. 232-33). Elizabeth Drews (1957), conducting a longitudinal study in East Lansing, Michigan, found high ability distributed proportionally among various ethnic, racial, and socio-economic groups quite at variance with the Terman findings thirty years earlier.

Douglas Bray, reporting for the Human Resources Studies at Columbia University, remarks, "A basic difficulty is that neither heredity nor environment can be measured. On the one hand, pure human strains are not available for experimentation. On the other, since we do not even know which environmental factors have a crucial influence on the development of the IQ, we are unable to weigh the differences between environments" (Bray, 1954, pp. 10-11). He recognizes that children differ in intellectual potential at birth, but by the time that this potential becomes measurable it has already been influenced by cultural opportunity. The differences reported from one cultural group to another suggest to Bray differences in environment, not differences in natural endowment.

As will be reported in the chapter on intelligence, many psychologists regard the intellectual component of genius, at least, as being more a matter of heredity than environment in the ratio of three-to-one. Lorge, in an address to the American Eugenics Society, tried to explain differences in IQ as being differences in the kind or quality of genes in the individual. These genes have not been identified, and all that we can say is that genes for intellectual ability are not simple characters as is color blindness. These genetic factors themselves have impact upon the individual's reaction to the environment. Lorge concludes: "An individual's performances are, in my opinion, determined by the tendencies in his genetic constitution, and by the experiences, activities and needs, he, because of his genetic make-up, seeks, utilizes, and satisfies. An individual's performance is a function of his genes, and what those genes cause him to do" (Lorge, 1941, pp. 206-7).

However, the relationship between hereditary and environmental influence is underscored by Lorge. "But even intellectual abilities must be given an environment rich in the opportunities for selection, utilization and satisfaction. . . . Superior intellectual abilities can be retarded or limited, or even harmed by an inadequate, unstimulating, or deficient environment. Even genetically superior seeds need cultivation" (*Ibid.*, p. 207). Maddox (1957), in a comprehensive summary of the issue, similarly underscores the "dynamic interaction" of heredity and environment. Because the variables cannot be isolated from each other, he regards further investigation of the issue as fruitless.

The natural causation of superior intelligence is also stressed by Lorge: "Superior intellectual ability is not a miracle. It is as natural as superiority in height or weight. Basically it is genetically constituted. The performance of the superior intellectual deviate will be, in part, conditioned by his environment and his education" (p. 208).

For persons concerned with education of the gifted, the conclusions seem to be: (1) superior ability is naturally caused; (2) both heredity and environment play a part; (3) since the school's realm is environmental enrichment, it must do all it can to help each individual attain the maximum of his ability as inherited and as modified by his total environment.

MOTIVATION AND PERSONALITY

It has become almost a truism that ability alone does not account for superior performance in life. Almost ruefully, Terman and Oden declare at the end of their twenty-five year follow-up, "At any rate, we have seen that intellect and achievement are far from perfectly correlated" (Terman and Oden, 1947, p. 352). Bray points out that "difference in performance does not prove that intelligence is innate; the differences between two groups may be due to early emotional and motivational experiences" (Bray, 1954, p. 9). Current studies of non-intellective factors in success stem from assumptions that achievement is based upon high ability as a minimum but that it must be supported by personality structure which includes a drive toward high-level performance.

Biographical material lends support to such assumptions. Did a Robert Louis Stevenson and a Franklin Delano Roosevelt achieve as much as they did in an effort to compensate for physical handicaps? Did blindness drive Milton on? did deafness goad Beethoven more than it hampered him? What inner qualities did these men possess which have been absent from the very large number of handicapped persons who have not reacted in this way?

Personality, of course, is itself the result of interacting heredity and environment. It is apparent, however, that it develops its own character in determining the individual's drive toward exceptional achievement.

"TO MADNESS NEAR ALLIED"?

One of the popular illusions about gifted personalities is the stereotype of the "mad genius." This may be a "sour grapes" reaction of the general population in envy of more gifted brethren, or it may disclose popular response to the non-conforming tendencies of creative personalities, their comparative disregard for the attitude of the public, and the intense drive toward closure which makes the creative worker oblivious at times to the world about him (see Chapter 5, Creativity). It is a far cry from these attitudes and tendencies to insanity, but a number of biographical studies completed at the end of the nineteenth century supported the "mad genius" theory. In *Absalom and Achitophel*, Dryden anticipated the approach of Lombroso and his followers when he wrote:

> Great wits are sure to madness near allied,
> And thin partitions do their bounds divide.

In 1891 Cesare Lombroso noted that "good sense travels on the well-worn paths; genius, never. And that is why the crowd, not altogether without reason, is so ready to treat great men as lunatics" (*The Man of Genius*, 1891, p. x). In the same year Nisbet's *The Insanity of Genius* (1891), another study of famous men, confirmed Lombroso's picture of an unusual proportion of madness among men of genius. These volumes enjoyed wide esteem, and it took the monumental study by C. M. Cox, *The Early Mental Traits of Three Hundred Geniuses* (Cox, 1926) to rebut these claims. Hollingworth cites Hirsch's analysis of the "negative view" of genius as "biologically linked with insanity, degeneracy and imbecility" from ancient to modern times. Hirsch sees the egalitarian expression of democratic sentiment as one strand. As a second he sees the efforts of "alienists, psychologists and psychiatrists" to establish not a causal relationship but to describe pathological states or abnormal emotions as conditions fomenting genius. A third is the Freudian hypothesis of fixation and sublimation where fixations of early infantile desires are sublimated into creative processes. And finally, he offers Adler's view of genius as compensation for feelings of inferiority. With these points of view Hirsch is not in agreement. He maintains the position that genius is qualitatively different from simple superiority, that there is no need to explain it as a pathological state of humanity, that "genius has a nature *sui generis*" (Hollingworth, 1942, pp. 278-82).

The longitudinal studies in the period between the two World Wars and numerous studies on characteristics of the gifted also do not support the assumption of "madness." Instead they indicate better-than-average emotional stability, good social adjustment, and a tendency toward earlier recovery from mental illness, possibly because of the greater intellectual resources of this group.

SOCIAL INFLUENCES ON THE DEVELOPMENT OF TALENT

THE IMMEDIATE CULTURE

The concentration of painters and poets in the Italian renaissance, the assemblage of dramatists in Elizabethan England, the concert of sculptors and philosophers in ancient Greece, the massed efforts of physical scientists in the past century demonstrate cultural periods that have featured simultaneous appearance of men of genius in a particular milieu and a particular field of endeavor. A phenomenon like the "flowering of New England" leads to an inference that human potentiality lurks always just beneath the surface, waiting for awakening in a friendly culture and thriving thereafter on the cross-fertilization of kindred souls. The immediate culture provides or denies motivation by the recognition it accords any particular gift. It encourages giftedness to the extent that it stimulates originality and it discourages gifted performance when it exerts pressures toward conformity. When the culture brings together spirits of like interests and high ability, it brings talent to flower. When it provides opportunity for exploration and time for creative work, the culture sets the physical stage for gifted expression. Two aspects of the *Zeitgeist* are of fundamental importance: how hospitable it is to extraordinary ability and intellectual distinction in general and what particular abilities and fields of performance it prizes at a given time.

Margaret Mead, from the perspective of a cultural anthropologist, takes a critical view of the contemporary American culture, finding prevailing attitudes toward success and high level performance distinctly negative. The gifted child, she maintains, grows up in a culture that has the wrong attitudes toward success and failure, luck and happiness, heredity and environment, and ability as a continuous or discontinuous variable. The American culture of today, she implies, places more value on luck than ability, exhibiting a "grudging willingness to recognize success within one's own field" (Mead, 1954, p. 211). She continues:

> The pressures for keeping on all fours with one's classmates, neighbors, business associates, which are increasing in American life, tend to be particularly felt in the school age groups, especially in the case of the child who shows intellectual or artistic gifts. (*Ibid.*)

In addition, she regards the culture as one which attempts to place all comparisons on a continuous scale, and she does not regard giftedness as a continuous variable. As a result, she claims "an appalling waste of first-rate talents while the slightly superior people just because they do have to work to get straight A's are forgiven" (*Ibid.*, p. 213).

A society rewards most lavishly the talents it prizes, and the greatest ability enters those fields where the rewards—recognition, adulation, power, or money—loom large. It is common to compare American achievement in business and industry with British achievement in governmental service. The differences are probably not accidental. The concept of civil service in England is such as to attract the greatest talents; to assert the same for the United States, despite many notable exceptions in government service, is scarcely realistic. In the United States industry and finance attract these talents. Small wonder, then, that American industry should be noted for creative and effective organization, and government operations for less flattering stereotypes.

Galbraith (1958) and Riesman (1950) are among those who see the United States moving from focus on production to focus on consumption, from manufacturing and agriculture to services. Our productive capacities in their opinion no longer require the single-minded attention that they once did. If this process is accelerated, there may be a decline in the demands of industry for the highest talents in production. Instead, sales, distribution, and advertising may increasingly drain off men and women of high ability.

We may, if this interpretation is correct, expect a continuing drain on the reservoir of talent that will prevent creative expression of the potential of many individuals. This drain takes several forms. In some cases young men and women of high ability will perceive the path to personal success through early termination of their formal education and immersion in occupations where the road to top achievement is through experience on the job. Obviously, the professional and scholarly fields can make no exclusive claim to high ability in a complex economy.

A second kind of drain occurs after the bachelor's or doctor's degree has been earned. Young people, like Tennyson's Northern Farmer, may not "marry for munny" but they may "go wheer munny is." Industry and government in their need for scientific and engineering ability often recruit high ability people for low level jobs, "stockpiling" them against future needs and sometimes effectively preventing any creative contribution by them. Bello, writing in *Fortune* (November 1958, p. 214), notes the fact that only 10 per cent of published research in physics, to take a single scientific field, comes from the thousands of physicists employed in industry.

Third, young people from high socio-economic families may find it difficult to give serious consideration to important fields of social service that are not regarded as upper-class occupations. It may be hard to reconcile the long hours of the physician, the modest pay of the professor, the limited resources of the research worker with the "captain of industry" or coupon-clipper role open to children in high status families.

Schools are frequently urged to develop a keen social conscience in high-ability children. Making full use of their power, these individuals may achieve what Maslow calls the "peak experience." In doing so they can also make a significant and necessary contribution to their society. On the other hand, schools must be realistic about existing monetary values and the powerful temptations to submerge creative impulses and productive potential in socially trivial occupations.

THE TEEN-AGE CULTURE

Students are influenced not only by the general values of the culture; they are apparently affected even more by the mores and attitudes of their peers. Sociologists are tending to identify a "teen-age society" or culture as a separate entity. Coleman (1962) and Tannenbaum (1962) have reported studies of adolescent attitudes toward academic superiority and achievement which indicate negative values toward intellectual performance of a high order. Tannenbaum sought out attitudes toward three attributes: academic brilliance, studiousness, and athletic achievement. His subjects did not indicate a preference between average intellect and academic brilliance, but they showed a marked distinction in favor of little effort over studiousness and in favor of athleticism over non-athleticism. Girls tended to favor non-studiousness and athleticism even more than boys. Tannenbaum concludes that

> . . . academic brilliance in and of itself is not a stigma in the adolescent world. However, when it is combined with relatively unacceptable attributes, it can penalize its possessor severely. The nonstudious athlete may demonstrate outstanding brainpower without fearing social derogation by peers; but a display of brilliance by one who is studious and indifferent to sports constitutes a definite status risk. The implied impression is that the brilliant student is an exceptionally prominent target for teen-age pressures to conform to certain behaviors and values. If so, there is danger of his deliberately masking his talent in order to relieve these pressures. (1962, p. 68) *

Tannenbaum's study was initiated in a New York City high school in a middle class neighborhood, and repeated in Denver and in rural New York state schools.

Coleman studied attitudes toward a number of attributes in nine schools that represented the major types of American communities as distinguished by size, urban-rural-suburban location, social class representation, and public-private operation. The major variables tested were desires of students to be most brilliant, most popular, or athletically outstanding (for girls, to be leaders in school activities). Some differences were noted from school to school, but in all schools, athleticism was the major ambition, popularity was second, and brilliance third. To these findings Coleman adds evidence to show the center of gravity moving from parents to peers in influencing adolescents' attitudes. Teachers were a poor third in this regard. It is therefore not surprising that the values of the "leading crowd" (those students regarded by others as setting the pace for the school society) were significant in affecting student opinion. In all schools the "leading crowd" had grades exceeding the average girls' and average boys' grades. The superiority of the leadership group, however, was greatest in those schools where grades were valued most. Stated in another way, where scholarship was most prized, the students who constituted the "leading crowd" had the greatest academic lead over their followers.

Particularly disturbing in both the Tannenbaum and Coleman studies was the agreement of the brightest students with the values of the group. They also regarded athletic prominence as most desirable and disparaged hard work in school subjects. In Coleman's words, "The culture

---

* From *Adolescent Attitudes toward Academic Brilliance*, by Abraham J. Tannenbaum. Copyright 1962 by Teachers College, Columbia University. Reprinted by permission of The Bureau of Publications, Teachers College, Columbia University.

has failed to encourage a self-image among those who are entitled to it by academic achievement." It "undercuts the desire of adolescents to think of themselves as intellectual," and exerts "a rather strong deterrent to academic achievement." Coleman concludes:

> If secondary education is to be successful, it must successfully compete with cars and sports and social activities for the adolescents' attention, in an open market. The adolescent is no longer a child, but will spend his energy in the ways he sees fit. It is up to the adult society to so structure secondary education that it captures his energy. (1961, p. 329)*

In the face of the apparent solidity of these studies, other signs give evidence of contrasting attitudes on the part of adolescents. School systems that operate special schools, special classes, or special programs for bright students find no shortage of applicants. In many cases, from ten to one hundred times as many students apply as can be accommodated. Colleges which make known their high admissions standards and awesome selectivity are bombarded with applications for entrance. Applications increase geometrically where students seek advanced placement classes and take the corresponding examinations. The science honors classes operated by many universities for high school students during the summer or on Saturdays are over-subscribed, and they, too, are forced into selectivity. A constantly increasing proportion of students graduate from high school and enter college. There is a remarkable shift of interest on the college scene away from the football-fraternity-prom queen end of the spectrum.

Both the disheartening studies of the adolescent culture and the more hopeful signs on the teen-age horizon merit serious consideration in studying provisions for educating the gifted. Nor should their significance for elementary education be missed. While younger children are more influenced by their parents, the influence of older siblings and comrades begins to take effect.

CREATIVITY COMES OF AGE

A heartening and unexpected result of Cold War anxiety has been a sudden rash of interest in creative performance and even a premium on nonconformity. While periods of anxiety normally produce a repressive atmosphere unfriendly to new and strange ideas, Sputnik's rocketing into the 1957 skies exploded into an awareness that the novel, the unheard of,

---

* From *The Adolescent Society*, by James S. Coleman. Copyright 1962 by the Free Press of Glencoe. Reprinted by permission of The Macmillan Company.

the "way-out," the intuitive, the imaginative, the intellectual, scientific, and academic were the new paths to national supremacy and security. Scholarly investigations into creative behavior, the creative personality, and the creative process were suddenly given publicity, and a prime mover of Madison Avenue advertising gave new impetus to a program for promotion of "brainstorming" (Osborn, 1957). Creativeness found its way out of music and art studios and became a byword in industry as well as in scientific and scholarly pursuits.

While there is always a danger in faddism, a more receptive atmosphere for creative endeavors bodes well in education of the gifted. First, it dictates a need to look critically at the probable effects of the multitude of proposals being offered to improve the schools. If the goal is greater creativeness, one cannot accept the return to more rigid educational patterns or the simple-minded multiplying of homework and pages covered in the textbook. Second, a fundamental concern with creativity prescribes consideration of the atmosphere of the school and the community. Openness and permissiveness acquire a new respectability. Third, education must take a direction oriented toward the future and the emergent rather than the bygone and the static as represented in the transmission of a past culture alone.

Not far removed from the theme of creativeness is a new emphasis on dynamic qualities in our national culture, or perhaps in Western Civilization itself. In the early 1960's the *New York Times* ran a series of articles by prominent men on national goals. John W. Gardner (1962) addressed himself to the topic of "Renewal in Societies and Men" in the Annual Report of the Carnegie Corporation in 1962. Perhaps this dialogue is motivated by fears of a Spenglerian "Decline of the West," perhaps by anxiety over competition with the communist countries. Whatever the cause, there is a growing conviction that America's future (and the world's) lies in growth, change, and renewal, not in simple stability or maintenance of the status quo. Gardner sees the relation between a "continuously renewing society," which has "built-in provisions for vigorous criticism," with the need for creative individuals. He argues, therefore, for opportunities for self-development, for freedom of the individual to "believe or doubt, agree or disagree" in his creative work. He seeks for the self-renewing man as indispensable to the self-renewing society. He describes this paragon as versatile, adaptive, highly motivated, possessing drive and conviction, and relentlessly urged onward by the sense that his own potentialities and the process of self-discovery never end. Other authorities might define the creative individual in similar terms. Still others would use these terms to describe maturity, self-actualization or genuine self-fulfillment.

The growth of popular and scholarly interest in creativeness and in dynamic aspects of our culture may indicate a new quality in the contemporary spirit of the times. Such a shift should have immediate as well as ultimate influence upon young people and their attitudes. It should be reinforced by planning in schools which will accommodate increased interest in creative and intellectual pursuits.

"NEGLECT OF THE GIFTED"

While it is fashionable to make schools the whipping boy in what is regarded as a crisis stemming from failure to realize the potential of the gifted, little has been dearer to the heart of the average pedagogue and school administrator than educating the outstanding student. Criticism comes in poor grace, moreover, from a community atmosphere which has rarely attached much kudos to the mantle of the teacher or professor. The forlorn efforts of frontier school teachers fighting the culture as they tried to help youngsters establish professional or intellectual goals have been sung in epics of the screen and television as well as in novels, poems, and the theatre. But teachers have had to carve out intellectual frontiers in metropolitan cities, in suburbia, and in well-established small towns as well.

Other factors may carry still more weight in the neglect of talent. Schools, particularly at higher levels, claim that they exist primarily to foster intellectual ability. Where the culture or the school itself discriminates against particular groups, streams are dammed up that might otherwise replenish the reservoir of talent. The report of the Commission on Specialized Talent indicated that only one-half of the top quarter of high school graduates complete a college program, that only 3 per cent capable of earning a Ph.D. go on to do so, and that only three-tenths of 1 per cent of top-ability women study for and secure a doctorate (Wolfle, 1954). A large proportion of the missing faces in higher education is attributable to lack of motivation or competing aspirations within the individual; part of it is chargeable to the failure of society to encourage this kind of application. However, an important part is due not simply to neglect but to actual discouragement by society. A major source of untapped ability lies in the ranks of superior women who are excluded from certain fields like physics and architecture or are more generally encouraged by our society to regard productive activity outside the home as less worthy than, and not compatible with, marriage and motherhood.

In addition, the ugly effects of racial and religious discrimination are increasingly brought into focus. While important strides in the right direction are being made, only a Pollyanna could overlook *de facto* exclusion or limited opportunities for Negroes, Orientals, Indians, Mexican-Americans, and Puerto Ricans in most sections of the country and for Catholics and Jews in some areas. Add to this the problems encountered by children from lower socio-economic backgrounds as documented in Warner, Havighurst, and Loeb's *Who Shall Be Educated?* (1944) and Hollingshead's *Elmtown's Youth* (1949).

Sometimes discrimination is applied unconsciously and unintentionally. Davis, Eells, Havighurst, and their colleagues have marshalled impressive evidence as to the cultural selection involved in intelligence testing (Eells, 1951). The partiality of intelligence tests, generally not recognized by the tester, automatically screens out many youngsters of high potential when tests are used to select children for special opportunities. School grades are subject to the same influences. Children who come from homes that promote middle class values, including upward-striving attitudes, respect for education and authority, punctuality, good manners, and acceptable speech, are likely to do better in schools which are normally operated by teachers with the same values than are children from homes with quite different value patterns.

Taken all in all, these limitations serve as artificial restrictions on the reservoir of talent. It is not enough simply to improve programs for children whose superiority is readily identifiable. It is equally important to make sure that no talent is being overlooked.

OBJECTIVES IN EDUCATION OF THE GIFTED

Education of gifted youngsters has for its purposes the same objectives as all education in a democracy: enrichment of the life of the individual and contribution to the advancement of society. The premise of giftedness, however, carries within itself suggestions as to significant differences in *degree* with respect both to individual growth and the social contribution.

Education is inevitably concerned with the individual; group experience may be a valuable *means* to learning, but learning must always be accomplished by the individual himself. In a democracy the individual is an end to be served by the state; in his free growth we have faith that he will live a fuller life and simultaneously contribute to the commonweal which the democratic state represents.

In the current era of perils arising from the Cold War conflict between East and West, from the threat of atomic destruction, from overpopulation, poverty, aggressiveness, and from the new nationalisms, it would be idle to ignore national needs for the most effective use of high ability. On the other hand, there is little reason to gear all education to the needs of the present and the past when what is needed are new, creative solutions for the future. "Tooling up" in the sciences, technology, and foreign languages may fill the gaps of the present. But will it also release creative potential in social sciences where contributions are so sorely needed to the arts of men in living and working together in peace? Can we forego new approaches to problems of values which may in the long run be the most practical of concerns if man is to survive? Murphy (1958) warns us that simple extrapolation of the trends that now exist can lead only to destruction. He sees our only salvation in "emergent" leaps forward that have characterized the creative enterprise of mankind in all times. To accomplish this leap forward education will have to focus on releasing creativity and not to filling existing slots. The goal must be, as Getzels says, "Man," not "Manpower":

> We are attempting to implement the paradox of applying the concept of Manpower to the self-realization of man. Early career lines, orderly training in narrow disciplines, stockpiles and stockpiles of engineers—these may give us a comfortable sense of neatness and security. But, last time out, the concept of the individual as Manpower got quite a licking from the concept of the individual as Man. . . . And so whether it be education in general or education of the gifted, I prefer to say: not Manpower, but Men—men in their infinite variety and complex personalities, in the unfolding of their desires and the unfettered expression of their own talents and of *all* their talents. (Getzels, 1957, p. 63) *

In a democracy, objectives in education of the gifted have to revolve around the belief that in serving the individual we serve society. The following objectives are therefore posited:

1. Education of the gifted aims to develop potential to the highest degree possible. In this task of releasing potential, education must broaden interests for purposes of exploration; it must identify talents whether illuminated or hidden by the immediate environment; it must design programs to maximize development of ability.

2. Education of the gifted must place heavy emphasis upon development of a "social conscience," a sense of responsibility to society which is the *noblesse oblige* of talent. Somehow the concept need be taught and learned that individual talent cannot be restricted to exploitation for personal self-aggrandizement. The good fortune of the individual is to be socially expressed in contribution to the culture in which talent is nurtured.

---

* Reprinted from "Social Values and Individual Motives," by Jacob W. Getzels, in *School Review*, Volume 65, Spring, 1957, The University of Chicago Press. Copyright 1957 by The University of Chicago.

3. Education of the gifted must reveal a sense of "the good life"—both in terms of social contribution and in terms of enjoyment of a full and self-fulfilling life. Narrow vocational specialization, a need of modern society, must be balanced with the roundedness of the Renaissance *homo universalis.*

4. Education of the gifted is not simply mastery of the cultural heritage; it is essentially a matter of developing creativity. The individual must start off in creative paths as early as possible. If the trend continues toward longer years in school, schools have to make possible more independent, less structured, and more creative work than in the past.

5. Education for the gifted should be broad enough to include talents of all kinds at all levels. But *programs for special ability* have to focus on unusual talent or they will become so diluted that they are not special programs at all. Schools have special responsibility in the intellectual-cognitive area; in other areas they supplement their own limited efforts by referring youngsters to other institutions.

6. Education of the gifted is inevitably concerned with the social milieu within which it operates. It depends upon, and therefore must help develop, a social atmosphere which is sensitive to, and appreciative of, intellectual superiority. In many American communities nothing short of a revolution of values is necessary. Sumptuary values must yield to respect for social service and cultural contributions. Such an orientation requires appreciation at both the student and adult levels.

7. A final objective is the development of a system for continuous evaluation of programs in school and community to develop ability. Periodic review is needed of identification procedures, of school and community opportunities, and of community attitudes toward superior intellectual performance.

SUMMARY

The major purpose in education of the gifted is release of the unique potential of exceptionally able persons. Fundamentally, we face the problem of individualizing education to the point where each young person is helped to fulfill his own special promise. The school has the task of educating *all* children and at the same time discharging its responsibility to *each* child. To the extent that schools succeed in individualizing instruction for all children, they succeed in enhancing education for the exceptional.

Genius may be viewed as extraordinary ability within the range of human capacities, or it may be viewed as so exceptional that it has nothing to do with more common potential. The Western ethical commitment to the worth of every human being and our inability to separate genius from the generality at early ages represent philosophical and practical grounds to comprehend education of the gifted within systems of education for all.

The heredity-environment issue also breaks down because it is impossible to separate the two components of the human being. The school's responsibility is to recognize the effect of environment and so to enhance the experience of each child in order that the fullest individual potential is developed.

Of the myriad gifts distributed in the world, intellectual potential is the particular province of the school. At least a modicum of intellectual power seems basic to success in all areas of endeavor. In the stresses of current competition with other nations, intellectual achievement has been given new attention as a necessary ingredient in the arts of national defense. In addition, intellectual development represents the community's primary charge to the schools in a long educational tradition.

Giftedness is not a question of ability alone—inherited or developed. It is very much tied to personality factors, such as motivation or "drive." The school cannot be concerned, therefore, with intellectual, artistic, and social abilities alone; it must take notice of personality factors to help each child develop his gifts.

Nor is giftedness limited to individual factors. It is within a culture that gifts flourish or wither. What the culture prizes, the culture achieves. Attitudes toward success, toward exceptional effort and performance, toward the new and original, toward different kinds of achievement— all these affect the aspirations of unusually talented people. The school necessarily operates within this framework and is successful to the extent that its aims coincide with the culture's—or to the extent that it can influence change toward the goals it seeks.

In their efforts to serve the individual and the culture, schools are likely to be most effective in education of the gifted if they focus on maximum development of the individual's potential. Wedded to this objective must be a genuine concern with concern for the social values that these brightest children develop. The goal cannot be limited to mastery of the cultural heritage of the past but must keep in view creative participation in the future. While human talents are myriad in their diversity, schools can be effective only if they are selective. They would, therefore, do best to reserve their major resources for work in the intellectual-cognitive area, their primary responsibility. Finally, schools must recognize the limited part they play in education. Since the cultural milieu is also a primary force, schools must be aware of the need to urge other social forces to a greater acceptance of intellectual achievement.

Chapter 2

Characteristics of Gifted Children

> *What a piece of work is a man! how*
> *noble in reason! how infinite in*
> *faculty! in form and moving how express*
> *and admirable! in action how like an*
> *angel! in apprehension how like a god!*
>
> —Shakespeare

Descriptions of greatness stud the literature of all nations. Accounting for the nature of genius is ever a fascinating theme. Tragedy, poetry, and even history, as "the biography of great men," take men of wide vision and noble daring as their story.

The advent of psychometrics in the present century made possible more objective analysis, recording of comparable data, and description of individuals of superior ability. Prior to the appearance of psychological tests, the characteristics of greatness could be described only "after the fact." After a man (or history) had established his greatness, then recollection, reminiscence, and memory might be employed to reconstruct his life and the details of his personality and abilities. The success of Binet's scales opened a new path—now ability might, hopefully, be *predicted*, and longitudinal studies could be planned and executed while young people with high scores were growing up. Reminiscence could be replaced with objective description. The impetus of the intelligence scales contributed also to the development of other measures on new, objective bases.

The most ambitious effort was the large scale research of Lewis M. Terman who directed the Stanford Genetic Studies of Genius identifying and studying one thousand elementary school children with IQ's of 140 and over. From 1921 until his death in 1956, Terman and his colleagues followed these persons with periodic follow-ups in 1927-28, 1936, 1940, 1945, 1951-2 and 1955. Objective measures and rating devices were employed to secure a mass of information that ranged from academic achievement, home background, physical development and health history, personality characteristics and special interests, to occupational adjustment and marital happiness in adult life. Wider use of intelligence testing in the decade following its introduction to the United States led to numerous studies relating physical, social, and personality characteristics to mental ability. Leta Hollingworth's, *Gifted Children: Their Nature and Nurture* (1926) summarizes much of this research which was completed prior to publication of her volume. Her work led her into contact with many extraordinarily bright children in New York City, particularly in P.S. 165 Manhattan and P.S. 500 (the Speyer School), and before her death she had collected twelve case studies of children with extremely rare IQ's exceeding 180. These studies are available in *Children Above 180 IQ* published posthumously in 1942. One of Paul Witty's early contributions to the literature of gifted children is *A Study of One Hundred Gifted Children* (1930). Sumption (1941) summarized findings about three hundred such children in Cleveland Major Work classes, and W. Drayton Lewis (1943) drew upon test data of 45,000 children in 36 states to describe family background and personality characteristics of 50 elementary school children with IQ's (Kuhlmann-Anderson) over 145 and 930 children with IQ's of 125-144.

Renewed interest since World War II has motivated new studies on characteristics of the gifted. These have involved studies that in some cases reinforce, in others dispute, the findings of earlier investigators (Goldberg, 1958). Ethnic, social, and economic background, reading interests, and intellectual behavior are some of the topics reported. Newly developed instruments have also been applied in study of the gifted. Some of these are projective tests of personality, "culture-fair" intelligence tests, and sociometric devices.

FAMILY BACKGROUND

Whether heredity or environment be the dominant factor, family background is important in shaping the values and motivating realization by the gifted child of his potential. Galton's title itself, *Hereditary Genius* (1869), indicates his own belief in familial influence. Comprehensive studies since the advent of more scientific identification procedures confirm the effect of the home without necessarily considering the heredity-environment controversy. Terman reported 182 families which contributed two or more children (siblings) who qualified for his research as having IQ's in the top 1 per cent. This is more than 1,200 times the number that pure chance would give (Terman, 1925, p. 110). He remarks, "That so many families contributed two or more means that something besides chance was operating, such as common ancestry, common environment, or more probably, both these influences" (Terman and Oden, 1947, pp. 17-18). In addition, he points to the superior attainments of many of the parents themselves as indicated by inclusion in *Who's Who*, holding important national offices and positions in colleges and industry, or having attained eminence in the arts.

Research on the occupational background of parents of the gifted tend to relate high occupational status to the rearing of gifted offspring. Terman classified the fathers' occupations as follows:

Professional	31.4 per cent
Semi-professional and business	50 per cent
Skilled work	11.8 per cent
Semi-skilled and unskilled work	6.8 per cent
(Terman, 1925, p.64) *	

Hollingworth corroborates this listing with findings reported in Wisconsin, New York, and in England. More recent evidence is not as clear-cut. Drews (1957) found that three-fourths of the gifted children she identified in East Lansing came from homes of skilled and unskilled workers and lower status clerical employees. At the same time the Quincy Youth Development Commission found "intellectual talent" in Quincy, Illinois, distributed unevenly in favor of the higher occupational groups (Bowman, 1956, pp. 20-21). The National Merit Corporation also "agrees that scholars come from hovels and palaces alike, but . . . finds that at least half of them come from homes which would be classified in the upper business or professional group" (Goldberg, 1958). The professional group, comprising 3 per cent of the population, supplies 30 per cent of the "scholars" (Holland and Stalnaker, 1958).

A disproportionately large number of first-born children appear among the gifted in all studies reported. Cattell's men of science, Terman's gifted, and a group identified by Cobb and Hollingworth, (1926, p. 180) all included more first-born than chance would dictate. More recently, Drews (1957) counted almost twice as many first-born among her bright adolescents as would be accounted for by chance. "When compared

---

* From *Mental and Physical Traits of a Thousand Gifted Children*, by Lewis M. Terman. Volume I, *Genetic Studies of Genius*. Copyright © 1925 by Stanford University Press. Reprinted by permission of Stanford University Press.

with middle and youngest children who test in the gifted range," Drews reports, "they appear to be superior, at least in motivation and self-esteem, even within this select group."

Another dimension of home background that has been investigated is the ethnic origin of the family. Terman's children came from "nearly all of the racial and nationality groups with any considerable representation in the cities canvassed" (Terman and Oden, 1947, p. 14), but he noted wide disparity in the proportions contributed by various groups. Repeated studies indicate larger proportions of high IQ children from native white, English, Scotch, and Jewish backgrounds, and smaller proportions from non-white and southern European origins (Terman, 1925, pp. 82-83; Hollingworth, 1926, p. 75).

It is not possible to determine whether the differences are inherent in the cultural groups or whether differential environments account for the apparent superiority of any particular group. However, some interesting studies have been completed which show (1) value differences to be more important than membership in given ethnic groups, and (2) a higher potential within low-scoring groups when environmental deprivation is taken into account. Strodtbeck's interesting research relating value patterns to differential success among ethnic groups in New Haven will be discussed in Chapter 3. Cultural deprivation may be even more pervasive in its influence.

The generally low performance of Negroes as a group on intelligence tests has led to a number of researches. Again, effects of heredity and environment cannot be isolated and identified, but the impact of environment seems to be borne out by a number of factors. Jenkins has contributed a number of studies which point to his conclusion "that race per se (at least as it is represented in the American Negro) is not a limiting factor in psychometric intelligence" (Jenkins, 1948, p. 400). Supporting evidence is found in 16 studies of 22,301 Negro children showing an IQ distribution of 0.3 per cent of 140 and over, 1 per cent at 130 and above. These proportions Jenkins regards as similar to those obtained in "normal" distribution for American school children. He remarks that these children manifest the same characteristics as do other children of very high IQ: "originality of expression, creative ability, and surpassing performance in school subjects. Some of these children, but not all, are greatly accelerated in school progress" (*Ibid.*). Of particular significance is the fact that all Negro children with IQ's over 160 were found in Northern or border state cities. It seems quite reasonable to expect that a similar distribution of ability ought to be found in Southern states where 80 per cent of the Negro population lives. Such children may not have been discovered in the South, according to Jenkins, because of the lack of opportunity and stimulation in their environment or because of a failure to utilize effective methods of identification. Jenkins sums up:

> The data of this article bring into sharp focus the limitations that our society places on the development of the highly gifted Negro. These superior deviates are nurtured in a culture in which racial inferiority of the Negro is a basic assumption. Consequently, they will typically experience throughout their lives educational, social, and occupational restrictions that must inevitably affect motivation and achievement. (Jenkins, 1948, p. 401).

Witty and Theman followed up in 1940 eighty-two mentally superior Negro youths whom Jenkins had identified in 1934 as having Binet IQ's ranging from 120 to 200. Achievement tests (Myers-Ruch High-School Progress Test and the Iowa Every-pupil Test in Understanding of Contemporary Affairs) indicated better-than-average performance but "not consonant with expectations based upon mental tests" given six years earlier. The range of scores ran from the thirteenth percentile on the Myers-Ruch and the sixth percentile on the Iowa to the ninety-ninth percentile on both tests. The median percentiles were 59 and 54 respectively despite the IQ range in the top decile. High school grades, relative standing in class (all but one in the top fifth), and interest in school were regarded as being as good as, or better than, those of comparable white students. Witty and Theman conclude:

> Although this group of gifted Negroes does not appear to have entirely lived up to its early promise in educational achievement as measured by standardized tests, it does rank high when all criteria of attainment are considered. In terms of the meager opportunity of some of these youth, this fact is surprising and gratifying. (Witty and Theman, 1943, p. 45)

Working with much younger children, Knoblock and Pasamanick report that Negro and white children who scored nearly the same in early intellectual and developmental potentials show greater variance at age three, when environmental factors begin to impinge. The researchers used the Gesell Developmental Test in studying three hundred children. They found a "marked racial divergence in adaptive and language behavior." The general developmental quotient and language ability rose in the white group, but fell among the non-whites. Knoblock and Pasamanick attribute this to less motivation toward learning in the non-white, generally low socio-economic homes, and greater deterrents such as more sickness, more working mothers, and lower nutrition (the *New York Times*, 1960).

In 1956 New York City instituted a "Demonstration Guidance Project" (later broadened and redesignated "Higher Horizons") which will be described more fully in Chapter 4 on Identification. This program is based on the assumption that cultural deprivation obstructs discovery of intellectual talent. It poses the probability that greater talent exists in the Negro and Puerto Rican population in New York City and elsewhere than may be found by conventional identification techniques. In this regard it questions the existence of racial differences and looks for contrary evidence that may come when children from these backgrounds are given environmental stimulation more nearly comparable to that of the white population (New York City, 1959b).

Bray (1954) states the problem provocatively in *Issues in the Study of Talent*. He notes the differential proportions of high IQ scores to be found in different ethnic, social, and economic groups in the United States and he questions the validity of these differences on statistical and biological grounds. Let us assume, he says, that the groups with the highest scores represent a maximum development currently possible given human potential, as it now stands, and optimal environmental conditions. If group A, for example, shows 2 per cent of its membership with scores over 135 while the national population stands at only 1 per cent, 2 per cent may be regarded as the potential for all groups if given equal opportunity and stimulation. Since the spread is actually of this order, Bray hypothesizes potential doubling of the reservoir of high ability in the United States. The New Haven Jewish-Italian study and the research on American Negroes make Bray's hypothesis appear reasonable.

To sum up, it would appear that Terman is on sound ground in his assertion, "No race or nationality has any monopoly on brains" (1947, p. 14). Recent research goes beyond this statement to suggest that varying proportions of high IQ children among different groups apparently reflect environmental differences rather than variation in innate ability. To educators this suggests (1) high ability is to be found in almost any family background; (2) when an inordinately low proportion is found, cultural deprivation is probably responsible. In the latter case, both school and the community at large have a formidable, but essential, job to do in compensating for an impoverished environment.

One final matter relative to family background: the quality of family living itself makes a difference. On the positive side Terman, Lewis, and Hollingworth cite evidence showing a high incidence of good family situations—low divorce rates, good emotional health, higher median income, more schooling—in the background of high scoring children. Some of the children also come from grossly inadequate homes. "Unfavorable living conditions appear to react very powerfully, and even disastrously, upon these very superior children," says Lewis of the ten children with poor backgrounds among his fifty cases of IQ's of 145 and over. Only one of the ten was well adjusted both personally and educationally. Most of the remainder suffered from both personal and educational maladjustment (Lewis, 1947). Frankel (1960) and Goldberg (1959) concur in relating poor family situations to underachievement in high school students. In addition, Strodtbeck relates "democratic" families to higher achievement, finding the home in which the mother shares in decisions a better stimulus to performance than that which the father rules autocratically (McClelland, 1958, pp. 181-84).

PHYSICAL CHARACTERISTICS

There is general agreement that intellectually gifted children are also blessed with good health and better-than-average physical development. Numerous studies accomplished in the 1920's attest to:

> Superior health of the mother during pregnancy
> Greater weight at birth
> Early dentition
> Learning to walk and talk early
> Fewer childhood illnesses
> Fewer physical defects except for defective vision in one-fourth more of the gifted children (Terman, 1925, p. 212)—perhaps a result of early and excessive reading!
> Higher average nutrition
> Greater height, weight, arm span, width of shoulders, hips, and strength of grip (Terman, 1925, p. 171)
> Superior motor control and motor ability (Terman, 1925, Chap. 7 and 8; Hollingworth, 1926, Chap. 4)
> Attractive appearance

Terman's 1955 follow-up indicates a persistence of good health in the adult life of the gifted. Better-than-average health is reported by his correspondents, generally, and the mortality of the group up to an average age of 44 was lower than that of the general American population (Terman and Oden, 1959, p. 29).

Despite evidence of physical superiority, the stereotype of the bright child as a bespectacled and puny weakling is hard to overcome. The impression may result from a mystical belief in compensation—that somehow the bright child has to pay for his mental superiority—or it may stem from the bright child's uneven development. The gifted child's

mental advancement generally outstrips considerably his physical superiority. That is to say, the ten-year-old with an IQ of 150 may operate
mentally on a fifteen-year level, but he is fortunate to hold his own physically with an eleven-year-old. Adults are likely to look for physical performance that matches the mental precocity and overlook actual age.
The effect is heightened when the child is accelerated in school. Comparison with *class*-mates rather than *age*-mates is inevitable, but unjust.
It is a rare sixteen-year-old high school senior who can compete equally
well on the football field with an eighteen-year-old.

SEX DIFFERENCES IN MENTAL ABILITY

The general tendency of girls to do better in school-work on the elementary and secondary levels raises the interesting question of possible
mental superiority of either sex. Test results actually seem to belie the
record of school achievement. If mental development were consistent
and homogeneous, statistics would justify little difference between the
sexes as to the age at which boys and girls begin to read, and that
difference would be in favor of the males. If scholastic aptitude, as measured by intelligence tests, were the only factor involved in academic
achievement, then, there would be slightly more male than female
valedictorians and salutatorians in high school classes.

Clark (1951) investigated sex differences on the California Tests of
Mental Maturity, using a large group of recent high school graduates.
The mean IQ for the group was 117. Women had slightly superior scores
in tests of memory, logical reasoning, and non-language factors. Men
were superior in numerical reasoning, spatial relationships, language
factors, and verbal concepts. The only variance, however, that was statistically different at the mean of the distribution was memory (women 4
percentile points higher). It is of interest to note that men evidence
greater standard deviations from the average, implying greater intra-
personal or trait differences except in spatial relationships and numerical
reasoning. Clark infers that separate sex test norms are not needed. If this
reasoning can be extended to other situations, little support, particularly
in the case of gifted children, is found for proposals to begin school work
with boys at an older age than with girls.

Miles (1954, p. 995) summarizes a number of studies on sex differences in mental ability. Terman's group showed a ratio of 121-100,
favoring boys, but Miles claims the Terman nominations procedure
operated in favor of boys. The problem is to secure a large enough
sample when one is seeking to generalize among persons representing
only 3 per cent or less of the population. Miles quotes eight large-scale

studies of high school and college students with IQ's above 140 or above the 97th percentile. In seven of these studies more boys than girls are identified. Here again Miles questions procedure by citing the effect of such "secondary factors" as "social motivation, physical endurance, fatigability in learning situations and examinations, and amount of practice or experience with different kinds of subject matter" (*Ibid.*, p. 996). The existence and amount of sex differences, she concludes, cannot be established until such factors are accounted for.

Hollingworth (1942, Chapter 3) finds great superiority fairly well divided between the sexes, although the number of people she could identify in the over-180 IQ range is obviously small. She summarized 19 published reports on tested children, of whom twelve were girls, seven boys. Her own testing led to twelve additional cases of whom four were girls and eight were boys. The total included sixteen girls and fifteen boys (*Ibid.*, p. 62).

For teachers, parents, and other educators the meaning seems to be clear. Exceptional ability (to a similar degree) is likely to be found in both sexes. At school ages when boys seem to achieve less well, causation is more apt to be found in the culture than in inherent sex differences. The task is to relate positively the concept of maleness with scholastic achievement among boys and adolescents.

EMOTIONAL STABILITY

The stereotype of the mad genius reflects an age-old association of unusual talent with the fringes of insanity. Chapter 1 traces briefly the history of the concept in modern times culminating in rejection of the mad genius thesis.

Terman devotes considerable attention to the problem of mental health in his follow-up studies and presents statistics on mental adjustment and emotional disorders in his gifted population. Ratings in 1940 and again in 1945 indicated "satisfactory adjustment" for about 80 per cent of the group, "some maladjustment" for about 15 per cent, "serious maladjustment without psychosis" 3.4 per cent in 1940 (4 per cent in 1945), and "serious maladjustment with psychosis" 0.8 per cent in 1940 (1.3 per cent in 1945). Comparison with the general population is difficult because of the absence of accurate statistics. Terman uses Pollock's expectancy figures based on the percentage of persons living at age eleven who will become insane by age thirty (roughly the age of the Terman group in 1921 and 1940) to show a somewhat better score for his group than for the general population. In addition, we must remember that the careful study of the Terman group has not been performed for the population as a whole, so that a greater proportion of mental illness in the selected group has no doubt been identified than is true of the public in general.

Study of the group at "mid-age" confirmed the "flower of manhood" study. In 1955, when the average age of the group was forty-four, the following results were reported:

	Per Cent	
	Men	*Women*
Satisfactory adjustment	68.8	65.9
Some maladjustment	22.3	25.1
Serious maladjustment without mental disease	6.2	6.0
Serious maladjustment involving hospitalization	2.7	3.0

(Terman and Oden, 1959, p. 37) *

Incidence of mental disease is slightly below expectancy for the gifted men and slightly above expectancy for the gifted women, but the reservations of the earlier study continue to hold.

Suicide rates, as one example of maladjustment, are also interesting:

	Per Cent	
	Men	*Women*
Terman's gifted group	1.2	0.7
General population (national)	1.7	0.6

Terman points out, however, that the gifted group's showing is actually better than this in comparison because they come from a population with higher than average suicide rates on three bases; the larger rate among higher-than-average socio-economic groups, among whites, among Californians (*Ibid.*, pp. 31-32).

Terman notes, too, that members of his group who have encountered serious maladjustment make a remarkably quick recovery. His conclusion:

> Superior intelligence does not appear to be a causal factor in
> mental disorders as found in this group but seems, rather, to have
> helped those affected to overcome their difficulties. The insight and
> intelligent cooperation shown by those who become mental patients

* From *The Gifted Group at Mid-Life*, by Lewis M. Terman and Melita H. Oden. Volume V, *Genetic Studies of Genius*. Copyright © 1959 by Stanford University Press. Reprinted by permission of Stanford University Press.

has almost certainly contributed to the improvement noted in several of the cases. (Terman and Oden, 1947, p. 108)[*]

Terman's records show also slight proportions of chorea, stuttering, delinquency, homosexuality, and alcoholism. The gifted are not without their problems, but they appear in less-than-average numbers.

While Hollingworth agrees with Terman on the generally superior emotional health of the highly intelligent, she is concerned with emotional problems that may arise because they find few congenial spirits with whom to communicate. She believes it very important for the gifted "to learn to suffer fools gladly," but she fears that the child with an IQ over 160 is doomed to relative isolation. "Such children," she says, "are ordinarily friendly and gregarious by nature, but their efforts at forming friendships tend to be defeated by the scarcity of like-minded contemporaries" (Hollingworth, 1942, p. 302).

More recently, Warren and Heist (1960) confirm findings of stability. These writers compared 659 men and 259 women taken from National Merit Scholarship winners in 1956 with undergraduates in general at the University of California and Michigan State University. On the Minnesota Multiphasic Inventory, no greater incidence of maladjustment was found. The scholarship winners showed greater originality, inventiveness, and resourcefulness. As in other studies of gifted individuals, the superior group tended to value theoretical and aesthetic rather than economic or utilitarian orientations.

Strang (1954) finds that the problems of the gifted are less than average, but a "supersensitive nervous system (or some other underlying condition) may be conducive to both emotional instability and creative intelligence." She sees some social maladjustment in IQ's over 170, including difficulty in relating to people whose abilities and backgrounds are so different.

Recent concentration on the effects of anxiety is reflected in the study by Feldhusen and Klausmeier (1962) of the relationship between anxiety and intelligence. The investigators tested 450 fifth grade children and found a negative correlation between scores on the Children's Manifest Anxiety Scale and IQ as measured by the Wechsler Intelligence Scale for Children. Correlations between anxiety and achievement were similarily negative. Higher correlations were found for girls than for boys. Feldhusen and Klausmeier suggest that children of greater ability are able to evaluate more adequately the dangers of a situation and are

---

[*] From *The Gifted Child Grows Up*, by Lewis M. Terman and Melita H. Oden. Volume IV, *Genetic Studies of Genius*. Copyright © 1947 by Stanford University Press. Reprinted by permission of Stanford University Press.

less affected by generalized fears. They also speculate on a chain effect in which low achievement generates anxiety which in turn prevents greater achievement.

Lewis' study on the characteristics of very superior children discloses a certain amount of maladjustment inferred from the BPC Personal Inventory and ratings of personality traits by teachers. As a group they show a superior adjustment and emotional stability. "The majority are very normal children making normal adjustments and there is no evidence here that abnormality or queerness is the typical characteristic. There is maladjustment to be sure, but it appears evident that their very superior ability has enabled them to adjust, in the majority of cases, to an educational system which we know neglects them" (Lewis, 1943, p. 309). Included in the maladjustment that was inferred from teacher ratings was a larger proportion of children with the highest intelligence quotients. Of the ten children with IQ's of 160 and over, six were judged to be somewhat maladjusted personally, and one educationally. Maladjustment was inferred from assignment by teachers of several of the following characteristics (not just one) to an individual child: "goody-goody," cute, destructive, domineering, day-dreaming, cruel, immature, oversensitive about self, slovenly, quarrelsome, unhappy, moody, and the like (pp. 306-7). Of the twelve children scoring between 150 and 160 only two showed similar signs.

Mensh (1950) has reviewed the literature on "Rorschach Study of the Gifted Child." He reports studies indicating that gifted children "on the average show good adjustment and only a very small per cent can be considered to be seriously maladjusted." When compared with a random group of adolescents, a gifted group tested by Davidson obtained high Rorschach scores in traits that show (1) "superior capacity to do abstract thinking, to generalize and to draw conclusions," (2) "possession of a rich inner life, or creative ability, and of maturity in relationship to oneself," (3) "the capacity to do original thinking, and to create and to use new concepts," (4) "unusual responsiveness to outer stimuli." Gair is reported, however, as concluding from Rorschach testing, " 'Possibly the emotional development of the superior seven-year-old children does not keep pace with their intellectual development' " (Mensh, 1950, pp. 10-11).

The observation of asymmetrical development parallels the comparison of physical with intellectual growth. It supports an old belief that the gifted child is a child first and a gifted mind second, and underlines Hollingworth's observation: "It is not realized that the child will actually remain in the period of immaturity as long as (or even perhaps a little longer than) the mediocre do, being simply superior to the latter at every point in the course of development *and also at maturity*" (Hollingworth, 1926, p. 162). To Professor Hollingworth this was a sign of superiority but not of precocity. The assumption of an all-round precocity is what leads to erroneous evaluations of the gifted child's conduct and emotional development.

SOCIAL DEVELOPMENT

Studies of gifted children apparently agree that intellectually gifted children seek out companions who are somewhat older and closer in intellectual maturity to them than are their own contemporaries. Terman assigned his group a "sociability" score based on play interests. The gifted group scored lower than the control group in selection among play activities judged to be non-social, mildly social, and markedly social. They also scored lower on the basis of preferences between relatively quiet and relatively active games. Terman attributes this in part to greater interest of bright children in mildly social games like anagrams, puzzles, chess and checkers which are unpopular with average children because of their intellectual demands. In part, he notes the handicap of accelerated children in more strenuous competitive sports (Terman, 1925, pp. 385-439). He notes also the possession by gifted children of far more favorable social preferences and social attitudes than characterize average children (*Ibid.*, pp. 491-92).

Terman's studies of social adjustment in adult life are favorable to the gifted. Incidence of marriage and age at marriage were about the same in 1940 as for the general population but considerably above that for the total college-educated population (Terman, 1947, pp. 224-30). The 1955 follow-up confirmed the earlier findings. At average age forty-four, 93 per cent of the men and 90 per cent of the women were married. The proportions of marriage are about the same for the gifted as for the total American population, but by middle age more college educated gifted women have married than have the women college graduates of comparable age in the total population (Terman, 1959, pp. 132-33).

Fertility rates are comparable to the general population. The average number of children per couple was 2.4 for the gifted group and 2.8 for the average family. The difference, however, may eventually be lessened or cancelled since, at the time of the study, two-thirds of the gifted women or wives of gifted men were of child-bearing age under forty-five, 10 per cent were in the thirty-five to thirty-nine age group, and 2 per cent were under thirty-five. The mean IQ of the children, interestingly, at 132.7 is considerably below the mean (151.6) of the gifted parents (*Ibid.*, pp. 139-41).

As might be expected a high proportion of the gifted married spouses who had a college education ranked high on the occupational scale. An effort was made to determine how happily married the gifted group was. On the basis of a schedule devised for the purpose, 85 per cent of the gifted group were estimated to be above average in this respect, as compared to 65 per cent for the total population (*Ibid.*, p. 136). While the tests could not be standardized on a large population, Terman interpreted the results in 1940 also to show "a slightly higher level of marital happiness, and a no less satisfactory sexual adjustment among gifted subjects than among less-gifted subjects" (Terman, 1947, p. 262). Divorce and separation figures for the total population are hard to secure and interpret, but Terman finds less divorce in the record of his gifted group (1959, pp. 133-34; 1947, pp. 224-30).

Mann (1957) undertook a study of children at the Colfax Elementary School in Pittsburgh to determine the pattern of friendships of children selected for special "workshops." Gifted children at Colfax spend approximately half the day in selected groups and half the day with unselected groups of age-mates. Mann discovered that gifted children tend to play with other gifted children after school. In sociometric tests, bright children choose and reject other bright children; other children choose and reject other children from their own group. The bright children and the unselected group tend to ignore each other.

Williams (1958) attempted to correlate intelligence with social acceptance, taking a population of almost nine hundred children, including 117 gifted children in three elementary schools in suburban Connecticut. To the group she administered achievement tests in order to secure a measure of academic performance, the California Test of Personality to measure social adjustment, and the Classroom Social Distance Scale (Cunningham, 1958, pp. 401-6) to measure acceptance by individuals of the class and by the class of individuals. She discovered "no appreciable differences in intelligence between high- and low-acceptees." Over four-fifths of the children who were well accepted by their classmates were achieving within or beyond what may be expected, but over three-fifths of the low-acceptance group were achieving below expectancy. She concluded that schools should make a greater effort to fulfill the needs of gifted children by strengthening their acceptability to other children, and thereby improving their performance. The high-acceptance children also extended greater acceptance *to* the group, and showed "greater permissiveness and a wider variety of channels for learning." They were more consistently satisfied with their interpersonal relationships.

Of interest are some of Williams' related observations. She inferred from her study that "all were powerfully concerned with themselves as children, not as special children"; that, like other children, they seek to use their body successfully, to love and to be loved, to be worthy members of the peer group. "It seems reasonable to conclude, then, that those engaged in seeking better opportunities for our gifted children might with profit look to the child first, and only subsequently to his gifts" (Williams, 1958, p. 220).

Other studies are either equally favorable to gifted children or they are non-committal. Lessinger and Martinson (1961) report that exceptional students at both junior and senior high school levels display accelerated personal and social maturity. They believe these young people may find more difficulty in peer group affiliation because of differences in maturity. Sheldon (1959), investigating isolation as a characteristic of highly gifted children under twelve years of age, concludes that isolation is a function of home and school factors, and not necessarily a concomitant of high intelligence. D. C. Smith (1962) is critical of many comparisons between bright and normal children because they confound the effects of socio-economic, educational, religious and other differences. By matching adolescent students for class, chronological age, sex, religion, and national background, he found that the only clear difference was a higher prevalence of independence and dominance among the gifted. Teachers, however, perceived the gifted as " 'more aggressive and rebellious.' " Smith concludes that no "inevitable associations" have been demonstrated between high IQ and personal-social characteristics.

Problems of social adjustment among accelerated children are often used to justify programs of non-acceleration. Proponents of acceleration, like Terman, note the temporary handicap to boys especially, but they argue the advantages of the "calculated risk" because of other values they attribute to acceleration. While the bright child may be somewhat precocious socially, it is idle to expect physical and emotional development as advanced as intellectual precocity evidenced by an IQ of 150 or more. Social acceptability is more likely to be pegged to physical and emotional maturation than to mental age alone.

Because physical competition is so much a part of the boy's establishment of a masculine role, acceleration is likely to prove a serious handicap in the crucial school years (a time of rapid physical growth) when two years' difference in size and strength may be quite marked. Until late in college, the disparity in physical development is likely to continue. Social adjustment and establishing the appropriate sex role in our culture are likely to suffer.

PERSONALITY TRAITS

Many studies have been performed to identify personality traits of the gifted. Many listings have been made, also, on a basis of the subjective feelings of writers. In both cases the reader of the study often feels that the investigator managed to find what he was looking for in the first case. The gifted child is found to have all the traits that one's mother assigns to him in her fondest dreams.

One of the more objective studies is an investigation by Simmons into the suggestibility of children "of exceptionally high intelligence quotients." Simmons (1940) found the bright children more resistive to suggestion. They were less easy to bend, slower to adopt opinions, and more tenacious of opinions once adopted. They proved less susceptible to influence and suggestion than individuals nearer to the norm in intelligence.

As part of their study of the winners ("scholars") in the National Merit Scholarship Corporation competition, Holland and Stalnaker (1958) sought out the values of the scholars. The young men set their sights on performance and pre-eminence: doing a good or necessary job, attaining a position of prominence or managerial responsibility. They showed little concern for either emotional or economic security, and they were not much interested in marriage, family, or aesthetics. The young women in the group showed a pattern closer to that of other females than to their male counterparts. They gave most weight to marriage and family life and placed lesser weights on work values, achievement, and vocational success. They showed little concern for the "self-centered values desired by males"—independence, recognition, and leadership.

A study by Ausubel (1951) on "prestige motivation" sought to determine the effects of competitive situations upon gifted children. Ausubel discovered that gifted children vary considerably in the relative degree of responsiveness to incentives concerning personal prestige or recognition. The students who are strongly motivated by considerations of personal prestige enjoy the competitive situation more. Children whose motivation is intrinsic (low concern for personal prestige and recognition) respond less to the competitive situation. No statistically significant differences were found between the high-prestige (competitive) children and the low-prestige (non-competitive) children in teacher or parent ratings on competitiveness or scholastic achievement. There was also a zero correlation between teacher ratings of competitiveness and cooperativeness. Ausubel finds "high prestige motivation not necessarily incompatible therefore with cooperativeness in group enterprises."

Drews (1957) asked the 150 gifted junior high school students in her study to furnish self-ratings. As a group, she reports, they seemed to be sure of themselves, rated themselves above average on ability, and chose higher level occupations than their average classmates. She notes "a built-in level of confidence, based on the reality of school grades and other comparisons with peers."

A considerable number of studies have assembled parent and teacher responses on the personality traits of gifted children. These responses tend to be quite saccharine, but they have one value in particular. They help dispel the notion that intellectual giftedness carries with it negative traits, and they purport to show, instead, that gifted children are responsible, altruistic, socially conscious, modest, creative, adventuresome, and sociable. Other characteristics attributed to the gifted are common sense, originality, a desire to know and to excel, self-confidence, a sense of humor, truthfulness, prudence, conscientiousness and leadership (Miles, 1954, p. 1005). Generally speaking, the gifted are less boastful, they cheat less, and they are more trustworthy (Terman, 1925, pp. 485-517). They are not considered especially forward, domineering, egotistical, or self-willed (Miles, 1954, p. 1005). They have a keen sense of personal responsibility; they are honest and resent injustice (Philadelphia, 1950, pp. 10-11). Hildreth (1938), seeking teacher notations on personality characteristics, found five times as many favorable notations for the gifted as the control group, and five times as many unfavorable comments on the controls. "Sense of humor," "willingness to face difficulties," "more independent and self-assured" were some of the favorable descriptions noted frequently of gifted children.

In considering teacher attitudes toward "gifted" children, it is important that terms be defined. Getzels and Jackson (see Chapter 5) distinguished between high IQ and high-creative youngsters in a private high school with an intellectually superior population. There was remarkably little overlapping of memberships between the high creative and the high IQ groups, but both groups did equally well on achievement tests. The high IQ group was judged to be more conforming to parent and teacher values; the high creative group indicated less conformity and considerable cynicism with respect to values held by adults. Particularly interesting is the ranking of students according to teacher preference. Without knowing how these students had scored on the two types of tests, teachers placed the high IQ's first, the students in neither high group second, and the high creatives last (Getzels and Jackson, 1962).

An interesting sidelight on moral values is thrown by Boehm's study (1962) of the relationship of moral development with respect to religion, social class and mental ability. Her test population consisted of 237 children in public and parochial (Catholic and Jewish) schools in Brooklyn. Using two of Piaget's stories and two original stories to reveal moral judgments, Boehm found that mental differences influence development of moral judgment but that social class membership is also critical. In general, middle-class children were able to make moral judgments earlier than working-class children. While brighter children in both class groups made moral judgments earlier, the differences between the gifted and average children were significantly greater in the middle- than in the lower-class group. Since practically all studies of gifted children reported in the pages of this volume feature a predominance of higher socio-economic families, the alleged superiority in moral values of gifted children may reflect differences in family background more than they do differences in intelligence.

ACADEMIC ACHIEVEMENT

Two important generalizations can be made from the studies of scholastic performance of the gifted. First, the high IQ group as a whole have superior academic records; second, their records in school at all levels do not exceed average performance to the same degree that their intelligence score exceeds the mean. The latter may reflect the uneven development of the intellectual prodigy.

One of the measures used frequently is that of grade placement. Terman found an average *progress* quotient of 114, meaning one year's acceleration in seven. Roughly speaking, the gifted were one year advanced in elementary school and two years in secondary school. With a reduction in acceleration as a school policy in the later 1930's and 1940's, it is conceivable that this quotient is further reduced. The progress quotient of 114, of course, appears to be a poor correlate of an intelligence quotient of 140 or higher, but the social, physical, and emotional development of the gifted would scarcely warrant greater acceleration than that which Terman discloses—and Terman (1954a) himself asks for nothing greater. Witty's study of *One Hundred Gifted Children* (1930) estimated an average progress quotient close to Terman's—116.

Scores on standardized achievement tests more closely approximate the IQ. Particularly in verbal areas there is a close relationship between the average IQ of 151.6 and the "subject quotient"—language usage 146.2, reading 145.3, spelling 140.2. Perhaps nothing more is revealed than the verbal loading of the intelligence test. Arithmetic quotient at 138.5 is not far behind (Terman, 1925, p. 295). On a general information test the gifted children do even better than in school subjects, probably due, says Terman, "to the fact that a child's stock of information is more dependent upon intellectual initiative and less upon formal school instruction" (*Ibid.*, p. 304). Apparently the child realizes his potential without placement at the level of his mental ability. The ten-year-old with an IQ of 150 would seem to achieve at the fourteen- or fifteen-year-old level in academic areas and general information (Achievement Quotient 140 to 150) while remaining with children of ten, eleven or twelve (Progress Quotient 114). Miles (1954, p. 999) reports studies attesting to superior performance in debating, history, composition, literature, grammar, general science, geography, civics, reading, and arithmetic. Bright children show their superiority most in areas requiring "verbal comprehension, usage and formulation" while they perform closer to the average in less intellectual pursuits such as physical training, sewing, penmanship, and industrial arts.

Still another agreement is in the area of individual differences. Profiles on achievement tests show performance as uneven, but not more so, than may be found in more typical cases. The difference lies in the generally higher level of the profile as a whole. "The score disparities in the various school subjects are similar and the gifted are no more one-sided than average children" (Miles, 1954, p. 1002). As a result, we may expect bright children to show strengths and weaknesses and to encounter difficulty at times within one or more areas of learning.

All, of course, is not a bed of roses. Terman found a considerable group of "non-achievers," and Lewis is concerned because so many children in the top one thousandth (99.9 percentile) on IQ tests fall below the top decile (under the 90th percentile) in elementary school subjects. He sees a "severe indictment of our present set up in the elementary school that less than half of these exceedingly able students . . . are obtaining scores in the top decile." More serious is the fact that many fall in the lower half of the academic distribution. Lewis' subjects with IQ scores of 145 and over seem to have achieved very little more than those in the range from 125-144 (Lewis, 1943, p. 308).

As might be expected, reading ability is developed early. In both Terman's and Witty's group from one-third to one-half of the children had begun to read before entering school. "Reading," says Miles (1954, p. 1003), "is the favorite pastime of the gifted children as well as their best-liked and easiest school subject." Gifted children as a whole read more and their reading interests range more widely than those of average children. They read more science, history, biography, travel, folk tales, informational fiction, poetry and drama, and they read less adventure, mystery, and emotional fiction proportionally (Terman, 1947, p. 39). While keeping a two-month reading record for his bright children, Terman discovered a volume of reading more than twice that of a control group. Terman calls the majority "inveterate readers." Boys read considerably more adventure stories than girls, and girls read far more stories of home and school life. Bright children of both sexes read more non-fiction than other children of the same age. Girls were more homogenous in their reading tastes than boys (Terman, 1925, pp. 447-49).

More recent studies show less favorable findings concerning the reading of bright children. Abraham (1957) reported that gifted children *can* read better and *do* read more but that their reading tastes are "limited, trite or poor." Goldberg (1958) cites a study by Kirshner in New York City junior high schools confirming this judgment: "They liked to read, but would not voluntarily tackle more difficult books than those read by average students." A need for guidance and direction of potential seems to be indicated.

In general bright children show a positive attitude toward school (Terman, Hollingworth, Jenkins, Sumption, Hildreth, Drews). It would be surprising if they did not, since the school, of all institutions, fosters most their special talents. Bright children relinquish quite early childish aspirations to be an airline stewardess, a truckdriver, or a movie heroine in favor of occupations that depend upon considerable years of schooling. Nor are they impervious to pressures in the culture which push in the direction of academic preparation. Drews (1957) reports, for example, three out of four gifted boys in junior high school aiming toward careers in science and engineering, while only 15 per cent of their less gifted classmates had such amibitions.

PLAY INTERESTS

In their play children tend to be children although some qualitative differences do appear when the play interests and activities of bright children are studied. Similarities to average children are greater than differences in studies reported by Terman (1925) and by Lehman and Witty (1927). Both Terman's "thousand" and Lehman and Witty's fifty matched pairs show the same interest in a wide diversity of active, social games. In general, boys like boys' games and girls like girls' games although Terman found that his girls from age eight to twelve were somewhat more masculine than the average in their play interests. Earlier in this chapter it was noted that gifted children showed a somewhat greater interest in quiet, intellectual games. Terman (1947, pp. 32-33) points out that this "does not necessarily mean the gifted are more inclined to be solitary; it may only mean that they are more resourceful in amusing themselves." Hollingworth (1926, p. 135) notes that bright children in the IQ range of 135-145 have the usual play interests, but that in the group scoring over 170 interests tend to be uncommon and children have trouble finding playmates with similar interests. In general bright children often spend as much time in play as do average children; their play time exceeds their reading and study time combined.

Some differences show up, however, in the range of 130 and up. Terman, testing play knowledge (information about games), assigned the gifted a "play quotient" of 136, meaning that the bright ten-year-old knew as much about games as the average thirteen-year-old. These children, as reported in other studies, know many games with an intellectual content, such as chess and bridge; they care less for sensori-motor games without a "score." They show interest in complicated, competitive games and in outdoor sports. Often problems arise because their interest in and knowledge about games outruns their physical growth and ability to compete with older children whose games they wish to share. Acceleration in the maturity of their play interests marks the bright children.

One of the intellectual play interests of children is found in the collections they keep. They usually manage twice the number of collections that other children do. Their collections tend to be larger in size and more scientific in nature.

Terman (1947, pp. 455-83) compares differences among various types of interests. In general, differences between bright and average children tend to be very great in intellectual interests, one-third as great in social interests, practically zero in activity interests. The correlations between these interests and achievements are in the same order, showing greatest comparability of intellectual interests with scholastic performance. Terman notes that the gifted are more enthusiastic about things in general. Lewis (1947, p. 304) found "no abnormality of interests for the group as a whole." Their tastes, however, were more extensive, and there was marked superiority in their interest in reading and music.

OCCUPATIONAL ADJUSTMENT

Drews' observation (1957) that three out of four of the gifted adolescent boys she studied were dreaming of careers as scientists or engineers has already been quoted. Her more recent work confirms Terman's and Hollingworth's earlier findings. Terman's experimental subjects "showed greater preference for professional and semi-professional occupations, for various kinds of public service, and for the arts" (Terman, 1947, p. 32). Terman cautions on the frequency of unrealistic ambitions held by pre-adolescents. Compared with the occupations of their fathers, however, "the ambitions of the control group were, intelligence considered, much more extravagant than those of the gifted" (*Ibid.*).

Hollingworth (1926), too, notes the lofty but often unrealistic ambitions of children in general. Lofty ambitions are not peculiar, then, to the gifted, but two desires appear among them which are rarely expressed by less gifted children. One is to be a learned person—zoologist, astronomer, mathematician; the other is to become a minister or a missionary. Hollingworth cites studies by Whipple and Coy, however, to document her thesis that not all bright children seek careers worthy of their ability—the child with IQ 130 who wished to be an electrician, and the 141 IQ who wanted to be a stenographer. Her conclusion:

> In general, the results of these studies suggest that the gifted need to have provided for them plenty of information about the various kinds of intellectual work which are needful in their day. Many of these children list ambitions which are below their capacity. (*Ibid.*, p. 140)

Conceivably, Drews' different findings indicate that more of this information is now being provided than in Professor Hollingworth's day.

Actually, the problem is of a different sort. It has been shown that children who score well on intelligence tests are scholastically well motivated and oriented toward professional preparation. The more important problem may be that of young people with high ability whose poorer motivation results both in lower IQ scores and ambitions for other vocations. Perhaps more adequate information need not be presented to the high IQ's. It may be that more adequate information and opportunity being presented to seemingly moderate IQ's may result in greater motivation toward higher occupational levels, scholastic effort, and consequently higher scores on intelligence tests.

As might be expected, the strongly motivated high IQ's do well in occupational adjustment. Terman (1959) lists formidable achievements as the total accomplishment of his group both in their thirties and forties. Median earned income at forty-four (1954) was $9,640, with 25 per cent of the group earning over $25,000. Occupational distribution follows:

Occupation	*Per Cent*
Professional	45.6
Managerial	40.7
Retail, clerical, skilled labor	10.9
Agriculture	1.6
Semi-skilled labor	1.2
Slightly skilled, unskilled	....
(*Ibid.*, p. 81)	

Of 329 men in the professions in 1955, 78 were lawyers, 57 members of college or university faculties, 55 engineers, 40 physicians in private practice, 27 chemists and physicists, 26 authors or journalists, 32 school administrators and teachers below college level, 7 clergymen, 7 geologists, 8 architects, 6 economists and 11 miscellaneous (*Ibid.*, p. 75). In general, income (as of 1954) correlates well with education except for the Ph.D.'s, whose median income of $8,917 trails the entire B.A. group at $9,850, the M.B.A.'s at $11,430, the LL.B's at $15,250 and the M.D.'s at $22,000. Those having only a high school education were earning $8,167 (*Ibid.*, pp. 81-95). A large number listed in *Who's Who*, authors of scholarly publications, and award winners are to be found in the Terman records.°

Not all of Terman's subjects are successful. Of 730 gifted boys, Terman and Oden compared the 150 most successful with the 150 least successful. The differences will be discussed in later treatment of achievement and motivation. While averaging just 3 IQ points below the high achievers, the low group had consistently less success in school, social adjustment, personality development, and occupational performance. Only 17 per cent of the low group were in the professional category as compared to 70 per cent for the high group (Terman, 1947, Chap. 23).

At the present point in the maturation of Terman's population, however, a note of scepticism begins to appear. In an article entitled, "The Vanishing Genius: Terman and the Stanford Study," Kreuter (1962) expresses a disillusionment she claims to find in Terman's own writings. She points to a gradual reduction in Terman's use of the word "genius" and to his increasing respect for the part environment plays in the development of ability. In contrast to the rosy statistics already presented, she points out that none of Terman's subjects has yet achieved distinction in the fine arts or more than moderate achievement in literature. Of more than one thousand potential "geniuses," there are only "several dozen" national figures and eight or nine internationally known personages at age forty-five to fifty. Finally, she concludes that Terman presents no evidence that the moderate achievers in his group are less intelligent than the high achievers.

Terman, like most investigators in the field, based research on characteristics of his population on an IQ computed at an early age in the child's life. Characteristics so identified cannot be more valid than the IQ as a measure of intelligence. Nor can the accuracy of the list be greater than the actual relationship between extraordinary achievement and "intelligence" at age ten or eleven, defined and measured as it was. Let us turn these statements around to underline their importance for education. Prediction of adult success on the basis of IQ continues to be extremely hazardous because (1) there are the many reasons (see Chapter 3) for being sceptical of the meaning of an IQ score; (2) it is not yet established that intelligence as currently measured is an important criterion in outstanding performance; (3) we are not at all sure what addi-

---

° From *The Gifted Group at Mid-Life*, by Lewis M. Terman and Melita H. Oden. Volume V, *Genetic Studies of Genius*. Copyright © 1959 by Stanford University Press. Reprinted by permission of Stanford University Press.

tional factors are necessary for high achievement. These reservations also mean that many of the characteristics listed may define Terman's (and similar) population(s), but that they do not necessarily portray the "gifted."

Because of this scepticism, research on characteristics of the gifted is being continued. New research is frequently based on more sophisticated ways of identifying a gifted population, on interest in new variables, and on more objective and sometimes more searching measures.

SUMMARY

Certain generalizations can be made from the many descriptive studies of intellectually gifted children. The outstanding trait is mental superiority, and this manifests itself in intellectual precocity, better-than-normal achievement in school, play interests that are seasoned with an intellectual content, playmates who are nearer their mental age than their chronological contemporaries, and occupational interests that capitalize upon their intellectual gifts.

Second, no "law of compensation" seems to apply; children do not make up for being bright by inadequacy in other areas. They are somewhat superior physically and they enjoy better-than-average physical and mental health. Although not without emotional problems, some of which may be related to their intellectual superiority, they are not "to madness near allied." Social adjustment, as measured by school friendships, marriage, and family life, is again above the average for our gifted population. Finally, they do not end up as failures ("early ripe, early rotten"), but do well in college and in adult life.

Third, they are still children. Their interest in play is not less than that of average children. They read books similar to those average children read—only more, and some that are "better." They want to be liked by their peers, and they apparently enjoy working and playing with youngsters of other levels of mental ability. They have the same emotional needs to love and be loved.

Fourth, their development is often asymmetrical. Their mental superiority is not matched in degree by physical, social, or emotional precocity. Problems may arise if assumptions of all-round maturity stem from advanced mental development. Herein lies a real danger of acceleration in school.

Fifth, intellectually gifted children seem to come from all kinds of family backgrounds. There is some degree of concentration in particular ethnic, religious, socio-economic, and occupational groups, but no group fails to produce some children who are extremely gifted. One guess is that the different proportions in different groups may result from differences in the environment, and particularly in the value patterns in the home.

These generalizations may, if held in mind, be helpful in identifying gifted children. They may also be of service in planning programs and conducting challenging and satisfying learning experiences for the gifted.

Chapter 3

Intelligence and Intelligence Testing

Whatever exists at all exists in some amount.
To know it thoroughly involves knowing
its quantity as well as its quality.

—E. L. Thorndike

Perhaps no measure used in education is more venerated or more pro-faned by the public than the IQ. On the positive side, this attitude reflects a readiness to accept a range of differences in intellectual ability and the possibility of measuring these differences. On the negative side, an unquestioning, almost idolatrous, attitude toward the measure reflects popular misunderstanding of the limitations of existing tests of mental ability.

It may be that the measure finds widespread acceptance simply because the need for such a measure is so great. Somehow, ability has to be identified and evaluated if education is to be truly adapted to individual differences. A highly specialized culture is constantly in need of differentiating devices in order to match pegs of infinite diversity with holes that are equally varied. The need for predicting probable achievement cannot be met without identifying (1) the nature of abilities needed, (2) the conditions under which ability culminates in achievement, and (3) individuals who have the necessary native ability or the required developed ability at some specified time prior to the beginning of specialized training.

Into this vacuum of need a host of intelligence tests have rushed since Binet and Simon published the first useful measure in 1905. Buros (1961) listed 238 intelligence tests in his bibliography of tests in print

50

in 1961. These tests are used to admit or to exclude pupils from public and private schools. They are used for classifying and placing students and also for hiring, assigning, and promoting employees. They are used to place men and women in the armed forces. Scholarships are in many cases awarded on the basis of such tests. Counselors use test results as a guide in advising students, and experts in remediation use them to determine the possibility of success in their efforts. Researchers use test scores as a way to measure growth if intelligence is a variable in their studies, and they also test scores to standardize and compare experimental populations.

Behind this widespread use of intelligence tests lie a number of assumptions, many of which are controversial. The basic assumption is that the test measures "intelligence." Obviously intelligence cannot be evaluated directly. Intelligence is manifested through behavior by the subject. Too many individuals use or cite test scores without ever asking what kinds of abilities are being assessed and whether they represent a reasonable sample of all intellectual skills. Even if the test does give a good sample of mental abilities, other questions need to be asked. These include statistical significance and limitations of the score, effects of the subject's test-motivation, impact of the subject's membership in a particular subculture, and the effects of personality factors such as anxiety on the subject's test scores in general. Of further importance is the relationship between scores on a particular test and performance in the school or job situation for which the test is being used. These considerations will be treated in later pages of this chapter.

Whether tests are used well or not, however, reliance on them indicates a general belief in the pervasive effect of intelligence. There is almost universal acceptance of the assumption that superior mental ability is the foundation for all exceptional work, although there may be disagreement on the level of superiority needed. Research and empirical evidence seem to support at least in a general way Spearman's postulate of a general factor (g) of intelligence which is common to all kinds of special ability. Evidence is found in the obvious mental superiority, at least in moderate degree, of leaders in all fields of endeavor. While it is true that intellectually gifted persons may or may not have superior special talents, outstanding people in all fields do show more than average mentality.

As a result, examination of intelligence is a necessary part of any study of education for the gifted. A number of questions intrude themselves and these will be discussed in the following pages. One of these questions is, "What is intelligence?" since the answer to this question determines the kind of efforts needed to develop intelligence as defined in the response. A second question is, "How can intelligence be measured?" since the identification of intelligence in the bud may be essential to the proper direction of educational resources. A third question is, "How much intelligence is required for superior achievement in a given field?" since we may assume different kinds of qualities as the essential background from which different kinds of talents spring.

DEFINITIONS OF INTELLIGENCE

Over the years a number of different and even contradictory concepts of intelligence have been developed. These concepts run the gamut from intelligence as a unitary factor, through intelligence as a group of basic mental abilities, to intelligence as a short-hand term for the layman, covering a multitude of varying, uncorrelated abilities that might better not be grouped under a single heading. Opinion continues to differ also as to the extent to which intelligence is inherited or influenced by environment and whether it is stable or subject to change.

Definitions of intelligence are also varied. Some writers are rapturous in their description:

> Intelligence of a high order is mysterious, manifold, fast-moving, luminous, tantalizing, and incredibly beautiful, like aurora borealis on a cool September night. (Hersey, 1959, p. 12)

Some are practical in their orientation:

> Intelligence learns how to do and how to get what is wanted.
> (Hollingworth, 1926, p. 28)

Some analytic:

> . . . the aggregate or global capacity of the individual to act purposely, to think rationally and to deal effectively with his environment. It is global because it characterizes the individual's behavior as a whole; it is an aggregate because it is composed of elements or abilities which, though not entirely independent, are qualitatively differentiable. (Wechsler, 1958, p. 7)

Some in terms of learning capacity:

> Intelligence is the ability to learn acts or to perform new acts that are functionally useful. (Getzels, 1954, p. 18)

One widely used definition has been Stoddard's:

> Intelligence is the ability to undertake activities that are characterized by (1) difficulty, (2) complexity, (3) abstractness, (4) economy, (5) adaptiveness to a goal, (6) social value, and (7) the

emergence of originals, and to maintain such activities under conditions that demand a concentration of energy and a resistance to emotional forces. (Stoddard, 1943, p. 504)

Lorge indicates that there are four ways of looking at intelligence: (1) *Biologically*, as the capacity to adjust consciously to problems and situations in life. (2) *Statistically*, as an analysis of performance on tests; the relationships among test scores. (3) *Educationally*, as the ability to learn. (4) *Empirically*, as good behavior, or the responses to situations from the point of view of truth or fact (Lorge, 1941).

COGNITIVE ONLY?

Many authors add to cognitive ability the matter of drive or motivation. Hersey comments on Hollingworth's definition: "This is a proper emphasis. What is wanted comes first; the capacity to get it is secondary. Intelligence without desire is of no use to society" (Hersey, 1959, p. 5). Wechsler includes in his concept of intelligence the configuration of abilities, drive and incentive. "It would seem that, so far as general intelligence is concerned, intellectual ability as such merely enters as a necessary minimum" (Wechsler, 1958, p. 7). Again, "Intelligence is all this and yet something more (more than g). It is the ability to utilize this energy or to exercise this ability in contextual situations—in situations that have context and purpose as well as form and meaning" (*Ibid.*, p. 11).

A GENERAL ABILITY?

Before the turn of the century there was general agreement that intelligence was general and inherited. The Binet tests were developed in the early years of the century on this basic assumption. Galton, and later Spearman, built a somewhat new concept in defining intelligence as basically a general ability (Spearman's g) determining more than one-half of a person's intellectual powers upon which a growing proportion of specialized capacities (s) develop in adulthood.

For some fifty years Burt has been defending this tradition vigorously in his definition of intelligence as "innate, general, cognitive ability." In arguing against the concept of mind as having no discernible structure or mind as comprising unrelated specialized abilities, Burt points to evidence in neurology, biology, and statistics. He cites, almost without exception, "positive and significant correlations between every form of cognitive activity." He defends the hypothesis of *supplementary* specialized abilities by citing "*well-marked clusters of augmented cor-*

relations confined to similar forms of cognitive activities, and leaving significant residuals after the general factor was removed. . . . The unavoidable inference is that *both* a 'general factor' *and* a number of 'group factors' must be at work" (Burt, 1955, p. 164).

Arguing that intelligence is cognitive, Burt rules out concerns for drive or "mental force" in defining intelligence. He sees a contrast "between the capacity for adapting, guiding, or directing mental activities, by means of discriminative and integrative processes, and the capacity for responding promptly, actively, and energetically" (p. 166). In order to maintain a viable definition of intelligence, he supports Spencer's antithesis between mental mechanism and mental force. Burt's conclusion confirms his threefold hypothesis:

> that there is a *general* factor making for efficiency in all mental activities, that this factor is essentially *cognitive* or directive, and that the greater part of the individual variance found in this factor is attributable to differences in *genetic* constitution. (*Ibid.,* p. 176) *

THE SEARCH FOR SPECIFIC FACTORS

In his classic and successful efforts to dethrone faculty psychology, Thorndike sought to replace mystical concepts of mind and intelligence with operational definitions that would be measurable and subject to scientific analysis. A result was the "connectionist" or "associationist" division of intelligence into three types—abstract or verbal; practical, involving facility in manipulating objects; and social, involving facility in dealing with human beings. Breaking this down still further, Thorndike developed the CAVD tests which will be described later in this chapter. It is not surprising that Thorndike opposed combining scores on separate parts of the test, representing specialized abilities, into a single score. Such a score would represent a single, general concept of intelligence which he could not accept.

The significant, positive correlations which exist among the various components of the CAVD tests are taken by Burt to support the g theory. Others, the Thurstones in particular, drew different conclusions. They found support for a theory of primary mental abilities—the idea that intelligence is made up of many factors and that these cluster into groups which they named "primary mental abilities."

Much current opinion combines elements in these three basic points of view. Something of a general factor in intelligence seems to be ac-

---

* From "The Evidence for the Concept of Intelligence," by Cyril Burt. *British Journal of Educational Psychology,* November, 1955. Reprinted by permission of Methuen and Co., Ltd., publishers.

cepted. As a way of measuring it, the primary mental abilities theory appears to have fairly broad acceptance. In recent years methods have been devised to produce a single score as representing combined achievement on the Thurstone tests.

IS "INTELLIGENCE" SIMPLY A POPULAR TERM?

The existence of many separate factors has been pushed quite far by Guilford and his associates. Guilford (1959) has sought to build a "structure of intellect" which hypothesizes from 90 to 120 different factors, more than 50 of which Guilford purportedly identifies. Constructing a three-dimensional model, Guilford plots on one side the materials or content dealt with by the individual, on the second side the operations which he employs, and on the third side the products of his intellectual activity. Content is divided among verbal (or semantic) and two types of non-verbal—figural and symbolic. Within these content categories, five operations may be performed: cognition (knowing information), memory, convergent thinking, divergent thinking, and evaluation. Six kinds of products are recognized: units of information, classes of units, relations between units, patterns or systems of information, transformations, and implications. Three kinds of content times five kinds of operations times six kinds of products yield 90 possible factors. Adding another class, behavioral intelligence, to the dimension of content, Guilford posits a possible 30 factors more. As a result, Guilford has come to regard *intelligence* as simply a semi-popular term, relying upon single-factor scores to do justice in describing an individual.

TESTS OF INTELLIGENCE

Instruments for the measurement of intelligence may be viewed as a logical outgrowth of nineteenth century faith in the methods of the natural sciences. Goslin (1963), in his attempt to place standardized testing in a "social perspective," provides a capsule history of test development. He regards a growing awareness of the possibility of measuring intelligence and the development of probability statistics in the last century as necessary foundations. To Galton he attributes both the concept of a continuous range of widely varying intellectual ability in the human species and contributions to statistical methods. In the latter he cites Galton's introduction of measurement in terms of deviations from a norm and his understanding of correlation later developed further by Pearson, his protege and colleague. Taken together, these contributions opened new vistas—the possibility of objective measurement of intelligence, the possibility of relating intelligence to achievement, and the ultimate possibility of using such measures for prediction. If successful, these efforts could achieve the goal, in Goslin's words, of determining "who should receive what kinds of training within the social system."

In the latter half of the nineteenth century a number of attempts were made to develop a reliable measure of intelligence culminating in the highly successful Binet-Simon test in 1905. Binet, in effect, made use of a sampling technique by posing to children problems requiring the use of abilities that represented intelligence to him. He hit upon a new idea, too, in arranging these problems in order of difficulty rather than in logical categories. As a result, persons administering the test had a simple scale for scoring test achievement. English translations were made by Goddard. In 1916 Terman published a revision which became known as the Stanford-Binet test. Terman held true to the fundamental conception of the original Binet scales, but he developed a new test with new items and a new scoring system. He introduced the idea of the Intelligence Quotient as a ratio between mental age and chronological age. For the first time specific instructions for administration and scoring were provided, and finally, Terman contributed to the test a set of norms based on a representative sample. The 1916 and 1937 editions of the Stanford-Binet have been used to classify an imposing number of American children. In 1960 a new edition appeared, substantially in the same format as its predecessors.

Binet and Henri, an associate, enumerated as functions of intelligence the following: the nature of mental images, imagination, attention, comprehension, suggestibility, aesthetic appreciation, moral sentiments, muscular strength, strength of will, motor skill, and visual judgment. Binet's conception of intelligence, says Freeman, "included mainly the following characteristics: ability to reason and judge well, to take and maintain a definite direction of thought, to adapt thinking to the attainment of a desirable end, and to be autocritical" (Freeman, 1955, p. 111). Later revisions of the Binet test adhered to the original ideas of the founder by giving heavy emphasis in the pre-school period to picture vocabulary, identifying objects by name, comparison and comprehension; to pictorial likeness and dislikeness, similarities, vocabulary, verbal absurdities, and abstract words at ages five to eleven; and from age twelve upward to vocabulary, absurdities, abstract words, proverbs, sentence building, and arithmetic reasoning. Less emphasis is given to manipulation of objects at all age levels, to problems of fact, to working with materials of concrete nature, to behaviors employing numerals.

Wechsler recognized the fact that the Binet test was overburdened with such items as vocabulary and abstract definitions. "It is for this reason," he noted, "that our scale is made up of performance as well as verbal items. An appraisal of general intelligence cannot be made on the basis of either alone" (Wechsler, 1941, p. 11).* Considerable use is made of the Wechsler Intelligence Scales for Children (WISC) and the Wechsler-Bellevue Intelligence Scale for Adolescents and Adults. As scales used in individual testing, these and the revised Binet have most acceptance as giving an accurate picture of intelligence. The Wechsler scales include tests on information, general comprehension, combined memory span for digits forwards and backward, similarities test, arithmetical reasoning, picture arrangements, picture completion, block design, object assembly, digit symbols, and vocabulary (an alternate item). Recognizing the "aggregate or global" quality of intelligence, Wechsler says, "The only thing we can ask of an intelligence scale is that it measures sufficient portions of intelligence to enable us to use it as a fairly reliable index of the individual's global capacity" (Wechsler, 1958, p. 14).** Wechsler attempts, too, to measure items Burt excludes from consideration in intelligence—"the subject's interest in doing the tasks set, his persistence in attacking them and his zest and desire to succeed" (*Ibid.*, p. 15).†

OTHER VIEWS, OTHER TESTS

Binet based his test on belief in intelligence as a general capacity. He was therefore less interested in significance of specific items per se than in the extent to which each part might measure the individual's general capacity. E. L. Thorndike and others differed from this position. They postulated not one intelligence, but many factors contributing to what we call intelligence. Thorndike's tests follow his own formulation of intelligence and center on four factors. The letters *C, A, V, D* in the popular name of the test each represent one specified kind of ability: *C*-sentence completion, *A*-arithmetic reasoning, *V*-vocabulary, *D*-following directions. Thorndike regarded these four as representing not the totality of intellectual abilities but a significant sampling of them (Thorndike, 1926).

Finally another middle position is found in the group factor theory

---

* Wechsler omitted this distinction in later editions of *The Measurement of Adult Intelligence*.

** From *The Measurement of Adult Intelligence*, Fourth Edition, by David Wechsler (Baltimore, Md., William and Wilkins). Copyright 1958 by David Wechsler. Reprinted by permission of David Wechsler.

† Horrocks (1964) provides comprehensive discussions of the Binet (Chap. 6) and Wechsler (Chap. 8) tests that are useful in appraising the suitability of these two individual measurement tests in a given situation.

of the Thurstones (1948). The Thurstones started by assuming a number of different abilities, but they further postulated grouping of these abilities in families which they called primary mental abilities. Both the Chicago and SRA tests of primary mental abilities are based on the following primary factors:

Number (N)	Ability to do numerical calculation rapidly and accurately
Verbal (V)	Verbal comprehension
Space (S)	Manipulation of objects imaginally in space
Word Fluency (W)	Thinking of isolated words at a rapid rate
Reasoning (R)	Discovery of principle in series of numbers or letters
Rote Memory (M)	Ability to memorize quickly

Three other abilities were named but not included: perceptual ability, induction, and deduction. Statistical treatment of large numbers of test scores utilizing the Primary Mental Tests seem to bear out Thurstones' contention. The low-to-moderate correlation among the six parts of the test indicate that separate abilities are involved. That some correlation is discovered indicates some family resemblances among the factors. To Freeman this signifies that, "These particular factors—such as the six 'primaries'—may well be conceived of as particular manifestations of a *general* ability rather than as 'primary' abilities" (Freeman, 1955, p. 80).

An interesting application of this theory is to be found in the recently developed Hunter Aptitude Scales for Gifted Children. Davis and Lesser (1959) approached the problem of devising a test for admission to the Hunter College Elementary School which is devoted to the education of intellectually superior children. Since the inception of the school as an experimental unit in the education of the gifted, individually administered Binet tests had been used to select students. Dissatisfaction with the narrow basis for selection encompassed in the Binet, and concern over the established effects of coaching on a test which is public property led the administration of the Elementary School to seek a test which would override these two limitations. Acting under a grant from the U.S. Office of Education, Davis and Lesser developed a test for four-to-five-year-olds designed to test superiority in any one of five items: space, vocabulary, number, reasoning, and science. Intercorrelations among the five tests, as administered to 110 children, averaged .44. As a further indication of genuine differences among these five abilities, of 57 children taking one form of the test, eleven children scored among the highest seven in only one test, five scored in the top seven on two tests, two scored in the top seven on three tests and two in the top seven on four tests. Comparable results were found in the second form of the test. On the two forms thirty-seven children scored within the top seven on one or more tests. Of these thirty-seven, none scored in the top group on all five tests, only four did so in four tests, and only five in three tests.

On the basis of the tests, six high scoring children in each group were admitted to the Elementary School prior to taking Binet tests. Thirty other children were admitted to a control group on the basis of Binets alone. After admission the experimental groups were given Binets and averaged 132 as compared with an IQ of 153 for the control group. Before beginning the school year, the two groups were given the SRA Primary Mental Abilities Test. Despite the 21-point difference in Binet IQ's, the experimental group means were significantly higher than the control group means in the Space, Verbal and Reasoning tests. The control group mean was slightly higher only in the Number test. At the end of the year, which included some specialized experiences based on different aptitudes as indicated in the Hunter Aptitude Scale, the PMA was repeated and "again the experimental-group means are significantly higher on all except the Number test, on which the mean is significantly lower" (Davis and Lesser, 1959 pp. 23-24a).

Two conclusions can be drawn from this research. One is that coaching vitiates the results of the Binet when administered in a highly competitive setting where parents set a high premium on a test score which determines admission to a very selective school. A second conclusion represents a far more important finding, if warranted—that selection on the basis of high special capacities may be more significant than admission on the basis of a high level of general intelligence.

Additional research with young children supports the possibility of identifying separate intellectual abilities at a very early age. Meyers and others (1962), testing a large number of six-year-olds in the Middle West, were able to establish differences among children possessing the following abilities: hand-eye psychomotor, perceptual, linguistic, spatial reasoning, and immediate memory. Their explorations led them to conclude that appropriate studies may well discover "a rather large array of factors," and that "differentiation of abilities is already well advanced" by the age of six.

Because of the relative ease of handling a single figure, the IQ as a single measure continues to be popular and is not likely to be replaced soon. Warrington and Saupe (1959) point out:

Although some of the newer differential batteries may be experiencing deserved popularity . . . the development and use of the venerable tests of general mental ability, or, more simply, intelligence, continue at the usual rate. While any conflict may have been more apparent than real, it nevertheless appears that publishers of differential batteries, having been unable to supplant single-score tests, have decided to recognize their value. For example, Psychological Corporation (Differential Aptitude Tests) and Science Research Associates (Primary Mental Abilities) have devised methods for combining parts into single scores. (Warrington and Saupe, 1959, p. 15)

The very fact that all intelligence tests, except the CAVD, result in a single score reflects a belief on the part of test makers that there is some general factor in intelligence. This general factor, so posited, justifies in their view combining scores on different parts of a given test into a single summary score.

Differences among theorists as to the nature of intelligence and its measurement must of necessity be interpreted when applied to an educational program. Some implications of the foregoing points of view might be the following:

1. To some extent a general factor seems to be present in intelligence. This makes limited use of intelligence testing possible. It justifies seeking various kinds of talent in a reservoir of somewhat superior intellect. It also makes possible, to a point, the selection of bright students and is a means of dealing with them on the basis of intellectual similarities.

2. On the basis of all theories, considerable differences in the kind of intellectual superiority may be found among students of generally high intelligence. This consideration argues against setting a very high score on general intelligence tests as a criterion of giftedness while arguing for the search for various specific abilities of exceptional degree superimposed upon a picture of generally superior intelligence. The first implication indicates the possibility of utilizing similarities in order to facilitate education. The second implication suggests the limited extent to which similarity may be assumed. Particularity of interest and talent dictates variety in programming and individuality in educational approach even among those identified as generally gifted.

THE OBJECTIONS TO INTELLIGENCE TESTING

Later developments have also resulted in lessening the significance of intelligence test scores. Myers indicates a shift in point of view from "measuring potential or native capacity to that of measuring aptitude for future academic work" (Myers, 1959, p. 150). He describes the Scholastic Aptitude Tests and the College Ability Tests as "tests of developed ability."

This caution is well advised in view of the growing chorus of unfavorable criticism against tests and an unthinking interpretation of test scores. John Hersey's pamphlet, *Intelligence, Choice and Consent,* scores the inadequacies of group tests (on theoretical grounds) as having not enough " 'top' to differentiate reliably between various degrees of remarkable talent" and as committing other crimes in operation:

> Many a child goes through life labeled with an I.Q., figured not to the nearest five or ten points but to an exact digit, based on a single unnamed group test given at a very early age, perhaps on a day when the child was functioning well but perhaps not, perhaps in a carefully controlled group situation but perhaps not, perhaps by a skillful teacher but perhaps not, perhaps scored accurately but perhaps not. (Hersey, 1959, p. 11)°

Hersey questions the psychological validity of tests, too, with regard to the populations against which norms are established, the neglect of sex differences in setting norms, oversimplified ways of arriving at IQ's, emphasis on speed, and the assumption that the IQ as measured is stable. He is expressing in more literary terms doubts earlier expressed by psychologists as well.

Guilford, for example, maintains that "psychology and psychologists since Binet have taken a much too restricted view of human intelligence." He points out:

> Too commonly a single score is the only information utilized, and this single score is usually dominated by variance in only one or two factors. . . . The list of factors that is to be presented in this article should clearly demonstrate the very limited information that a single score can give concerning an individual, and on the other hand, the rich possibilities that those factors offer for more complete and more meaningful assessments of the intellects of persons. (Guilford, 1956, p. 267)

Getzels (1954) expresses increasing scepticism as to the value of a single intelligence test score. He believes we are moving toward multiple evaluations in order to select able leaders, including personality characteristics, and special artistic and social talents.

OTHER THAN INTELLECTIVE FACTORS

Edgar Doll, in a whimsical article, "The Four IQ's," adds three important dimensions to the intelligence quotient in seeking the constitution of high ability. These are *inner quest*—the individual's search for values which is reflected in his aspirations; the *ideal qualities*—traits of personality; the *innate quirks*—obstacles which lie between the individual and fulfillment of the *inner quest* (Doll, 1957). Maddox in England asserts:

> The practical consequence of taking test scores as the best measure of innate ability is that those who are not sophisticated enough to maintain the distinction between 'intelligence' and 'tested intelligence' may use 'innate ability' as a first and sufficient explanation of poor performance; whereas poor performance, particularly that of older underprivileged children in verbal tests, for example, may result equally from any one of the five factors listed by Eells. (Maddox, 1957, p. 174)*

The five factors cited from Eells (1951) are: difference in genetic ability, developmental factors, cultural bias in test items, test motivation, and test-work habits or test skills. The last three items are environmental and tend to penalize certain sub-groups in the culture. These sub-groups are specific ethnic cultures, lower socio-economic segments, and certain racial groups.

CULTURAL IMPACT ON TEST SCORES

Davis, Eells, and their collaborators have given particular attention to the cultural content of intelligence tests (Eells, 1951). They are concerned with administration of tests to culturally deprived children who have not been represented in the population upon which the test was standardized. Cattell (1958) in his "culture-free" test, and Davis and Eells in their test of general intelligence have attempted to reduce the cultural bias which seems to affect all tests.**

The Davis group points out that Binet validated his test against school achievement scores. Binet assumed that all children in his sample had the same cultural and social motivations since they all came from work-

---

* From "Nature-Nurture Balance Sheets," by H. Maddox. *British Journal of Educational Psychology*, November, 1957. Reprinted by permission of Methuen and Co., Ltd., publishers.

** Horrocks (1964) indicates culture-fair qualities of the Goodenough (Draw-a-Man) Intelligence Test, the Raven Progressive Matrices and the Leiter International Performance Scale as well as the Cattell and Davis-Eells Tests (pp. 271-96).

ing-class neighborhoods. Yet, the Davis committee, in its study, found substantial differences in upward-mobile values within the working class. Terman in his Binet revisions and Otis in the Army Alpha also validated their scores against school achievement. Otis selected only those problems which distinguish retarded pupils, and these youngsters are found overwhelmingly in lower socio-economic groups. Similarly, Binet, Otis, and Terman rejected "problems on which lower socio-economic groups are equal to or superior to the top socio-economic groups" (Eells, 1951 pp. 33-34). Davis considers other tests as well and concludes, "There has been no adequate research carried out to effect (a) the discovery of problems and symbols that are equally familiar and motivating to all socio-economic groups or (b) the discovery of the proportion of items that favor rural as compared to urban groups" (*Ibid.*, p. 37).*

Validation of intelligence tests against school achievement may fail to consider that school achievement depends largely upon traits of character rather than upon mental capacity—attention, drive, a positive attitude toward schooling, and a desire for success in the middle-class culture. Lack of this drive causes children of low socio-economic groups to do poorly in their school work (*Ibid.*). Tests using such validation, therefore, would seem to correlate with the requisite traits of character related to a middle-class culture rather than to mental ability which it is the purpose of the test to identify.

Davis felt sure that there must be youngsters who do not show up well on intelligence tests but who do have skill in solving problems that "suggest potentialities for further education if the school had broad enough goals to utilize talents of these kinds" (*Ibid.*, p. 43).

Ralph W. Tyler, a member of the Davis committee, suggests:

> We shall need to study the kinds of problems these children (lower class) attack; the ways in which they attack these problems; the respects in which their solutions are more or less appropriate; the ways in which the problems are symbolized by different children —whether in words or in other forms; and, eventually, to devise ways of testing for a wide range of problem-solving abilities, so that we can identify in children a more complete range of potentialities for meeting new situations, that is, abilities to learn. (Eells, p. 46)

ATTEMPTS TO DEVELOP A CULTURE-FAIR TEST

The challenge is to develop a test which can measure intelligence isolated from cultural influences. Because verbal ability is related to cul-

---

* Reprinted from *Intelligence and Cultural Differences,* by Kenneth Eells, Allison Davis, et al. by permission of The University of Chicago Press. Copyright 1951 by The University of Chicago.

tural factors, some efforts in this direction have used the nonverbal tests. The New York City Demonstration Guidance Project (Higher Horizons), for example, revealed a significant superiority in using the Wechsler non-verbal test to identify its population. Unfortunately, because verbal factors are so involved in intellectual giftedness, it has not been possible to develop a non-verbal test with high enough "ceiling." In 1964 the New York City Public Schools discontinued use of standard intelligence tests because of possible cultural bias and commissioned a test publisher to proceed with development of a new culture-fair test.

The Davis-Eells tests (1953) represent an effort to implement the point of view of its authors as already described. The tests are relatively new and as yet have not established their superiority over established tests with respect to neutralizing cultural differences. Several studies have been made but they are not encouraging.* One, carried out by Tate and Voss, tested 1,200 pupils, employing as subjects two classes each of children in urban and rural; 4th, 5th, and 6th grade; white and Negro schools in Pennsylvania and South Carolina.** Davis-Eells test results were compared with scores on the California Tests of Mental Maturity, both language and non-language forms. The Davis-Eells tests discriminated between white rural and urban more sharply than did either California test. The means of Negro sections were substantially below those for white sections, with the Davis-Eells differences falling between the differences of the California language (greatest differences) and the California non-language tests (least differences).

The intermediate test employed contains 62 items classified in four subtests: probabilities, money, best-way, and picture analogies. The test does not require reading but it is not limited to non-verbal or performance type items. It calls for responses to oral questions and pictured situations. An effort is made to avoid content in questions and pictures which would be more familiar to urban children of one socio-economic class than another. Items are excluded which, on logical grounds, are believed to discriminate against children from certain socio-economic backgrounds. An effort is made to equalize motivation by selecting content and pictures of interest to all children.

The test manual indicates that the tests were constructed to elicit "correct associations, the logical classification of concepts, the discrimination of crucial differences, the definition of analogous relationships, the draw-

---

  * Ludlow (1956), Altus (1956), and Coleman and Ward (1955) present negative evidence on the "fairness" of the Davis-Eells tests to lower class children.
  ** Rural Negro schools could not be found in Pennsylvania, resulting in 42 rather than 48 different groups.

ing of reasonable inferences, the organization of a problem into a meaningful pattern, the gaining of insight, and the mental activity of foreseeing a solution" (Davis and Eells, 1953).

The Davis-Eells test was deemed to measure some aspects of problem solving not measured by other tests. Tate and Voss after experimental use of the test, concur with Rosenblum, Keller, and Papnia (Rosenblum and others, 1955) that lower-class failures result not from unfamiliarity with test content but from "failure to make correct associations, discriminate crucial differences, connect elements of probability in a meaningful manner—in short, failure to abstract. The test did not tend to reveal a 'hidden intellectual potential' missed by other tests" (Tate and Voss, 1956, p. 385).

EQUAL POTENTIAL IN ALL GROUPS?

Starting from a set of assumptions apparently close to those of Davis, Bray explores the possibility that we are missing much potential in the reservoir of talent because of the cultural overlay that motivates some children and anesthetizes others. Let us, says Bray in his provocative little volume, *Issues in the Study of Talent* (1954), take whatever ethnic, cultural, or economic group which shows the highest proportion of young people with IQ's over 125. Understanding the impartiality with which nature distributes her favors, may we not assume that this maximum presence of high intellectual ability in a particular group ought to be matched by a similar percentage in every other group *given the same cultural advantages?* These same cultural advantages, obviously, are not limited to museum trips, books in the home library, and college degrees in the family, but encompass more important factors such as the values of the sub-culture.

Strodtbeck (McClelland, 1958, Chapter 4) draws on studies of the value systems of differing cultures in his research on social mobility and the differential achievement of first generation Italian and Jewish children born in the United States. He hypothesizes that the following make a difference with respect to eventual personal achievement: a belief in an orderly world as contrasted with a faith in "Destiny"—luck or fate; a willingness to leave home to make one's way in life; a preference for individual rather than collective credit for work that is done. As a *general* rule he finds the former set of values more characteristic of first or second generation Jewish families in America than in Italian families of similarly recent immigrant background. In comparing the two ethnic groups, Strodtbeck finds substantial differences in average achievement and relates this to typical value patterns. However, most revealing is his assertion that where Italian and Jewish families share the same values, differences disappear in the achievement of the two groups!

Identification of talent, as these two researchers explore the matter, seems not to be restricted to an "innate intelligence." Value systems, the sub-culture, and the pattern of motivation which the individual learns from his sub-culture seem to play an important part in realizing unusual potential.

THE TEST AS A "SELF-FULFILLING PROPHECY"

Goslin introduces still another caution in the use and interpretation of test scores. He points out that a child who does well on an aptitude or achievement test is likely to be given special instruction or encouragement while the child who does poorly is likely instead to receive attention which lowers his self-esteem. Through additional opportunities and a raised level of aspiration the high-scorer's chances of achievement are increased. As a result of negative reinforcement, the low-scorer's achievement motivation and subsequent performance are likely to be further reduced (Goslin, 1963, pp. 156-57).

UNEVEN DEVELOPMENT; UNSTABLE IQ'S

Another caveat in the use of intelligence tests arises from two factors disclosed by longitudinal studies. One of these is the uneven emergence of differential abilities encompassed in the term intelligence. The other is the relative instability of the IQ.

As we use intelligence tests to identify superior intellect, a number of sobering considerations are in order. One pitfall is implied in Nancy Bayley's studies with young children indicating considerable variation in each child's score as he grew older.

Bayley (NSSE, 1940) suggested four hypotheses to explain these variable rates in summarizing her work for the National Society for the Study of Education Thirty-Ninth Yearbook, Part II:

(1) Intelligence is fundamentally innate, but its growth is irregular because it is the resultant of numerous functions that develop both concomitantly and successively, each growing out of previously established abilities but developing in its own way.

(2) Although inherently stable, intelligence as measured is inconstant because the composition of the tests varies, stressing different abilities at different ages.

(3) Rate of increase cannot be predicted because it is variable.

(4) Variations in rates of mental growth are the result of differing

environmental influences, either beneficial or detrimental, which act on the growing organism differently at different stages of its development.

Or, the last assumption in combination with any one of the first three (NSSE, 1940, p. 30).

When intelligence tests are repeated within a short period of time, a certain constancy in scores is noted. Writing more recently, Bayley remarks, "This very stability of scores over certain short periods of the life span led to the assumption that intelligence is a basic entity which changes only by accretions and decrements in quantity with childhood growth, adult stability and senescent decline. . . . It is not a position held for long by those who have been actively engaged in studying the nature of intelligence and its growth" (Bayley, 1955, p. 805). Most pernicious has been the tendency of the uninformed to extrapolate either beyond or below the scores on the assumption that the IQ is a stable score. The Berkeley Growth Study and the Guidance Study records are cited by Bayley to show very low correlations between scores in infancy and scores at eight years of age. When scores of high school students (age 14 to 18) were compared with their scores as pre-schoolers, the correlation for boys was .67, for girls .34. She concludes that there is

> little hope of ever being able to measure a stable and predictable intellectual factor in the very young. I am inclined to think that the major reason for this failure rests in the nature of intelligence itself. I see no reason why we should continue to think of intelligence as an integrated (or simple) entity or capacity which grows throughout childhood by steady accretions. (*Ibid.*, p. 807)

Instead, Bayley sees a changing organization of mental factors. She believes that something akin to g appears soon after the second or third year so that by age five or six higher correlations with later test scores may be found. To explain this shift Bayley points to varied and complex factors that influence intellectual growth—inherent capacities for growth, the emotional climate in which the individual grows, and the material climate encompassing "opportunities for experience and learning and the extent to which these opportunities are continuously geared to his capacity to respond and to make use of them" (*Ibid.*, pp. 813-14).

On the opposite end of the age distribution, interesting findings are available with respect to continuing increases in intelligence in maturity. Terman and Oden disclose increments in their re-tests of the thousand persons they followed from childhood to middle age. During a twelve-year interval in which the subjects moved from their mid-thirties to their late forties, both the gifted subjects and their less gifted (on an average) spouses advanced half a standard deviation on the Concept Mastery test (Terman and Oden, 1959, p. 77). Owens, checking Army Alpha tests thirty-one years after their administration in World War I, also found a plus .55 SD increase. Finally, Nisbet in England, testing 141 graduates at average ages of twenty-two and one-half years and forty-seven years found a similar upscoring, concluding "that such persons do not give evidence of decline in test performance at least up to the later forties" (Nisbet, 1957, p. 190).

NATURE OR NURTURE

All the foregoing findings tend to reopen the question of heredity and environment as influences upon intelligence. Perhaps nothing is less exciting to experienced students in psychology and education than the old nature-nurture controversy which is forever being warmed up again and served anew. Yet, the devoted researchers who continue to cultivate what is just an old chestnut to many of their colleagues, occasionally throw new light on an old subject. The Thirty-Ninth Yearbook of the National Society for the Study of Education devoted two volumes to examination of new findings in the 1930's, and by and large reinforced earlier thinking. A strong minority viewpoint was expressed by persons reporting on studies at the University of Iowa concerning the effect of nursery school attendance on intelligence scores, but the large majority of writers in the Yearbook attempted to demolish a hypothesis of environmental influence. In general, they seemed to agree that intelligence is relatively unaffected by environment except where environmental differences are gross. The assumption is that the intelligence quotient is hereditary and relatively static, that whatever differences show up over a period of years are due to a function of testing, not to actual changes in intelligence.

Paul Witty differed sharply from this majority view in the Yearbook and expressed his point of view cogently again in the following year in *School and Society*. Witty points out, "Again and again, it has been shown that changes of large magnitude occur much more frequently than one would assume" (Witty, 1941, p. 153). He cites studies showing a shift of 20 or more points in 16 per cent of the cases rather than the one or two in one thousand that we might statistically expect. He also calls attention to the fact that longitudinal studies show a decreasing correlation between initial and re-tests as the time interval between the two increases. Here, environment seems to be having a very evident effect.

Nancy Bayley's previously mentioned studies with very young children illustrate the cumulative effect of environment. Testing children from one month to ten years, Bayley found among infants a small negative correlation between intelligence scores and environmental factors like the school achievement of the parents, social rating, family income, father's occupation, and social-economic status. But as the environment became more obtrusive and the child grew older there was a consistent increase in the correlations between the child's intelligence score and these environmental factors (NSSE, 1940, II, 12-13).

Lorge adds his support to belief in environmental influence on IQ scores. Although he indicates belief that IQ differences represent differences in genetic make-up of the individual, he recognizes environmental impact upon testing. "Intelligence," he says, "can never be measured directly. It can only be inferred from indirect observations of the performances hypothesized to be intellectual in origin. . . . Tests of intelligence measure a person's ability to deal with aspects of his environment in terms of values in his environment at the time and up to the time of testing. . . . Intelligence as measured by intelligence tests, therefore is operationally environmental, and only inferentially biological." Accuracy in measurement depends, moreover, upon rapport with the examiner, upon opportunity in the child's life to secure maximum benefit from an environment, and upon having lived in an environment "within the scope of the standardization of the instrument" (Lorge, 1941, p. 205).

All of this adds up to dissatisfaction on Witty's part with intelligence tests:

> It seems, then, that the intelligence test cannot fairly be said to be measuring "inborn" intelligence, for its results are highly modifiable at every age level. Moreover, as the interval grows, the unreliability of the scores increases. Accordingly, the IQ from an intelligence test appears almost useless, as has been pointed out, for individual diagnosis and prediction. (Witty, 1941, p. 155)°

Such a point of view seems to contradict that of Burt who insists that intelligence is an *innate* as well as a general, cognitive ability. "The evidence," he maintains, "indicates that at least 75 per cent of the measurable variance (based on carefully checked assessments) is attributable to differences in genetic constitution, and less than 25 per cent to environmental conditions" (Burt, 1955, p. 177). His British colleague, Maddox, could scarcely differ more directly:

> It seems that an environmental emphasis (which is more characteristic of America than of Britain), has come about, not as Burt

---

° From "Evaluation of the Nature-Nurture Controversy," by Paul Witty. *School and Society*, September 6, 1941. Reprinted by permission of the Society for the Advancement of Education, Inc.

suggests, because of changes in fashion, but because investigators have failed to produce convincing evidence about the genetic components of intelligence. . . . Interest in the nature-nurture problem has declined because investigators have been unable to frame experiments to settle their disagreements: the problem has come to be regarded as 'metaphysical' since hypothetical concepts such as 'innate ability' cannot be operationally defined. (Maddox, 1957, pp. 166-67) *

In order to by-pass the problem, Maddox indicates that American test constructors simply regard tests as work samples predictive of scholastic performance. "The crude dualism heredity *versus* environment has now given way to attempts to partition test variance into hereditary and environmental contributions" (*Ibid.*, p. 167). The problem is additionally complicated when one turns to exceptional children growing up in exceptional environments. Whatever may be true of ordinary children in ordinary environments, environmental effects in the case of children from underprivileged groups may be far different.

CREATIVITY AS A FACTOR IN INTELLIGENCE

In existing tests remarkably little attention has been given to recent concern with originality and creativity as factors in high intelligence. Research by Getzels and Jackson underlines this gap between new theory and current testing practice. Getzels and Jackson (1960a) set up experimental groups comprising 449 students in a Midwestern private secondary school, representing the school's total population. Standard intelligence test scores were compared with five creativity measures taken or adapted from Guilford and Cattell or constructed especially for the study. The creativity measures included word association, suggestions of uses for things, finding hidden geometric forms in more complex patterns, suggesting new endings for fables, and designing as many numerical problems as possible from sets of given information. The High Creativity group were defined as those with scores in the top 20 per cent on the creativity measures and they were compared with the High Intelligence group, comprising those with the top 20 per cent on the standard intelligence test. Two experimental groups were set up: a High Creativity group with scores in the top 20 per cent on the creativity measures but below the top 20 per cent in IQ, and a High Intelligence Group comprising individuals in the top 20 per cent of IQ's but

---

* From "Nature-Nurture Balance Sheets," by H. Maddox. *British Journal of Educational Psychology*, November, 1957. Reprinted by permission of Methuen and Co., Ltd., publishers.

below the top 20 per cent on the creativity measures. The High IQ group had a mean IQ of 150, the High Creative Group had a mean IQ of 127. School achievement means for the two groups were respectively 55.00 and 56.27—in favor of the lower IQ but higher creative group! Correlations between the five creativity measures and IQ ranged from 0 to .56.

Various inferences may be drawn from these statistics. One, creativeness is more closely related than intelligence to teacher approval and school achievement. Two, creativity is related to higher motivation. Three, intelligence may represent a threshold type of variable. Four, creativity is an important part of intelligence but it is not measured on the three instruments used—Binet, WISC and Henmon-Nelson. Number one is refuted by further findings in the study. If the inference is drawn that the creative youngster pleases the teacher more and therefore does better in school despite his lower intelligence score, this conclusion is denied by the data gathered as to teacher preference. Teacher preference ratings gave the high intelligence group a significantly greater edge over the high creatives. Another assumption, that higher motivation might account for the apparent "overachievement" of the high creatives, is similarly discounted by the lack of significance in differences of Need Achievement scores between the two groups.*

The third and fourth inferences seem more tenable. A variety of sources agree that high achievement in various fields depends upon intelligence scores well above average yet not in Terman's very superior or "near-genius" class. Special interest, specific abilities, and very strong motivation seem necessary for the individual of any ability beyond this "well-above-average" threshold, or floor, and it is of little significance just how far above the threshold the individual may be. Getzels and Jackson's research may support such an argument with respect to creativity. Creativity may be a more important factor than differences measured on conventional intelligence tests in accounting for very superior performance among persons who exceed the threshold.

There is a growing body of opinion to support the fourth inference, that creativity is itself a factor in intelligence. The Minnesota Studies of Creative Thinking in Early School Years conducted research similar to Getzels and Jackson's and reported similar results with children in grades one through six in the University of Minnesota Elementary School. Identifying high-creative and high-IQ children as did Getzels and Jackson, the research team headed by Torrance found "no significant differences between the means of the IQ and the Creative groups on any

---

* McClelland *n:Achievement* stimulus-pictures were used to measure this variable.

of the measures of achievement" (Torrance, 1960, p. 24). Replications of this study in other Minnesota schools have reinforced this finding.

Ways of defining creativity that are applicable in test construction are just now becoming available. Further refinement of the term is needed and measures need to be developed and then included in testing. Until that time, intelligence test scores may have to be regarded as incomplete and faulty with respect to creativity, an important manifestation of intelligence.

Guilford, looking at Binet's validation of his tests against school achievement, doubts the coverage by intelligence tests of creative ability. "Operationally, then, intelligence has been the ability . . . to master reading and arithmetic and similar subjects. These subjects are not conspicuously demanding of creative talent. The content of intelligence tests reveals little of obviously creative nature" (Guilford, 1950, p. 447).

ANXIETY AS ANOTHER SOURCE OF ERROR

Sarason (1960, pp. 265-68) indicates still another consideration necessary in interpreting test scores. In his study of anxiety in elementary school children, he notes variance in test anxiety exhibited by children. He points out that "the potentialities of the high-anxious child are not likely to be discerned by conventional testing procedures." The inferior performance of low-ability, low-anxious children is likely to be immediately apparent in a low score, but a child of high ability who is overanxious is likely to perform at a level of mediocrity which is simply ignored. Sarason says:

> These effects are perhaps least apparent when one tests the *bright but anxious* child whose absolute level of performance may be more than adequate (for example, his school grades and achievement-test scores may be well above average). When this child is compared to the bright but nonanxious child, we see more clearly the interfering effects of anxiety. (Sarason, 1959, p. 27)

SUMMARY: INTELLIGENCE TESTING AND ITS SIGNIFICANCE

In summary it may be well to note that the intelligence test measures far more than innate or developed ability. Much of what it measures is extraneous and obscures the subject's actual intellectual potential. The long listing offered by Goslin (1963, pp. 132-52) indicates the many factors impinging on a test score which becloud its meaning:

Innate Factors
  1. General ability
  2. Special inherited abilities
Background and Environment
  3. Cultural background
  4. Formal training
  5. Experience with similar tests
  6. General health
Personality
  7. Achievement motivation
  8. Interest in test problems
  9. Anxiety
Situational Factors
  10. Perceived importance of the test
  11. Morale of the individual
  12. Physical condition of the examinee
  13. Interference from the environment
  14. Influence of the tester
Test Demands
  15. Specific abilities required
  16. Speed of response required
  17. Misleading items
Random Variation
  18. Guessing
  19. Clerical errors.°

Since the tester is usually interested in measuring only items 1 and 2 and occasionally 3 and 4, note must be taken of some 15 extraneous factors which distort the meaning of scores that are derived.

There is considerable practical significance in what may seem to be a theoretical discussion to this point of intelligence testing. Current indications reveal a relative condition of "saturation" in identifying superior ability and motivating college attendance among culturally favored subcultures in our population. At the same time, *other* groups suffer an awesome loss of potential. In some upper income suburban areas the question may well be, "Why are so many children of indifferent ability being pushed toward college attendance?" while in underprivileged environments one asks, "Why are half of the college-capable graduates not going on to college?"

° From *The Search for Ability*, by David A. Goslin. Copyright 1963 by Russell Sage Foundation. Reprinted by permission of Russell Sage Foundation.

The socially important problem is inherent in the latter type of situation. More and more evidence is adduced to indicate a heavy cultural encrustation in various population pockets which prevents identification of youngsters of high potential. These youngsters will continue to be overlooked as long as intelligence tests are given undue weight and the limitations of the tests are not faced up to realistically. The ease with which an IQ may be used to separate the milk from the cream is all too tempting. Certainly intelligence tests have values in bringing strengths and weaknesses of individual children to the attention of teachers and parents. But it is just as certain that many children will be overlooked or wrongly typed if the score is accepted at face value. Accordingly scepticism is prescribed if:

(1) There is reason to expect cultural handicaps for any particular youngster or group of youngsters who are being tested

(2) Tests are not repeated frequently enough to account for uneven maturation of different intellectual factors that are included

(3) No measure of creativity is included

(4) Supplementary measurement of critical thinking is omitted

Finally, a last sceptical word should be expressed concerning the utilization of the test and test score. If scores are used for segregating groups, what implications are intended for the development of potential? Classification is no substitute for individualization. What each child can be is more important than what the mean of a segregated group is. Witty's conclusion remains remarkably valid:

> It is evident, then, that an acceptable criterion for "giftedness" must be sought primarily outside of provinces covered by the intelligence test. It appears that "giftedness" can be estimated only by observation of a child's behavior. The child whose performance is consistently remarkable in any potentially valuable area might well be considered gifted; he should be given the opportunity that his attainment warrants for nurture and continuous growth, but his development should not be predicted or his future attainment prescribed, except as increased growth necessitates adaptations and changes. (Witty, 1941, p. 156)

A last word of caution with respect to testing should be uttered. Witty's strictures on intelligence testing have already been cited. He advises the direction of effort toward development of each student's ability, rather than toward narrow identification alone. He apparently agrees with Sandburg that speed may be bred in the foal but that a dark horse often wins. McClelland approaching the problem from a somewhat different angle explains the danger of an approach which places emphasis on talent potential as the fixed attribute of a few. "Emphasis," he says, "should shift from identifying talent potential to studying the process by which talent becomes actual, by which it develops" (McClelland, 1958, p. 25). Putting all one's eggs in the basket of intelligence tests may be most inappropriate in a mobile society like ours where it is difficult to predict what values, abilities, and motives may be required.

Chapter 4

Identification of Exceptional Ability

Speed is born with the foal—sometimes.
Always some dark horse never heard of before
is coming under the wire a winner.

—Carl Sandburg

If ability could be developed simply by exposing the able to opportunity in a rich environment, there would be little need to fret about identifying high potential. Ability being present could seize upon opportunity and flower accordingly in time. In such a situation schools would have only to offer a wealth of challenge and a variety of stimulating learning experiences. The able youngsters would do the rest.

Unfortunately, this automatic development of talent is mere wishful thinking. We are concerned about potential that is not realized, about high level ability wasted in low level pursuits, about drab lives spreading out before people who might live more richly, and about unfilled needs in a society demanding more top level competences than are apparently at hand. One of the keys to the problem lies in early identification of young people with talents so that they may move ahead with the arduous preparation required in high level careers. Early identification may provide the motivation necessary for strenuous effort. Perhaps it can be used to level obstacles of a cultural, educational, or financial nature as well.

The efforts to identify and deal differently with gifted individuals in school runs counter to the American folklore of equality and brotherhood, at least on the surface. In our assertions that all men are equal, we often overlook the fact that all men are also different. Failure to identify young people with hidden but genuine potential may result in denying them the opportunity which is equal in its challenge to less demanding opportunities presented to less able contemporaries.

The democratic ethos does not require foregoing efforts to identify ability. It requires that we look below the surface and give full value to ability that may be submerged in unequal environments. The Rockefeller Brothers Fund report on *The Pursuit of Excellence* states well the issue of democracy in the identification of students with exceptional ability:

> First, we must not make the mistake of adopting a narrow or constricting view of excellence. *Our conception of excellence must enhance many kinds of achievement at many levels. . . .*
>
> Second, we must not assume that native capacity is the sole ingredient in superior performance . . . a product of ability and motivation and character. . . .
>
> Finally, we must recognize that judgments of difference in talent are not judgments of differences in human worth.
>
> To sum up, it is possible for us to cultivate the ideal of excellence while retaining the moral values of equality. (Rockefeller, 1958, pp. 16-17) *

USING INTELLIGENCE TESTS INTELLIGENTLY

Preceding chapters have set forth the values and limitations of intelligence testing, and the characteristics of gifted persons have been described in some detail because identification is dependent upon a combination of testing and recognition of the characteristics of unusual ability. The intelligence quotient is one index of intellectual ability. Other instruments are necessary because of occasional inadequacy, inaccuracy, or inappropriateness of the IQ score. On the basis of his exhaustive search for high intelligence subjects in California, Terman estimated that he had uncovered 80 per cent, possibly 90 per cent of the children in the top percentile of intellectual performance. The remainder, he assumed, were not discoverable because their superior ability was hidden by shyness, laziness, inferior adaptability, or slow school progress (Terman, 1925, p. 33). Our problem today continues to be one of seeking out the 10 or 20 per cent who are hard to find. We have also to refine techniques in order to recognize those comparable to Terman's sample, and we need to inquire whether the Terman technique was broad enough to include the full breadth of talents that comprise giftedness.

With all these qualifications on the use of intelligence tests in mind, we may look at circumstances in which they are used or may be used. So long as schools are restricted to budgets requiring large group procedures, group intelligence tests will continue to serve as a primary screening device. In some schools children with high scores on the group test are subsequently given an individual test. In a few schools all children are given the individual test. Because of the expense of administering individual tests, some school systems try to replace it with an average of two or more group tests. While the individual test has some advantages over the group test, both types are subject to the criticisms expressed in Chapter 3 of intelligence tests and their administration.

TEACHER OBSERVATION

Because of the limitations noted in intelligence testing, other mechanisms are an obvious need. Most easily available, of course, are teacher judgments and, after a few years of schooling, teacher ratings. While Terman reported with some discouragement that teachers were right only half the time in selecting children of high mental endowment (as tested by the Stanford-Binet), he was gratified with the 50 per cent that he could include in his roster. Since that time (the early 1920's), efforts have been made to provide teachers with clues to help them identify exceptional pupils. Many school districts and professional associations have published lists of characteristics that may serve as keys. Chapter 2 of this volume may be so used.

One of the most systematic efforts to locate special talents has been that of the Quincy Youth Development Project. Starting in 1951, the project set out to explore the resource-potential inherent in a community to develop exceptional ability in its children and to remedy the maladjustment of handicapped children. The Quincy Youth Development Commission was established to cooperate with a research team from the University of Chicago. Tests were administered to an experimental group in the fourth grade and a control group in the sixth grade with the purpose of identifying talent and handicaps, and noting the effects of a planned program over the course of ten years.

The Quincy Project sought to identify gifts in the following areas: intellectual ability, scientific ability, leadership ability, creative ability, artistic talent, writing talent, dramatic talent, musical talent, mechanical skills and physical skills. Teachers were provided with a handbook that described a number of characteristic behaviors of each of these abilities. They were then given "ability rosters" for each gift. All children in the class were listed on the roster. The teacher was instructed to utilize one behavior and to consider how well each child met the description. Children outstanding in this regard—about 10 per cent was suggested—were to be scored "1" for the behavior. The teacher was then asked to take the next behavior and rate all children for this category. After considering all of the characteristic behaviors for a given ability, the teacher added up the "1's" given to each child, entered the total and noted the behaviors on which the child scored high. These lists of behavior represent an excellent guide for teacher observation (De Haan and Kough, 1956, pp. 19-54).

It is of interest that teacher analysis of observed behavior precedes other recommended techniques that are included in the Quincy study. For general intelligence, both general intelligence tests and differential mental ability scales are recommended. In addition, informal analysis through tests and games is suggested (see section below on work samples). In science, observation is supplemented by use of cumulative records, standardized achievement and interest tests. To assess leadership potential various types of sociometric devices round out teacher observation. Work samples play an important part in creativity, art, writing, music, and mechanical skills.

Piekarz (*In* Robinson, 1954) suggests that the teacher look for certain distinguishing characteristics in the early childhood program. In group activities gifted children show leadership in solving problems, foreseeing difficulties, and anticipating outcomes. They are resourceful in overcoming difficulties. They show unusual command of language and a large vocabulary. They are self-confident and unafraid to try new things. What they do in their spare time they follow through to completion, and they find distant goals motivating, not discouraging. In observing the child by himself the teacher should look for a show of independence and initiative. The kinds of books he selects to read, or to have read to him, and his interest in reading may be revealing. Hobbies after the age of seven or eight may also give some clue to unusual interest or ability. The teacher may be able to judge his work qualitatively by looking for attention to details and attempts at refinement. "Insatiable curiosity" is one of the characteristic attributes of the gifted child (*Ibid.*, pp. 22-23).

As the child grows older, Calhoun (*In* Robinson, 1954) notes these characteristics of the bright child in the intermediate grades: a wide vocabulary, more scope in social relationships, a greater range and intensity of interests than is normally seen, and creative expression in music and art. He suggests the use of "situational tests" in identifying ability. Many children participate in the following, but greater interest and more effective work is shown by the gifted pupil in making scrap books, museum field trips, voluntary reading, bulletin board displays, selection of radio and television programs, creative writing, dramatics, writing music, reading poetry aloud, making maps, independent research, and responsiveness to humor (*Ibid.*, pp. 27-28).

At the secondary level the North Central Association (1958) in its Superior and Talented Student Project suggests the following behavior characteristics to help teachers screen their students:

1. The student learns rapidly and easily.
2. He uses a great deal of common sense and practical knowledge.
3. He reasons things out, thinks clearly, recognizes relationships, and comprehends meanings.
4. He retains what he has heard or read without much rote drill.
5. He knows about many things of which most students are unaware.
6. He has a large vocabulary, which he uses easily and accurately.
7. He can read books that are one or more years in advance of the rest of the class.
8. He performs difficult mental tasks.
9. He asks many questions and has a wide range of interests.
10. He does some academic work one or more years in advance of the class.
11. He is original in his thinking, uses good but unusual methods.
12. He is alert, keenly observant, and responds quickly. (North Central Association, 1958, pp. 8-9)

Many of the characteristics that identify able learners elude currently available aptitude and achievement tests and the quantitative measures which they produce. For example, Getzels urges consideration of the following "intellectual characteristics of the able learners":

1. He has greater curiosity and is not content with mere rote repetition.
2. He is more exploratory and is likely to want to go beyond the limits of a particular problem or the arbitrary restrictions of a particular lesson unit.
3. He is more autonomous and is likely to want to work out problems independently.
4. He is more abstract in his thinking and is likely to want to generalize from particulars to principles.
5. He is more creative and is likely to be impelled to add something original or imaginative of his own to a given problem or classroom project. (Getzels, 1954, p. 21)*

---

* Reprinted from "Distinctive Characteristics of Able Learners," by Jacob W. Getzels, in *Promoting Maximal Reading Growth among Able Learners*, edited by Helen M. Robinson, Supplementary Educational Monographs No. 81, by permission of The University of Chicago Press. Copyright 1954 by The University of Chicago.

Numerous checklists are available for teachers. All require subjective, qualitative ratings. All require highly relative judgments. The ability to learn and remember new things is always stressed. Seeing relationships, being able to work with abstractions, and high verbal ability as expressed in speech and reading are other characteristics that alert the teacher to the possible presence of intellectual giftedness. Because of the nature of school programs the teacher is in a rare position to see such signs as no one else can.

PITFALLS IN TEACHER OBSERVATION

Certain pitfalls, however, have to be avoided as the teacher seeks to ascertain particular ability on the part of any child. Working with thirty or more children in a group, the teacher can easily assume giftedness where only glibness exists. The child who has an attractive personality sometimes wins the teacher over to the extent that the personality assessment influences the evaluation of ability. The amenable, obliging, docile child also has cards stacked in his favor. Conformity to teacher patterns and demands is more welcome in a crowded room than a continuous display of rebelliousness. It is much easier to recognize talent in the well-behaved, obliging, attractive, verbal child than in the non-conforming, rebellious, unprepossessing, withdrawing child. Small wonder, then, that Getzels and Jackson (1958) should find that teachers much preferred the high IQ group with conforming tendencies to the high creative group who were more independent and sometimes cynical.

Other factors that obstruct identification also cloud the perception of the teacher. The teacher generally sees the child, not his background. Frequently, however, the teacher is evaluating the effects of his background and not the child's native ability. The child from the culturally rich home needs relatively little ability to outshine the youngster from the home that is on the wrong side of the cultural tracks. In addition, the teacher often has no way of distinguishing between the youngster's own ability and drive and the extent to which the child is achieving as a result of Mother or Dad's coaching or pressure. To a certain point assistance may not matter, since ultimately we are interested in how well the individual *employs* his gifts. However, there are numerous cases where the early bloom fades inexplicably or where early promise settles into under-achievement or resentment. If genuine ability is not present, at some point, parental assistance and pressure cease to help and the child who has been mistakenly selected for more complex intellectual tasks finds himself lost and frustrated. Sometimes, unfortunately, genuine ability rebels when the child becomes aware that he is merely an alter ego for an ambitious parent seeking to lead a second life. This awareness often comes in adolescence with an awakening sense of self, and the adolescent asserts a rejection of his parents' values. Repudiating the academic values of an ambitious parent can result in serious underachievement.

PAST ACHIEVEMENT

At the high school and college level no single index gives as high a correlation with later academic performance as school grades. School grades share with achievement tests the advantage of including a built-in measure of persistence, drive, and study skills. While there are fundamental differences between elementary school and secondary school, between high school and college, it is also true that there are many basic similarities in the over-all educational process. For similar reasons the publishers of the Scholastic Aptitude Tests regard their tests as indicators of *developed* ability. Motivational factors are therein tested in their effects. The advantage of the school grades over the aptitude tests lies in the fact that they reflect a teacher's experience with a given student over an extended period—a semester, a year, or more. The aptitude test may have the advantage of standardization and objective scoring but is always a more limited sample of the individual's performance and experience. Two more types of evidence that are valuable in identification, therefore, are the child's accumulated school performance and the scores of standardized achievement tests.

Of all academic achievements, the most generally useful in predicting later performance is reading skill. There are various reasons why this should be true. Conventional definitions of intelligence lean heavily on verbal, abstract, symbolic, relational items. All of these are involved in reading. Considerable overlapping is to be found between some definitions of intelligence and the components of reading skill. Moreover, since the usual way of validating intelligence and aptitude tests is to judge their predictive value in scholastic performance, it is not strange that reading should be of paramount importance since it is the basic means to success in the upper academic reaches. While it is true that not all good readers do well in college, poor readers find it difficult simply to survive there.

One caution must also be observed. The success of using reading scores in predicting academic success carries with it its own limitation. So long as we limit intelligence to verbal types of behavior we find a high correlation with reading ability. So long as we define giftedness as success in verbal undertakings dependent upon reading, we find a high correlation between performance and reading ability. If, however, we broaden our concept of intelligence to include such things as creativity, social leadership, spatial perception, numerical concepts, and computation, reading skills play a somewhat less central role. Also, if we use as our criterion successful vocational application, personal development, social responsibility, and emotional adjustment, correlations with reading skills are also likely to be rather low.

The same conclusion is to be found here as in the employment of intelligence tests. The scores reported are helpful indices but they relate to limited facets of giftedness. The child with the unusual reading score must certainly be considered for inclusion in any intellectually gifted group. But the failure to achieve a high reading score is not necessarily a sign that other intellectual abilities are absent.

CHILDREN AND PARENTS AS SOURCES

A number of other methods are also of value in seeking to identify gifted boys and girls. Children reveal themselves in many contexts. In addition to the school environment, interaction with other children and activities in the home provides a reservoir of information. Sometimes teachers are surprised to note realistic appraisals of children by their friends. For some time, sociometry has depended for information about social interaction upon children's choice and rejection of each other. The familiar sociogram gives us an interesting picture of social leadership. In intellectual fields children are also able at times to spot superior ability. The "grind" may not be the star in a sociogram but he is often the center of attraction when homework has to be done—or when correct answers are sought surreptitiously during a test.

Among the members of a highly selected group, however, rank order is not always apparent to the children. Brumbaugh (1955) secured some interesting but inaccurate responses from eleven-year-olds in the Hunter College Elementary School (all children above 135 IQ; median 150) when she asked them, "What is an IQ?" She obtained results that were still more startling when the pupils were asked to guess which children in the class had the highest IQ's. In most cases there was little accurate perception of relative brightness in the classes she interviewed.

With more mature perspective, parents may be in a better position to judge exceptional ability although consanguineity may not be the best guarantee of objectivity. Parents may not be expected to give a dispassionate appraisal, but their efforts may be given some direction through use of checklists to indicate the kinds of activities their children engage in. Brumbaugh and Roshco (1959) have developed the following checklist for parents. It may also be used as the basis for a conference between parent and teacher:

1. Did your child walk and talk earlier than most other children of his age and sex?
2. Did he show a comparatively early interest in words?
3. Does he have an exceptionally large vocabulary for his age?
4. Did he show an early interest in reading?
5. Did he show an early interest in clocks, calendars, jigsaw puzzles?
6. Did he show an early interest in numbers?
7. Does he express curiosity about many things?
8. Does he have more stamina and strength than other children of his age and sex?
9. Does he tend to associate with children older than himself?
10. Does he act as a leader among children of his own age?
11. Does he have a good memory?
12. Does he show unusual reasoning power?
13. Does he have an unusual capacity for planning and organizing?
14. Does he relate information gained in the past to new knowledge that he acquires?
15. Does he show more interest in creative effort and new activities than in routine and repetitive tasks?
16. Does he try to excel in almost everything he does?
17. Does he concentrate on a single activity for a prolonged period without getting bored?
18. Does he usually have a number of interests that keep him busy?
19. Does he persist in his efforts in the face of unexpected difficulties?
20. Does he figure out his own solutions to problems and show uncommon "common sense?"
21. Does he have a sense of humor that is advanced for his age?
22. Does he show sensitivity to the feelings of others?
23. Does he show a comparatively early interest in God, religion, and questions of right and wrong?
24. Does he make collections that are more advanced or unusual than those of others in his age group?
25. Does he show an intense interest in some artistic activity, such as drawing, singing, dancing, writing, playing a musical instrument?
26. Does he make up stories that are vivid and dramatic or relate his experiences with a great deal of exact detail?
27. Does he like puzzles and various kinds of "problem" games?
28. Does he have exceptional ability in mathematics?
29. Does he show an unusual interest in science or mechanics?
30. Does he show awareness of things that are new or novel?

(Brumbaugh and Roscho, 1959, pp. 43-44)[*]

LOOKING FOR HIDDEN POTENTIAL

Identification procedures must be viewed in the light of purposes to be served by the search for special ability. Test scores generally indicate which young people have *already* "arrived" or which young people are well on their way. These individuals do not represent a problem of identification. In addition, being easily found, they are readily served. The problem lies in those children and youth who *ought* to be on the way but who are prevented by personal, cultural, or educational handicaps. If the purpose of identification is to group together children who are already reading better than their classmates, the reading test is an effective instrument. If the purpose is to find those youngsters who ought to be reading well, the reading test by itself proves to be too limited.

A second determinant of identification procedures is the nature of the program for which children are being selected. If the purpose is to establish classes which will be taking farther flights into academic areas with verbal material, achievement and intelligence tests as now constituted represent a viable approach. On the basis of past success, future achievement in comparable activities can be predicted. If the aim, however, is to stimulate creative abilities and to encourage originality, the conventional tests yield few valid clues. Again, we return to the Chicago and Minnesota findings that high intelligence (as defined by scores on existing tests) and high creativity are not synonymous (see Chapters 3 and 5).

The important jobs in identification—finding potential that has not yet been nourished, and discovering talents that do not necessarily correlate strongly with school achievement—remain a challenge. Attention to the purposes of identification and to the nature of the school program that makes identification necessary may prevent wasting resources on inappropriate procedures and instruments.

WHAT DEGREE OF ABILITY, WHAT RANGE OF TALENTS?

One of the basic decisions to be made in identification is the degree of superiority to be sought. In the discussion of definitions of giftedness in Chapter 1, differences in perspective were presented. One may seek individuals more than three standard deviations above the mean of intellectual ability—the top one-half of 1 per cent—and be assured that those included will do extremely well academically with few exceptions. But at the same time one must recognize that so narrow a selection will exclude a very large number of extremely capable individuals because of (1) the standard error of the instrument employed, (2) qualitative inadequacies of all existing tests, (3) personal differences among subjects not related to intellectual ability alone but affecting scores on tests, (4) cultural differences among subjects which contaminate the scores on aptitude and achievement tests. In very large communities, a highly selective criterion (top one-half or 1 per cent, top 2 or 3 per cent) is frequently used, with the rationalization that able children who are excluded still have the opportunity to learn in a rich program offered to all students in the school system. Their chief loss, it is claimed, is in exclusion from association with bright children only which is effected by grouping. Moreover, there is research that questions the academic value of grouping itself (see Chapter 13, Grouping).

In all but the largest communities selection of the very exceptional group is not even a matter of choice but is simply not feasible. One-half of 1 per cent yields only fifteen children in a school district of three thousand pupils. Even 3 per cent gives a group of only 90 scholars in all 12 grades. A large high school of one thousand pupils normally enrolls but 30 students with IQ's over 130 (to take the simplest distinction). Unless a community is large enough to bring together children from more than one school it is rarely possible to assemble as many as 25 students for a class of the top one-half per cent or even top 3 per cent in ability. But organizational reasons are not the only rationale for widening the range of ability to be identified. In terms of intellectually gifted students the primary aim of education in the common schools is preparation for college. While some students survive in college with average intelligence, by and large, students who do well in college average above 115 IQ. This fact justifies many school districts in including in their "gifted" group the top fifth of the intelligence distribution.* This is substantially the recommendation of James Conant (1959) in his report, *The American High School*. It should be apparent, however, that a school program geared to very exceptional ability may be too rigorous for the top fifth, and that teachers planning work for the top fifth may not adequately involve the top half-per cent if all youngsters in the class are treated as a group.

Not only is the range of abilities at issue; there is also the problem of the range of talents that ought to be included. The facile assumption that all students of superior *general* ability ought to be identified ignores

---

* It is of interest to note that in the period from 1957 to 1964 the Chicago Public Schools gradually shifted the cut-off point for special classes downward, arriving at the conclusion that the program should embrace 15 to 20 per cent of the school population. This shift followed a general reduction in the proportion of children with very high IQ's accompanying population changes in the "inner city" common throughout the United States (Chicago Public Schools, 1964, pp. 6-10, 72).

the fact that a large number of individuals might be added who show special promise in any *one* field—science, mathematics, linguistics, writing, dramatics, speech, music, art, industrial arts, retail selling, bookkeeping, typewriting, etc.,—but whose general ability is undistinguished. Conversely, students may be found who do very well in general but who have no outstanding talent in any one field. In the past we have generally taken the student with the high general average and excluded the student with unusual special ability if limited to a single field. This may merely indicate unwillingness to accept the specialized nature of our times and occupations.

ISSUES IN IDENTIFYING TALENT

McClelland (1958) takes a critical view of the whole of identification procedures as currently employed. He feels that not enough objective information has been accumulated on a scientific basis. He sets forth a number of issues in identification of talent whereon research is needed. One problem arises from our assumption that abilities are static—that a talent discovered at age ten will be constant ten, twenty, thirty years later. Actually the problem of prediction is complicated because potential varies over a period of time in proportion to opportunity for development and use. Second, McClelland points out that we have few functional analyses of superior performance in any walk of life. If we had these analyses we could recognize the components that are necessary for success and use them in identifying potential superiority. Without them, we remain very much in the dark.

For the most part we employ measures that have a high correlation with success in school. While this kind of instrument predicts success in school and college relatively well, unfortunately the correlation with success in life is not encouraging. This is true simply because there is "a lack of fit between performance in school and later life" (McClelland, 1958, p. 8).

Third, a normal way of identifying characteristics necessary for success is to analyze the life and performance of persons eminent in their field. Such analysis is made after these persons have attained their position. Did these persons show the same characteristics and behave in the same manner prior to their achievement of success? Not what they are now, but what they were in the early period is necessary for us to know if we are to identify potential achievers at a future time. Again the information for early identification is not available.

Fourth, McClelland raises an interesting question which is shared by others. "What evidence," he asks, "is there that intelligence is not a threshold type of variable; that once a person has a certain minimal level of intelligence his performance beyond that point is uncorrelated with his ability? Several studies suggest that if such a minimal level is set fairly high, ability may no longer play a crucial role in success" (*Ibid.*, pp. 12-13). This question is reinforced by observation that virtuosi in various fields may show high, but not exceptional intelligence. Brandwein (1955), in *The Gifted Student as a Future Scientist*, suggests that selection of science potential begins with a somewhat higher-than-average intelligence but must be reinforced by spatial perception and a strong interest in science.

All of these uncertainties led McClelland to the conclusion that we are barking up the wrong tree in seeking to identify talent with our crude methods. We should shift, he suggests, "to studying the process by which talent becomes actual, by which it develops" (1958, p. 25). Failing to do so, we place emphasis on talent potential as the fixed attribute of a very small number of people. Were we to learn more about the process of developing talents we might include many more people in our efforts and we might bring many and greater gifts to fruition. Anne Hoppock (1958), speaking for the Association for Childhood Education, expresses a similar point of view. Tax-supported schools, she points out, are designed for all the children of all the people. Each parent has the right to expect the school will value his child and help him become his best self. "By seeking the undiscovered resources which lie within every child, we best assure the identification of very able children. . . . Perhaps the most effective way to find the creative potentialities of children is to put them in an environment which encourages them to behave creatively" (Hoppock, 1958, p. 7).

To assist in the development of a framework for research on the conditions and outcomes necessary for identification and development of superior ability, McClelland suggests the format in Table I. Research that fills in such a chart for eminent performance in specific fields such as medicine, law, or teaching is needed if competent identification is to be achieved.

RECOGNITION OF SPECIAL ABILITIES

Traditional concern with the "universal man," the "well-rounded individual," and "liberal education" often obscures the fact that people have special abilities and operate as specialists in their daily tasks. No one will quarrel with the lofty educational ideal expressed by the individual of broad culture and wide-ranging interests and abilities. No one will deny the desirability of broadly educated physicists and versatile

Table I.

Illustrative Analysis of the Determinants of Performance Considered "Talented" in Terms of Its Desired Effects

A	B	C	D
Antecedent Conditions	produce A person with certain characteristics	who interacts with A situation with certain characteristics	to produce performance with desired outcomes
Heredity Cultural Values Family structure Socio-economic status Parent attitudes	Abilities Emotional stability Values Motives Characteristic modes of response (traits)	Working conditions skills required values required motives required stability required Type of persons in the situation	Work efficiency Occupational rank School grades Community service Good morale Successful leadership Social effectiveness

(McClelland, 1958, p. 5) *

* From *Talent and Society*, by David C. McClelland and others. Copyright 1958 by D. Van Nostrand Company, Inc. Reprinted with permission of D. Van Nostrand Company, Inc.

humanists, but neither can society afford to reject the gifts that come from the narrow physicist who has but minor interest in society and the arts or from the linguist who is scientifically illiterate. Anderson notes, "We can say with some assurance that the human being possesses many special abilities which are uncorrelated, or correlated to such a slight degree that one cannot be predicted from the other" (J. Anderson, 1960, p. 21).

What this signifies in identification of talent is the need to seek out special interests and abilities whether or not they are related to high general ability. Chapter 3, Intelligence and Intelligence Testing, has presented the challenge of factorial analysis to theories of intelligence as a unitary, general capacity. If one accepts the factorial thesis, then one seeks to identify individuals showing high ability in those factors that are related to success in particular fields. For example, space perception correlates well with scientific training and performance. A high general intelligence score that omits space perception is not as helpful as it might be in predicting science aptitude. A high general score and a low space perception score do not augur well for success in science. A high space perception score, accompanied by other factors important in science, would be more promising than a general score alone. The discovery of low to moderate correlations among various factors on tests such as the CAVD and the Differential Aptitude Test batteries supports greater utilization of scores on individual factors than is now the case.

The multi-factor approach also questions the validity of various identification procedures in use in elementary and secondary schools. First, the reliance upon single cumulative scores from general intelligence tests appear to be excessive. While high general intelligence is perhaps identified, no doubt many children are excluded who show moderate general ability but who have unusual talents in specific fields. Second, establishing high *average* grades as a screening device for special programs in the school or in particular subjects raises the same question. Honor schools often enroll many students in some special classes where they show only the barest interest. They are there because of general grade averages and aptitude scores. Third, admission to colleges and to special programs in colleges on the basis of general aptitude tests or high school averages is subject to the same criticism. A high general mediocrity may be pre-empting opportunity which should be afforded to high special abilities that are not also favored with high performance in non-related fields.

What is needed, therefore, is some means to identify special ability in particular fields. Having identified such ability, schools must then find some way of fully challenging this ability whether it is accompanied by superior general intelligence or not. The old assumption that everyone in secondary schools and colleges must be exposed to the same dose of the cultural heritage violates this point of view. Somehow we have to find academically respectable ways of exempting Einsteins, Edisons, and Churchills from requirements that have little meaning for them instead of subjecting them to regimes that prevent their potential from revealing itself.

INTEREST AS A SIGN OF POTENTIAL

Ways of identifying special abilities attracted the efforts of a Science Study Group established at the University School at The Ohio State University in 1958. First the group adopted the following criteria by which they might select "manifestations of talents":

> (1) they (manifestations of talent) should apply to talent of all kinds; (2) they should be specific enough for quantitative treatment . . . ; (3) they should be discrete enough so that there is no confusion about what is meant; (4) they should be expressable in verbal terms—that is, be able to be described behaviorally; and (5) they should be few enough in number so that the full range can be held in mind. (Schmieder, 1959, p. 1) [*]

On this basis the group selected six manifestations which, by implication, "define talent as an intensity of interest along with the skills, understandings, and commitments that come when this intensity is long continued" (*Ibid.*). The six manifestations follow:

(1) prolonged pursuit of an interest
(2) great amount of time devoted to an interest
(3) active search for information and ideas—that is, expanding to ever-broadened understandings
(4) multiplicity of related interests in the field
(5) degree of self-initiated interests or concerns
(6) accumulation of an unusual degree of skill and understanding.
(*Ibid.*)

The cardinal place of interest and self-selection by the individual is revealing. It confirms Brandwein's (1955) finding at Forest Hills High School in New York when he sought to identify students with special ability in science. Students were invited to apply for a special program if they were interested; in addition, teachers were asked to nominate

---

[*] From *Fostering and Developing Science Talent*, by Fred J. Schmieder. Columbus, Ohio, Center for School Experimentation, The Ohio State University, 1959. Reprinted with permission of Fred J. Schmieder.

students and records of school performance were examined. In 90 per cent of the cases students coming into the new program identified themselves. Only 10 per cent were added as a result of teacher nomination.

These two examples also serve to support arguments for avoiding restrictive identification procedures. These arguments (see McClelland above) assert our inability with available instruments to distinguish accurately young people of high promise. Instead, support is found for broadening the range of opportunity. In organization of special classes, the range of ability may be extended in order to include students showing unusual interest.

A second inference may also be drawn from the use of interest as a primary identifying factor. It is all good and well to utilize interest when children come from equally stimulating cultures into the school situation. What of the "mute, inglorious Miltons" who have never had the opportunity to develop an interest in the Muse? While certainly the school is helped by interests already developed, the school represents in many areas the only medium through which new interests may be awakened. Before it can assess potential, then, for many individuals and in many areas of study the school must first present rich opportunities for experience. On the basis of a fair chance in specific areas, pupils can develop and show interests which the school can evaluate for future promise. For "culturally deprived" populations the school has a particularly challenging—and socially responsible—task.

INDIVIDUAL INTELLECTIVE FACTORS

How, then, does one proceed to identify these special factors in intelligence and other special abilities? One does not, of course, simply discard the general intelligence test, scores on the Binet and Wechsler-Bellevue scales, or the general results of group tests. One means of broadening procedures is to consider scores on non-verbal tests and on tests claiming to be "culture-fair." High scores on these tests may serve to increase the reservoir of exceptional potential. Second, one may attempt to devise tests such as the Hunter Aptitude Scales for Gifted Children (Davis and Lesser, 1959) to identify exceptional scores in factors for which one is looking in pre-reading age groups. With older children one may employ group tests to yield separate scores for individual factors. These include the Thorndike CAVD tests, the Differential Aptitude Tests, the California Tests of Mental Maturity, the Kuhlmann-Anderson Intelligence Tests, and the Terman-McNemar Test among others. Although total scores are available on these tests, attention should be focused on very high scores on any of the sub-tests or separate factors.

ACHIEVEMENT IN INDIVIDUAL AREAS

Achievement is a sign of ability motivated within a favorable, supporting environment. Accordingly, high scores in particular areas of achievement also identify special ability, although some children will be missed because of low motivation or cultural handicaps. High scores in any single area on the usual standardized achievement test may also be regarded as one sign of potential. These tests have the advantage of being free from human bias which may color any one teacher's evaluation of a given child's ability—for better or for worse! Here again, it is the high score on an individual test that we are looking for, not the high "profile."

TEACHER OPINION

Teacher judgment and school grades also help to increase the size of a gifted population. The "human element" may affect judgment, but sympathetic observation often uncovers ability hidden by negative motivational or cultural effects. A perceptive teacher is often able to discern *interest* and *potential* that are more a promise than an actuality while the test is limited to performance in the present. Once again, it is more significant to learn that Jenny is a "whiz" in history than to discover that she is a very mediocre scholar in all other areas.

An interesting instance of teacher sensitivity to special talent is manifested in a study by Pegnato and Birch (1959) in a Pittsburgh junior high school enrolling 1,400 students. Teachers in the school were asked to name students whom they regarded as gifted. They selected the following:

    154 as "gifted" (no further definition)
    137 as outstanding in music (71) or art (66)
     82 for leadership qualities (home room or student council officers)
    179 as outstanding in mathematics

Of the nominees, 450 had IQ scores over 115; 334 had earned achievement test scores three or more grades above their grade placement. Of considerable interest is the fact that teachers named 781 individual children out of the total of 1,400 as gifted in one way or another.

SPECIAL TESTS

Special tests are also helpful. The Watson-Glaser Critical-Thinking Appraisal does not correlate very highly with general intelligence test scores. It may therefore be looked to for identification of a group of students who would be ignored on an IQ basis alone. The Test of Critical Thinking in Social Science serves the same purpose. Burton, Kimball, and Wing list and annotate other tests that shed some light on critical thinking ability in general and critical analysis in literature, natural sciences and the social sciences (Burton, 1960, pp. 439-44).

In such fields as music and art, tests that are truly predictive of later performance would meet a very real need. Some tests (Lewerenz Test of Fundamental Ability in Visual Art, Horn Art Aptitude Inventory, Seashore Measure of Music Talent, Drake Musical Memory Test, Kwal-wasser-Ruch Test of Musical Accomplishment, Meier Art Judgment Test) are available and have been used more or less extensively for a number of years. Unfortunately, they give a rather rough estimate of success. To some extent they are affected by the fact that one may know a great deal *about* particular areas without being able to *do* anything oneself. One of the main values of these tests is the indication of interest that familiarity suggests.

In testing for social leadership qualities the Quincy Youth Development Project devised a "Behavior Description Chart" to guide teachers in their observation. The chart is organized into eighteen sets of descriptive statements with five statements in each set. For each set the teacher is asked to mark the statement which is most and least descriptive of the child he is evaluating. As indicated in the example that follows, it is not obvious which statement represents maximum leadership:

    A. Quarrelsome
    B. Likes jobs which give him responsibility
    C. Avoids games
    D. Does his share, but does not seek leadership
    E. Is usually courteous to other children
                (Bowman, 1953, pp. 132-4)

A more widely used method of identifying leadership is to utilize children's choices as expressed in sociograms. Asking children to name two or three classmates whom they would choose as friends, whom they would like to play particular games with, whom they would join on specified committees, whom they would want to work with on particular jobs, whom they would like to sit next to—such questions yield information on simple popularity or information on children's perceptions as to the helpfulness of other children. Recognizing that the responses may say as much about the child replying as about the children chosen, the questioner may in any case distill interesting information about leadership roles as perceived by a child's contemporaries.

Still another technique is that used by Gardner and Thompson (1956) working with college students at Syracuse University. In interviews students were asked to rank fraternity brothers in order to determine various social characteristics and their effect upon goup morale and pro- ductivity. They were assisted (or "forced") in this process by being asked first to select the highest and lowest member with respect to a given attribute such as loyal friendship, and then to name another who would seem to be "just about average." The student was then asked to name another fraternity brother who ranked in between the top and the average member, and a fourth brother who ranked in between the bot- tom and the average member. This device served to set up four quartiles, and the student then ranked remaining members in order as being more or less loyal (the attribute in this example) than the five students selected as reference points by the respondent himself (Gardner and Thompson, 1956, pp. 30-38).

The four scales used in the Syracuse research are of interest in attempt- ing to come to grips with the elusive elements that comprise social leadership. They were designated as Playmirth (members with whom the respondent enjoys spending an evening for fun), Succorance (per- sons he regards as helpful and sympathetic in an emergency), Achieve- ment-recognition (persons whose company is valued as helping to secure recognition from others for purpose of achievement), and Affiliation (persons valued for their loyal friendship). The technique described for a college population, but variations may be worth exploring for use with younger students. This technique was employed as an improve- ment over the simple sociogram since it forced attention to all members of the group and was not limited only to those who came easily to mind. Nor was it limited to the most noticeable members (for good or ill) in the group.

Considerable experimentation is in process on the identification of social leaders, for in social, business, and politcal affairs it is often such a leader who secures action. No clear evidence is yet available which indicates predictive value of the devices being tested.

IDENTIFICATION IN INDIVIDUAL SUBJECT AREAS

Specialists in each of the academic areas are concerned with predictive devices that may help identify potential in their areas. Accordingly, as one reads any of the professional journals devoted to a particular area one finds results of such efforts. One of the more helpful sources is the series of booklets being published by the Academically Talented Student Project of the National Education Association. Relevant sections are to be found in currently completed bulletins on English (NEA, 1960b), Modern Foreign Languages (NEA, 1960c), Social Studies (NEA, 1960e), Mathematics (NEA, 1959a), Science (NEA, 1959b), Administration (NEA, 1960a), Art (NEA, 1961b), and Music (NEA, 1960d).

Specialists in most subject areas recommend employment of general intelligence tests, achievement tests in their own area, teacher grades, and teacher opinions. They urge consideration of items such as the following:

> Use and comprehension of a wide vocabulary
> Ability to learn easily and rapidly and an eagerness to do so
> Long attention span for difficult material
> Asking of meaningful questions and intellectual curiosity in general
> Broad interests high-lighted by intensive interest in a subject area or
>   in careers related to the subject
> Ability in intellectual operations such as generalization, comparison,
>   understanding relationships, handling abstractions and critical
>   thinking
> Originality, creativity, and imagination
> Retention of learnings
> Dislike of routine, drill or rote, memory exercises
> Ability to work independently
> Ability to work with others
> Power of self-appraisal and self-criticism and a self-motivating
>   quality.

In addition, as might be expected, specialists ask for particular competences in areas related to their subject. These are considered in some detail in later chapters in this volume which deal with individual subject areas.

WORK SAMPLES

In many fields the only valid reflection of potential is through early expression of promise. While some tests exist in fields like music, art, and creative writing, auditions and examinations of sample products yield results that correlate much better with success. New York City maintains two special high schools dealing with some such fields, an academic high school called the High School of Music and Art, and a vocational high school called the High School of Performing Arts. These schools select their students partly by auditions in dramatics, dance, and musical performance (vocal or instrumental) and by evaluation of artistic creations. Judges are generally persons from the performing arts who voluntarily give their time to select young people who show promise of talent. Emphasis is not on the finished product but on the glimpses of originality, inventiveness, feeling, and creativeness that distinguish the artist of the future from the person who can turn in a well-trained but uninspired performance. New York City as a center for the arts is able to provide a milieu and personnel. Each community has to seek out professional and lay expertise that is available in order to supplement judgment of teachers with exceptional background and artistic taste.

The performance criterion has the merit of assessing motivation, persistence, and ability to learn, as well as aptitude. However, it suffers even more than most standardized tests in reflecting the opportunities and handicaps of the child's environment.

In academic areas also the work sample is important. Originality and creativity in writing are more likely to appear in a student's work than on a standardized test, although some general picture of creative perspective may be forthcoming from the ingenious measures recently tested in research projects at the University of Chicago, University of Minnesota, Hunter College, and a few other centers. Since there are signs that creativeness may often be particular rather than general, the work sample is a desirable supplement to the new tests. The sample shows creativeness in a specific application.

What is true in writing is true in regard to the way in which a student approaches a problem in mathematics or a social-political-economic situation which invites fresh insight.

It is of interest that performance is the best criterion that foreign language specialists can offer to identify exceptional ability in linguistic talent. Urging the initiation of foreign language in the third grade if at all possible, they recommend results of early learning as the measure of ability to proceed further (NEA, 1960c).

One of the interesting assumptions underlying exhibits at science fairs and the project report in the Westinghouse Science Talent Search is the belief that a boy or girl will show potential and originality more in the projects he undertakes than in any other way. In industrial arts, vocational fields, and home economics the work sample again is a primary way of judging promise.

DeHaan and Kough suggest some interesting situations in which performance can be observed. Games testing memory, general information, and ability to reorient oneself are offered as informal means of checking general intelligence. Creativity is evidenced in listing quickly all the things that students may think of which share a particular quality (such as all things that are round), in imagining "what happens if" some peculiar event were to take place, in suggesting improvements in common objects, or in listing multiple uses for common objects. Identification of dramatic talent may be fostered by observing efforts at pantomime, at acting out a story, or at reading a play aloud (DeHaan and Kough, 1956, v. 1, pp. 21-46). The Quincy Youth Development Project, to which DeHaan and Kough contributed, sought to locate art aptitude by rating four drawings that students submitted. One was a draw-a-man assignment with instructions carefully standardized. Other drawings were of a schoolroom, a scenic picture, and a favorite subject. The jury looked for representational ability, line technique, area technique, flexibility of objects, compositional unity, color, artistic movement (path of viewer's vision), creative liberty and communicativeness, rating each of these on a five-point scale (Bowman, 1953, pp. 43-44).

A parallel performance test was employed in identifying writing ability. Children were asked to write four papers and given a modified thematic apperception test. The four papers included narration of a "most exciting event," description of "the person I would like to be like," a letter to grandmother, and the weaving of a story around any four of some twenty word pictures (two-word phrases, like "magic pebble") presented to the children. The efforts were again given to a jury for analysis (*Ibid.*, p. 46).

A very important problem in the employment of work samples is establishing criteria for analysis. Unfortunately, the prize in some science fairs is awarded for nothing more inspired than a beautifully copied drawing from a textbook or other source. This is more likely to happen when judges are poorly instructed and the objectives of the fair are not clearly understood. More typical would be the performance of the artists evaluating applicants at New York's School for Performing Arts where signs of originality, insight, and professional sparkle take precedence over a polished performance alone. Suggested criteria follow:

1. Does the work show signs of fresh viewpoint or insight?
2. Does the technique indicate individuality and initiative in attempting to solve the problem undertaken?
3. Does the work show persistence in attempting to solve the problem? Is there effort to work out details as well as the broad pattern?
4. Is the subject imitative or does it show a fresh sensitivity to beauty, to problems in the area or to possibilities of the medium employed?
5. Is something of a "professional" verve foreshadowed?
6. Is nothing more evident than patient practice and conformity to a given model?

7. Is there any sign of "protest" against customary practices, procedures, solutions, or ideas?
8. Is there any sign that the work would have been accomplished without the external motivation of a contest?
9. Is there evidence of capacity for self-criticism, self-evaluation, and subsequent, independent improvement?

SUMMARY

Where special programs can be offered to selected groups it will always be necessary to identify promise. To sum up ideas set forth in this chapter, the following procedure may be attempted:

1. Endeavor to identify intellective and personal factors necessary for high performance in the field under consideration. Establish a "threshold IQ" if possible and build upon this a percentile or score level for particular intellectual factors that appear necessary.
2. Administer intelligence tests that give both a general and special factor score.
3. Secure some measure of general creativity and attempt this with the group.
4. Invite volunteers to apply in order to secure an important measure of interest through self selection.
5. Secure teacher recommendations.
6. Consult student grades in the particular area and in related subjects.
7. Employ any special tests which give a measure of achievement, interest, or aptitude.
8. Seek out work samples in the particular area. If possible form a qualified jury to evaluate the samples.
9. Identify students who apparently have had no opportunity to develop interest or skill in the area. Expose these students to exploratory experiences. Include the top fifth (or tenth, or fiftieth, or whatever fraction school policy establishes) of the exploratory students in the special program on a tryout basis. Provide for volunteers from this group, too, after they have had a chance to "get their feet wet."
10. Keep the special group open for students who may later be identified, and permit students who feel they have made a mistake to withdraw.

Perhaps the most important conclusion to draw is that life and education are the best means of identification. Tests and other measures are only a very halting kind of shorthand. Anderson states this point of view effectively:

> From the developmental point of view it is also clear that a good and universal program of education for children between the ages of five and seventeen years offers the best opportunity for the systematic exploration of talent because it covers substantial portions of the period of growth and permits children to find themselves through contact with stimulating materials and ideas. Hence from a developmental point of view, short-term tests and measures complement education rather than become the primary device for locating talent. (J. Anderson, 1960, pp. 23-24)

Chapter 5

Creativity as an Aspect of Giftedness

*Out of the meaningless practical shapes of all that is living or
lifeless
Joined with the artist's eye, new life, new form, new colour.*

—T. S. Eliot

Avid to learn, receptive to the environment, stimulating to his teachers, the bright child constantly tempts parents and educators to try to make him over in their own image. Here is the learner apt for absorption of the cultural heritage, its graces as well as its substance. Here is the student who can and who will "work hard," "apply" himself, "buckle down," and "meet standards." For him the extra subject, the accelerated program, the longer assignment, the polished skill seem appropriate, for he is the child who will and who can respond.

The appropriateness of such procedures, however, has to be measured against the aims of our culture and its schools. Academic achievement in the realm of the customary disciplines is certainly valuable, but there are some who would question this goal as the only value to be sought. Gardner Murphy, in his provocative volume, *Human Potentialities* (1958), raises serious objection. He has little doubt of the ability of gifted youngsters to absorb the heritage. This, he says, is not the need of our times when civilization walks a tightrope between catastrophe and glory. We have a pressing need "to see in perspective where the major areas for fresh creations exist; in particular to discover those areas in which curiosity about the social order, eagerness to understand man's

101

predicament, may be capable of highest development, in order that an educational process attuned to the need for full utilization of such a capacity may do its work while there is time" (p. 109).*

More important than learning to apply the old is releasing man's potential to design the new. More important than slow progress by extrapolating into the future from the past is the rapid jump forward or the adoption of new directions in a creative process similar to a biological mutation. Murphy sees no hope in any tendencies now afoot for resolving the international tensions that have beset the world increasingly since the turn of the century. New and creative ideas, dramatically different and not continuous with our current thinking, will be needed to break existing stalemates. Murphy seems devoutly to believe that man has the necessary equipment, biological and social, continuously to develop such creative responses:

> Because man has this rich potentiality for sensory, motor, intellectual experience, and has to combine all this in fresh acts of cultural creativeness, he is doing nothing more than realizing these potentialities when he writes *Macbeth* or flies a plane at Kitty Hawk. And it is not only human to invent oneself out of one world into another; it is also human to keep moving toward a destination which is not set within man's present nature but keeps changing as the nature of his environment changes. (*Ibid.,* p. 316)

This point of view is shared by Sinnott (*in* Anderson, 1959, pp. 27-28) who regards life itself as a creative process. In biological forms below man, Sinnott sees life as conservative and rigidly fixed in its genetic constitution. This rigidity is found in man's *physical* structure, too, but in the complexity of the human brain Sinnott finds infinite possibilities of new mental patterns. He regards imagination as the basic formative quality of life emerging from rigid physical limitations to express itself in high creativity.

Creativity, like Motherhood and Fatherland, will find few adversaries, but differences exist in the approach to its development and release. One argument is that creativeness is a function of adult performance, that in youth one gets ready. One needs experience, understanding, knowledge, and skill. One needs the tools of humankind as arms. This is the basic justification for considering education as the transmission of the cultural heritage, for prescribing a curriculum determined by experts, for requiring more learning, and more "coverage" for the able. The counter-argument stems from a belief that creativeness is an aspect of person-

---

* From *Human Potentialities*, by Gardner Murphy. Copyright 1958 by Basic Books, Inc. Reprinted with permission of Basic Books, Inc.

ality and intelligence that stems from birth or early childhood, that creativeness is learned and therefore may be encouraged or inhibited by the environment. Such an argument justifies "progressive" school programs, permissive environments, student participation in establishing goals, and exploratory activities as part of an educational program for creativeness.

The release of creativity is thus argued on social grounds, on the needs of the world in time of crisis for original, "emergent" approaches rather than the extension of trends already established. The importance of the issue, however, lies not only in social need—the manpower concept—but also in individual self-realization—the development of man, as an ideal. Helping the gifted individual truly to realize his own gifts, his own being, depends upon release of unique and creative powers.

CREATIVITY AND INTELLECTUAL GIFTEDNESS

Implicit in the preceding statement and in the thoughts of many persons concerned with education of the gifted is the assumption that creativity is one aspect of giftedness. Taylor (1959) indicates that such an assumption depends upon the definition of intelligence that is employed. When high scores on current intelligence tests are taken as the criterion of giftedness, creative ability is not necessarily found among the population regarded as gifted. In such a case, the word *gifted* apparently is attached "to high academic performance in school-like activities which are often not very creative in nature." As a result, Taylor suggests that we may more accurately posit the existence of numerous different types of giftedness, one of which is the high IQ. Different kinds of creativeness may make up a whole class of other gifts, and still other types—such as planning, evaluation, decision making, communication—may also exist separately.

Guilford (1950) relates this shortcoming in intelligence tests to the history of psychological research on the theory of learning. Much research, he points out, has been done with lower animals in which signs of creativeness are almost non-existent. In addition, the effort to "scientize" and quantify resulted in developing learning theories formulated so as to cover phenomena that lend themselves to ordering in a logical scheme. Unfortunately, what may have proved feasible has not proved comprehensive as well, and it is time that learning theory take into consideration such matters as insight and creative activity. Guilford describes how Binet validated his tests against achievement in school subjects, primarily reading and arithmetic, subjects which are "not conspicuously demanding of creative talent. The content of intelligence tests reveals little of an obviously creative nature." (Guilford, 1950, p. 447).

This analysis may help explain the source of Leta Hollingworth's (1942) puzzlement when she discovered that only one-third of her very high IQ subjects displayed any remarkable creativity. Most of Terman's thousand most gifted subjects also are apparently making their way effectively through life, but a disappointingly small number have distinguished themselves in creative performance. In more recent years efforts have been made to apply objective measures in order to compare the scores of individuals on intelligence and creativity tests. Getzels and Jackson (1962, pp. 20-22) found remarkably little overlapping between high intelligence (IQ) and high creativity groups when they tested the young people in a private high school with an intellectually superior population. Torrance (1962, pp. 59-63), testing children in elementary schools, noted an overlapping of only 30 per cent of students who scored within the top 20 per cent on both IQ and creativity measures. On the other hand, Simpson and Martinson (1961), studying gifted children in California, observe that "the IQ as an identification criterion locates individuals of great variety and virtuosity." They question the view that a high IQ is more a mark of conformity to the school and its academic demands than it is a sign of creativity.

Actually, an accommodation of the two views—that IQ does or does not correlate with creativeness—is possible. Barron (1961) indicates that the correlation of the two factors over the whole range of ability is approximately +.40, but that the correlation between intelligence and creativity among individuals with IQ's over 120 is only +.10. The Simpson-Martinson study apparently covers creativity within the whole range of ability; Getzels and Jackson, Terman, and Hollingworth worked only within the narrow limits of high ability. MacKinnon (1961) computed a correlation for creative architests of −.08 between scores on Terman's Concept Mastery Test and tests of creativeness. For creative scientists, the correlation was −.07. Taken together, all these findings support the generalization that a moderately high level of intelligence is necessary for creative work, "but beyond that point being more or less intelligent does not crucially determine the level of a person's creativeness" (MacKinnon, 1961a, p. 89).

Taylor, Murphy, and others have long noted the relatively low creative component in school and college work. Intelligence tests have been validated against academic performance. A tight little circle has been closed in which intelligence and academic performance are equated and creativity excluded. Small wonder, then, that a low relationship exists between academic performance and adult success. To the extent that creativity may be needed in adult enterprise (and Taylor presents some evidence to bear this out) a solution may lie in greater recognition of creative ability and the revamping of academic programs so that creative behavior may be nurtured.

DEFINING CREATIVENESS

In seeking to secure nominations of creative students from faculty members at the University of Nebraska, Drevdahl presented the following definition to his colleagues:

> Creativity is the capacity of persons to produce compositions, products, or ideas of any sort which are essentially new or novel, and previously unknown to the producer. It can be imaginative activity, or thought synthesis, where the product is not mere summation. It may involve the forming of new patterns and combinations of information derived from past experience, and the transplanting of old relationships to new situations, and may involve the generation of new correlates. It must be purposeful or goal directed, not mere idle fantasy—although it need not have immediate practical application or be a perfect and complete product. It may take the form of an artistic, literary or scientific production or may be of a procedural or methodological nature. (Drevdahl, 1956, p. 22) °

A number of other definitions have been offered. Torrance (1962) sums up many of them by noting that almost all involve production of something new or original and a process that includes four elements: sensing some kind of deficiency, formulating ideas or hypotheses, testing hypotheses, and communicating results. In the Interdisciplinary Symposia on Creativity (Anderson, 1959), Dow, Fromm, Maslow, Rogers, and May agree in addition on a greater emphasis on self-aware-ness, the sense of "I," "not primarily to discover something new, but to experience in such a way that the experience originates in me" (Fromm, p. 50). Maslow (p. 89) appears to equate his concept of the "peak experience" with "self-actualizing creativeness." Rogers (pp. 71-72) defines the creative process as "the emergence in action of a novel relational product growing out of the uniqueness of the individual on the one hand and the materials, events, people or circumstances of his life on the other." He finds the necessary motivation to creativity in the tendency of "man to actualize himself to become his potentialities,"

° From "Factors of Importance for Creativity," by John E. Drevdahl. Reprinted with permission from *Journal of Clinical Psychology*, January, 1956.

"the urge to expand, extend, develop, mature—the tendency to express and activate all the capacities of the organism."

In attempting to define creativity we shall find it useful to employ four perspectives suggested by Mooney. He points out that creativeness is variously considered in relation to (1) the product created, (2) the process of creating, (3) the person of the creator, and (4) the environment in which the creative work is done (Mooney, 1957).

THE CREATIVE PRODUCT

Obviously, creativity must ultimately be manifested through performance or expression. To be sure, distinctions have to be made. A scientific discovery, for example, may be historically creative—like Salk's polio vaccine, or it may be personally creative—like the high school student's unaided discovery that the difference between squares of consecutive integers increases by 2. Russell draws the distinction well:

> Home and school can consider creative thinking (a) as a discovery which is fresh for the child himself, involving self-realization, (b) as the production of ideas or materials which contribute to the pleasure or welfare of the group to which the child belongs, and (c) as a comparatively rare, original contribution to the culture, a contribution which only a few gifted individuals can make. Obviously, homes and schools are more concerned with the first two types of creative activity, but in so doing they may be paving the way for the third type of contribution. (Russell, 1956, p. 384)*

Distinctions between major and minor gifts in creativity must also be recognized, since failure to do so might eliminate all but works in the class of *Hamlet* and the "Mona Lisa." This may be carried to the opposite extreme where every learning act is regarded as creative. Such is Kilpatrick's claim that all learning is creative since in learning the child achieves some new insight or reorganizes his experience in a way that is new for him.

There is some merit in Kilpatrick's view because it makes the term less cabalistic, less the prerogative of the favored few. Burton, on the other hand, distinguishes between creativity and learning as the difference between what the child learns to create himself and the discovery of what others have learned. "Learning," he says, "is more the process of discovery than creation. Through discovery of what others have learned the child learns to create himself, but that learning is not necessarily

---

* From *Children's Thinking*, by David Russell. Copyright © 1956 by Ginn and Company. Reprinted through the courtesy of Blaisdell Publishing Company, a division of Ginn and Company.

creative" (Burton, 1952, pp. 480-82). There are limitations, too, to a definition of creativity that becomes as broad as learning, for it ceases to be helpful in identifying a factor whose discovery is needed for maximum development.

Generally speaking, there is considerable agreement on the following attributes of the creative *product*:

> Novelty or originality of contribution; either new for the individual or new for the culture; the contribution may represent a product, a method, or a new insight into a problem.
> Social value; since objective criteria are difficult to apply, the contribution has to merit acceptance by some group of people at some point in time (Meer and Stein, 1955)
> An intellectual content and background, but not restricted to areas of intellectual endeavor; intelligence is viewed as a necessary but not a sufficient condition in itself.

CREATIVITY AS A PROCESS

A highly creative product ought to stem from a creative process. Teacher and parent are more likely to see the process in its early stages than they are to see an extraordinary product. If the process has its own characteristics and if these can be identified, it would behoove the teacher or parent to assist in developing the process.

One form of the process is described as creative thinking. Russell (1956, Chap. 11) places emphasis on self-discovery, perceptual and integrative factors in the chapter he devotes to creative thinking. Guilford (1957) distinguishes between convergent and divergent thinking on the basis of directedness in the process. Convergent thinking points toward the one acceptable solution. "Divergent thinking . . . (is) characterized . . . as being less goal bound. There is freedom to go off in different directions. . . . Rejecting the old solution and striking out in some new direction is necessary, and the resourceful organism will more probably succeed." (Guilford, 1957, p. 9). Working with Guilford's distinction, Getzels and Jackson define creative thought as "goal directed, easily flexible, manipulation of knowledge in a wide variety of novel or original ways." In the process they note such factors as adaptive flexibility, associational fluency, and perhaps most important, originality.

The nature of divergent thinking is to be found also in the mental activity we often call fantasy. Getzels and Jackson noted the greater use by their high-creative subjects of stimulus-free themes and unexpected endings. Their divergent thinking was further exemplified in humor, playfulness, and greater use of incongruities. They also noted: "The creative adolescent seems to possess the ability to free himself from the unusual, to 'diverge' from the customary. He seems to enjoy the risk and uncertainty of the unknown" (Getzels and Jackson, 1959, p. 56).

Crutchfield (1961), on the other hand, declines to attribute all creativity to divergent thinking. He finds differences in the characteristics of the "so-called creative process" in accordance with the nature of the creative task involved. Divergent thinking is found in some, convergent thinking in others. Crutchfield insists that the creative process is not mysterious, that it is not a single unitary process with sharply defined or sequential stages, and that considerable analysis of the process is still needed.

Mooney (1954) identifies four elements in the creative process as he observes the individual in relation to (1) the extension of his experiencing, (2) the focussing of his experiencing, (3) the management of his actions during experiencing, and (4) the derivation of significance from his experiencing. As catchwords for these four aspects, Mooney suggests *openness, self-realization, control,* and *aesthetic evaluation.* The "openness" criterion is discussed later in this chapter. The second element involves, in Mooney's words "focus through self-differentiation and self-realization," a willingness to be different about things, a persistent inquiry into the meaning of the individual's own life. "Control" involves a self-discipline but also a mastery of the materials and tools of one's work. Finally, significance is derived in terms of aesthetics—harmony of form and function, pattern, order. Presumably these functions may characterize intellectual as well as artistic performance.

Leuba (1958) helps to throw some light on the question of why some people are more open to experience than others. He relates a factor of increased stimulation to creative effort. He questions the assumption that people do things to reduce such needs as curiosity and tension, but feels that much behavior arises in order to increase these stimulations. He formulates a "principle of optimal stimulation," "that those activities are strengthened and tend to predominate which raise stimulation from inadequate levels toward an optimal one." Accordingly, he notes that students "do not ordinarily seem to study in order to reduce drives, anxieties, or tensions; on the contrary, they seem to learn most effectively what is stimulating and exciting to them" (Leuba, 1958, pp. 139-40). One might assume from Leuba's hypothesis that the creative individuals are those with a maximum of curiosity, those who seek stimulation and develop a maximum of autonomous interest and activity because of the stimulation they find in the process.

The effort to identify observable factors in the creative process extends from relatively simple analyses to the more recent work of Guilford and his associates where 14 factors are identified and 53 tests employed to measure aspects of these factors. Guilford's (1950) first hypothesis included sensitivity to problems, ideational fluency (fluidity of ideas), flexibility of set (ability to change tack, to shift from one frame of reference to another when "first guesses" do not work out), ideational novelty (fluidity of new ideas, new solutions), synthesizing ability, analyzing ability, reorganizing or redefining ability (rearranging materials and ideas in new ways to meet new needs), span of ideational structure and evaluating ability. At first, Guilford suggested these as possible factors in creative scientific work, but later study by his group has apparently established a conviction that these factors apply in other fields as well. The fourteen factors listed by the group as factors in creative thinking include such general abilities as verbal comprehension, numerical facility, perceptual speed, visualization, and general reasoning. Perhaps more specific to creativity are other factors they list: word fluency, associational fluency, ideational fluency, closure, originality, redefinition, adaptive flexibility, spontaneous flexibility, and sensitivity to problems (R. Wilson, 1954).

Viktor Lowenfeld and his associates sought independently at Pennsylvania State University to find measurable criteria responsible for creativeness. Focussing on art rather than science, Lowenfeld (1958) points out "that both investigations, after exploring numerous possible criteria, arrived at almost exactly the same eight criteria of creativity." "This would, then, as far as our data are concerned, establish that *creativeness in the arts has common attributes with creativeness in the sciences*" (*Ibid.*). Lowenfeld lists the following "eight attributes of creativity which significantly differentiate creative from less- or noncreative persons in both investigations":

1. Sensitivity to problems
2. Fluency of ideas (the number of different ideas which a person may have when thinking of using a single item, for example)
3. Flexibility (the individual's ability to adjust quickly to new situations)
4. Originality (uncommonness of verbal and sensory responses)
5. Redefinition and the ability to rearrange (redefining a material by using it in a new way or by giving it a new meaning)
6. Analysis or the ability to abstract (starting with the whole and arriving at details)
7. Synthesis and closure (combining of several elements to form a new whole)

8. Coherence of organization ("that part of creativity most closely related to aesthetics, for aesthetic growth appears to be responsible for the changes from a chaos on the lower end of the continuum to the most complete harmonious organization on the upper end." *Ibid.*, pp. 539-40) °

While noting the similarity between creativity in the arts and in the sciences, we should also do well to take note of MacKinnon's (1961b, p. 6) distinction between the two areas. In the sciences, he indicates, the creative product is not related to the creator. The creator is a person who acts largely as a mediator between externally defined needs and goals. He operates on some aspect of the environment to produce a novel and appropriate product, but he adds little of himself as a result. By contrast, the artist develops a product that is clearly an expression of his inner states, of his needs, perceptions, and evaluations. Considering the polar distinction between internal and external, between self and environment, one cannot but wonder at the many similarities discovered both in the creative process and the creative personality in the two areas.

STAGES IN CREATIVE PERFORMANCE

Attention to the creative act itself has been focussed in an attempt to order various stages within the act. Using somewhat different terminology in order to express slightly different insights, several writers seem to agree on the following elements:

1. Sensitivity to a problem or to a theme for expression. Psychologists relate this to openness to experience, to adventurousness, to a willingness to explore in realms of the unknown. The willingness to extend experience is involved in the desire to understand both what is going on inside oneself and in the environment, and in interest in new ideas, fresh perspectives, and experimentation (Mooney, 1956). Murphy refers to "sensitiveness, the presence of a need that satisfies itself and feeds upon more and more material of a certain type—color, space, relations, tone, rhythm. As satiation occurs, the need sets itself a bigger, more complex goal of the same type; and the individual *learns to create*" (1947, p. 466). This sensitiveness may be perceptual, involving sensory qualities, but it may also be conceptual, concerned with relations that are interpersonal or abstract. The highly sensitive person becomes more and more involved in these experiences until he is inexorably driven to find new forms or ideas.

° From "Current Research on Creativity," by Viktor Lowenfeld. Reprinted with permission from *National Education Association Journal*, November, 1958.

2. A period of "incubation" (Wallas), "accumulation" (Murphy), or "searching" (DeHaan and Havighurst) follows the initial sensitivity or preparation. The individual adds to his background, centers his action for fulfillment (Mooney), begins to order, organize, and refine his increasing store of experience.

3. A moment of creative insight (DeHaan) occurs which provides the necessary organization, the new form, the new ideas as if *de novo*, but actually as the culmination of subconscious processes that have all along been paralleling the conscious. Murphy and Wallas refer to this event as illumination:

> . . . usually in a moment of excited self-direction toward the goal, an integration of the accumulated material takes place in which both conscious and subconscious storehouses of experience are drawn from. A whole that is the answer to the long quest is made manifest in a moment often characterized by *illumination*. (Murphy, 1947, p. 466) °

4. A period of confirmation (DeHaan), polishing (Murphy), or verification (Wallas) is necessary to complete the creative act. The new insight, idea, form, tone, composition, or solution needs testing, elaboration, or extension. "As the need and achievement are relived again and again, it becomes clear that the need is not perfectly fulfilled or that secondary needs are still frustrated and the work of art or of science is accordingly hammered out until it is more adequate." (*Ibid.*)

Scepticism as to the ordering of elements in the creative act may indeed be appropriate. Certainly the occurrence of insight or illumination may appear at any point in the sequence; it may also characterize each of the four stages.

The imaginative burst of insight is the element that reflects a sense of mystery in the process. For this reason investigators are concerned with the role of fantasy in the creative process and the factor of fantasy in the personality structure of creative doers and thinkers.

Russell (1956, p. 309) quotes Vinacke's attempt to analyze stages in imaginative thought. He defines four steps. The first is simple play and enjoyment of the activity; this is followed by interpretation and appreciation. Fantasy gives way to more serious efforts as "guidance of action" leads to anticipation and planning. Finally, constructive or creative thoughts ranging from fantasy to problem-solving may lead to closure.

Murphy has given considerable attention to "subliminal" fantasy and

---

° From *Personality*, by Gardner Murphy. Copyright 1947 by Harper & Brothers. Reprinted with permission of Harper & Row, Publishers.

dream components in creative action. He quotes F. W. H. Myers' phrase, "subliminal uprush," as defining the "process of being over-whelmed by accumulated unconscious or subliminal material. . . . Ex-actly the right set, together with a vast fund of relevant material . . . may be touched off by a slight or even a subliminal cue, so that one reacts to many relevant phases of a problem at once (1947, pp. 460-61). Murphy cites, too, Prince's concept of the coconscious, that material in the unconscious which has been building up simultaneously with ma-terial in the conscious mind is suddenly released or made available. He suggests that such a concept may explain what he calls elsewhere "dream creativeness"—the claim by Robert Louis Stevenson, Coleridge, and various other writers and scholars that their inspiration arrived in dreams while asleep. Murphy makes the following guess:

> Partly because the outer world is not there to say no, partly be-cause the senses can contribute only a few and feeble interferences, partly because none has at his disposal the entire material of his life, and partly because no critical standards, no acid test can be invoked, the dream typically reaches heights and spreads out over areas which the disciplined mind of the civilized adult would not dare to scan. (*Ibid.*, p. 426)

Ghiselin (1952) provides a fascinating interpretation of the role of the unconscious and "self-surrender" to the inner promptings of imagination in his introduction to an anthology of accounts of the creative process at work by eminent scientists, authors, and scholars.

Working on a less poetic level, Crutchfield (1961) inquires into the conditions necessary for inception of the creative process. He insists that the task has to be the person's *own* problem, one that he experi-ences intensively as his concern, and not one assigned to him by others. He needs the freedom, thereafter, to discover, to select and to define elements for himself, with a sense that things as they are don't "fit." The creative process involves "some effective transformation or reorganiza-tion of cognitive elements." Then, Crutchfield cites these conditions as necessary for the transformation: that the elements be available, that they be selectively activated, contiguous, salient, free, and fitting.

THE CREATIVE PERSON

A third way to look at creativity is to study the creative person him-self. This view starts from the assumption that the creative product is neither a happy accident nor simply the result of faithful pursuit of the proper methodology; creative work is seen as the expression of creative personality. The fact that few great men have been limited to a single contribution supports this point of view. Now, since the school can scarcely expect to help its immature clientele produce works of creative authority, conceivably its greatest contribution can be in the direction of fostering the development of creative personalities.

One issue that arises is whether creativity is a unique phenomenon or a matter of degree. In the latter case a continuum would be assumed wherein some small amount of creativeness is found in even the least original of mortals. While admitting that the supreme heights of creative endeavor are scaled by few individuals in a century, Russell (1956, pp. 306-8) joins a large band who deny that only the bright child, only the genius can create. Creativity, he says, may be found at all levels of intelligence. The editors of New York City's *Curriculum and Materials* concur: "Creativity is widely distributed. It is not confined to one geographical area, the gifted, or any ethnic or social group" (New York City, 1959c). A democratic ethos based on the belief that a divine spark gives worth and dignity to every human being must start from such an assumption. From a practical point of view as well, the absence of established instruments for identifying creativeness at an early age argues in favor of assuming the existence of some creative ability in every pupil. Crutchfield (1961) also assumes that every human being is in some way creative. Despite wide individual differences, Crutchfield focusses on the pragmatic consideration that the actual creative performance of every person falls far short of his potential. Guilford (1962) agrees. He concedes that heredity may establish lines of development, but notes that individuals rarely realize their full development in any respect. He expresses faith that there is considerable room for improvement in creativity as well as in other native abilities, however limited by heredity.

Factor analysis employed to describe creativity is utilized in describing the creative person as well. A number of studies have used some method of identifying creative persons and have then measured the distinctive characteristics of these subjects. Barron, for example, worked with a group of one hundred Air Force captains, administering a test of originality and then forming two groups for purposes of comparison on a basis of high and low scores on the originality measure. To justify his procedure he remarked, "There is good reason for believing . . . that originality is almost habitual with persons who produce a really singular insight" (Barron, 1955, p. 478). He defined originality as the capacity for producing adaptive responses which are original, and he found evidence to support the following hypotheses:

> That original persons prefer complexity and some degree of apparent imbalance in phenomena.
> That original persons are more complex psychodynamically and have greater personal scope.
> That original persons are more independent in their judgments.

That original persons are more self-assertive and dominant.
That original persons reject suppression as a mechanism for the
control of impulses. (*Ibid.*, p. 484)

Drevdahl employed a population of undergraduate and graduate
students at the University of Nebraska in order to compare personality
characteristics, intelligence, and creativity ratings. On the basis of the
definition cited on page 105 above, faculty members nominated their
highly creative students. Drevdahl then administered a number of tests
to them and drew the following conclusions:

Creative persons are superior in verbal facility, fluency, flexibility,
and originality.
Creative persons are more withdrawn and quiescent. Creative
artists are somewhat more radical and self-sufficient than creative
scientists or non-creatives.
The art group are more sensitive emotionally, more bohemian.
Individuality or non-conformity appear to be desirable for creativity. (Drevdahl, 1956, p. 26)

Some studies of creative children and adolescents add perspective on
the nature of creative personality. Getzels and Jackson (1962, pp. 33-
60) discovered high academic achievement as one characteristic. Contrasting their high-creativity group of adolescents with the high intelligence (i.e., high IQ) group, they discovered that academic achievement
was quite similar in the two groups despite an average difference of 23
points in IQ scores. Although they scored as high on standardized tests,
the high creatives were not rated as well as the high intelligence group,
nor above the average for the school, when teachers expressed preferences for students in terms of the degree to which they would enjoy
having individual students in their class. In rating qualities they would
prefer for themselves—character, emotional stability, goal directedness,
creativity, wide range of interests, high marks, high IQ, and sense of
humor—the high IQ and high creative groups produced rankings which
were very similar except for one significant difference. The high creatives ranked a sense of humor second; the high IQ's ranked it last in the
group of eight characteristics.

Correlations determined by Getzels and Jackson between the qualities that students prefer for themselves and those which they believe
teachers to value are also provocative of conjecture. The high IQ's
showed a positive correlation of .67 between their choices and their idea
of teacher values. The high creatives showed a minus .25 correlation in
this comparison. This may reflect the failure of the high creatives to win

teacher approval to the same extent as the high IQ's. It may result either from rejection of the teacher's values or a feeling of rejection by the teacher.

Both the high-intelligence and the high creative groups seem to believe that their values are closer than are the teacher's to qualities needed for success in adult life. Correlation coefficients between qualities they desire for themselves and those they feel necessary for adult success follow:

High IQ's .... .91

High creatives .... .10

The correlation for the creatives proves to be very low, indicating perhaps that they take themselves less seriously than the high IQ's, perhaps that they are in rebellion against adult values, or perhaps that they are both more idealistic and more cynical than the high IQ's.

One of the widely noted personality characteristics is regarded by some as eccentricity, by others as non-conformism. Griffin (1958) reports her analysis of "movement responses" in Rorschach tests of persons of established creative accomplishment. Such responses, according to the Rorschach manual, should indicate "more individualized intelligence, greater creative ability, more 'inner life,' stable affective reactions, less adaptability to reality, more intensive than extensive rapport." Griffin reports her concurrence with other investigators in finding creative individuals scoring low in this area and therefore *not* less adaptive to reality.

Russell (1956, p. 76) rejects the view that creativity is related to revolt; he regards creative endeavor as representing progress along an indicated path rather than rebellion from it. Murphy admits that factors exist which involve nervous wear and tear for the highly creative individual. The craving for experience and expression is intense. The drive to achieve a solution for a particular problem may take the individual out of context with most of his environment. He may be so engrossed in himself that he considers himself above the normal conventions of health and society. He experiences inevitable frustrations in moving forward in new areas. Yet, "all of this does not in the least mean that most geniuses are abnormal; only that nervous wear and tear are not uncommonly associated with high creativeness" (Murphy, 1947, pp. 467-69).

Murphy is quite consistent on this point, for he sees emotional well being as a product and a process in creative work:

> It is, after all, realization of self that actualizes the potential that keeps hand and brain at work. Whatever incompleteness or *frustra-*

tion gnaws at the heart may give fire or fury to the effort—but *fulfillment*, rather than frustration, may also lead on to finer fulfillments. If the organized skills and the passion for experience are there, then, paradoxically, both defeat and victory may lead on to new victory. (Murphy, 1958, p. 133) °

Drevdahl and Cattell (1958), in testing a large number of established artists and scientists, attribute to them "what Riesman classifies as the autonomous person who both thinks and acts differently from the apparently unthinking average." Their analysis of 153 creative artists and writers indicated that they "differed from the normal population in being more intelligent, emotionally more mature (ego strength), dominant, adventurous, emotionally sensitive, bohemian, radical, self-sufficient and of a higher ergic-tension." On a test of sixteen personality factors devised by Cattell, the writer-artist group was found to be similar to a creative scientist population tested by Cattell and Drevdahl in another study. They do confirm, however, the contention that creative persons may hold themselves above customary conventions: "Conformity, concern for propriety, adherence to social standards and dictates are somewhat lacking in our experimental population" (p. 109).

Additional studies by Fromm (*in* Anderson, 1959), Barron (1961), MacKinnon (1961a), Gough (1961), Crutchfield (1961), Taylor (1961), Drews (1962), and Arnold (1961) serve to confirm the picture of the creative person already presented. A composite of these reports would reveal the following characteristics:

A positive view of self, leading to freedom from defensiveness and toward a capacity for self-actualization; psychiatric stability which takes stress and turmoil in stride

A sense of commitment, of full involvement; a sense of destiny about oneself; a strong drive toward achievement for its own sake; a sense of strong personal goals and attendant direction of energy in their pursuit

An openness to experience: in relation to the environment, to other people and to one's own inner life; a willingness to admit to consciousness aspects of inner experience that are denied by others, and a drive to express them; intuitive perception and thought

Cognitive capacities of an extraordinary nature reflecting strong theoretical values, a preference for the complex, asymmetrical,

---

° From *Human Potentialities*, by Gardner Murphy. Copyright 1958 by Basic Books, Inc. Reprinted with permission of Basic Books, Inc.

and unordered; a capacity to entertain many ideas simultaneously; independence of judgment; unwillingness to accept any
stage as final

A balance between intellectuality and emotionality; strong aesthetic interests and orientation; freedom from excessive restraint
of impulse; high aesthetic sensitivity

Autonomy in the face of social pressure; an ability to maintain one's
integrity reflecting limited concern for the reaction of others;
achievement via independence rather than conformity; independence in thought and action; relative freedom from conventional restraints on interests.

The most ambitious effort to describe creative personality is found
in Mooney's "Indices of Creative Behavior". Mooney (1953) collected
266 criteria of this kind (e.g. No. 75, "He likes to feel things and perceive things directly"; No. 19, "He is aware of his own vitality"; No. 79,
"He is highly perceptive of some aspects of his environment.") and then
classified them under headings related to his conceptual framework for
identifying creative talent (Mooney, 1957). He suggests two major
rubrics: Self Orientation, and Orientation to Others. The following
headings and sub-heads are used in his organization:

Part I. Self Orientation

1. Openness for the reception and extension of experience: direct
   and spontaneous experiencing; openness to self, environment,
   life, growth and emergence, the unknown, and ideas
2. Movement toward the differentiation and realization of self:
   reaching beyond conformity, asserting independence, realizing
   uniqueness, creating self and world
3. Disciplined management of means to significant experience:
   selection of vital work, concentration of effort, conservation of
   energy, control of work, management of materials, self-management
4. Esthetic ordering of the forms of experience: reflective turn of
   mind, sensitivity to harmonies of relationships; feeling way
   through; structuring toward simplicity and unity; sensing of
   analogies; concern for vital forms; autonomy of ideas; acceptance
   and productive use of the unconscious; awareness of values,
   purposes, assumptions; positive, concrete, vivid, relative thought

Part II. Orientation to Others

1. Openness for the reception and extension of experience with
   others: openness in feeling toward others, openness in feeling

of others toward him, protection of a system of openness in
interpersonal relations, openness to learning about human nature
2. Disciplined management of means to significant experience with
   people: skills used in dealing with others, concepts underlying
   his dealings with others, self-management. (Mooney, 1953)*

The indices that Mooney lists should be helpful as parents, teachers
and other adults (1) seek to identify creative behavior, and (2) work
with young people in helping them develop behavior patterns that tend
toward creative expression. These criteria certainly broaden the notion
of creativity as commonly held and reinforce the assumption that creativeness, in varying degrees, may inhere in all or in most human beings.
To this extent, they may serve as some of the more important goals in
education.

TESTING FOR CREATIVITY

One of the interesting by-products of the effort to identify specific
factors in creativeness has been the development of ingenious devices
to measure hypothesized factors. Seeking evidence for as many as sixteen different factors, Guilford and his colleagues devised 53 separate
tests and were satisfied that they had established fourteen of the sixteen factors. Cattell, Thurstone, Jackson, Getzels, Torrance, Wilson,
and Barron are only some of the investigators who have developed measures for such factors as fluency, sensitivity to problems, closure (or redefinition), facility, humor, perceptual speed, and flexibility of set.
Getzels and Jackson (1962, pp. 198-208) utilized in their study a
group of five measures of creativity, some of which were constructed by
Guilford and Cattell. The five measures were: (1) word association,
asking for as many definitions as possible of common stimulus words;
(2) uses for common things, with responses scored according to the
number and unusual quality of suggested uses for so common and versatile a thing as a brick; (3) hidden shapes, seeking for perception of
a given geometric form concealed in a more complex form or pattern;
(4) fables, seeking for cleverness in suggested endings (moralistic,
humorous or sad) for uncompleted fables; (5) make-up problems,
searching for variety in the number of problems that the subject could
pose, given paragraphs with a number of numerical statements.
Barron used Guilford's unusual uses test and seven others in seeking

---

* From *A Preliminary Listing of Indices of Creative Behavior*, by Ross L. Mooney.
Columbus, Ohio, Bureau of Educational Research, The Ohio State University. Reprinted with permission of Ross L. Mooney.

to measure originality among his group of Air Force captains. A Consequences Test (write what would happen if certain changes were suddenly to take place in a given situation) and a Plot Title Test (provide titles for given stories) were also borrowed from Guilford to identify cleverness and novelty in approach. In addition, the Rorschach and Thematic Apperception Test were administered to measure originality of response. Anagrams were employed to measure both originality and correctness of solutions. Subjects used as many words as possible in a given list in making up a story as still another test of originality. Finally achromatic inkblots were presented, with high scores assigned to the more infrequent responses. All tests called for free responses in order to provide a maximum area of free operation, reflecting Torrance's scepticism as to the possibility of developing "multiple-choice or other objective-type tests which will take full account of individual differences in creative thinking" (Torrance, 1960a). Ratings on six of the eight tests Barron employed correlated to a high degree with independent observers' ratings, but the Rorschach and the inkblots showed low correlations (Barron, 1955).

Guilford and his associates have probably been most assiduous in seeking to test for highly specific factors. Working with 410 Air Cadets and student officers, they designed their 53 separate tests. As an example of their procedure, the following were tests employed to measure ideational fluency, one of their fourteen factors: plot titles, consequences, common situations, brick uses, impossibilities, and sentence analysis.

Torrance and his group working at the University of Minnesota have attempted to adapt a number of tests to children of elementary school age and have also introduced a number of tests of their own. They discovered that they could successfully administer both to children in grades four to six and to college students adaptations of Guilford's tests of unusual uses (substituting a tin can for a brick), impossibilities, consequences, problems, improvements, and situations. They developed a battery in which children were aked to suggest improvements in certain toys so that they would be "more fun to play with." Torrance and Radig built an "Ask-and-Guess Test" showing a situation such as Tom, the Piper's Son, stealing a pig and being chased by some one. "The subject is asked to think of all the questions he can about what is happening, questions which cannot be answered by looking at the picture. Then he is asked to think of all of the possible things which could have caused the action and finally to list all of the possible consequences" (Torrance, 1959; 1962).

The Minnesota group also developed two non-verbal tests: (1) presenting a geometrical figure and asking the subject to sketch objects using the figure as the main element in the design, and (2) looking for non-essential details which a child introduces in drawing a picture of a house, tree, or person (adaptation of Buck's H-T-P Test).

The tests have been used to secure scores on factors also sought by other investigators: ideational fluency, spontaneous flexibility, inventiveness (called "inventivlevel"), and constructiveness. Torrance indicates the group "had no intention of getting into the psychometric business" when they initiated their studies of creative thinking, but "are being seduced" into standardizing the "batteries of fairly promising measures" which they have thus far developed (Torrance, 1960).

For the teacher in the classroom or even for the school administrator, many of these tests may not be available or practicable. One may expect that the same criticisms applied to various intelligence measures may be made of these tests: first, that the effort invested in identification of a few might better go into developing the potential of a higher number of students; second, that any test is subject to the effects of cultural background which may enhance the apparent creativity of some and hide the potential of others; third, that it is difficult to devise any test for which all subjects will be equally motivated. However, the tests serve a real purpose in rescuing creativity as a concept from the realm of mystery and miracles. The tests indicate that factors which may be identified are involved, and they suggest that that which may be measured may also be improved by schools and other social institutions.

Teachers, of course, may justifiably want to experiment with the tests described as giving more of an objective picture than observation alone provides. That identification of gifted youngsters still depends upon the teacher's role as an observer is indicated by the following suggestions given to teachers in New York City:

Creative Potential—Clues to Look For

Children who show these characteristics have creative potential:

Satisfaction in activities which challenge and call for new and different approaches.

Self-discipline, persistence, and sustained concentration.

Ability to go beyond the facts and to discern new implications, to imagine and to speculate.

Originality in going beyond what is now accepted and looking forward to what may be accepted later.

Flexibility and spontaneity that are tied to a goal or purpose.

Ability to enter wholeheartedly and personally into an experience.

Ability to find some unity in apparent diversity, to perceive struc-
ture or to create a new design, to discover similarities and to
relate or connect things.
Sensitive perception of some aspects of the world of nature and of
man.
Auditory imagery as vivid as actual tonal perception.
High abstract and verbal intelligence, and inventiveness.
Awareness of, and concern about, unsolved problems.
Fluency of thought; capacity to evaluate the quality and logic of
ideas.
Ability to analyze, to abstract and to synthesize.
Rugged mental health and stability. (New York City, 1959)

THE CREATIVE ENVIRONMENT

A fourth perspective on creativity is the environment which fosters
creative personality and behavior. This perspective is most meaningful
to teachers and others who work with children because it is in enhancing the environment that they can make their greatest contribution to
education for creativeness. The environment, of course, includes both
the immediate influences that affect the child, and the creative artist
and the culture itself as it encourages or inhibits creative behavior.

In "Creativity and Culture," Stein (1953) develops a strong relationship between the two elements in his title. He takes what he calls a
"bipolar view," assuming that an interaction between individual and
environment is crucial to creative endeavor. "A creative work," he says,
"is a novel work that is accepted as tenable or useful or satisfying *by a
group in time.*" The "culture fosters creativity to the extent that it provides an individual with the opportunity to experience its many facets.
A culture that limits the freedom of a person to study in one or a variety
of areas cuts down his opportunity to pick out the gaps that exist in the
culture and also keeps him from learning the necessary media of communicating his feelings or ideas." (Stein, 1953, p. 312).

In an interesting inquiry into "Environment and Creativity," Taylor
(1961) looks into relationships between superior and subordinate, the
effects of the group on the individual, the influence of "the organization,"
and the culture or *Zeitgeist.* For the working engineer or scientist, the
relationship between superior and subordinate is regarded as the most
important single factor in creative productivity. Creative effort depends
upon an environment in which a man is free to make honest mistakes.
While some studies of the group and its effect on the individual show
greater productivity for the individual working alone, Taylor insists
that the nature of the particular group is critical. In some instances,

individuals may feel that they can be creative only when they work in the group with which they identify. In considering the effects on the individual of "the organization," Taylor draws on Simon and March's "law" that programmed activity tends to drive out unprogrammed activity. He makes the inference that the organization reduces time available for creative effort to the extent that it imposes increasing demands on the creative worker for programmed activities (assigned tasks). Finally, Taylor notes effects of the subculture as it operates through the socio-economic class, and the influence of the larger culture through the *Zeitgeist* or spirit of the times.

For creativity to exist, says Stein, three things are essential: (1) a person who is sensitive to the gaps in his culture and who is able to develop solutions to close the gap; (2) means of communication which are available to that person; (3) an audience which will be receptive to him and to his solutions.

We find mingled pessimism and optimism concerning the availability of these solutions. A number of voices are being heard that bemoan an apparent tendency for creativity to be submerged in organization. Whytes' *Organization Man*, and Riesman's other-directed contemporaries are counterparts of fears expressed in the Rockefeller Brothers Fund report, *The Pursuit of Excellence*, and in the more scholarly formulations of Murphy and Mooney. Technological society means more than the standardization of mechanical parts. It seems to impose upon us a need to do as others do. The concentration of power, industry, and population which characterizes modern life seems to promote group enterprise, group methods, group discussion, sometimes at the expense of individual enterprise, thought, and invention. "Mass production and mass education," says Smith (1957), tend to stifle individual thinking and individual expression." Mooney is troubled with obstacles to creative endeavor that arise from three sources. One is the interdependence in contemporary industrial society that makes being different, original, or dissident more difficult. A second is our "outside enemies"—imagined and real fears that enforce conformity upon us to protect us from such enemies as domestic and foreign adversaries in the Cold War, for example. A third is "inward inexperience," the fact that we are so unpracticed in taking a long, hard look at ourselves (Mooney, 1956). We are so accustomed to our struggle with the outside environment that we do not know ourselves well enough to stand up as individuals so that each of us may dare to realize his unique potential.

Murphy, while recognizing the threats of group life, also contemplates its strengths. He finds a group or "corporate character" of the thinking process in all creative eras. He says we "need to understand both the forces underlying highly focused creative activity of a genius and forces underlying culture-wide creativity which has characterized some people for long periods. . . . Where there is a generation of creators . . . there is mutual stimulation and release through understanding" (Murphy, 1947, pp. 454-55). Perhaps Murphy is challenging us to forego romantic nostalgia, recognize the potential that exists at any time, and "be up and doing."

It seems obvious to recognize current emphases (but has it ever been different?) on what is correct, on good taste and on the "well-adjusted." Riesman implies greater freedom to be "self-differentiating" (Mooney's term) in a past era marked by greater inner-directedness. Yet the witch trials of Salem, the tyranny of the small town, and the pressures of pioneer life were all very powerful stimuli toward conformity in earlier times. Recent creative surges in nuclear physics, modern mathematics, architecture, and sculpture, to name but a few fields selected at random, seem to confirm Murphy's assertion of "culture-wide creativity" and the assumption of ever present creativity in fields that are given kudos by the culture.

THE SCHOOL AND CREATIVE GROWTH

Among a host of community influences the school has a most important role to play in the development or inhibition of the creative disposition. The school (or any institution, for that matter) may serve to raise high barriers such as those mentioned. "Much more than a limited restraining effect" is feared by Murphy. "There is always the possibility of a critical interference with the integrative process by which the many free components in a free personality flow together at the time of the first great explorations in life" (1958, p. 169). Accordingly, he advises provision in schools of special facilities for recognition and encouragment of highly creative persons. It is not enough to urge students to think creatively. They must be encouraged to associate freely with creative peers in fellowship with daring and inspired teachers. He describes a sequence: "First, support, a hand to hold; then a few steps alone; then a race against time to see how much a short life can yield" (p. 168).

Russell points out that young children are often creative in language, construction, play, graphic, and dramatic activities. These creative tendencies are associated with other characteristics such as ease of emotional response, lack of conventional knowledge, and comparative freedom to experiment. Creative thinking in children ranges from highly personal, imaginative productions to solutions of special problems in not unusual ways. The personal, autistic dimension decreases, however, in favor of more highly directed problem-solving as tasks are set by the school and these replace self-initiated and self-directed activity. The child is caught between demands of spontaneity and conformity (1956, Chap. 11). "Childhood and creativity often go together," Russell says. "One of the consequences of growing up is that people begin to behave in rubrics, to act in terms of stereotypes" (*Ibid.*, p. 328). Smith concurs: "An inhibited and restricted child learns to imitate and will soon content himself with following set patterns in life rather than to take the initiative to think through his problems for himself. . . . To think creatively each child must identify himself with his own experiences. In fact, he must experience intensely himself" (Smith, 1957, p. 76).

Torrance lists "a number of factors which appear to block the development of creative thinking abilities":

> Premature attempts to eliminate fantasy ("Many teachers and parents regard fantasies as something unhealthy and to be eliminated.")
>
> Restrictions on manipulativeness and curiosity ("a significant relationship between degree of manipulation and quality and quantity of inventive responses")
>
> Overemphasis on sex roles ("The high degree of sensitivity involved in creative thinking has a distinctly *feminine* character in our society; the independence and autonomy required has a distinctly masculine character.")
>
> Overemphasis on prevention of frustration
>
> Induction of fear and timidity ("We have been unable to evoke a maximum performance from some subjects because of their fear and timidity.")
>
> Emphasis on verbal skills ("The school's overemphasis on verbal skills and insufficient emphasis on problem solving . . .") (Torrance, 1959, p. 314)

In a later publication, Torrance (1962) lists other "problems in maintaining creativity." Many of these problems arise from personal relationships with parents, teachers or classmates. Included are "sanctions against divergency"—the feeling of others that they are threatened when creative children express their uniqueness. Equally difficult for others to accept is the creative child's preference to learn on his own, to find his unique identity (in a sense, to be different), to attempt difficult tasks and dangerous activities. Torrance adds these factors together to speak of the "psychological estrangement of creative children."

The problem of recognition is mentioned by many writers. Henry (1957) is concerned with recognition because he believes that creativity, like other learnings, needs to be reinforced. He makes the following hypotheses concerning "*pre*-creativity" in elementary school children:

> Creativity is probably associated with responses not customarily reinforced.
> Creativity is associated with heterogeneity of responses. . . .
> Creativity is accidental (unplanned, unscheduled) behavior in a social organization.
> Creative responses are inadvertently reinforced.

Henry seems convinced that creativity has to fight against odds in asserting itself in childhood. "It would seem to be the nature of creativity and novelty in children that it begins as an accidental, customarily unreinforced, response, occurring in a matrix of standardized behavior, and that in the beginning it tends to survive by eluding the cultural controls, by appearing undetected amid the cultural stereotypes. One might say that *in the beginning creative activity is like a criminal eluding the police by losing himself in the crowd*" (Henry, 1957, p. 152). He regards the creative response as being in essence an error, a deviation from required homogeneity, which is rewarded. On the basis of this reinforcement, the deviation from the pattern tends to spread or generalize.

The school would seem to be caught on the horns of a dilemma. On one side is the matter of maximum free, independent growth, the attainment of which seems consonant with growth in creative power. On the other side are the needs to maintain a cultural heritage, to set learning assignments, to "acculturate" the individual. In this lie hazards of conformism and limiting creative growth and behavior.

To guide schools in fostering creative development, Drews (1962) suggests certain conditions which facilitate the burgeoning of talent, and these may be applied to creativity as well. The conditions include expectancy of original and superior work, encouragement, provision of models in school and community, giving of awards, freedom to develop, and psychological acceptance of originality and superior performance. Torrance (1962, Chap. 8) puts emphasis on rewarding diverse contributions, developing minimum skills, utilizing opportunities, and developing values and purposes. In recognition of possible obstacles, he advocates reducing overemphasis on sex roles, avoiding equation of divergency with mental illness, reducing isolation, and helping youngsters to cope with anxieties or fears.

DeHaan and Havighurst, analyzing specific activities in schools provide a list of procedures that stifle activities and a second list which promote creative effort. On the negative side:

1. High standards of achievement for low level work
2. Inflexible assignments and methods of work
3. Impatience of adults
4. Conformity to group standards of mediocrity
5. The teacher's attitude (De Haan, 1957, pp. 171-72)

On the positive side they suggest procedures to develop creativity:

1. Encourage the gifted child to be productive.
2. Make extra time available.
3. Provide stimulation to produce and perform.
4. Provide materials.
5. Serve as an audience.
6. Help children become more sensitive to their own inner needs and problems in the environment.
7. Employ activities to stimulate creativity.
8. Assist in extra-curricular activities.
9. Inform parents of child's abilities.
10. Refer child and parents to other agencies that can assist.
11. Help find scholarships, contests, awards. (*Ibid.*, pp. 174-79)*

Other writers confirm or extend the preceding list of what the schools ought to do. Guilford (1950) believes we need more understanding of the nature of thinking. Upon such understanding we might build knowledge of what specific steps to take in order to teach students to think. Murphy (1947) looks for "a pattern of creative skills . . . which may be gained by persistent practice." The school should be able to help students discover and manipulate their sensory experience "so as to restructure their relations, to complicate them, and to improvise new ones." Russell (1956, pp. 380-87) suggests the school may help in the building of a background of related experiences and afford "accessibility of a variety of materials, time and a permissive atmosphere for creative work, and a teacher who has had experience in creative activities." He adduces evidence that appreciation as well as performance of a creative sort can also be encouraged in the classroom or other group situations.

Some suggestions are available for emphasis on specific skills, presumably involved in creative performance. Moreno (1962) sees a need for "spontaneity training" and advocates the use of psychodrama to release creativity in children and adolescents. He gives examples of such procedures in teaching communication skills, foreign languages, and even vocational skills.

---

* Reprinted from *Educating Gifted Children*, by Robert F. DeHaan and Robert J. Havighurst, by permission of The University of Chicago Press. Copyright 1957 by The University of Chicago

Various authors have given attention to development of sensitivity, including both sense perception and intuitive perception. Carlson (1960) recommends such training at the early childhood level, and urges a balance between impression and expression. MacKinnon (1961a, p. 92) says frankly that we do not know how much educational method can do to foster the development of intuitive perception and intuitive thinking. However, he ventures the guess that rote learning, emphasis on various facts per se, and memorization reinforce sense perception, while other methods may contribute to strengthening intuitive perception and thinking. These methods include, he suggests, efforts to transfer from one subject to another, efforts to seek out common principles that relate facts in different disciplines, stress on analogies, metaphors and symbols, and exercises in "imaginative play."

In suggesting criteria for evaluation of programs aiming at creative development, Hilgard (*In* Anderson, 1959) also prescribes a recipe for method. These criteria include the following:

1. *Initiation* of inquiry by students on their own
2. Opportunity to take responsibility for creative work, to exhibit it, and to take satisfaction even "in small evidences of creativity"
3. Judging the student's original work in terms of individual progress rather than group norms
4. Time for substantial involvement in "idiosyncratic specialization"
5. Evidence of yearly progress toward diversity of talent rather than conformity. Self-initiation, recognition and satisfaction, individual goals, time for "divergent" activity, and progress toward diversity are Hilgard's key words in growth toward creativeness (Anderson, 1959, p. 180).

Drews (1962) argues the merits of discovery as a way of learning and cites the work of Beberman in the University of Illinois Curriculum Studies in Mathematics. The "open-ended" experiment in science would be another illustration of this approach.

Torrance (1962) follows a similar track in underscoring the individual learning styles of different persons. In a study in four quite different school environments, Torrance compared how well creative subjects learned in situations exhibiting learning by memory as contrasted with situations where pupil initiative and discovery were presumably more in evidence. He noted that highly creative students learned as much as high IQ students, but not in all schools. "Apparently highly creative individuals prefer to learn creatively rather than by authority and when given an opportunity to learn in that way achieve as well as their more intelligent but less creative peers" (p. 63). With Torrance, Getzels and

Jackson (1962, pp. 124-30) distinguish between IQ and creativeness, between remembering and discovering, between information and knowledge.

While there is a tendency to underscore process in learning rather than the subject-matter absorbed, MacKinnon (1961) indicates the need to have a large body of facts as well as reasoning skills in order to establish the widest possible set of relationships among facts. He notes the complementary nature of theoretical and aesthetic values held by creative persons and urges school attention both to the cognitive search for truth and the aesthetic search for beauty.

Taylor (1962), writing on "The Effects of Instructional Media on Creativity," offers some insights that spread from media to the whole realm of instruction. He starts from a general concern with the impression normally given in complex technological aids of omniscience, of a closed universe, and of single ways to do things. He seeks, instead, ways of using new media and instruction in general so that students develop a picture of an open universe where new questions are always possible, where solutions are not permanently fixed, and where individual learning styles and problem-solving strategies are encouraged. To do this, he would like discussion and recitation techniques to recognize bold, intuitive leaps as well as systematic steps forward. He wants all students to see that new ideas cannot be judged solely by present-day common-sense notions. He urges development of evaluative methods that don't "program" or fence students in, therein reducing their chances to be creative. Instruction should recognize the need for a rich inner life, for creative reception as well as creative expression, and for the development of a sense of genuine involvement on the part of students. On the surface teaching by television and programmed instruction threaten such goals. Taylor implies other, more creative possibilities in the use of the new technology if educators will establish and seek an objective of creativeness.

Concern for creative development necessitates fundamental rethinking in programs—even programs for the gifted—which have traditionally revolved about conventional definitions of intelligence and giftedness. Torrance (1962, pp. 193-203) indicates the sweeping nature of needed reforms. A program that really focussed on creativity would first of all have to reorient identification procedures so that measures of creativeness were added to conventional IQ scores. Second, there would have to be a rethinking of objectives of the curriculum and of particular courses so as to include creative thinking. For example, Torrance cites a study of social studies units in high schools in which the teachers classified their work as 70.7 per cent cognitive, 5.3 per cent memorizing,

18.7 per cent convergent thinking, 1.7 per cent divergent thinking, and 3.6 per cent evaluative. While the proportions may vary in other subjects, the small portion allowed for divergent thinking suggests the scope of reform necessary. Third, change is needed in the curriculum so that students may learn creatively much of what they now learn by authority. Fourth, new methods and materials must be developed to foster creative growth and to stimulate students to learn creatively. Fifth, new measures of achievement must be devised to include assessment of creative thinking in the year's learning performance. Finally, teacher-pupil relationships have to be reviewed to discover ways for rewarding creative thought.

THE TEACHER AND CREATIVE GROWTH

Because of the impact of school climate, models and interpersonal relationships, the teacher would seem to play a large part in the encouragement or inhibition of creative tendencies. Carlson (1960) and Torrance (1960b) prescribe a teacher who is himself a fully functioning, self-actualizing person. They seek a teacher who is sensitive, resourceful, flexible, willing to get off the beaten track. His view of himself must be so positive that he can relate constructively to others and particularly to creative students who may be so self-consciously different as to seem obnoxious at times. This positive view of self is probably necessary, moreover, to avoid regarding the unusual student as a threat. To inspire sensitivity and intuitive perception on the part of his proteges, the teacher must exhibit the openness to experience he is trying to foster in others. He must share the theoretical and aesthetic orientations of his gifted students if he is to be able to partake in their creative discourse.

Torrance is interested, too, in the teacher's function as a guide. He lists the following roles that the teacher plays: a "refuge" against the slings, woes, and criticism of the world, a sponsor or patron, a guide in understanding difference from other people, a listener for communing ideas, a resource for recognition of creative talent (Torrance, 1962, pp. 8-14).

Rasey (1956) indicates the need for shift in role-concept on the part of teachers from that of "imparter of knowledge" to that of "creator." She sees the teacher as a stage manager and scene shifter leading the child into areas rich in experience.

Dangers to creative development are also related to the figure of the teacher. Henry (1957) points to the assumption generally made that greater attention to children's needs and reduced distance between the teacher and children provide ideal conditions for creativity. But of all needs, the child's need for love is the strongest. If the teacher's love is administered in a uniform way, the child tends to abandon his heterogeneous (creative) behavior in order to obtain the affection of the teacher. Thus, he is likely to "stay in line" to satisfy his need for love—and it may be the teacher who is apparently giving greatest attention to children's needs who may serve most, though unintentionally, to stifle creativity.

GUIDELINES IN SCHOOL APPROACHES TO CREATIVITY

From the foregoing analyses of the creative process, creative product, creative personality, and environmental factors essential to creativity, a number of guidelines may be inferred to assist school personnel in fostering creative development.

One of the initial phases in creating has been identified as opening windows on experience. Lowenfeld seeks to encourage spontaneity of expression and resulting ability to take advantage of a given situation in developing new ones. The mind, he says, seems never to stand still, but maintains a "chain reaction" in response to the initial stimulus. In children the initial response may well be found in fantasy:

> As soon as phantasy is translated into some form of expression through the intuitive power of the creator, it ceases to be mere phantasy. Educationally, this is of great significance because it answers the often placed question of how far we should go in stimulating the phantasy of children without "overstimulating" them. We cannot go far enough as long as the child uses it and turns it into concrete and factual material, such as his creations. It is the intuitive quality of the imagery of the gifts which does not stop without this great fulfillment. (Lowenfeld, 1956, p. 17) *

Russell (1956), too, believes that fantasy, wishes, and dreams are involved in imaginative thought. He raises the practical question as to the extent to which these can flourish in a busy classroom of 30 or 35 children. He suggests planning of certain quiet periods during the day with a chance for children to read, write, draw, or rest—and be open to the dream-fantasy-wish process.

Stimulation through a rich environment appears to be a universal recipe in the education for creative expression and interpretation of experience. The maintenance of spontaneity is part of this. If the first guideline is the maintenance of a rich environment, the second is freedom from a completely structured situation which gives the child little opportunity for creative endeavor. Patterning the responses of children,

---

* From "The Case of the Gifted Child," by Viktor Lowenfeld. Reprinted with permission from *School Arts*, April, 1956.

setting endless tasks for children to perform, asking for illustration rather than free expression in art forms: these leave the child little opportunity to explore his own world of imagination, dream, and aspiration.

A third guideline is recognition given to the creative child. The psychological principle of reinforcement through reward is applied here. School and home are advised to look at creativity in children as a process rather than as a product—to expect what is personally original to the child, not what is historically new to human civilization. The child should be helped to sense personal satisfaction in being creative.

A fourth guideline recognizes closure, redefinition, or reorganization of experience in creative behavior. Russell (1956, p. 385) emphasizes the importance of both the perceptual and the integrative factors in creative thinking. To the teacher this may suggest the value of placing emphasis on helping youngsters see relationships, contrasts and sequences.

A fifth guideline counsels recognition of group contributions to individual creativity. While the group can exert tyrannical control that represses originality, it can also stimulate certain types of creative thinking. Both Murphy and Russell have pointed to the interpersonal stimulation that comes from groups working simultaneously on similar problems or similar media. The theoretical justification for the committee approach to problems is the expectation that new syntheses may appear as a result of group endeavor. These outcomes may be quite different from any of the ideas that the individuals in the group originally introduced.

Sixth guideline is recognition of the role of self-discovery in creativity. In expressing his own unique thoughts, the individual may be regarded as ultimately finding himself. Mooney describes this process as self-realization and self-differentiation. An inference that teachers and parents may draw is that a path to development of creative activity is assisting children to find themselves. Such discovery may come through creative play or dramatics or through any other activity that helps develop a sense of self (Russell, 1956, p. 385). Hopkins declares, "Each child must be free to create the new meanings necessary to release and emerge himself. Children must understand through use of personal empirical observation the process of their own creativeness which is their own life fulfillment" (Hopkins, 1956, p. 282).

Seventh guideline underscores the importance of readiness as a factor in creativeness as in other human processes. Readiness is approached through environmental stimulation, but also through what Murphy calls "the inner logic of material and the inner logic of human personality in relation to the structure of material" (Murphy, 1958, p. 166).

To Murphy creativeness represents a developmental process that follows the growth of the child. In the early years he sees childlike fantasy and the delight of the child in "sensory values, meanings, pursuit of curiosity, delight in uniformities and laws" (*Ibid.*, p. 162). As the child grows older he notes a "great burst of fresh enthusiasm which sweeps like wildfire through the minds of those boys and girls who want to know, to control, who want to get hold of meanings, who want to grow in and through this strange, exciting, challenging environment" (p. 165). With John Fiske, he points out that the gradual prolongation in our culture of infancy permits mankind a span of years for the enrichment of creative potentialities before the responsibilities of adulthood arrive. These adolescent years, with childish fantasy not far in the background, with enthusiasm at a fever pitch, are the years when one may hope for uniquely creative endeavor. The tragedy of the period is that adolescence is often wasted in drilling into young people "standardized information and skills—skills often picked up incidentally in adolescence much more easily if creative discovery has been fostered in the first years of the latency period [childhood]" (p. 166). To teachers and curriculum planners the significance of this point of view is strong. Emphasis on learning for college entrance, on skills for future use, may blot out a time in life which is uniquely adapted to initiating creative outlooks and endeavors.

Eighth, the importance of the community has to be recognized as a stimulus to creative effort and as an environment which reinforces or represses divergent thought and expression. The school which arrogates to itself the whole of educational planning and operation assumes a needlessly heavy burden of responsibility and closes the door on far richer resources than any school could ever have. Access must be had not only to the activities and facilities of the school, but also to communication with actively creating individuals in the community, farms, industry, libraries, museums, and the physical environment of the total milieu.

The teacher, of course, is the crucial figure in the school environment. Strang (*in* Witty, 1959, pp. 24-25) underlines the need for teachers "who maintain an attitude of inquiry, who do not know all the answers." She seeks the teacher who "is alert to creative sparks in his pupils. He watches, listens, and perceives potentialities, notices children who want to do the original thing, who put ideas together in new relations."

Comparable to the influence of the teacher is the atmosphere of the school and the classroom. Hopkins (1956) defines "creative climate" as involving: an atmosphere in which each person receives a maximum acceptance by direct empathy; ways of working which enable each child to remove fears that stem from authoritarian experiences, which help the child locate new areas of interest; freedom for the child to create new meaning necessary to release and further his own emergence as an individual. Strang seeks a school atmosphere which "demands order and discipline while it offers opportunities for initiative and originality." Such an atmosphere assures a quiet background for contemplation, exploration, and performance. It protects the child from the intrusions of disorder and from the inhibiting effects of prohibitions raised at every point by too strict a discipline.

SUMMARY

In the education of gifted children there is probably no objective more important than the development of creative ability. From the perspective of the individual there is the need, challenge, opportunity, and responsibility to help each person become all that he possibly may. His essential individuality is to be found in his originality rather than his adaptation to a culture, his assimilation of the heritage, however desirable these may be as *means* to the end of individual development. From the perspective of society there is little point in concentrating attention on education of the gifted unless the very able are being helped to create something new, to add something to the culture, and not simply to maintain it as they have received it.

To assist in development of creativity, educators can draw upon a rapidly developing body of research. Perhaps the greatest contribution comes from an attitude that creativity is not so mysterious that it defies study and analysis. As a result, recent investigation appears to confirm the existence of specific, observable factors within the global concept of creativeness. Ingenious tests have been developed which measure these factors with some reliability, and these factors are found to undergird creative work in dissimilar fields. In addition to defining creativity as a personal characteristic, research has had some success in describing the creative process and in distinguishing stages in this process. Investigations into the nature of the creative personality have uncovered a body of information which may also assist educators in developing characteristics essential to the realization of creative potential.

Research on creativity has been performed in school situations also. Provocative evidence has already been gathered on relationships among creativeness, intelligence test scores, and school achievement. This research indicates a need to reevaluate reliance upon the IQ, even as a predictor of scholastic performance. Investigators are concerned about measured attitudes of teachers toward children with high creative potential. There is growing emphasis upon the impact of the school environment, methods and materials on children, and their attitude toward creativity.

The extent to which creative potential is released may well serve as a fundamental criterion in judging the effectiveness of any program that purports to promote giftedness. Against such a criterion one must evaluate all of the controversial proposals that are made. Does acceleration by shortening the period of formal school attendance hasten self-realization in the independence of adulthood and thereby enhance creative behavior? Or does acceleration place emphasis upon more rapid mastery of the heritage and thereby eliminate opportunities arising in a less hurried schedule for creative thought or playful fantasy? Does homogeneous grouping ensure the play of one creative mind against another? Or does homogeneous grouping promote conformity to teacher-imposed standards? Do suggestions to increase the academic load and homework of secondary school students enforce a richer and more stimulating environment? Or does the greater load preclude unstructured, independent, creative activities? Does a more rigidly prescriptive curriculum guarantee tools with which to work? Or does prescription violate principles of "controlled freedom" for creative talent?

Too often new proposals are made on a basis of what seemed to work in some mythically golden era in the past or on a basis of personal predilection or vested interest. In education of the gifted, as in other areas, objectives and criteria are of basic import. One such criterion is the contribution made by any proposal to development of individuals who will be creative in living their own lives and in facing the pressing needs of our times.

Chapter 6

Planning Programs for Gifted Students

*The whole art of teaching is only the
art of awakening the natural curiosity
of young minds for the purpose of
satisfying them afterwards.*

—Anatole France

Americans look to the schools for all kinds of miracles in the education and rearing of their children. We have a traditional faith in education as a pathway to success, a panacea for social ills, and an instrument for adjustment of the unfortunate. For the gifted child, schools hold the greatest promise of all since human talents and capacities are not in full-flower at birth. The more sophisticated the gifts, the more they need assiduous development in order to reach fruition. To say that the school owes a special responsibility to the intellectually gifted might imply neglect of the schools' obligation to every child as an individual. It is true, however, that schools are strategically organized to bring intellectual capacities to full bloom and to assist in the development of various special abilities as well.

Education of the gifted is one application of the doctrine of adapting programs to individual differences and needs. The Southern Regional Project for Education of the Gifted (1962) provides a well-reasoned rationale to justify special education for gifted students. In its manual for program improvement, five underlying assumptions are listed:

1. Gifted children as a group differ from others in learning ability; they learn faster and remember more, and they tend to think more deeply with and about what they learn.

2. As adults, gifted persons tend to remain similarly advanced beyond the average and tend to assume distinctive social roles
   as leaders in the reconstruction and advancement of whatever
   lines of activity they engage in.

3. The regular school curriculum only barely approximates the
   demands of either the greater learning capacity or the anticipated social roles of gifted persons.

4. An educational program *can* be devised which *does* more adequately meet these basic demands, and which on the whole
   being uniquely suited to the gifted is both unnecessary for and
   impossible of accomplishment by students of lesser ability.

5. Differentiated educational provisions for the gifted promise to
   discover more gifted persons, to improve their education, and
   to launch them earlier into their chosen careers so that society
   as well as the persons themselves, may enjoy longer the fruits of
   their productive and creative labors.

                                    (Southern Regional Project, 1962, p. 22)*

Some schools and some teachers are more successful in making this
kind of adaptation than others. A number of schools have reported practices or are exploring programs that appear to be unusually successful
in individualizing instruction at the upper ends of ability scales. This
chapter is concerned with principles of planning such programs at the
elementary, secondary, and college levels. Succeeding chapters will
discuss specific programs at these levels and in the commonly required
subject areas.

PRINCIPLES FOR PLANNING

Education of the gifted represents a point in the continuum of education of all students. In planning special programs this idea should be
kept in mind since too many enthusiasts plead that the gifted represent a
special case. They imply that schooling of the gifted warrants the offhand
rejection of all research in education and psychology in general. If a
particular curriculum is effective for most students one should assume
that appropriate modification rather than outright rejection is desirable
for the gifted. If given methods have proved their worth for the total
student population, it is likely that these methods will work with the
gifted if they are adapted in the light of established differences between

---

* From *The Gifted Student: A Manual for Program Development*, by the Southern Regional Project for the Education of the Gifted. Reprinted with permission of
the Southern Regional Education Board.

the gifted and the average. Conversely, if various procedures or materials have not proved successful with most students, one ought not to assume that they will work better with the gifted unless there is good evidence to show that failure in the past has been due to intellectual difficulty of the material. It is no secret that much curricular deadwood lingers long because of tradition or sentiment. What has seemed boring or useless to the average pupil is likely to strike the gifted child in the same way. A first principle that may be enunciated, therefore, in planning programs for exceptional students, is that these programs must be based on sound educational and psychological foundations that can be supported by research rather than tradition and sentiment.

Second, education takes place in a culture, both in a global and national setting and in a local community or neighborhood. Education of the gifted has to take into consideration community attitudes toward exceptional performance in any field and in academic fields in particular. The goals that are set have to be consistent with what the nation and the community want for children. Where there are differences between the national aspiration, community attitudes, and professional hopes, the profession has two choices. It may accept lower standards or it may work for change in community attitudes toward learning and indirectly for change in national cultural aspirations as well. The design for education of the gifted cannot be limited to the school and to children; it must include a program of community orientation and participation.

Third, education of the gifted is founded upon a good program of education for all students. It is not separate from the total program and it is certainly not in competition with it. There is no point in contrasting what is spent for the palsied child with what is spent for the intellectually gifted. There is no justification in arguing that the best teachers should be assigned to the gifted. Education for any group of students can be no better than the total educational program of a school district. No child is ever a member of the special group alone. Not every gifted child is identified for special treatment. The program for the gifted should be a suitable capstone of a strong, effective, and seemly educational arch, not a glittering mansion in an educational slum.

Fourth, the program should express a clearly reasoned philosophy of education of the gifted. This philosophy should include the educational outcomes that represent goals for each gifted child as well as the objectives of the school system. What kind of individual are we trying to develop in terms of personal qualities and achievement? What kinds of programs are we trying to establish to produce this kind of individual? Williams presents an interesting selection of statements on objectives in Chapter VIII of the National Society for the Study of Education's Yearbook, *Education for the Gifted* (NSSE, 1957, pp. 147-54). The objectives in a single school are exemplified in Hildreth's account (1952) of the program at Hunter College Elementary School. Common to most statements is the ideal of educating a person who will live a life that provides for a maximum of self-realization and social contribution. Other goals include a sense of social responsibility, creativeness, versatility and breadth of interest, depth of information and understanding, effective thinking and personal happiness.

Fifth, the program should place heavy emphasis on the identification of potential. The school should have a systematic approach to the discovery of talent, but it must also give attention to means of identifying abilities that are hidden by under-achievement, lack of motivation, and cultural handicaps. The identification program, as indicated in Chapter 4, must supplement the customary testing devices with a broad exploratory program and with the sympathetic eyes of teachers who are alert to the faintest glimmer of potential.

Sixth, as an integral part of an educational system, a special program for the gifted has to provide for fluid communication and movement of teachers and pupils inside and outside the program. All teachers should have a chance to teach in the program if they wish, and no teachers or administrators should be identified with this program as their vested interest. When special classes are set up, teachers and pupils should not lose sight of the fact that identification and assignment procedures are rarely perfect. Some exceptional youngsters will remain outside the special program; in some school systems the policy decision may reject special classes altogether. In either case the teacher can expect to have some very able students in "regular" classes.

Seventh, focus has to be placed on instruction and curriculum. Administrative devices like acceleration and grouping may have some purpose, but what really counts ultimately is what happens to the bright youngster in the classroom—and what he is stimulated to do by himself. The heart of any program, therefore, has to be the cooperative faculty planning and the individual teacher operation that make new and better learning experiences available to young people. Teachers need time for this kind of planning, and they need the means for study, visiting, and exchange of ideas if they are to conduct continuously improving programs. While the administrator is often solely responsible for securing the material means, while he is regarded as the kingpin in making the administrative or organizational adjustments, his greatest contribution comes in the leadership that he gives to his professional staff in cooperative planning of enriched programs for gifted students.

Eighth, one of the most important jobs of instructional and guidance personnel is to consider problems of motivation and underachievement. As indicated in Chapter 16 lack of motivation is the most frequent cause of failure to develop potential ability. A systematic program needs to be planned to develop and maintain high levels of aspiration in the hearts of gifted pupils. In some communities the culture may make this effort unnecessary; in others the values of the community culture may be the chief bar to the achievement of promise.

Underachievement is often related to low motivation but is also frequently caused by other factors as described in Chapter 16. No agency is as well equipped as the school to recognize underachievement or to take steps to do something about it. Identifying underachieving pupils is in itself an excellent argument for more rapid extension of guidance services to elementary schools and the improvement of guidance in secondary schools. One of the major services in a program for the gifted, then, is the development of motivation and the early recognition of underachievement.

Ninth, while the school assumes its own responsibility for the development of talent, it also recognizes the role of other agencies in the community. Youth-serving agencies, private and public, formal and informal, are able to provide facilities, services, and an environment which are different from the schools'. Various individuals, working outside institutional frameworks, often have still other valuable services to offer. Industry and social organization in the community are yet other sources. Schools should recognize the many facets to development of ability and share with other agencies and individuals in coordinating activities. In this way maximum use may be made of a community's resources to develop high potential.

Tenth, a program needs continuity. Special attention to able youngsters at only the high school level may come too late. Underachievement and the development of motivation set in much earlier. Stimulation in elementary school alone may result in boredom in a junior high school which recognizes only one level of ability. A special program in junior high school needs to build on something positive in elementary school and something constructive in senior high. It is distressing to note the example of some school systems which have introduced foreign language into the elementary school without planning continued study in junior high.

Eleventh, bricks are not made without straw. There is no point in casting envious glances at per-pupil costs in the case of mental and physical handicaps or in attempting to justify greater (or less) expenditure for the gifted than for the average. Additional funds are not spent because the children are brighter and therefore worth greater expenditure. Extra funds can be asked only when the faculty wants to do specific things with exceptional youngstes because these specific things have the best educational potential. Funds are asked for these learning experiences and not for the gifted students *qua* gifted students. So also may some high cost activities be requested for average and slow students. The budget should be planned in terms of the experiences planned, not in terms of cost-per-pupil segregated on an ability basis. What is important here is not a specially high budget for exceptional students but a total educational budget adequate to a program for developing the individual potential of all students in the school system.

Both in terms of personnel and budget it is important to remember that education of the gifted simply extends the principle of individual opportunity to cases of extraordinary ability. For this reason the "separatist" position of many writers on special education should be viewed critically. For administrative purposes it is often necessary to segregate costs of particular parts of the school program. Sometimes, when there is special interest in education of the handicapped or the gifted, it is easier to secure special funds in these areas than it is to secure funds for the total school program. Ultimately, however, it is of little service to either the handicapped or the gifted to be setting up completely separate programs, to make unchangeable identification, to establish vested interests and little empires, to develop petty jealousies and animosities, and eventually to create "sitting ducks" in splendid isolation which are inviting targets for ill-intentioned critics of all or part of the school system.

A FRAMEWORK IN CURRICULUM DEVELOPMENT

A basic component in education of the gifted is the curriculum framework within which the teacher operates and the curriculum planning which he does within the overall pattern. Earlier consideration of the characteristics of gifted children and their learning patterns suggests some of the guidelines that are discussed below. Whether the teacher is planning for children in his own classes or whether he is a member of a committee planning programs for superior children, he may find these suggestions helpful.

Gifted Children are Children Still. The basic needs and drives of children do not change because they have superior intellectual power, nor is a new psychology of learning called for. Research supporting the "activity" approach and unit procedures has proved just as valid for bright children as for others. When bright children remain with their classmates in cross-sections of the school population, unit organization makes individual learning at a suitable pace and depth more feasible than do older classroom routines. Segregated groups, such as Hunter Elementary's, Cleveland's Major Work Classes, and the Colfax Workshops, also attest to the superiority of unit planning. The integration of learning experiences is as much desired for the gifted as for the general, perhaps more so, because of the greater urge on the part of bright children to see relationships, to understand why things are as they are.

Because bright children function as children rather than as disembodied brains, it is useful to do program planning in terms of the "developmental needs" concept that Havighurst has explored (1953) or the "persistent life situations" of Stratemeyer and her colleagues (1957). Havighurst's thesis is that every person faces particular developmental tasks at a particular time of life. Successful mastery of these tasks "leads to happiness and success with other tasks, while failure leads to unhappiness in the individual, disapproval by society, and difficulty with later tasks" (1953, p. 6). Havighurst lists the following tasks as those of the elementary school years:

1. Learning physical skills necessary for ordinary games
2. Building wholesome attitudes toward oneself as a growing organism
3. Learning to get along with age-mates
4. Learning an appropriate masculine or feminine social role
5. Developing fundamental skills in reading, writing, and calculating
6. Developing concepts necessary for everyday living
7. Developing conscience, morality, and a scale of values
8. Achieving personal independence
9. Developing attitudes toward social groups and institutions (*Ibid.*, pp. 15-28)

The adolescent, says Havighurst, faces the following tasks:

1. Achieving new and more mature relations with age-mates of both sexes
2. Achieving a masculine or feminine social role
3. Accepting one's physique and using the body effectively
4. Achieving emotional independence of parents and other adults
5. Achieving assurance of economic independence
6. Selecting and preparing for an occupation
7. Preparing for marriage and family life
8. Developing intellectual skills and concepts necessary for civic competence

    9. Desiring and achieving socially responsible behavior
   10. Acquiring a set of values and an ethical system as a guide to
       behavior *(Ibid.,* pp. 33-71)°

In designing a curriculum for gifted students these tasks ought to be kept in mind. Books and academic achievement are no substitute for these goals. Havighurst maintains that these tasks need be accomplished in childhood and adolescence or failure to do so will stand in the way of adequate living ever after. The school curriculum has to take these tasks into consideration. It should not encourage bright children to substitute other gratifications even though scholastic success is pleasing to the teacher and to parents. More important than such temporary accomplishment is the possibility that underachievement at a later date may result from poor emotional adjustment which in turn reflects failure to get on with these developmental tasks at the proper time.

Of interest, too, is the framework suggested by Stratemeyer. Her thesis is that the child, the adolescent, and the adult face certain persisting situations in life at successively more mature levels. She proposes that the curriculum be organized around these situations since they compose the important learning and living activities of children and adults. She offers a schema which sums up these situations:

EDUCATION IN OUR DEMOCRACY

means

development of individual understanding and responsibility

in dealing with

INDIVIDUAL AND GROUP SITUATIONS OF EVERYDAY LIVING

by providing

MAXIMUM GROWTH IN INDIVIDUAL CAPACITIES AND
SOCIAL PARTICIPATION

as the learner grows in ability to deal with

ENVIRONMENTAL FACTORS AND FORCES

(Stratemeyer, 1957, p. 147)°°

   The individual and group situations include the family, civic and social activities, work, leisure and spiritual life. Individual capacities subsume

---

° From *Human Development and Education,* by Robert J. Havighurst. Copyright © 1953 by Longmans, Green and Company. Reprinted through the courtesy of David McKay Company, Inc.
°° From *Developing a Curriculum for Modern Living,* Second Edition, by Florence B. Stratemeyer and others. Copyright 1957. Reprinted with permission of the Bureau of Publications, Teachers College, Columbia University.

health, intellectual power, moral choices, aesthetic expression and appreciation. Social participation involves person-to-person relations, group membership and intergroup relations. Environmental factors and forces include natural phenomena, technological resources and economic-social-political structures and forces (*Ibid.*).

The paragraph above suggests a functional listing of subject-matter for children, adolescents or adults. It is cited here as one of the "social processes" curriculum organizations which have been recommended in the past thirty years. In education of the gifted it has particular significance since it is based on the premise that the conventional subjects themselves are not enough, that some meaning has to come from them, and that "more of the same" is not truly "enrichment." The task in education of gifted children is not simply to add more reading, more arithmetic, more science, but to help the bright child find greater meaning in the life about him. One way is to begin with Havighurst's list or Stratemeyer's schema (or any variant thereof), and to examine curriculum offerings in the light of these suggestions. New experiences may then be introduced which contribute to the achievement of goals which the faculty selects. Stratemeyer presents a comprehensive list of persistent life situations that illustrates increasing maturity levels in experiences which the school can provide (*Ibid.*, pp. 155-321).

The Place of the "Fundamentals," Drill, and Routine. A large part of elementary education is devoted to mastery of what we term the "fundamentals": reading, writing, arithmetic, geography, American History, and some smattering of world history and science. Hollingworth was convinced from her studies that the bright child learned what was presented to him in half the time alloted and that the exceptionally able learned the content of the elementary curriculum in just one-fourth of the time needed by average pupils. Where little was done to enrich the curriculum or accelerate the pupil, in her opinion, from one-half to three-quarters of his time was wasted.

The problem of excessive time devoted to drill affects the junior and senior high schools also. Differential learning rates in secondary schools spread farther and farther. The typical two or three year spread in ability in the primary grades may grow to a five or six year spread in any senior high school grade. The teacher necessarily concerns himself with whatever he regards as "fundamentals" or "minimum essentials" in his specialty. What is necessary practice for the majority, however, becomes routine drill for the bright student who is merely "going through the motions." While some time spent in overlearning may be justified, much of the bright child's time might better be spent in extensive learning rather than unnecessarily intensive practice. Where uniform examinations, such as the New York State Regents tests, are given, the temptation is great to coach the bright student endlessly so that he may earn a score from 95 to 100. Some of the time might be more effectively used if the student were less well drilled and exposed instead to more independent study, creative expression, or other new experiences in the same field.

These strictures on unnecessary drill are not meant to disparage effective mastery of essential learnings. On the average, bright youngsters do well in basic tool areas as well as in special fields of interests. But averages apart, many a bright student is found who has been permitted to move along in blissful ignorance of fundamental computation processes, of the elements of sentence structure or of simple historical facts. Sometimes bright students are denied the opportunity of further education because of these deficiencies. The teacher's job is to make sure the child develops the needed background, but also to move him along when he has the necessary competence.

In the public schools the major aim is stimulation to further study. Every teacher faces at some time apparent conflicts between coverage of content and stimulation of independent interest and activity. With the bright child there is a temptation to push rapidly on in the subject matter of a particular discipline, to assign more homework, to learn more facts, to develop more concepts. To some extent this constitutes enrichment. So long as the child is interested, even excited over the new learnings, enrichment may be genuine. After a certain point, however, the teacher's or child's effort to cover more and more subject matter may become compulsive and ignore natural limits to learning. If this becomes true, verbalism rather than learning may take place, and this spurious type of achievement may be expected to evaporate rapidly.

A different approach involves the realization that the child has a long learning career ahead of him, persisting, one would hope, as long as life itself. As the child matures, his ability to grasp material increases. One semester in college may produce more understanding than two in high school. Many college departments proceed on the assumption that the student who has completed some high school work in their area may be enrolled in the same section as students who have had no exposure at all in high school. If these assumptions are realistic, apparently elementary and secondary schools have greater responsibility in stimulating interest and building study methods in particular fields than they do in covering the area itself.

These considerations may be of assistance to the teacher who would like to make use of independent study, pupil participation in planning, committee activity, and other devices which give promise of developing a greater sense of involvement or commitment in learning. These devices often result in more intensive work in a particular portion of the curriculum but they may also prevent equal coverage of all topics in a given course of study. In the long run greater value is to be found in stimulating abiding interests than in premature coverage at a low level of student involvement.

A major goal in education of the gifted should be development of independence, originality, and a desire for creative expression. One necessary condition is the growth of self-direction. A second is encouragement of initiative in solution of problems. A third is opportunity for expressive activity. Obstacles include an excess of prescription in the program of the bright child. Because he absorbs information so well, because he is generally willing to perform whatever task the teacher assigns to him, the temptation is to load him up with more and more teacher-directed activities. He takes another major subject; he learns a foreign language at an early age; he is given private instruction on a musical instrument, in dancing, horseback riding, or astronomy. In particular subject areas the teacher suggests (requires) that he read additional books, write additional reports, undertake additional projects. A good case can be made for each of these experiences. However, add them together and there is no breathing space for the child. If he is forever meeting the expectations of others—his parents and teachers—can he ever become truly self-directing? To meet this need, schools at all levels, from primary grades through the university, are offering programs of independent study. If the student is self-starting, all the better; if not, the teacher helps him get started, is available for consultation when necessary, helps to set requirements so that the youngster will not simply "coast."

"Piling on" academic solids also results frequently in reducing the bright child's opportunities to explore in expressive fields at his own rate. Art, music, industrial arts, home economics are often sacrificed to make way for additional elective work in academic fields characterized by study and recitation rather than creative expression. Under such a regimen the bright student may never learn what satisfactions reside in these expressive fields. Lacking these experiences, he may forever feel unprepared and inept when opportunities in the arts offer themselves.

Time for independent and artistic activity, not additional assignments and a heavier load, is the key to development of self-direction and creative interests.

Nothing is more important in the education of the intellectually gifted than the maintenance of intellectual challenge. Activities need be continually evaluated: are they routine or stimulating? Do they aim merely at correctness or do they combine correctness with the challenge of new elements? Are activities alloted more time than is necessary simply because tradition assigns a given number of weeks (days or periods) to a particular topic? The emphasis must be on *quality* rather than *quantity*. High standards need be employed for high ability students.

Related to maintaining intellectual challenge is the value placed on intellectual achievement. An intellectual snobbery that patronizes or ignores social, artistic, and physical values is not rewarding. But in a child and adolescent culture which values highly athletic prowess and social success, and in an adult culture which proclaims loudly its economic values, the school has a special responsibility to hold intellectual values high. Incentives to achievement and rewards for achievement must be provided.

A basic purpose in all grades and in all courses is the development of critical thinking. Reflective, analytical, creative, and critical modes of thought are characteristic of the intellectually gifted. While thinking cannot be taught in a vacuum, ability to use thought processes is a more important outcome than any of the content of the curriculum. Like "education" in the old saw, modes of thought are the residual after the content of schooling is forgotten. No school, however advanced or demanding, can predict the content needs of its students; all schools can confidently predict needs to think effectively. Because the bright student has exceptional potential in this direction, teachers have a particular interest in placing primary focus on development of clear thinking rather than on content for its own sake. Again, it is necessary to concentrate on basic needs rather than on the temptation to cover a mass of material.

Of primary importance is the social orientation of individual achievement. To this point we have been looking at the potential of the intellectually gifted. Equally pressing are the uses to which this potential is put. While intellectual abilities may, in a sense, "come naturally," a sensitive social conscience has to be nurtured carefully. The cue may come from the conservation-minded farmer who has learned to regard ownership of his fertile lands as a stewardship. He holds in his care a valuable resource to use wisely, with a sense of social responsibility as well as personal enhancement. School and society are charged to develop a similar sense of social obligation among those endowed with unusual mental ability. The intellectual gift can be used for good or evil. When used for good it has enormous possibilities. A fundamental goal in education of the gifted must be building an awareness of social responsibility in using the unusual ability with which the talented are gifted.

Balance and breadth are essential ingredients in the curriculum of the gifted. Educating the "universal man" a la da Vinci may not always be a possibility. Striving to enrich the life of every child is within the reach of the school. For the bright child, this entails a responsibility to extend opportunities to explore in a variety of fields, in artistic and manipulative fields as well as in academic areas. Single-minded pursuit of intellectual goals is not sufficient justification for reducing exposure to physical activities and athletics, to home economics and industrial arts, to the fine arts, or to commercial subjects. One reads with chagrin of such decisions being forced upon high school students in particular to a greater and greater extent. Like any other child, the bright child has great needs for expression and for emotional release. He has also the potential of gaining more from the "non-academic" activities than the average. Certainly the bright child should not be forced into these experiences in a vain attempt at "all-aroundness," but the school should provide the proper exposure and assist in the development of sufficient skill to make further experience satisfying.

Exposure to many kinds of experience assures a balance in the child's educational diet which is as needful for the bright child as for others. Balance should characterize several dimensions: intellectual and emotional ; mental and physical; individual and social; critical and creative; work and play. To expect every bright child to excel in every area is to wish a horse for every beggar. To require satisfactory performance in all areas is not realistic. To make opportunities for wide experience possible, however, is the responsibility of the school.

Flexibility rather than uniformity should characterize the curriculum. Variety of offerings rather than a narrow curriculum based upon outmoded traditions facilitates the flexibility that is needed to meet individual needs and interests. The goal in a program for the gifted should be an extremely rich environment from which guided choices can be made. There is no objective evidence to support any of the favorite programs of much publicized pundits. Three years of a foreign language, four years of English, three years of social studies, the "new" mathematics, integrated arts, advanced placement courses: one may find evidence of the value of each of these, but no one can argue seriously that any one is an absolutely essential key to success, even to academic success. Instead of tailoring the prodigy to fit the pattern, perhaps we should consider the possibility of tailoring the pattern to fit the prodigy. Commitment to narrowly prescribed courses does not provide such flexibility. Teachers and school administrators should have freedom to depart from accepted norms in building an exceptional program that is maximally effective for an exceptional child.

While grouping for some purposes may be justified in educating the gifted, schools must provide a total environment that stimulates the variety of life in America's highly pluralistic society. There is little support for development of an intellectual elite that will have few contacts with persons not so endowed. The school must put its own characteristic value on intellectual performance. It is not justified, however, in developing intellectual snobbery. The neighborhood elementary school and the comprehensive secondary school continue to have much to justify them in the American tradition and on the American scene.

The teacher is the key figure in education; he is just as central to the education of the gifted. The teacher serves not only as a mentor but as a model of intellectual interest and intellectual achievement. His basic role is not to convey information, but to stimulate intellectual interests and develop high standards of achievement and social concern. Choice of teachers cannot be left to chance or rotation. Choice, however, cannot be made only of the "best" teachers. Or, if choice is made of the "best" teachers, "best" must be defined as "best for the gifted," just as other teachers need to be assigned as "best" for the handicapped or for children in general. For the gifted, "best" will mean not necessarily the most learned or the person with the highest degrees; it will mean the ability to stimulate the gifted to maximum learning.

GUIDELINES

An interesting test of some of the foregoing principles of operation is to be found in a comprehensive checklist that Passow and Brooks (1960) have developed for study and evaluation of provisions for educating the gifted. They suggest use of the list not only to check current provisions but to stimulate attention on the part of school faculties to improving programs for talented students. Almost one hundred rating items are included in the following areas:

1. How is talent defined?
2. How is ability identified?
3. Is continuous assessment provided?
4. How is articulation with other school units provided?
5. What are the policy and provisions on grouping?
6. What are policy and provisions for acceleration?
7. How is instruction adapted for the gifted?
8. How is balance in the program provided?
9. What special equipment and facilities are available?
10. What provisions are made for guidance and counseling?
11. How are personnel and materiel resources in the community employed?

12. What provisions are made for in-service training of teachers and other personnel working with the gifted?

SUMMARY

Education of the gifted is an extension of adapting instruction to the needs of the individual. Education of the gifted can be no better than the totality of educational provisions in the community. Neither the general nor the special case can be dealt with in the absence of positive attitudes of the community toward education and intellectual endeavor.

Programs of education for the gifted should be informed by a general philosophy of education and with respect to special aims intended for the gifted. Of primary importance. are provisions for identification of intellectually superior students, taking into account limitations of testing programs, and considering the differential effects on children's development of atypical neighborhoods and communities. Following identification, programs developed for the gifted must be closely related to the full program of the school with good communication between teachers and students in special programs and those in the remainder of the school or school system.

Certain administrative devices make some contribution toward improving instruction of the gifted, but major emphasis has to be placed upon curriculum, instruction and guidance in order to achieve maximum effectiveness in any program. Of particular importance is motivation of gifted students so that they may achieve results consistent with their potential. In this effort the school should recognize the possible contribution of resources in the community and should make use of them. In the school as in the community there is the need for selection and utilization of properly trained and stimulating persons, and the provision of an adequate budget. Unifying these various features should be continuity in planning and continuity in educational provisions.

Various guidelines are suggested in planning instruction of highly able students. Gifted children must be viewed as children first. They have normal developmental needs; they face the same tasks in growing up in our culture as do other children. If a functional curriculum is of value to all students, it should be pursued with gifted students as well. The ability to survive should not be taken as justification for imposition of procedures that research has proved to be ineffective in the past. Bright children have perhaps greater need of mastery of fundamentals than others, but their earlier achievement should be recognized. They need a modicum of practice, but not drill beyond establishment of appropriate levels of competence.

In subject matter the aim should not be encyclopedic coverage but stimulation of interest and arousal of motivation for continued study. A major goal is development of independence in learning; methods should develop the ability of students to work by themselves and should not be restricted to completion of ever more detailed assignments by the teacher. Critical thinking should stand high in the aims to be achieved. As potential leaders of the community bright youngsters stand more in need than others of a sense of social responsibility.

The program should be characterized by balance and breadth, but opportunity for specialization in keeping with the child's interests should appear early. Emphasis on all-round development should be tempered by recognition that bright children may also have special spheres of interest and special blind spots, and that they should not be deprived of opportunity to pursue their special strengths because of poorer performance in areas of weakness. Such an approach requires flexibility in the curriculum. Continuity in provisions for the gifted involve continuity in instruction, in the curriculum, and in guidance. Finally, recognition of the strategic role of instruction in education of the gifted underlines the importance of the teacher as the key figure in the gifted child's intellectual growth.

Chapter 7

Patterns in Education of the Gifted

The belief that all genuine education comes about through experience does not mean that all experiences are genuinely or equally educative.

—John Dewey

The sudden burst of interest in the 1950's in education of the gifted resulted in the appearance in educational journals and in popular magazines of a rash of articles describing special programs at various levels in school systems. A number of surveys have also appeared which summarize some of the more promising practices. Examples of these are *A Survey of the Education of Gifted Children* by Havighurst and others (1955), *Practical Programs for the Gifted* by Kough (1960), and *Programs for the Gifted, A Case Book in Secondary Education,* by Everett and others (1961). The reader will find some detailed information of interest about particular programs in each of these volumes. This chapter is divided into four sections which attempt to consolidate information about particular programs into patterns of education at the elementary, junior high, senior high, and college levels respectively. The ideas that are fundamental to each of these patterns should be observed in making choices between various alternatives in establishing programs for the gifted in the classroom or in the school system.

SPECIAL PROVISIONS FOR GIFTED CHILDREN IN ELEMENTARY SCHOOLS

Despite preoccupation with the needs of meeting problems raised by an explosion in school population in the past half century, school systems have done considerable exploration of special programs for gifted boys and girls in elementary schools. Programs range in nature from enrichment of the curriculum in regular classes to the establishment of a special school with special learning experiences. Some of the changes are administrative in nature, some instructional.

Administrative devices range in the following order of specialization:

1. The selective school that serves gifted children only
2. The neighborhood school which operates a few special classrooms for bright youngsters
3. The school which organizes special programs for bright children for only part of the day
4. The school which provides special experiences just once or twice a week for selected students
5. The school which makes no administrative provision other than consultant service to teachers who want to enrich the program for the few outstanding pupils in their classrooms.

In addition, some schools provide for acceleration through the school program by early admission to school, by grade skipping, or by combining two years' work in one (or three years' work in two). The teacher, of course, works within the framework he finds, but in many cases teachers have a voice in determining the framework or in altering it. Since teachers working with gifted students are often invited to share in such decisions, it is important that they be familiar with research and exploratory practices that are administrative as well as instructional.

ACCELERATION IN ELEMENTARY SCHOOL

The merits and problems of acceleration are discussed in Chapter 14. The elementary school is the scene of a large part of the acceleration that takes place during a child's schooling. Early entrance (admitting bright children to a first-grade program at age five) is being advocated vigorously in some parts of the country. It has the advantage of not telescoping the elementary program on the one hand and of enabling the greatest enrichment on the other. Unfortunately, it suffers from two important handicaps—the difficulty of making judgments as to ability before the child has entered a formal school program and a problem of policy in most school districts where parents are eager for early attendance by their children. Parents often press the school board to make exceptions for tots who miss the deadline for admission by a week, a month, three months, or even half a year. "Holding the line" for children of average ability becomes more difficult when exceptions are made, albeit for those regarded as "gifted."

Acceleration is accomplished in a variety of ways. In some schools an individual teacher notes early reading and other signs of precocity on the part of one or two children in the first or second grade, discusses the situation with the principal or other supervisor, and decides to give the child advanced work so that he may "skip" the next grade when promotion time comes. This informal type of acceleration program is probably the most prevalent. In some very large schools teachers note exceptional youngsters in kindergarten and the first grade and nominate these children for a special class grouping in the second grade. Sometimes this process is undertaken at high grade levels as well. The children who are selected are then exposed to a curriculum that involves the work of two grades in one year, and those who do well are accelerated by a double promotion at the end of the year. Occasionally a child is moved ahead in the middle of the year either on the individual basis first described or on the group basis just presented. Finally, some school systems have made use of summer school activity to accelerate selected children who have succeeded in an abbreviated version of the next year's work in special summer classes. While never widespread, the program has had its chief appeal in school systems that at the time employed semi-annual promotion. The summer activities could be more realistically related to a semester's than to a year's work.

Whatever the mechanism, it seems likely that acceleration will continue to be used to some extent in elementary schools, particulary where other ways of helping the gifted child are not feasible. The elementary school is not restricted by two basic facts of life that limit acceleration in secondary school: fundamental physical and social changes that accompany and follow puberty, and departmental organization of the school which highlights uneven performance of youngsters. Physical and social differences of the accelerated child are less likely to be noticeable in elementary school. The self-contained classroom is more likely to focus attention on general superiority rather than the ups and downs of a particular child's work in a number of subject areas.

SPECIAL PROGRAMS

Perhaps the best known programs for gifted children in elementary schools are those of the Hunter College Elementary School (New York City), the Cleveland Major Work Program and the Colfax (Pittsburgh) Elementary School, each typifying a different approach. The Hunter school is a special school for intellectually gifted children only. The Cleveland program brings together in specified school centers children of special ability. In a sense they operate as a "school within a school" in the building they attend. The Colfax program groups gifted children together for half the day and disperses them for the second half with the whole spread of ability to be found in an elementary school. Some schools refer to this last type of program as "partial segregation."

All of these programs are large city programs. They are facilitated by a city's concentration of population. Drawing upon only part of the island of Manhattan, the Hunter Elementary School is able to bring together 450 children with IQ's (Binet) of 135 and up, averaging 150. In the nation as a whole, this distribution represents one per cent of the population. Theoretically, then, a special school as selective as Hunter would depend upon a total elementary school population in the district of around 45,000 assuming that all parents of qualified children wanted them to participate. To give an idea of the concentration needed to support such a school, the total population in the area served by Hunter College Elementary School is in excess of one million.

The Colfax School in Pittsburgh is a large school, enrolling twelve hundred students in what the principal calls "a good, middle-class community" in which many of the parents are college graduates (NSSE, 1958, p. 240). In this school five workshops for gifted children, one at each grade level except the first two, are organized. A minimum IQ of 130 is required. Since 10 per cent of the children are in workshops and normal distribution would yield less than 3 per cent over 130 IQ, apparently the population upon which the school draws is not typical but reflects the neighborhood segregation which is characteristic of large cities.

The Cleveland Major Work Classes are established in approximately one-third of the city's schools. Children of high ability may attend one of these schools rather than their neighborhood school if suitable transportation arrangements exist. Again we find a program which is possible only when more than the normal proportion of very bright students can be assembled in one school.

The Hunter College Elementary School (Hildreth, 1952) admits boys and girls on the basis of individually administered intelligence tests. Those scoring highest are brought to school for an interview with the principal so that some estimate of social and emotional maturity for an advanced program can be made. A small number of children are admitted to a nursery school at age three and to the kindergarten at age four. These children continue through the six years of the graded program, and they are joined by a much larger number of five-year-olds for a combination kindergarten-first grade program. In essence the program is one of early admission.* Some acceleration takes place thereafter, but

---

* Since 1961, the one year's difference in admission age has been reduced to six months.

it is limited to the most exceptional cases, rarely more than one in a grade.

Children at Hunter engage in a program that includes an increasing amount of specialization as they grow older. By and large, they remain with their own teacher through the first grade. Thereafter, they have their "core" experiences—language arts, social studies, and mathematics with their home room teacher, but they go to other teachers for a foreign language, science, art, music, physical education, and industrial arts one or more periods a week. The class group, which averages 29, is split into two halves for most specialties. Some coordinated planning takes place between the home room and special teachers. Grade groups, two or three classes on a single level, plan together such activities as assemblies which the children write and produce, and field trips that may involve the entire grade. For many years a club period was conducted once a week with all children participating. The club program was terminated in 1960 in order to reduce fractionizing of the school day.

The school serves as the laboratory school for Hunter College which operates a large teacher education program, but the College also maintains close relations with the New York City and suburban schools for observation and student teaching. Hunter College Elementary School, however, has the distinction of serving in an experimental and research capacity both for teacher education and for education of the gifted. A closed circuit television system facilitates observation in the elementary school both by undergraduates and by teachers in the graduate program who are extending their competence in working with gifted children.*

The Colfax School attempted to serve its bright youngsters at first by providing two hourly sessions each week when boys and girls in the upper grades met with an enrichment teacher. This did not prove effective because of problems of coordinating activities with the teachers from whose classes the selected children came. The next step was to organize a club period for all students at which time the gifted children attended the enrichment classes. Here a problem arose because the bright children were those especially interested in participating in the club activities. Finally, the workshop program was developed. Bright children are enrolled in a workshop for half the day for their basic academic subjects. In the other half of the day they meet in ungrouped classes "for those activities that are less likely to bring out individual learning capacity." The latter include art, music, physical training, dramatics, and library classes as well as such activities as class parties and community programs (Pregler, 1954). Both the early program at Colfax

---

* In 1965 substantial changes in policy were effected in order to serve the needs of the city's urban population. New policy bases admission on the basis of observation of children in day-care centers. Use of intelligence tests as the major criterion was discontinued since they tended to exclude lower income and minority ethnic groups.

(two or three periods a week) and the current program (half of each school day) are the plans being used most widely in the United States.

Major Work Classes were established in Cleveland Elementary Schools in 1921 and have been extended since to junior and senior high schools as well. Elementary schools in Cleveland are authorized to establish Major Work Classes if they can enroll enough students who qualify. Children are assigned a "Probable Learning Rate" by the Cleveland Bureau of Educational Research, and this screening plus an IQ (Binet) of 125 or greater are used for admission. Approximately one-third of the elementary schools in Cleveland have Major Work Classes, drawing students at times from more than the immediate neighborhood. Classes often extend over more than one grade in order to bring together enough pupils who meet the minimum IQ criterion. These students remain together for the entire day but share in all-school activities like clubs, parties, assemblies, and community functions with other students (Hall, 1956). New York City's Intellectually Gifted Classes operate on a similar basis (New York City, 1959a, pp. 10-15).

These three organizations share a single point of view in addressing their efforts to children who are *intellectually gifted in general* as defined by individual or group intelligence tests. Some less ambitious programs also operate on the same basis. A number of schools scattered all over the country provide special instruction one or more periods a week for intellectually gifted children who are temporarily withdrawn from their regular class and meet other bright children either in their own school or in another.

Some schools, however, are seeking special kinds of giftedness and offering special kinds of programs on the same "part-time" basis. Portland, Oregon, for example, selects children who have a special bent for science, literature, music, art, and other specialities and brings each special group together to work on its own area of interest. Some school systems provide for these meetings, at times, in places other than the school. Reading groups, for instance, in Los Angeles meet in the public library with a librarian who has special interest in children and competence in stimulating reading at ever more mature and satisfying levels. In all these cases children are separated from their classmates for only a small portion of the week. Often they bring back to their class interesting material to share with their fellows. The simplicity of such organization makes identification less important and less necessary. It opens the path to self-identification by display of interest.

One final administrative device is worth noting—the operation of summer school classes for advanced pupils. Some school systems explored the use of summer schools as a mechanism of acceleration in the 1920's, but practically all such programs were dropped during the Depression in the 'thirties. In the 'fifties again new interest burgeoned in summer programs, although they were not often related to acceleration. Some programs such as that in Darien, Connecticut, started as an effort to provide stimulating intellectual fare to boys and girls during the summer with only a tenuous relationship to the public school system. Most summer programs are at the secondary level, but occasional classes for younger children are found. Obvious dangers are inherent in a program which maintains the conventional pressures of the school year. These dangers can be obviated when summer work is not taken for "credit" or promotion, but where the sole purpose is extending interest in areas of the child's choice. Emphasis in such an approach should be on individual and group projects, recreational reading, independent work, and creative activities. The Chicago Public Schools (1964, p. 22) have undertaken significant explorations since 1960 in providing special summer session classes for children in culturally deprived areas. These schools enroll children in relatively small classes grouped according to ability. A program of challenging learning activities encompasses opportunities for expression in literature, mathematics, creative writing, and speech. The professional staff sees far-reaching implications for gifted pupils as well as for other children coming from disadvantaged backgrounds.

JUNIOR HIGH SCHOOL PROGRAMS FOR THE GIFTED

One historical objective of the junior high school that has been largely left behind and one current objective that presently shapes the early years of secondary education characterize the major approaches to education of the gifted in junior high schools today. The first of these is acceleration, the second a combination of exploration and enrichment.

A major purpose in establishment of junior high schools in the early decades of the twentieth century was speeding the progress of young people through school as suggested by the name of one of the committees urging the new school organization, the Committee on the Economy of Time. Then, as now, many of the seventh and eighth grades were used to consolidate learnings of earlier years rather than to approach new subject matter. The junior high school was first proposed to telescope some of this review and to begin secondary education at an earlier age. In the course of time this objective was dropped. Increased concern with social development, a broadened school curriculum, and increased knowledge within most disciplines have served to fill to the brim the three years of junior high school. In place of an effort to save time, junior high schools turned to use of the time available for a broader, richer, more diverse program under the names of exploration and enrichment.

For the gifted, however, a few communities have attempted to preserve the goal of acceleration, and some of these have tried at the same time to diversify and enrich a program telescoped to two years or to five semesters. A much larger number have sought instead to expose bright students to additional experiences in academic areas, to social development through increased co-curricular activities and student organization, and to a more diversified program through offering increased opportunity in art, music, industrial arts, and pre-vocational subjects.

The New York City and Baltimore public schools have been outstanding exponents of acceleration. The New York City program offered Rapid Advancement classes to children of superior ability from World War I until shortly after World War II. Children in the top quarter of their group were permitted to complete the three year program in two. Surveys of results were not encouraging and recommendations for discontinuing the program were made (New York City, 1939, pp. 40-41). Soon after World War II, the Rapid Advancement classes were replaced with the Special Progress program. Since many of the RA students had apparently been accelerated more than was good for them, more rigid standards of admission were established for the SP classes. These included an IQ of 130 on group tests, a reading level one year above grade and an arithmetic level half a year over normal. More detailed description will be found in the chapter on acceleration. Baltimore has followed a similar program of acceleration in its junior high schools.

Even in New York City, however, sentiment is expressed against this automatic acceleration. Since the brightest children were being siphoned out of the three-year program, teachers felt obliged to recommend the two-year program for all eligible students, and parents felt they had no right to keep their boys and girls, if sufficiently gifted, in classes from which top ability had been skimmed. In 1960, an alternative program was developed, and parents of bright children were given a choice of enrolling them either in a two-year Special Progress or a three-year Special Progress class. Plans were developed for an especially challenging three-year program so that bright students would gain sufficiently more from it to warrant the additional year.

"Enrichment" at the junior high school level in most school districts is an amalgam of accelerated subject matter, extended subject content, additional academic experiences, leadership opportunities, and exploration in non-academic areas. With the blessing of the College Entrance Examination Board's Commission on Mathematics, ninth grade algebra as modified by the "new mathematics" is becoming standard fare for bright students in the eighth grade. General science is being completed in the eighth grade, and the regular high school course in biology or earth science is found in the gifted student's ninth grade program. More advanced literature is attempted in the English class and a higher level of written work is expected. The social studies program is more likely to vary in maturity of approach than in the subject matter itself. Students are introduced to a modern foreign language via the audio-lingual approach in the seventh grade and some acceleration may be expected where adequate articulation with senior high school language instruction is effected.

Programs for gifted young adolescents do not depend upon junior high school organization. St. Louis provides a program for grades 5 to 8 in its eight-grade elementary schools that parallels programs already described on the elementary level. Children are selected for special programs on the basis of an IQ score of 130 or higher (Binet) and achievement up to grade level in arithmetic, language arts, and reading. They then complete the normal eight-year curriculum by the end of the seventh grade. In addition, they take conversational French for three years and textbook French for one year. In grade 8 they study ninth grade English, Algebra, French, and Science. Testing before admission to high school determines whether they will receive a half or full credit or no credit whatsoever for the ninth grade work. And as in many junior high school programs for the gifted, the boys take a limited program in industrial arts and the girls in homemaking (one year only) (Kough, 1960, pp. 102-3).

In some junior high schools the heavy academic load precludes any real effort to explore in expressive art forms or even to dabble in household skills. A sounder program provides time for art, music, home economics, wood and metal shops, ceramics, leathercraft, and the like. In some cases these programs are soft-pedaled for the intellectually superior since they are not likely to represent vocational possibilities. For the mentally superior child, however, vocational exploration in these areas should lead to cultural development, to personal enrichment that comes from the joy of doing or the delight of self-expression. The school must forever keep before it the goal of educating the man, not of training manpower. On a ultilitarian level, typewriting and possibly shorthand for personal use in higher education may be as important to the bright student as typewriting and stenography to another young person as tools for making a living.

The boy or girl in junior high school enters a phase where the family yields to the peer group as a center of interest. There is a growing self-assurance and a gradual drive for independence from adult control. Group activities in the classroom, co-curricular activities in the club

period or after school, sports, journalism, and dramatics all provide opportunities for the early adolescent to try his wings socially, both with
students of his own sex and with the opposite sex so lately regarded as a
bore or a menace.

To Havighurst (1953), with his theory of "developmental tasks," these
social and physical activities represent necessary learnings. If not learned
at this stage, the individual may remain an adolescent forever. The
school takes the best hours of the day and provides the greatest opportunities for social interaction and social growth. It has to accept responsibilities, therefore, to provide opportunities and guidance in social development. Since all young people face the same developmental tasks in
our culture, the school stands on shaky ground if it short-circuits these
experiences for bright children, asserting their greater need to get on
with academic affairs. Social and emotional immaturity may be a greater
hazard to ultimate academic success than the time taken in junior high
school to assure this growth. The child with a heavier class program may
be limited in such a way. The child who spends but two years in a
junior high school has one year less than his contemporaries to develop a
leadership role in various co-curricular functions.

One further word of caution needs to be expressed. A common assumption lies behind the policy of reaching up for high school subject matter
and pushing it down into the junior high school. This is the assumption
that education is a matter of mastering the subject disciplines as organized, and that beginning them early assures earlier mastery. A competing
assumption places a dynamic learner in a dynamic culture at the center
of the educational operation. The needs, interests, and purposes of the
learner and the culture are central, and the disciplines represent resources upon which the learner draws in achieving his purposes. Many
persons believe that the second assumption operates for the average
or slow learner but that the first assumption should determine the program for the bright. Actually, evidence does not support this distinction.
The Eight-Year Study of the Progressive Education Association (Aikin,
1942) established quite well the value to the bright student of the more
modern approach. This study, which matched graduates of thirty experimental high schools with as many control schools, showed the greater
success in colleges of students who had taken part in the more permissive
programs. Going back to past programs because they have an aura of
academic respectability is apparently no favor to the bright young people
in our schools.

Junior high school programs that will be effective have to do more than
imitate programs at higher levels which have no great record of success.
Certain criteria have to be considered and met. For example, will study

of organized biology in the ninth year do more to stimulate creative thinking in science than a less structured laboratory science program where students have greater freedom to explore ideas and test them by experimentation? Will study of algebra or *Ivanhoe* a year earlier lead to greater interest in mathematics or literature and a sense of commitment to further study? Will heavy homework assignments lead to greater independent exploration and study? Will heavier reliance on the old assign-study-recite-test method develop the values that are claimed for pupil-teacher planning and group activities in the classroom? Will renewed emphasis on grammatical constructions be effective now when no evidence has been found to support this kind of study in the past? All proposals have to be examined critically. In the matter of educating the gifted it is all too easy to be blinded by appearances of "solidity," and academic respectability. Many proposals carrying such a countenance are simply flights into the past in utter disregard of evidence that discredited them long ago.

SENIOR HIGH SCHOOL PROGRAMS FOR THE ACADEMICALLY TALENTED

Senior high schools afford a variety of administrative adaptations for gifted young people by reason of certain characteristics and traditions of the high school. One of these is the size of urban high schools which generally assures to the bright boy or girl the company of other youngsters of similar ability. A second is departmental organization. This facilitates specialization in programming to accompany specialization in intellectual abilities. A third is the tradition of variable grouping either by assignment or through election of particular courses. Fourth, is the guidance programs which were initiated in high schools as a result of the Vocational Education acts started in 1917. Guidance personnel are to be found in all but the smallest high schools (and here the principal takes responsibility), but they are not found in similar proportions in junior high schools and they are the exception rather than the rule in elementary schools.

High schools in the United States started as the successors of the European Grammar Schools and were, initially and by tradition, institutions for the elite. Only after 1900 were there as many as 10 per cent of the fourteen- to seventeen-year-olds enrolled. Not until the second half of the century did as many as 50 per cent of the eighteen-year-olds complete a high school program. However, the major attention of secondary school educators from World War I to the end of World War II was necessarily riveted to the manifold problems involved in extending high school education to all the children of all the people. To say that the gifted were neglected in this period is an overstatement, but it would be equally inaccurate to say that they received the same attention as mythical averages, drop-outs, and the mentally retarded. New attention has been given to this group since 1950. Some old procedures have been reinstituted and a number of new approaches have been explored.

PROGRAMS ACTUALLY TAKEN AND DESIRED BY ABLE STUDENTS

Applbaum's study (1959) of winners of awards offered by the Merit Scholarship Corporation provides an interesting summary of the educational program offered to academically superior students. Questionnaires were returned by almost two thousand of the Merit Winners and by one thousand principals of participating schools. Practically all (96 per cent) were well enough motivated to go to college. Very few had ever been accelerated. About 90 per cent were over seventeen when they were graduated from high school; 81 per cent were not accelerated in high school; 90 per cent took six years to complete the six-year junior-senior high school course. Applbaum interprets the lack of acceleration to mean that students and principals alike are more interested in profitable use of time while in high school than in reducing the usual time for completion of high school. Both students and principals indicated a preference for enrichment over all other special provisions for the gifted.

A comparison of programs actually in operation with those recommended was secured by asking for free response to questions on special provisions now utilized and special provisions recommended. More than 1 per cent of principals reported the following provisions in effect:

	(Per Cent)
Advanced courses on an elective basis; accelerated courses; honors courses; college preparatory courses	53.6
Heavier load	12.7
Special leadership opportunities	6.6
Different teaching methods through core, field trips, etc.	4.4
Use of facilities in near-by colleges; extension courses; auditors in colleges	3.5
Special recognition and honors; memberships in scholarship clubs and honor societies	4.8
Individualized instruction	3.0
Special projects	3.0
Interschool and intraschool scholastic contests	2.7

The following were recommended:

(Per Cent)

Advanced courses; college level courses; honors courses; accelerated courses; correspondence courses; creative writing courses; college preparatory courses — 42.5

Small classes — 10.4

Special field trips — 2.4

Academic freedom — 2.3

Special projects — 1.8

Individualized instruction — 1.8*

(Applbaum, 1959, pp. 36-37)

Fewer than 1 per cent of the principals reported the following as existing or recommended them for the future: more home, community, school understanding; reading clinics and other remedial classes; work experiences; voluntary attendance; after school, evening, Saturday, and summer classes; completely different curriculum; correspondence courses; school within a school organization; exchange students program; special recognition and honors; leadership training; heavier load; college style programming; special high school; use of college facilities; creation of better climate between gifted and other students; more rigid control of program for gifted; more remuneration for teachers of gifted; reducing load for gifted; consolidating schools to provide larger number of gifted in one school. It is apparent that the 53.6 per cent reporting, and the 42.5 per cent recommending, enriched courses represent a tremendous majority over those reporting or recommending other solutions.

A California study investigated principals' reactions to programs for the gifted. Allison summarized the following "needs of the gifted child" reported by 33 of 45 selected high school principals:

1. Extension of experience through special assignments, clubs, laboratories, or library
2. Enrichment of regular classes
3. Guidance and counseling
4. Special classes or special school
5. Acceleration within the college prep program
6. Acceleration
7. Extensive use of community resources

---

* From "A Survey of Special Provisions for the Education of Academically Superior Students," by Morris J. Applbaum. Reprinted by permission from the *Bulletin of the National Association of Secondary-School Principals*, October, 1959. Copyright: Washington, D.C.

He listed the following provisions for the gifted reported by these principals:

1. Inspiration, stimulation, and encouragement to excel
2. Appropriate guidance in the early career
3. Ability to overcome apathy and boredom
4. Opportunity for exploration at an early age
5. Sympathetic response from peer group
6. Encouragement to attend college
7. Adequate social adjustment
8. Financial aid

(Allison, 1959, pp. 102-103) °

ABILITY GROUPING

Ability grouping in various forms is perhaps the most pervasive administrative adaptation employed in attempting to educate more effectively with the academically talented. The commonest application of this approach is the use of multiple curricula in a high school. Theoretically, the academic, general, commercial, and vocational courses are geared to career interests. It is no secret, however, than in practice students are steered into one curriculum or another on the basis of ability rather than vocational objective. Small high schools, of course, cannot afford the luxury of this differentiation of program and students. Many large high schools now reject a premature typing of students and the rigidity that normally characterizes the multiple curricula organization. In place of this organization these schools adhere to individual programming, and students are likely to select courses on the basis of need or interest rather than on ability alone.

A second type of grouping operates informally and without conscious action on the part of school authorities. This is to be found in the elective program. While some students, because of career considerations, will select courses where they can expect but meager success, most students size up their own strengths and weaknesses and choose electives where they feel confident of their ability. In this type of grouping self-selection is the rule.

Grouping through electives, however, does not affect approximately half of the student's program—the required courses in English, Social Studies, Mathematics, Science, Music, and Art. A good case can be made for organizing these courses on the basis of cross sections of the student

---

° From "California Principals Study a Curriculum for the Gifted," by Harold Allison. Reprinted by permission from the *Bulletin of the National Association of Secondary-School Principals*, February, 1959. Copyright: Washington, D.C.

population rather than on ability levels. Evidence can be cited to support either type of organization. Accommodating individual differences in the completely heterogeneous group is difficult, probably more difficult than in a group where the ability spread has been deliberately limited. Dealing adequately with individuals who differ widely requires small classes. Many school districts have attempted to avoid the large expenditure involved in reducing class size by organizing classes on a basis of ability and claiming an automatic adaptation to individual differences. Such adaptation of course is nominal only if not accompanied by changes in curriculum and method as well.

SPECIAL HIGH SCHOOLS FOR THE GIFTED

Ability grouping in secondary schools takes various forms. It is at its most extreme in specialized high schools, such as Baltimore Polytechnical and several schools in New York City.* These schools are highly selective in enrolling students because of the heavy pressure for admission. They claim to be general high schools with a strong bias toward college entrance. However, they capitalize upon a student's interest in a particular area in order to stimulate his total educational development and to encourage pursuit of his special interest, ability, or talent. Except for Performing Arts which is organized as a vocational high school, all these schools send more than 90 per cent of their graduates to college. Some of these schools enroll only the top 1 per cent in intellectual ability. They are obviously possible only in a large city with tens of thousands of high school students and a well-developed public transportation system since students should be able to come from all parts of the school district.

Perhaps the strongest feature of the specialized high school is its student body. There is constant contact of the student with others of equal ability. High ability is taken for granted, and high performance can be demanded of all students. Since students learn so much from each other, strong cultural interests are likely to grow from the mutual stimulation these young people provide for each other. There is no penalty for sterling achievement, no shame attached to the "grind" who studies hard.

An unfortunate concomitant of grouping all these gifted youngsters together seems to be the highly competitve atmosphere that is engendered. Despite efforts by teachers and administrators to counteract this

---

* Hunter College High School, Stuyvesant High School, Bronx High School of Science, High School of Music and Art, High School of Performing Arts, and Brooklyn Technical High School. Even more highly specialized is the the Novosibirsky Boarding School of Mathematics and Physics in Siberia where some three hundred winners of competitive examinations took an experimental curriculum in mathematics in 1962-63 (Soviet, 1963).

competitiveness, students of these schools invariably decry an overly competitive environment when they are asked to evaluate their school. Some students of moderately high ability are discouraged by competition with others of exceptional talent. A phenomenon which often occurs in college or the graduate school is thus found much earlier, and more destructively, in the specialized high school.

The group from whom leadership comes, both academically and socially, tends also to be attenuated in the specialized school. Students of moderate leadership ability are lost in brighter constellations. In the powerful massing of tremendous leadership potential only outstanding talent has the opportunity for expression. The loss of moderate leadership ability is disturbing because there is need for many degrees of leadership, for more leaders, including those of modest skill, as well as for the most unusual.

HONORS SCHOOLS AND HONORS CLASSES

Most school systems are not of the mammoth size that can foster specialized high schools. Some of the larger cities will accordingly concentrate top ability students in a few high schools where they become a school-within-a-school. Such an honors group can also be organized in a single high school of some size in a single-high school community. In either case, a group of students are selected on a basis of aptitude and achievement tests, school records, and teacher recommendations. Generally the 130 IQ criterion yields too small a group, and some fraction such as one-fifth or one-fourth of the group is used instead (IQ 125, 120, or 115, depending upon the size of the school and the selectivity feasible). These students are then scheduled together for as many of their classes as possible. Efforts are made to assign teachers with the greatest interest and competence in working with the academically superior.

This type of honors school operates on the same principle of general intellectual superiority as does the specialized school. There is not much reason to expect consistently high performance in every academic field. As the group becomes less highly selected this consistency across fields becomes less and less likely. Students may be made to feel guilty or inadequate because of mediocre performance in particular fields when there is no real evidence to support capacity for equally high achievement in all fields.

The honors school has one distinct advantage over the specialized school. Housed in the same building with all their brothers, honors students have more opportunity to assume leadership roles. Conversely, the whole school finds plenty of yeast in its dough. The specialized school, on the other hand, tends to rob other neighborhood high schools of a real source of talent. In the Bronx, for example, Bronx High School of Science students win a disproportionate share of awards such as the New York State Regents Scholarships, while nearby high schools can boast of proportionally few award winners. Moreover, teachers in these other schools decry the absence from their class of the spark that is struck by a few bright students. Extracurricular activities also tend to be less exciting and less well led.

Many schools recognize the variation of abilities within any student and accordingly organize honors classes in individual subjects rather than honors schools. The student scheduled for an honors section in English may thus be placed in an unselected science course. He is challenged to do well in his area of special ability, but he is not required to keep up with budding genius in subjects where he is a duffer. He need not fly with the eagles and swim with the fishes at the same time.

While ability grouping seems logical under philosophical examination, it has yet to establish itself empirically. Abramson (1959) completed a study in New York City comparing the graduates of a specialized school with those of an honors school and honors classes in neighborhood schools and finally with graduates of schools with unselected classes. Keeping intellectual ability constant from one group to the other, Abramson discovered that there were no substantial differences in first- and second-year college performance among graduates of different types of schools. Some efforts are made to explain this failure to distinguish among them. One line of reasoning suggests that comparison of college grades is not enough, that there are other fundamental values where differences might perhaps be found—in cultural interests, for example. Second, one may point out that it was the school organization only that was investigated. We do not know that there were any differences in school program, and obviously it is program rather than organization that makes the difference. Since New York State schools feel obliged to give assiduous attention to preparation for the uniform Regents examinations, it is possible that the program remains the same regardless of changes in grouping. On the other hand, both of these explanations may be regarded as rationalizations in the eternal warfare between the advocates of grouping and the advocates of scholastic cross-sections.

ACCELERATION IN HIGH SCHOOL

A second approach to providing for the gifted in senior high schools revolves around acceleration. Generally, high schools have set inflexible requirements expressed in Carnegie units. Regardless of depth of understanding and the amount of subject matter digested, a student may earn no more and no less than one Carnegie unit for a course taken five periods a week for 36 weeks (two semesters). The high school sets a minimum goal of 16, 17 or 18 units for four years' work. No acceleration is possible. The student may, however, accumulate units a bit more rapidly if he takes more than the usual number of courses each year and/or attends summer school. Such a program may see the bright youngster through high school more rapidly but it assures nothing in the way of greater challenge in each of the standard courses he must accumulate.

For many years the University of Chicago has been willing to admit especially well qualified students at the end of the eleventh rather than the twelfth grade. In the 1950's the Fund for the Advacement of Education (1957) sponsored wider utilization of this plan and a number of high school and colleges entered into a joint agreement resulting in early admission to college of a limited number of students. These students made excellent academic records and good social adjustments in college. The program, however, has failed to spread, possibly because high school students want to graduate with their class, possibly because of the belief of high school staffs that they can provide better for the gifted than the typically overcrowded, depersonalized lower divisions of the large colleges, possibly because of stereotypes we hold as to the desirable age at which the young person spreads his wings and goes off to college leaving the protection of his home.

Better accepted and enjoying widespread popularity is the Advanced Placement program operating under sponsorship of the College Entrance Examination Board and the Fund for the Advancement of Education. The College Entrance Board reports the initiation of the program in this manner:

> The Advanced Placement Program traces its origin to the General Education in School and College Committee Report and to the Committee Reports of the School and College Study of Admission with Advanced Standing. As an activity of the College Board it retains the flexible and responsive character of an exploratory project. Supported from 1952 to 1955 by the Fund for the Advancement of Education, the School and College Study did four things. It assisted in the organization of new college-level courses in a small group of public and independent schools; it examined the students who took these courses; it effected an agreement among 12, and later 15, colleges to give credit and placement to students who did satisfactory work in these courses and examinations; it sponsored conferences for school and college teachers. As the Study progressed, additional schools equipped to do such work set up advanced courses

and their graduates entered colleges and universities throughout the country.

(College Entrance Examinations Board, 1958, p. 7)

From a small beginning involving a score of high schools and colleges the program has widened each year, reaching in 1959-60, 890 schools; 10,531 students; and 567 colleges. Since students may take more than one Advanced Placement course, 14,158 examinations were administered (College Entrance Examinations Board, 1960). High schools that participate establish college-level courses for highly able students. Course suggestions are worked out by committees of college and high school teachers. At the end of the year students take examinations prepared by the same committees. Individual colleges set their own score on the examinations as the criterion for allowing college credit for the course. Some participating colleges do not allow credit toward a degree but waive requirement of the freshman course for students making a B or better on the examination. The program now covers advanced courses in the following 11 fields: American History, Biology, Chemistry, European History, French, German, Latin, Literature and English Composition, Mathematics, Physics, and Spanish. More complete treatment of the Advanced Placement Program will be found in Chapter 14 on Acceleration.

PROBLEM OF THE SMALL HIGH SCHOOL

The small high school (under one hundred students in each grade) suffers from a number of handicaps in educating intellectually talented adolescents: insufficient numbers of bright students for mutual stimulation; insufficient courses to provide for specialization; dependence upon the broad background of a few teachers responsible for instruction in several subjects; problems of scheduling for challenging experiences for a very small group; location in areas normally remote from rich cultural resources.

Where transportation permits, reorganization of school districts is desirable in order to assemble a larger number of students under one school roof. Often this solution is not feasible because of geographic and economic factors. Sometimes it is only community sentiments which stand in the way. In either case the obligation remains to do something to challenge bright students. A number of different expedients have been explored.

One solution is to bring together outstanding students from several high schools for one or two half-days a week. Vocational schools serving a wide area have done this for some time and may provide a good example. In Lewis County, New York, academically gifted students from six high schools meet one afternoon a week in a Youth Seminar. The county director of personnel services, a guidance counselor, and a homemaking teacher are the core of the faculty and they draw upon other teachers as needed. In general the group takes topics from the common learning fields—language and social studies—since these assure the common student background needed.

Some small schools consolidate forces in another way. One supervisory district in Orange County, New York, makes use of the community college in the county seat on Saturday mornings. A weekly class has been organized, drawing outstanding students in mathematics and science for presentations by mathematicians and scientists in industry, colleges, and government.

A third approach is possible through the use of new tools in learning. Learning foreign languages from a television teacher may be a far cry from conversing with one's teacher in class in the language being studied. For a student who has no opportunity for the latter, however, television may be an acceptable substitute. Helpful, too, are programs like the Sunrise Semester and Continental Classroom programs that bring into the student's home advanced material for which demand in his small school is not adequate. Language laboratories for teaching foreign languages, teaching machines, scrambled books, and the correspondence courses that have been with us for a long time also represent possible learning resources, particularly in schools limited in their student body and personnel. However, some motivation is needed, some opportunity to talk about what one is doing by oneself. The principal, guidance counselor, or a sympathetic teacher is an essential advisor in the use of these impersonal techniques.

HOMEWORK

A controversial matter in education for many years has been the assignment of work to be done at home. The limitations of the commonly stereotyped homework assignment are well known. There has been frequent criticism of assignments which are routine and uninteresting, or which demand greater insight and experience than the student can muster. Such a picture, of course, need be neither accurate nor universal. In a study of the effects of homework assignment on scholastic success, W. Anderson (1946) discovered that students of better than average ability made higher scores in English, social studies, and mathematics when they were given homework than did a control group that was freed of homework assignments. The students doing homework showed a better sense of direction in class and an ability to work with less teacher direction than did the non-study groups.

Apparently, the problem centers not so much on whether homework shall be assigned but on the type of homework that shall be assigned. Woolever (1955), doing research in science education, suggests the use of laboratory homework with simple equipment available in the home in place of the less imaginative verbal assignments done from a textbook alone. His study of superior high school students revealed a preference for the following types of assignments: research reports, arguing a controversial issue, using their own ideas, reading books of their own choice, doing experiments at home, and solving problems.

The Superior and Talented Student Project of the North Central Association notes the tendency of inexperienced or less skilled teachers to utilize the less stimulating and more burdensome assignments. Editors of their newsletter comment:

> The problem of quantity rather than quality assignments has been difficult to overcome. When it is suggested that assignments are sometimes long or inappropriate, they react by asking if they should be watered down. This isn't the point; the point is to stimulate students with ability. (STS News, 1960, p. 35)

SUMMER, EVENING, AND SATURDAY PROGRAMS

For the youngster who is avid to learn, the school day, the school week, and the school year seem absurdly short. Limiting the ablest student to the resources of the school, however excellent, may not fully extend him. Many schools are reaching out for assistance to resources in the community—professional people and scholars in nearby universities and in local industry, workers in government agencies, homemakers with extraordinary competences, and retired persons.

A number of school systems have been able to work out desirable relationships with local universities. In a few cases exceptional high school students are able to enroll for a course or two in the regular college program while they are still attending high school. More typical are special opportunities worked out cooperatively where selected students participate in a weekly evening program, a Saturday session, or a summer program. The University of Rochester (New York), for example, conducted a seminar in the 1957-58 school year for twenty-six students from 19 school districts in its area. In addition, for many years the University has worked cooperatively with Rochester high schools. The program is free to meet the needs and utilize the opportunities of the situation and is not directed toward college credit. Reed College provides college resources for the Portland High Schools (Oregon) during the school day, and the two organizations plan cooperatively the program for gifted children in that city. Colgate has offered a summer workshop for students in Oneida County (New York). The University of Texas played host to twenty-eight budding chemists from 14 Texas high schools in the summer of 1956. Summarizing activities over a three-year period, Miami University (Ohio) issued a comprehensive report in 1961 of its University Study Program for Superior High School Students, operating both during the summer and the academic year (Miami, 1961). The list might be extended considerably, but the few examples cited indicate one pattern of school-college cooperation. Summer sessions help schools in noncollege communities; year-round opportunities may be developed in college towns.

A unique kind of summer offering was initiated in 1963 in North Carolina under the sponsorship of Governor Terry Sanford with the assistance of the Carnegie Corporation and local businessmen ("The Governor's School," 1964). A special school was organized on the campus of Salem College in Winston-Salem and enrolled four hundred talented high school students who were to enter their junior or senior year the following September. The student body, coming from 85 counties in the state, comprised 140 boys and girls in the performing arts and 260 in academic areas. In an eight-week session, the students gave time to a major subject, a second area of particular interest, and two afternoons a week to seminars based on the Great Books. While the work in major areas and the residential experience were significant events in the lives of these young people coming from a diversity of backgrounds, the Great Books seminars were regarded by Franklin Keller, the consultant in performing arts, as less than successful.* The school seems to have succeeded in providing a "peak experience" for exceptionally gifted students in areas of low population density.

The summer and year-round programs offer contrasting values. Generally the weekly seminar adopts an area of common interest or plays host to speakers who serve as guides in the exploration of a number of professions and disciplines. The summer workshop provides an opportunity for more concentrated pursuit of a better defined interest. The Oneida County-Colgate workshop, for example, offered laboratory work in science or a combination foreign language-international relations program. Forty-four students worked on scientific research projects four hours daily for six weeks. Sixty-two students took a language course in a language laboratory two hours daily for six weeks and divided the

---

* Address, Metropolitan Association for Study of the Gifted, New York City, March 17, 1964.

remaining two hours between foreign policy and interpretation of literature as one option and creative writing and speech and dramatics as a second option. The typical "teaching unit" was a team composed of a college and high school teacher (Young, 1959).

A second type of university cooperation takes place under governmental auspices. The National Science Foundation has sponsored each year a number of science and mathematics seminar-research programs for high school students on a number of college campuses in various parts of the country. Generally the host and planning agency is a particular college department, and the department normally provides the instructors as well. These programs include both summer courses and offerings on Saturdays during the school year. High school credit is normally not involved.

The Joe Berg Foundation (Chicago) has for a number of years urged industries with scientific personnel to spearhead the formation of science seminars for interested high school students. A number of schools have affiliated themselves with local Joe Berg committees. Scientists and engineers working in the community join with school leaders to develop after-school seminars for students selected by written examination after recommendation by their principal or teachers. Some firms open laboratory facilities to participating students to pursue individual projects. Local seminars have been established in many parts of the country including Los Gatos, California; Rochester, New York; Elkins Park, Pennsylvania; Annapolis, Maryland; and Sheboygan, Wisconsin. The Foundation provides materials to assist local committees in organizing and developing programs (Joe Berg Foundation).

COLLEGE PROVISIONS FOR GIFTED STUDENTS

While college programs are by definition devoted to students of high intellectual ability, colleges may also fail the gifted by neglecting to adapt to individual differences in the higher reaches of the ability spectrum. Cole has detailed experimentation in some colleges to vary the curriculum for exceptional students, but he is critical of "too many colleges" for "supplying every customer with a standardized product regardless of his interests and abilities." He continues:

> The standard curriculum may be satisfactory for the standard student, but at many institutions there are too many students who are bored with the work they are taking, duplicating material poorly learned in secondary school, being led slowly along the path of learning when they have the ability to race ahead of the pack. (Cole, 1958, p. 25)

As in specially selected classes in elementary and secondary schools, college classes normally represent a wide range of ability. Using the IQ as a criterion, we note that a score of 110 to 115 is generally regarded as adequate to attain a degree in college. Many states require their state universities and colleges to admit any high school student who applies, thus reducing the minimum IQ for a portion of the entrants. From this minimum, scores spread all the way to maximums of 180 and beyond. The spread is likely to be extended as colleges necessarily respond to the desires of an ever increasing proportion of high school graduates to attend. One solution is to erect high barriers and develop highly selective standards. A second solution, more likely to be employed, is to admit a larger number of applicants and to adapt the college program to the needs and abilities of a heterogeneous group. In either case, the gifted student needs to be treated differently than the "standard student" Cole depicts.

In providing for the superior student, colleges have generally followed one or the other of two philosophies. One approach regards college as primarily a preparation for adult endeavor. The needs of any one student is seen as roughly similar to any other's. Special ability is recognized by accelerating progress through a fairly standard curriculum. The second approach puts value on the college experience itself. The time spent in college rather than the program is kept standard. The able student is exposed to a deeper, more enriched program in the four years that he spends in college.

ACCELERATED PROGRESS

Programs of acceleration that affect college students actually begin in high school. The Early Admission and Advanced Placement Programs, initiated in 1951 and 1952 respectively, have already been described. By truncating the fourth year of the high school program (Early Admissions) and by improving articulation between courses in high school and college (Advanced Placement), these programs may reduce the student's time in formal schooling by a year or more.

A third type of acceleration that involves high school work is the credit-by-examination system at the University of Buffalo, the University of Illinois, and the Ohio State University among others. Entering students may take examinations in freshman courses without taking the courses themselves. If they receive a grade of B or better on the examination they are granted credit for the course. Buffalo has been following this system since the 1930's, providing some guidance for superior students in high school preparing for the examinations. The University reports about 60 per cent of the students passing examinations in a variety of subjects. Moreover, students who passed nine or more semester hours work by examination have proved superior to the entire freshman class in their college grades. They apparently were not handicapped when taking advanced courses in college without taking their prerequisite work in the same institution (Pressey, 1949, pp. 123-24). In addition to credit-by-examination for entering freshmen, various universities permit students at all levels to earn credits in the same way.

While sallies into acceleration at the college level are apparently justified, there are few signs of any effective growth of these practices. Despite Lehman's (1953) statistics on early age of stellar achievement, America seems wedded to the idea of an invariable four-year term for college. Such being the case, efforts to make the four years more meaningful for the bright student may have more effect in the long run. These efforts include such matters as elective offerings, special programs, independent study, guidance, and experimental teaching methods.

ELECTIVE OFFERINGS

A common response to inquiries concerning provisions for exceptional students is citation of rich elective offerings listed in the college catalog. Theoretically, the student may seek courses sufficiently rigorous to challenge his ability and meet his academic needs. Questions that remain unanswered include (1) What provisions are made in the area of required courses? (2) Are students helped to meet students of similarly high ability through some form of grouping? (3) Are instructors able to maintain high standards of content and challenge or must they temper their instruction to a lower average? (4) What is done to motivate students to seek courses of difficulty rather than "snap courses" leading to straight *A's* and honors upon graduation?

HONORS PROGRAMS

Electives alone do not answer these questions. Since 1958 the Inter-University Committee on the Superior Student has been publishing a newsletter, *The Superior Student*, which serves as a clearinghouse for exchange of information on honors programs, one of the most widely advocated solutions to the problem. J. W. Cohen, director of the Committee and editor of the newsletter, makes certain recommendations in the development of an honors program:

> First, plans for superior students should start as early as possible, preferably by recruiting them on admission to college. . . . Late

bloomers would . . . enter the program whenever evidence of their worthiness was forthcoming.

Second, the lower division is as crucial for Honors as the upper, perhaps more so. A general, or college, Honors program should therefore exercise its influence long before specialization starts in the upper division. The challenge to deeper perspectives should begin at once. . . .

Third, full-fledged departmental Honors programs should accompany the general or college program. . . .

Fourth, a multiplicity of approaches is needed to meet the variety of superior students in any large university. In the general or college Honors there should be made available from the beginning of the student's career, Honors groups and seminars of all kinds, Honors colloquia, specially designed courses, independent studies, and summer projects. . . . As far as possible the technique of Honors groups and colloquia should be that of the conference. . . .

Fifth, an Honors Council, a director and a counseling staff should be established for the administration of the program as it affects superior students and faculty. . . .

Finally, examination procedures, written and oral, should be worked out in a form appropriate to stated aims, both in general and departmental programs. On the basis of these examinations, final awards should be determined. (Cohen, 1958, pp. 4-5) [*]

The Honors program claims to be the answer to the student's contentment with mediocre performance, to anti-intellectualism and the attraction of non-academic activities on the campus, and to the pursuit of grades as ends in themselves. "The superior student is actively sought out and brought to a fuller consciousness of his potentialities. He is under continuous challenge and stimulation to develop and maintain an Honors outlook in all of his work, in purposive scholarship and growing cultural insights" (*Ibid.*, p. 7).

Under the aegis of honors programs, some interesting developments are taking place in areas where there has been a great need for some time. One of these is required courses outside the student's specialization. Often the generally superior student is regarded by the instructor as one with all the non-majors in the course. Slobodkin (1958) tells of an inter-disciplinary science honors course at the University of Michigan for superior non-science majors. The responsibility of science depart-

---

[*] From "On Honors Programs," by J. W. Cohen. Reprinted with permission from *Superior Student*, November, 1958.

ments for education of the scientifically literate citizen as well as the future scientist is apparently taken seriously in this case. Individualization of graduate programs as well as the baccalaureate may be found in descriptions in various issues of *The Superior Student* of honors in a medical school (Kansas University) and the graduate program in history (Emory University).

An interesting overview of the honors program is found in a memorandum submitted to the Swarthmore Faculty Curriculum Committee by Dean W. C. H. Prentice (1959). Prentice states three aims: better teaching, achievement of a concentrated or intensive educational experience, and freedom of the student from class attendance and "all the paraphernalia of daily assignments and recitation." The last includes freedom for self-direction by the student and liberation from the tempo of other students. Prentice states as "standard techniques" the employment of small classes, eight students or fewer, and the holding of long sessions—four or five hours—but only once a week. The following features of the Swarthmore program are regarded as distinctive:

1. The student does all of his work under the new method of study, leaving behind the practices of course work not only in his major but in everything that he is taking.
2. He spends two full years in the program instead of one or two semesters at the end.
3. He is expected to stand examinations in each of the areas in which he has worked, and the examinations themselves have unusual conditions.
   a. The examinations are given by professors from other institutions.
   b. These terminal examinations are the only ones that have any bearing on the student's standing.
   c. All of the examinations are taken at the same time, at the end of the entire period of four semesters.
   d. The examinations are both written and oral.
   e. The final assessment of the student is made by a conference of examiners rather than by the averaging of grades. (*Ibid.*, p. 13) *

Problems of identification loom as large at the college level as at the common school level. Riley suggests the following as qualities by which gifted students may be identified:

a. Extraordinary memory
b. High level of abstract thinking

---

* From "The Honors Program at Swarthmore College," by W. C. H. Prentice. Reprinted with permission from *Superior Student*, April, 1959.

   c. The ability to apply knowledge and illuminate experience
   d. Intellectual curiosity
   e. Intellectual honesty
   f. Persistent goal-directed behavior
   g. Facility of expression and discriminating vocabulary
   h. Variety of interests
   i. Physical well-being
   j. Pattern of sound values. (Riley, 1959, p. 10) *

Riley expresses her conviction that motivation is the first step in identification since an individual's top performance depends upon his efforts
to do his best. To provide such motivation she advocates personal guidance and association of the student with others of high ability in special
sections, seminars, and colloquies. The importance of vital and challenging teachers is also noted.

INDEPENDENT STUDY

A number of colleges have for a long time made available to very
superior students the privilege of independent study under a senior faculty member in place of a stipulated number of elective credits. This
opportunity has generally been reserved to seniors. Coming at the student's initiative, these programs have been extremely few in number.

New emphasis upon the need to develop independence in study and
to permit independent sallies into fields of interest has reinforced the
effort motivated by expedience to provide for larger numbers of students
on college campuses. Accordingly additional colleges are exploring
independent study, and several are extending independent study privi-
leges to lower division students and to required courses in the general
education program.

In 1957 Bonthius, Davis, and Drushal published a survey of independent study programs. They report programs in one quarter of the
nation's colleges and a number of different approaches in these institutions. Some colleges involve only a portion of the student body in independent work; a few enroll all students in such activity for a small
fraction of their college course. The general pattern finds the student
following a program of reading or laboratory work more or less on his
own. Generally he presents only a final report on his work (Bonthius,
1957).

Related to independent study is the tutorial system practiced for centuries in England and utilized for many years at Harvard. A number of
colleges have more recently instituted plans of this type. Students are

---

* From "Finding and Launching the Superior Student," by Susan B. Riley. Reprinted with permission from *Superior Student,* January, 1959.

assigned to a tutor, plan a program of work with him, and meet with him periodically as individuals to discuss their studies, to present and review reports. Closer supervision by the tutor distinguishes tutorials from independent study, but the student's activity is otherwise quite similar.

Programs of independent study do not find universal acceptance. Many faculty members question the ability of the college student to pursue with profit an independent program. Some professors prefer more systematic immersion of the student in a program that is designed and conducted in the more conventional manner by the instructor. They are fearful of the student's enthusiasm for a particular topic if concentration on it causes gaps in other areas. Still others place high value on the interchange and cross-fertilization that takes place in a college class. They see the student missing this kind of stimulation and insight when independent study takes the place of thoughtful seminars and discussion groups.

The tutorial system is in part open to the same criticism. In addition problems arise from the assignment of tutors. Their economic situation normally impels colleges to assign junior staff members or graduate assistants as tutors. At times these young men and women are wonderfully stimulating mentors and excellent models with whom the student can readily identify. Often, however, they lack sufficient depth and have had limited contact with students. Sometimes they are so ardently pursuing their own doctorate or other research project that they give too little time to their tutees. Where senior staff members are assigned, sometimes they are able to involve students in their own scholarly pursuits. Sometimes, unfortunately, they are too preoccupied with their own concerns to regard the tutee as more than a burden. At any rate, the quality of personal relationship which develops between tutor and tutee can spell the difference between a highly stimulating and a deadening experience. Interaction with other students and a planned curriculum are not present to mediate between the two parties.

EFFECTIVE USE OF EXISTING SERVICES

Honors and independent study programs represent methods of developing greater curricular flexibility. Faculties employing them recognize the wide spread of abilities in their students and adapt the curriculum to these differences. Other ways of providing flexibility include exempting students from particular requirements or adjusting requirements to the particular strengths and weaknesses of individual students. Adaptations in curriculum may be accompanied also by more stimulating teaching methods and better directed guidance services.

Criticism of deficiencies in the traditional lecture system is widespread. A medium which deals with a large group of students as if they were all mentally equal is not likely to challenge exceptional members of the group. Nor is the best use made of the professor's mettle in a procedure which denies students the opportunity to test their understanding through discussion with classmates and the instructor. Emphasis is placed increasingly on the small section, on discussion, on Socratic dialogue. It is conceivable that so-called teaching machines may also make a contribution if they provide to bright students an opportunity to accomplish more quickly the learning tasks that are routine or factual in nature. If the "scrambled book" or other automated devices can relieve the instructor of these simple jobs, more resources may be available for the relatively expensive discussion group of small size.

Increased attention is being given, too, to the guidance needs of the superior students. Concern of guidance personnel in this area is not new, but on most campuses first attention has had to be given to those students in danger of being dropped for poor work. Honors programs at some colleges are enhanced with additional guidance personnel in order to promote learning on the campus as well as to untangle personal problems and offer career counseling. The freshman leaves the relatively protective secondary school for the large college campus where nobody seems to be interested in him. He may be separated from family direction for the first time. He may feel—and may actually be—lost in an unfamiliar crowd. Superior intelligence is probably of some help, but interested guidance personnel have an important role to play. Someone has to find the better students and keep them from discouragement or disillusionment, from developing a rationale of getting by with the least effort. Someone may be needed to help the young man or woman keep his focus on academic goals so that he doesn't dissipate his energies on social, recreational, and athletic activities alone. Someone should help the student arrive at a realistic appraisal of his own potential. Effective guidance may keep the bright student from wasting his time, dropping out of college too early, or simply muddling through.

Students of college age are already in those years when the most productive talents of all times have begun to make their important contributions to civilization. Colleges have but two choices. One is to locate bright students and accelerate them through a standard curriculum as fast as their ability will carry them so that they may get on with their work. A second is so to organize college studies that the outstanding student has the independence he needs to put his potential seriously to work while still in college. Ultimately this means that the college has to make available to the outstanding student what it makes available to its faculty —the opportunity not only to study as an academic neophyte but also the privilege of contributing as a scholar and researcher. It should be possible for a student to became an academic adult even before commencement.

COMMUNITY RESOURCES FOR THE GIFTED

Obviously the formal schooling process is only part of an individual's education. The more gifted he is, the more he is likely to learn informally through daily contacts with the environment.

The general attitude of the culture toward intellectual activity is likely to be as potent a factor as specific provisions for the development of talent. The communication media available contribute both to the general atmosphere and specific learnings in the community. Newspapers, periodicals, television, radio, and motion pictures are powerful influences on the young. Despite the standardization that results from the spread of national news chains, distribution channels and broadcasting networks, considerable variation may be found from community to community in the substance presented through mass media. A realistic concern with education of the gifted must extend to the quality of these resources in each locality.

Various institutions in the community have a high potential for contributing to the promotion of intellectual excellence. Many library systems are not content simply to provide a depository of printed matter. Special reading programs for very young children, reading circles, book review clubs, lecture series, writing or dramatics groups operate under library auspices in a number of communities. In the same way, museums often make the most intensive use possible of their resources by sponsoring creative as well as appreciative activity. Young people's groups in the arts, in history, archaeology, and natural sciences may be found under the aegis of local museums. Religious organizations as well, by stimulating intellectual and creative ability, may challenge the curiosity, ingenuity, and mental power of bright young people. The library, museum and church appeal to young persons on the basis of special interests, and interest is the catalyst in the employment of ability. In some cases, as in the Cleveland Major Work program, community groups have been the main force behind the initiation of school programs for the gifted.

Business, argiculture, and professional groups also are often able to contribute to development of special ability. Opportunities for try-out experiences in business and professional offices can open wide vistas of vocational choice to young people. The financial resources of the business community often operate through service club programs to sponsor scholarships for students in high school and college. Programs like Junior

Achievement, helping young people organize and operate small businesses, provide an incentive for involvement in business activities that may lead to better understanding of economics and human relationships. Support of formal learning programs after school, on weekends and in the summer represents a more direct contribution to education of able students.

Health and psychological services in the community, while not focussed on the gifted, make their special contribution to bright students. An excellent school program for the gifted may fail in individual cases if not bolstered by agencies meeting these other needs. Such services also represent possible career exploration opportunities for youngsters with special interests.

Groups of responsible adults in a number of communities have organized special associations for improving the education of the gifted. These groups often include professional educational personnel as well as parents and other interested persons. While the hazard of misdirected enthusiasm is always present, the possibility of coordinated activity also exists. School and community leaders can work together to study the need of the gifted, the variety of possible programs, and the provision of opportunities in school and community to develop the maximum potential of each child in its service area.

SUMMARY

At the elementary, secondary, and college level, certain policies are apparently pursued in common. At all levels the major drive is to enrich the educational experience of students of superior intellectual ability. Different approaches may be encountered at all levels, depending upon the attitude in each institution or community as to the relative values of acceleration and homogenous grouping. While there is no agreement on the kind of acceleration that results in earlier graduation from a particular school level or completion of formal education itself, there is agreement on the need to accelerate the studies offered to students of high potential. At times this is achieved by providing greater breadth in given areas, sometimes by adding new areas of learning, and sometimes by moving more rapidly through the content of particular disciplines. Emphasis is placed on maintaining a high degree of challenge for the bright student and avoiding the boredom that might result from a restricted educational diet which offers him no greater scope or variety than is offered to the average student. At the same time there is fairly general acceptance that "more of the same" does not represent an improvement.

At all levels certain problems appear to be constant. One is identifying bright students who somehow have not yet revealed their potential. Second is providing a program with sufficient stimulation within a framework which does not put the bright student out of contact with the remainder of his class. A third is maintenance of motivation at a high level in order to avoid the phenomenon of underachievement which seems to affect both schools and colleges alike. One may also note an apparent conflict between maximum coverage of the cultural heritage and the development of programs which place considerable emphasis on independent study by the student.

Educational institutions are approaching these problems in different ways. In some cases they are merely returning to educational procedures of the past. These emphasize the elite nature of the school population and impose upon students traditional curriculum organization and subject matter of the past. Some institutions are attempting to make a major transformation in order to secure greater individualization of instruction for students all along the line. Some are adding special opportunities for gifted students or are grouping the highly able together. They hope that this administrative device will foster comparable adaptation by the teacher in his methods and the curriculum and a desirable amount of mutual stimulation on the part of bright students. Some institutions are experimenting on methods of improving articulation with institutions at the next higher level in order to provide advanced opportunities for their bright students. In all, a considerable amount of exploration and experimentation may be observed which, if continued, augurs well for development of programs of continuously improving quality for students of superior ability.

Chapter 8

Thinking

Thinking in its lower grades is comparable to paper money, and in its higher forms it is a kind of poetry.

—Havelock Ellis

No task in the education of the gifted offers more promise than the teaching of thinking. A growing body of evidence supports the hypothesis that thinking can be taught, and a variety of materials is being developed to help the teacher in this function. Renewed research on the part of psychologists into thinking indicates the possibility that we are on the threshold of improved understanding of thought processes. Without in any way disparaging the role of information in the curriculum, there is substantial agreement among both the liberals and conservatives in educational theory that the teaching of thinking—and its direction toward socially desirable goals—is the main purpose of education. By definition the intellectually gifted are the most likely to make great gains in learning to think. Thus, an ultimate objective in educating the gifted, regardless of age level or subject, is the teaching of critical and creative thinking.

Psychologists with widely differing orientations are currently coming to grips with the phenomenon of cognition. The 1964 Yearbook of the National Society for the Study of Education summarizes efforts of behaviorists to build the concept of a mediating cognition that is interposed between stimulus and response, and of Gestaltists to refine their concept of cognition from their initial statement of insight. Both camps apparently accept some aspects of personality theory which focus on the integrative functions of the ego, motivation, and social influences.

184

The work of psychologists is being reinforced by developments in information theory. Communication systems are being studied in terms of the internal coding and recording of inputs, as well as the more conventional analysis of inputs and outputs alone. This attention to internal operations corresponds to the behaviorists' concern with a mediating process in cognition and the Gestaltists' concept of a dynamic personality. The eventual result, hopefully, is the development of more sophisticated understanding of the thinking process, and this in turn should lead to more effective teaching of thinking.

DEFINING THINKING FOR EDUCATIONAL PURPOSES

Attention to thinking is no new phenomenon. The dawn of consciousness, in all probability, brought with it wonderment about the major process of consciousness—thought. However thought takes various paths—undirected reflection, criticism, imaginative fancy, problem solving, and so on. Burton, Kimball, and Wing (1960, p. v) start with this definition:

> Thinking results when there is persistent effort to examine the evidence which supports any belief, solution, or conclusion which is suggested for acceptance, together with the implications and further conclusions of the evidence.[*]

They then list the following kinds of thinking: problem solving, as in the sciences; logical inference as in mathematics; making and supporting value judgments; stating and supporting goals, policies and decisions; critical analysis, and creative development of ideas (Burton, 1960, vi-vii). Ennis (1963) lists a number of "aspects" of critical thinking which are useful in analysis of this highly general term. He lists deduction, assumption finding, definition, explanation, determining reliability of evidence and authorities, generalization, hypothesis testing, evaluating theories, detecting ambiguities, and detecting over-vague and over-specific statements. It should be evident from these two efforts at classification that thinking takes many forms but that it is possible to be specific about particular thought processes. It is this possibility of clearer definition that makes programs for training in a particular thought process feasible. Thinking in general need not be a vague goal of the total curriculum; particular thought processes can instead shape the content and method of specific subjects to some extent.

---

[*] From: *Education for Effective Thinking*, by William H. Burton, Roland B. Kimball, and Richard L. Wing. Copyright © 1960, Appleton-Century-Crofts, Inc. Reprinted by permission of Appleton-Century-Crofts.

Investigations into Thought Processes. Efforts to teach problem solving in the schools evidence the pervasive effect of Dewey's statement of five steps of a complete act of thought in *How We Think.* These include the awareness of a problem, definition and location of the problem, making a hypothesis, elaborating and checking the hypothesis through reasoning, and testing the hypothesis in action. These steps may be useful in suggesting processes for school training. In fact, Burton, Kimball, and Wing organize their volume on *Education for Effective Thinking* (1960) around several of these steps. However, these steps also appear to be an oversimplification, particularly in view of more recent research into the complex phenomenon of thought.

Forming concepts. Considerable attention is being given, for example, to concept formation and stages in the development of thought processes. Piaget is concerned with the way in which children develop a "basic repertory" of concepts. Other psychologists are beginning to go beyond the initial acquisition of concepts to the matter of how these concepts function (Thomson, 1959). Piaget (1953) has described a series of developmental stages, starting with a sensori-motor period from birth to two years of age, a period of "pre-operational" thought from two to four, of "intuitive" thought from four to seven, of "concrete operations" from eight to eleven, and of "propositional or formal operations" from eleven to fourteen. In the intuitive thought period the four-to-seven-year-old begins to use signs for absent objects, to understand means-ends relationships, and to develop a firmer grip on the distinction between real and imagined events. In the elementary school years, the child is said to form clear-cut operations—concepts of classes, relations, numbers. Ideas of space, time, and a material world in which everything has a place in relation to everything else begin to emerge. After eleven, the child crosses a threshold where he becomes able to deal with concepts and generalizations not tied to concrete objects. Such an analysis should be extremely useful to teachers in defining the limits of their program and also indicating the developing need as the child grows for more stimulating, more demanding operations. Even the gifted child cannot be pushed beyond his developmental status; nor should he be allowed to stagnate at a level below.

That such neat formulations as Piaget's are open to question is revealed in the investigations of Wann, Dorn, and Liddle (1962) reported in *Fostering Intellectual Development in Young Children.* Their research with three hundred children in nursery schools leads them to believe that more can be done and more should be done intellectually with children from the age of three to six. They challenge Piaget's thesis that no formal deductions are possible under the age of seven or eight. Wann and his group found these young children ready to build concepts from their observation of the world about them. They declare that the aim of building concepts about their world should serve as the key element in selecting educational experiences for young children. A quotation from this report is indeeed suggestive in planning programs for the gifted:

> The readiness of young children for challenging intellectual experiences was evident throughout the study. The young children were eager to gather information to apply in their conversation and their play situations. They were attempting to see relationships, to make generalizations, to discriminate, to classify. They were interested in faraway in time and in space. There was an interest in causality as well as concern and sometimes confusion in distinguishing between naturalistic and magical explanations for various phenomena. The children were observing the scientific world about them with much curiosity. They were actively using concepts of quantity, of size, of space, of number. These children were using words beautifully, metaphorically, humorously and nonsensically. They were struggling to communicate with others and trying to learn to hear and understand what others were saying to them. (Wann, 1962, p. 98) *

Do we live to think or think to live? Still another aspect of thought being explored is its very reason for being. Much psychology of the current era is predicated on a needs-reduction theory; i.e., practically all behavior is related to removing some need—hunger, pain, loneliness. This point of view is being challenged sharply by a more dynamic personality theory which sees man as seeking stimulation rather than quiescence. Getzels (NSSE, 1964, pp. 240-67) speaks for an increasing group of scholars when he suggests that there may be "not only viscerogenic needs to be satisfied by satiation, but also neurogenic needs to be gratified by stimulation, i.e., needs for excitement, novelty, and the opportunity to deal with the problematic" (p. 256). Wright and Kagan (1963) voice the same sentiment when they assert that "human motivations to be rational, to be correct, to structure information efficiently, ... are always present." Unlike hunger, thirst, pain, or sex, these motives are not dependent upon deprivations. Such a position is freed from limiting thought to situations of perplexity, as Dewey assumed, and permits the educator to place focus on thought for its own sake. Here again one sees special implications in educating the intellectually gifted.

Cognitive style. Interesting research is also directed toward differ-

---

* From *Fostering Intellectual Development in Young Children*, by Kenneth Wann, Miriam S. Dorn, and Elizabeth Liddle. Copyright 1962. Reprinted with permission of the Bureau of Publications, Teachers College, Columbia University.

ences in "cognitive style." Not only do individuals differ in thinking
power; they also differ in the way they approach a problem requiring
thought. Bloom and Broder (1950), reporting on their efforts to improve
problem-solving processes of students at the University of Chicago,
placed their focus on the efficiency with which the individual arrives at
a solution, the extent to which he brings in extraneous material, the
extent to which he is swayed by external considerations, and the extent
to which he can pursue a particular line of attack. They discovered individual differences in understanding the nature of the problem, in understanding ideas contained in the problem, in the general approach to the
solution of problems and in attitudes toward problem solving. They
noted that directions seemingly clear to some students were misleading
to others; that some students had difficulty in organizing their thoughts
in any systematic way.

Kagan, Moss, and Sigel (1960) analyzed performance on tests of
cognitive ability, classifying what they described as "conceptual style"
and "cognitive style." Their identification of characteristic patterns of
individual subjects led them to posit the possibility of ultimate discovery
of links between cognitive processes and personality variables.

Bruner, Goodnow, and Austin (1958) devised and developed an ingenious experiment to identify the "strategies" used by individuals in
a task which involved formation of a concept. Their research led to the
conclusion that different subjects used identifiable, characteristic ways
of approaching their problem.

French (ETS, 1963) administered 15 cognitive tests to 177 high school
and college students in an effort to discover differences in the way that
subjects approach test items. He secured information of the problem
solving approaches of his group and used this information to devise 17
ways of dividing the group into contrasting pairs. Roughly, half the
students in each pair were found to use one problem-solving style, while
the other half used a "distinctively different" style. He offers as an
example the difference between an "analytic" approach and a "visual"
approach to a problem of space perception. To educators, this should
suggest the possibility of identifying specific skills in problem solving
and developing programs to teach these skills. Different kinds of giftedness may result in different kinds of learning.

Gallagher and Lucito (1961), comparing the sub-test patterns of
gifted, average, and retarded children on the Wechsler Intelligence
Scales for Children, report different intellectual *patterns* as well as differences in intellectual *ability*. Here again the existence of different approaches in thinking is manifest.

All of these inquiries into "style" in cognitive processes combine to
question any view of thinking which is monolithic. Just as scientists have

long argued that there is more than one scientific method, there is more than one approach to thinking, more than one set of cognitive operations. When the teacher gives specific attention to instruction in thinking, therefore, he must encourage more than one approach and seek to develop manifold styles in cognition.

Divergent and Convergent. Focus on different styles in thinking helps to illumine discussions of divergent and convergent thinking. Guilford (1951, 1957), in his analyses of creative thinking and "structure of the intellect," introduced the distinction between convergent thinking which uses systematic reasoning processes in a search for the "right answer," and divergent thinking which is marked by fluency, flexibility, originality, and elaboration in a process that is more "free wheeling" and imaginative. In a sense, convergent thinking uses facts to solve problems while divergent thinking is free to develop its own data, raise its own questions or take new directions. To some extent, these types of thinking should be considered as characteristic styles or modes for given individuals, not as better and poorer approaches to problems.

Male and Female. Sex differences also affect cognitive style. Reporting on a number of studies, Waetjen (1963) indicates that as early as eight years old girls are more dependent upon the visual environment while boys act more on internal cues; that males and females hold different perceptions of self and others; that males are more aware of cognitive factors and females of emotional factors in a given situation. Here again monolithic views of thinking are questioned.

Inquirers into the nature of thinking and cognitive processes freely admit that they are only beginning to scratch the surface of an extremely profound topic. However, an important first step has been taken in efforts to break down into viable research units a process which has heretofore remained too molar to approach profitably. Piaget's work on concept formation and developmental stages, numerous investigations into cognitive styles, and studies of cognition in school as well as laboratory settings give promise of increased understanding of the thinking process. Recently these efforts have been reinforced using computers that can simultaneously deal with the numerous complex inputs needed to simulate thought (Carnegie, 1962). Together, these approaches may yield the understanding fundamental to development of effective school programs for teaching of thinking.

TEACHING OF THINKING IN THE SCHOOLS

The improvement of thinking has long been a goal of education. Burton, Kimball, and Wing (1960, pp. 283-93) present a brief resume of efforts to achieve this objective, starting with college courses in formal logic which traditionally have had little effect on thinking. In secondary schools before World War I "faculty psychology" supported the claim that various subjects developed particular competences like the "faculty" of thinking, and that this formal discipline would be automatically transferred for use in meeting various problems in life. While some laymen continue to argue the virtues of certain subjects because of their supposed intellectual rigor and attendant "discipline," competent psychologists and educators no longer accept this theory. Herbart, who helped to dethrone formal discipline in the mid-nineteenth century, offered his own "five formal steps" of learning and thinking. These combined inductive and deductive processes and played an important part in the training of American teachers until quite recent times. Unfortunately, these became hopelessly formalized. Burton criticizes the tendency to put too great trust in a formula and to overlook the pluralistic nature of thinking processes discussed in preceding pages of this volume.

Burton, Kimball, and Wing also summarize more modern research on methods of teaching critical thinking in secondary schools in science courses, mathematics, language arts, and social studies (*Ibid.*, pp. 297-305). The following table presents methods which they regard as established by reliable research:

In biology:
1. Instruction on the scientific method with special consideration of the subordinate concepts which are involved in the formulation of the hypothesis or generalization
2. Study of experimental procedures, identification of experimental factors
3. Study of résumés of experiments, writing conclusions from data read about
4. Discussion of conclusions thus reached by other class members with regard to accuracy, completeness, and the degree to which the conclusions go beyond the data

In chemistry:
1. Student selection and planning of experiments
2. Encouragement of students to:
   a. Recognize the value of controlled experiments
   b. Recognize basic assumptions
   c. Make clear records
   d. Use good laboratory techniques and careful observation
   e. Draw conclusions of their own from data they collect

In geometry:
1. Establishment of theorems inductively
2. Study of definition

3. Study of assumptions
4. Study of inductive proof
5. Study of factors which determine valid conclusions
6. Presentation of above matters in nonmathematical contexts—for example, advertisements, news reports, magazine articles, and selections from the history of science

In algebra:
1. Development of algebraic principles through method of self-discovery
2. Application of certain algebraic principles to nonmathematical materials
3. Discussion of extrapolation and interpolation of the data

In language arts, use of the following units:
1. Recognition of the need for definition
2. Logic and the weight of evidence
3. The nature of probable inference
4. Deductive and inductive inference
5. Logic and the method of science and characteristics of scientific attitudes
6. Prejudice as a factor making for "crooked thinking"
7. Values and logic
8. Propaganda and "crooked thinking"
9. Reading methods, as prescribed by William Gray

In social studies:
1. Propaganda analysis when reinforced by above units
(Burton, 1960, pp. 306-7) *

These findings give support to teachers who put emphasis on scientific method and logical analysis, on experimental procedures and discovery by the student, and on the application of rational methods learned in a course to the world at large.

NEW EXPERIMENTS IN TEACHING OF THINKING

A number of more recent inquiries confirm Burton's summary and also explore new areas.

Inquiry Training. Suchman (1960) in the late 1950's developed a program and materials for "inquiry training," acting on the assumption that a method of inquiry can be taught and that it is transferable from one

---

* From: *Education for Effective Thinking*, by William H. Burton, Roland B. Kimball, and Richard L. Wing. Copyright © 1960, Appleton-Century-Crofts, Inc. Reprinted by permission of Appleton-Century-Crofts.

kind of problem situation to another. Suchman and his associates began their program with short films of physics demonstrations which present problems of cause and effect. Children in elementary schools view the films and then try to solve these problems with questions through which they gather data and perform imaginary experiments. The teacher normally responds to questions with a simple "yes" or "no" or "That's your hunch (hypothesis); how would you test it?" These sessions are interspersed with discussions in which the pupils analyze their processes. The purpose is to teach strategies and tactics of scientific inquiry. Films have also been prepared for use in economics and physiology. Suchman describes his objectives in this manner:

> Inquiry training is designed to supplement the ordinary science classroom activities. It gives the child a plan of operation that will help him to discover causal factors of physical change through his own initiative and control, and not to depend on the explanations and interpretations of teachers or other knowledgeable adults. He learns to formulate hypotheses, to test them through a verbal form of controlled experimentation, and to interpret the results. In a nutshell, the program is aimed at making pupils more *independent, systematic, empirical,* and *inductive* in their approach to problems of science. (Suchman, 1960, p. 42) *

The rationale behind inquiry training is a conviction of the potency of discovery as a method of learning. Suchman finds value in discovery because he regards the experience of data gathering as "intrinsically rewarding," because discovery strengthens the child's faith in the regularity of the universe, because the self-confidence that comes from discovery leads the child to make "creative intuitive leaps," and because practice makes perfect in use of the inductive, logical processes involved in discovery (1961, p. 148). The close relationship between inquiry training and discovery is seen in the title of the article quoted: "Inquiry Training: Building Skills for Autonomous Discovery." In brief, Suchman aims at a triple goal: training in scientific method, training in thinking, and development of learner autonomy.

Suchman was able to show significant results in training fifth-grade children in inquiry skills over a fifteen week period. Most of the pupils in his research became "more productive in their design and use of verification and experimentation." They showed growth toward "a fairly consistent strategy" which they were able to transfer to new problem situations. Finally, says Suchman, "They make fewer untested assump-

---

* From "Inquiry Training in the Elementary School," by J. Richard Suchman. Reprinted with permission from *Science Teacher*, November, 1960.

tions; they formulate and test more hypotheses; and they perform more controlled vs. uncontrolled experiments in the course of their inquiry" (1960, p. 47).

Primary grade vistas. Reference has already been made to the study of Wann, Dorn, and Liddle (1962) with children of pre-school age. In this project, the investigators sought to discover the information children have about their world, how they use their information, the nature of their concepts, and their ability to use intellectual processes involved in conceptualization. They found that children have ways of understanding their world. Children want to know about the phenomena that surround them and also about the world beyond the here and now. They want to understand the "demands of social living," and they want to know about language. What was especially revealing in the study was the children's readiness to deal with concepts. Wann, Dorn, and Liddle found evidence even with young children to support Bruner's thesis that key concepts and fundamental structures should be used as "indicators of facts or information that should be taught." This research lends strength to the idea that concept development should be an important goal in working with pre-school children as well as with their older siblings, and that training in thinking cannot begin too early.

Also at primary school level, Shotka (1960) reports an interesting unit with first grade school in a private school for gifted children. She modifies an outline for critical thinking in secondary school for use in the first grade, by simplifying vocabulary and level of operation:

1. See and state a problem.
2. Recognize what can be taken for granted.
3. Assume what is true for the sake of testing.
4. Give reasons for testing.
5. Get evidence: reading (by teacher); looking about us for answers; talking to parents and people in a position to help us.
6. Evaluate the evidence by: finding bias, validity, reliability.
7. Put findings together and organize them.
8. Draw conclusions.

Miss Shotka takes the conventional unit on the home and community helpers to help children sharpen their thinking, to form concepts, to gather data, and to evaluate ideas and evidence. She urges other teachers to follow three procedures: to encourage children to express ideas in general as well as concrete terms ("vegetables" for "peas and beans"), to encourage children to give reasons for ideas they express, and to encourage children to voice their own evaluations and appreciations.

Convergent vs. *Divergent.* A study by Gallagher (NSSE, 1964, p. 191) offers provocative results on teaching for convergent vs. divergent thinking. At the junior high school level a slight increase in divergent questions by the teacher led to a large increase in divergent thought production by students. An example of a divergent question used is: "What would have happened if the United States had been settled from West to East, rather than from East to West?" Apparently a planned strategy by the teacher can make a substantial impact upon the nature of his students' thinking. Imaginative approaches *can* be taught.

Teaching Creative Thinking. Can creative thinking be "taught" in the primary grades? In training businessmen in creativeness, Osborn (1957) developed a series of questions to guide them in imagining new products. Torrance (1963) applied these in the primary grades to help children "dream up" new toys. Some of these questions follow:

> What would happen if we made it larger? smaller? What could we add? subtract? substitute for part of it? What would happen if we gave it motion? odor? light? sound? color?
> What would happen if we changed the shape? (Torrance, 1963, pp. 137-38)

Torrance divided his population of 375 children from two schools into four groups. Two conditions of training were compared—training in the use of Osborne's questions versus no training. Two sets of instruction were used—motivation to produce as many new ideas as possible versus motivation to produce clever, original, unusual ideas. One trained group and one untrained group were given the first set of instructions. The other trained group and the other untrained group were given the second set of instructions. Except for the first grade children, significant differences were found favoring the trained group for each set of instructions. Significant differences were also found for the instructions to produce clever, original, unusual ideas—*both* in the quality of ideas offered and in the number of ideas. The latter finding is contrary to Osborn's belief that an increase in number of ideas brings with it automatically an increase in quality. Torrance's conclusion:

> . . . pupils in the primary grades, with the possible exception of the first grade, can in a short period be taught a set of principles that will enable them to produce more and better ideas than they would have without training. The results provide no support for motivating pupils in the primary grades to produce a quantity of ideas without consideration for quality. (Torrance, 1961, p. 41) °

Analysis of verbal behavior: Additional promise for the teaching of thinking is offered in the outcomes of a study at the University of Illinois

___
° From "Priming Creative Thinking in the Primary Grades," by E. Paul Torrance. Reprinted with permission from *Elementary School Journal,* October, 1961. Copyright 1961 by The University of Chicago.

of logical processes observed in classroom sessions (Aschner, 1963). Tapescripts were made of more than two hundred sessions in grades 7 to 12, and four major processes suggested by Guilford's work were identified and scored: cognitive memory, convergent thinking, evaluative thinking, and divergent thinking. In the record of verbal behavior, routine directions by the teacher and convergent thinking were observed much more frequently than the other operations which appeared in descending order as listed. Very few remarks were scored as exhibiting divergent thinking. As part of the project, a sophisticated procedure was developed to identify specified types of thought operations. Of potential value to the teacher is this focus on particular types of thinking rather than on an intangible molar approach. The technique of analyzing verbal behavior on the basis of intellective processes is also important in the clues it gives for directing emphasis in the classroom. Finally, the discovery of an imbalance between memorization and more creative thinking acts suggests serious need for reconsidering teaching methods.

Numerous studies, in addition, may be found in professional literature of teaching projects to improve thinking skills. While there is a wide range in the objectivity of these reports, in general, one finds much reason to confirm the assumption that thinking can be approached directly in the classroom. Moreover, an increasing effort is found to range beyond a rather primitive kind of academic problem-solving into more critical analyses of thought processes and creative production.

"PRESCRIPTIONS" FOR TEACHING OF THINKING

A substantial array of materials is available for teachers who are interested in making direct contributions to the quality of their students' thinking. Some of these suggestions for teachers come from rational analyses of the thought processes and inference of paths leading to their enhancement. Some are the outcome of the authors' own experimentation. Others arise from comprehensive study of research findings with conclusions based upon the writers' generalizations therefrom. The pages that follow include concerns with the teacher himself, the classroom environment, the learner's attitudes, and development of specified thought processes.

THE TEACHER AND THE TEACHING OF THINKING

Obviously, the teacher is a key factor in an area of learning where process, skills, and attitudes are more important than a specific core of information to be taught. The teacher is not confined in his contribution to deliberate instructional activities; he also serves as a model of critical thinking and perhaps, on occasion, of divergent and creative thought as well.

The general atmosphere of the classroom must be carefully prepared if students are to feel free to range widely and creatively in their thinking. This, too, the teacher affects intimately. Suchman (1963) sets certain conditions that are essential for development of learner "autonomy." The teacher, he says must present "open" problems—concrete situations where the answer is not to be found by simple appeal to authority in the form of teacher or textbook. He must give the learner freedom to "operate." He should provide an environment which is responsive to the child's questing. He has to help the student become aware of processes in thinking and must guide the learner to look at problems in new ways.

The teacher can profit also by recognizing blocks to development of autonomy as Suchman sees them. The teacher who controls every item in the classroom leaves no door open for experimentation. The teacher who rewards only mechanical repetition of learnings (the "approved solution") does not encourage "storage and retrieval" of learnings in creative style. Presenting convergent problems only limits opportunity for autonomy which is characteristically divergent at least in part. Employing the wrong motivational systems—ego reinforcement, praise and blame, considerations of one's role with peers in the classroom—may be self-defeating. On the other hand, intrinsic motivation, the heart of autonomy, is tied to the cognitive process itself: thinking for the sake of thinking. Finally, teaching the child in a "data poor situation" (one devoid of opportunity to find necessary information) keeps the child dependent rather than making him autonomous.

Relying on these observations, Suchman makes a plea for a shift in classroom activity. He urges less teaching of generalizations and conclusions exclusively. What is needed, he says, is to give the child a chance to arrive at theory through his own transactions with the environment. Teach inquiry skills, he exhorts; don't control them. Cease teaching "directively" from a teacher-dominated curriculum; instead, teach "responsively" to the child's searching and theorizing.

Wann, Dorn, and Liddle (1962), working with pre-school children rather than Suchman's middle graders, define the role of the teacher in intellectual development in a similar manner. They see the teacher's function as "observing and listening, supporting and extending, selecting and planning." The key to intellectual development, they say, lies in the ability young children have to extend and clarify their understandings of the world. The school's task is to provide "a variety of materials for manipulation and experimentation, opportunities to acquire information about many things in the environment, and help in the process of problem-solving and conceptualization" (Wann, 1962 p. 140).

To this, Wann and his associates relate the need for the teacher to understand the structure of the disciplines upon which they draw. For this reason they list the key concepts in science, social science and language which should inform instruction in these fields. Teacher training for concept development, therefore, seems to depend upon the teacher's being able to conceptualize the material he is teaching.

ESSENTIAL ATTITUDES

Thinking, of course, is not a bloodless affair involving simply a mechanical manipulation of information and concepts. Perception of the world about us depends upon attitudes we bring to our observation. Formation of concepts from what we see also involves selective and interpretive processes that stem from attitudinal factors.

Burton, Kimball, and Wing (1960, pp. 38-41) present a list of critical attitudes necessary for good thinking. These attitudes (presented with suggestions for their development) include the following:

Intellectual curiosity
Intellectual honesty, acceptance of responsibility for the thinking
    process and its results
Objectivity
Intelligent scepticism or suspension of judgment
Openmindedness
Conviction of universal cause-and-effect relationships
Disposition to be systematic
Flexibility
Persistence
Decisiveness

Where thinking in the group situation is involved, the authors identify other appropriate attitudes: respect for another's view, candor and expectancy of candor on the part of others, and careful listening.

Development of these attitudes stems from experience in using the intellect to solve problems, to analyze situations, to evaluate ideas and materials, and to produce new thoughts. As in other learning areas, the teacher has to pay careful attention to development of attitudes as important concomitants of specific learning experiences.

THOUGHT PROCESSES:

ASSOCIATIVE THINKING, MEMORY, FANTASY

Most commonly exercised of thought processes in conventional school work is associative thinking and recall (reproduction of material presented). Recent developments stress more sophisticated and creative intellectual functions; yet it would be idle to disparage the part of simple, associative learning operations in learning the many useful and necessary parts of the cultural heritage. Certainly there is no justification to base the major part of formal learning on memory, but some training in memory skills is useful to bright as well as to slow and average learners. For this purpose, useful suggestions may be found in most of the available "how to study" manuals, particularly at the secondary and college levels.

In recent decades fantasy has begun to achieve a new recognition. Far from viewing fantasy as an obstacle in the development of critical thinking, Russell (1956, pp. 223-24) points to the place of fantasy in the child's development both as it merges into the "creative, imaginative thinking of childhood," and as it gives clues to the teacher for better understanding of the child. He cites the "contributions to mental health of fantasy expression in dramatic play, painting, writing and sociodrama."* In addition, new emphasis on creativity and divergent thinking has raised an aura of respectability and even pragmatic utilitarianism around the once-suspect world of dream and fantasy. Chapter 5, Creativity, focuses on this thought process.

Associative thinking is being cast in a new light in learning, however, as behavioristic psychology itself takes on something of a new hue. As behaviorists direct fresh attention to habit, strength, drive, and incentive motivation (NSSE, 1964, p. 32), emphasis in associative learning and reproductive thinking is moving toward the old Gestalt concerns with goal-seeking behavior, purpose, and meaningfulness to the learner. While recognizing the gifted child's skill in memorative activities, the teacher should nonetheless make use of the facilitating effect of purpose.

CONCEPT FORMATION

As indicated in the early pages of this chapter, psychologists are trying to come to grips with the basic element of thought—the formation of

---

* From *Children's Thinking*, by David Russell. Copyright © 1956 by Ginn and Company. Reprinted through the courtesy of Blaisdell Publishing Company, a division of Ginn and Company.

concepts. Meanwhile, at all grade levels, teachers are necessarily involved with the process and product of concept development. Hullfish and Smith (1961), distinguish between perceptual and conceptual levels of learning. They assert the tendency in education to focus on percept and to neglect the important generalizing activity which is the essence of conceptualization. They argue, therefore, the importance of seeking out relationships. At a more advanced level, one can recognize a widespread conviction of the need to focus on concepts rather than individual facts in the enthusiastic reception of Bruner's "structure of knowledge" approach.

There is general agreement that human beings develop concepts gradually in their effort to find meaning in the many individual phenomena of existence by working out systems of relationships. Because experience is never final, concepts change with the experience, direct or vicarious, of the individual. Perceptualists will insist upon the individual nature of perception, and, therefore, of concept development. They will also stress the importance of the learner's current state (his openness to experience, acceptance of self and others, present frame of reference, for example) in receiving percepts and forming concepts. Thus, the teacher has to be concerned both with the learner and with what he can do to help organize the world of possible observations.

In organizing materials for concept development, the teacher needs to draw upon a rich and diversified environment. He has to be concerned with individual items in the environment as parts of classes of things and ideas because he is ultimately concerned with the kind of generalization that a concept represents. At all points, learners need encouragement to develop and express concepts, "ideas" of things, and not simply to remain at a level of perception of individual phenomena. This may be done best if students can use all media of expression available to them —words, pictures, models, music, dramatization, pantomime.

Russell (1956, p. 246) identifies errors in concept formation that provide useful guidance for teachers. He points to (1) errors in percepts from which concepts emerge, (2) confusion between images and memories aroused during recall, (3) lack of experience to check or validate generalizations reached, (4) set or suggestibility caused by certain factors in the environment, and (5) overconfidence in results of one's observation and conceptual thinking (*Ibid.*, p. 246). Of importance to the teacher in guiding learning is repeated emphasis on actual experience, accurate observation, and clear thinking in arriving both at percepts and concepts. From experiences in naming, counting, measuring, discriminating, abstracting, and generalizing, the child formulates concepts. In doing so, perception, memory, and even imagination play a part. Teacher and pupil alike have to be aware of the impact of emotional factors, tensions, and needs if concept development is to be reality oriented.

Burton, Kimball, and Wing present three suggestive "serious errors in aim and method of teaching" in their rich chapter on "The Role of Concepts in Thinking." They bid the teacher avoid the following pitfalls:

> "1. Concepts are given out ready-made." (Assume that telling equals teaching and that hearing equals understanding)
> "2. Activities and experiences are not carried through to the level of concept derivation." (Much activity in process but little intellectualization)
> "3. The learner is allowed to remain submerged in specifics." (Facts for facts' sake)
>
> (Burton, 1960, p. 165)*

Finally, teachers are advised to recognize the danger of verbalization and to probe for genuine understanding of concepts that are expressed by learners.

PROBLEM SOLVING

Thought as problem solving in education dates back to Dewey's classic formulation of a five-step definition of problem solving in *How We Think* (1910). Russell (1956, p. 256) presents a breakdown in chart form of steps in problem solving taken from Dewey's work in 1910, Burt in 1928, Gray in 1935, Johnson in 1944, Polya in 1945, Humphrey in 1948, Bloom in 1950, Burack in 1950, and Vinacke in 1952. Practically all include initiation in perplexity, sensitivity to a problem, recognizing or formulating a problem. They move on to exploration of the problem and developing hypotheses. Next are some kind of ratiocination and/or gathering of data in order to test the hypotheses. Finally there is some evaluation of hypotheses and generalizations in the light of data gathered, subjective evaluation or reasoning. Some authors also include references to a flash of insight, free play of thought, trial and error, and elimination of sources of error. In general, there is a recognition that these steps represent analyses after the fact, and that some of them may be telescoped and none of them need occur in the order noted. The value of these analyses lies in suggesting areas for training of students.

Burton, Kimball, and Wing (1960), for example, organize suggestions for teachers under rubrics of major phases in problem solving as they see it. First, they recommend procedures to help students find, identify, and

---

*From: *Education for Effective Thinking*, by William H. Burton, Roland B. Kimball, and Richard L. Wing. Copyright © 1960, Appleton-Century-Crofts, Inc. Reprinted by permission of Appleton-Century-Crofts.

clarify problems and to help students stay with the problem chosen. These include providing opportunities and practice in stating problems growing out of their own needs, discussing the requirements of a good problem statement, intervening to help simplify the problem if it gets beyond the experience and information of the pupils, and asking questions to direct attention to specific points if class thinking reaches an impasse. The teacher will also find pointed suggestions to employ in order to help clarify problems, to stay on a particular problem, and, most important, to encourage questioning and to stimulate curiosity.

In furthering the emergence of hypotheses ("the origin of conclusions"), Burton *et al.* give these general guidelines for use in the classroom: 1. re-examine the original situation; 2. "cast about" deliberately in one's background of experience and reading; 3. consider carefully one's natural predilections, biases and prejudices; 4. set the problem aside temporarily. Specific suggestions are again provided for the teacher.

Substantial treatment is given, too, to the "nature, source and use" of facts in thinking. Criteria for verifiability of facts, sources and methods of obtaining facts, and the values and dangers of using personal experience as distinguished from experience under controlled observation are considered in turn. Procedures for guiding the analysis of experience should be useful to the teacher interested in direct attention to teaching of thinking.

Some light on abilities needed for problem-solving is found in the efforts of Bloom and Broder (1950) to help college students in this process. Certain fundamental differences were observed in the comparison of students who succeeded and those who failed in problem-solving. The successful students showed an ability to solve problems as presented; the others were more likely to misinterpret directions and to give solutions to the wrong problems. The high scorers showed an understanding of the ideas in the problem, with notable differences between the two groups in bringing relevant knowledge to bear, in realizing fully implications of ideas in the problem, in relating reading and lecture notes to the problems, and in using relevant knowledge at their command. In their general approach to solution of problems, the successful students showed greater thought about the problem. They exhibited more careful and systematic thinking about the problem, and a greater ability to follow through a process of reasoning. Finally, their attitude toward the solution of problems was more positive—in attention given to reasoning, in confidence in their ability to solve problems, and in their reducing the role of personal considerations in arriving at a solution (*Ibid.*, pp. 26-32). The skills and attitudes associated by Bloom and

Broder with high performance in problem solving are suggestive goals for the teacher aiming at improvement of pupils' thinking for problem solving.

In problem solving, Russell indicates that there is no "age of reason" which children must attain before they can attack problems. However, very young children cannot be expected to succeed with highly verbalized problems; therefore, they should encounter non-verbal situations. Russell reminds us that not all problem-solving is intellectual in nature. "Children are often impetuous in problem-solving, jumping from awareness of a problem to some solution without any intervening steps, influenced by their emotional reactions rather than by knowledge of logical steps in thinking" (p. 279). He cites evidence that children do not follow a series of organized steps like Dewey's; instead they break down the major problem into a series of subordinate problems, and eventually solve the problem by integrating their subordinate solutions. Parents and teachers can give positive assistance at various stages in problem-solving:

by calling attention to material in the stimulus situation which the children may not perceive
by assisting children in using the inductive-deductive method
by encouraging children to raise questions and to check sources
by providing opportunities for observation
by calling attention to personal factors in situations which may color the use of reason
by helping children recognize common errors in logic

The teaching of scientific method as such may be helpful with older children. "Testing solutions in action" is suggested as an "antidote" to excessive verbalization in problem-solving (*Ibid.*, pp. 375-76).

Because problem solving is so commonly accepted an objective and method in education, it is easy to succumb to a formal routine and to glorify lifeless application of formulas as a more rigorous and sophisticated process. Getzels (NSSE, 1964, pp. 241-42) makes an important distinction between presented and discovered problems which can help prevent application of the term to routine drills. He identifies eight different types of problems, starting with the most common where the problem is known and where there is a standard method known to the student of solving problems. This is the usual exercise in arithmetic texts and classrooms. Getzels moves from this to situations where the problem itself has to be discovered, where the method of solution is known but has to be discovered, and finally where the problem has to be identified and no known method for solution is known to the student or to others. These represent "a range of problems involving various degrees of what is known and unknown, requiring various degrees of innovation and crea- tiveness for solution" (*Ibid.*, p. 242). To the teacher this represents an implicit suggestion to replace pat "problems" with situations that are truly problematical in nature. As this is done, Getzels suggests that hard and fast distinctions between "reasoning" and "imagining" are likely to be blurred: "Thinking, reasoning, imagining, reflecting, judging, con- ceiving, and problem-solving are close kin to each other when one is dealing with the 'unknown'" (*Ibid.*).

CRITICAL THINKING

A general phase of intellectual activity which cuts across many thought processes is critical thinking. Methods of logical analysis, inference, de- duction, induction, and evaluation are commonly included. Various authors suggest policies and procedures for development of critical thinking, organized in keeping with their particular analyses of the think- ing process.

Marksberry (1963) recommends provision of opportunities for growth in intellectual abilities and skills through improvement of comprehen- sion, application, analysis, and evaluation. To enhance comprehension, she urges a program in schools aimed at avoiding careless generaliza- tion, preventing confusion of words with their meaning, using who-what- when-where "indexes", locating events and persons specifically in time, avoiding vague and overworked words, and documenting statements. To the teacher she gives this advice: avoid use of directive language which tends to stifle inquiry, and ask questions which require interpre- tive answers. In helping children "derive sets of abstract relations," she advocates emphasis on Dewey's five steps (which she refers to as the "hypothetico-deductive method"): identification of the problem, formu- lation of hypotheses, deducting consequences of the hypotheses, gather- ing more data if necessary, and drawing conclusions.

Russell considers critical thinking as involving four conditions: knowl- edge of a field in which thinking is being done; a general attitude of questioning or suspended judgment; some application of methods of logical analysis or scientific inquiry; taking action in light of this analysis or inquiry. Some writers add a measure of belief and other affective fac- tors (1956, p. 283). Russell arrives at this definition: "the process of examining both concrete and verbal materials in the light of related objective evidence, comparing the object or statement with some norm or standard, and concluding or acting upon the judgment then made" (p. 285). He notes the development of tests of critical thinking by Ed- wards, Johnson, Raths, Taba, Terman, Tyler, Watson and Glaser, and

Wood, but little agreement on items that should be included in these tests.

Russell advises teachers that encouraging children to question statements and evaluate work products provides the most frequent opportunity for critical thinking in school work. Because critical thinking involves a complex of abilities, children should encounter a wide range of concrete and verbal materials. Thinking in critical terms is a function of the total school program and not of any specific area. The teacher's attitude is crucial. He must regard critical thought as an important "objective of instruction, must allow time for discussion of controversial issues, must see that all sides of a question are presented and must emphasize the process of working toward an answer rather than the correctness of the answer itself" (Russell, 1956, p. 303).

Burton, Kimball, and Wing (1960) give detailed consideration to inference (the "heart of thinking"), deduction, induction, sampling, analogy, and evaluation. The listing of logical fallacies (pp. 212-23) will be helpful to teachers planning specific units on critical thinking. The teacher who wants to make a direct attack on critical thinking will find their chapter on general methods in teaching for thinking helpful. This chapter includes description of a number of teaching units: conventional problem-solving units dealing with explanation, discovery and verification; normative units, dealing with value systems; units on criticism, and the case-study method. Guidelines for teaching of creative thinking are also offered.

Hullfish and Smith posit "reflective thinking" (1961) as "the method of education." In doing so they present to the teacher a working discussion of the "tools" of thinking and language—inference and fallacy, meaning and language, and the conceptual response. An important part of their volume is their insistence on the relationship between values and thought processes. While advocating careful attention to the development of skills in thinking, they insist that these be informed by beliefs oriented toward democracy, a sense of individual dignity and worth, and freedom of thought and expression.

Hullfish and Smith assert: "The fact is that a 'right answer' has no greater educative value than a wrong one." (p. 197) They then provide suggestions for the teacher to guide an "inquiry into meanings," advocating a kind of Socratic questioning technique. The inquiry into meanings is reinforced in the authors' recommendations by essential relationship of trust between teacher and students, by testing of meanings, by an effort to find structure in learning in the sense of Dewey's reconstruction of experience (or Bruner's idea of the structure of disciplines), and by focussing on "real life experiences" and "real life problems" in the classroom. But even in the most traditional of situations the teacher can make a start by seeking greater reflectiveness in examinations, summaries, outlining, planning, illustration, and student writing.

OPEN TERRITORY

While schools have for a long time focussed attention on critical thinking, many questions remain unanswered. Ennis (1963) asks for research in the following areas: further refinement of the concept of critical thinking; discovering more accurately the capabilities of children to learn to think critically; conduct of developmental studies in the growth of children's thinking; determination of subject matters particularly suited to different aspects of critical thinking; and development of a theory of critical thinking and education therefrom.

Getzels (NSSE, 1964, pp. 265-66) enumerates six instructional issues that revolve around teaching for problem-solving which are equally relevant to other thought processes. First, he is concerned with the distinction between presented and discovered problems, between "puzzlers" posed by the teacher or text and problematic situations uncovered and explored by students themselves. Second, he is concerned with the employment of Piaget's "stages" in the development of thinking. How should education for thinking be adapted to these stages, with differences in the processes available to children in the pre-school, early childhood, pre-adolescent, and adolescent periods? Third, now that diverse investigators have established different "styles" in cognition, how can we determine what effect individual styles have on learning, and how can we accommodate teaching to these differences? Fourth, there is an apparent paradox between teaching for creative thinking and teaching for critical thinking, between the impulsive and the rational. How is this paradox to be resolved in the classroom? Fifth, the human being seems to be both stimulus-reducing and stimulus-seeking in his behavior. Will this insight affect school programs based on a needs-reduction theory? Will new hope be found for academically rigorous programs centered on belief in students' desires to learn for learning's sake itself? Finally, two major directions may be observed in current instructional innovation: on the one hand, development of new curriculum materials like the new proposals in natural sciences and mathematics; on the other hand, proposals for direct approaches to inquiry training like the Suchman program and to creative thinking like the Osborn procedures. Which of these represent a more valid approach; if an eclectic design is possible, how are the two to be combined?

The Getzels statement is indeed a provocative summary of the many open areas in study of thinking for the enhancement of school programs. Little that is concrete is available for wholesale adoption by a teacher or curriculum committee. A whole new vista, however, is opening which promises genuine enrichment of the curriculum in general and a particular enhancement of programs for the intellectually gifted.

SUMMARY

The teaching of thinking is a fascinating subject in the education of gifted children because it is in this area that the intellectually superior children should indeed excel. Recent work in psychology gives promise of more precise understanding of the thinking process. School programs for the improvement of thinking may draw fresh sustenance from new developments in cognitive theory, studies of motivation, recognition of differences in cognitive style, and inquiries into patterns of development of the intellectual processes.

Teaching of thinking is not a new program in schools at various levels. A stream of research has been growing steadily which supports direct efforts at the improvement of thinking. In particular subject areas, there is evidence in favor of specified methods and processes as goals of instruction. New investigations open wider potentials for work with children and adolescents. They yield the promise of increasingly meaningful and sophisticated work in improvement of thought processes with gifted students.

A body of literature exists which offers many suggestions to teachers for general operation in the teaching of thinking. In addition, specific help is available as teachers approach more specific processes—associative thought and fantasy, concept formation, problem solving, and critical thinking. Creative thinking has received little consideration in this chapter because of attention elsewhere in this volume.

Except for limited projects, teaching of thinking will go on in the context of other school experiences—as part of large projects or in the framework of particular subjects and units. It is hoped that the material of this chapter can provide one important goal and some perspective in consideration of planning curricula for the gifted in the learning areas of the chapters that follow.

Chapter 9

Language Arts for the Gifted Student

Reading maketh a full man, conference a ready man, and writing an exact man.

—Francis Bacon

The verbal nature of most school programs places primary focus on language development of the gifted. To some extent this focus simply reflects the bookish orientation of formal education. Perhaps more important is the continuing, and probably increasing, significance of verbal and symbolic factors both in scholarly and business endeavors. The growing demand for more formal education in many vocational and professional fields places increasing weight upon more effective language skills for the gifted. This chapter will consider aspects of language arts in elementary and secondary schools including the foreign language program.

Elementary School Programs

READING

Many intellectually gifted children enter the first grade at six years of age already reading. Some are already reading when they enter kindergarten at five. Others who have the capacity for early reading are not doing so simply because the environment has not given them adequate motivation or opportunity. Still others, despite their general ability, will develop reading ability at a later date.

In no part of the school program is as much attention given to differential progress as in reading in the elementary school. Appropriate instruction in the primary grades should result in an individualized approach for bright children that dispenses with readiness programs for the early readers and curtails time spent in readiness for those showing ability to get on with actual reading. On the other hand, where the teacher suspects that genuine ability is disguised by cultural handicaps, definite need may be apparent for more time than usual on extending the pupil's background of experience. Grouping early readers together within the classroom may help them share their new-found skill with others, thus avoiding an unnecessary preparatory program.

Even more important is the availability of a wide range of materials to suit the interests and capabilities of the children. The problem of providing material at the children's interest level while respecting the limits of their reading vocabulary affects all children, but it is aggravated for the gifted. In the first few grades the speaking vocabulary and concepts that children use and understand far outstrip their reading vocabulary. While the authors of the standard reading series have done wonders in using limited sight vocabularies to tell stories that have some interest and humor, no textbook representative can seriously claim that the content of the readers stretches the intellect, imagination, or curiosity —except for reading skill—of the average six- and seven-year-old, let alone the gifted child. It is also true that the content of many stories prepared as "children's literature" is not up to the interest level of bright pupils.

The primitive reading ability of the young child can be supplemented by other means that bring him literature he can understand but which he cannot yet read. In the first two grades there remains good reason for the teacher to read to gifted children so that reading matter of all kinds can be used which meets their interests. In addition, a well-stocked classroom and school library should include more challenging material than that which is simply "at grade level." The reading lists prepared by the Association for Childhood Education, the National Council of Teachers of English, the American Library Association, and the annotations in the *Children's Catalogue* provide guidance in selecting books for library shelves. Many state departments of education and local school systems also publish valuable bibliographies.

The general aims in reading instruction have particular relevance in teaching the gifted. Basic is the development of strong and worthwhile interests in reading. For the gifted more than anyone else, reading represents the major avenue of learning and a fruitful source of enjoyment and enriched living. Second is the development of fundamental skills for independence in reading, such as word perception and recognition. Earlier independence can be expected of the gifted, and they can make more use of independence in reading. Third is the development of comprehension which is not limited to reading in a narrow sense but is a function of thinking in general. In order to read complex material or to read critically one must develop the ability to think critically and maintain attitudes necessary for clear thinking. A most important part of reading development for the gifted is building habits, skills, and attitudes that are part of thinking in general.

In all three of these aims the integral relationship between reading and other communication arts—writing, listening, speaking, and utilization of the mass media—is important. Coordinating these other aspects of communication with reading is especially rewarding when working with the gifted because of their greater scope in all verbal fields. For the gifted as well as for other children, reading is not to be taught in a vacuum; it is to be taught as part of a total communication program. Communication processes and products have value in themselves but they also facilitate learning in all subject areas. Accordingly, much reading instruction and growth will be done in conjunction with the teaching of social studies, science, mathematics, and other areas. When working with the gifted, teachers can take advantage of superior verbal powers to promote greater learning through independent reading of text, supplementary, and reference materials. They must also be prepared to teach special reading skills needed in these areas if children are to be successful in independent study efforts.

In the primary grades children with special ability should get off to a flying start in the enjoyment of reading, both from their own perusal of pre-primer, primer, and "easy reader" books, and from hearing the teacher read a host of interesting stories and informative paragraphs and articles. Teachers should bear in mind the devastating criticism of John Hersey and others concerning the content of basic readers as far as interest is concerned and should bring in as much other material as possible. Two provocative criticisms of the reading series are (1) the lack of masculine interest for the boys and (2) the middle class orientation of practically all series used in schools. Introduction of mechanical, scientific, sports, or cowboy motifs as found in many of the inexpensive little picture books prepared for children is one way of attacking the first problem. A number of authors have written stories about lower class backgrounds and minority ethnic groups in recent years; these may be found in listings such as the American Council on Education's *Reading Ladders for Human Relations.*

READING SKILLS FOR THE GIFTED

As children build up impetus in striving for independence in reading, the teacher can be helpful in hastening introduction to various forms of word analysis. The rapid accumulation of sight vocabulary by the gifted warrants early exposure first to phonetic and second to structural analysis. It seems particularly wasteful not to give the gifted child these tools of independence as soon as their interest and sight vocabulary warrant. The use of context clues as an aid in perception is a normal concomitant of building the sight vocabulary even in pre-primers. Finally, the most sophisticated source of word analysis can be tapped with the gifted while they are still in elementary school. This is the recognition of words by their derivation from other languages. Slowly and gradually children can build a familiarity with the most important roots coming from Latin, Greek, and French. Where a foreign language is taught in elementary school, this approach has the greatest possibility of effective use.

In the middle and upper grades specific study techniques enter the reading curriculum of bright children. These include the following:

1. Determining the purpose of reading a particular item and adapting one's method of reading to this purpose
2. Increasing ability to comprehend difficult material: finding the main idea, ordering ideas in sequence, relating details to the ideas they elaborate
3. Responding actively to reading materials: drawing inferences, seeing relationships, arriving at conclusions
4. Reacting critically to material: discriminating among sources, weighing the validity of information presented, selecting what is important and relevant, distinguishing fact from opinion, turning to other sources to check accuracy and significance of material read
5. Locating information: using table of contents and index in book; employment of dictionary, glossary, encyclopedia, atlas and other reference works; reading maps, charts, graphs, and tables; use of library tools such as the card catalogue and periodical guides
6. Note-taking in reading reference material and following discussions
7. Organizing material read or heard; outlining and writing summaries

8. Learning ways to remember important material: selecting facts worth remembering, practicing recall, reorganizing material in different ways, utilizing mnemonic devices

All of these skills have relevance for every child. Since they are related to superior verbal ability, they have a special future value and are more meaningful even in elementary grades for the intellectually gifted.

IMPROVEMENT OF READING

It is a truism that one learns to read by reading. Part of the school's and the parents' responsibility is to implant the desire to read, to make reading rewarding, and to ensure that the pleasures derived from reading have at least an even chance in competition with the lures of television, the movies, and other time-consuming media. Availability of interesting and enriching reading material at home and in school is, of course, essential. The school library and the community library should be familiar haunts for the bright child, but they become so only as teachers and parents provide time and make the necessary arrangements. Reading, like other good habits, is "catching." Parents build their children's interest in reading when they select books for themselves on the family trip to the library while also helping the children make their own choices. The teacher can do the same when he takes his class or a few pupils to the school library. The teacher's occasional references to adult books and magazine articles which he has just read reinforce the growth of a positive attitude toward reading as a desirable and pleasurable activity.

There are other specific things that the teacher can do to stimulate interest in reading. A genuine stimulus can come through "outside" reading in class. Least enriching and most boring, however, is the book report for extra credit. It is far better to act out brief dramatizations when three or four children have read the same book or story. Children can also be arranged in small groups for sessions of shared story telling based on books most recently read. Art and construction activities can be related to books as well as to other themes. Children may be encouraged to do creative writing on a topic suggested by a book they have read. They may compile a list of favorite books recommended for Christmas or birthday gifts. The social instincts of children support the use of devices where individual reading can result in group activity and recognition.

There is general agreement that even gifted children benefit from a planned program of instruction as indicated above. Superior ability does not warrant a "just let them alone" approach, but rather promises greater achievement where instruction is provided. Independence, how-

ever, can be encouraged. Strang recommends that bright pupils be
allowed to make reading plans of their own. The teacher provides access
to materials of value and guides the child's reading according to the plan
the pupil is following (*In* Robinson, 1954, p. 8).

Some bright children, unfortunately, will be found who experience
real difficulty in reading. In some cases particular school conditions or
culturally inhibiting environments are at fault, but in most cases deep-
seated emotional causes are found to exist. A complicating factor lies in
the fact that retardation in reading generally hides the existence of
superior ability, since reading is taken as a sign of ability in its own right
and since reading is often involved in other measures of talent. Where
high ability is suspected despite poor reading achievement, the teacher
should seek assistance in appraising both the child's real ability and the
causes of his reading handicap.

Finally, there is a problem of balance in the life of the child. The
stereotype of the bookworm is well known. Some bright children do find
escape in books; some compensate for real or imagined inferiority in
other fields by turning to reading; some simply become so engrossed in
reading that they have time for little else. The teacher who is academically oriented by virtue of his training may unwittingly encourage pupils
to neglect other aspects of their development. On the other hand, Strang
notes that a much larger number of pupils find their reading time is
usurped by other activities, and that this competition from other areas
is greatest at age twelve or thirteen when reading activity might be at its
maximum (*Ibid.*, p. 9).

Of particular importance is the choice of books in the bright child's
free reading. Larrick's *A Teacher's Guide to Children's Books* (1963)
clothes the bare bones of a book list with many readable suggestions for
enhancing children's reading activities. "Acceleration," in the sense of
reading adult books, is a poor solution for a twelve-year-old with eighteen-year-old reading ability. In deploring a diet of Hemingway, Dreiser,
Faulkner, and O'Neill for fifth and sixth graders, Sattley (1960) notes
"the lack of knowledge among parents and teachers of the wonderful
world of books, existing today which are meaningful, challenging, and
important to young people." She recognizes the appeal that some adult
books will have for children, and she does not advocate forbidding these
books to children. However, she feels that the girl who is immersed in
Gone with the Wind and the boy who is entranced with *Moby Dick*
ought not to be missing at the same time the books that have greater
meaning for children of their own age. Mr. Popper, Mary Poppins, Dr.
Doolittle, and Freddy, the Detective, are part of the social, as well as the

literary, life of the fourth and fifth graders, she says. She suggests the following "principles of reading guidance" for the child:

> To broaden and deepen boys' and girls' experiences through reading; to fit the book to the child, not the child to the book; to recognize that every age has its masterpieces, and to set the masterpieces of the present and of the past into reasonable perspective; to challenge but not push; to be wise and patient enough to wait for the child's own pattern of growth to unfold. (Sattlee, 1960, pp. 1, 4)

OTHER LANGUAGE ARTS

The general policy that undergirds the approach to reading is valid, too, in other phases of the language arts program. This policy involves acceleration of the learning sequence, enrichment of learning at all points of the sequence both in quality and quantity, use of more varied and more advanced materials, encouragement of creative leanings, and consideration of the probable academic orientation that practically all bright children will be taking until they are twenty years old or older.

WRITING

The bright child generally enters the first grade able to write capital, and sometimes small, letters in manuscript. He is interested in doing more with his skill, but his muscular coordination is not likely to be much advanced over that of average children. While it is true that sight reading vocabulary is woefully behind the child's thought and speaking ability, his writing skills are even less developed. The teacher's first aid to bright kindergartners and first graders is service as an amanuensis, "printing" stories at the child's dictation, writing captions for pictures the child has drawn or painted, helping the children to compose and then to write down little poems. One teacher in a school for the gifted found it possible to hectograph a monthly magazine which included some contributions from each of the six-year-olds in her class.

Perhaps the most trying aspect of writing in the primary grades is the large gap between the child's creative ideas and the primitive state of his handwriting and spelling skills. Two apparently contradictory but actually supplementary approaches are suggested. The child bursting with ideas to express may be more easily persuaded of the value of handwriting skills and spelling knowledge. Necessary practice may accordingly be more easily motivated. On the other hand, the child's urge to express himself should not be dampened by discouraging insistence upon correctness for its own sake. Ultimately, of course, high standards of expression—both content and form—should be demanded of the capable student, but early efforts should be greeted with appreciation of what the child is trying to say rather than blue-penciling of the inevitable errors that reflect the discrepancy between the child's ideas and his expressive techniques.

Wyatt (1962) reports studies of various facets of creative writing. There is some agreement that children through grade nine write better on derived topics than from their personal experience. This may imply that children should not be expected to be "self-starters" before senior high school. Young children improve when the teacher reads aloud their compositions. They also show growth when they are able to read their own work to their classmates. For gifted children there is a positive correlation between the amount of reading done and the complexity of sentence structure they attempt. This complexity, however, presents problems since children are often not able to punctuate or capitalize properly, and sentence structure errors increase precisely in the years (upper elementary) when the desire for complex expression outruns ability to handle complex sentences on paper. Many errors seem to relate to sentence structure and general writing competence. As a result, isolated drills rarely improve the elementary pupil's writing. Wyatt suggests the need for a number of studies on creative writing, including evaluation of programs (1) where focus is placed on specific mechanisms needing improvement rather than on a general program for the whole class; (2) where emphasis is placed on increased writing rather than on drills; (3) where children are given more freedom to use their imagination in compositions, and (4) where grouping based on writing ability is employed experimentally.

Unfortunately, the elementary school teacher has to make a distinction between correctness in practice exercises and correctness in creative expression. As the child becomes more mature in his skills the distinction may gradually be blurred and eventually discarded. Some teachers are successful in making this transition by finding ways to "publish" the child's work and therefore by giving him incentive to perfect spelling and usage and to improve handwriting while still expressing himself creatively. Class magazines, letters to visitors, notes to parents and adult friends, and bulletin board displays are some common devices used.

Obviously sustained practice is needed to develop handwriting, whether manuscript or cursive, which is legible, attractive, and rapid enough not to discourage the writer. Recognizing the bright child's early impatience with drill, the teacher must seek varied applications that carry some meaning and immediate usefulness to the child. Understanding the part that knowledge of progress plays in learning, the teacher can help the child develop a system for himself of recording his own improvement. This can take the form of a portfolio with work samples, a table showing marks received or the number of errors noted, or a chart that indicates the time taken to write a given number of words. There is no reason to adopt for gifted children a different sequence in manuscript and cursive writing than is used with other children. Muscular coordination is not much advanced, and grade-for-grade, the gifted child may have poorer coordination since he is likely to be somewhat accelerated and therefore younger than other children in the same grade. There is a good argument to retain manuscript writing for several years so that the child need not make a change when he is at last developing some facility in writing down his ideas.

Teachers in special classes for the gifted find a primer size typewriter especially valuable for children in the primary grades, both for reading and writing. In the middle grades there is some research supporting the introduction of typewriting as a skill in itself and for the contribution that it apparently makes to academic progress. Few bright children will become typists or stenographers, but typewriting has become almost a necessity in college, and practically all children of high intellectual ability may be expected to enroll eventually. While children should not be encouraged to regard typewriting as an alternative to development of skill in handwriting, there is good reason to introduce typewriting as part of the enrichment program for gifted pupils.

SPELLING

Much that is said of handwriting applies to spelling as well. Since English spelling is not strictly phonetic, spelling involves considerable memorization and drill as well as the application of rules and logic. A combination of phonetics, rules, and ratiocination through derivation can help to put spelling on a rational rather than on a memorative basis alone. Enrichment in spelling involves not only the introduction of more difficult words but also exploration into reasons why words are spelled as they are.

Good practice in teaching spelling to the gifted is comparable to good spelling practice in general. The keeping of individual word lists is an obvious necessity when one considers the futility of stress on any particular words beyond the three thousand in most frequent use. While the first three thousand appear in the spoken and written vocabulary of a large proportion of the people, any individual words beyond that may be used by only 1 or 2 per cent of the literate population. Horn declares that a "law of diminishing returns operates very markedly after a few hundred words have been taught," and suggests that only the three thousand words of highest frequency in his *Basic Writing Vocabulary* (1926) be taught formally (Horn, 1950, p. 1253). Instead of formal drills on established spelling lists—over and beyond the most frequently used words, and particularly the words most commonly misspelled, the "spelling demons"—emphasis should be placed on spelling words that the individual child uses or on new words that come up in connection with new subject matter. An important goal should be improved use of the dictionary as a resource in solving spelling problems.

Second, the futility of drill on words already spelled properly should be considered. The gifted, no more than the average, should not be wasting time copying five or ten times a word they have never misspelled. There is validity in the common use of spelling pre-tests by teachers and excusing pupils from practice on words they spell right initially.

Third, spelling should be integrated with word study, reading, and writing. New words encountered in reading or needed in writing should lead to the dictionary and then to use by pupils in their own speech and writing. Emphasis upon creative and colorful use of words may eliminate elements of drudgery in word study and spelling. If pupils are learning a foreign language, English spelling can often be traced to forms in the language from which the word was taken. However, even in the absence of study of foreign languages, dictionary listing of derivations ought to be regarded and discussed when bright children are studying both meaning and spelling.

GRAMMAR AND USAGE

Except at the most sophisticated levels, usage is a matter of habit. A large proportion of bright children may be expected from homes where good language habits prevail. These children are not likely to make common errors in speech or writing. As a matter of fact, it sometimes happens that such a child will never consider using "he don't" until he is confused by the choice of right and wrong that confronts him in a workbook. Children coming from culturally deprived homes, however, may not be so fortunate, and their occasional lapses in usage are the more noticeable because of the obvious contrast between their thought and expression.

Learning rules of grammar is sometimes advocated as the proper procedure to correct poor language habits. Research does not support this point of view, probably because expression is more a matter of habit than of reason. Particularly in the elementary school, emphasis should be first on the right form and on tactful ways of correcting the pupil when he makes errors. If correction results in inhibiting expression because of the young child's sensitivity when he is just beginning to speak to a large group of other children or when he is beginning to write, the teacher has to "temper the wind to the shorn lamb" and seek expression first and correctness later.

For the gifted as well as for the average the recommendation of the National Council of Teachers of English carries meaning:

> Concerted attack on individual items of usage in the intermediate grades helps greatly in clearing the way for more mature elements of speech and writing in later years. Crucial matters of literacy should come first. Niceties such as the distinction between *can* and *may* have no place in the program of pupils still saying *I seen it* and *I done it*. Labeling the parts of speech has proved in one research study after another, both in this country and in Great Britain, to be futile so far as its effect on speech and writing is concerned. Intermediate-grade pupils should have practice in the *use* of language, not in the classification of forms. This does not mean that the teacher may not refer to a word as a verb or pronoun and that some children will not use the terms after her. It means that instruction will be focused on improvement in the pupils' own speech and writing. (NCTE, 1954, p. 238) *

Of considerable value in teaching usage are the lists developed by Pooley (1946) and confirmed by the National Council of Teachers of English which distinguish among school levels at which certain forms should be taught and those at which these forms should be deferred for greater maturity.

As children grow in maturity, the "enriching" aspect of correcting usage and written language involves introduction to grammatical explanations of correct usage and language structure. There is no basis to suppose, however, that routine drills on parts of speech, the three types of dependent clauses, and diagramming of sentences will have any greater attractiveness to bright than to slow students unless they can see some usefulness in them—and unless their language concepts are advanced enough for them to understand what is being taught. After all, it is not the slow or average student who turns up in college, having forgotten all that was taught to him as "grammar," and claiming that he

---

was never taught it. It is the verbally superior student who is admitted to college. Even for the above-average group, formal instruction in grammar apparently does not succeed. Grammatical concepts have to justify a place in the curriculum on the basis of correcting errors or enriching the language of the pupil, not simply as a value in themselves. The teacher who finds a meaningful approach, however, is more likely to succeed in teaching this abstract material to bright students than to others.

SPEECH AND LISTENING

Most frequently used of the language arts are speech and listening. The teacher can make a genuine contribution in these areas to the education and life of academically talented pupils. Concern for speaking ranges all the way from correction of mechanical speech defects to developing self-confidence in speaking before the child's own class and larger groups of children and adults.

Most bright children in elementary school have a speaking vocabulary, a sentence structure, and a speech pattern which is related to their mental advancement. Some few, however, will be found with infantilisms at age five and six and even later. Many need to learn voice projection. Lisping, lalling, and stuttering are not eliminated by the simple fact of intellectual giftedness. Because speech is a matter of habit, the elementary school does well to attack these problems as early as it can effectively do so. It must, however, start with the purpose of developing interest in oral activities and a sense of adequacy in children as they try to express themselves in speech. As in writing, emphasis must be on content rather than on form. The young child is not limited in speech activities as he is in writing by the need to learn a new medium that makes both conceptual and muscular demands. He has been speaking words since he was one year old, sentences soon thereafter. The bright child who has not been culturally handicapped can already express himself with considerable skill in kindergarten. The school draws him out, provides experiences that challenge oral expression, stimulates creative ways of saying what is on the child's mind, and finally (not least, but veritably *last*) builds an idea of standards of expression.

Throughout the elementary school there is gradual development of speech activities. "Sharing periods" in the primary years grow into more ambitious reports on individual activities and projects in the intermediate grades. Dramatic play and creative dramatics help to bring shy children out of their shell since more attention is focussed on the situation and the group than on the individual child and his speaking skill. Choral reading should start when children can first speak simple poems in unison and should grow into more finished productions that draw out the full drama and music of the poem or play. Skill in conversation grows as children are permitted to work and speak together informally.

Discussion skills start in small group activity, perhaps springing from a reading group, perhaps from the job of a committee working on one aspect of a class unit. By and large, the teacher recognizes the need for small groups and small audiences to provide maximum participation for each pupil and to afford a setting for speaking which is more natural than speaking before the entire class. Taking part in "buzz" groups, serving as the discussion leader, and reporting for the group, help to develop specific discussion skills.

Speech defects ought to be ferreted out for correction as early as possible. Until the child develops some confidence in himself, it is often hazardous to focus attention on errors. When the teacher senses that the child possesses enough assurance, efforts should be undertaken to correct infantile letter substitutions, harsh, thin, or nasal voice quality, lisps, lalls, stuttering, careless articulation and the like. If a speech correctionist is available, referral is often desirable. Whether a correctionist can be called or not, the teacher must assist in the process of correction. Care should be taken to avoid embarrassing the child who needs help. If defects are extremely noticeable and even painful to the listener, other children have to learn to be patient, understanding and sympathetic. To ignore poor or inadequate speech patterns, however, is extremely unfair to the gifted child whose general verbal excellence may be eclipsed by a speech problem.

Particular attention should be given, too, to the child from a culturally limiting background. One of the most obvious signs of cultural handicaps is to be found in the child's speech pattern. Generally slovenly or illiterate speech may grow in English-speaking homes; unidiomatic, poorly inflected speech may reflect a non-English speaking home. For the child who has unusual intellectual capacity, an inadequate language pattern can become an insuperable handicap. Often the school is the only agency that can help. Too often it is an oasis where children make their only contact with appropriate English.

Because of the verbal nature of our culture, listening, viewing, and observing are basic methods of learning. The child listens with varying degrees of participation. Sometimes he is barely conscious of what goes on around him; sometimes he half listens, as to Mother's eternal demand that he pick up his toys or clothes. Sometimes he seems to be absorbing what is said but not reacting. At other times he responds by digging into his own experience in order to relate what is said to what he has knowledge of. Sometimes he goes farther; he asks questions, voices his own opinion, or starts his own line of independent thinking. The later activities represent more sophisticated levels of operation. In this direction all children, but especially bright children, should be guided through discussion.

To develop this kind of thoughtful listening, the teacher will find a variety of techniques useful. He may provoke thought by asking questions. He may organize activities that demand knowledge of what has been said or read aloud. He may ask for creative elaboration on a theme that has been set forth. He should never be satisfied with mere parroting back of material.

There are other aspects to listening beyond the classroom. Children spend long hours with the mass media, particularly television. While the effect may often be intellectually soporific, guidance can make the experience more stimulating. Without disparaging the child's choice of programs, the teacher can encourage thoughtful reaction to what is shown. He can call for inventive parody of what is seen and heard. He can go beyond this to class discussion of what makes a "good," an "exciting," an "informative" program for boys and girls. Ultimately, by recognizing the child's right to choose childish programs, he may help the pupil to choose the best of the fare that is offered and to move in the direction of more mature choices. In addition he may succeed in encouraging children to consider the balance of time spent on television viewing, outdoor play, and free reading. Comic books, motion pictures, and radio may be approached in the same way as television.

Language Arts in Secondary Schools

The language arts program in secondary schools is of fundamental importance to the gifted both because of the basic necessity of communications skills for persons in leadership and because of the potential of the gifted to profit from advanced instruction in utilitarian and aesthetic elements of the program. In 1953 the National Council of Teachers of English established a Committee on English for High School Students of Superior Ability which stated special objectives in language arts for the intellectually gifted student:

> Since many academically talented students will find themselves in positions of responsibility when they are adults, the English teacher anticipates their language needs in public speaking, discussion, research, professional writing, and other areas requiring communication skills of an advanced nature. Therefore bright students are taught the history, structure, imperfections, and beauty of language. They are taught to consider how the context of time, place,

and medium can affect the meaning of words and how audiences with diverse interests may react in different ways to the same words. Pupils are taught the devious techniques by which some speakers and writers use language to conceal their intent, to distort truth, and to prevent straight thinking. . . . In brief, language instruction helps these pupils to do creative and original thinking, as well as to communicate ideas accurately and honestly. (NEA, 1960b, pp. 8-9) °

Emphasis is placed on the development of communication skills and on refinement of thought processes. In addition, the superior intelligence of the gifted student makes possible the appreciation at higher thought and higher aesthetic levels of literary and informational reading. The challenge falls to the teacher of the gifted to place emphasis on these objectives which are relevant to the ability of the superior pupil. In meeting this challenge the teacher will find the report of the Committee on English for Students of Superior Ability, published as the bulletin on English by the National Education Association Project on the Academically Talented Student (NEA, 1960b), a useful guide. Of particular interest to the English teacher should be the chapter by Cohen and Coryell, "English Studies," in *Educating Superior Students* (Cohen, 1935, pp. 56-98).

The committee of the English Council makes a number of recommendations for organization of programs for students with special ability in English. These include:

1. Ability grouping, with small seminar groups for students in the top 3 per cent
2. Limitation of drill on routine correctness as determined by early administration of diagnostic tests
3. Setting of more advanced goals and more rigorous standards of expression for the gifted
4. A literature program that is characterized by reading of original works in their entirety, by attention to broad cultural goals, and by integration of objectives in reading and literature
5. A goal of effective expression with appropriate emphasis on both creative and expository writing and speech. (NEA, 1960b, pp. 119-20)

Differences in school philosophy from community to community and differences in school size ensure the coexistence of homogeneous and heterogeneous grouping for all of the foreseeable future. The individual

---

° From *English for the Academically Talented Student in the Secondary School*, by the National Education Association and the National Council for the Teachers of English. Copyright 1960 by the National Education Association. Reprinted with permission of the National Education Association.

teacher is not able to make such decisions himself but faces the group he meets, of narrow or wide ability range, intent upon doing the best he can for each student. The goals that have been stated can be met for the bright student under either type of organization, and the English Teachers Committee itself admits that there is no research evidence to establish definitively the superiority of either type of grouping (*Ibid.*, p. 83).

If special classes are established, Gordon and Freudenreich (quoted in NEA, 1960b, p. 27) suggest one criterion that applies universally— "the factor of eagerness to take the course, not to get the credit, but to do the work. Such eagerness indicates more than ambition; it indicates the consciousness of needing and being ready for a more challenging course of study." This readiness is evinced, they say, in avid reading, in familiarity with the classics, in writing, in contact with the performing arts, museums, and lectures.

Independent work and small group activities are to be recommended under both types of grouping. So, too, is the organization of broad units which encourage students to pursue their interest in a particular field as far as their ability will take them. There is considerable agreement among authorities in the teaching of English that the study of literature should be organized around broad themes, that a particular play or novel or essay should be studied in relation to some fundamental ethical idea or social problem or in comparison with other literature of the same type. *Julius Caesar*, for example, may be studied by a bright class in conjunction with plays having similar themes; or, it may be studied in the context of struggle for power and compared with Robert Penn Warren's *All the King's Men*.

The broad unit calls for class, small group, and individual planning which challenge the bright student's ability to contribute. Group and individual projects that are part of the unit call for independent work and for leadership in small group activity. Individual competence can be developed and expressed through oral reports, dramatization, creative writing based on group or individual activity, and panel discussions on particular aspects of the work studied. When the class is relatively homogeneous, a consistently high level of performance may be expected. In heterogeneous groups the range of performance may mirror the range of ability, and there is no need, if properly guided, for ability to remain hidden under the proverbial "bushel."

READING IN JUNIOR AND SENIOR HIGH SCHOOL

In the long sweep from the seventh to the twelfth grade superior students ought to make striking gains in their reading ability and sophistication. The basic reading skills should be well established, and so should an interest in reading. Where this is not true, the teacher should look for causes of underachievement and attempt to remedy the situation. In a few cases the cause of reading retardation may be simple and "mechanical," and limited work in remedial reading may suffice. Certainly it is worth trying again if there are signs that somehow the student has new motivation and is ready for a fresh and more promising start. Generally, however, the intellectually gifted student who is not reading well represents a more serious problem, and the help of a reading specialist and a psychological case study may well be in order.

Where lack of motivation is at the root of the problem, the teacher may make some contribution by helping the student to recognize the value of reading (and other language arts). But more specific to the student's perception than the general goals of English are daily assignments; English specialists urge emphasis on the purpose and importance of every assignment which is given. This emphasis should include suggestions on how to study and how to read the material assigned. Supervised study periods provide opportunity for observation of and work with individual students. Consultation with other teachers may reveal special interests that may serve as a focus for improvement in English. The teacher can help the student set goals for his own improvement so that he competes realistically with himself rather than futilely with the budding Hemingway of Lincoln Junior High School. Conferences with parents and enlisting the underachieving student in extra-class activities are also recommended as techniques to improve motivation and performance (NEA, 1960b, pp. 46-49).

For most gifted students the need is for development rather than remediation. Reading skills, even in the junior high school, should be incorporated into the literature program and should not be used to justify time spent on material of dubious literary value. Such integration may be attempted in recognition of the fact that not all work of literary merit need be difficult. Some of Saroyan's short stories and Jack London's dog legends, for example, may serve the dual reading-literature needs of bright students in the seventh and eighth grades. Distinction among reading approaches for different types of reading material and different purposes in reading is one of the lessons to be learned in secondary school years. The appreciation of literary qualities and critical analysis while reading fall to the English teacher. To teachers in all other subject areas fall responsibilities for teaching the specific vocabulary and concepts of their areas and particular reading modes that are relevant to their subjects.

Reading by gifted students makes possible relatively sophisticated analysis and discussion of the material read. Certainly there is no literary gem in the secondary school curriculum which must be read for its own sake only, for the particular pearls of wisdom that are found therein and without which a cultured life might not be worth living. Various schools report instead emphasis on philosophical, semantic, social, and ethical elements as well as literary qualities. The Mt. Lebanon High School (Pennsylvania), for example, distributes to a special class studying *Moby Dick* a reading list organized around these themes: The Problem of Evil, The Consequences of Sin, A Search for Faith, The Sea, and other allegorical works (NEA 1960b, pp. 72-73). Some schools introduce units on semantics for bright students in various high school grades. Many agree on gearing their study of literature to an understanding of contemporary society, of psychological motivation, of the development of the cultural heritage, and of other cultures past and present. Some few schools suggest to students for individual reading books that may have personal value in understanding and facing their own problems. Witty (1956) encourages and describes this process in relating reading to the developmental tasks of adolescents. An excellent source book for teachers in helping young people to choose reading of value and interest to them is Hanna and McAllister's *Books, Young People and Reading Guidance* (1960).

Advanced Placement programs in English normally center around the study of literature. Materials are generally selected from one or more of the college-level anthologies, sometimes a textbook on rhetoric, and these are supplemented with selected individual titles and paperback anthologies, generally of poetry. While there seems to be a drive to gain academic respectability by emphasis on the older classics, authors studied range all the way from Aeschylus and Homer through Shakespeare and Bacon to Ibsen and Tolstoi, James Joyce, and Hemingway.

In brief, the literature program for bright students should aim at personal values in enriching the life of young people through reading; it should seek utilitarian values in improvement of reading skills; it should focus upon more general intellectual values in emphasis on the thinking process.

EXPOSITORY AND CREATIVE WRITING

The English teacher has a special interest in the boy or girl who shows some spark of originality and creativity in his writing. He has a responsibility to nurture this spark whenever it is found but also to develop competence of all verbally gifted students in workaday, expository writing that is essential for school and college work in all subjects. In addition, he may make some contribution to expository skills on a high level for students who may some day be reporting scholarly work in their special area of interest.

Perhaps the most important thing the English teacher can do is to build and maintain interest in writing. Too commonly high level personnel loathe the prospect of any writing assignment. There is room for suspicion that severe blue-pencilling in high school days and routine writing chores contribute to this distaste for written expression. To the English teacher falls the delicate job of synchronizing student interest and adult standards. Primary focus of adolescent student and professional adult alike is on the content of what is said and not upon form. On the contrary, what distinguishes the English teacher's job is precisely his role-concept which puts emphasis on correct—or even exciting—form. Yet, to maintain the adolescent's interest in improving his style and technique the teacher has to indicate primary interest in the content of a theme and his desire to help the student say more effectively what he wants to say.

USING GRAMMAR TO IMPROVE WRITING

The Council of Teachers of English holds out hope to the teacher of the gifted who sees in grammar a tool for improvement of writing:

> Knowledge of systematic grammar is likely to prove most useful, not to the less able students, but rather to the more able. To *learn* systematic grammar, he has to apply the principles to his own speech or writing and to the speech or writing of others. Such ability to grasp principles and to apply them readily to new sets of facts is stronger in some students than in others. In the brightest student, this ability is often his most noticeable characteristic. (NCTE, 1956, p. 368) *

However, the Council of Teachers of English warns, the brighter students are usually those who have the least trouble with problems of good English usage, and diagnostic testing early each year should eliminate from study and drill items which have already been mastered (NEA, 1960b, p. 120).

At the secondary level, therefore, systematic grammar teaching assumes a role different from that in elementary school. The greater maturity of the student and his increased reading and linguistic experience

---

* From: *The English Language Arts in the Secondary School*, prepared by The Commission on the English Curriculum of the National Council of Teachers of English. Copyright © 1956, Appleton-Century-Crofts, Inc. Reprinted by permission of Appleton-Century-Crofts.

justify more concerted attention to the structure of language. In addition, his verbal gifts give promise that grammatical analysis may be employed in practice as he writes and speaks. Furthermore, the demand of the foreign language teacher for familiarity with grammatical terms begins to make sense for both student and teacher. The student is now able to apply knowledge of structure to a different language. The teacher of a second language needs gradually to draw more on knowledge of the structure of language. Yet there is still no justification for teaching, out of context, formalized, routine drills that apparently have no direct usefulness.

Instead of learning grammar as a dead and perfect science, the student can experience a more valuable study if the teacher will approach grammar as the structure of living and changing language. How rules of grammar were developed, the mistakes that grammarians have made in formulating these rules, how language grows and develops, the growth of structural linguistics—these topics will stimulate greater interest in linguistics and the nuances of language than workbook exercises. Hugh Sykes Davies' *Grammar without Tears* (1953) and Pooley's *Teaching English Usage* (1946) contain stimulating material on this subject for student and teacher alike.

THE SECONDARY SPELLER

In the teaching of spelling to bright students in secondary schools, principles of operation at earlier levels may be extended. Early diagnosis should eliminate study of words, rules, and approaches which represent no genuine problem. While individual "demons" may need to be studied as single words, students in junior and senior high school should be employing clues from phonetic and structural analysis and from a growing understanding of morphological changes and relationships that stem from a word's derivation from another language. While spelling in English often appears capricious, students should accumulate a stock of information and understanding which serve to explain the surface peculiarities of English orthography. Some study in context of Latin roots and how these roots change in transformation to English seems essential to good spelling which is not restricted to memorization of individual words alone. Boys and girls studying either French or Latin can assume leadership in study of differences in structure when the word is derived directly from Latin as compared with words coming from Latin via French. The dictionary is the basic resource for words coming from the multitude of languages that provide a smaller proportion of roots. The dictionary should be used not simply to find correct form but to discover how English spelling copies and differs from the language of a word's origin. In this way use of the dictionary accounts not only for a greater number of words but for enriched understanding of the spelling (and meaning) of words studied.

Except for the small number of words that are commonly misspelled, at the high school level, any given word list has little utility. The only values of such lists for bright students lie in the way in which they may be used. These values accrue if emphasis is placed on the process of looking words up, on understanding the reasons why a word is spelled as it is, and on developing a habit of being *sure* about spelling of a word rather than being content with guessing. However, the same values can be built through the maintenance of individual spelling and vocabulary lists. These approaches may ultimately have more meaning for the student than a few thousand words selected by the teacher or curriculum director from the half million or more that make up the English language.

WRITING, TYPEWRITING, AND STENOGRAPHY

As children grow into adolescence their muscular coordination improves. This coordination, added to accumulated writing experience, should produce a higher level of penmanship. While improvement is made and should be demanded, the desire and need of the student to get his ideas onto paper rapidly often results in almost illegible scribbling. Some students find continued use of manuscript of value, and this ought not to be discouraged if the student can maintain legibility and develop adequate speed. At least a modicum of legibility, neatness, and aesthetic appearance ought to be demanded in handwriting since the bright student will need to do considerable writing in high school, college, and adult life.

On the other hand, there is no justification for condescending attitudes toward typewriting and stenography as school experiences for bright children. The college student who cannot type with reasonable efficiency is handicapped to some extent. The college student who can use some kind of shorthand has a definite advantage in the many note-taking situations required of him. Unfortunately, in many junior high schools bright students are shunted into still another academic class when typewriting might have greater ultimate value in learning academic subjects at a later date. Stenography is generally reserved for students in the commercial curriculum and is regarded as vocational only.

Actually, there is need to re-evaluate offerings in both these fields. Some schools differentiate between typing that is meant as pre-vocational and typing for personal use. Perhaps the framework in which secondary schools operate where the Carnegie Unit establishes every subject as a daily period every week for a school year (or half a unit for a semester) accounts for the small number of bright students who receive instruction in these areas. It is hard to refute opinions that such a course represents an inordinate proportion of the bright child's school year. What is needed in typing is some sort of compromise which gives the student a few periods of instruction in typewriting and then provides for practice in free periods or at home. Because of the need to maintain skill, a typewriter at home is an essential, and assistance to a poor student in securing a machine may be no less significant than other, more ambitious scholarship aids.

In shorthand also there is need to reconsider conventional offerings. The student who is going to become a stenographer may well need one of the systems which uses its own symbols and requires a fairly long period for development of skill and speed at a high level. The college-bound student will need to write quickly but not at the same speed as the professional stenographer. Some colleges have made available to their students courses on methods which employ the conventional alphabet for the most part. Six or eight weekly lessons generally suffice to give the student the basic knowledge. Concerted use in taking notes from lectures and from readings generally suffices to develop a speed of eighty words or more per minute. There is no obvious reason that militates against offering such a voluntary course in free periods or after school in secondary schools as well.

CREATIVE WRITING

Adolescence presents a concatenation of circumstances that encourages creative expression as in no other period of life. On the technical side the young person is at last developing enough competence in mechanical skills to be able to express himself on paper. Psychologically, the adolescent is in a period marked by wonder, sensitivity, and idealism. While more aware than the child of attitudes of others toward him, he is less self-conscious than the adult. The need to assert himself as an individual, to tell all the world he is growing up, may also encourage self-expression. Many lyric masterpieces in world literature have come from youths in their late teens.

The English teacher in junior and senior high may accordingly look for both interest and marked achievement in creative writing. Some few young people will be found with a particular interest in writing for its own sake, with motivation toward writing careers, whether realistic or not. A larger number of bright students will respond to stimulation toward creative expression as amateurs—just for the fun of it or for the therapeutic values of self-expression. The need of the adolescent to "find himself," to locate his own position in the wide universe, to develop a sense of values may be explored through writing—narrative, lyric, dramatic, or expository. Some of the perplexing but pressing problems of the adolescent provide the dramatic or philosophic stuff of literature: conflict between generations as the child grows up in his own family; the individual caught between desires to conform and to rebel; the young person struggling to find meaning in life; the effort to establish spiritual as well as economic independence; relations with brothers and sisters and relations with peers outside one's family; the advent of romantic love; alertness to social wrongs; loyalty to community, to region, to nation, to humanity.

Since these concerns are so often the themes of the world's great literature, one can readily see the desirability of relating the reading to the writing program. The good reader will find provocative parallels in *The Bible, The Way of All Flesh, Of Human Bondage, Hamlet, The Grapes of Wrath, A Farewell to Arms, Arrowsmith, Joseph and His Brothers,* and a host of volumes available in paperback reprints as well as on library shelves. In this area, as in many others, the distinction between education for all and education for the gifted is the same. The difference lies in quality rather than in kind; deeper understanding, greater sensitivity, and more articulate expression may be expected.

To encourage this expression secondary schools use various devices. One is to provide for publications channels—school and class papers and literary journals which invite creative expression and reward it through recognition. A second is to provide for interchange among interested students. This may be a small writing group in an individual class with whom the teacher meets periodically—sometimes while the rest of the class is otherwise engaged, sometimes in free periods, after school, or in the homes of teachers and students. A third is to provide an established forum for exchange of ideas—a writing club, poetry club, playwrights' company, journalism group, radio and television workshop. Many schools provide elective courses for students in English in their junior and senior year so that they may choose, if interested, a Creative Writing or similarly named class. Some schools cooperate with interested writers in the community who are willing to sponsor off-campus junior writers groups. In many communities the public library serves as the meeting place for aspiring writers, and a librarian utilizes his knowledge of books to further the taste of young people for writing. The essential elements are common to all: an adult who can stimulate young people to write and who can give some guidance in expressive techniques; a forum for exchange of ideas and mutual encouragement and cross-fertilization; a method of publishing or at least reading aloud the products that ensue. Regular English classes in the high school can conceivably meet these conditions, too.

SPEECH

The verbal felicity of the intellectually gifted may make a section on speech seem superfluous. Yet it would be fallacious to assume that a reading-writing program is adequate to the needs either of those generally gifted or of those with special talents in the language arts. Speech programs for the gifted run the gamut from corrective and generally developmental programs to the offering of highly specialized training for boys and girls who show promise of genuine talent in public speaking, dramatics, and radio and television presentation. A basic competence in self-expression is essential to performance in a variety of fields that attract the intellectually gifted. Superior ability in verbal presentation and in discussion skills contributes to leadership in the same fields. Thus, a high standard of speech effectiveness has to be set for bright students in general and not simply for those who may specialize in speech activities.

Speech patterns, of course, reflect the family and community background of the student. If the school is indeed discovering all the high potential in its student body it will include boys and girls "from the wrong side of the tracks." An especially difficult problem is found here since the pattern which teachers regard as simply adequate may be viewed by the adolescent, his friends and family as overly elegant or even sissified. The student may need to develop two modes of language—one for school and one for his neighborhood. Such bifurcation requires greater sophistication than may be generally expected of children and adolescents. Even if the youngster tries hard to develop an acceptable speech pattern for formal situations, his customary use of undesired standards militates against real change.

In junior and senior high school oral communication plays an important part in the transactions of every class, in school activities, and in social life outside the school. Many classes are almost completely oral events. Reciting, debate, committee activity, reports, and panel discussion are to be found in almost all subjects. The teacher expects oral participation to reflect superiority in the area he teaches. The opportunity is present for spoken expression in each field of strength. In English and speech classes greater emphasis can be placed on the improvement of oral effectiveness whatever the speech situation. In this way, the teacher of speech contributes to achievement in all areas. Choral speaking, reading plays and other literature aloud, and various forum type activities represent opportunities for both corrective and developmental work.

The importance of small group discussions in all spheres of life puts emphasis on skill in group process. Participation in "buzz" sessions, leading discussion groups, recording and reporting for one's group are skills that depend upon practice at all school levels.

More extensive oral projects in the class challenge higher levels of expression. Putting on a play, staging a debate, presenting an assembly program, reporting to other classes or to parents on particular experiences, conducting a club meeting, simulating a radio program or, in fact, presenting a program on radio or television—all these activities are within the ken of junior and senior high school classes within a very wide range of maturity levels. Some of these activities are carried on outside of class. In senior high school, co-curricular activities, honors classes and electives in speech activities provide an emphasis that is often not available in the "regular" English class.

A fundamental concern, however, in education of the gifted in secondary schools is the special competence in speech needed by the scientist, the historian, the lawyer, and the physician as well as by the person whose vocation lies in speech fields. The student aiming at the former careers is likely to be so wrapped up in his own field that he is not likely to enroll in special speech activities, curricular or otherwise. To such a student opportunities for oral presentation and group discussion have to be available both within his special field of interest—for he has to learn to express himself well in that context—and within the regular English class where somewhat more attention may be given to form because of the English teacher's special training. On the one hand is the need for improvement of technical speech; on the other, emphasis is needed on expression of thought, on organization of a topic, on stimulating and maintaining interest, on "reaching" one's audience, on creative and imaginative expression even in purely expository speech.

Foreign Languages

Foreign languages have found their way into elementary and secondary programs for intellectually gifted students via two routes. One is the search for "horizontal" enrichment—the addition of new material at the elementary level that would not entail acceleration ("vertical" enrichment). The second has been a response to demands for foreign language training to fill a gap in national skills. Both approaches have, ultimately, to be interpreted in the light of contributions they make to the development of individual potential and creative living.

The "classical" elementary programs for the gifted have offered foreign languages in early grades for many years. These include Cleveland's Major Work programs and the Hunter College Elementary School. In the latter, French or German is studied one or two days a week with a special teacher starting when the children are seven years old. All instruction is given in the language that is studied. A conversational approach is used. Instruction is continuous to the end of the sixth grade. At that point boys and girls may continue with the same language in junior high school. Because they are grouped with students coming from other elementary schools not offering foreign language instruction, articulation is difficult for these and other children with previous language training. The youngsters have the benefit of greater readiness and knowledge, but it is not generally possible to build directly upon it in terms of the secondary school curriculum. If the arguments of foreign language specialists hold, these children are far more likely, because of early exposure to conversational use, to master thoroughly a second or even a third language.

Sumption (1941), evaluating the Cleveland program, reports initial enthusiasm of boys and girls in the Major Works Classes for their foreign language. When novelty wears off and the need for sustained practice begins, interest apparently declines. By the third year, one-third of the students remain devoted, one-third begin to object, and one-third are slightly uninterested. Gifted or not, the children are part of a broader environment which makes little use of other tongues. What may seem "enriching" to the teacher or administrator, may not prove, in practice, to enrich the life of an eight-year-old.

One caution, then, ought to be observed. Foreign languages may be of considerable value and interest to many pupils in elementary and secondary schools. It is doubtful whether the statement can be extended to *all* students, or even to all gifted students. Specialization of intellectual abilities argues against prescription in languages as it does against required programs in science or mathematics. We should be interested, therefore, in foreign language programs offered as a matter of choice, rather than as a matter of course, to gifted students. Of some assistance to teachers may be the new Modern Language Aptitude Test developed at Harvard University which is apparently being used with a measure of success to predict ability to master a second language.

A committee of the Modern Language Association and the NEA Project on the Academically Talented Student prepared in 1960 a bulletin on teaching foreign languages (NEA, 1960c). The group recommended a ten-year program beginning in grade three, with an alternative six-year program beginning in grade seven, and a four-year program beginning in grade nine.

The ten-year program begins with an audio-lingual program in grades 3, 4 and 5 for fifteen minutes each day. In grade 6 the fifteen-minute period turns to formal structure drills without grammatical explanation. Grade 7 provides a full period three times a week, brings in grammatical elements, an organized reading program and introduction to writing. Laboratory facilities are recommended at this level, too. In grades 8 to 12 the program is intensified and extended in the direction of full competence in speaking, writing, and reading, including literary materials.

The six- and four-year programs attempt to follow the same organization, except that less time is left for the conversational introduction in the longer program. The ten-year program is preferred for two reasons: "It results in a notably higher degree of linguistic control and it exposes the student, for ten highly formative years, to concepts of another culture and civilization" (NEA, 1960c, pp. 40-62).

From the point of view of the linguist, the early beginning is essential, "preferably not later than the third grade." The skill to learn unfamiliar sounds by imitation with an accent as good as the teacher's declines, it is claimed, at about the age of ten (*Ibid.*, p. 14). In addition, a program in grades 3 to 5 may provide the best kind of screening device for selecting students with the necessary language ability to go ahead and students with extraordinary ability who ought to be urged to expend special effort. This selection via exploration is in line with ideas developed in many areas in Chapter 3 on identification of special ability. A major drawback after the glitter of novelty has tarnished is lack of opportunity to use the language. Another is the child's sense of personal involvement which may not be as great as that of the teacher who is straining to meet national manpower needs in international affairs.

Conversational approach to a foreign language requires a higher level of teacher competence than does the older focus on reading knowledge, grammatical structure, and translation. The purpose of early instruction is to establish authentic speech patterns. The importance of the teacher-as-model is basic. If a teacher who can "speak like a native" is not available, the program may be self-defeating. Personnel may be recruited from outside the school or school system. A person not trained as a teacher may work with the teacher in giving language instruction. A special language teacher may be needed even in schools that adhere to the self-contained classroom otherwise.

Since 1958 foreign languages have been taught in special classes for intellectually gifted children in grades 4 to 6 in a score of elementary schools in New York City. A guide based on the experience of the first teachers in these classes lists the following aims:

> To pronounce foreign sounds correctly
> To understand simple expressions in the foreign language
> To say simple things in the foreign language
> To follow directions given in the foreign language
> To acquire a vocabulary of five hundred useful words
> To sing a half dozen familiar songs.

(Stiassni, 1959, p. 2)

The approach in the program is conversational, making use of objects, pictures, and charts. Writing is restricted to keeping a record of new words in a notebook. Spoken language is used almost exclusively, with much reliance on songs and games. The basic learning technique is imitation and frequent repetition of the spoken model.

Certain aids are available to supplement the efforts of a competent teacher. Publishers are experimenting with a series of motion pictures making use of native speakers or highly fluent American teachers to provide an example and to lead pattern drills. Printed text material, in other cases, has been organized to accompany recordings or tapes. The Modern Language Association is sponsoring some materials of this kind.

An increasing number of schools may be found with fully equipped language laboratories. Basically these laboratories are facilities for playing tape recordings of language instruction, for recording the student's response, and for playing back to the student his own speech in the new language. The fully equipped laboratory provides for group instruction as well as individual practice. It has a library of tapes that permit the student to move ahead at his own speed. However, any school can provide the basic components inexpensively. Tape and disc recordings are readily available for purchase. Playback equipment and a tape recorder for the student to record his own voice are the minimum essentials.

Other types of assistance are found in the mass media. Foreign language broadcasts or lessons via commercial or educational television channels provide additional practice for the student. As students increase in ability, they may gradually learn from and appreciate the fine motion pictures produced abroad. Many of these films provide a realistic picture of another culture in its native habitat; in addition, they are of value in teaching the language.

Ideally the language laboratory, television, and motion pictures supplement the teacher who speaks the foreign language with an authentic accent. Unfortunately there are not enough teachers of foreign languages available to supply all the high schools in the United States, let alone junior high schools and elementary schools. Where the fully competent teacher cannot be found, consideration should be given to use of these other media as substitutes.

Certain issues in teaching foreign languages remain unresolved. One of these is the selection of languages to be taught. As an aid to mastery of particular disciplines, a small number of western European languages traditionally taught seem to be adequate. The Soviet Union's giant strides in scientific fields argue for introduction of Russian. The language as a tool for scholarship, however, is only one purpose. Problems of international understanding and the needs of diplomacy and commerce argue the case for all of the languages that may be found in the universe. School systems have to make choices; they are restricted by the training of their personnel or by availability of additional personnel in doing so. Their only consolation is the claim of linguists that learning a second language makes learning of still other languages an easier matter.

A second problem is the place of classical languages in the foreign language program. Conversational approaches tend to downgrade the study of Latin. Claims of classicists as to the fundamental nature of Latin are in apparent conflict with advocacy by modern language specialists of early study of currently spoken languages.

A third problem is the place of general language courses and the approach to foreign languages as a study of the structure of language. This approach focuses more on linguistic study and understanding of other cultures than on the mastery of a single language. However, its customary exposure of students to a smattering of several languages sometimes helps the student select the language he will later study with some persistence.

In education of the gifted, one should distingush between foreign languages as a special area of study and foreign languages as "enrichment" to fill the time of students who have time left over from prescribed studies. There is little point in denying the importance of study of foreign languages in their own right. As an automatic addition to the diet of every intellectually superior student, however, foreign languages should be subjected to the normal criteria of aptitude, interest, and even utility. The bright student with little aptitude for foreign languages should not have to struggle with them as a stumbling block in the way of other studies.

SUMMARY

Language arts are of fundamental importance to the intellectually gifted student. They occupy a large fraction of the time spent in formal education. They represent both a means to achievement in other areas and an area for accomplishment in themselves. For the gifted student basic concerns must include establishment of fundamental learnings, progress at a pace consistent with the learner's ability, development of tastes and interests, as well as skills and techniques. The teacher of language arts has the opportunity to help youngsters build necessary competences for achievement in all areas and a cultural background that may enrich all of the student's life.

Chapter 10

Social Studies and Social Education

> *Know then thyself, presume not God to scan;*
> *The proper study of mankind is man.*
>
> —Alexander Pope

No area lends itself so well to enrichment for the gifted as does social studies. One can vary infinitely the degree of sophistication in approaching problems in history, government, economics, sociology, geography, and anthropology—or in attacking issues of human relationships which cut across a number of these disciplines. Since all of this may be done without vexatious problems of acceleration and without recourse to mere busywork, social studies presents a potential for ideal adaptation to gifted students. The major requirement is that the teacher regard the social studies as a broad area which is not circumscribed by the facts set forth in the course of study or the textbook. For the bright child these limited statements of "content" may represent not a totality but simply a springboard from which to leap into more mature study.

Education for citizenship and development of background in the social sciences are joint objectives for all students, including the intellectually superior. The problem in social studies for the gifted is not one of framework but rather one of method and materials. The probable leaders of the maturing generation need to be building an especially strong sense of social responsibility; in addition, they will need, and should be capable of, greater achievement in the social sciences.

ELEMENTARY SOCIAL STUDIES

In terms of method in the elementary school, there is general agreement that the unit, project, or activity approach meets the requirements

237

of the more able learner. Proper handling of a unit gives the bright student an opportunity to share in planning, gives him independence in study, and enables differential contributions in keeping with differences in ability, interest, and scholastic sophistication. Organization of committees on a basis of particular jobs to do normally provides a cross-section of abilities. In the cross section, the able student has the opportunity to develop leadership qualities as he contributes to the work and organization of his committee.

One problem that faces the teacher and curriculum planner is the difficulty of matching social studies content to the immaturity and inexperience of elementary school students, gifted or not. Responses of bright children to instruction may be deceptive. There is the danger of regarding their ability to verbalize as genuine understanding when a considerable gap may, in fact, exist between genuine comprehension and glib utterance of complex concepts. Research pointing to the rather late maturation of a time sense suggests the inadvisability of accelerated study of chronological history (NCSS, 1953, p. 201). Understanding of social and international problems also requires greater maturity. The key to curriculum development for the gifted in elementary social studies would seem not to be accelerated content (as it sometimes may in other areas), but rather the exploration of fields currently employed which enrich understanding of the scene about us. Hollingworth proposed imaginative organization of a familiar content as one way of meeting this problem. She advocated the development of units on the evolution of common things in our environment, a proposal that was put to use during the life of the Speyer School experiment in New York City (Greenberg, 1941).

Suggestions by the New York State Elementary Curriculum Bureau are representative of the kinds of enrichment activities recommended for gifted students:

1. Trace a series of historical events showing relationships and possible generalizations.
2. Study the origin of our food supply, laws, government, or other ideas as a basis for understanding the evolution of our culture.
3. Make a map showing early travel routes in a particular area and another of the same area showing highways, rail and air routes now in use.
4. Compile a list of special skills used by employees in certain vital industries.
5. Make a chart showing the designs of early coins tracing their evolution to present day coins. Write a history of the first use of money.

6. Write and help produce plays and puppet shows on topics in citizenship or topics of interest in the other fields of social studies.
7. Make a scrapbook, posters, paintings, murals, etc. on topics of interest related to the social studies.
8. Prepare special reports, going more deeply into subjects or events than may be possible in the regular classroom program.
9. Do independent research into causes and effects of selected events in history or the effect of geography on historical events.
10. Prepare short biographies of the lives of famous people—especially related to events or places currently under study. (New York State, 1958, p. 27) [*]

SKILLS IN SOCIAL STUDIES

The citizen's need for information about the social scene in which he lives is apparent. Equally important to the student are skills which can make him self-propelling in searching out information on his own. These skills are especially meaningful for the bright student since he can employ them in independent study earlier than the average boy or girl. In developing these skills, the teacher of bright children will find helpful the Twenty-fourth Yearbook of the National Council for the Social Studies, *Skills in Social Studies* (1953, and Revised Edition, 1963). The Council focuses upon skills for citizenship, skills in human relations, critical thinking and problem solving, locating and gathering of information, organizing and evaluating information, reading and listening, speaking and writing, interpreting materials in graphic form, developing a time sense and chronology, and participating in group undertakings. The volume is addressed to all levels of teaching and suggests activities that may be used in the classroom as well as goals to be sought. Of particular interest are chapters by Fraser and Johns on developing a program for learning of skills and on grade placement. The latter chapter (NCSS, 1963, Chapter 15) helps the teacher avoid attempting the impossible while still planning some acceleration of learning.

Social studies in the schools are intimately related to the reading program. In the early grades social studies themes are employed in reading materials. In later grades social studies make their contribution to development of skill in reading non-fictional material. In almost all grades social studies depend upon the reading that pupils do—in textbooks, in supplementary materials, in newspapers, periodicals and reference

[*] From *Curriculum Adaptations for the Gifted*, by the Bureau of Elementary Curriculum Development, New York State Department of Education. Copyright 1958. Reprinted with permission of the Bureau of Elementary Curriculum Development.

sources. While gifted students in general do well both in reading and social studies, the teacher can enhance progress in both areas by facing realistically problems of reading in social studies.

A characteristic learning problem in social studies arises when young children are confronted with abstract concepts or events that are remote in time or space. These two concerns are linked here as a single problem because they both involve development of experiential bases for words, ideas, and generalizations. The matter of providing concrete referents for concepts is at the heart of the teaching of reading. The ability of the gifted student to verbalize should not mislead the teacher into an overestimate of his actual comprehension.

Huus (NCSS, 1963, Chapter 6) lists sources of reading difficulty in typical social studies material. A large number of concepts are to be found in a relatively small space. The nature of social studies material changes with rapidity that bewilders the learner. Yesterday's "facts" are today regarded as erroneous interpretations. Often a welter of ideas is presented with no clue as to their relative importance. Information is offered in a complicated style; sentences are often inverted; familiar words are used in strange ways; technical terms are inevitable. In addition, in the middle grades children are confronted with a shift from a fictional to an objective approach in the writing of social studies texts. The author is generally an expert immersed in his field; sometimes he forgets that the interest he has generated over the years has yet to be matched by a learner who is currently apathetic. Finally, there is a problem of space. Each year history brings additions; nothing is erased. Result: treatments are often too brief for full understanding by the young reader.

Knowing the sources of difficulty, the teacher can help students begin to overcome them. Throughout the common school years, young people need help in abstracting ideas from printed material. Huus suggests particular contributions as the responsibility of social studies. These include vocabulary development, differential reading rates, formation of relationships, and expanding concepts. In these areas the teacher can find work with gifted students especially rewarding. The verbally superior student can respond more successfully to study of the specific meaning of words as used in the social sciences, to the introduction of new words necessarily involved in studying foreign cultures and times past, to puzzling out phrases and abstract terms requiring interpretation. With the exigencies of college work in the offing, students need to distinguish between skimming, cursory reading, study of materials, and critical reading. They need to develop skills in each of these approaches and to learn when to employ them. How to study is an essential complex of skills closely related to these reading procedures, to taking notes, to outlining material and organizing it.

For the process of organizing material, Huus suggests help to the student in forming relationships in content they read—relationships inherent in the organization of the matter, cause-and-effect relationships, relationships organized by space or time criteria, relationships involving the importance of ideas, and application to personal experience. Finally, the opportunity to help students expand their concepts lies in encouraging wide and extensive reading. The social studies teacher contributes through the books he brings into class, the jackets he displays on bulletin boards, the books he recommends to the librarian for purchase, the titles he recommends, the selections he reads orally to students, and the radio and television programs he suggests that may lead to further reading. Additional ideas on reading in the social studies may be found in booklets issued by the National Council for the Social Studies at the elementary (Fay, 1961) and secondary (Preston, 1963) levels.

Some of the skills in social studies may be approached a bit earlier and more intensively with gifted pupils. Concrete materials such as maps and globes lend themselves to study in elementary school, including the making of simple maps of the school neighborhood as early as the first grade. As children demonstrate understanding, more involved concepts may be introduced. These include understanding of map scales and computing distance, locating places on maps and globes by latitude and longitude, reading map signs and symbols, and comparing maps to draw inferences.

Learning how to study is a skill to which social studies may make an important contribution at all school levels. In social studies, where reading is a fundamental tool, the student may become independent at an earlier stage than in mathematics and science where process development and experimentation require greater teacher guidance. Thus, the child who has learned to read precociously may be ready to go off on his own quite early in social studies. Study skills are best learned "on the job"—in the process of learning. Emphasis may be more effectively placed on methods while studying a specific topic than on abstract skill development in a unit on "How to Study." The gifted student in particular may benefit from assistance in ways to locate material, to study these materials, to appraise them, and to utilize them. Study skills requiring special attention include taking notes, outlining, abstracting, and summarizing material. These are skills that need continuous refinement from elementary grades all the way through graduate school. In addition, the elementary and secondary school student need assistance in reading maps and in interpreting statistical presentations in the form of graphs, tables, charts, and pictograms.

Use of reference materials such as the dictionary, junior encyclopedias, and atlases also begins early for bright children. A classroom set of such items is often necessary when many gifted children are grouped together. This does not preclude use of a central library in the school but reduces the necessity for minor detours to the library in the midst of some scholastic journey.

The school library, of course, should be a much richer repository of material than the classroom, and library skills need early development. How to find books in the library, where to locate periodical material, how to use vertical files crammed full of pictures, pamphlets, and ephemeral items—these are part of the learning tasks in elementary school that help children find information they seek in the present but also arm them with tools that will serve them well when their greater maturity permits exploration into more profound topics. The teacher's responsibility is to help children develop these skills in a context of meaning by suggesting areas for research or ways of finding answers to questions pupils ask.

SOCIAL STUDIES AND THE TEACHING OF THINKING

Because social studies deal with open-ended problems and issues that are within the knowledge of school children, genuine opportunities exist for improving the quality of children's thinking. Gifted children, like other children, do not arrive at a state of pure reason all at once. Among small children an absolutist tendency dominates. Things are all black or all white. Children tend to be egocentric. Their limited experience interposes no objection to their belief that their dad can lick any other dad on the block, that their toys are the best, that their family's religion and political persuasions are the truest. Add to these limitations the child's confusion of real and not-real, of objective and subjective, of dream world and real world. These three erroneous attitudes are joined by immaturity in two other important respects. The ability to generalize and abstract are present from an early age, but this ability apparently develops very slowly. Finally, abstract relationships, such as cause-and-effect, are not well understood in early childhood (Burton, 1960, p. 336).

Ultimately maturation and experience reduce fallacious approaches to thinking and the ability to handle abstractions grows. Particularly gratifying development may be observed in intellectually gifted children. However, it is necessary to recognize that growth from immature to mature thinking represents a continuum rather than two sharply defined poles with children either at one end or the other. Especially notable is the fact that children—and grown-ups, too—will think critically, objectively, without prejudice and avoiding fallacies, in some areas and not in others. The mixture of logic and illogic is one of the attributes we use to describe childhood and childishness.

To the elementary teacher this means (1) he may expect even the bright child's thinking to exhibit egocentrism (everything I have is the best), a failure to distinguish real from not-real, and a failure to perceive relative degrees between absolute poles; (2) he can expect in early years a very primitive ability to deal with abstractions; (3) he will be able to see with the passage of time improvement in both these areas; (4) he can stimulate growth by giving attention to the child's thought processes. In secondary schools the teacher should find fallacious thinking giving way to increasing powers of abstraction among gifted children. He will be able, moreover, to direct specific learning activities toward improvement of thinking as well as guide student thought in particular learning areas.

The teacher helps to develop effective thinking in four ways: by providing experiences in critical thinking, by helping learners build a store of pertinent knowledge and facts, by helping students master the processes of reasoning, and by stimulating and guiding the growth of attitudes essential to clear thinking (Carr, 1938, p. 1228). The National Council for the Social Studies urges the teacher to avoid certain obstacles to critical thinking which are commonly found in schools:

> Emphasis on rote memorization of facts; on drills divorced from practical application; on busy work, such as the meaningless filling in of workbooks; on rewards for agreeing with the teacher; on penalties for independent thinking challenging the status quo; on problems without meaning to the pupils—all such emphases tend to stultify thinking and to deaden curiosity, which is the wellspring of thinking. (NCSS, 1953, p. 49)

Burton, Kimball, and Wing have attempted to suggest particular devices that elementary and secondary school teachers can employ in teaching thinking. They take two approaches basically, both of which are relevant in social studies programs. One is orientation of units and content that are conventionally used in such a way that major emphasis is given to thought processes. The other introduces special units that are concerned with thinking and with fallacies that interfere with effective thought. The first approach involves choice of conventional problem-solving units. Emphasis is placed on units which deal with explanation of phenomena or conditions, with discovery of a new generalization or new process, with verification of the worth or advantages of a substance or theory, and with the weighing of evidence in cases where experimentation is not feasible. A second type of unit they suggest is termed "normative"—investigation of values in field where controversy abounds: for example, the topic "Should we have socialized medicine?" A third type they call "units of criticism." Study of the validity of statements being made or heard is the substance of such a unit which gets down to analysis of the logic of a statement itself, of the weight that the speaker or writer brings to his statement, of fallacies in thinking that may be discovered, of the author's use of propaganda devices, and of the author's distinction between fact and opinion. Finally, Burton, Kimball, and Wing suggest use of a "case-study" method. What is sought here is a detailed account of events leading up to some type of difficult problem (Burton, 1960, pp. 310-23).

In addition to focus on thinking in handling the usual content, Burton, Kimball, and Wing advocate introduction of specific units on thinking in the social studies curriculum. Such units may center around the collection of data, fallacies, semantics, and propaganda devices (Burton, *op. cit.*, p. 368). Propaganda analysis has found its way into social studies in many schools since the early efforts of the Institute for Propaganda Analysis in the 1930's. Children as well as adults are constantly subjected to a barrage of propaganda from political, economic, and advertising sources through the ubiquitous mass media. It is not difficult to awaken interest of gifted students in analyzing the claims that are constantly being urged upon them. The gifted student, again, has particular competence for handling the analytic thought processes involved.

The National Council for the Social Studies suggests a series of activities that may be introduced in social studies classrooms to study propaganda devices (NCSS, 1963, pp. 85-91), and teachers will find valuable the *Analysis of Propaganda* by Hummell and Huntress (1949).

GROUP PROCESSES

While attention to individual thinking is primary, focus on group processes in thinking is also much desired. The gifted young person is already a member of informal and formal groups and is destined, with his less gifted fellows, to participate in vocational, political, economic, religious, and social group activities. Understanding of group processes can help the intellectually gifted exert leadership through which their ability may bear the fruit of its promise. Teachers should have some familiarity with the imposing body of literature on group dynamics which developed in the late 1940's and 1950's. Especially valuable is Hare's *Handbook of Small Group Research* (1962).

There is substantial evidence indicating superior productivity when a group gives its attention to problems which are often tackled by individuals. Russell (1956, p. 267) cites research which shows that pairs or groups of students solve more problems than individuals though they may take more time in the process. Groups seem to learn more than individuals, and they seem to make more accurate judgments as a group than as individuals. Obviously a group brings more to any given situation than can an individual. The group represents to an individual an arena where he can learn to work with others, respecting their ideas and finding out how to attract their attention to his opinions and contributions.

Because groups do not always function in a constructive manner, training for group membership and activity is desirable. In the protected school environment, boys and girls can take part in group situations and later reconstruct and analyze their activity under the guidance of a perceptive teacher. Young people can learn to identify roles that persons play in a group—supportive, aggressive, withdrawing, contributing, compromising, questioning—(Benne and Sheats, 1948, pp. 98-106) and improve their own performance as a result of this awareness. They can learn to place themselves in the other fellow's position (role playing) and thus develop the tolerance needed for effective cooperative discussion and thinking. They can explore the place of "hidden agenda" in influencing the thinking and opinion of individuals in a group. Students may also learn how to hammer out consensus rather than adopting unworkable solutions on the basis of bare majorities. In the process they learn what it means to be a group member and how to help the group pursue ends that the members seek.

A distinction is commonly made between two functions of leadership: one is advancement of the group toward its goals; a second is the enhancement of personal relationships within the group. DeHaan labels persons performing these two functions as the "task specialist" and the "socioemotional specialist" respectively (NSSE, 1957, pp. 141-143). Schools normally give major attention to the first function. Muessig and Rogers (NCSS, 1963, Chapter 12) define five goals in helping young people to fulfill the second fuction as well:

Ability to feel for others, to empathize with them, to be sensitive to their needs, problems and aspirations

Ability to examine one's own feelings, values, capabilities, and shortcomings with an eye toward developing a healthy, mature and realistic self-concept

Ability to see people as individuals rather than as stereotyped members of particular groups

Ability to balance facts and feelings, the intellectual and emotional

Ability to work effectively with others as a member of a group.

These objectives have special significance for the gifted, since their capabilities often lure them into single-minded pursuit of group or individual goals without giving adequate attention to personal feelings of members of the group. The teacher can make an important contribution to the personal development and effectiveness of the bright student if he can help him combine the "task" and "socioemotional" leadership functions.

FOCUS ON CONCEPT FORMATION AND GENERALIZATION

A central problem in the teaching of social studies is the relative positions of facts and concepts, or information and generalizations. Obviously, the specific and the general are interrelated. The gifted student, however, is better endowed to organize facts into meaningful relationships and generalizations. For some time there has been a perceptible movement in geography away from name-and-place geography as important in itself toward development of the important concepts that describe man's relationship to his physical and geographical environment. The bright student, no doubt, can memorize more state capitals and longer lists of industrial products of particular regions than can other boys and girls. The waste, however, seems all the greater if such facts are not supportive of important generalizations on the interdependence of the regions of the world, on the relationship of man to climate, on the reciprocal influences of man and environment. Studies of reasons why certain cultures have developed as they have in particular geographic settings may be more meaningful than learning the agricultural products of the area and the population of its valleys and cities.

History as well lends itself to more critical thinking than learning the dates and places of men and events in isolation. For one thing, it would seem a pity if bright children were not exposed to the historian's method as an example of critical thinking. How are historical facts established? What goes into the weaving of historical theories? Why do explanations of great historical movements change from time to time? What establishes the authority of a historian? What is fact and what opinion in a history book? Excellent sources for the secondary school teacher are the bulletins prepared by the Service Center for Teachers of History (1957 ff.), operating as an arm of the American Historical Association.

An especially good guide for the teacher who wishes to emphasize the development of important ideas is *A Guide to Content in the Social Studies* (NCSS, 1958) which defines basic themes that may direct the choice of content and provide a framework in organizing factual material. Prepared by a committee of the National Council for the Social Studies, the *Guide* lists these themes:

1. The intelligent uses of the forces of nature
2. Recognition and understanding of world interdependence
3. Recognition of the dignity and worth of the individual
4. The use of intelligence to improve human living
5. The vitalization of our democracy through an intelligent use of our public educational facilities
6. The intelligent acceptance, by individuals and groups, of responsibility for achieving democratic social action
7. Increasing the effectiveness of the family as a basic social institution
8. The effective development of moral and spiritual values
9. The intelligent and responsible sharing of power in order to attain justice
10. The intelligent utilization of scarce resources to attain the widest general well-being
11. Achievement of adequate horizons of loyalty
12. Cooperation in the interest of peace and welfare
13. Achieving a balance between social stability and social change
14. Widening and deepening the ability to live more richly°

SPECIAL PROGRAMS IN SECONDARY SOCIAL STUDIES

Social studies have dual aims for gifted students in secondary schools. First, for bright students in general they must develop more than an ordinary understanding of social problems and principles. Second, they must provide the exploratory experiences that stimulate development of social scientists in embryo. The National Education Association Project on the Academically Talented Student and the National Council for the Social Studies have developed a policy statement for the gifted student in high school. For these young people a minimum of three years of social studies is urged in grades nine to twelve, with at least half of the program devoted to study of non-American areas. History is conceived broadly to include economic, social, cultural, and intellectual developments as well as conventional political studies. Procedures should be planned to introduce the talented student to the methods of the social sciences. The cognitive gifts of the academically talented student call for a curriculum which is conceptual in nature, emphasizing not factual content alone but facts as they contribute to the development of ideas and concepts. In addition, the ability to deal with concepts should lead to

---

° From *A Guide to Content in the Social Studies,* by the National Council for the Social Studies. Reprinted with permission of the National Council for the Social Studies.

interdisciplinary courses and units, and to studies that correlate history with literature, science, or art. A judicious selection of materials is urged in order to give depth and richness of treatment precedence over mere coverage. Various degrees of independent work should be introduced demanding responsibility on the part of superior students for pursuing their own study. The tutorial approach, contract methods and less frequent meetings of the class may be combined with a requirement of "wide and discriminating reading in both primary and secondary courses and rigorous training in research and writing" (NEA, 1960e, pp. 22-26).

To implement their recommendations, the joint committee proposed the following social studies curriculum:

Grades 9 and 10:

World History and Geography—the Western World

or World History and Geography—Asia

or Introduction to the Social Sciences (an introduction to the techniques, subject matter and perspectives of anthropology, sociology, economics and political science)

Grades 11 and 12:

Required: American History and Government

Option A: Introduction to the social sciences (an adaptation of the 9th-10th grade course for more mature students)

Option B: Electives: Modern European History (advanced placement); Far Eastern History; The Middle East; History of Great Britain and the Commonwealth; Latin American History; Africa; International Relations; Economics; Sociology; Psychology; Seminars in the history of ideas, contemporary problems, great issues, world cultures, etc.

Modern European History, British History, and the Seminars are recommended as one year courses, the remainder for one-half year (*Ibid.*, pp. 26-30).

The committee advocates the use of ability grouping wherever possible. Klein suggests the following qualities as criteria to employ in selecting students for advanced study:

1. A searching and open mind toward social problems and data
2. Social sensitivity, a genuine interest in people and in the consequences of social interaction, and respect for and appreciation of other people's ideas and ethical values.
3. Capacity for critical judgment, with particular reference to the assessment of human behavior

4. Emotional balance and a sense of perspective in evaluating the evidence of social science
5. Imagination, the ability to project one's self into social situations that differ in time and place from one's own
6. A sense of time and the ability to see events in their relationship to other events that precede and follow
7. The ability to carry on research in social problems, to perceive the limits of a problem, to secure data, to weigh evidence, to formulate hypotheses, to reach meaningful conclusions, and to organize the results effectively for written or oral presentation (NEA, 1960e, p. 16)

Classroom procedures include some variations on normally recommended methodology with an eye to the special ability of the gifted. These include: problem solving; forums, debates, and panel discussions; field trips; collateral reading in depth and breadth; critical use of modern mass media; and individual research reports. Of particular interest are the committee's suggestions for enriched reading in the social sciences. These include materials for illustration and dramatization, source items for factual detail about historical periods, specialized references at a mature level, interpretation of reading for documentary analysis, reading of contemporary accounts and reading that exemplifies historical method and other social science methodology (*Ibid.*, pp. 31-43).

Apart from the committees organized in various subject fields by the NEA Project on the Academically Talented Student, the only systematic approach to instruction of the gifted at the secondary level has been that published twenty-five years earlier by the Association of First Assistants (Department Chairmen) in the High Schools of New York City. This association published a volume, *Educating Superior Students*, in 1935 with chapters on each of fourteen subjects. Steinberg, in the chapter on History and Civics, urges use of Morrison's "mastery unit technique," an adaptation of the contract plan (Cohen and Coryell, 1935, pp. 115-16). Students are given work sheets which guide them in study of a topic from basic texts to supplementary reading and library work, culminating in the writing and presentation of individual or committee reports. Steinberg reports about two-thirds of the time spent in individual work. The contract plan is a technique which continues to be used in a number of schools conducting special classes for selected students.

A successor to the contract plan is probably the less formalized writing of short and long research papers as a part of courses that provide for more group discussion and interaction than the Morrison plan. Use of long papers representing a semester's work should come only after careful appraisal of the students' background, maturity, and interest. Even the gifted student at the secondary level often needs the closer guidance that can accompany more frequent submission of shorter research units. The danger arises, too, of excessive attention to form rather than to content and thought processes employed.

FIRST-HAND EXPERIENCES IN SOCIAL STUDIES

Original research is not beyond the abilities of secondary school students. Explorations in local history frequently are given the town's blessings. Often material is available if someone will only go out and gather it in. High school students may uncover such material by interviewing descendants of the older families in the community, by examining archives in the city hall or county court house, and by thumbing through old newspapers. Community studies represent a parallel opportunity in the field of sociology and economics. Follow-up studies of a class of graduates or a group of drop-outs from high school may yield information as valuable to the school board as to the researchers. A study of adolescent use of leisure time or the availability of recreational resources can have special meaning to a high school class. Other studies may be done on voter registration, trends in home building, and the utilization and care of natural resources.

Of value in stemming growth of meaningless verbalization is the use of "laboratory practices in citizenship" being advocated by the Citizenship Education Project (1958) and other agencies interested in practical citizenship. Recognizing the need to make abstract concepts of citizenship come alive through concrete activities, the Project has stimulated the development of numerous direct learning experiences in connection with "premises" of American democracy that the Project staff has formulated. These activities stem all the way from developing a school historical museum to campaigns urging voter registration and organizing school traffic courts. Of particular application at the secondary level are some of the ideas noted in publications of the Project. These may be adapted for elementary schools as well. Here, again, a good idea for students in general proves to be especially valuable in developing leadership and knowledge for the gifted.

Field trips for gifted students should be planned with special care because of the greater learning potential of the participants. Simple "rubber-necking" or sight-seeing is scarcely excusable considering the large amount of time consumed in direct experience as contrasted with reading or listening. Bright youngsters need direct experience as much as other students, but they should be guided into more profound generalization and greater understanding of relationships. The trip to a saw mill should not simply be an example of an industrial process with focus on the steps in lumber production from forest to consumer. Technological, social, economic, and ethical issues give the trip significance, interest and challenge. Speakers from the saw mill management or local labor leaders should be asked to explore such issues with students rather than dwelling upon the industrial marvels of high pressure water power and saws that turn at "x" revolutions per minute. Planning sessions with students that precede the field trip ought to outline issues about which information can be sought.

Extra-class activities can also enrich the social studies curriculum for the gifted. Current events, clubs, debating, junior local history societies, United Nations assemblies, and local junior UN associations enlist the participation of students with social-science interests. Careers in the social sciences may be encouraged by "internship" programs where students engage in work experiences centered in local government offices. A few communities have explored placement of volunteers in government offices and various social service agencies so that students can secure the benefits of work experience and gain some knowledge of careers in these fields.

THE TEACHER OF SOCIAL STUDIES

In the social studies the competence of the teacher becomes especially significant. There is a need to draw upon many disciplines and to relate them to the needs, interests, and problems of the young. There is the problem of handling controversial material of a sensitive nature to many communities. There is the need to avoid doctrinaire treatment in order to stimulate critical thinking by students and to avoid propagandizing.

A large majority of teachers of social studies come to their profession with majors in history. The specialization of most universities does not permit as wide a spread in other social sciences as the history major will need to teach social studies with distinction. The gifted need a teacher who will continue his academic work and broaden it, and who will also read widely in many fields.

In addition to enhancing his scholarship, the teacher must also maintain an active interest in civic activities. In this way he is able to give students a fresh orientation to actual problems of citizenship. He may also wish to participate in civic, social, and political activity and thereby serve as a model of active civic participation. The danger of accusations of partisan activity is, of course, real. The teacher must himself be skillful, and he must also depend upon support from school leadership.

In elementary schools teachers face the need of continuous updating of background in all fields. Identification of some teachers in each school as special resources in social studies may help direct interested students to them. Other teachers may also use these specialists for assistance. In addition, a continuous in-service program in the school district can help elementary school teachers widen their foundation in the social sciences and gain fresh perspectives with new developments in current scholarship. Exchange teachers and exchange students from other countries may also serve as an especially rich resource.

NEW HORIZONS IN SOCIAL STUDIES

New programs on a large scale were instituted in the early 1960's to reconsider social studies programs in the schools. The United States Office of Education initiated Project Social Studies with research and demonstration centers on a number of university campuses. The National Science Foundation followed its earlier programs in mathematics and the sciences with a course content improvement program in the social studies that may be parallel to its predecessors in scope and impact. The National Council for the Social Studies cooperated with the American Council of Learned Societies to produce an important volume entitled *The Social Studies and the Social Sciences.** The College Entrance Examination Board instituted an examination of social studies programs that may have an effect similar to work sponsored by the Board in mathematics. In addition, professional associations in geography, anthropology and economics have supported projects for improvement of the curriculum in their respective areas in elementary and secondary schools. Because of the academic orientation of most of these studies, there is strong potential in them for the improvement of social studies programs for the gifted.

SUMMARY

At the elementary and secondary levels, social studies are part of the common experience of all students. The program is oriented toward citizenship needs rather than academic specilization. The bright student should draw from these experiences values qualitatively different from those of the average boy or girl. All share a program of social education aimed at more effective participation in group life of the family, community, nation, and the world. The gifted student is more likely than most to ascend to positions of leadership in community life. He has a greater need to operate effectively as a group member and occasionally

---

* Harcourt, Brace & World, Inc., 1962.

as a group leader. While a social conscience is desirable for all students, for potential leaders it is essential if our society is to maintain itself and move forward. Finally, the bright student can utilize more fully in citizenship activities the learnings in social sciences which are the subject matter of the social studies.

While citizenship is a primary aim for all students, scholarship in the social sciences per se has special meaning for the intellectually gifted. A firm grounding in these disciplines should be established in elementary and secondary schools, so that the student who has an aptitude for the social sciences may move early into a mature specialization in college. Interested students in high school should learn of career opportunities and national needs for historians, political scientists, sociologists, economists, anthropologists, geographers, and psychologists. The common school program gives its primary emphasis to social studies as general education; for the gifted, preparation for specialization must also be considered.

Chapter 11

Science and Mathematics for the Gifted

> *We are on the threshold of utter disaster or unprecedentedly glorious achievement. No previous age has been fraught with problems so momentous; and it is to science that we must look for a happy issue.*

—Bertrand Russell

The era of atomic energy, rockets, and space satellites has made the nation acutely aware of science. The ubiquitous competition with Soviet Russia has accentuated pressures on schools to upgrade their programs in science, particularly where students with scientific ability are concerned. As a matter of fact, practically all new proposals in science and mathematics in recent years have centered about curricula suitable mainly for the highly gifted. In one respect these demands have been healthy: they have placed in sharp focus the need for curriculum reorganization in science, a notably weak field prior to 1950 in elementary schools, and in mathematics, a field in which teaching at the secondary level had not changed materially for two centuries. These same demands, however, have not been quite so wholesome when they have tended to impair a balanced educational diet. Nor can these pressures be viewed with equanimity when they impose the same program on all students nor when they "guide" into shortage areas all students of moderate ability whether they have superior interest and competence in other areas or not.*

---

* From the point of view of the gifted, uniform requirements are always invidious because they invite dilution of the required program in order to make it even moderately viable as fare for every student.

IDENTIFICATION OF SCIENCE APTITUDE

Considerable research has been done in the identification of scientific aptitudes in young children. Lesser (1962) summarizes efforts to define talent in science, noting differences among investigators as to (1) the existence of scientific aptitude as a definable entity, and (2) the components of this aptitude if it may be defined. Some investigators are convinced that science talent is not a single trait but that it is an "aspect of high general intelligence which emerges through environmental stimulation and available opportunities for development." Others believe such a trait exists but disagree as to its components which include some of the following: "sensitivity to problems, ability to develop novel ideas, and the ability to evaluate" (Guilford, 1950); "specialized and persistent curiosity, alertness in detecting inconsistencies, and a high degree of mechanical-mindedness" (Subarsky, 1948); "industry, devotion to work, energy and initiative" (Cole, 1956); and "spatial visualization, manipulative ability, ability to plan and design a study, and ability to communicate" (Super and Bachrach, 1957).

Biographical approaches have also been used in efforts to identify elements in scientific achievement. Roe (1953) studied elements in family background and individual development of eminent scientists. Knapp and Goodrich (1952) checked on educational backgrounds of individuals listed in *American Men of Science* and discovered unexpected proportions of scientists coming from particular undergraduate institutions. One may infer from these data that individual abilities tell only part of the story, that stimulation in particular educational programs is of great significance. Brandwein (1955), studying high school students, established three categories which suggest bases for identification. These include, first, "genetic factors"—high level verbal and mathematical ability, and adequate sensory and neuro-muscular control. Second are "predisposing factors"—persistence, willingness to work on a task overtime, to withstand discomfort, and to face failure; and "questing," a search for new ideas that comes from marked dissatisfaction with present explanations of how the world works. Third are "activating factors"—opportunities for further training and the accessibility of an inspiring teacher. The first factors are constitutional—cognitive and physical abilities that are "natural," rather than acquired. The second factors are conative—emotional, motivational. The third factor is environmental—the contribution of the culture to the ability and the willingness of the individual. By providing students with opportunities to work independently at Forest Hills High School (New York) in science activities, Brandwein and his colleagues set in motion a mechanism for self-identification which is regarded as one of the more effective types of selection. These opportunities include working in laboratories in free periods during school hours or before and after school, preparing instructional materials for teachers, assisting the science teacher, helping maintain a science museum and vivarium, joining in such co-curricular activities as science clubs, and preparing a science journal.

Early identification of students with aptitude in science is commonly advocated. Since interest and self-direction seem to be important elements in science achievement, University School at Ohio State University made a study through student autobiographies of factors in the development of science interests. The study identified the following as important factors:

1. Attitude of teachers and parents toward the child's questions
2. The influence of family and friends
3. The value of mass media of communication, trips to museums, hobbies and games, books, chemistry sets and other materials, particularly as provided for in the home
4. The child's own curiosity, desire to create, ambition and determination
5. The role of organizations and special events
6. The content and structure of the science program or individual courses in science
7. Methods and activities employed in the science program or in individual courses
8. The role of the laboratory and its equipment for use in experimentation and the development of special projects, both in and out of school
9. The place of outdoor education
10. The role of mathematics
11. The concern shown for the high ability student
12. The effectiveness of the teacher (Schmieder, 1959, pp. 9-23).*

Definition of the adjective "early" in early identification apparently relates to the level at which the writer operates. At the Hunter College Elementary School, Davis and Lesser report on one project predicting science ability at the five-year level (F. Davis, 1959) and on another testing for ability at the seven-to-eight-year level (Lesser, 1962). In the year following testing, the tests appear to have had predictive validity. The research was not extended far enough in time to evaluate prediction

* From *Fostering and Developing Science Talent*, by Fred J. Schmieder. Columbus, Ohio, Center for School Experimentation, The Ohio State University, 1959. Reprinted with permission of Fred J. Schmieder.

over a longer period. Brandwein (1955) and Bloom (1955), working in the senior high school, speak of "early" identification at the ninth and tenth grade level (ages thirteen to fifteen). There is no necessary conflict between identification at one age or another. It is noteworthy that Bloom and Brandwein place heavy emphasis on interest and self-selection. These elements no doubt reflect the same aptitude and environmental factors that produce high scores in the tests administered at earlier ages.

OBJECTIVES IN SCIENCE FOR THE GIFTED

Objectives emphasized in science are found in the areas of information, attitude, skills, and application. Certainly an important goal in education of the gifted is understanding the world we live in from a scientific point of view. Small bits of information are learned and interpreted in the light of concepts, generalizations and principles. The bright child may be expected to accumulate a larger store of information but also to have greater facility in handling the abstractions to which this information contributes and by which the details are explained. Learning scientific attitudes and methods contributes a major outcome both for the future scientist and the future layman. While teaching critical thinking with verbal materials is basic in social studies and language arts, in science critical thinking takes concrete form where experimentation and more direct cause-to-effect relationships can be seen. DeHurd suggests ten skills that should accrue:

1. Reading and interpreting science writings
2. Locating authoritative sources of science information
3. Performing suitable experiments for testing ideas
4. Using the tools and techniques of science
5. Recognizing the pertinency and adequacy of data
6. Making valid inferences and predictions from data
7. Recognizing and evaluating assumptions underlying techniques and processes used in solving problems
8. Expressing ideas qualitatively and quantitatively
9. Using the knowledge of science for responsible social action
10. Seeking new relationships and ideas from known facts and concepts. (NSSE, 1960, p. 37)

Throughout, emphasis should be on concept formation rather than accumulation of information per se, and on discovery as a primary

---

* From *Rethinking Science Education*, Fifty-ninth Yearbook, Part I, of the National Society for the Study of Education (Chicago, The University of Chicago Press). Copyright 1960 by Herman G. Richey. Reprinted with permission of Herman G. Richey.

method of learning. Schwab (1962) expresses this point of view eloquently in "The Teaching of Science as Enquiry," stressing the tentative
nature of scientific knowledge and the dangers of presenting information in science as permanently established and unassailable.

MOTIVATING INTEREST IN SCIENCE

An important problem in a society that is more entranced by technological wonders than by the science which makes them possible is motivating interest in science careers. Based on its biographical study of
young people with an interest in science, the Ohio State University
School committee listed the following implications for school personnel:

1. Students must be permitted and have sufficient opportunity to
   ask questions; parents should be encouraged to adopt a healthy
   attitude toward their children's questions.
2. The teacher needs to know his students' home background and
   its impact.
3. Field trips, mass media, publications should enrich the program.
4. The school program should aim at promoting and developing
   the student's curiosity, desire to create, and determination to
   succeed; early experiences are essential.
5. The science program should provide an outlet for the student's
   desire to be creative, utilizing in-school and out-of-school organizations and events.
6. Methods and activities should provide for actual experiences in
   problem solving, independent discovery, drawing conclusions,
   using the library and other resources.
7. Participation should be encouraged in outdoor activities, such as
   camping and hiking.
8. The science and mathematics programs should work together
   to assure developing interest in both fields.
9. The high-ability student should feel either through method
   within a course or through program organization that he is moving along and accomplishing worth-while things.
10. The teacher is a key person in fostering and developing interest
    and talent and should be carefully chosen for teaching assign-
    ments (adapted from Schmieder, 1959, pp. 34-35)

An important element in experimental programs at elementary and
secondary levels is the effort to stimulate interest in science as a field of
study. Bloom, Brandwein, and others stress opportunities for first-hand
experience, for actual handling of the materials of science and for student exposure to experiments that are truly open-ended. The essence
of science is not in following a laboratory manual, cookbook style, but
in reaching for what is still—to the student—unknown. The efforts by

Roe and others to categorize the backgrounds of working scientists is an effort to seek out environmental factors which motivate commitment to scientific work.

ELEMENTARY SCHOOL SCIENCE PROGRAMS

Rapid strides are being made in improvement of science education at the elementary level. School districts with the necessary resources recognize the inadequate preparation in the past of most teachers for the teaching of science. Accordingly, summer workshops and in-service courses in science during the school year have been offered in many places and have been generally well attended. Colleges of education, moreover, have been stepping up their science requirements for elementary school teachers and providing instruction in methods of teaching science. Under the auspices of the National Science Foundation, special summer workshops have enrolled elementary as well as secondary science teachers in the study of new subject matter and teaching techniques.

In one sense, then, elementary science education may be said to be improving. General betterment brings with it improved offerings for the gifted. In another sense, a basic problem in elementary school science remains unsolved. It is idle not to recognize the feeling of inadequacy that many elementary teachers continue to feel in this area. Actually the problem is dual in nature, involving both limited background in science and inadequate preparation in science education. Not having studied the problems of science teaching, such a teacher is likely to confuse science information with science education. Science in his hands becomes simply another set of facts to be absorbed. All students, gifted or not, depend upon much improved programs of science preparation for teachers.

A good science program at the elementary level takes steps toward achieving the various objectives of a science program anywhere. Nowhere do children exhibit more curiosity than in the elementary school. Helping children to find answers to their many questions of how things work and why they work as they do is the beginning of an organized view of the scientist's universe. Guiding them in small experiments aims not only at discovery of a solution but also at appreciation of experimental method and critical thinking. A basic purpose running throughout the teaching of science should be the stimulation of interest in science as a subject and as a method. Obviously the most effective teacher is one who is himself interested and who is himself well equipped to guide scientific inquiry.*

---

* The reader is referred to Suchman's work on inquiry training which is discussed briefly in Chapter 8.

Blough and Blackwood in publications of the U.S. Office of Education suggest numerous experiences of value at the elementary level, and they list easily available, inexpensive material that may be used in experimentation. Other suggestions are to be found in publications of the National Science Teachers Association. If the gifted child is to see more in science than just another variety of book-learning, facilities for scientific exploration are essential. Movable science tables are available which are equipped with their own water and gas supply and with electrical outlets that may be connected to a wall socket. Flat surfaces such as long tables and wide window ledges are needed to set up projects. Finally, space has to be provided for storage of the students' uncompleted projects as well as for the teachers' supplies.

In addition to regular classroom work in science, the student with a special interest in science has opportunities to participate in science fairs that have sprung up in the wake of the Science Talent Search. Here again, required participation by every child in the class waters down rather than enriches the program. Everyone is urged (or directed) to bring in a project, and the teacher has little time, accordingly, to work with a handful of students instead. If the teacher were to concentrate upon the few children truly interested, he might draw them out, discover their special areas of enthusiasm, and suggest to them ideas for projects which they might then push farther. In the absence of such guidance, children too often depend upon parents for the idea and for its execution, too.

In viewing elementary science patterns, the committee preparing the National Society for the Study of Education 1960 Yearbook on science defined behavioral objectives related to (a) knowledge and understanding, (b) skill and competence, (c) attitude and interest, and (d) action patterns. The committee explained:

> With respect to *knowledge and understanding*, a primary-grade child is able to generalize in simple terms about seasonal changes; their effect upon the way people eat, dress, and live, and their effect upon plant and animal life. An intermediate-grade child has knowledge of electrical phenomena and understands the uses of common appliances. An upper-grade child should have an understanding of the universality of change and some of its causes.

> Regarding *skill and competence*, a primary child should be careful in crossing streets, should play safely, and should know how to deal with fire. In the intermediate period, a child is able to use simple scientific apparatus. . . . In the upper grades a child knows how to repair a variety of appliances and simple machines. . . .

> As to *attitudes and interests*, a primary-child should exhibit inquisitiveness with regard to all aspects of his environment. In the intermediate

grades, children should be interested in learning the simple scientific principles of sound, light, heat, electricity and magnetism.

Finally, in the *action pattern* of a primary child, there should be evidence that he asks sensible questions as he seeks to satisfy his curiosity . . . The intermediate-grade child goes to reliable sources of information and collects data. He helps keep home and school premises clean, sanitary, and orderly. In the upper grades, for example, a child uses scientific information in a broad range of activities about the home relating to appliances, equipment, gardens, furnace, ventilation, and conservation (NSSE, 1960, pp. 115-17).°

Starting from these premises for all children, the committee expresses an expectation that gifted children will learn more science quantitatively, but that qualitatively purposes remain the same. Emphasis on individual differences, however, will capitalize on "rare opportunities to challenge children of varying intellectual abilities and interests. *If there is one unique purpose* in teaching bright children, it is to keep their interest in science alive so that many of them will choose to pursue careers in science, mathematics, and engineering" (Italics added; *Ibid.*, p. 117).

Basically, elementary science helps the child to find answers to his questions about the environment. But science *asks* questions as well. Children of ability should be encouraged to ask *why* a given answer is correct so that they may build an understanding of basic concepts and principles. Generalization, conceptualization, and abstraction are a peculiar forte of the intellectually gifted child. To allow learning to fall short of this stage is to neglect the culminating step in the bright child's learning. Obviously, however, principles and generalization represent a last step, not a first step, even in the exploration, discovery, and concept-formation of the gifted.

Mechanisms in this process are the science curriculum of the elementary school, the science corner in the classroom which invites reading and experimentation in science, clubs that form through interest in space, electricity, or plant-life, participation in science fairs, building science museums, and laboratory work within and outside the curriculum. To staff such programs, a few schools provide a special science teacher or borrow him from the secondary schools. In the Hunter College Elementary School a special science teacher meets every child from age six up in a specially equipped laboratory once or twice a week. Classes are divided so that the teacher is able to conduct a genuine laboratory program with

---

° From *Rethinking Science Education*, Fifty-ninth Yearbook, Part I, of the National Society for the Study of Education (Chicago, University of Chicago Press). Copyright 1960 by Herman G. Richey. Reprinted with permission of Herman G. Richey.

a group of twelve to fifteen students. A major problem is the limited time each student has for science in this kind of organization.

Some schools find able science teachers on their regular staff and free these persons at stated times to work with children showing special interest in science. Some school systems provide science consultants who serve individual schools either as experts working with the teachers or as itinerant special teachers working directly with groups of children. It is indeed short-sighted, however, not to recognize the inadequacy of the average teacher's preparation for an active program in science marked by genuine student exploration and discovery. And such an active program should certainly take precedence over a book-oriented program which simply stresses mastery of science information.

The availability of leadership personnel often dictates the organization of science opportunities. If a special teacher is available, a project room can be maintained full time in the elementary school. Children can be scheduled to work in such a room as part of their regular program. They can also visit the room to work on individual projects as their class program may permit. If no one teacher can give a major portion of his time to science instruction, a club period once or twice a week may make it possible for the teachers especially interested in science to guide boys and girls who choose to join the radio, electricity, astronomy, or greenhouse club. If an outside consultant visits a few times during the week, children with special interest may be excused from their regular class activities to work with the consultant. If the consultant works with teachers only, provisions for individual scientific activity should be made in the framework of the class daily program. Any of these alternatives can be effective if sparked with the enthusiasm and competence of personnel assigned to it.

JUNIOR HIGH SCHOOL SCIENCE

At the junior high school level, the student is ready for an organized approach to science. Recent recommendations (New York City, 1960) urge a two-year general science program in grades 7 and 8 and the beginning of a specialized science course—earth science or biology—in the ninth grade. A committee in New York City, seeking to replace a two-year accelerated program with a three-year enriched program in the junior high school recommended such an organization but placed equivalent stress on method. The committee urges the "open ended" approach to laboratory work, describing it in these words: "It will involve having pupils themselves recognize the problems needing to be solved, delimiting the problems into smaller problems, and then their suggesting laboratory procedures for seeking answers to these problems" (*Ibid.*, Science Section, p. 3). They recommend not only school activities but small experiments at home, field trips, and reading of accounts of original research that are of appropriate simplicity. Such accounts are to be found in the Alembic Club reprints (Edinburgh, E. and S. Livingston, Ltd.). A good example of methodology in a problem-solving experiment in junior high school is provided in the report (*Ibid.*, pp. 11-14).

The conventional club program in junior high school provides administrative opportunity for special interest activities that are science-related. Hobbies such as radio and photography are obvious centers for club organization. If the school has (or can acquire) such facilities as greenhouses, gardens, or observatories, these facilities can attract groups of pupils into clubs. In addition, all such activities can be incorporated into a single club, if personnel and equipment make it possible for students to work simultaneously on a variety of interests. The club, however, should make project and experiment activity possible; it should not be limited to discussion of experiences outside the club or to an academic study of science information. The basic purpose remains that of building firmer interest in science activity and study.

The strengthening of programs in elementary science is leading to speculation as to its eventual effect on the junior high school program. It is conceivable that practically all the general science customarily taught in junior high school will be covered in the elementary school. Many science educators question moving high school type courses in biology, physics, chemistry, geology, or astronomy to grades seven and eight. It is apparent that continuing examination of the junior high school science curriculum will be needed. The effort to provide a program that relates scientific information and scientific method to the child's life and environment will probably be continued. Greater emphasis on problem solving by the students themselves is suggested as one way of upgrading the program while retaining the same general approach. A second would involve more advanced probing into the applications of science. A third would put more stress, for bright children at least, upon theoretical elements that come closer to the systematic approach of conventional high school science.

SCIENCE IN SENIOR HIGH SCHOOL

At the senior high school level, experimentation with course offerings is bearing fruit in biology and the physical sciences. The professional associations in these fields in the late 1950's gave new attention to revisions that would bring science offerings up to date, and simultaneously provide more challenge and interest to the gifted. These programs are still experimental. They are marked by greater emphasis upon laboratory procedures that approximate more closely the work of the scientist in research where he is genuinely seeking an unknown result. Far more equipment and more extensive storage space are needed for student activity and student projects than has been planned even in the newer high school buildings. An earlier trend to replace student experimentation with teacher demonstration or motion pictures has apparently been forgotten. Emphasis is not upon *coverage* but upon depth of experience, appreciation of scientific method, and stimulation of interest in scientific activity.

Curricular offerings are marked in some places by differentiating science experiences according to the interests and abilities of learners. Chemistry, for example, is offered on several levels—an applied, layman's chemistry which is not intended for college preparatory students; a descriptive, somewhat theoretical chemistry which is meant for the college bound student who displays no special interest in science; and a rigorous quantitative, theoretical chemistry which will be directly preparatory for chemistry specialization in college. Similar adjustments are made in some schools in biology and physics. Where possible, special project classes are offered to students so that they may work with some independence in small numbers under the guidance of a teacher competent to direct research activities.

Sad experience with the conventional, unimaginative, science programs of the past argues for a high degree of ability grouping in the future. Before a full commitment is made to ability grouping, it is necessary to explore more attractive and meaningful programs with a broad spread of ability. The lifeless courses that imitated college types have, over the years, repelled high school students. Because a year or more of organized "laboratory science" was required, many schools watered down their science program in an effort to help students "pass" courses which were not inherently meaningful. A better solution might have been to upgrade courses by individualizing the approach within each class. In addition content might have been modernized. The objectives of science education as indicated earlier ought to have stimulated development of courses no longer imitative of higher level programs.

Few efforts of this kind have been made. Some exploration, however, has been attempted in diversifying courses, using ability grouping as a basic principle. Distinctions have been made in some cases between science-for-the-citizen and science-for-the-scientist offerings. Such an approach has the merit of providing a sufficiently challenging program for the more able who are already identified. For those not identified, however, the school may find itself providing a less stimulating course that prevents later self-discovery by the student or identification by the school.

A number of patterns are to be found. Pupils showing little aptitude in science take general science through the ninth grade, followed by a one-year elective in what purports to be a "laboratory" course in biology, physics, or chemistry. The less able students, if grouped together, are likely to have more demonstration and less experimentation. "Laboratory" exercises often turn out to be cook-book type practices where the student is required to produce the results called for by the "recipe" in his workbook. A few schools have substituted advanced general science for physical science requirements. Some have instituted courses of some interest in the applied physics or applied chemistry area.

Providing for the non-science student in this way, schools have felt free to provide more rigorous courses for the more able. A common approach is to omit ninth grade general science and to plunge directly into an organized program of biology or earth science. In a sense this procedure represents acceleration. In addition, the selected grouping apparently makes more feasible a course that is more quantitative and theoretical. More laboratory work is also offered. Some schools are working with "open ended" experiments rather than the cook-book type. In addition to the usual kind of college preparatory science courses, honors courses are offered in the larger schools to students of exceptional ability and interest. These courses may simply delve more deeply into college level work, but frequently they provide opportunity for individual exploration, project work, library research and the "open-ended" approach. Brandwein (1955) describes features of such an "operational approach for science-oriented students": honors courses in biology, physics, and chemistry, advanced science offerings, career guidance and extracurricular activities in science. Activities include "original" research, laboratory techniques, operation of laboratory equipment, skills in shopwork, library research, mathematics, exhibits, reports of students' own work, seminar sessions, participation in the Science Talent Search and Advanced Placement work.

Club programs provide additional chances for students to share burgeoning interests in science. Programs normally include opportunities to pursue individual projects, presentations by experts on the faculty and from outside the school, participation in competitions such as science fairs, and reports on research in special areas of interest.

At the senior high school level the growing competence and accumulated knowledge of the exceptional student in science make possible a number of first-hand experiences in science. Some schools stimulate such students' participation in science by permitting them to serve as laboratory assistants in unassigned periods. Some school science rooms are enriched with models, diagrams, and collections that superior students have made. In some cases students have marked nature trails in the wooded sections of the school grounds, of adjacent city parks, or of nearby hillsides in rural and mountain areas. School camps provide unusual opportunities for junior naturalists, foresters, zoologists, botanists, and geologists. All of these activities may be regarded as informal kinds of work experience. A more advanced kind of work experience is found in actual placement of students, during or after school or on Saturdays, with clinics and industrial research departments, in the offices of physicians and health departments, and in science laboratories in the community.

Visits to science facilities in the community—university, governmental, or industrial—are used to stimulate interest and develop some basis for understanding. Bringing science resource personnel into the classroom can provide both stimulation and new learning.

Statements made by New York City high school science chairmen in 1935 continue to hold true: "Growth in physical science is chiefly made through contact with science apparatus and inspiring, sympathetic teachers." ". . . pupils in physical science need, more than all else, first-hand experience with science materials and scientific literature . . . opportunity to do individual work in verification, problem solving, and research work within their abilities" (Cohen, 1935, pp. 268, 277).

CURRICULUM PROPOSALS BY PROFESSIONAL GROUPS

The resurgence of interest in high school science in the 1950's, stemming from international crises in the emerging "space age," found expression in fundamental reconsideration of course content by science and teacher groups. Professional associations in physics, chemistry, and biology as well as the National Science Teachers Association brought together scholars and teachers to update curricula, to refresh teacher backgrounds in science, and to develop material both for students and for teacher training. These programs are of particular concern in educating the gifted since their primary emphasis is on college-preparatory science and on the higher ability within this selected group.

The group that got its study off the ground first was the Physical Sciences Study Committee, starting in November 1956 with a grant from the National Science Foundation to Massachusetts Institute of

Technology.* The Committee related its work to that of a committee of the American Institute of Physics, the American Association of Physics Teachers and the National Science Teachers Association. In the course of its activities, the Physical Sciences Study Committee prepared a series of new texts and motion pictures for use by high school students, a syllabus and monographs for teachers, and a number of annual institutes (supported by the National Science Foundation) for physics teachers. Twelve such institutes for familiarizing teachers with new developments were operated, for example, in the summer of 1960. A result of this concerted activity was that six hundred high schools were already using PSSC materials in 1960-61.

The National Science Teachers Association has made available a considerable quantity of publications to assist teachers in enriching their program. These include material at both the elementary and secondary level such as science project pamphlets, bibliographies, lists of free and inexpensive materials, and clearinghouse pamphlets on teaching suggestions. The last include *New Developments in High School Science Teaching* (1960) and the annual STAR (Science Teaching Achievement Recognition) abstracts which report selected successful teaching techniques each year. Teachers of the gifted who are seeking ways to enrich science programs may look for considerable assistance to their professional associations.

Parallel developments have taken place in biology and chemistry. Supported again by the National Science Foundation, the American Institute of Biological Sciences organized the Biological Sciences Curriculum Study in 1958 and by 1960 had developed textbooks for trial use in secondary schools attempting three different organizations of biological material. The American Chemistry Society has produced a chemistry course on 16 mm. film which should have value in those schools not able to secure adequate chemistry personnel, and in other schools as a stimulating supplement to competent teachers. Two new curricula are available in Chemistry—the Chemical Bond Approach and the Chemical Education Materials Study. Commercial publishers have produced texts for all these new programs.

ADVANCED PLACEMENT SCIENCE COURSES

In Science as in other areas, considerable experimentation has been done with Advanced Placement Courses. The Advanced Placement

---

* Excellent reports of developments in curricula in the Sciences and Mathematics sponsored by the National Science Foundation are to be found in the Spring 1962 issue of *School Review*.

Bulletin carries the following remarks concerning work in Biology and Chemistry:

> An advanced course in biology may be either a single intensive course or a second course presupposing an earlier beginning course. In any case, it should provide a more mature presentation of content and more extensive laboratory experience than is usual. . . .

> The following important considerations should shape the presentation of an advanced course in biology. The fact that fundamental principles apply to both plants and animals should be emphasized. The overall approach should be dynamic, making constant reference to functional morphology. Evolution should be a fundamental theme or framework of the course, and the interdependence of organism and environment should receive constant attention with stress on animal adaptations and behavior. Living materials, and field work if feasible, should be an integral part of the laboratory work (CEEB, 1958, p. 25).*

> The advanced chemistry course should be planned to meet the objectives of a general chemistry course on the college level . . . Beginning general chemistry (in college) is conceived as an introduction to chemistry. It concerns itself with the fundamental assumptions and the *logical structure* of chemistry.

> The students should attain such a competence in *dealing with simple chemical problems* that they will feel a *justifiable self-confidence* within these fields.

> The emphasis is on chemistry as an intellectual subject and on the rigorous training in fundamentals needed in preparation for future work in it or in related fields.

> The advanced work in chemistry should not displace any other part of the basic curriculum for any student. . . . Some secondary schools have successfully given the advanced level chemistry as the first course, allowing 10 to 12 periods of chemistry per week. (*Ibid.*, p. 37)

In physics, the Advanced Placement Program distinguishes among three different types of physics courses at the college level—a descriptive physics course which is aimed at the student who will probably take no additional courses in the area; a second course, more quantitative and more rigorous, depending upon algebraic and trigonometric handling of

---

* From *Advanced Placement Syllabus*, College Entrance Examination Board, Princeton, New Jersey. Copyright 1958. Reprinted with permission of College Entrance Examination Board.

principles in physics and a third type which is still more rigorous and depends upon the methods of calculus in formulating physical principles and applying them to physical problems. Advanced Placement work is suggested to offer the second type of program at the high school level. But students who may specialize in physics or engineering are advised not to take Advanced Placement work in physics, but rather to "place primary effort upon preparing themselves for the Advanced Placement Examination in Mathematics (which includes calculus)" (*Ibid.*, pp. 117-19). Since Advanced Placement courses are intended precisely for the kind of student who would need the third type of course, secondary school teachers and administrators might do well to capitalize on the candor of the Advanced Placement Bulletin and look to other fields for accelerated college work.

OTHER PROVISIONS FOR THE GIFTED IN SCIENCE

Various alternatives to the Advanced Placement Program are found in secondary school offerings. In addition to the four-year sequence for grades 9 to 12, some schools offer electives so that interested students may take two science courses in their third or fourth year or both. Electives suggested by the National Science Teachers Association committee working on the NEA Academically Talented Student Project include microbiology, field biology, advanced general chemistry, atomic physics, electronics and electricity, geophysics, a fourth year of mathematics, history of science, astronomy, earth science, and geochemistry. Of a different type are suggested science seminars or science research courses which permit variation from the typical course pattern and perhaps greater personal involvement of the student in scientific endeavor (NEA, 1959b, pp. 13-14, 53).

The committee of the National Science Teachers Association participating in the NEA Academically Talented Student Project declares that there is no one best curriculum, no one best way to organize subject matter. Instead the committee suggests "nine fundamental guidelines for the selection and organization of subject matter." These guidelines follow:

> The content should be developed in the light of contemporary scientific thinking and theorizing. As often as possible, pupils should glimpse the frontiers of scientific investigation. They should come to understand that neither our knowledge nor our understanding is static. . . .
>
> Content areas should be developed in depth. To this end, a few well-chosen areas should be studied, and the emphasis should be on

better quality of teaching and learning rather than on covering a great diversity of subject matter. . . .

The over-all science program for the talented should be planned carefully to assure continuity of the program from the elementary school through college. . . . Such articulation should avoid the needless repetition of subject matter. . . .

Science content should be developed in such a way that pupils have many opportunities to work with science materials, equipment, and apparatus. . . . The choice and development of content areas should be planned to reveal the relationships among the sciences. . . .

The science program should be planned for the early and increasing application of mathematics to the precise formulation of scientific relationships and to the application of scientific laws and principles. . . .

The teaching of science should be concentrated increasingly on the development of the concepts, principles, broad generalizations, and great issues of science rather than on the accumulation of unrelated facts. . . .

Full advantage should be taken of the science resources of the community for enriching and supplementing the science program for talented students. . . .

Science should be taught in such a way as to reveal the influence of science in such other areas of culture as politics, economics, world outlook, standard of living, and the influence of these areas in the development of science. Recognition of the social responsibility of science should be developed. (*Ibid.*, pp. 14-25) *

The bulletin setting forth these guidelines illustrates from topics in junior and senior high school science how these suggestions may be carried out in practice.

RESOURCES FOR SCIENCE PROGRAMS

Bricks, of course, are not made without straw. The teacher needs the material and the time to do a stimulating job. In addition to the usual science materials, if students are doing individual projects, the teacher needs a budget and a petty cash fund for ready purchase of necessary items. He needs work space and storage space for students. If these can

---

* From *Science for the Academically Talented Student in the Secondary School,* by the National Education Association Project on the Academically Talented Student and the National Science Teachers Association. Copyright 1959 by the National Education Association. Reprinted with permission of the National Education Association.

be provided apart from the regular laboratory, individual projects and independent work will not conflict with the normal school routines. Some of the tools typically found in a wood shop or machine shop are also needed for construction in science research projects.

At the elementary school level, Martin and others recommend adequate space for children to work, read, experiment, set up, and leave occasional long-term projects or exhibits. They call for a work counter with storage cabinets beneath it, electric outlets, running water, bulletin boards, and a display case. Some source of heat is also needed.

At the secondary level, Martin suggests locating science rooms in close proximity for sharing of common teaching materials. Movable furniture and placement of utilities along the sides of the room provide desirable flexibility. Space is needed for storage as well as activity. Project areas should be equipped with proper tools and supplies for construction and repair of science apparatus. Facilities should include areas for reading of printed material. Auxiliary rooms should include storage-preparation areas, a darkroom and office for the science teacher (NSSE, 1960, pp. 235-38).

Not all science work is done in a laboratory. In the upper grades there may be increasing employment of library resources. Science reference materials and books dealing with the history of science have an important place either in the school library or in a special collection housed in the science rooms. Books like those in the Traveling High School Library of the American Association for the Advancement of Science, the Alembic Club reprints, and scientific periodicals should be included.

If the science teacher is to carry a normal number of classes, he needs assistance in the laboratory, both for preparation of his regular classes and for the supervision of students doing independent work. The previously noted committee of the Science Teachers Association suggests that "competent, paid laboratory assistance may be drawn from the ranks of qualified members of the community, such as retired personnel, housewives, and college students, or from among qualified high-school students" (NEA, 1959b, p. 47). Even with such assistance, the teacher who would like to guide individual experimentation cannot give the necessary help when his class exceeds the recommended limit of fifteen to twenty students.

NON-SCHOOL PROGRAMS

One source of assistance comes not inside but outside school hours and the normal school framework. Concern on the part of governmental, scientific, and industrial leadership has led to development of programs after school, on weekends and during the summer which provide science experiences both for students and teachers. Several universities extend such informal assistance—speakers, seminars, organized courses, summer programs, and after-school laboratory experiences—to neighboring school systems or to individual high school students. The largest summer program for high school students is sponsored by the National Science Foundation which supported intensive experiences in science and mathematics for approximately 7,500 high school students on college campuses throughout the United States in 1964. Additional programs of a similar type are sponsored on Saturdays during the academic year. The Joe Berg Foundation* has mobilized industrial scientists in a number of communities to provide in-school or out-of-school leadership for young people of scientific bent. Science institutes are offered to teachers by the Federal Government to update their training; at Oak Ridge a program is geared to the teacher who wants special background in nuclear physics. Some industrial firms provide work experience in summers for science teachers as well as for students. In larger communities the teacher can often find such assistance already organized. In smaller communities the teacher may be able to mobilize unused resources, or he may find ways of joining with teachers from other schools to organize regional seminars during school days or on weekends for students in sparsely settled areas. Such a program in rural New York State, for example, has been able to provide an unusual Saturday morning experience in science and mathematics for students in all of one county, drawing upon qualified leadership personnel who are willing to undertake the necessary travel on the weekend.

Mathematics

The mathematics program in education of the gifted has suffered from two factors in the educational scene. One has been the static nature of secondary school mathematics in the United States for approximately two centuries and an unimaginative approach to arithmetic in the elementary school that was confined to routine drill on computation. The second has been a greater loss for bright students in mathematics than in other areas as a result of broadening the population base in schools without individualizing instruction. Both of these factors, fortunately, are now the subject of intensive treatment.

ELEMENTARY PROGRAMS

Elementary mathematics in the past quarter-century has benefited from the "meaningful" mathematics approach. Emphasis placed on un-

---

* 1712 South Michigan Avenue, Chicago 16, Ill.

derstanding of mathematical processes rather than on computation alone has moved elementary programs in the direction most valuable to intellectually gifted children. Their ability to comprehend, apply, and generalize, and their lesser need for drill combine to support a program that places stress on mathematical and social meaning. Some recent programs are "getting out from under" an exclusive stress on social applications. Instead, greater balance and more challenge result from putting primary emphasis on the meaning of the mathematics itself—the number system and the processes employed to utilize number. Certainly, in the case of the gifted child, the school cannot rest satisfied simply with accurate manipulation of numbers; more important for present appreciation and later development is understanding of why and how number systems "work."

Authorities in the field distinguish among four levels of pupil operation: manipulation of objects in quantity; "laboratory" procedures in discovering and understanding arithmetical processes as a result of working with real or representational objects; symbolic learning that bypasses the slower handling of real objects; and the use of short cuts and equivalent operations to arrive at solutions. Obviously all children need some of all four of these approaches to learning, but the gifted child should not be kept busy with idle manipulation when he is ready to move on to more abstract functions. The bright child may be expected to advance at an earlier date to symbolic operation alone, but this "early date" may not arrive much before junior high school.

A word of caution is necessary before plunging too rapidly into advanced studies with the gifted child. It is a truism that not all of a child's intellectual powers develop evenly. Verbal, mathematical, reasoning, spatial and other factors have been identified as distinct functions, and correlations among them are not always high. What, then, if a child has been identified as an intellectually gifted youngster on the basis of the Binet? The test is admittedly heavily weighted toward verbal ability. What happens is what might be predicted. In special school programs where admission depends upon a high Binet score, mathematics is the area where children are most likely not to perform at anticipated levels. High ability in *mathematics*, accordingly, is not always present in the high IQ child. A combination of factors is needed to predict this ability; these include the intelligence quotient, but also reading ability and interest, vocabulary, previous arithemic achievement, and such general characteristics as intellectual curiosity and perseverance.

Education of the mathematically gifted child, then, takes on two facets: education of the mathematically gifted leading possibly to careers in mathematics, and education of the generally gifted to have as much appreciation of mathematics as possible for the intelligent layman. If children are selected for special attention on a general basis, a wide variety of mathematical abilities will be present and a variety of content and method will be necessary.

Emphasis on *useful* mathematics in the years before World War II led to development of curricula that were limited by the uses of mathematics observed in children's or adults' activities. Such a program drew immediate protest from some quarters. Not what uses are currently made, but what uses *might* be made if adults knew more mathematics—this was the criterion that critics suggested. Schools should be concerned with enriching life, not with maintaining an impoverished status quo. Brownell (1941) experimented with first and second graders and came up with an impressive list of useful mathematical topics within the range of six- and seven-year-olds if they were but exposed to a richer mathematical environment.

The gifted child's superiority in abstract operations make the more recent approach in organizing the mathematics curriculum especially relevant. Emphasis is placed on the role of mental discovery by children of the meaning, nature, and structure of the number system; on arithmetic as a language of quantitative thought and action; on the mathematical meanings involved in computation; on mental analysis and computation; on the development of "self-imposed standards of critical thinking and accurate computation" both in and out of school. An important objective is a growing "appreciation for and interest in arithmetic as an indispensable language and functional resource in industry, commerce and the sciences" (Shane, 1958, pp. 229-30). The School Mathematics Study Group, having initiated its program of revision at the secondary level, has more recently turned to elementary programs starting at the fourth grade. Other groups and individuals working at a number of centers are also giving their attention to introducing the language of modern mathematics in the elementary school.

ENRICHMENT

Enrichment in mathematics involves both the introduction of new topics and acceleration through earlier study of topics normally taken at a higher grade level. To some extent introduction of new topics also anticipates work at higher levels and results in acceleration as well. Hollingworth insisted that the bright child could learn the usual elementary school curriculum in one-half the time normally provided, the very bright child in one-quarter the time. The surplus one-half or three-quarters can be used in various ways. One is acceleration. A second is enrichment through increasing the number and complexity of applications or enrichment through introduction of related but different topics.

A third is to be found in the intensification of the learning experience. Some authorities distinguish among three levels of teaching in mathematics—for appreciation, for understanding, and for mastery. Since the mathematically oriented child is capable of the third level, one may well assume that the surplus of available time will go partly toward developing mastery. Such a statement should not be interpreted to justify long periods of involved drills. The child should be able to perform basic operations, to understand their rationale, and to compute without making errors. Beyond this point, further drill brings diminishing returns. Gradually, slide rules, tables, logarithms, and mechanical computers should be introduced.

Review of recommended programs of enrichment reflects agreement that topics should come largely from modern mathematics. There is little tendency to increase complexity of problems and intricacy of manipulation in conventional areas. Excellent sources for the teacher are the Twenty-seventh Yearbook of the National Council of Teachers of Mathematics which deals with enrichment in elementary and junior high schools and the Twenty-eighth which treats enrichment in senior high school and the transition to college mathematics.

Enrichment topics in the elementary school should be related to overall goals of the mathematics program. Grossnickle (*in* Fliegler, 1961) recommends the following attainment for the gifted in mathematics by the end of the sixth grade: fundamental principles governing structure of the system of numeration; commutative, associative, and distributive laws; inverse processes, meaning of reciprocals, representation of division as a fraction; identity elements. Flagg lists the following topics as the content of a special program in the fifth and sixth grades (later extended to seventh and eighth as well) for gifted children in the laboratory school of the Illinois State Normal University: "(a) historical topics; algorithms formerly used, development of numerals, other numeration systems; (b) exponents—meaning, use in analyzing place value and in scientific notation; (c) bases other than the ten; analysis of place value, operations; (d) sets and sentences; equalities and inequalities; (e) number systems; natural numbers, integers (positive and negative), rational numbers; laws governing operations; (f) number line representations and graphing; (g) prime numbers and factors; (h) tests for divisibility and why they 'work' " (Flagg, 1962, p. 381). Flagg also indicates that gradual extension of the "new mathematics in elementary schools is beginning to preempt some of these topics for the general program for all students. As a result the Illinois Normal program for gifted children changes as needed to maintain a high level of challenge for the special classes.

At the junior high school level, topics recommended overlap with those of the elementary school because of the need for more sophisticated treatment of these topics and because of a generally fluid situation arising from current introduction of new approaches in mathematics. Some topics suggested include history of numbers, numeration in bases other than ten, prime and composite numbers, inverse operations, statistics and graphs, probability, set theory, rational and irrational numbers, and phases of plane geometry.

New curricular proposals in elementary mathematics include experimental materials which should be helpful to the teacher of gifted children seeking direction. The following programs are of particular interest:

> School Mathematics Study Group project on elementary mathematics; Director: E. C. Begle, Stanford University. Materials published by Stanford University Press.

> University of Illinois Committee on School Mathematics; Director: David A. Page, University of Illinois. Materials published by University of Illinois Press.

> Syracuse University Madison Project; Director: Robert Davis, Syracuse University.

> Geometry for Primary Grades; Director: Newton Hawley, Stanford University.

> Sets and Numbers (Primary Grades) and Experimental Project in Logic (Intermediate Grades); Director: Patrick Suppes, Stanford University.

> Greater Cleveland Mathematics Program; Director: George Baird, Educational Research of Greater Cleveland (75 Public Square, Cleveland 13, Ohio).

Supporting the flourishing activity in curriculum development has been a surge in the printing of materials for students and teachers by professional organizations and commercial publishers. The National Council of Teachers of Mathematics has prepared a number of books and pamphlets, some for teachers, some for students, some for both, which present new topics and curriculum developments. L. W. Singer (*New Mathematical Library*) and Webster (*Exploring Mathematics on Your Own*) have published series of booklets for use by students. Row-Peterson has prepared a group of 16 page pamphlets for pupils in grades 3 to 6. Other publishers are reorienting their textbook series in keeping with new developments. In addition, there is a rapidly growing list of supplementary books for students on the themes of "fun in mathematics," mathematical puzzles, paper folding (topology), codes, numeration, and mathematical history. These materials potentially build understanding and a background of information while contributing a sense of wonder and excitement to students independently pursuing their interest in mathematics.

ACCELERATION

The most commonly observed characteristic of gifted children is their precocity in handling abstractions inherent in mathematics. One may expect, therefore, earlier readiness of many bright children for mathematics at all levels. Since mathematics is probably more sequential in its organization than is any other subject, it would seem likely that more rapid progress through the sequence is appropriate. Enrichment in mathematics at the elementary level necessarily entails acceleration in learning both the processes and social arithmetic of the first eight grades. In many schools and in most textbook series, careful gradation has been planned. It would seem perfectly proper to follow the sequences that have been laid out. It would seem equally improper to subject a child who already has a good knowledge of number meanings and a high level of mental arithmetical ability to the laborious tracing of numbers in the first two grades and the invention of "number stories" to illustrate their meaning. Similarly, a child who is already doing subtraction and addition with three-place numbers at home ought not to be limited to the addition facts with sums to 9 or subtraction facts with minuends to 6 because these standards represent optimum grade placement for the average. While readiness programs in reading and arithmetic are indeed important, the gifted child who enters school with experience in both these areas is likely to be discouraged and disappointed if his appetite to learn new things is ignored.

By and large, the child who is ready for multiplication, division, fractions, ratios, or decimals ought not to be held up simply because a given topic belongs to the next grade. The teacher of bright children, of course, is likely to get in curricular difficulties if he truly seeks to enrich the program in a district where the course of study is extremely rigid. If children with genuine ability in mathematics are to be given the opportunity they need, a more flexible view of curriculum has to be taken. This entails organization of small groups in the heterogeneous class that can move at a faster pace. It also calls for articulation as these children move to the next class so that they need not backtrack or tread water while the rest of the class catches up. Ultimately, the elementary school child will "run out" of elementary school topics, and ways of introducing junior high school math need to be found. The same cross-over will be experienced toward the end of junior and senior high school where normal course offerings will be inadequate. In homogeneous groupings, the same situation arises, but the atypicality of an entire class may simplify necessary adjustments.

Various alternatives are open when the school needs to look to the next school level in order to provide suitable opportunities. Some communities make available the more advanced work in the lower school program, utilizing teachers with special background or borrowing teachers from the next higher level. Some communities say impliedly, "You've learned all we can teach you in this organization. Now we will transfer you to the next level at an earlier age." Some communities keep their bright children with their age group but provide them with a period or two in the building at the next higher level where they study their special interest with older students. Thus, some fifth and sixth graders may be found in the high school one period a day, and some high school students in a nearby college. In no subject is the problem more apparent than in mathematics because of the sequential nature of the discipline. There is a certain point beyond which addition of two-column numbers cannot be "enriched."

THE TEACHER OF MATHEMATICS IN ELEMENTARY SCHOOL

Fundamental changes are taking place in elementary as well as in secondary mathematics. An important problem in instituting more challenging programs will be the preparation of teachers, particularly in elementary school where few teachers have extensive background in this area. Some school systems may be successful in updating the mathematics training of large proportions of their elementary teachers. Others may have to depend upon use of specialized mathematics teachers in elementary schools. Some may have to limp along until they have gradually replaced retiring teachers with new teachers who have themselves studied modern mathematics in high school and college.

Proposals in the 1960's to departmentalize upper grades arose, no doubt, in part from observation of the inadequacy in mathematics of many classroom teachers assigned to teaching all subjects. Before departmentalization is accepted as a solution considerable research data of a substantial nature are needed. A study by Gibbs and Matala (1961) does not support the use of special teachers either in urban or rural situations for science and mathematics in grades 5 and 6. Testing the use of special teachers in different communities, they reported "no difference in insights and understandings gained in science and in mathematics" as class organization and school systems were compared. The particular personnel available in a given school district, rather than a fixed policy on specialization, seems to provide the best guide, until further evidence is at hand, in determing the approach to be used in teaching mathematics to especially apt pupils.

The teacher himself, rather than the type of organization, was found by Gibbs and Matala to be significant in changes of interest on the part of pupils. If children gifted in mathematics are to enjoy opportunities in newer areas, they will need teachers who are qualified to lead them in the study of new material. In-service workshops, graduate courses on university campuses or at extension centers, and reading of the multitude of attractive materials available offer avenues to teachers to update their training. School districts interested in their gifted students should provide resources and facilities to assist in this continuing professional growth.

NEW SECONDARY SCHOOL PROGRAMS

Recommendations made in 1959 by the Commission on Mathematics of the College Entrance Examination Board promise considerable impact on secondary school programs. Following four years of study, the Commission presented the following "nine-point program for college-capable students":

1. Strong preparation, *both* in concepts *and* in skills, for college mathematics at the level of calculus and analytic geometry
2. Understanding of the nature and role of deductive reasoning—in algebra, as well as in geometry
3. Appreciation of mathematical structure ("patterns")—for example, properties of natural, rational, real, and complex numbers
4. Judicious use of unifying ideas—sets, variables, functions, and relations
5. Treatment of inequalities along with equations
6. Incorporation with plane geometry of some coordinate geometry, and essentials of solid geometry and space preception
7. Introduction in grade 11 of fundamental trigonometry—centered on coordinates, vectors, and complex numbers
8. Emphasis in grade 12 on elementary functions (polynomials, exponential, circular)
9. Recommendation of additional alternative units for grade 12: *either* introductory probability with statistical applications, *or* an introduction to modern algebra. (CEEB, 1959, p. iii) [*]

---

[*] From *Program for College Preparatory Mathematics,* by Commission on Mathematics. Copyright 1959 by College Entrance Examination Board. Reprinted with permission of College Entrance Examination Board.

Leaving the construction of new programs in grades 7 and 8 to other committees studying the problem (School Mathematics Study Group with headquarters first at Yale and later at Stanford, the University of Maryland Mathematics Project, the University of Illinois Committee on School Mathematics, and curriculum committees of the National Council of Teachers of Mathematics), the Commission seeks at the end of the ninth grade:

> Skills, concepts and factual knowledge covering:
>   The number system and the decimal representation of numbers
>   The elementary operations with integers, decimal fractions, and
>   simple fractions
>   The vocabulary and ideas of elementary intuitive geometry
>   The use of algebraic symbolism in formulas and simple equations
>   The beginnings of graphical representation of data, of formulas,
>   and of simple equations. (CEEB, 1958, p. 107)

The Commission suggests a framework built on the established foundation:

> Grade 9: "Increased attention to algebra . . . with an equally earnest recommendation that the point of view from which the material is presented be that of contemporary mathematics." "Introduction of instruction in deductive reasoning"

> Grade 10: Geometry, with three-fold objectives: "acquisition of information about geometric figures in the plane and in space"; "understanding of the deductive method as a way of thinking"; "opportunities for original and creative thinking by students." To accomplish this, a reduction in the number of theorems studied; introduction of coordinate geometry; treatment of certain material in solid geometry "along with analogous content of plane geometry"

> Grade 11: Material from advanced algebra and trigonometry: Continued work on basic concepts and skills; linear functions: radicals; quadratic function; quadratic equations; systems of equations; exponents and logarithms; series; number fields; plane vectors; coordinate trigonometry and vectors; trigonometric formulas

> Grade 12: Three possible programs:
>   "(1) Elementary Functions, first semester; Introductory Probability with Statistical Applications, second semester.
>   (2) Elementary Functions, first semester; Introduction to Modern Algebra, second semester.

(3) Elementary Functions and Selected Topics: Elementary functions enlarged to a full year by additional topics."
(CEEB, 1959, pp. 18-46) *

Within these general outlines modifications may be made that introduce modern mathematics recommendations coming from various groups studying the problem. Suggestions in some detail are also to be found in the bulletin on mathematics of the Project on the Academically Talented Student (NEA, 1959a, pp. 22-32).

While considerable pressure has been generated to increase greatly the number of students enrolled in advanced mathematics courses, Conant suggests the need for restraint. A high level of intellectual ability is needed for advanced study in mathematics. If more than 15 per cent of the students are enrolled in these courses, says Conant (1959), efforts to extend such study will be self-defeating. The instructor will not be able to bring students along without diluting the challenge of the course. It might be wise to limit the group to top ability in mathematics (see Chapter 4) and not to top intellectual ability if one gives credence to specialization in intellectual functions.

Such reasoning lends support to ability grouping in secondary mathematics programs. Grouping of this kind generally results naturally when students have choices between general mathematics and college preparatory programs at the lower grade levels. It is extended in the junior and senior years when elective arrangements provide for self-selection. However, requiring all college preparatory students to take three or four years of mathematics might swell enrollments and lower the quality of advanced courses. Such extension would result in an unhappy experience for bright students who are mathematically inept while impoverishing the courses for the mathematically talented.

In mathematics, as in other areas, experiences outside the classroom can spur individual initiative, study, and commitment. Some schools organize mathematics clubs and even mathematics teams which enter into friendly competition with teams from other schools. Emphasis should be placed on creative thinking and extension of interest rather than on competition for its own sake only. Students may develop mathematical exhibits which illustrate projects upon which they have worked, and these may be displayed in mathematics and science fairs. Some mathematics projects are listed in "Thousands of Science Projects" published by the Science Clubs of America (Washington, D.C., Science

---

* From *Program for College Preparatory Mathematics,* by Commission on Mathematics. Copyright 1959 by College Entrance Examination Board. Reprinted with permission of College Entrance Examination Board.

Service, 1719 N. Street, N.W.). The Academically Talented Student Project also calls attention to the contests of the Mathematical Association of America and the Society of Actuaries, and to enrichment materials published by the National Council of Teachers of Mathematics (NEA, 1959a, pp. 33-36).

New developments in secondary mathematics also require some fresh study and review by teachers of mathematics. The Talented Student Project advises the teacher of the mathematically gifted to "refresh his knowledge in the area of analysis (the calculus and analytic geometry) and to catch up with some work in modern algebra." Recommendations include such topics as elementary concepts of sets and their applications in elementary mathematics; logic and symbolic logic, especially as related to geometry; probability and statistics; the number system; a modern concept of functions; and topics in modern algebra, such as groups, rings and fields (*Ibid.*, pp. 41-42). Secondary school mathematics teachers will find considerable assistance in the volume of Appendices with which The College Entrance Examination Board Commission on Mathematics followed up its recommendations for a new program in senior high schools (CEEB, 1959a).

At this time a revolution appears to be growing in the teaching of mathematics. Almost all efforts in the 1950's have been in the direction of a more challenging program for mathematically talented students. Many of the new proposals are likely to seem hopelessly beyond the average student. The major asset of new recommendations, however, lies in the many new ideas that will be within the scope of gifted boys and girls. Another is the excitement it promises to teachers working with new materials and to the students who will be the beneficiaries of their enthusiasm.

SUMMARY

Both science and mathematics education have made large steps forward as a result of large scale assistance provided by the National Science Foundation and other public and private agencies. This effort has borne fruit in proposals for significant changes at all levels in both these major areas. New curricula have been established, and they have been accompanied by new materials and special training of teachers, largely at the expense of the Federal Government. Of particular interest to those interested in the intellectually gifted is the focus of these programs on children with special abilities in each field. It is no longer accurate to charge that programs do not exist to challenge the mathematically and scientifically talented student. On the contrary, new offerings at the elementary, secondary, and collegiate levels provide enough material to stretch the powers of the very best students and sometimes, unfortunately, to overwhelm them.

The new programs in these fields have certain points in common. There is an emphasis on concept development. The programs focus upon developing the ability to generalize as well as upon the learning of important generalizations already established. Proponents of new approaches advocate the method of "discovery" in both science and mathematics. "Inquiry" is transformed into a system, methodology or strategy that may be transposed from field to field.

Distinction is also made between mathematics or science for the citizen and mathematics or science for the specialist. For the former, proposals include an understanding of basic concepts and of the structure of the discipline involved. For the latter, advanced programs once reserved for more mature students are offered at each school level.

Public interest in these fields is reflected both in special activities in the school and in new opportunities in the community. Science honors programs capture the interest of students in weekend and summer sessions. Business, government, and professional groups sponsor science fairs, mathematics contests, study groups, and seminars for students in secondary schools.

In mathematics and the sciences, opportunities for the gifted abound. Schools can give direction to these efforts through appropriate motivation and identification of talent, through revision of programs, and through stimulating the growth of their professional staffs.

Chapter 12

The Fine Arts

A thing of beauty is a joy forever:
Its loveliness increases; it will never
Pass into nothingness.

—Keats

Perhaps the most serious defect in many proposals for the gifted made in recent years has been neglect of the arts, both fine and practical, in the effort to shore up the "academic" part of the curriculum. Added "solids" had to displace something else, of course, and the result was less time in the curriculum of the gifted for music, art, industrial arts, home economics, typing, commercial areas, vocational shops and agriculture. Unfortunately, this action was predicated upon armchair logic rather than research.

Evidence gathered in the widespread Eight-Year Study (Aikin, 1942), in the parallel study by the Southern Association (Jenkyns, 1946), and in at least one statewide study (Katterle and Craig, 1955) does not support heavy reliance upon formal studies or emphasis on traditional "solids" as the only, or even the best, way to prepare gifted students for successful work in college. The Eight-Year and Southern Association studies revealed superior performance in college on the part of graduates of the most liberal high school curricula. Katterle and Craig, in the State of Washington, showed the absence of relationship between the pattern of courses taken by their students and their later success in college. Instead, application and achievement in high school, regardless of courses taken, correlated well with achievement in college, regardless of major selected. Loading more "heavy" subjects on the student has no discoverable justification in research.

VALUES FOR THE GIFTED CHILD

For the gifted student, the fine and practical arts have the same values they do for other students. In addition, while there is no high correlation between intellectual superiority and artistic talent, proportionally more talent is to be found in the intellectually gifted than in average groups (NEA, 1961b). Any discussion of these areas, then, must consider both their general values for the gifted student and special training for the young person with an unusual talent. This chapter will be devoted to art and music only. They are selected because of their own importance but also as exemplars of the case for other "minor" subjects. The reader is referred to publications of professional societies in the other fields for study of special programs in those areas.

The general values of art and music are of particular significance in working with bright students because of the typical responsiveness of the gifted. Programs for these young people should stress expression both for its own sake and for the release of tension. Improved perception of both sound and visual stimuli add to general as well as artistic objectives in education. Appreciation of the cultural heritage and the development of taste are likelier of attainment with the bright student than with others.

The NEA Academically Talented Student Project in its booklet on art (1961b) views certain negative characteristics in the contemporary culture which may be corrected by greater emphasis on art. Included in these are factors that inhibit creativity such as the loss of individuality and pressures toward conformity. Others, like the time of tension and anxiety we live in, affect emotional health. Our values are influenced by the dominance of science and technology and by an overconcern with materialism. Yet these humanly neutral or humanly negative factors coexist with a longer life span and more leisure. Art and the other fields that stress the aesthetic, emotional, and expressional experiences can make a genuine contribution toward greater creativeness, emotional stability, a more humanistic set of values, and richer use of leisure in a life that is fuller and longer.

THE ARTS IN EDUCATION FOR CREATIVITY

Of basic importance is the possibility that the fine arts may promote a general creativeness that can transfer to the able student's fields of major interest. The factors of creativity identified by Guilford (1950), Lowenfeld (1958), and others would appear to be susceptible of edu-

286

cational development. *Openness to experience* appears to be a primary quality required for creative work. The art and music teacher can make notable contributions to this openness as they give training in perception and encourage artistic expression of thought. McFee (1961) discloses that teachers can prepare children for more complex visual tasks by helping them understand the nature of new things they meet. She sees a reciprocal relationship between cognitive understanding and visual perception. We see more as we know more about an object; we learn more as we look to see more. The fine and practical arts are media for increasing the sensitivity of individuals to the world around them. This sensitivity is regarded by many as the first step in creativity.

Another factor in creativeness is defined as *ideational flexibility*. The world of the arts is essentially one that has been created by artists and composers who have seen and heard the universe in ways different from those of their contemporaries. An important task in art education is helping students to recognize that brightness, color, size, and shape are not rigidities but qualities that vary with the viewer's perspective, the environment, and other conditions. What was dissonance in Beethoven's music to his contemporaries was glorious harmony to later generations. If transfer of training is possible, development of a general cognitive and perceptual flexibility may be promoted through this approach in the arts.

Ideational fluency as well as flexibility is regarded as an important factor in creativeness. This factor is defined as the ability to respond to a stimulus with a multiplicity of ideas featuring both quantity and originality. The arts have a potential contribution in various ways. First, the variety of non-verbal media offers many possible frames of reference for thought and its expression. In addition to the use of a verbal language, graphic, and musical symbols provide new modes of communication. Second, the non-literal perspective of the arts encourages an emotional as well as an intellectual reaction to a stimulus or problem situation. In a sense, existentialist modes of attack are added to a priori, realist, and experimentalist approaches. But in addition to these theoretical interpretations, the arts have as their basic mode in education a challenge to the learner to create, to develop new things, new ideas. While the mode of most subjects is convergent, arriving at the "right" answer, the mode of the arts is divergent, requiring *different* answers. Here, too, an important problem is transfer. Only as all teachers in a school recognize the place of divergent thinking, is it possible for the art and music teacher to make an impact which is not isolated and limited to the art or music room. Moreover, neither art nor music is intrinsically divergent in its approach. If the aim is to copy a picture with exactitude or to paint a scene only as the teacher sees it, if emphasis in music is restricted to controlled performance of music written by others, art and music can also become simple exercises in reinforcement of rigidity, devoted to the least possible originality and variety of response.

Finally, it is not possible to dissociate creativity from a creative product. Somewhere along the line the individual has to persist through to the solution of his problem. He has to exhibit what Lowenfeld (1958) calls "coherence of organization". He has to subject his work to his own critical evaluation. In art and music we are not involved in an area of "right answers" or predetermined solutions. The need is therefore greater for the individual to arrive at his own synthesis, his own organization, his own conclusion, his own product. Evaluation must be partially subjective and individual, more than a question of being right or wrong in the teacher's eyes. While such experiences are not uncommon in creative writing (also a fine art), they are extremely rare in most academic subject matters. A curriculum that deliberately restricts the fine arts experience reduces *ipso facto* the exposure of students to creative experience. There is reason to believe that such experience might develop a kind of autonomy in meeting new problems, responding with a variety of hypotheses, organizing solutions, and applying self-evaluation.

OBJECTIVES IN ART FOR THE GIFTED

Beginning with finger paint, plasticene and tempera in kindergarten, art activities account for a large part of the early childhood school program, but gradually they decline in time and importance assigned to them. Too often free expressive finger painting gives way in the intermediate grades to illustration of social studies themes and the designing of covers for projects in various areas. In such a framework, the intellectually gifted child is likely to limit himself merely to workmanlike illustration of themes in the content of subjects he has studied. Such efforts fail to achieve important values in art when the emphasis is intellectual rather than aesthetic, emotion-expressing, or tension-releasing. In the junior high school the student is likely to have a year or two in graphic arts and perhaps crafts. In the senior high school, unless the student can elect art work—a practice generally discouraged for bright students—no further formal exposure to the world of art is likely. As indicated in the previous pages, the gifted student deserves and needs more than this.

What are important goals in art education for the intellectually superior? These are some desired objectives:

Development of visual sensitivity and powers of observation. Formal education tends to stress verbal elements and to neglect the senses.

In art, students can be helped to see more detail in their world; to become more aware of form, space and color; to relate in new ways to their environment. The intellectually gifted student in particular can learn to supplement cognitive with visual, tactile, and aural ways of knowing and understanding. To the bright student who is not going to be an artist, visual sensitivity may be equally important in fields like mathematics, science, and engineering where spatial perception, for example, is an established predictor of aptitude.

Acquisition of a non-verbal system of cognition and communication. Verbal communication is the primary means of learning in formal education, but reinforcement with other media may prevent substitution of verbalism for meaning. Ideas may be organized visually as well as verbally. Poetically, Lowenfeld says, "For our children art should become their friend to whom they turn with their joys and sorrows, their fears and frustrations, whenever words become inadequate" (Lowenfeld, 1957, p. 55).

Development of aesthetic attitudes in work and recreation. The concept of art-for-art's sake is a good example of autonomous motivation that sooner or later must be developed in the student's field of major interest if exceptional outcomes are to eventuate. The mathematician's concept of an "elegant" solution is another way of expressing this aesthetic attitude toward work. Interest in the process and product themselves without regard to external rewards is an attitude characteristic of the artist.

Opportunity for experimentation and innovation in various art media as an apperceptive background for creativity in other fields as well.

Establishment of self-identity through satisfying individual performance. In the thrill of executing one's own conception the individual "finds" himself as a unique, worthwhile being. Add to this an appreciation of his right to be different, and a basis for creative work is laid.

Opportunity for expression *qua* expression: for presonal enjoyment, for emotional release, for constructive expression of emotions. This goal constitutes the main objection to an art program which is restricted to illustration and the consequent denial of expression for its own sake.

Development of attitudes and skills in self-criticism and evaluation which come from assessment of one's own efforts according to one's own purposes and utilizing one's own criteria. The criteria in art are not externally imposed as they are in most academic fields. The student can combine reason and emotion in developing his own evaluative processes.

Development of aesthetic standards in life both as a producer and consumer.

Becoming familiar with our culture's art heritage, recognizing art as a growing, eternally changing process, frame of reference, and product.

Appreciation of the function of art in life, past and contemporary. Art objects are never viewed as discrete items, but as part of a whole complex.

Relating art to science, history, literature, and music.

The last three of these objectives are avowedly academic. They represent only a small part of the art program and represent no substitute for direct art experiences. An art program which is expressive only, however, restricts the potential art learnings of the bright young person.

THE ART CURRICULUM FOR THE GIFTED

As in the case of other talents, the intellectually gifted is only slightly more likely than other students to be artistically gifted. The artistic elite are likely to exceed the population norm for intelligence but may or may not be in a rarefied intellectual stratum. An art curriculum for bright students must therefore comprehend a wide spread in art abilities. At the upper end it can include provisions for the artistically superior whether they are of high intelligence or not. In general, selective devices for art aptitude have not been triumphantly successful. Most authorities believe that evaluation of work samples by competent judges is the best way of predicting talent.

Certain guidelines may be set forth in providing art experiences for the intellectually gifted. First, art should not be viewed as a program of busy work for slow students who have difficulty with the verbal medium. The bright student has as much need for art experiences as the slow student, and he can do more with them. In the elementary school, the pupil should therefore have a balanced program which includes both creative and correlated art work in all possible media. He needs specific instruction, not just the provision of time and materials. Second, the pupil should have the opportunity to work directly with art specialists who can give more direction and provide more challenge than the generally trained classroom teacher. If he needs more time than is normally assigned to art, this time should be "stolen," judicially, from the schedule. He should not be denied the art experience in order to make up work in other, "more important" areas. Third, a specific program of art experiences should be designed which includes planned attention to perception training, to form, color, design, size, and space orientation; to experimentation with different media in two and three dimensions; to consideration of art in daily living; to the beginnings of relating art to history; to the development of artistic taste as a consumer; to the planning and completion of art projects with specific attention to self-evaluation; to the development of skill in presenting ideas visually in the process of illustration.

SPECIAL ART OPPORTUNITIES

Attention must also be directed to the student who is gifted as an artist. If he is also intellectually superior, it is all the more necessary that he have time to pursue his artistic gift and not be loaded down exclusively with academic electives. Elective programs with considerable challenge, and under a highly stimulating teacher, should be available for the talented art prospect regardless of his IQ. Of particular interest are after school and Saturday classes provided by art museums in a number of cities where young people with unusual interest are able to further their explorations in a number of media, sometimes with the help of practicing artists.

How does one identify the gifted art student if standardized tests are of small value?* Lowenfeld (1957, pp. 421-22) recommends examination of the child's art work in search of the following distinctive factors: fluency of imagination and expression, highly developed sensibility (in areas like movement, space, color), intuitive quality of imagination; directness of expression, and a high degree of self-identification with the subject-matter and the medium employed. On the negative side, there would be the absence of rigidity, of stereotyped expression, of endless repetition of the same theme. These criteria are admittedly subjective. A person who is an artist himself is in the best position to judge. Lally and La Brant note that the gifted child seems to be more sensitive to sensory stimuli than the average and that he thinks in terms of visual

---

* A number of tests are available, including the Graves Design Judgment Test, the Horn Art Aptitude Inventory, the Knauber Art Ability Test, and the Meier Art Test: Art Judgment. Predictive validity is not high. Mendelowitz (1953) points out that art testing is more likely to discover the child who does not have ability than the one who does.

images. While all children are exposed to creative work in the primary grades, Lally and La Brant remark that the truly talented child continues his interest even in later years when the atmosphere may be unsympathetic to artistic expression (AAGC, 1951).

Opportunities to display work in school and out have to be contrived. In many communities art shows and outdoor art fairs invite contributions from local high schools. In others, the school should take the lead in organizing such events. Certainly, no after-school gathering in the school, whether adult or student body, should take place without art products prominently in display. The attractive entry lobbies and display cases in most new schools provide a natural facility for such exhibits. In addition, the vast amounts of flat, unadorned wall areas in most new schools cry out for artistic display of some kind.

Just as no good school exists without a library, no good school ought to forego a collection of paintings and sculpture. Berger (1959) gives an interesting account of how Tottenville High School in New York City went about building its own collection through selection and purchase by a faculty-student committee. The Seattle Public Schools have arranged with the Public Library for a continuously rotating collection of prints that are mounted on uniform size mats and hung in interchangeable frames throughout the school district. Excellent prints are available at low cost and add variety to original paintings which a school may also purchase.

Many secondary schools are equipped with rather good art rooms, providing facilities for work in a variety of media. Extending the program to all students beyond the eighth grade would demand additional rooms in most cases. Two further items are needed in most schools. One of these is expanded space for storage of student art work, both two- and three-dimensional. Too often, storage limitations restrict students to work that can be completed at a single sitting. A second need is a small studio area where students can work independently. Such areas might be small workshops separated by glass from the adjacent art room (a smaller version of the typing room adjacent to the stenography or bookkeeping room), or an alcove in the art room set off by a partial partition or other architectural feature from the main part of the art workshop.

THE ART TEACHER

In the elementary school the art teacher is most likely to be the homeroom teacher who is responsible for practically all areas of learning. The number of teachers who have had considerable exposure to art is likely to be quite small, with perhaps proportionally more art majors in early childhood education than beyond. As part of certification requirements most elementary school teachers have had some exposure to art education. This background should be weighed against the criteria that Lowenfeld (1957) sets for the art teacher: personality characteristics marked by creativeness, a high degree of sensitivity, and flexible relationships to the environment; empathic abilities to put himself in the place of his students as they work with art; an understanding of the needs of his pupils; creative activity on his own part. Lowenfeld advocates creative activity for the teacher for two reasons: to develop insight into children's thought and experience, and to build skill in thinking and creating in different mediums (*Ibid.*, p. 77). Since few teachers are likely to meet the criterion of creative art activity, the availability of excellent consultant service in each school is important. Frequent studio work with an art specialist present is also desirable.

In secondary schools if art is taught at all, normally a properly prepared teacher is on hand. Unfortunately, in small high schools (enrollment under two hundred), art is the subject most frequently omitted. When it is taught, it is often taught with the left hand by a teacher whose major interest is elsewhere. In larger schools where a full-time art teacher or an art department functions, the situation is potentially more favorable. However, the need for creative, stimulating, secure personnel persists. Making time available to students so that they may have an improved art program is no less severe a need.

MUSIC FOR THE GIFTED

The music curriculum for the intellectually gifted is composed of various elements. There is the division already mentioned between the intellectually superior and the musically gifted, with considerable overlapping since many musically gifted are also in the intellectual elite. Obviously there must be some distinction between programs for the intellectually gifted and programs for the musically exceptional.

The general music program for the intellectually superior students should give attention to vocal and instrumental performance, listening, and some limited experience in musical composition. Mursell (1956) states the orientation of the program as musical growth for all. He puts primary value on helping children "respond creatively in their dealings with music."

Pitts (1944) stresses the need in the elementary school to place emphasis on children and their development rather than on technique and performance. She looks at music as expression, communication, and experience whose purpose is to "enlarge the personality and enrich the social living of all." Music provides a medium for self-realization through expression and performance. Group musical undertakings represent a means to extend social effectiveness through enhancing a sense of belonging, through "willing subordination of self for mutually valued purposes," and through learning to respect the differences in individual capacities. But music in the elementary school is not limited to performance: there is also the beginning of a listening and creating program which hopefully will lead to furthering productiveness in the arts in our culture. While these are values to be achieved for all children in elementary school, it should be evident that they are particularly meaningful to the bright student and open to the fullest achievement by him.

At the secondary school level, the administrator and music teacher will find an excellent guide in the NEA pamphlet, *Music for the Academically Talented Student*, prepared by a committee of the Music Educators National Conference (NEA, 1960 d). This bulletin attempts to focus important principles in music instructions on the special needs of bright students. Building upon the intellectual resources of these young people, the committee establishes a number of objectives, including the following:

> Ability to recognize and understand form in music
> Deeper insight into meanings
> Greater skill in performing and/or listening
> Determination of taste by discriminating judgment of value rather
>   than by whim
> Initiative and independent activity in musical fields

The committee's list of desired outcomes implies curriculum content as well:

> Growing familiarity with important music of all periods and styles
> Increasing understanding of interior design of music
> Knowledge of stylistic characteristics distinguishing music of one
>   period from another
> Understanding of development of the orchestra and its instruments
> Knowledge of most significant characteristics of major forms of
>   music
> Understanding of the role of music as medium of communication in
>   history and function of music in contemporary life
> Knowledge of scientific and mathematical bases of music; of relation-
>   ships between significant musical, artistic and literary works
> Realization that music is expressive of intrinsic values, and increas-
>   ing self-identification with both music and those values

Recognition of values distinguishing artistic music from music which
  is merely entertaining
Increasing knowledge of critical works and reference sources for
  music. (NEA, 1960 d)

While most of these outcomes are cognitive rather than aesthetic in
their expression, the bulletin emphasizes at various points that performing and listening are indispensable for musical growth. No studies
about music can substitute for direct experience with music. "Although
the music education of academically talented students should be intellectually oriented," the committee continues, "it should also help them
to develop emotionally. . . . The ability to hear everything there is to be
heard in a piece of music . . . is of greater value than memorized knowledge of biographical data concerning its composer. The academically
talented student should be given every encouragement and opportunity
to participate in creative activities and in independent study" (*Ibid.*,
pp. 99-100).

In music, as in other fields, the task of the educator is to avoid the
temptation of over-intellectualizing experiences for the bright student.
To make of music purely an intellectual exercise robs music of one of
its special properties and makes it only another academic study. Pitts
(1944) notes that music represents a medium for direct expression of
emotion without the intermediary symbols of language. This quality
should not be diminished by undue intellectualization or verbalizing.

SCHEDULE PROBLEMS

Since music, like other arts, should be viewed as having special qualities desirable for all students, the matter of scheduling becomes a prime
concern. The six-period day with hour-long classes has much to com-
mend it, but such an organization too often militates against art or
music in the program of the college-bound student. Educators in these
fields believe that students should be able to continue this work throughout their school career, a conviction that contrasts sharply with current
practice which may limit students to a single semester (or less) in art
and music in the senior high school and a single year in junior high
school. A number of alternatives are offered, including the following:

An eight-period day with 45-minute periods
Experimentation with schedules so that alternatives to the Carnegie
  unit may be explored; programming students of high ability for
  other patterns than the five-days-a-week routine for each major
  subject

Under existing schedules, programming exceptional students simultaneously for music and another subject, each student making
his own decision as to which course to attend each day (see NEA,
1960 d)

Use of drill time not needed by the able student in various subjects
for independent studio work in art or for individual performance
or listening in music

Reconsidering the total pattern of the school curriculum, giving
more balanced attention to the fine arts

THE MUSIC TEACHER

Of primary concern is the teacher of music, himself. While the values
of the self-contained classroom in the elementary school are acknowl-
edged, the limitations of the "common branches" teacher in dealing with
music must also be recognized. Certainly everything that can be done
should be done to develop competence for every teacher in music education. Only a small minority of teachers, however, may be expected to
achieve the necessary enthusiasm for music, literacy in the field, and
competence in performance and teaching others to perform. To
confront the able student with less is to take the "bite," the challenge
and the stimulation out of music education. The most expert teaching
and the richest possible background are needed to ensure that music will
be a satisfying emotional and stimulating intellectual experience. These
strictures, of course, must be related to the age of the pupil. The music
specialist may be successful working as a consultant with the classroom
teacher in early childhood programs, although more will be needed
for the child who shows promise of being a virtuoso musician. In the
intermediate grades, periodic exposure to a genuine expert in music
should supplement experiences in the classroom. In the upper grades
and in secondary schools, the music specialist is essential.

The music teacher must be competent to conduct a program which
includes performance, composition, and both the aesthetic and intellectual sides of listening. The last of these specifications calls for a
teacher who is broadly trained and not simply an excellent musician.
The teacher must also have the time to manage these experiences. Pressures on the teacher to provide performing groups for the community
—marching bands, choirs to perform at public events, music festival
competitions—inevitably get in the way of serious attention to listening
programs and creative work with music. The pressure of numbers may
be equally inexorable. The music teacher who has to meet very large
groups for "General Music" is severely limited in his efforts to employ
the individualization that is essential.

OTHER RESOURCES

Facilities and other resources are also a necessary consideration. Independent and individual work require adequate listening posts or booths in a music center or library, practice rooms for individual and small group performance, and listening. A comfortable room for informal groups to "browse" through musical selections is highly desirable.

Even more essential than the school's treasury of music, however, is the community's offerings. The restricted musical fare available on radio and television in most parts of the United States is a sad commentary on the failure of school music programs in the past to develop a demand for serious music. Except for the very large cities, concert performances, even of touring artists, occur but a few times in the year. Communities concerned about the education of their gifted youngsters must recognize that provision of a library, a literary group, a Saturday morning science seminar, and a dramatics group are not enough. Good music, too, has to be broadly available. There is need for community pressures to secure some prime radio and television time on local stations and networks for this purpose. Development of subsidized musical series for sustained programs in middle-sized communities is another desirable project.

THE MUSICALLY TALENTED

Over and above the music program for the generally gifted is the problem of special training for the musically talented and the musically gifted.* Early identification of the musically talented is indeed difficult. Existing standardized measures have not shown any marked value in predicting exceptional ability. Growth of the voice and musculature are too unpredictable to foreshadow vocal or instrumental performance of high quality in maturity. Lally and La Brant (AAGC, 1951) warn against exploiting the young player. Frequently, they say, a willingness to entertain and imitate adult behavior are mistaken for talent. The best evidence of musical ability lies in a deep and persistent interest in music itself. Sur and Schuller (1958) add qualities suggested by the Pennsylvania Music Educators: superior aural sensitivity and sensory equipment, well-above average mentality, imagination, and outstanding singing voice or digital manipulability.

Whether special training for the musically talented is a function of the

---

* The Music Educators (NEA 1960 d) assign the top 25 per cent in music ability to the talented group, and the top 2 to 3 per cent to the gifted group.

public schools or of private conservatories is a matter for policy-making in each school district. Some systems will want to provide opportunity for the greatest possible development for this special gift, as for intellectual ability, up to age eighteen, and at a level commensurate with the ability of the student. A city as large as New York is able to afford special schools—the High School of Music and Art and the High School of Performing Arts—for students of unusual ability. Other systems may regard this kind of education as basically the job of the conservatory and special music teacher. Except for the very select gifted group who give promise of becoming the performers and virtuosi of tomorrow, the school should be able to give strong assistance to the musically talented group. At some point, however, a line has to be drawn as to the services reasonably expected of the public school. In the large city with multiple resources available, both in terms of instruction and scholarship assistance, it is much more feasible to draw such a line than in the small community where the public school music teachers are the only available resource. At what point it becomes desirable to send the gifted child from a small community to a locale and institution with richer resources is again a matter of public policy and family attitudes.

A number of specialized provisions are feasible in high school for musically talented students. Sur and Schuller (1958) recommend such devices as the music honors program in the University of Wisconsin High School, establishment of a music major in high school, allowance of credit for private music instruction, use of student conductors for musical groups, and offering advanced courses. The music major would take advanced courses in Applied Music, Music Theory, Music History, and Music Literature, and would, in addition, participate in special choral and instrumental ensembles. Honors work could include individual projects such as listening to and analyzing musical works, writing compositions for performances by the school orchestra, chorus or string groups, and practicing solo performances for special concerts. Sur and Schuller, however, caution against imbalance in the student's program if early over-specialization results in obstructing general educational development or college admission.

To the intellectually gifted student, music can be an avenue for creative expression and a means to develop factors that are part of a general creativity. It can represent a source of tremendous emotional satisfaction in performance and listening. Participation in vocal and instrumental groups generally provides high quality emotional and social values. In addition, a valuable intellectual component is present in the appreciation, performance and creation of music. It is important that schools recognize but not overplay the intellectual values in music education.

More important is it that schools guarantee to each child the opportunity for rich musical experiences in the face of academic pressures that compete for his time and attention.

SUMMARY

Art and music represent but two of the non-academic areas which offer a major contribution to the intellectually gifted student. Together with dance, physical activities, and the applied arts, they afford personal expression, emotional release, deep involvement, creative achievement and satisfaction. In Barkan's words (1955), the arts may be viewed as means for communion and communication alike. In contrast to procedures in the conventional subject matters, in the arts the learner is central and the process is as important as the product.

Because of all these values, the arts are highly important to the gifted student. Proposals which sacrifice the aesthetic and expressive component to an increased intellectual imbalance must be viewed critically. A healthier emphasis would be to insist on strengthening the artistic component in the education of the gifted students so that it might make its maximum contribution to their growth.

Chapter 13

Ability Grouping

*Good company and good discourse
are the very sinews of virtue.*

—Izaak Walton

No administrative device proposed for education of the gifted is argued more frequently or more heatedly than ability grouping. Polls of teachers' opinion, particularly at the secondary school level, indicate strong support for such practice. If educational problems could be solved purely by processes of ratiocination, no solution would appear more reasonable than grouping children in special classes according to their academic potential. Almost without exception, professional and lay advocates of intensified programs for the gifted call for ability grouping. On the other hand, many leaders of the educational profession in universities and school systems emphatically oppose ability grouping on social and philosophical grounds. Differences are not resolved by research evidence which is inconclusive. No consistent support can be found for either position, and reports from study to study are in conflict with each other.

Problems associated with grouping are complicated by disagreements on definition of the gifted and by questions of feasibility of grouping in most communities. The typical American school district operates with a single high school enrolling fewer than five hundred students, a junior high school of comparable size, and two or three elementary schools. In many cases further consolidation of school districts is not a practicable solution because of distances involved in transportation of children. A school district with some three thousand children (far larger than average) would normally enroll only fifteen students in 12 grades who fall in the top one-half of 1 per cent of the intelligence distribution. There would be thirty in the top 1 per cent; seventy-five in the group more than two standard deviations above the mean (2½ per cent); 480 (16 per cent) in the group more than one standard deviation above the mean—those generally regarded as having sufficient potential to complete college. The last group, if the distribution curve is smooth for the whole population, would include about forty students in each grade in such a school district.

It is at this point in considering the hypothetical distribution of a school district population that the problem of definition and the problem of feasibility intersect. A sufficient number of exceptional students must be available to justify special classes. By this criterion, feasibility can mean the top 1 per cent in some mammoth school districts like New York City. In others it is the top tenth, top fifth, top quarter, top third or even top half of the student body. As a larger and larger fraction is included in the group designated as gifted, obviously the nature of exceptionality is more and more diluted. At some point, one must ask whether the work that can be done in the broadened group is truly different from that which can be done in a random sampling. If not, why go to the trouble of grouping with its attendant dangers of labeling children as able or unable? Why undertake such risks in view of the obvious inadequacy of existing identification measures if little can be accomplished by doing so?

Not only is the range of ability a matter of concern: the diversity of abilities that are nurtured also needs definition. If one is to accept Witty's commonly accepted definition—consistently outstanding performance in a socially useful field of endeavor, even a narrow range of ability in a large number of fields can comprise a very large number of students. Unfortunately, there is little point in selecting students outstanding in ten different measures and then grouping them all together. Their only common trait may be their exceptionality; otherwise, their interests, backgrounds, aptitudes, and developed abilities may be even more widely scattered than in a class chosen at random ("heterogeneous").

There are, therefore, two necessary pre-conditions to consideration of ability grouping. One is agreement upon the definition of individual talents to be developed in the school. Second is presence in the school of sufficiently large numbers of genuinely outstanding students with a particular talent.

GROUPING: THEORY AND PRACTICE

Ability grouping has been advocated for more than a century as a logical solution to problems of instruction arising from the wide range of learning potential in a system of universal education. The introduction of graded classes in American public schools in the middle of the nineteenth century constituted a first step in this direction by reducing differences based on age and experience in school. Ultimately, however, a growing awareness emerged that wide individual differences persisted despite the new system of grade grouping.

A host of schemes have been attempted for grouping children by ability either in their assignment to classes in a school or in the organization of groups within a class. Shane describes thirty-five different grouping methods that have been employed (Shane, 1960; NSSE, 1962, page 49). Since local factors suit one type of grouping better to a given community than to another, the list should be helpful to schools studying their grouping practices.

An important approach to the problem of individual differences in class instruction is found in the programs called "laboratory plans" by Wilhelms (1958) in his summary of grouping practices in the United States. These began with the individual progress plans pioneered by Preston Search in Pueblo in 1890 and Frederic Burk at San Francisco State College in 1913. Carleton Washburne, a student of Burk's, developed the Winnetka Plan shortly after World War I. Parkhurst's Dalton Plan and Morrison's Unit plan were other contemporaries in the 1920's. All these plans share a single approach: individualization through varying the rate of progress with focus on the individual student working alone on an assigned task. Current proposals for use of programmed instruction and teaching machines are strikingly parallel to these "contract" plans.

A second method introduced to individualize instruction focused on varying the program through a group rather than an individual approach. This was the introduction of fast and slow tracks in Cambridge in the 1890's, in Batavia, shortly thereafter, and in North Denver in the 1900's. Batavia provided two teachers in a single room that accommodated eighty pupils, with one teacher assigned to the fast, one to the slow learners. North Denver's program was similar but is put its primary emphasis on the bright pupils.

Popularization of the Army General Classification Test in the effort to identify ability rapidly during World War I stimulated interest in intelligence testing. One of the products of the "scientific" movement in education in the 1920's was the spread of ability grouping based on such tests. Detroit led the way with its "XYZ" groups in 1919, enrolling the top 20 per cent in its "X" classes, the middle 60 per cent in the "Y" classes, and the bottom 20 per cent in the "Z" classes. Many other cities developed similar patterns. Variations on the theme included multiple-track grouping where students in the several tracks covered a given course of study at differential rates, and "platoon" grouping where departmentalization in the elementary school could be employed to separate out diverse ability groups.

Evidence on the effectiveness of ability grouping at the time was not at all clear. Grouping apparently made its greatest contribution to low ability groups. The striking rise in efficiency of teaching or learning which was expected never materialized, perhaps because grouping in the 1920's and 1930's was not normally accompanied by differentiation of method or curriculum. Pupils, teachers, parents, and administrators were generally favorable to grouping practices except that low-ability children in some cases apparently developed more negative attitudes toward schools. Ability grouping lost much of its early acceptance after 1935 but did not disappear. With increasing evidence accumulating on the variability of any group, the word "homogeneous" lost some of its charm. In addition, there was a growing interest in diversity and pluralism. Development of "needs theories" in the 1930's and 1940's put emphasis on multi-faceted personality development and unique individual goals in place of a single-minded focus on academic competence and "minimum essentials" in the earlier decade.

In the 1950's intensification of the Cold War between East and West and the rivalry of the opposing camps in space technology encouraged the view that concern with personality and emotional well-being are secondary to other national defense needs. Many academicians, laymen, and some educators rushed to argue the return to a glorified, if unreal, past when academic standards were high, competition ruled the day, and a proper emphasis was placed on education of the elite. Since practically all students must be educated through high school today, they urged the employment of nicely defined grouping procedures which would separate the fit from the unfit. Surveys in the 1960's in urban school systems show ability grouping to be the prevailing procedure. Throughout the nation ability grouping seems to be spreading although new research does not support this return to the past any more than previous research found evidence to maintain such grouping policies.

GROUPING THE GIFTED

In time, attention to grouping spread from the general problem of the normal range of ability to the special problem of the very able learners alone. In Cleveland, the efforts of a community group eventuated in 1921 in the organization of Major Work classes for selected children who spent half the day working together in the primary academic areas. In the other half day, these children were dispersed among the whole school population for art, music, physical education, lunch, and assembly periods. In New York City two classes were organized for intellectually gifted children as a pioneer effort in 1922; a special experimental program was conducted in the Speyer School (Greenberg and Bruner, 1941), and a concerted program over the years has developed special "Intellectually Gifted Classes" involving as many as 24,500 children in 279 elementary schools in 1963. These classes meet together for the whole day, providing contact with other children only in all-school activities. Programs similar to Cleveland's or New York's have grown in a number of cities since 1950.

Still more selective than the special class in the neighborhood school is the special school for gifted children. At the elementary level, the Hunter College Elementary School and a few private schools represent conscious efforts to limit quite narrowly the range of intellectual ability. The Hunter School, utilizing individual intelligence tests that are described more fully in Chapter 7, enrolls children who rank in the 99th percentile on the tests employed. At the secondary level, New York City, Baltimore, and Boston have operated, for many years, high schools with highly selected student personnel. These range from the top 1 per cent in academic aptitude to somewhat larger proportions both on intelligence test scores and on measures of other abilities such as musical performance and artistic production. Less deliberate selection of intellectually superior students is made by a number of university laboratory schools which tend indirectly to be selective of the *families* of the children who attend by giving first priority to children of faculty members.

More typical is the neighborhood school with the normally wide range of ability. Since urban secondary schools tend to be large institutions, both junior and senior high schools have sufficient numbers to have developed traditions of grouping students by ability and curriculum. A few cities offer accelerated junior high school programs to specially grouped students of high ability. In senior high schools many school systems offer honor classes to students of demonstrated ability in individual subjects. Some high schools operate honor schools as separate units within the large framework. Students selected for the honor school have most of their academic work together throughout the day.*

Many school systems do not provide special classes in the regular curriculum for gifted students. Instead they provide "opportunity"

---

* An interesting variant on the Honors School is Chicago's "100" program. Fifty high schools identify their 100 most academically able students (25 in each grade), and maintain a "special and continuous program of motivation, guidance, and honors classes" for them. In addition to more challenging academic work, these young people are given "broadened opportunities for leadership and socialization" and special orientation for college admission and scholarship examinations (Chicago Public Schools, 1964, pp. 23-24).

classes during the day, in the evening, on Saturdays, or during the summer in addition to the normal school program. Only highly gifted students are invited to attend such classes. In the elementary school, children from a cluster of schools in Los Angeles, for example, meet together one morning or afternoon a week for a special class in science or a session with an interested librarian in the public library. At the high school level, the University of Rochester is one of several which offer special evening seminars during the academic year for selected high school students.

OTHER BASES FOR GROUPING

Ability grouping is by no means the only type of separation offered in efforts to facilitate teaching and learning. Other types of grouping accept the separatist principle of ability grouping but propose different criteria. Olson's concept of organismic age has led to a proposal of grouping on the basis of organismic age, a concept which adds various physiological, social, and personal factors to the intellectual determinant alone. Another method relies almost exclusively on social maturity, and a third combines the child's social maturity and the personality of the teachers available for the groups being formed.

Current interest in the ungraded elementary school unit, primary or intermediate, suggests the possible value to the gifted child of a group which is not limited to a narrow age range. An increasing number of schools are trying out the ungraded primary unit in particular. Children aged six, seven, or eight may be grouped in a single three-year unit. They may move to the next unit after two, three, or four years depending upon readiness for more mature work and associations. Advocates of the plan argue the strength of its contribution to brighter pupils.

So long as formal educational procedures are organized on a group basis, experimentation with methods of grouping may be expected. The summary of research that follows, however, indicates quite clearly that grouping is at best a facilitative device. Without accompanying changes in curriculum, method, and materials, adaptations in grouping practices are not likely to produce major transformations.

RESEARCH ON GROUPING

REVIEWS OF RESEARCH

The intensive study of ability grouping in the 1920's and 1930's and renewed study of grouping starting in the 1950's produced a number of reviews of research that are useful to educators concerned with the effectiveness of different grouping patterns. Cornell's summary (NSSE, 1936) reported the inconclusive nature of research on ability grouping in the earlier period. Ekstrom (1961) published a critical review of experimental studies of homogeneous grouping that covers the more recent period. Eash (1961) pointed up differences in values considered in the later research. Wrightstone (1957) summarized pertinent research in the NEA series of pamphlets on "What Research Says to the Teacher."

In her summary of research on grouping, Cornell reported the consensus of reviewers "that the experimental evidence as to the achievement status of pupils under a plan of ability grouping is inconclusive" (NSSE, 1936, p. 295). There was some agreement that homogeneous grouping is favorable to the achievement of slow groups, with dubious or unfavorable results for average and bright groups. The possibility of a faster pace in covering a given amount of work was suggested for bright groups. Both gains *and* losses were reported for homogeneous grouping in English, geometry, and English History. In reading, total educational achievement, Latin, and algebra, the evidence is either inconclusive or favorable to ability grouping.

Most studies had been affected by the desire to restrict variables in the studies to grouping alone. To do so, teachers had generally been asked to employ the same curriculum and the same methods with experimental and control groups. In those cases where curriculum and method adaptations accompanied changes in grouping, a total effect favorable to homogeneous grouping was apparent. Cornell summarized:

> The results of ability grouping seem to depend less upon the fact of grouping itself than upon the philosophy behind the grouping, the accuracy with which grouping is made for the purposes intended, the differentiations in content, method, and speed, and the technique of the teacher, as well as upon more general environmental influences. (NSSE, 1936, p. 304)

A later review of research on grouping (Ekstrom, 1961) supported earlier conclusions with respect to contradictory findings. In general, where curriculum, method, and materials were not varied, grouping failed to make any significant difference. In some studies no difference was shown in conventional areas, but little effort had been made to measure gains where curriculum content had been enriched. Eash and Wrightstone, in general, supported the conclusions of Cornell and Ekstrom.

CRITIQUES OF RESEARCH ON GROUPING

Various reviewers of research in this area have suggested reasons for the inconclusiveness of evidence reported. Wrightstone relates difficulties in grouping itself to problems of research on grouping. The chief difficulty, he says, has been to find a suitable basis for ability grouping:

> Various measures, such as intelligence test ratings, achievement in reading, average achievement in several subjects, or teachers' marks, have been used as criteria. Experience and research have shown that any one of these factors, when considered alone, is seldom satisfactory. Moreover, several factors used together do not reduce materially the range of differences in a class of 30 or more. It is doubtful that any "perfect" combination of factors exists tho various types of grouping within the classroom have value. (Wrightstone, 1957, p. 6)

Wrightstone cites research claims that attribute grouping difficulties to two erroneous assumptions: that achievement in school subjects depends almost entirely upon intelligence; that the relation between intelligence and achievement is static. Yet, the facts are widely known that children with a given intelligence test score will vary widely in achievement in the various school subjects. In addition, "Pupil motivation, attitudes, interests, and teaching practices provide a dynamic, not a static, relationship between intelligence and achievement" (*Ibid.*, p. 7).

Passow (1962) underscores the difficulty of generalizing from research that has been reported. Studies that have been completed are often not comparable for a variety of reasons. These include variations in scope, aim, or purpose of the studies; variations in the number of students, number of groups and size of classes involved; and variations in duration of the studies. Moreover, in some research curriculum is differentiated; in others it is not. Efforts to hold teacher competence constant are not always apparent. Methods of selecting students and the means of matching experimental and control groups frequently do not follow standards that are essential for unequivocal research findings. In addition, measures used to evaluate growth vary in validity from study to study.

Cornell, writing a quarter-century earlier, centered her criticism on the absence of adequate measures to evaluate many of the alleged desirable or undesirable results of grouping. She was particularly concerned with the failure to measure objectively effects that may be the most important—habits of thinking, work habits and social attitudes. While some progress has been made in measurement of the less tangible results of education, Cornell's statement is still generally valid. She calls attention, too, to a problem that is always a vexatious one in educational research, that it is "virtually impossible to maintain a situation in which all factors except the experimental one are kept under control for a sufficient length of time" (NSSE, 1936).

Ekstrom's criticism of research efforts is important in guiding new research:

> Controlled experimental studies comparing the effectiveness of homogeneous and heterogeneous grouping, as evaluated by student achievement, showed a great variety of experimental designs and no consistent pattern of results. Many experiments failed to control the type of teaching and to provide differentiation of teaching according to ability levels. Poor experimental design, such as the use of available data only and the use of matched pairs of subjects on unwarranted assumptions of similarity, made many studies less effective. (Ekstrom, 1961, p. 223) *

Ekstrom agrees with Passow and Cornell that positive results favoring homogeneous groups were found in those experiments "that specifically provided for differentiation of teaching methods and materials for groups at each ability level."

SOME SPECIFIED RESEARCH STUDIES

Among the welter of studies on grouping, a few have been selected for discussion in this chapter because of their unusual interest, including studies of special programs for the gifted, and some large scale efforts in New York City, Stockholm, and England. These investigations reflect the pattern of disagreement to be found in general in research on grouping.

Findings favorable to ability grouping. Some direct and some inferential evidence has been accumulated which seems to give clear support to homogeneous grouping for gifted students. Sumption (1941) attempted a comprehensive study of Cleveland's Major Work program which includes both grouping and curriculum factors, although these are not differentiated in the study. He reached by questionnaire 263 individuals who had studied in Major Work classes. He then compared (1) a control group of 65 students with high intelligence test scores (mean I.Q. 126.5) who had not been in Major Work classes with (2) 65 students (mean I.Q. 127.2) who had spent two or three years in Major Work classes and (3) 65 students (mean I.Q. 127.6) who had studied from four to twelve years in Major Work classes. The only evaluative device used was the questionnaire, and some question must be raised therefore as to validity and objectivity. However, Sumption inferred from the

---

* Reprinted from "Experimental Studies of Homogeneous Grouping: A Critical Review," by Ruth B. Ekstrom, in *School Review,* Volume 69, Summer, 1961, by permission of The University of Chicago Press. Copyright 1961 by The University of Chicago.

returns superiority for Major Work scholars in social responsibility, leadership, opportunity to discover aptitudes, self-expressive activities, and career ambitions. In addition these students had won a greater number of scholarships and honors. The Major Works graduates reported wider participation in leisure-time activities and significant differences in reading interests and activities. Little difference was found in vocational adjustment, physical, and mental health. The respondents felt that they had made no sacrifice in fundamental knowledge and skills. In face of the difficulty of measuring many intangible values claimed for grouping, the questionnaire results represent an effort to make comparisons in such areas. Unfortunately no standardized or objectified comparisons are cited in the study.

Justman's comparison (1952) of children in New York City's normal progress and special progress junior high school classes invites an inference based on the narrower grouping generally of students in special progress classes. Children in the special progress classes completed the two year program with academic achievement as good as the normal progress classses made in three years. While this more rapid attainment may be attributed to acceleration alone, there is room to infer some contribution as a result of greater homogeneity of the classes.

In a state-wide study of programs for the gifted in California, Simpson and Martinson (1961) reported on the effects of 17 different administrative and instructional approaches including acceleration, special grouping, and special attention in regular classes. Where special programs were provided, there was uniformly higher achievement than in matched control groups. There were no decrements in the number of friendships or in the interpersonal status level of 929 pupils in the program. Simpson and Martinson reported gains in personal-social attributes. Unfortunately, it is necessary to attribute these positive effects to the total situation rather than to grouping alone.

Despite the dearth of substantial and unchallenged evidence, observers of highly specialized schools and classes are most often convinced of the greater challenge, stimulation, and motivation in these "homogenized" environments. MacLean (1956, p. 217) comments: "Cross-fertilization of ideas develops at a rapid rate and brings clarification of concepts. There is vigorous growth in the feel for tools and the mastery of skills and techniques. Psychologically, expanding achievement brings a feeling of confidence, security, and adequacy. The pace of learning is swift; the range of attempt and accomplishment wide, and of comprehension deep." While admitting arrogance, snobbery, boredom, indifference, and superficiality are a danger if segregation is poorly done, Mac-

Lean notes that these effects also accrue when bright children are forced to move at a snail's pace in heterogeneous classes. The system should not be condemned because it is sometimes operated badly.

Teacher attitudes toward grouping. There is a surface logic in ability grouping which is attractive to many lay observers and professionals alike. If students are taught in groups, it seems only reasonable that organizing groups according to abilities would be the most efficient way to learn. The NEA Research Division (1961) polled a nation-wide sample of teachers in elementary and secondary schools in 1960 and discovered a two-to-one preference in elementary schools and ten-to-one choice in secondary schools supporting ability grouping. The results were tabulated as follows:

	Elementary (per cent)	Secondary (per cent)
Approve of grouping	57.6	87.3
Disapprove of grouping	33.1	8.6
Don't know	9.3	4.1

A breakdown was also made for teachers who had taught under ability grouping and those who had not:

	Elementary (per cent)			Secondary (per cent)		
	Had not taught under A.G.	Had — taught under A.G.	Had taught under both plans	Had not taught under A.G.	Had — taught under A.G.	Had taught under both plans
Approve	46.1	78.8	63.3	81.8	87.3	90.5
Disapprove	36.9	17.7	33.3	8.5	9.8	8.1
Don't know	17.0	3.5	3.4	9.7	2.9	1.4

(NEA Research Division, 1961)*

These findings are representative of other studies which show that the closer the individual is to the classroom the more he favors grouping. Thus, teachers are most strongly in favor, administrators less, and college professors of education least. It seems significant that teachers at both levels who have taught under ability grouping are more favorably dis-

---

* From "Teacher Opinion Poll." Reprinted with permission from *National Education Association Journal*, April, 1961.

posed than those who have not. The large difference between elementary and secondary teachers may be explained on at least two bases: (1) the elementary school teacher has contact with the same students for practically the full school day; he has more time, therefore, to individualize his work; (2) the elementary school teacher is more concerned with the child's total development than with achievement in a single subject.

Negative Evidence: New York City. New York City's Bureau of Educational Research has reported extensive studies of the effects of grouping in elementary and secondary schools. Abramson (1959) summarized a high school follow-up study which compared college records in the first two years of high ability graduates in 1955 from four types of high school organization: a specialized high school, an honors school within a neighborhood school, honors classes (students enrolled in one or two such classes) within a neighborhood school, and a school with heterogenous classes. The students were grouped in three levels: IQ 115-124, 125-134, 135-160. Students scoring above 160 were not included in the comparison. At the end of the freshman year and again at the end of the sophomore year in college, the grade point averages of students coming from more and less highly selective classes showed no differences. The only significant difference was found among levels of intelligence. There were no significant differences in honors or awards won, either, except by levels of intelligence. Abramson summarizes:

> The major conclusion derived from the findings of this investigation is that, when compared by the measures of achievement which were used, no superiority of preparation for college can be claimed for either the specialized high school or the honor-class program as contrasted with the comprehensive high school which had grouped students heterogeneously. The over-all achievement of students, as indicated by grade-point averages and honors, is associated with their level of intelligence rather than with the particular high school they attended. (Abramson, 1959, p. 180)

He concludes that the lack of evidence to support ability grouping suggests that further research on the education of the academically gifted should be centered on curriculum and methods of teaching.

The elementary school study (Goldberg and Passow, 1962) involved about 2,200 children in 86 classes in 45 different elementary schools. Children were assigned to fifteen kinds of groups which differed in their spread of ability. On the basis of Otis (Alpha Form) IQ scores measured in the third grade, children were divided into five groups: IQ's of 130 and higher, 120-129, 110-119, 100-109, and under 100. These levels were systematically combined in order to yield some groups that had high scorers only, some low scorers only and some with different combinations of high, middle and low. The classes remained together for the two-year duration of the project and were tested at the beginning of the fifth grade and at the end of the sixth grade. Efforts were made to measure academic achievement, interests, self-appraisal, attitudes toward school, attitudes toward more and less able classmates, friendship and leadership status and creative writing. The pupils' teachers in the fifth and sixth grades rated each child on a variety of traits in addition. The following results were reported:

> Achievement tests provided measures in nine areas, including reading, language, arithmetic, social studies, science, and work-study skills. On all but the science, social studies, and arithmetic computation tests, the increments in achievement were seriously limited for the higher ability students by the test ceilings. For all five ability levels taken together, achievement increments in social studies, reading, vocabulary and the three areas of arithmetic were significantly greater in the broad-range than the medium and narrow-range classes. However, the differences were generally small and for no one group were they significant in more than two or three of the subjects tested. In general, if the data for the five ability levels are considered as a whole, the indications are that the broad-range patterns (four or five ability levels) show the largest mean increment in achievement, followed by the narrow-range patterns (one or two ability levels). The smallest increments were observed in the medium-range (three ability levels) groups. (Passow and Goldberg, 1961, p. 4) *

What of the comparative achievement of students in any one level as found in different groups? Children in the three middle ability groups (IQ 100-109, 110-119, and 120-129) did equally well whether they were at the top, in the middle or at the bottom of the ability range in their class. Children in all ability levels did better in science and social studies when some gifted students (IQ 130 and over) were in the group. On the other hand, the presence of children of low-average ability also had a positive effect on the arithmetic scores of all children in a group.

In general, the differences found in achievement among students of like ability were found to vary but little as a result of the pattern of grouping employed. The bright student did as well or better in a group with a

---

* From *The Talented Youth Project: A Progress Report, 1961*, by A. Harry Passow and Miriam L. Goldberg. Horace Mann-Lincoln Institute of School Experimentation Interim Reports. Reprinted with permission of The Talented Youth Project, Teachers College, Columbia University.

wide range of ability as he did in a group for bright youngsters only.*
The researchers concluded that grouping per se showed little effect upon
achievement. More important seemed to be differences in the teacher's
techniques, content and personality.

To explain the apparent ineffectiveness of grouping efforts in the New
York City research, various observations have been made. The usual
(and often valid) explanation is offered that measuring instruments did
not cover the possible changes in attitude, interest, and breadth of learning which may have taken place. Perhaps more significant, in light of
the Stockholm research which is reported below, is the observation that
an unforeseen effect resulted from research efforts to limit variables in
the study. Schools in predominantly white, middle class neighborhoods
were chosen in order to limit the effect of variations in cultural, ethnic,
social, and economic factors. It is conceivable that children from such
a background are not significantly affected by grouping practices when
they attend a school whose values are consonant with those of their families.

Hamilton, Ohio. A smaller-scale study by Edmiston and Benfer in
Hamilton, Ohio, in 1948 produced strikingly similar results. Children in
the fifth and sixth grades in four schools were organized in 16 groups,
eight narrow- and eight wide-ability groups on the basis of intelligence
test scores. Average IQ of the groups was almost identical, but the
range of the narrow groups was 29 IQ points as compared with 41 for
the wide groups. The schools made use of special reading teachers, each
of whom had two wide- and two narrow-ability groups. Using the Stanford reading tests over a six month period, average growth of the wide
group was 8.54 as compared with 8.02 for the narrow group. The authors
expressed a belief that organization of special classes for the very slow
learners now obviated the necessity for further ability grouping (Edmiston and Benfer, 1949).

Studies in England. In England, as in New York City, it is curious to
note new research which does not support policies of ability grouping
that have been maintained for many years. Daniels (1961) reports on
comparison of streamed (ability-grouped) and unstreamed schools in

---

* It should be noted, however, that the study lost some of its precision because
of shifts in IQ that occurred between the tests in the third grade which were used
for identification of the groups and the tests in the sixth grade. On the third grade
tests, 39 per cent of the sample scored 120 or higher; on the sixth grade tests (Otis,
Beta form), 69 per cent of the sample scored at this level. As a result, some of the
narrow-range patterns became in effect broad-range groups. The changes in IQ
were not ascribed to grouping, but to qualities of the Alpha and Beta forms which
were used. There was a greater relationship between the third grade reading test
and the Beta form than between the Alpha in the third grade and the Beta (Hage,
1960).

two local educational authorities, where school size, IQ distribution, social-economic status, and staff quality were regarded as equal. Students were matched by IQ scores. In the unstreamed schools, the mean IQ was increased significantly (3 points); greater increases were recorded in reading, English, and arithmetic, and there was a decreased dispersion in scores throughout, indicating that slower children were being helped most.

Pidgeon (1960) has described the "National Survey of the Ability and Attainment of Children at Three Age Levels" and has made comparisons[*] with studies of results in Australia, Canada, Scotland, South Africa, India, and California. Pidgeon is surprised to discover greater variability of scores in countries like England which practice streaming to the greatest extent. He regards the spreading out of levels as being the opposite of what is normally claimed for grouping systems. In addition, he cites disturbing evidence indicating (1) that the average transfer in England from one stream to another is only 2.3 per cent each year in contrast with teacher estimate of annual change of 17 per cent; (2) that there is a "self-fulfilling prophecy" that accompanies grouping: slower children tend to do better when wrongly assigned to the brighter groups, and they tend to make less progress and leave school early when assigned to the slow groups. In addition, social class factors seem to enter the picture. Somehow 11 per cent more middle class children were found in the brighter stream than was expected from their ability; 26 per cent fewer middle class children were found in the slower stream than might be expected. Pidgeon's conclusion is that streaming interferes with individualization of pace and activity in English schools.

ABILITY GROUPING AND SOCIAL CLASS

Husen and Svensson (1960) seized upon reorganization of the Stockholm schools in 1955 to make a long-desired comparison of achievement of students in selective and comprehensive groups. In doing so, they gathered some fascinating data concerning differential effects of grouping upon students coming from varied social class backgrounds. In 1955 comprehensive schools were established for the south end of Stockholm, but the north end retained its traditional dual system. In the data that follow, students in the comprehensive schools in the south end are referred to as "undifferentiated." Those selected for the *realskola* in grades 5 and 6 in the north end are referred to as the "plus select" (high ability) group; those who remained in reorganized classes in elementary

---

[*] Lecture, Metropolitan Association for the Study of the Gifted, New York City, March 5, 1963.

schools are referred to as "minus select" (low ability). In the two grades, 2,755 students were compared in terms of type of school organization and social class. Intelligence tests, two reading comprehension tests, writing tests, and two arithmetic tests were administered with the following results:

Intelligence tests: Lower class children made significantly different gains in the following order: plus select, undifferentiated, minus select. Middle and upper class children showed about the same intelligence differences from age 11 to 13 regardless of the type of school organization.

Reading Comprehension I: No significant differences when social class factor was held constant. Reading Comprehension II: Children in lower and middle classes showed a significant tendency to respond more definitely to the plus-select environment. This responsiveness to the select milieu showed up more clearly among pupils on average and high achievement levels.

Writing tests: Children showed more skill in tests of structure in writing ("structurization") in the plus-select schools. Children from upper and middle class homes made gains in spelling regardless of school organization. Lower class children made the greatest gains when they were placed in plus-select and undifferentiated classrooms.

Arithmetic approximations: Children in plus-select schools made the most progress. Computation: no significant group differences were found.

The results indicate little differentiation of effect upon upper class children when placed in any of the three types of school organization. Middle class children also show little effect except for one part of the reading test. In five of the seven tests, however, children of manual workers profited more from the plus-select milieu.

Husen and Svensson infer from these results no superiority for the selective school except for the lower-class child. They summarize with these statements:

> Children from the culturally less privileged homes responded most strongly to selective academic-type teaching. Children from homes of higher status apparently are receiving full intellectual stimulation outside the school.
> . . . the minus-select classes tended to be less stimulating than the undifferentiated classes . . . There seemed to be no pedagogic advantage in grouping together pupils of average or below-average capacity. (Husen and Svensson, 1960, p. 49) [*]

---

[*] Reprinted from "Pedagogic Milieu and Development of Intellectual Skills," by Torsten Husen and Nils-Eric Svensson, in *School Review*, Volume 68, Spring, 1960, by permission of The University of Chicago Press. Copyright 1960 by The University of Chicago.

The study challenges the assumption that it is the above-average children who are hampered most by undifferentiated classes. In the words of the investigators, "This alleged superiority of the selective or academic-type of pedagogic milieu is not strongly supported by the present study" (*Ibid.*).

It is well to note that the population of the plus-select schools, while including a few lower class children, was predominantly upper class. The reverse was true of the minus-select schools. One cannot overlook the possibility that a factor in the greater achievement of lower class pupils in the upper class school was the contagion of different values with respect to education on the part of middle and upper class families. Adherence to such values by upper and middle class children may explain comparable achievement regardless of their school assignment.

Transfer these inferences from the Stockholm study to the New York City studies. May one assume that a reason for so few differences in school achievement either in elementary school or college lies in the uniform values toward education held by the groups being studied? Is it conceivable that parallel studies in New York and other cities cutting across cultural and class lines would show differential response to grouping? Would a child from an underprivileged background show greater achievement if placed in a high ability group which was culturally privileged than if he were retained in a lower social class group with questionable attitudes toward education in general? Placement of some children in schools not in their own neighborhoods (either as a move toward integration or in an effort to solve school housing problems) makes possible some interesting research in this direction. Interesting results might also come from comparison of underprivileged students who are given scholarships to upper class private schools with students of equal ability who remain in their own neighborhood.

SUB-GROUPS, FLEXIBLE GROUPING, AND INTEREST

Some research findings are available on grouping policies not based on ability alone. Daisy M. Jones (1948) reported "An Experiment in Adaptation to Individual Differences" in Richmond, Indiana, where the variable was the class-as-a-single-group compared with the class working in small groups. The experimental group (small groups) used individualized materials regardless of grade levels; the control group used mainly the materials assigned to its grade level (fourth). Over a nine-month period there was a significant superiority in growth for the experimental grouping in reading, arithmetic, spelling, and general average. The greatest difference was reported for slow and average children. For children with IQ above 110, the differences were not significant. Apparently, superior children are less dependent "on individ-ualization of instruction and guidance from their teacher than are their less capable classmates" (D. Jones, 1948, p. 270).

Holmes and Harvey (1956) have compared permanent and flexible grouping *within* third, fourth, and sixth grade classrooms in San Diego that were not homogeneously grouped. Arithmetic and sociometric tests were administered. No significant differences were found in arithmetic growth, in attitudes toward arithmetic, or in social structure of the groups whether the classes remained in their original groups through-out the year or whether the teacher continuously rearranged them. Com-parisons were also made of children of comparable ability in these groups. Again, no significant differences were found. In this situation, at least, it mattered little whether grouping was effected just once during the year or whether it was kept flexible.

Interest may be of greater significance than general academic aptitude even in the grouping of students of high ability. MacLean (1956) de-scribes a provocative comparison made by Lazarus in a California high school. An "enriched and accelerated" class in reading and creative writ-ing had been formed, and extraordinary achievement was reported for a group formed on the basis of interest despite a wide spread in intelli-gence test scores whose median was 104. As a result of an article in a popular magazine, many additional pupils with high IQ's sought admis-sion to the course. The new group had an IQ range of 110 to 150 with a median of 120, but it did not perform as well as the earlier group's literary output either in quantity or quality. MacLean comments, "We have here an illustration of a sound principle of counseling psychology that high ability with little or no interest achieves far below moderate ability with high interest" (1956, p. 216).

PHILOSOPHICAL COMMITMENTS AND PSYCHOLOGICAL CONCERNS

Grouping is not simply a matter of tradition and research. Grouping expresses philosophic commitments in education and conclusions from psychological inquiry. While the needs of gifted children may be in some ways different from those of other pupils, the basic philosophical commitments of a given culture still apply, and giftedness does not in some magic way free a child from the operation of psychological prin-ciples.

Grouping policies reflect a community's idea of the purposes of edu-cation—or the lack of any clear idea as to the aims its schools should pursue. They reflect also concepts of democracy, equality of opportunity, human dignity, and the pursuit of excellence. The method of grouping employed may also say much about a community's attitudes toward conformity and diversity.

Schools in the 1920's made the assumptions that efficient teaching of subject matter was the primary goal and that tests of intelligence could be used as the primary determinant in grouping learners. Social stresses in the 1930's and new educational viewpoints challenged adherence to these limited objectives for the schools and contributed to the discard of ability grouping in many places. Alberty and Brim, writing in the National Society for the Study of Education yearbook on Grouping (NSSE, 1936, pp. 123-29), set forth a totally different concept of educational objectives. The goals they asserted were "intelligent purposing in personal and social life, social sensitivity, ability to think, integration of personality, and creative self-expression." "Social sensitivity," they said, ". . . calls for a sympathetic understanding of all individuals, whether they possess many or few talents. Social planning requires the cooperation of all, of whatever type or level of learning." To accomplish these tasks, they cited the need for basic reorganization of schools, curricula, and methods. Instead of equal ability groups, they predicted that small groups would be formed in terms of interests and activities, subordinated to the problem at hand and the educational goals in view. They could see such groups changing frequently as new problems and activities might demand.

In place of intelligence scores, Brim and Alberty, accordingly, proposed other criteria in determining grouping policy. Would the policy stem from the concept of a changing, "open" universe and aim therefore at developing flexibility to meet changing conditions? Would it guide students toward intelligent self-direction? Would it develop a socially responsible philosophy of living? Would it reinforce a trend away from deadly uniformity? Would it facilitate individualization of instruction while conserving the values of group activities? Would it recognize the child as a dynamic organism and facilitate growth of the "whole child"? Would it promote such values in education as socialization, creativeness, ability to think, growth of interests, and integration of personality?

SOCIAL COHESION IN A DEMOCRACY

Implicit in Alberty and Brim's statement of purposes of education were their attitudes toward education in a democracy. Concern with social cohesiveness in the traumatic 1930's led to demands for educational devices that would stress the common interests of citizens rather than their individual differences. These demands were consistent with the heritage of public education in the United States as a unifying influence in a country with the greatest diversity of ethnic backgrounds the world had yet seen. Grouping policies must always be consistent with the goal of social and civic unity as a basic purpose in American education. These policies must also square with premises concerning the fundamental equality of all human beings and equal opportunity for all men.

Advocates of ability grouping commonly make a distinction between equality and egalitarianism. They assert, with good reason, that equality of opportunity does not mean the same opportunity for all. They criticize heterogeneous grouping as providing the same educational fare for those who need it and those who do not, for those who can benefit from it, and for those who cannot. Yet it is an over-simplification to claim that differentiation of educational opportunity is necessarily dependent upon ability grouping in all (or most) subjects at all (or most) grade levels. Research evidence does not support the claim that ability grouping necessarily provides greater differentiation than other methods of grouping.

Taking note of citizenship needs, some authorities advocate ability grouping in all academic subjects in secondary schools except social studies where the need is recognized to develop mutual understanding among all elements in the body politic. Not all social studies representatives are pleased with this exclusion, and they present the same arguments for ability grouping as do specialists in other fields. A compromise such as that suggested by Conant in his study of American high schools (1959) would group students by ability for their study of American and world history but organize cross-sectional groups for twelfth-year classes in Problems of American Democracy.

Many educational theorists continue their support of heterogeneity despite renewed pressures in the 1960's toward establishing simplistic academic goals and forming narrow ability groups as the best way to meet them. The new pressure to return to old procedures is stoutly resisted by some educators whose policy is described as follows by Wilhelms:

1. Greater commitment to welfare of the individual pupil; a genuine search for the kind of group in which a child will do his best and grow in a well-rounded manner; movement from ability grouping to grouping based on such factors as interest and need
2. Less faith in any one criterion; IQ as an aid rather than a final determinant; greater weight given to judgments of teachers and counselors
3. Growing recognition of variability
4. Viewing ability grouping as a concession to mediocre teaching

5. Increased value placed on diversity and deliberate use of grouping to encourage diversity
6. Limiting ability grouping in high school to areas of greatest need, such as English
7. Increase in concern for differentiation of content and method at several levels
8. Reduced need for further grouping in the regular classroom as a result of development of classes for the mentally retarded. (Adapted from Wilhelms, 1958, pp. 8-11)[*]

Persons who are committed to development of democratic values and skills as an important goal of American education have to face a number of issues in evaluating grouping proposals. Will the method of grouping employed lead to appropriate respect for the dignity of other persons? Will it develop the student's self-respect and a sense of his own dignity? Will it lead to social sensitivity, civic responsibility, sympathy for others? Will it lead to a sense of civic unity or separateness? Just as research evidence does not establish the superiority of ability grouping for intellectual achievement, it does not paint a clear picture of democracy in the heterogeneous classroom or anti-democratic outcomes in classes that are relatively homogeneous. Obviously, much more study is needed.

It is important, however, to note a striking correlation between upper class membership and enrollment in high ability classes, between particular ethnic backgrounds and particular ability group placement. Methods used to identify ability groups are unfortunately sensitive to these social distinctions as well. Using exisiting identification measures, school leaders may find social integration and ability grouping antithetical. In some cities parents seek out special schools or special classes for children as a covert form of social segregation.

CREATIVENESS, CONFORMITY, AND DIVERSITY

Growing emphasis in the Space Age on creativeness has led to concern over the effects that grouping may have on the conformity-diversity axis. In general, opponents of ability grouping take the position that grouping tempts teachers and administrators to regard their "homogeneous" groups as units rather than as collections of unique personalities. On the other hand, the diversity of a heterogeneous group cannot be overlooked. It is on this basis that some authorities explain the surprisingly superior

[*] From "The Nature of Classroom Grouping for Learning," by Fred R. Wilhelms. Paper prepared for discussion group, 1958 Annual Conference of Association for Supervision and Curriculum Development. Reprinted with permission of Fred R. Wilhelms.

achievement of gifted students in the broadest range groups in some researches.

Academic achievement is not affected in this way only, however. Ability grouping is being criticized as a pressure toward conformity upon students in terms of career goals, personality, attitudes toward learning, and in the very act of thinking itself. It is significant that the writers in the National Society for the Study of Education yearbook on *Individualizing Instruction* (1962) regard ability grouping and individualization as incompatible. In another publication, Wolfle notes reduced variability among the group members as an effect of grouping procedures. He cites these examples of pressures toward conformity: uniform lesson assignments, and identification of superior students through standardized tests of general ability, grade-point averages, and class rank (Wolfle, 1960). The tendency "to emphasize cognitive skills: the ability to remember, to solve problems conventionally (as the textbook and teacher solve them) and otherwise to be a 'lesson learner' " is regarded as an obstacle to individualization and development of creativeness (NSSE, 1962, p. 28).

PSYCHOLOGICAL CONCERNS

Philosophical commitments apart, grouping procedures should be consistent with psychological information available on the nature of learners, of children in groups, and the social and emotional effects of various grouping practices.

Human variability. Of primary importance is the wealth of information that psychology has assembled on the variability of human beings. Hardin (1959, pp. 186-187) has summarized in table form differences among human beings with respect to various physiological factors. He calculates a "factor of variation" by dividing the maximum by the minimum score for a given physical quality within the normal range. This factor varies from 2 for phosphate concentration in the blood, to 8 for the minimum percentage of alcohol in the blood that is intoxicating, to 42 for minimum perceptible movement in peripheral vision. As an illustration of variability, one individual may have 42 times the peripheral vision of another; one may show an intoxicating percentage of alcohol in his blood after imbibing only one-eighth the alcohol that another does.

In psychological rather than physical factors, similar variations are found. In the school situation, teachers and administrators have discovered repeatedly that selection of children on the basis of one or two variables such as reading comprehension or an intelligence quotient may have no relevance with respect to ability in arithmetic, art, music, social studies, or physical activities. In addition, the IQ as a predictor of academic performance has been challenged by recent research on creativeness by Torrance (1960a)) and Getzels and Jackson (1959) in different situations with children of different age levels. In both cases researchers compared "low IQ-high creative" children with "high IQ-low creative" children. Grouping by "intelligence" can be successful only if the many variables that constitute intelligence are included in a test score, and only if there is a high degree of correlation among these variables, a proposition which is denied by all the evidence available. There is a general consensus that the various expedients which have been attempted reduce variability in a class by a rather small fraction. To state the fact in a different way, variability in a "homogeneous" class is only slightly less than the variability in a class grouped by chance.

Intellect as part of personality. Modern psychology, of course, no longer supports the unspoken assumption that intelligence "flies solo." Featherstone (1940) points to two unwarranted assumptions that are implicit in many grouping plans: (1) that all other traits are closely associated with the intellect; (2) that needs which cannot be met through intellectual channels merit little consideration. All of the emphasis of psychiatry since Freud has been to stress the fundamental importance and pervasive influence of the emotions. There is little doubt that operation of the intellect is very much circumscribed by emotional factors, often unconscious. Identification of a group in terms of high IQ gives data only on some intellectual factors; it gives no insight into instruction required except in intellectual matters. Yet, every group has problems related to volition, emotions, and social adjustment that must be met by other than intellectual processes.

Recognizing the dynamic quality of learning and the individual nature of perception, Featherstone insists that a curriculum does not exist outside or apart from the pupil. Psychologically speaking, there must be a curriculum for each individual. Mass teaching of gifted pupils is no better than mass teaching of average pupils. If grouping leads to a facile assumption of homogeneity, to glossing over of individual differences, it can be only a negative influence in teaching. The studies showing greater effectiveness of wide ability groups may serve only to corroborate this point of view.

Social attitudes. Much information is still needed on the social effects of ability grouping. Advocates of such procedures insist that no snobbery exists on the basis of statements from gifted children (Hunter College Elementary School, 1958, p. 2). This is indeed a questionable statement in view of claims by other persons that children in the elite school situations display at times insufferable conceit and condescension toward

other children. Obviously, a child bright enough to be selected for a
highly elite group is bright enough to give the socially acceptable answer
when asked for his self-appraisal or reaction to others. Horace Mann's
study of children (1957) in the Colfax Elementary School is not unequivocal but it is of interest. He studied the play choices and the personal preferences of children in a school where the bright children spend
half the day in heterogeneous situations. Being of elementary school age,
the children tended to play after school with other children living near
their homes regardless of school grouping. In response to sociometric
devices children tended to select and to reject other children in their
own school group. Either they didn't know other children as well or
they didn't think of them as working partners (equals?) in the choice
situations Mann presented.

Abraham and Edith Luchins (1948) studied the grouping system in
New York City elementary schools to detect effects on attitude formation. Children in New York City are assigned in most cases to classes
with a hyphenated number where the first number indicates the grade
and the second the ability level as determined by intelligence test and/or
reading scores, for example, 4-1, 4-2, 4-3. In most cases the "1" class
is the top ability group, the "2" class next, and so on. Children in the
fourth, fifth and sixth grades were interviewed. A high percentage of
children in all ability groups indicated their belief that their parents
would prefer them to be in the 1-class. Most children in the 1-class
would not give up their 1-class membership even if the teacher in
the 2-class were "better and kinder." A majority of the other children
would place teacher qualities above class status. A high percentage of
children in the 1-classes frequently would not play with or choose friends
from children in the 2-classes. Children in the lower ability classes would
in most cases choose without respect to class. The Luchins indicate evidence of feelings of inferiority and frustration on the part of children in
the 2-classes. These people regard the bright children as snobbish. The
Luchins conclude with a judgment that "homogeneous grouping seemed
to help create a kind of caste-system in the school," and that it reinforced the overemphasis on grades, honors, promotion, and competition.

Maxine Mann (1960) performed a similar study in the midwest with
102 children grouped in four ability levels in the fifth grade. When children were asked which group they were in, practically all children in
the middle groups (second and third) identified their group by their
teacher's name. Almost two thirds of the children in Section One identified their group as the "high," "top" or "best" fifth grade class. Two-
thirds of Section Four identified themselves by saying they were in the
"low," or "lower" fifth grade rather than using conventionally their

teacher's name to identify the class. Reasons children gave for their own placement were revealing. Half the children in the two middle groups gave "I do not know" as the answer and an additional quarter gave the non-committal "They put me here" or an equivalent. None of the top and bottom groups "didn't know." Five-sixths of the top group used "positive terms of ability or achievement"—" 'I'm smart,' " " 'I worked hard,' " " 'We can work a little faster.' " Three-fourths of the low group used "negative terms of ability or achievement": " 'I am too dumb,' " " 'I can't think good,' " " 'Most of us are lazy,' " " 'We aren't smart.' " In the top group, 21 of the 30 pupils used "I" ability reasons (describing themselves) for their placement; 3 gave "we" ability reasons (describing the group). In the bottom group, 6 of the 18 gave "I" ability reasons; 7 gave "we" ability reasons. Mann found evidence in her study that disturbed her concerning the effects of grouping policy on the self-concept students were developing. Eash (1961) comments:

> The evidence is fairly conclusive that grouping practices in a school can assist in developing social situations that influence the student's perception of self, his sense of dignity and worth, and his attitudes toward other children. In view of this, grouping practices should be concerned with furthering the establishment of social climates that will encourage the intellectual, social and personal development of every child without detrimental effects on individual children. (*Ibid.*, p. 431)

Intercultural research findings about grouping. Perhaps most pervasive of the social effects of ability grouping is the unconscious social stratification which so frequently ensues. Evidence concerning social and civic attitudes of children raised in socially homogeneous environments is not available. However, most authorities on intercultural education advance the hypothesis that broad understanding depends upon varied and daily exposure to children of other ethnic, cultural, social, and economic groups than their own. This assumption seems plausible, at least on the surface. Grouping practices that restrict contacts ought to be questioned unless valid evidence to the contrary becomes available. What is most interesting in education of the gifted is the Swedish research which shows that children from lower socio-economic levels are likely to be most adversely affected when restricted to low ability groups.

Shaftel (1962) in a review of research on education for cross-cultural understanding reflects concern for social and personal goals that depend upon the individual's breadth of personal contact. She cites a study by Coelho (1962) of students abroad which indicates the necessity of the kind of education " 'that would increase the probability of broadening the basis of an individual's self esteem, reality-testing, self-knowledge, and range of compassionate concern for others.' " One may indeed question grouping procedures which limit the social and ethnic range of classmates in the interest of alleged academic homogeneity. A study by Bronfenbrenner, "On the American Child," (1961) describes children coming from achievement oriented families as excelling in performance and goal-directedness but also as being more aggressive, tense, domineering, and cruel. Concentration of such children in a single class could conceivably—although evidence is not yet available in the literature—result in superior academic performance, but the negative personal qualities might be too great a price to pay.

Unfortunately, Bronfenbrenner's study corroborates inferences to be drawn both from Maxine Mann's research reported earlier and from an interesting study of grouping in England. Rudd studied "The Psychological Effects of Streaming by Attainment" (1958) on 180 children entering the same selective central school at eleven years of age in London. The control group was composed of 90 children who remained in their original groups for two years. The experimental group was divided into three streams (ability groups) with transfers made from group to group after each half-yearly examination period. No significant differences were discovered in achievement or in attitudes toward examinations, school work, or school life in general. In the streamed groups, however, there were fewer social contributions made by the pupils (volunteering to bring in information, offering to help other pupils, for example), more copying of work, more aggressive behavior and less attention to work. An interesting behavior difference was found in comparing the A stream (high) and C stream (low). The A stream conformed to authority while achieving only a low degree of social cohesion. By contrast the C stream appeared to be "comrades in adversity" with higher frequencies of both minor misdemeanors and social contributions. Social cohesion of the non-streamed control group was markedly higher.

RECOMMENDATIONS

The conclusion is inescapable that administrative provisions merely set the limits within which the teacher may work with his students. Adjustment to individual differences is the function of the teacher and the resources he has available to him. He may arrange for grouping within the classroom with instructional, remedial, or social ends in view. Groups may be organized on a basis of ability to give some gifted students especially challenging opportunities while slower students are working on mastery of lower level work. Groups may be organized around particular interests where fast and slow students work together in keeping with their own potentials. Where useful, laboratory plans such as the Dalton and Morrison contracts may be pursued by individual students or the whole class. Assignments may be differentiated either through individual tailoring, through organization of sub-groups in the class, or through making of maximum and minimum assignments with students encouraged to work at the most meaningful level. Cocurricular projects in the activity period or after school invite an informal, voluntary grouping which normally combines interest and ability factors.

The many educational advantages of group instruction assure its continuance for a long time. The problem of individual variation within the group will remain as long as learners are taught in groups. Decisions as to the use of ability grouping should be made after consideration of the following questions:

1. Is it really desirable to limit variability for the purpose of the desired instruction?
2. To what extent will proposed plans actually reduce variability in specified dimensions?
3. Are defensible instruments for selection available? What factors are being controlled? What factors are left for uncontrolled variability?
4. What measures will be used to insure individualization *within* the group? (Too often, when grouping comes in, individualization flies out.)
5. How will curriculum, methods and materials be differentiated between and within groups?
6. Will methods of selecting groups increase pressure on students toward conformity as they strive to be selected?
7. What is the likely social effect of grouping? Will social segregation patterns in the community be reinforced or mitigated? What will be the effect on existing friendship groups? Will attitudes toward other individuals and other ability groups deteriorate? Will groups of children be assembled who are overly self-centered and self-seeking?
8. What are the likely personal effects of grouping? How will grouping affect children's self-concepts?
9. What provisions will be made to keep grouping flexible in recognition of the unevenness in human development?
10. What arrangements are being made to secure objective evidence on academic, social, and personal effects of the policies under consideration?

While the evidence on grouping remains equivocal, there is reason to believe that ability grouping may be warranted in special situations under special circumstances. The nature of these special situations and circumstances is implicit in the answer given to the questions above. When ability grouping is employed, certain conditions should be met:

Grouping should be employed for highly specific learning outcomes.

Special grouping, if employed, should not be limited to a few academic specialties which are closely interrelated; students with talents in a wide variety of areas should have the same opportunity for distinction and specialized assistance.

Students should be assigned to special groups only where their abilities are distinctive; they should have the opportunity to work with "the generality" where their talents are smaller.

Criteria for grouping should include all contributing factors to outstanding achievement in a particular field; use of a single measure like IQ or reading scores should be avoided; interest should be given a leading place as an identifying factor.

Special groups should be based upon highly distinctive ability and unquestioned interest; broadening the ability and interest base in order to assemble a larger number of students may defeat the original purpose of grouping.

Any effort to set up ability groups must be accompanied by genuine efforts to adapt curriculum, methods, and instructional materials.

Guidance services should be expanded to improve identification procedures, to explore with students problems of motivation, and to extend opportunities for further enrichment beyond the school program to able students.

SUMMARY

The reviews of Cornell, Eash, Ekstrom, and Wrightstone agree on the relative lack of consistent evidence supporting any one kind of grouping. They report, apparently, some slight superiority for ability grouping, but its effects are greatest for dull children, less for average children, and least for gifted children. Some recent studies (for example, New York City, Passow and Goldberg, 1961) go still farther and see an actual negative effect of ability grouping on the most able children.

At any rate, the effects of grouping appear to be related to the breadth of the group "homogeneously" organized. Wrightstone indicates that variability in achievement in grades with three ability groups is about 83 per cent of that in groups organized by chance. If there are only two ability groups, variability is reduced by only 7 per cent. Studies have not been reported on reduced variability for very highly selected groups. If one may extrapolate with some validity from the two- and three-ability group reductions, classes that select the top 1 per cent, the top 10 per cent, the top 15 per cent on one measure or another, may show a further reduction in variability. If this reduction is desired, reasons of population size and concentration argue employment of ability grouping in secondary schools and in large cities more than in elementary schools and smaller communities.

It is entirely possible that confused research results stem from failure to distinguish among possibilities in school districts related to size of the population. Obviously if variability is going to be reduced by only a minor fraction, effective ability grouping is limited and will not result in any great academic efficiency. This being the case, it seems unwise to risk the social and personal hazards which have been posited and in some cases demonstrated. In very large schools or very large school districts, educational authorities may have to decide between academic and social values or devise procedures that mediate between the two and obviate the necessity to make a choice.

There is also agreement that grouping in itself is only a facilitating device. Substantial increments in learning come, apparently, only when grouping is used to promote differentiation in classroom method, in the curriculum that develops, in guidance provided and in materials employed.

Chapter 14

Acceleration

The lamp of genius burns quicker than the lamp of life.

—Schiller

No paradox is more striking in the education of the gifted than the inconsistency between research findings on acceleration and the failure of our society to reduce the time spent by superior students in formal education. More evidence will be found favoring acceleration than homogeneous grouping or particular enrichment devices; yet acceleration is the least practiced instrument in educating the gifted. Apparently those values which favor a standard period of dependency and formal education for young people in our culture are stronger than demands for early achievement because of social need. These values seem stronger, too, than the individual's desires for early independence or his drive to create.

The years spent in school, of course, are not determined by school authorities. School boards work within confines established by the economy and by attitudes toward educating the young which reflect the nation's economic needs. In the United States for at least two generations our society has been able to forego the productive efforts of adolescents and of approximately one-fourth of young adults of college age. Our traditions of equal opportunity and of individual betterment through education have influenced public and private decisions to keep young people who can be spared in school. Not only have they been permitted to attend school, school attendance laws have steadily pushed upward the age at which they have been required to go to school. Moreover, public and

328

private means have been employed to encourage college attendance of young people beyond the compulsory school age.

These factors of social policy and individual sentiment have been reinforced by the economic structure. Labor-saving devices have sharply reduced the need for unskilled labor and have increased the need for semi-skilled, skilled, and professional services. Employers, able to choose older and better educated entry workers, are unwilling to hire less responsible, more poorly educated boys and girls leaving school at an earlier age. Labor leaders are firm advocates of a high compulsory school age because they recognize the tendency of children in the poorer economic groups to withdraw from school earliest. They see the children of their union members as needing education the most and getting it the least. Also, with a necessary eye on economics, they are not eager to see the labor market glutted with unprepared workers who always represent a threat to the maintenance of adequate wage scales.

While the gifted children are themselves not likely to be the early withdrawals from school, they are affected by legislation and attitudes that have grown up to protect the average. If society can afford to keep the average young man in high school until he is eighteen, ought the talented student to be rushed through to complete at sixteen? If the culture keeps the moderately bright student in college till twenty-two, ought the very superior be put to work—with a B.A.—at nineteen? Some parents take pride in early graduation of their children; others have a feeling akin to guilt, sensing an obligation to support their children until the more typical school leaving ages. These cultural values that obstruct greater use of acceleration are likely to be reinforced rather than weakened, and the paradox of minimal acceleration despite evidence supporting the practice is likely to be maintained.

Acceleration, however limited, is a part of education at all levels. Early admission to kindergarten or the first grade will be found in a number of school systems. Grade skipping in elementary schools is practiced less frequently than once was the case but is still in evidence. Many schools provide for completion of two years' work in one—or three years' in two—at the elementary and junior high school levels. In senior high school and college acceleration will rarely be found to include completion of particular courses or grades in less than standard time. Instead, acceleration results almost exclusively from assumption by the student of a heavier program than usual or enrollment in summer school work. In a few cases admission to college prior to completion of the senior year (sometimes, even the junior year) is allowed. Some colleges will give course credit on the basis of examination. Finally, some students secure college credit, and possibly earlier graduation from college, as a result of completing Advanced Placement courses—in essence taking college work in high school in lieu of the normal high school curriculum.

Table A. ADMINISTRATIVE PROCEDURES FOR ACCELERATION

School Level	Procedure Employed
Kindergarten to Grade 6	Early Admission Grade Skipping Combined Grades (3 years in 2, or 2 years in 1)
Junior High School	Combined Grades (3 years in 2 or in 2½)
Senior High School	Early Graduation through (1) taking more courses per semester, (2) enrollment in summer school
College	Articulation Policy· in relation to high school Early Admission (after sophomore or junior year in high school) Advanced Placement with college credit for college level courses taken in high school Credit for courses by examination Early Graduation through taking heavy program or summer school work

THE CASE FOR ACCELERATION

The argument for acceleration is mounted from several different sectors. One is based on biographical studies which establish the early age at which the most creative contributions to human civilization have been made. Others are social needs, individual development, and educational research and statistics.

AGE AND ACHIEVEMENT

What part of life represents a man's prime? Which years are the most productive? Can any generalization be made as to the age at which the great men of all times have made their most notable contributions? Harvey Lehman in a volume entitled *Age and Achievement* (1953) summarizes the fascinating results of a monumental study of outstanding men in many walks of life and their achievements. Lehman's technique was to assemble a panel of outstanding scholars or performers in each field and to secure a listing of persons whom they regarded as the great men and women in their profession. In the same way he secured a judgment of the outstanding works of these eminent people. Lehman then attempted to relate productive and creative output to the age of the individual being studied. As one might guess, lyric poets, athletes, and actresses are reported as doing their greatest work in the early adult years. Less expected are statistics concerning the most productive years of philosophers, educators and social scientists. Lehman's figures which follow indicate the period of greatest productivity in various fields:

Field	Age at which very superior contributions were made at greatest average rate:
Physical sciences, mathematics, inventions	
Chemistry	26-30
Mathematics	30-34
Physics	30-34
Electronics	30-34
Practical inventions	30-34
Surgical techniques	30-39
Geology	35-39
Astronomy	35-39
Biological sciences	
Botany	30-34
Classical descriptions of disease	30-34
Genetics	30-39
Entomology	30-39
Musical Composition	30-39
Literary works	under 45
Philosophy	
Logic	35-39
Metaphysics	40-44
Social philosophy	36-44
Social Sciences	
Political Science	30-39
Economics	30-39
Educational Theory and Practice	35-39
Psychology	30-39

Art

Painting (oil)	32-36
Painting (oil, American)	40-44
Sculpture (American)	35-39
Modern Architecture	40-44

Some contributions may be made only after excellence has been recognized. Accordingly, the following categories are related to much higher ages:

Earned income over $50,000 annually	60-64
Commercial and industrial leaders	65-69
Presidents, American colleges and universities	50-54
United States Presidents	55-59
Ambassadors	60-64
Senators	60-64
Head of the Army	60-64

Lehman concludes:

> It remains clear that the genius does not function equally well throughout the years of adulthood. Superior creativity rises relatively rapidly to a maximum which occurs usually in the thirties and then falls off slowly. (Lehman, 1953, p. 330) *

Pressey (1962) confirms Lehman's statistics with his observation that recent research indicates a high correlation between early earning of the doctorate and professional success. The median age for earning the doctorate is 26.1 for members of the American Academy of Sciences, and 25.0 for winners of Nobel prizes in physics and chemistry.

The implications of this research for education should be reasonably clear. If superior ability is to bear fruit, it must be helped to flower early. Independent work in the field of special interest must be available as early as the late teens, perhaps.

Many writers assume from these conclusions that the only justifiable educational method is acceleration. Actually, two choices are available. One, assuming that the student must always be the student and never the scholar while in school, is acceleration up to two or more years through high school, an abbreviated undergraduate program, and, if desired, a doctorate in two additional years. The young man or woman of exceptional ability, on this basis might leave high school at fourteen or

---

* From *Age and Achievement*, by Harvey C. Lehman (Princeton University Press, Princeton, N. J.). Copyright 1953 by American Philosophical Society. Reprinted with permission of American Philosophical Society.

fifteen and earn his doctor's degree before reaching twenty. This would leave him the prime years for original work and major achievement. Pressey (1962) quotes an unnamed college president as saying, "I think it is almost criminal to let people stay in the role of student any longer than is absolutely necessary."

A second solution requires greater adjustment in schools and colleges, but is probably more acceptable within our social framework. The objective desired is to maximize an individual's period of productivity, not necessarily to reduce his formal education. Nothing in the current *modus operandi* actually prohibits independent work and adult achievement by students while still in college or graduate school. Indeed, the aim of the dissertation in the Ph.D. program is initiation of such serious endeavor. What stands in the way is not a set of regulations. The bar is simply a stereotyped way of looking at a student, what he does in school, his relationship to his teachers and the degree of independence given to him for individual work. Thus, the situation is not as easy as changing regulations or altering a framework. It is the more difficult one of changing the concept of being a student.

Let us imagine, however, an accelerated program of adult achievement rather than an accelerated progress through the grades and degrees. A boy is identified as having unusual interest in science while still in the third grade. He is given special instruction in science and permitted to do simple laboratory work in the remaining elementary grades. In junior high school he plunges early into high school sciences and is encouraged to work on projects of his own. In high school he does college level work either at a nearby university or through special instruction in the high school.* He is not required to mark time in courses where he shows little interest or aptitude but is invited to use laboratory and project rooms for individual experimentation. In college he moves directly into advanced work and undertakes an honors program that gives him considerable time and opportunity to explore his own ideas and those his advisors suggest. Actually, he pursues a doctoral level program as an undergraduate, and a curriculum is tailored to meet his needs. Normal degree requirements are adapted to give him maximum time for individual work without doing excessive violence to the aims of general educa-

---

* The Chicago Public Schools (1964) have institutionalized a procedure of this type through "place-out" in the ninth grade and Advanced Placement classes in high school. Able ninth-graders may pass over individual freshman high school courses in areas where they demonstrate proficiency by examination. Of three thousand boys and girls "placing-out" in various subjects in 1963, many of them had taken special early morning classes in a nearby high school while still attending the last year in an eight-grade elementary school. Advanced Placement courses are described later in this chapter.

tion. As a doctoral candidate, he is freed to do work of major importance, with the sponsorship, guidance, and facilities of a university available to him, but without the irksome routines, requirements, and examinations that stand in the way of serious achievement. In this way, the student is functioning as an adult for several years before receiving a doctorate, but he is not required to live, work, and play with fellow students older and more worldly wise.

HISTORICAL PRECEDENTS

Acceleration was the first administrative device employed in providing specially for the gifted. St. Louis inaugurated a program of flexible promotion in the elementary school in 1868, providing for more rapid completion of the usual subject matter and without skipping over any parts. A number of variants of acceleration were introduced in school systems throughout the United States from that time until 1930. The variants included grade skipping (double promotion), promotion upon completion of stated work, double track systems (bright children completing elementary school one or two years earlier than usual), combining of grades, and early entrance.

That no system of acceleration affected any large group of pupils was evident in the comments of President Eliot of Harvard in 1888. "The average age of admission to Harvard College has been rising for sixty years past, and has now reached the extravagant limit of eighteen years and ten months," Eliot told the annual meeting of the National Education Association (Pressey, 1949, p. 5).* This concern, echoed by other educators before the turn of the century, led ultimately to formation of the NEA Committee on the Economy of Time and a succession of reports from various committees culminating in formation of junior high schools. An early purpose of the new school unit was reduction of time spent in elementary and secondary schools. Some cities, like Baltimore, New York, and Worcester (Massachusetts) did provide for two-year completion of the three-year program by superior students. By and large, however, schools systems found there was more to be done with young adolescents. They provided more work in fundamental areas, exploration, guidance, and extra-curricular activities and did not reduce the twelve-year common school term.

At the high school and college level little recognition has been given to the ability of bright students to learn more rapidly. The year, semester,

---

* In 1932 the average was still as high as eighteen years and eight months. In 1960 the median age of high school graduates was 18.1, and the median college freshman was 18.9.

or quarter are rigidly enforced for fast and slow learner alike. A few concessions are made. In many institutions superior students are permitted to take a heavier load and accordingly to graduate a semester or a year earlier than average. Experimentation with early admissions programs has resulted in permitting a few high school juniors, and even some sophomores, to enter college a year or two before high school graduation. Advanced Placement makes possible college level work in high school. Colleges which credit such work toward college graduation enable the student to finish his college work somewhat earlier. Finally, credit by examination in a few colleges opens another path to earlier accumulation of the necessary credits. Discussion of some of these specific programs follows.

EARLY ADMISSION TO ELEMENTARY SCHOOL

Readiness to learn does not come for all children at the same time. Readiness for a formal school program or even for reading as a major activity in primary grades is just as variable. School administrators are under continuous pressure to make exceptions when an age-date is set rigidly for first enrollment, whether kindergarten admission is set for those reaching the fifth birthday by September, November, January or May. Unfortunately, the pressure comes not only in behalf of children who are mentally and socially precocious. Parents who want their children in school early for a variety of reasons, justified or not, mount the same pressure and force school boards into adopting rigid admission dates for their own self-preservation. Only as a school system develops effective, objective, and impartial procedures of identification, can it afford to make exceptions for the intellectually gifted.

Some schools, despite this problem, have been able to administer programs of early admission. Worcester (1956) has made a careful study of such programs. He cites reports of early admission in Brookline, Massachusetts, Pittsburgh, and Berks County, Pennsylvania, and a number of school districts in Nebraska. In Brookline, IQ was used as the criterion for entrance. The early entrants did better throughout school after kindergarten. They were not physically distinguishable from the children of typical grade age. They were less often referred for personality, emotional, or social problems. Pittsburgh used 130 IQ as its criterion and reported positive results. Muller (1950) completed a study in 1955 of elementary students admitted to public schools under the requirements of the Nebraska program of early attendance. Teachers evaluated achievement, health, coordination, acceptance, leadership, attitudes, and emotional adjustment of 4,275 children. "Results of this study," says

Worcester, "are unequivocal. If a child is ready mentally, it is clearly to his advantage to enter school even though he be slightly younger, chronologically, than the average" (Worcester, 1956, p. 27).

Since its reorganization as a school for the gifted in 1941, Hunter College Elementary School has admitted children to its nursery school at age three, its kindergarten at age four and its elementary program at age five.* Individually administered Stanford-Binet tests have been used, and children have been admitted from the top down in order of IQ. Generally, this selection has resulted in a class average of 150 and minimum scores around 135. An interview with the principal or an admissions committee and observation of the child at informal play with a few mates are used to establish adequate social maturity. The five-year-olds normally enjoy a combined kindergarten-first grade program. With few exceptions there is no additional acceleration in the six grade program. Children benefit from enrollment in classes where practically all their classmates are of the same age.

Early admission programs are of value because they are adapted to the readiness of children. They are limited in effectiveness by the accuracy of identification procedures employed. Correlations between IQ scores in the pre-school period and scores in early adolescence are low enough to cast some doubt upon the use of such a criterion by itself. A second value of the early admission program is the greater likelihood that the entrant will pursue an undisturbed course in elementary school. Further acceleration is rarely employed. Instead there is every reason to develop a truly enriched program.

DOUBLE PROMOTION AND COMBINING GRADES

The most common form of acceleration in elementary schools is rapid progress through skipping of grades or completing three grades in two years or two grades in one year. Little educational justification is asserted for skipping grades. Where the device is used, it is employed frankly as the simplest solution to the obvious boredom of a bright child. For a short time after skipping, the child will find some challenge. Within a few short months, he usually finds himself ahead of his new classmates. He has had to change old friends for new. He is now likely to find himself among the smallest children in the room.

A type of acceleration that finds greater acceptance is one that follows a definite plan. In kindergarten, first or second grade, children are identified who may benefit from acceleration. They are grouped together, and

---

* A general revision in the program in 1959 increased the admission age by six months, halving the previous acceleration.

as a unit will cover the curriculum of the next two or three years in less than the normal time. This kind of acceleration will be found in many parts of the country in elementary and junior high schools.

The advantage of rapid progress through combined grades lies in the systematic quality of the program. Work is not short-circuited or telescoped. Children do not have to adjust to continually changing class groups. The ability of the bright child to learn faster is put to use. Unfortunately, the rapid progress program encourages the teacher to concentrate on coverage of content rather than the individual learner. Rapid coverage also limits time that might be spent on individual projects, on following up promising leads in learning, and on flexibility in the curriculum essential to genuine pupil-teacher planning. Education becomes something to rush through, rather than an experience to savor, to broaden, to deepen, and to enrich.

Possibilities for acceleration also inhere in the ungraded primary or intermediate grade unit which has been growing in various parts of the country. Children remain in a basic group, generally for the three years of the primary or intermediate grades. During this period they are helped to make individual progress and to meet individual goals. If they achieve the academic objectives of the primary grades, or the intermediate grades, in less than the usual time, promotion from the completed unit may occur at the end of two years. It is of interest to note that the Chicago Public Schools (1964) see in their program of this type (labelled "the continuous development plan") a possible successor to grade-skipping in Chicago which is gradually declining.

ACCELERATION IN HIGH SCHOOL AND COLLEGE

The methods used for acceleration in high school and college are described in the chapter on high school and college programs. One result is to put sharper focus on the bright student and his educational needs. Advanced Placement courses and college follow-ups generally represent a much enriched program for the student. Early admission of non-graduates from high school to college can eliminate some repetition of work that results from poor articulation.

Pressey (1949) argues effectively against acceleration which is limited to assumption of heavier loads and summer study. Unfortunately, each student earns exactly one unit, no more and no less, regardless of the quality of his achievement, for 36 weeks of a subject studied five periods a week. What is needed is some qualitative method of record keeping and course offering which will break the lockstep inherent in the Carnegie unit. If acceleration is at all desirable, early graduation at either level should depend upon quality of learning, not on the number of periods spent in class. Credit by examination, use of comprehensive examinations, acceptance of honors projects, and employment of "contract" systems are possible devices to facilitate variable progress through high school and college.

WHEN TO ACCELERATE

Most of the acceleration that is practiced takes place in the first nine years of school. There is good reason for this to be so. Keys argues the case in this way:

> It is in the elementary grades that the need is greatest, for the modern high school affords other opportunities for enrichment and adaptation through its differentiated curricula and student activities. Adjustment to classmates older than oneself is probably made most easily when early in one's schooling, before friendships and *crowds* are too strongly established. Moreover, there is less danger of important content being permanently missed when a lower grade is passed over. (Keys, 1942, p. 254) [*]

Because different children mature differently, if acceleration is to be employed it will take place when it seems most appropriate. Criteria should include academic achievement, some measure of physical age and an evaluation of social maturity and emotional stability. Intelligence and achievement scores, checked against teacher grades, should indicate ability that would place the student in approximately the top quarter of the grade to which he is being accelerated. Physical data should include height, weight, and strength measurements and appropriate information on sexual maturation. It is to be expected that the accelerated student may not equal the norms of an older age group. At times a "calculated risk" despite marked physical immaturity may seem worth taking, but school authorities, parents and the pupil should all be aware of the situation as it is and as it may affect the pupil. Because of possible tensions that may accompany acceleration, signs of emotional immaturity should be respected as an important caution. Social development may not impose an insuperable bar, but signs of immaturity should either negate acceleration or occasion careful orientation of the student, his parents and teachers.

There is almost universal agreement on two years as the upper limit of acceleration prior to college. Further acceleration in college should

---

[*] From "Should We Accelerate the Bright?" by Noel Keys. Reprinted with permission from *Journal of Exceptional Children*, May, 1942.

probably depend upon the student's career plans. A very superior student might enter college at sixteen and satisfactorily complete a B.A. program by eighteen, if permitted to do so. If he is immediately to enter graduate work, this might be an acceptable pattern. If he is seeking to enter into employement dependent upon college graduation, his youth is likely to serve as a barrier and a longer, enriched college program would stand him in better stead. Keys speaks for practically all writers on the subject when he says:

> Given an intelligence quotient above 140, therefore, with health and other factors reasonably favorable and the need for lengthy professional training in prospect, school practice should aim at entrance to college or university around the sixteenth birthday for the man, and up to half a year younger in the case of the brilliant girl. Owing to earlier maturation in women, the underage girl enjoys a distinct advantage in social relationships over the underage boy. With acceleration exceeding two and a half years, the risk of social maladjustment increases, but there is abundant evidence that under exceptional circumstances and in the absence of special class facilities, advancement by as much as three years may be the best solution. The writer would hesitate to advise more than that. (Keys, 1942, pp. 254, 269)

RESEARCH SUPPORTING ACCELERATION

Numerous studies can be cited to show the absence of deleterious effects resulting from acceleration and the presence of a variety of advantages. In only rare instances can negative research evidence be found. Nevertheless, there is little reason to doubt the accuracy of Wilson's research findings that half of the school administrators whom he surveyed object to accelerating children of IQ 135 or higher (F. T. Wilson, 1954). One of every three college professors of education takes the same position.

On the basis of his study of some 1,400 gifted persons over a long period of time, Terman concluded that "the accelerates in my gifted group have made a decidedly better record than the non-accelerates" (quoted in Pressey, 1949, p. 18). Terman compared members of his group with respect to educational record, social adjustment, health, marital adjustment, and vocational success. Three sub-groups were compared: those graduating from high school up to age fifteen and one-half, those graduating from fifteen and one-half to sixteen and one-half, those graduating at sixteen and one-half and older. The Binet IQs secured in childhood were only slightly different, but the most accelerated did considerably better than the other two groups on Terman's

Concept Mastery test when it was administered twenty years later. Educationally, there was a consistent superiority of the most accelerated over the moderately accelerated and of the moderately accelerated over the least accelerated. The most accelerated had a higher proportion graduating from college, more average grades of *B* or better, more graduation honors, and more study at the graduate level. Socially, the least accelerated had a slight edge: in a rating of "satisfactory" by a field worker while the group was in high school, on the number of college activities, and on a rating of all-round adjustment when the group was about age thirty. The health record of the most accelerated was superior. More of the men in the most accelerated group were married in 1945 when the group was approaching thirty-five, but more of the least accelerated women were married. Both the men and the women in the most accelerated group married at an earlier age. The most accelerated had had considerably fewer divorces. Twice as large a proportion of the most accelerated men as of the non-accelerates were rated in Terman's A (top) category on vocational success.

Looking at the total picture, Terman concluded that the influence of school acceleration in causing social maladjustment has been greatly exaggerated. His comments are instructive:

> There is no doubt that maladjustment does result in individual cases, but our data indicate that in a majority of subjects the maladjustment consists of a temporary feeling of inferiority which is later overcome. The important thing is to consider each child as a special case. (Terman and Oden, 1947, p. 275) [*]

> Controversy . . . hinges on the relative weight that should be given to intellectual and social values in the educative process. . . . [A considerable proportion of non-accelerants] languished in idleness throughout the grades and high school and failed to develop the ambition of habits of work necessary to make them successful in college. The question is, how much risk of social maladjustment one can afford to take in order to keep the gifted child at school tasks difficult enough to command his attention and respect. The data here reviewed indicate that the risk of maladjustment is less than is commonly believed. . . . The disadvantage is usually temporary. Moreover handicaps of social immaturity would not be so great if a larger proportion of the gifted were promoted rapidly so that the underage child would not feel so conspicuous. (*Ibid.*, pp. 279-81)

---

[*] Reprinted from *The Gifted Child Grows Up*, Vol. IV, *Genetic Studies of Genius*, by Lewis M. Terman and Melita H. Oden with permission of the publishers, Stanford University Press. Copyright 1947 by the Board of Trustees of Leland Stanford Junior University.

These social problems of acceleration Terman regarded as a calculated risk, particularly since later social adjustment of the group was encouraging. In view of the greater academic and occupational success of the accelerates and of the greater span of prime productive years before them, Terman concluded that the risk was worth taking. As a general rule he advocated one year's acceleration for students with IQ over 135 to permit college entrance by age seventeen, and concluded further that the majority would be better off to enter at sixteen (*Ibid.*, pp. 265-81).

Pressey assembles an impressive body of evidence supporting rapid progress of the gifted in his volume *Educational Acceleration* (1949). He cites studies in colleges (Minnesota, Columbia, Dartmouth, College of the City of New York, Pennsylvania, Buffalo and Barnard) from 1913 to 1939, all of which indicate greater academic success and persistence to graduation of students entering college at sixteen or younger as compared with students of normal or above-normal age (*Ibid.*, Chap. 2). He points to evidence of better-than-average participation by the accelerants in athletics and other extra-curricular activities. Studies are also quoted which attest to superior performance of students in elementary, junior and senior high schools in Massachusetts, Illinois, Missouri, Wisconsin, Pennsylvania, Kentucky, and California.

In this volume Pressey also reports on his own research in an experimental program of college acceleration in wartime (1942-1945) at The Ohio State University. The accelerated students earned considerably better academic records than a paired control group but took part somewhat less in social activities. A much larger proportion of the accelerates remained in college and completed their work for a degree (*Ibid.*, Chap. VI). A follow-up ten years later by Flesher and Pressey compared 104 women accelerates and 104 women non-accelerates among graduates in the original group. The accelerates undertook advanced study to a greater extent, earning graduate degrees in a two-to-one ratio over the control group. Also, almost twice as many of the accelerates continued their career after marriage. Slight differences are to be found in the proportion of the control group married and in the number of children born to them. Flesher and Pressey discount this difference because of the year's difference in age between the groups and the likely compensation for the small difference in that one year (Flesher, 1955).

Pressey was impressed with the fact that only one-third of the students who were invited to attempt the accelerated program availed themselves of the opportunity. "Educational convention," he notes, "puts a premium on the educational lock step." He looks to "greater flexibility of programs and better guidance" so that superior students will capitalize upon their ability to move faster than the academic programs which "appear to be paced for the average student" (Pressey, 1949, p. 91).

Still another important study of acceleration is reported by Keys in *The Underage Student in High School and College: Educational and Social Adjustments* (1938). Keys compared the growth of 348 students entering the University of California between 1922 and 1930 at sixteen and one-half years or less with a control group seventeen years of age or older at entrance. He also studied 133 boys and girls in Oakland who had been accelerated from three to five semesters.

The accelerated college group showed "large and significant superiority on practically all points of scholastic distinction"—grade point average, number elected to Phi Beta Kappa, scholarships earned, membership in honor societies. They tended to graduate in less than the average time. More completed the work for the Bachelor's degree; more qualified for teaching certificates; more continued on into graduate study; more entered professions; fewer went into business careers. At one point Keys' group differs from Terman's and Pressey's. Of the women in the Keys group 59 per cent were married at age twenty-five while only 38 per cent of the control group were. Keys sought his groups' reaction to their college program in four areas: benefit from instruction, physical health, social relations, and emotional adjustment. The accelerates provided more favorable response on instruction and health; the control group gave more favorable replies in the social and emotional realms. Keys concedes that social relations proved "most difficult for males entering at 14 or 15."

At the high school level, accelerates (averaging twenty months younger than controls who were matched by sex, socio-economic status, grade placement and IQ) scored higher in academic achievement, study habits and scholarship. Comparisons were made among three IQ groups —high (136 and up), middle (120-135), and low (under 120)—with equal representation of accelerates and controls in the second and third group. *Pairs* could not be found for the very high accelerated group. The accelerates participated more in the athletic program, with the higher IQ accelerates taking greater part than accelerates with somewhat lower IQ scores. The top IQ group did not hold more school offices than the middle group. Accelerates in the bottom IQ group fared not so well, and Keys concludes that acceleration for pupils under 120 IQ is seldom advisable. Employment of the Bernreuter personality scales led to the conclusion that sociability on the Bernreuter is "more a function of intelligence than age." Students' estimates of their own general happiness favored the accelerates. Thus, the Keys study reinforces other studies as regards student attitude toward their own acceleration. A strong minority dissents, but about three accelerants out of four react favorably to their rapid promotion in the past.

In New York City the rapid progress system in the junior high schools has at times been a matter of controversy. In 1939 a committee established to study the city's junior high schools recommended "a study of the situation that will result in reducing or eliminating acceleration and in providing a course of study better adapted to the needs of the pupils" (New York City, 1939, p. 41). Changes in the junior high school curriculum over the years had resulted in equating the ninth year program to that of the first year in senior high schools. As a result, all of the acceleration was accomplished in the seventh year of Rapid Advancement classes, with seventh and eighth grades telescoped into a single year. The Committee reported:

> . . . there can be little or no justification for this procedure. In the first place, the present generation of pupils is younger by a year or more than former pupils. There is less need for acceleration. On the contrary, there is every reason for keeping our bright pupils in the junior high school until they are old enough to make the social adjustments that are so valuable to the high school pupil. In too many instances, bright pupils pass through high school and even college too immature socially and intellectually to derive the best advantages from the instruction offered. Furthermore, completing a two-year course in one year generally results in giving to the bright pupils a course in minimum essentials when what they need is an enriched course of study. (*Ibid.*, p. 41)

Rapid Advancement classes had been established in 1923 to enroll the top 15 per cent of students in intellectual ability. Report card ratings were used to select students for the special classes. Either the selection, the general rationale or the abbreviated program was faulty, however. In 1932 one principal was able to show conclusively that his top group of normal pupils in a three year program ranked higher on standardized tests than certain Rapid Advancement classes. In 1946 rapid advancement was reduced from one year to one semester after a number of years in which the reduced acceleration had been permissive.

Shortly thereafter the accelerated program was reorganized under a new name and under a system of more rigorous selection. Special Progress classes were established which returned to the principle of a full year's acceleration. Starting at first with somewhat lower standards, the program moved in 1949 to a minimum IQ of 130, with a reading level of 8.5, arithmetic 8.0, chronological age eleven, and an adjudged social maturity of twelve years. The New York City Bureau of Educational Research undertook a study of the effects of the Special Progress classes comparing achievement of equated graduates of normal and accelerated programs in the tenth grade of a special school of gifted students. Justman (1953) reported for the Bureau marked similarity in achievement between the accelerated and normal progress groups, no significant difference in grades on the New York State Regents' examinations at the end of the tenth grade. The conclusion: Intellectually gifted accelerates are able to complete the tenth year course of study at the Bronx High School of Science with no appreciable loss when contrasted with equally gifted pupils from elementary schools or junior high school normal progress classes.

Another study in New York City matched 74 "Special Progress" (2 year program) with 82 "Normal Progress" (3 year program) students of equated mental ability in 1949-50 (Justman, 1952). Academic achievement was measured in terms of reading, computation, mathematics, science, social studies, work-study habits, and creativity in language arts. Personal and social adjustment, interests and attitudes comprised other axes of the study. Despite the year's difference in age, there were no significant differences in reading, computation, or creative writing. The accelerated group was significantly superior in mathematics, science, social studies and some work-study skills. Statistical differences were not found in the non-academic factors—in social adjustment, personal adjustment, attitudes, or interests. Justman concludes:

> In general the only area in which any advantage is associated with placement in a Special Progress group is that of academic achievement. . . . On the basis of the evidence resulting from this study it is clear that the segregation of intellectually gifted pupils in homogeneous Special Progress groups is not without value. The acceleration of such pupils by a period of one year on the junior high level is not accompanied by any marked loss in those areas to which the program of acceleration was directed. On the contrary, the concomitant gain in academic achievement may be looked upon as a strong argument in favor of the retention of such classes within the framework of the junior high school. (Justman, 1952, p. 40)°

It is important, however, to keep one qualification in mind. The average IQ of students in both studies reported upon place them in the top 2 to 3 per cent of the population. These studies took place after New York City had limited acceleration in junior high school to students scoring over 130. The average IQ in the Bronx High School of Science study was actually 143. New York City's earlier dissatisfaction with Rapid Advance-

---

From "A Comparison of the Functioning of Intellectually Gifted Pupils Enrolled in Special Progress and Normal Progress Classes in Junior High School," by Joseph Justman (Board of Education, New York City, 1952). Reprinted with permission of Joseph Justman.

ment classes that were not so selective indicates the need for extreme caution in undertaking a program of acceleration.

SOCIAL AND PERSONAL ADJUSTMENT

The parents' primary objection to acceleration is often based on fears of social maladjustment, even if temporary, as Terman described. The New York City studies just cited may not give a complete picture since the youngsters studied were in the ninth and tenth grades. At age thirteen to fiftteeen, personal and social disparities due to age may not be important to the average youngster since he is still not the highly social creature that he becomes a few years later. Engle (1938) reports on a study of personal and social adjustment in high school and college. The results of the Early Admissions program of the Fund for the Advancement of Education (The Fund, 1957) may also be significant.

Engle selected one hundred matched pairs in three Indiana high schools and the University of Indiana, equating his pairs on four bases: sex, grade, intelligence, and school marks. Each pair had one student who was one or more years younger than normal for his grade and one student who was at age-grade level. For evidence he used personality schedule scores (Cowan Adolescent Personality Schedule), a short questionnaire on the effect of skipping on social adjustment, and a listing of activities participated in by the subjects. The high school accelerants showed a slightly lower score for maladjustment than did the non-accelerants; the college accelerants showed slightly higher maladjustment. In the absence of statistical significance, Engle concluded that there was "no apparent relationship between scores on the personality schedule and age of entry."

When related to attitude toward acceleration, much larger differences were found on the adjustment scale. High school boys and girls and university men and women who regarded acceleration as a handicap all showed much higher maladjustment scores than students who were favorable to acceleration. Oddly enough, those who considered acceleration a handicap were at least as active socially as those who were not critical of acceleration. On the whole, however, there was no statistical significance in the amount of social activities of the accelerates and non-accelerates. When compared with students of their own age, accelerates were at least as active as others socially.

Opinions solicited concerning acceleration included the following kinds of problems:

> Difficulties resulting from home conditions, with parents putting too much emphasis on the age factor
> Difficulties in relationships with the opposite sex

Difficulties in general social relationships
Resentment at being considered "different" from classmates.

The questionnaire, however, indicated a decrease in such difficulties with maturation. This finding supports Terman's viewpoint that the social handicaps of acceleration are only temporary.

As part of the Early Admission to College program sponsored by the Fund for the Advacement of Education, from 1951 to 1954 twelve colleges admitted 1,350 students who, with a few exceptions, were under sixteen and one-half years of age. The majority had finished only the tenth or eleventh grade. They were known as "Fund Scholars," and each student had a two-year financial grant. The participating colleges were the University of Chicago, which had already maintained such a program for many years, Columbia, Wisconsin, Yale, Fisk, Goucher, Lafayette, Louisville, Morehouse, Oberlin, Shimer, and Utah. Shimer admitted a cross section (no special criterion) of students to the Early Admission group. The other colleges attempted to refine their selection procedures in keeping with the early age of the entrants that was sought. Additional achievement tests were administered beyond those normally required. High school records were considered. Behavioral case histories were studied if available. An effort was made to assess maturity and emotional stability in the customary interview. Some colleges made judgments as to stature and appearance to avoid excessive differences between the early entrants and the rest of the college population.

The colleges adopted different policies in providing for the special group on campus. Fisk established a program which separated the Scholars most sharply from the normal college population. A new basic college was organized with a special curriculum and faculty and a separate dormitory governed by its own regulations. At Louisville and Utah most students lived at home. At Wisconsin the Scholars stayed in rooming houses. In the remaining colleges they mingled in the regular dormitories with other students. Except for Fisk, Scholars were subject to the same social regulations as were other students, but they were barred or discouraged from joining fraternities because of their age. Guidance was uneven, ranging from clinical counseling and psychiatric service to more common patterns of dormitory advising and informal assistance from individual faculty members. Scholars were encouraged to participate in sports and other extra-curricular programs.

Evaluation included three aspects: academic performance, student reaction to the progam, and social and emotional adjustment. Comparisons were made between the Scholars and the total college population and between the Scholars and matched groups. At Shimer which experimented with a cross section of ability, no superiority was shown. Acceleration of all college preparatory students would accordingly seem inadvisable. At the other colleges, the Scholars' grades on the Area Tests of the Graduate Record Examination were higher than those of their total class, a finding to be expected as a result of the careful selection process. However, most of the experimental group also exceeded the scores of the comparison group who were older and who had completed one or two more years of work in high school. Whether the Scholars would have done even better if they had also completed high school is an intriguing question but, of course, indeterminate. The colleges had admitted a few students on completion of tenth grade, most after the eleventh grade, and a few high school graduates. Those who had finished eleventh grade work performed best on the examination. The youngest group did not do as well as the middle group, but earned higher scores than the high school graduates.

Richard Pearson of the College Entrance Examination Board studied personal reactions to the program by an analysis of essays written by 184 Scholars and 173 matched comparison students in the spring of 1955. Nine out of ten of the successful Scholars approved the program, finding greater intellectual challenge and less waste of time through repetition. Selected because of earlier academic achievement, they found few problems in academic adjustment. Elements of scholastic independence, such as study habits, planning one's own time schedule and handling college course organization and methods of teaching, presented no greater problem to the Scholars than to the control group. Personal and social problems, however, were more acute among the Scholars than the comparison group. Problems were aggravated whenever the Scholars were identified and separated by administrative action. "They had somewhat more difficulty than the comparison students in overcoming shyness and making friends. The boys found it almost impossible to get dates, since the girls were older, whereas the girls found their youth an advantage" (NSSE, 1958, p. 329). The scholars recommended abandonment of special treatment practices for early entrants, more effective orientation programs, and more adequate counseling.

A team of three psychiatrists experienced with college students studied the emotional and social adjustment of the Scholars. They reported "that the proportion of the Scholars with characterological difficulties, neuroses, or psychoses in no case exceeded that among college students in general and, in some institutions, was below expectations"(*Ibid.*, p. 330).

The Early Admissions study underlines the nature of the acceleration paradox. With the exception of social problems encountered by accelerated students (particularly boys) in college, all the advantages appear to be on the side of rapid progress. Despite this evidence, however, there is little disposition on the part of colleges, high schools, parents, or students to support extension of the system to other colleges.

ADVANCED PLACEMENT PROGRAM

Far more acceptable to students, the public, and educators has been the Advanced Placement Program (see Chapter 7). Initiated in 1952 by the Fund for the Advancement of Education, the program provides for acceleration of *learnings* in high school without offering earlier admission to college. Selected students follow syllabi developed for the College Entrance Examination Board by committees of high school teachers and college instructors. At the close of the year students write examinations prepared and scored by similar committees for the College Board. Participating colleges establish their own passing grades and extend college credit to entering students on this basis. Some colleges exempt students from parallel requirements in college instead of giving credit toward a degree. In these ways the student may accelerate progress toward a degree or make room for a richer curriculum. That this pattern has proved more acceptable than the Early Admissions operation may be seen in the increase in the number of students taking Advanced Placement examinations from a few score in 1953 to more than 10,000 in 1960 and more than 21,000 in 1963.

Students are generally selected for Advanced Placement classes on the basis of grades and teacher recommendations. Most schools permit a student to take no more than two such courses. Classes are generally kept small, and the teacher is often given a lighter teaching schedule so that he may undertake the additional preparation necessary for a truly advanced course. In anticipation of the college level course in the senior year, some schools start advanced work as early as the sophomore year so that students will have completed the normal high school curriculum in selected courses before the senior year begins.

The stimulation of taking a college level course should be a real incentive to an able high school senior. Students who plan to attend colleges which typically group freshmen in very large lecture sections may profit greatly from study of the same material with a high school teacher in a small class. Obviously the library resources of high schools that offer such programs have to be very much reinforced. In some cases exposure to the unique point of view or prized procedures of particular college departments may be more valuable to the student.

It is important to note that there is no magic in the course's being a college level course. Students in honors courses in high schools are unspoiled enough to point out that stimulation comes not from the "honors" label, but from the quality of teaching experienced. One director of an honors school notes with annoyance occasional misinterpretation of the "college level" designation of Advanced Placement work. At times, he notes, the highly stimulating discussion leader at the high school level feels that he must turn to the formal lectures he remembers from college when he is assigned to teach a college level course. The scintillating discussion then gives way to a mediocre or pedestrian lecture.

Another consideration is the substitution of the Advanced Placement syllabus for local planning that may have merits of its own. The various subject committees have tried to keep their syllabi general to allow for differences in individual teacher planning. However, the focus is upon coverage of a particular college course. Those schools which have used their honors courses for seminars in which students shared in planning may prefer adhering to their more flexible design. Schools which encouraged individual study as part of honors programs will also have reason to retain their pattern. Generally speaking, the Advanced Placement rationale puts its primary value on earlier completion of specific course content.

Some ardent advocates of Advanced Placement are themselves frank in noting dangers in the program. Henry W. Bragdon, associated with the program from its inception, is hopeful that it will help increasingly to discover untapped abilities, that there will be less drudgery in secondary education, and that curricula will be closer to individual needs and ambitions. He sees hazards ahead, however, as he notes overemphasis on the prestige value of advanced placement. Some schools are devoting too much time to advanced classes at the expense of individualization. There is the temptation for students to limit their program to courses where advanced credit may be earned, and to avoid new courses, experimental programs and such areas as art, music and drama where examinations have not yet been set up. He concludes:

> This problem gives me a case of acute pedagogical schizophrenia. On the one hand I believe in the Advanced Placement Program as it is, and think the examinations central. On the other, I believe in experimentation and think that singing madrigals is fully as educational as solving equations. I suspect that the way out, if there is a way out, lies in minimizing the credit-cum-acceleration attractions of advanced placement and playing up the aspect of enrichment. (Bragdon, 1960, p. 20)

The major point to be made in this chapter, however, is the contrasting appeal of the Early Admissions and Advanced Placement programs. The greater spread of the latter program implies support for the thesis that accelerated learning and accelerated independence in schools and college are a more feasible mode of operation in our culture than accelerated promotion and graduation.

NEGATIVE REACTIONS

Dissenting from the evidence gathered in various research projects, many persons continue to question the educational effects of acceleration. Often their argument is based on concerns of individual and social development where objective measures are notably lacking. They may say with some conviction that the evidence marshalled in favor of acceleration omits serious evaluation in those areas.

Rothman and Levine state the case against acceleration persuasively in an article entitled "From Little League to Ivy League" (1963). They see in this practice reflections of parental pressure pushing the child toward adulthood before he is ready. The effort to save time, they fear, eliminates creativity and discovery as methods of learning. Play for play's sake disappears, and the growing child is deprived of his chance to be a child. Instead he must fit a mold of achievement which predisposes to conformity. To be an individual, to become a social being is one of the major tasks for young children, they say, and warn, "What is omitted must be fulfilled even at a later and less appropriate date." Their conclusion, and one to note well in this chapter on acceleration: "Stop pushing!"

SUMMARY

Despite social forces that oppose acceleration of superior children toward early completion of formal schooling, the weight of research evidence is in favor of acceleration. Acceleration may be accomplished at any level of the school system and may be effected in a number of ways. Methods include early admission to elementary school, grade skipping, combining grades in order to reduce time, shortening the duration of the junior high school program, assumption of heavier programs and summer study in senior high school and college, early admission to college prior to high school graduation, and credit by examination while in college. When standards for acceleration are kept sufficiently rigorous, advanced students generally maintain a greater interest in school, earn higher grades, persist in school until completion in greater numbers and go on to graduate study in greater proportion. Emotional problems are not encountered to any greater degree. Participation in extracurricular activities does not suffer, but social adjustment above the junior high school level presents a greater problem for accelerated boys. Accelerates in great majority give their approval to the program of rapid advancement. Studies indicate that the social inferiority suffered by underage boys is only temporary and that eventual adjustment, when measured by age of marriage and marital happiness, is not affected.

Authorities generally agree that acceleration should not exceed two years in the twelve-year common school program. Physical age and social maturity should be considered as well as academic achievement in accelerating a student.

In the face of common opposition to acceleration of the child in his progress through school, the alternative of accelerating learnings and independence in school may be a viable one. The idea of "advanced placement" of subject matter throughout a student's school career could conceivably result in completion of the normal elementary school, high school, and college curriculum before graduation from each level. In college and graduate schools such a procedure might result in the student's embarking upon adult and independent study, research, and professional activity while still enrolled at the university. At any rate, schools face two choices: changing public and professional attitudes toward early graduation or providing genuine acceleration toward adult activities while the student is still in school.

Chapter 15

Guidance

There is a tide in the affairs of men,
Which, taken at the flood, leads to fortune;
Omitted, all the voyage of their life
Is bound in shallows and in miseries.

—Shakespeare

Most of the normal functions of a school guidance program have particular relevance in education of the gifted. Identification of strengths and weaknesses, assistance in arriving at educational and vocational decisions, counseling in the face of emotional and social problems, providing information to the faculty as a basis for curriculum adaptation, helping the student to understand and to accept himself and others, evaluating growth—all of these have specific significance for the gifted learner because he shares the common problems of his age group and faces still others that arise from the uniqueness of his gifts.

Widespread concern has been expressed by national commissions, professional societies, and individuals over the failure of a large proportion of students with high ability to continue their education after high school. Of the 40 per cent of students who do not complete high school, a significant proportion are in the top 10 per cent of ability as measured by aptitude tests (Wolfle, 1954). One fifth of the top third of students taking the National Merit Scholarship examinations in 1958 did not enter college as full-time students (Holland, 1962).

There is a tendency to attribute this loss of potential to inadequate guidance services. Terman and Oden (1954b), noting that 15 per cent of their top percentile group did not enter college and that 30 per cent did not graduate, cited the following as the two most important reasons: (1) failure to identify ability, (2) failure to provide an appropriate school program when high ability was discovered. Passow (1956)

352

charges that guidance and educational procedures fall short in motivating able youth either to work up to capacity in high school or to develop college goals. Lack of desire for college training is seen as second only to lack of finances as a major reason for leaving school after high school graduation. Chapter 16 in this volume on Motivation and Underachievement attempts to set the problem in a broader framework. Studies are cited which indicate that guidance alone produces no miraculous cure. However, it seems reasonable to suppose that effective guidance procedures should make observable contribution toward better self-assessment and career planning. French (1959) states the case in positive terms when he notes that "as the guidance services of secondary schools improve, a larger percentage of the students with high academic ability enter college."

The assumptions underlying faith in the efficacy of guidance services include the following:

(1) Adequate guidance services will provide for continuing identification of able students.

(2) Adequate guidance services will cause students to develop strong academic motivation and high-level career aspirations.

(3) Proper identification and follow-up of gifted students will produce useful adaptation of the curriculum.

(4) A combination of the first three effects will result in greater college attendance by able students.

As a result of this pattern of thinking a number of projects have developed around guidance as a central motif. These include the projects on underachievement at De Witt Clinton High School (Goldberg, 1959) and Evanston High School (Fair, 1959), the Demonstration Guidance Project in New York City (Hillson and Myers, 1961, and Schreiber, 1958), and the Superior and Talented Student Project of the North Central Association of Colleges and Secondary Schools (North Central Association, 1958, 1959). In addition, research studies are reported by McCarthy (1957) and Ohlsen and Proff (1960) on employing group guidance procedures to reduce underachievement. Some of the results are encouraging, some not conclusive, but design and implementation of these projects are evidence of a strong commitment to guidance as an important process in education of the gifted.

Premature withdrawal from school and underachievement are generally viewed as problems of educational or vocational guidance. Actually these phenomena reflect personal problems of emotional and social adjustment as well as adaptation to academic demands. Personal counseling is, therefore, no less essential for gifted students than for others. In addition the gifted may have some problems peculiar to their giftedness. Counseling involves parents as well, where both career motivation and personal problems are concerned. This chapter will therefore discuss the major tasks of guidance personnel in meeting the needs of the gifted: personal counseling, educational and vocational guidance, working with parents. Identification of the gifted is an essential function in education and guidance; for this topic the reader should refer to the chapter on Identification.

SCHOOL GUIDANCE SERVICES

School systems should provide a systematic program for guidance of the gifted as part of their total guidance procedures. The *Guidance* booklet of the NEA Academically Talented Student Project lists clearly the responsibilities of guidance services to gifted students. First, guidance personnel should provide necessary information for the school to work effectively with its more gifted pupils. This information includes listings of students to indicate the range of abilities and the number of students in these ranges and data on special talents and individual skill deficiencies. With student personnel information, counselors can help interpret individual students to their teachers, particularly where discrepancies between ability and achievement exist. A second responsibility of guidance workers is to assist in curriculum development. Knowledge of individual students, their range of abilities, and career needs equips the counselor to make unique contributions in planning school programs and in developing new studies. Third, guidance workers offer counseling to superior students as well as to the more obvious and demanding cases of failure and misconduct. This counseling includes efforts to enrich the student's opportunities outside of school in fields such as art and science;* efforts to avert development of undesirable attitudes toward oneself and others; assistance to gifted students in setting standards for themselves; help in winning acceptance in group activities as members and leaders; and understanding of the need for drill and discipline in basic skills (NEA, 1961e, pp. 56-59).

Guidance, of course, is a continuous process, and the need for guidance does not wait upon the establishment of designated guidance departments or guidance counselors. In the elementary school no less than in secondary school and college, a process of appraisal is necessary to identify needs, problems, general ability, and special talents. There is the need for all teachers to understand their students' personal and fam-

---

* A comprehensive list of summer opportunities is to be found in the NEA Academically Talented Student Project booklet on Guidance (NEA 1961e, pp. 100-41).

ily problems. Principals, school nurses, social workers, and school psychologists as well as guidance workers can help teachers understand such problem situations at all levels. Schools have to provide an emotional climate which is conducive to learning. Effective guidance services can help develop such conditions. At all levels there is the need for sympathetic and expert interviews to appraise ability, performance, emotional adjustment, and to stimulate interest in scholastic achievement.

These functions are common to guidance services in all schools. As the child progresses to the junior high school, adolescent developmental problems emerge. Assistance may be needed in establishing proper relations with peers of both sexes. Discovery and development of new interests becomes more important. Orientation to a new kind of school organization is needed. Curriculum choices have to be made.

In senior high school the student has to develop a concept of his appropriate sex role. He may need help in moving toward emotional independence from his parents and toward assumption of adult roles economically and socially. Post-high school educational and vocational plans become necessary. To assist him, the student needs to develop a realistic self-concept and to make use of it in planning for current and future activities.

These guidance needs characterize all young people, not the gifted alone. Guidance for the gifted takes on special significance because of the greater dependence of the gifted on formal education for realization of their potential. Rothney and Koopman regard guidance of the gifted as capable of highly effective results because the gifted "are capable of participating more fully in the analysis of data about themselves and of coming to more clearly thought-out decisions" (NSSE, 1958, p. 360).

It is important to recognize that these all-important guidance functions are not accomplished by counselors alone. All the adults with whom youngsters come in contact are potential sources of guidance. Boys and girls adopt certain adults, consciously or unconsciously, as models. They seek advice and information from these models and also from other adults whom they respect even though they do not wish to follow their example. Much guidance comes from experiences that young people have and the inferences they draw from this experience. Books—fiction and factual, television, radio, and motion pictures afford a mass of information, ideas and attitudes which affect the learning and decisions of young people. The school should make efforts to maximize the usefulness of all these sources. The reader will find valuable suggestions in a comprehensive list Endicott has prepared of community resources and activities that may contribute to guidance programs (Endicott, 1961, pp. 59-61).

PERSONAL PROBLEMS OF THE GIFTED

The oft-repeated truism that gifted children are children first is not without merit. It implies that gifted children share the emotional needs and personal problems of other children at any given stage of development. In addition other problems may be anticipated which arise from the uniqueness which the outstanding child enjoys by definition. Moreover, many of the needs common to all children are somewhat modified by the atypicality of the gifted.

Like other children, the gifted experience need for love and affection, for emotional and physical security, for a sense of belonging. Like others, the gifted child wants to be needed and accepted as an individual. Gifted children share the common needs to be free from unusual fears and from excessive feelings of guilt. They have to experience a sense of achievement, self-acceptance, and a feeling of their own worth.

The special gifts of these children depend upon emotional security for maximum realization. While history records the performance of many geniuses in the face of severe physical deprivation and emotional disturbance, there is available a considerable body of evidence to support the thesis that frustration and deprivation are most likely to thwart achievement, self-realization, free expression, and creative output in all areas. Maslow (ASCD, 1962) describes the integration of emotionally healthy people in whom "the conative, the cognitive, the affective and the motor are less separated from each other" and work "collaboratively without conflict to the same ends." Satisfaction of higher order needs in particular, says Maslow (1954, Chapter 8), depends upon positive conditions in the familial, economic, political, and educational environment.

Discouragement, neurotic fears, self-abasement close the individual off from experience. He is likely to become rigid intellectually as well as emotionally, to expend excessive effort in defending a negative self-concept, suspicious of or hostile to others, and incapable of making contact with reality. All of these characteristics are the opposite of the goal of self-actualization which is essential for the realization of the promise of giftedness. "High level wellness," to use Dunn's term, is more than absence of disorder; it implies functioning fully and enjoying the utmost of one's potential (Dunn, 1961).

EMOTIONAL SUPPORT IN THE HOME

The uniqueness of the gifted increases the need for understanding on the part of parents and other adults upon whom the gifted child depends. He needs to be understood not only as a child but as an unusual child. He needs to have special opportunities in order to develop his uncommon potential. But at the same time that his unusual abilities are recognized, he has to feel that he is loved simply as a member of the family, of the community, and not only because of his special abilities— loved for who he is rather than for what he can do. Some parents, unhappily, seek status through their children's performance. The parent with a heavy emotional investment in his child, with a great compulsion to see his child achieve in unusual ways, can easily lead the child to believe that he is valued only for the satisfaction that he brings to his parent.

Quite an opposite danger is also possible. Some parents of gifted children openly resent the obvious superiority of their offspring. Some unusual children make their way over obstacles raised at home or despite the sheer indifference of their families. This problem may be aggravated when the child's siblings are much less talented. Provision of special opportunties that far exceed anything the parent himself experienced as a child, provision of opportunities not afforded other children in the family, may raise serious problems to the child and to the family as well. The school and other community agencies may have to help the parents understand the unusual nature of their gifted child in such circumstances; school and community may have to supplement educational opportunities provided by the family.

In addition, economic and cultural poverty may severely limit the development of the unusual child because of cultural limitations. The family may not be aware of the potential of a given child.* If aware, financial restrictions may stand in the way of offering anything more than the most meagre opportunities. Self-support and contribution to the family's resources may be so urgent that nothing but the most immediate goals can be entertained. Assistance from community agencies and scholarship support may be essential if gifts requiring advanced training and delayed earning are to be realized.

SPECIAL PROBLEMS OF EXCEPTIONALITY

While the emotional needs common to all children are basic for the gifted as well, the "higher order" needs postulated by Maslow may be even more significant for consideration in guidance of the gifted. Maslow includes in this classification needs for information, for understanding, for beauty and for self-actualization. Maslow regards these needs as developing later in the human species than the physiological and inter-

---

* Cheyney (1962) reports a study in Ohio of five hundred sets of parents of children with IQ's of 125 and above which shows greater awareness of children's gifts among lower socio-economic (93 per cent) than higher socio-economic (69 per cent) groups. In all, 82 per cent of the parents were so aware. Special opportunities were provided for 87 per cent of upper class, but only 69 per cent of the lower class gifted children.

personal needs, but he claims that gratification of the higher needs produces "more desirable subjective results—more profound happiness, serenity, richness of inner life." These needs are modified by the culture, by reality and by possibility and are accordingly subject to education in the broadest sense (Maslow 1954, Chapter 8). Exposure and training develop interests that become autonomous and acquire the driving force of emotional needs. Development of such autonomous interests in this way may actually represent in itself a prescription for the education of the gifted, for this is the ultimate goal of education. In the realm of these higher order needs the school plays a strategic goal. Many of the traditional goals of the school are related both to the stimulation and the satisfaction of needs for information, understanding and beauty. As the school, through curriculum and guidance alike, helps the student find himself, it may make a contribution toward self-actualization. In all cases more than a dry-as-dust approach to subject-matter and guidance is obviously needed.

As the child enters school and more fully into a peer society, and as he negotiates the course of school life, new problems arise for him that grow out of his special talents. One of these is a result of the uneven development of the intellectually gifted child. Able to operate academically with children several years older, he is still functioning emotionally, socially, and physically at a level relatively close to his own chronological age. Adults have to be ready to accept reactions that are sophisticated in one sphere and childish in another. An adjustment of the bright child to his peers is similarly necessary. He has to learn to cope with unusual praises and unusual demands. He has to accept his own difference from others in some fields. Both modesty and realism in appraising his own ability and comparing himself with others are necessary. Adult guidance should help the gifted child to view himself wholesomely and also to see himself as his peers see him.

Because potential "clamors to be used," the intellectually superior child develops interests different from those of his peers. These range from a simple interest in reading itself and different choices of reading matter to greater concern for values as the child passes through adolescence. While his classmates are avidly pursuing the box-scores and batting averages, the gifted adolescent may become more immersed in problems of individual and social ethics, in philosophical and religious issues. Who man is, how he came to be, the meaning of death, divine and civil justice, social and economic problems find a responsive spark and sometimes set off passionate searches. Often they lead to doctrinaire and revolutionary stances on the part of the bright youngster. The adolescent often identifies with a hero, living or dead, whom he adopts. Guidance takes many forms in addition to the conventional interview. The child finds guidance through stimulating classroom discussions, sympathetic chatting with a respected "model" in school or community, encountering new questions, discovering fresh perspectives, consulting recommended reading that aims to develop broader human understanding, and introduction to responsible religious, civic, and social action groups.

Building social relationships with peers is a developmental task that acquires increasing importance as the child matures and progresses through school. The gifted child's sense of difference is probably no asset in a period when all children, facing disquieting and new problems, place a high value on conformity. Parents and teachers should do all they can to help a child make necessary social adjustments without encouraging him to hide his special ability under a bushel basket of conformism. A child's uniqueness in his special talent may be more easily accepted by others if he is able to relate with them on a basis of parity in social and sports activities. Family activities should not be skewed to a child's special interests but should include a balancing concern with broader fields. Daddy has to help Johnny improve his pitching and batting as well as his mind. A casual (but approving) attitude toward the child's special gifts should prevail. This should include modesty as well as a realistic appraisal.

Some of the devices used in group dynamics training may be effective in helping young people in their problems of social adjustment. Role-playing so that the child can see differing points of view may be useful. Understanding the emotional motivation of other persons, their "hidden agenda" may also help. Recognizing the different functions that individuals play in a group may deter an individual from perpetually playing the dissident, the questioner, the improver upon ideas of others. More constructive roles in pushing group purposes forward should be identified, and students can be helped to play such parts as they learn to identify more with the group and its goals and seek less attention for themselves. Ability carries with it a potential for leadership, but leadership has to be accepted by the group, and the leaders have to be acceptable to the group. Young people need guidance in learning to function effectively in group situations.

Part of the social adjustment necessary in childhood and adolescence is development of appropriate sex roles and suitable relationships with the other sex. To some small extent this may involve a larger problem for intellectually gifted children. Typically there is less differentiation in interests among bright children according to sex. Bright boys are likely to be as interested in reading and poetry as girls; bright girls are as likely to be interested in mathematics and science as boys. Unkind labeling by peers of such boys as "sissies" or such girls as "tomboys" does not help them in their relationships with either sex. Again, helping these young people develop basic play and social competences in areas other than their area of exceptionality should contribute to greater acceptance and understanding by others.

Terman and Hollingworth gave careful attention to problems that arise because of extraordinary intellectual ability. Hollingworth in studying children with IQ's over 180 had occasion to note the differences in social adjustment of children who were moderately superior from those who were highly exceptional. She noted a tendency for children above 170 IQ to play and work by themselves more than those around 140. She characterized the moderately superior as possessing an "optimum intelligence" in terms of personal happiness and adjustment to society. The tendency of extremely bright children to pursue interests like reading that are carried on in solitude aggravates the problem of "alienation" from peers in her opinion (Hollingworth, 1942, pp. 263-65). Terman and Oden noted some maladjustment in the middle teens for the group over 170 IQ. They also indicated a greater disparity for this group between ability and school achievement, although they raised the question of the adequacy of school measures in evaluating achievement as a possible explanation (Terman and Oden, 1947, pp. 289-94). Strang (1954) raises the same question of social maladjustment and problems of human relations as a result of high exceptionality. Guidance of exceptional children has to include utilization of some of this superior potential in solution of problems of human relations, in understanding and accepting oneself and others as human beings.

GIFTEDNESS AND MENTAL HEALTH

Investigators are in general agreement on the superior mental health of intellectually gifted persons. A lower incidence of minor and serious emotional disorders is reported in the studies of Terman, Hollingworth, and Lewis. In addition, the superior resources of gifted persons result in more frequent and more rapid recovery from mental illness. However, the gifted group as well as others do succumb to stresses and strains, and some of these are accentuated by giftedness itself. In addition to the type of problem already mentioned, Strang cites strains that grow out of the creative intensity of many persons of high ability. There is a faint echo of the ancient theme of "genius to madness near allied" in her observation: "It is possible that an intense creativity may cause nervous strain and tension, and that a super-sensitive nervous system (or some other underlying condition) may be conducive to both emotional instability and creative intelligence" (Strang, 1954, p. 217). While the picture of queer conduct arising out of complete absorption by the scientist, philosopher, or artist is much exaggerated in the many caricatures that exist, there is some reason to believe that contact with reality is sometimes lost.

Another problem Strang discusses is the feelings of inferiority which oddly enough often affect the gifted. High ability leads to a high level of aspiration. At times the level is set hopelessly high and the individual debases his own self-concept as a result of failure to achieve the impossible goals he has set for himself. Among students in school and college, often the student is not aware that he is attempting things far beyond his maturity. Pressures from the home, middle and upper class expectations of top level academic performance, and ambitions for admission to highly selective colleges add to the child's own hopes, sometimes unreasonable. Often the school itself adds to this pressure. Strang notes that sometimes a high level of anxiety and fear of failure may produce a disorganized effect on the child's performance.

In the classroom problems of the gifted may be exhibited in different ways. At one extreme is a marked sense of inferiority stemming from failure to meet a hopeless level of aspiration. At the other is immodesty that may be seen in a painful *amour propre*, in intellectual bullying of other children, or in flights into intellectual pursuits to escape from inadequacy in physical and social situations. Some writers note a love of argumentation (NEA, 1961e). Where anxiety leads to rigidity and a form of intellectual paralysis, poor academic achievement will result. Gallagher and Crowder (1957) note that the emotional problems of gifted children are generally of the "non-irritating" variety. "They do not generally have emotional problems of sufficient magnitude to disturb their teachers, parents or peer groups. In short their problems are not one of commission but omission" (Gallagher, 1957, p. 318).

Grotberg's study (1962) of institutionalized gifted persons (median age thirty-four) may be helpful to school personnel in their efforts to forestall emotional problems. Comparing patients with IQ's over 120 with patients of lower ability, Grotberg discovered that half the women and three-quarters of the men in the superior group showed a greater perception of failure, that the group showed a negative attitude toward work and that they reported resistance to parental pressure. The adjustment advantage they had enjoyed in youth was apparently lost in adulthood. Grotberg suggests the following implications for schools: (1) that greater attention be given attitudes toward work; (2) that gifted pupils be helped to deal with failure; (3) that they be guided in developing a self-concept and ideal consonant with their own promise; (4) that schools work more closely with parents; (5) that schools work with gifted students to continue their education and develop in accordance with their promise.

PROBLEMS REPORTED BY GIFTED STUDENTS

As part of its program to stimulate aspirations to attend college among the more able high school students, the North Central Superior and Talented Student Project conducted a problem survey among more than two thousand students in a nineteen-state area. Endicott (1961, Chap. 3) reports the responses of representative high school juniors of superior ability on a "Problems and Plans" checklist, classifying them as problems of school adjustment, problems concerning future plans, home and family problems, and social and personal problems. Endicott's summary (1961, p. 22) follows:

Problems of Superior Students 943 Boys and 1,093 Girls	Students Who Checked "Very Important to Me"	Students Who Checked "Of Some Importance"	Students Who Checked "Not Important"
	(Per Cent)		
1. Discovering special abilities	57	33	10
2. Vocational choice	53	32	15
3. Study habits and reading	47	34	19
4. Self expression	46	41	13
5. Choice of high school subjects	45	33	22
6. College expenses	45	29	26
7. Personal appearance	38	34	28
8. Choices regarding college	38	33	29
9. Relations with parents and family	35	28	37
10. Personal standards of conduct	35	31	34
11. Getting enough sleep	33	34	33
12. Relations with teachers	32	35	33
13. Emotional problems	31	33	36
14. Part-time employment	30	29	41
15. Relations with other students	29	35	36*

* From *Guiding Superior and Talented High School Students,* by Frank S. Endicott. Copyright 1961. Reprinted with permission of Superior and Talented Student Project, North Central Association of Colleges and Secondary Schools, Chicago, Illinois.

The preponderance of problems on Endicott's list are of an external nature rather than problems of an internal, emotional kind. Most of the problems stated by these students are of the kind that teachers and counselors can deal with at their own level of training. While this inference is encouraging, the reader should keep in mind the tendency of students to respond to questionnaires in a way they believe their teachers want them to react. They may accordingly have given more attention to the perceived interests of their teachers than to their own deeper problems.

To the extent that the questionnaire responses may be taken at face value, they seem to indicate that the more able student has adjusted to his superiority by the time he is a junior and that he is concentrating on making the best use of his intellectual gift. In comparing Endicott's findings with those of Terman, Hollingworth and others, it is important to keep in mind the differences among the populations studied. The North Central group is identified as the top 25 per cent of the high school population. Terman's group was the very much more attenuated top one per cent of the total population. Hollingworth discusses young people in the top 2 to 3 per cent and also the highly exceptional one in a hundred thousand. Not every student of college ability shares either the talents or the personal and educational problems of the top 1 per cent.

CHOOSING A CAREER

The emphasis in our activist culture is not simply on *being* gifted but on the uses to which gifts are put. For this reason it is not surprising that the North Central juniors checked problems relating to the discovery and cultivation of aptitudes as the top six items in their list. One may also anticipate the focus of counseling experts on vocational choice. Rothney and Koopman (NSSE, 1958, Chapter 14) declare:

> Counseling of the gifted does not differ in nature from counseling of other students, but it does vary in its demands on the counselor. Interviews will be concerned primarily with the strengths and limitations of the gifted child and about his current and future opportunities. (*Ibid.*, p. 348)

Rothney and Koopman go on to say that guidance of the gifted varies from the usual primarily with respect to educational and vocational counseling, to assistance given to students in "self-appraisal and self-conceptualization", and to helping students cope with unusual pressures from parents, teachers, peers and others.

Vocational guidance of the gifted student differs in several ways from the more usual career counseling. The counselor, parent, and teacher should be aware of the potentially greater loss when the gifted student is not helped to find a niche where he may do his most satisfying, creative, and socially constructive work. The problem is not simply avoiding occupational dead ends; it is finding careers sufficiently open-ended to challenge the worker's full ability. Because of this job requirement, the gifted student faces a range of career possibilities much more limited than that implied in the blithe assumption that he can do anything.

In addition, the gifted student faces the problem of the pyramid, of the extremely small amount of "room at the top." The actor who is simply "adequate" goes unemployed. The musician who is described as "competent" plays few solos. Political and industrial leaders assert the need for creative, extraordinary scientists and engineers, not simply those who follow the formulas and blueprints of others. The truly gifted student faces a problem of competition which scarcely exists at the skilled trade or clerical level.

Vocational guidance of the gifted begins with discovery of interests and talents. First the student needs help in finding himself. He has to set his sights at an appropriate level so that he is not doomed to disappointment on one hand or restricted by too low a ceiling on the other. Part of this process is self-appraisal; the other part is job-analysis. Because of the bewildering specialization that characterizes contemporary industries and professions, the student needs much information concerning families of occupations and their many subdivisions. Students can gain much by meeting persons who are engaged in their possible vocational choice; they would be still the wiser with some opportunity to try their wings at a low altitude in the chosen career constellation.

Just as preparation for a career and adjustment to an occupation involve far more than the specific skills required, vocational guidance includes much more than consideration of a particular occupation and the technical preparation for it. It is admittedly fatuous to speak of vocational guidance in the early school years; yet the picture the child begins to develop of his own powers, his personal worth, his ability to interact with others, influences in large measure his later vocational aspirations. The beginnings of vocational guidance are found in efforts to help the child view his powers and limitations realistically.

Study of career possibilities is part of the curriculum of many junior high schools. For some students this study may be quite late. Experiences in the home and community, family traditions, contacts with adults in various occupations, vicarious experiences in reading, in attending to movies, radio or television may have led pre-adolescents to rather firm vocational commitments. Most elementary school teachers report having arrived at their career choice while still in elementary school themselves. For other students study of careers in junior high school is precocious. The world of work is still far off. Unsophisticated interests center vaguely on such "romantic" roles as airline stewardesses, baseball players, and rocket pilots. Obviously, readiness to explore vocations is as essential as readiness in a reading program. Parents and school personnel need to distinguish passing interests from careers with some real potential. Rather than encourage early decisions, they should work for good basic preparation, sound work habits, and development of strong interests in broad occupational fields. Freehill (1961, pp. 356-58) outlines three elements in vocational planning for the gifted: self evaluation, vocational knowledge, and willingness to formulate a plan. He urges the need of guidance personnel to become more sophisticated since an intelligent career choice involves understanding of personalities, knowledge of value systems, ability to help the student to relate to his self-image, and knowledge about occupations (*Ibid.*, p. 367).

Academically gifted students are not often ready to select a career while in secondary school. They should be encouraged to consider the relatively undifferentiated goal of college attendance, however, with more specific professional choices left open. The intention to attend college should come quite early. Studies of college attendance indicate that a generalized family expectation of college study is more highly correlated with attendance than such other factors as finances, geographic location, and social position. Since children start in school at an early age, the school is in a strategic position to initiate or reinforce the expectation of college in the future.

As young people indicate an interest in specific careers or simply in gainful employment, the school should be able to provide sources of information. A considerable literature is developing on career choices open to young people at various levels of vocational competence. The counselor or teacher should be able to direct students to pamphlets or to persons who can supply facts on availability of particular jobs in particular areas, the demand for persons with such training, personal qualifications necessary, the kind of training needed, the nature of the work, expected remuneration, and the like.

Haller and Miller (1961) have done some interesting research on the "level of occupational aspiration" which reinforces other observations on the importance of the self concept and related factors in determining career goals and career choices. Using the Occupational Aspiration Scale which they devised, Haller and Miller found aspiration related to concept of self, to the subject's role concept, and to the style of life related to the occupation he chose. The subject's image of himself with respect to success and achievement correlated at a high level with his level of aspiration. If schools are interested in encouraging students to undertake various pursuits they can contribute to this outcome by helping students see themselves as succeful performers in such activities. They must also help students see the occupation as a prestige-bearing one. These conclusions are especially meaningful as schools work with neighborhood sub-cultures that are apathetic to, or ignorant of, scholarly preparation and its potential contribution and rewards.

Students in secondary schools should not be hurried into career decisions. General goals, such as college attendance, scientific study, and teaching, are more tenable than early specialization both because of the constantly changing nature of our industry and because of the many changes of mind that are the right of a young person with the whole wide world before him. Academic choices are required all along the route. The secondary school student should be advised not to make choices that close off possibilities that may still seem desirable. Premature specialization and failure to meet general requirements for a whole family of occupations may result in sealing off the future rather than keeping it open until a wiser choice might be made.

While the student is keeping his future open, however, the school should help him explore the world of work in many ways so that his eventual choice is based on as broad a sampling as possible. Cooperative work experience with school supervision represents an excellent firsthand approach. Part-time casual jobs also have some value. Volunteer work in community agencies and governmental services offers a glimpse of employment in numerous related fields. Speakers, biographies, novels, and visits to occupational milieus are still other channels for the flow of occupational information. All of these should be accompanied by simultaneous appraisal and self-appraisal of the students' own potential and interests. In this effort some of the available aptitude and interest inventories provide a point of departure which can be interpreted in the light of the students' performance in school and out and against a backdrop of personal observations made by teachers, counselors, parents, and adult friends.

The NEA Academically Talented Youth Project (1961e) lists the following desirable outcomes of a vocational counseling program:

> To help the student acquire a sound concept of himself
> To help the academically talented student widen his horizons to the varied possibilities that his talents indicate
> To help the student keep career paths wide and open-ended

To encourage educational planning and career goals that recognize human adaptability of the able to the changes of fast-moving economic and career patterns (NEA, 1961e, pp. 77-78) *

EDUCATIONAL COUNSELING

For most gifted students school experiences represent the major means for development of their ability. Positive attitudes toward school and a positive concept of themselves as scholars are as important as appropriate choices of subjects and curricula. An important goal of education throughout school years and particularly in the early grades is development of an interest in academic activities for their own sake and an appreciation of the fact that today's world demands advanced scholastic training for high level employment. Objectives of educational counseling should include development of appropriate self-confidence in school work, acquisition of efficient work-study habits, appraisal of academic strengths and weaknesses, correction of deficiencies in basic skills, exploration of a variety of academic specialities, selection of programs and courses based on ability and career needs, and choice of appropriate specialized schools and colleges. Failure to meet these objectives raises the problems of educational guidance: low motivation, retardation in certain skill areas, premature specialization and its opposite—an inability to define career objectives even at an advanced stage.**

The normal tools of counseling are employed in guidance of the gifted. Use of aptitude and achievement tests call to the attention of teachers performance of children which sometimes belies their actual ability. Interest inventories may give some clues for the direction of counselors and teachers who are helping young people make educational choices. Cumulative record folders which include anecdotal records and personality ratings provide another source of information. Personal interaction between counselor or teacher and the student is essential in the process of helping the student to find himself and to plan an educational program which will be uniquely meaningful to him. Contacts with other personnel on the school scene, with parents and with other adults in the community who know the student provide still more information about the boy or girl which can be useful in educational planning. Follow-up

---

* From *Guidance for the Academically Talented Student* by National Education Association and American Personnel and Guidance Association. Copyright 1961 by National Education Association. Reprinted with permission of National Education Association.

** For discussion of the role of guidance in approaching problems of motivation and underachievement, the reader is asked to turn to Chapter 16.

after the student leaves the school can help in the graduate's educational achievement and may give new light in dealing with other children.

Sometimes the most effective guidance takes place without the presence of the counselor or homeroom teacher. Try-out experiences are of special value to young people. Exploratory courses often provide opportunities to investigate new worlds—mechanical, academic, artistic. Much of the junior high school program is set up with this avowed purpose. More specialized work in senior high school as well gives the student a chance to determine whether tentative decisions he made in junior high school are really valid for him. Much exploration should also take place at the elementary school level. The gifted pupil, in the time he does not need for the conventional curriculum, should have the opportunity to try his wings with more advanced mathematics, science, art media, musical performance and appreciation, literature, creative writing, dramatics, social sciences, and industrial arts. Laboratories, shops, and studios where the youngster can work under minimal supervision provide excellent settings for such exploration. Foreign language laboratories and programmed materials may also be employed by gifted students for independent self-discovery. At the secondary level special seminars on a university campus and supervised correspondence courses also provide opportunities for exploration.

In high school students are often asked to make choices which may have long-term effects. The choice of a language can be more intelligent if a student knows early in his educational career what his future specialization will be. Decisions to take more or less mathematics and science may affect admission to, or performance in, certain technical and engineering schools, although important studies exist which show that the nature of application is more important than the specific course pattern a student takes. The counselor may help the student avoid disproportionate emphasis on academic areas, music, vocational agriculture, business subjects or homemaking. Current pressures weigh heavily in the direction of traditional academic areas, but the argument against imbalance affects mathematics, science, and foreign languages as much as it does the so-called minors.

Still another area of concern in secondary schools is cocurricular activities. Generally gifted students take more than average part in athletics, club activities, journalism, dramatics, and school service functions. The counselor who is concerned with the student's social development and leadership potential encourages this kind of activity. A problem arises, however, in the danger of "overscheduling." With more varied interests, the gifted adolescent is likely to commit himself to far more activities than seem wise. Such students should be helped to select a few activities that carry special meaning for them. They should then be urged to make major contributions to these activities rather than to spread themselves thin in a host of unimportant events, functions, and organizations. The value of cocurricular activities in providing balance through social and physical activities should also be recognized. Not all cocurricular time should be given to the science team for a student interested in science, but some balance between the field of specialization and other kinds of participation should be advised. Some schools set an arbitrary limit on the number of each student's cocurricular activities. It is hard, however, to find an adolescent who has "killed himself" from over-participation. Better than an arbitrary quantitative limit might be counseling toward a deeper involvement in a limited number of activities.

Some cities make available special schools for gifted students at the secondary level or special programs within the neighborhood junior and senior high school. In these cases teachers and counselors have to appraise the readiness of students for such selective situations and the probable impact upon the child. A common observation of such schools is their highly competitive character. Competition seems to be in the air in the selective school or the selective program regardless of the teachers' efforts to soft-pedal it.* Often chronological acceleration is a part of such programs. The individual student must be appraised in the light of his readiness for a highly competitive situation or acceleration. In addition, a problem arises for children who are moderately gifted. Such children who are obviously better than average in unselected classes may find themselves outclassed in a special program and may become discouraged.

CHOOSING A COLLEGE

The approach of graduation from high school brings with it the problem of selecting a college. Even for the gifted student, a particular college's all-round excellence is not enough to qualify that college as the best school for him. Because of a number of factors some students do better in a small college than a large one; some need the resources of the large university campus. Some schools have academic traditions of a high order; some put much emphasis on social development. Some students need the opportunity to get far away from parental over-protection. Some do better when they are close to home or in a college that provides for day students only. Some departments in some colleges put their major emphasis on graduate research activities and give only minor

---

* The college counselor in one of these schools has remarked, "If a fifty cent prize were offered for the high score on a three-hour test, half our children would take it."

attention to undergraduates. Some colleges make special provision for students who have had enriched programs in high school; others lump together all comers in anonymous lecture sections of large size. Some colleges provide close supervision of student activities; some provide almost complete freedom. These differences affect entering freshmen differently. The high school counselor can assemble information about individual schools and individual students in order to recommend appropriate college choices for each student.

Finally, many students fail to go to college because of their families' limited finances. Guidance offices normally assemble as much information as they can about scholarship opportunities. In some cases schools raise their own scholarship funds to assist students who do not receive other grants. Guidance personnel should have secured over a long period of time necessary information on the ability of each gifted child's family to send him to college. Where resources are insufficient, the student and his family should be given information on sources of assistance that are available. Efforts should be made to find part-time employment for students who need it as well as to secure available scholarships. Men's and women's service and civic organizations in the community are often a willing source of funds or employment opportunities. The guidance personnel in the school are most likely to know the needs of gifted students who are on the point of dropping out of school or who despair of financial resources to go to college. They should take the lead in helping the needy student help himself.

Most high schools maintain a considerable library of information for students about colleges. Materials should include a good sampling of catalogues, particularly those attended most by students in the area, sample college applications, directories of colleges, books and pamphlets dealing with career choices and scholarship information. *High Potential*, a publication of the New York State Education Department Bureau of Guidance, carries valuable bibliographies for students. Some of the more frequently used sources follow:

1. *Information about Colleges*
   American Council on Education. *American Universities and Colleges.* Washington, D. C., The Council, 1956.
   Bowles, Frank H. *How to Get into College*, New York, E. P. Dutton, 1958.
   Brownstein, Samuel C. *College Bound: Planning for College and Career.* Great Neck, N. Y., Barron's Educational Series, 1957.
   Brownstein, S. C., and Weiner, Mitchel. *How to Prepare for College Entrance Examinations.* Great Neck, N. Y., Barron's Educational Series, 1957.

College Entrance Examination Board. *College Handbook.* Princeton, N. J., Educational Testing Service, 1957.

Fine, Benjamin. *Fine's American College Counselor and Guide.* New York, Prentice-Hall, 1958-59.

Landis, Paul H. *So This Is College.* New York, McGraw-Hill, 1954.

Lovejoy, Clarence D. *Lovejoy's College Guide.* New York, Simon and Schuster, 1959.

McReynolds, John W. *How to Plan for College and What to Do When You Get There.* New York, Simon and Schuster, 1956.

Resnick, William C., and Heller, David H. *On Your Own in College.* Columbus, Ohio, Charles E. Merrill, 1963.

Ruby, Normie, and Ruby, Harold. *Stairway to College.* Boston, Porter Sargent, 1955.

Shosteck, Robert, *College Finder.* Washington, D. C., B'nai B'rith Vocational Service, 1955.

Sifferd, Calvin S. *College and You.* Bloomington, Ill., McKnight and McKnight Publishing Co., 1952.

U. S. Office of Education. *Accredited Higher Institutions.* Washington, D. C., Government Printing Office, 1960-61.

Wilson, Eugene S., and Bucher, Charles A. *College Ahead!* New York, Harcourt, Brace, 1958.

2. *Scholarship Information*

Feingold, S. Norman. *Scholarships, Fellowships and Loans.* Cambridge, Mass., Bellman Publishing Co., 1955.

Lovejoy, Clarence D., and Jones, Theodore S. *Lovejoy-Jones College Scholarship Guide.* New York, Simon and Schuster, 1957.

National Merit Scholarship Program. Evanston, Ill., National Merit Scholarship Corp.

National Scholarship Service and Fund for Negro Students. *Bulletins.* The Service, 6 East 82 Street, New York, N. Y. 10026.

New York State Education Department, *Opening the Door to College Study.* Albany, N.Y., The Department, 1959.

COLLEGE TRANSITION PROGRAMS

Of particular interest to academically gifted students are summer programs on college campuses offered as a transition to college. With the assistance of the National Science Foundation approximately seven thousand secondary school students were able to participate in tuition-free training in the summer of 1962. The Summer Science Training Program for Secondary School Students has offered to high ability students science and mathematics programs beyond those normally available in high schools. Students participating in these programs have received financial aid equivalent to a maximum of 50 per cent of the estimated travel and subsistence costs.

The programs subsidized by the National Science Foundation are obviously limited to highly selected students. In addition, a much larger number of high school juniors, seniors, and immediate graduates are welcome to enroll in regular or special courses in nearby colleges. Some colleges have entered into special agreements with schools in adjacent counties in order to serve students still enrolled in high school with special courses. These courses normally carry no credit but provide an enormous amount of stimulation and academic motivation for participating students. A few colleges in urban areas extend these programs into the school year and offer seminars in after-school hours or on weekends for interested students of superior ability. Apart from Summer Science Training Programs, the New York City Schools *Curriculum and Materials* has listed the following opportunities for college transition study for high school students in New York State, for example:

Summer workshop for endorsed high school applicants in dance, theatre and art

Summer Institute for Junior Engineers and Scientists

Appropriate level courses in languages for high school students with excellent academic records

Computer Math Program for able school students

High school reading and study skills

High School Experimental Program for students with college potential but not eligible to be admitted to full-time standing

Essentials of Science; Essentials of Mathematics; Basic College Skills

Courses in printing, crafts, photography, and a Reading Laboratory

College credit program for selected high school students

Special summer program in humanities, science and mathematics for able high school students who have completed junior year

The value of these programs as exploratory experiences for students is apparent. No less important is their contribution as a transition for high school students to the mysterious groves of Academe.

WORKING WITH PARENTS OF THE GIFTED

Counselors who have worked with gifted children recognize the need for working with the parents of these children as well. Gifted students are as sensitive to parental influences as any children. Parents provide the biological inheritance which sets the limits within which ability operates; they are responsible for the physical environment; they determine the emotional setting in which the child is reared; almost exclusively they provide learning situations for the infant, and they continue to furnish learning opportunities for many years although they begin to share this function more and more with other persons and agencies; their values permeate the home environment, and these values are most important in the establishment of levels of aspiration by family members. Terman, Hollingworth, Miles, and others report an extremely high proportion of supportive family backgrounds in their studies of gifted children.* Because of the very pervasive influence of the family, this is indeed encouraging. However, one may well consider how great an obstacle to achievement negative family situations constitute in other cases.

Deep interest in the gifted in recent years has resulted in publication of a number of excellent volumes for parents of highly able children. Brumbaugh and Roscho's *Your Gifted Child*, (1959), Strang's *Helping Your Gifted Child* (1960) and DeHaan's *Guidelines for Parents of Capable Youth* (1961) are valuable sources to recommend to parents. They are also useful to school personnel in representing to them the concerns and perspectives of parents of gifted children.

THE QUESTIONS PARENTS ASK

Parents ask many of the same questions teachers ask about gifted children. First, they want to know how they may ascertain whether their child is truly unusual in his abilities. Second, they want to know how they may help at home in developing these abilities, what help should be given before school years, in elementary school, secondary school, and even in college and beyond. They ask what out-of-school opportunities should be provided to enrich the school experience. They want to know how to determine whether the child's school is giving him the best possible program. They ask for assistance in selecting special high schools, special high school programs, and appropriate college choices for their child. They fear, generally, that their child is not working up to his capacity, and they want to know what the school can do and what they should do to motivate him to greater effort. They ask for recommended activities that may contribute to their child's admission to the highly selective colleges. The volumes already cited will help parents find answers to some of these questions.

For identification of special ability, parents often have to be disabused of ready belief in the magical qualities of intelligence and aptitude tests. They should be informed of some of the common signs of intellectual

---

* One should note, however, that these are the families of *identified* gifted children. It is quite possible that many potentially gifted children are never discovered because of negative home conditions.

superiority: walking, talking, and reading at an early age; possession of an unusual vocabulary for the child's age; development of many interests and a long interest span; high level performance in intellectual activities such as reasoning, generalizing, and working with ideas; evidence of intellectual curiosity; facility in listening to, understanding, and carrying out directions; demonstrating a good memory; penetrating quickly to the heart of problems; possessing an extensive store of information; showing originality in expression and in attacking problems; sensing what is really significant in a situation. These are signs that a parent may look for, expecting increasing quality at higher age levels. The parent should also be cautioned that these are *general* signs, that any specific child may still be gifted even though he learned to walk or talk at a relatively late age.

In addition, the criterion of early performance has to be hedged with a question concerning the way in which the child first showed new achievements. In evaluating ability, it makes a difference whether the child has learned to read by himself or whether he has at last responded to careful, and perhaps tedious, coaching by his parents. So, too, "number facts" and science information may indicate unusual native ability or simply premature "teaching" by the parents. Coaching is a factor not only in observing performance but also in interpreting intelligence tests taken at an early age. In some cases special school opportunities are open only to children with high scores on intelligence tests. Parents, seeking the best educational situation for their children, at times, coach children, particularly on the better known tests, and may succeed in helping a child score some ten or twenty points higher than would otherwise be warranted. Parents should be cautioned on pushing children into situations where their real ability may be very much below that of their classmates.

Parents also ask, quite legitimately, for the test results and their significance when children take standardized tests in school. There is general agreement that a raw score (IQ 142, e.g.) ought not to be given, but that the parent should instead be told the percentile band in which the score falls. Thus, a parent would not be told that his ten-year-old has the mind of a fourteen-year-old, but that Johnny's score was in the top 1 per cent (or top 5 per cent if the school prefers a more conservative interpretation) of scores for children Johnny's age. While there is some danger of inflating the ego of Johnny's parents and hazarding vanity on Johnny's part, the counselor is more interested in the parents' understanding of Johnny's true ability so that every desirable step be taken to help Johnny realize his potential. Reporting and interpreting aptitude and achievement scores may follow the same pattern. In all cases, an effort should be made to help the parent understand the approximate nature of the measure employed and the margin of error that exists.

CONTRIBUTIONS TO SCHOOL LEARNING

Parents of preschoolers are often anxious concerning permissible teaching of school matter to their youngsters. The major contribution that parents can make is to provide a rich and stimulating environment that is supportive and non-threatening. Every child ought to have parents and other adults read to him, tell him stories, teach him songs, help him learn to play games, provide toys that invite both mental and motor development, take him to zoos, parks, and museums, provide picture books and other easy reading material, supply simple art materials like paint, crayons, and clay, introduce him to simple puzzles, and furnish special activities where warranted such as nursery school, dance, art or music lessons. The gifted child should be able to derive more from these opportunities than other children. His response will be one of the important signs of his superior ability.

One of the results of these stimulating experiences will be the child's efforts to go beyond what is immediately presented. Ultimately the child is not satisfied to be read to; he wants to learn to read himself. He wants to be able to count and perhaps perform other mathematical operations. He wants to sing, to play an instrument, to draw, to paint, to sculpt. To the parent who worries lest he be anticipating school activities, Strang says, "If a child seems to be handling a situation effectively, let him go ahead. If he seems eager to read or to do things you think are too difficult for him, let him try. Following his lead is quite different from forcing him into activities for which he is not yet ready" (Strang, 1960, p. 93). The task of the parent is not to force the precocious child into a lockstep. He helps the child develop his abilities, without putting pressure on the child to do so, and he tries to keep teacher and principal posted on the child's development. The basic principle is that the school adjusts to the learner, not that the learner be held back in order to meet a predetermined schedule of learnings.

THE HOME AS A FORCE IN LEARNING

The parents' greatest contribution, however, is more likely to lie in fields that do not overlap the functions of the school. As man lives not by meat and drink alone, the child grows not by books and school work alone. Emphasis in schools is appropriately placed first on academic matters. Physical development, social growth, and emotional maturity represent areas where the home's contribution is potentially much greater.

Consider how important physical play skills are to boys and adolescents. The father who helps his son to catch and bat better may simultaneously be contributing to his scholastic achievement by relieving him of concern over real or imagined inferiority. The many sports and play activities that claim the time and effort of boys and girls represent opportunities for parental assistance—through provision of facilities and equipment and through instruction if needed.

The home, also, provides the backdrop for social growth throughout childhood and in a large part of adolescence. The parent can help by providing physical facilities for social interaction, by supervising play relationships, by helping children develop insight into problems of social adjustment. In addition, parents can help children make their entree into social clubs and hobby groups by encouraging membership in youth-serving agencies like Y's, scouts, and neighborhood associations. They contribute to their own children, though less directly, by volunteering to serve as adult leaders of youth groups where the need for adult assistance is perennial. Finally, the home serves even more by example than it does by precept. Mature social relationships exhibited by parents with their peers serve as a model for children. Adult friends coming into the family circle provide experience for youngsters in relating to persons older than they.

Emotional maturity also reflects the family more than any other single element in the child's life. The home where parents are mature and stable makes a greater contribution than the home which is intellectually febrile but emotionally threatening. Parents have to be sensitive to the emotional needs of their children. They have to be realistic about what they can do and what they cannot do as parents so that their own feelings of guilt do not contaminate the whole family atmosphere. Parents, as well as children, have to be free on occasion to "blow off steam." The total picture of family life, however, has to be one of maturity on the part of parents, affectionate acceptance of children with their foibles as well as their talents, love for each child for what he is rather than for the kudos he brings his parents. The family portrait also depicts support for all family members in their contacts with each other and with the outside world, the setting of reasonable but demanding standards of achievement, the establishment of aspirations appropriate for each individual, and the growth of values that combine individual excellence and social responsibility.

Some specific activities in the family relate in a general, but important, way to total scholastic achievement. The home is a very real cultural milieu and as such sets sights for children. The home is a place where books and journals are read frequently or rarely, where a particular quality of reading matter is to be found. The music that is heard at home may simply duplicate what is poured out in juke boxes and radios anywhere, or it may open new horizons in folk music, opera, or the symphonic repertory. Conversation in the home can vary from occasional grunts and gossip, to discussion of children's interests, adult concerns, sports, the day's news, ethical issues, and the arts. Teachers of kindergartners in some deprived areas report that their children appear to have picked up almost no speaking skills or vocabulary at home. Teachers in other areas have to impose severe limits on overly verbal children.

"Doing things" with children is still another positive contribution that is no less important for not being directly related to a curriculum. Cooking, baking, building small objects, making papier-mâché animals, painting (house painting or *objets d'art*), finger painting, gardening, just tinkering around, are educational activities for children and fun for parents (except when adults inherit the major share of cleaning up). When the parent asks what he can do to help his child in school, mentioning activities of this kind represents more than a facetious answer.

"Going places" with children is another parental contribution that need not be tied to this week's social studies unit. In effect, the parent is being asked to widen his child's cultural horizon. Field-tripping resembles in this regard the other experiences already mentioned. Parks, libraries (pity the poor child whose parent says he hasn't been in a library in twenty years!), museums, walks through sections of the city, visits to nearby historical sites, shopping in the neighborhood or large commercial center, churches of many faiths, rivers, lakes, mines, forests, farms, all represent educational resources. Many are accessible easily and without cost to any family. Vacation trips, family camping, county and state fairs, plays, concerts, and such activities represent other rewarding experiences but must obviously be geared to a family's income. Choices have to be made, and the family should focus upon things to do and places to visit that extend the child's horizons, not simply upon those things which the child has found pleasurable in the past and wishes to repeat endlessly. Activities that truly engage the parents' interest as well are doubly valuable since the child catches the reflected values of adults.

As children grow older they seek help with school assignments that may be troubling. Help that the parents offer should be in the direction of making the child independent. The parent is most helpful when he avoids providing the answers and instead helps to clarify questions. Once again, the parent has to find his joy in the child's growth, not in the child's perfection. If the child is bright, he is bright enough to try to make his parent do his work for him. If the parent is bright, he will give the child cues that help him do his work for himself. As the child progresses through school, it may become more and more difficult for the parent to provide any direct help to the child. The parent can, however, help secure necessary resources: access to libraries, a modicum of reference works in the home, a place to study, and facilities to store study and reference materials.

What reference materials should a home provide? Gifted children ought to have available, to begin with, a dictionary intended for a school level above their current grade placement—a junior level dictionary in the primary grades, an intermediate level dictionary in the upper elementary grades, a collegiate dictionary in secondary school, an unabridged beyond that. A junior level encyclopedia is useful through elementary school; it supplements a senior encyclopedia through junior high school. While these reference works are expensive when purchased new, used or old edition dictionaries and encyclopedias may be purchased in the larger cities or by mail for 20 to 30 per cent of the price when new. Newspapers and magazines coming into the home are important sources of current reference. The book review sections of the larger newspapers periodically publish useful lists of paperback editions for establishing inexpensive reference collections in selected fields of scholarship. Since no home can have more than a small sampling, however, children should learn to make frequent use of the public library and not develop a dependence upon a limited home library.

As the child progresses through high school, his attention is directed toward choice of an institution for higher education. Far more important than the parents' affinity for a particular college is their manifest expectation over the years that their child will go to college. Given this expectation and a responsive commitment on the child's part, parents may help supplement school information on college possibilities. Parents may assist (but not take over) in writing to colleges for information. They can devote vacation time to touring a few college campuses that are within ready access. They can seek opinions from other parents with children in college. Finally, they can help their children be mindful of deadline dates for submitting applications, taking examinations, and seeking interviews. In an era when there are impossible pressures for admission on the prestige colleges, parents can utilize their greater maturity to help their children view the problem of admission and rejection realistically. They will frequently find valuable assistance available in the person of the college admission adviser in the high school.

At all points in the child's life the parent serves as a guide, unconsciously, to vocational choice. The parent's attitude toward his own work serves as an important stimulus to follow in his footsteps or as a warning to do otherwise. The attitudes of both parents toward the careers of relatives and friends who are seen in the home help to form the child's response to other vocations. How the parents view different occupational levels—unskilled and skilled labor, agriculture, sales and white collar jobs, business management, government service and the professions—helps to mold general attitudes toward classes of occupations. Parents often need advice on setting realistic, attainable goals for their gifted children; sometimes they need to be counseled not to permit children to set their sights too low. In all cases, parents and teachers alike have to be aware of the immense variety of challenging, rewarding careers that are open in our economy, many of which are outside the average person's knowledge. Parents should be advised of vocational counseling services in the school and community.

And finally a word for those homes where such parental assistance or interest is not available. In such cases identification of the gifted by community agencies like the school, public welfare departments, churches, and social service organizations becomes imperative for children of all ability levels. Obviously, no institution can truly serve *in loco parentis*. The obligation is none the less a heavy one to cultivate the full possibilities of human existence. While the school may counsel the parent who is willing and able to help his talented child, it must also do all that it can to find supplements or substitutes for the parent who cannot do so.

SUMMARY

Guidance services perform functions in schools which touch the gifted in many ways. It is conceivable that these services may often be critical in directing development of high potential. There is no evidence that guidance alone will work wonders, but specific contributions are seen at various points.

Identification of high potential often requires the best skills and instruments that guidance services can provide. Even where the existence of giftedness is already clear, the need remains to identify specific strengths and weaknesses as keys to educational planning.

Gifted persons, like all others, have their share of personal problems, some aggravated by the uniqueness of their talents. Competent guidance services are needed to help the gifted come to terms with these problems so that they will not obstruct self-fulfillment and the realization of unusual potential. Whether viewed as the achievement of "high-level wellness" or the maintenance of mental hygiene, the objective is one which often demands highly sophisticated guidance services.

The more unique the student's gifts, the more important that educational planning be guided on a personal, individualized basis. Educational guidance of the gifted means direction of planning around the individual's gifts and needs rather than enforcing conformity to externally established patterns. Of first importance are establishment of worthwhile goals and development of motivation adequate to the necessarily delayed realization of complex career objectives. Planning for college is almost always a part of this process.

Because of the nature of intellectual superiority, educational and vocational guidance are multiply intertwined. Superior ability does not simply mean free choice among a number of the usual careers. Instead it involves seeking out very particular areas where a special gift bears its maximum yield. Such areas are likely to provide few openings, and to demand very high levels of excellence and lengthy training. Identifying ability and interest, furnishing information and providing opportunities for exploration are imperatives in vocational guidance.

Parents as well as their gifted children are part of the guidance process. Parents may seek help in providing an optimum growth environment for their children. In some cases parents need to be awakened to the promise of their children and the need to contribute more effectively to realization of that promise. Working with parents is not the exclusive concern of guidance personnel, but guidance functions in many cases cannot be performed effectively except through contact with the home.

The burden of this volume is that education of the gifted is an extension of individualization in education. The importance of guidance of the gifted may be seen in the fact that guidance services are the school's primary instrument in individualization.

Chapter 16

Motivation and Underachievement

And that one Talent which is death to hide,
Log'd with me useless . . .

—Milton

Milton bemoaning his blindness is a tragic thought. Impelled by a stern sense of mission, Milton struggled on. The poems which are called the "work of his maturity" followed his blindness by a decade and more. How may one explain, by way of contrast, the phenomenon of thousands of youth of high ability, with no visible handicaps, who never fulfill their promise?

Numerous compilations have been made which attest to the failure of able young persons to exploit their talents. Warner, Havighurst, and Loeb (1944) estimated that the number of students with requisite ability who do not attend college equals the number of students with lower ability who do enroll in the ivied halls.* Their judgment is that half of the students who do not enter college exceed in ability half of the students who do attend. Wolfle, making a survey for the learned societies, found the following percentage of college graduates among the indicated levels of ability:

---

* Obviously there is "room at the top" in fields not requiring college attendance. Present employment trends, however, suggest that the non-college man is handicapped in most areas when high intellectual ability is needed.

Level	Per Cent Graduated from College
Top 0.1 per cent	69
Top 1 per cent	59
Top 5 per cent	49
Top 10 per cent	42
Top 20 per cent	34

(Wolfle, 1954, p. 149)

In general, all students in these distributions are considered capable of completing a college course; yet only 1 in 3 graduated. Other studies paint pictures that are similarly bleak.

A number of alternative explanations may be made. One of these is that intelligence scores and high school grades are not adequate predictors of college success. The chapter on intelligence testing reports studies that cast considerable doubt on popular testing instruments. The omission of important factors in intelligence tests (creativity and social leadership, to mention but two), the neglect of conative factors (persistence and motivation, for example) support the following thesis. While many students possess relatively high verbal capabilities, they may not have the total qualities necessary for persistence and success in college. In brief, because of high verbal ability, they are overrated. This explanation probably applies to some "underachievers," but it does not seem adequate for the large number of cases of low achievement.

ECONOMIC DETERMINISM

A second explanation that has more currency centers upon financial limitations. College attendance is expensive. Costs for tuition and room and board continue to rise. In low income families there is a sacrifice of potential income from the youth who goes to college rather than to work.

Do these obstacles in fact deter able students from attending college? The evidence is circumstantial and contradictory. On the one hand we know that high school graduates who must live away from home to attend college enroll in smaller proportion than do graduates who are able to live at home while attending a commuting college. We know that tuition-free institutions enroll a larger proportion of children from low income families than do colleges with moderate or high fees. Millett (1952), reasoning from the effect of veteran scholarships after World War II, discovered no greater increase of college attendance among low income groups than among more favored groups as a result of government assistance. Mulligan (1951) also found cultural factors more influential than economic factors. He noted that children from white collar and skilled groups who fail to go on to college are frequently the victims of economics, but that children of farming, semi-skilled, and unskilled groups are more likely to be deterred by cultural tradition than by finances. Apparently the aspirations of a group are more effective than socio-economic status in motivation toward academic achievement and college attendance.

Cole's study (1956) of able students revealed a large percentage who attributed their failure to enroll in college to financial handicaps. On the other hand, Cole indicated greater relationship between parental occupation and college attendance than between socio-economic status and further study. Questioning the top 30 per cent of almost 33,000 high school seniors, Cole discovered that 12 per cent of those not going to college gave finances as the reason. A much larger proportion, 25 per cent of the high ability boys and 45 per cent of the brightest girls indicated simply the lack of a college goal in their plans for the future. Almost one tenth of the boys and one fifth of the girls said they had no interest in higher education (Cole, 1955).

Havighurst presents two statistical tables underlining a relationship between social class and college attendance rather than the desired relationship between ability and college enrollment:

Percentage of Social Class Groups Entering College

Social Class	Per Cent of total group	Entrants to college (percentage)			
		1920 (est)	1940 (est)	1960 (est) male	female
Upper, upper middle	10	40	80	85	70
Lower middle	30	10	20	55	35
Upper lower	40	2	5	25	18
Lower lower	20	0	0	10	5

Intellectual Ability and College Entrance
(Source: *American Higher Education in the 1960's*. Columbus, Ohio State University Press, 1960).

Quartile of Scholastic Aptitude	Percentage			
	Enter College		Do Not Enter College	
	Male	Female	Male	Female
I (top)	19	14	6	11
II	15	9	10	16
III	4	3	21	22
IV	2	1	23	24

(*In* Shertzer, 1960, pp. 228 and 229)[*]

[*] From: Bruce Shertzer, editor. *Working With Superior Students* (Chicago: Science Research Associates, Inc., 1960). Reprinted with permission.

The first table shows marked differences among social classes in college attendance but is hopeful in terms of the increasing proportion of lower class students enrolling. The second table reveals 10 per cent of graduates in the bottom half enrolling in college while 43 per cent in the top half do not. Both tables show clearly the smaller proportion of girls who enter, particularly girls of high ability and low social class.

A study of high ability high school seniors in New York State not planning to attend college showed comparable but not coinciding results. Among the top 20 per cent, the father's occupation rather than the child's ability "appeared to determine in large part who would go on to college after high school, who would attend a four-year degree-granting institution rather than a junior college and who would select a local college rather than one located outside the State" (Bienenstok, 1957, p. 161). In all occupational categories girls cited lack of interest more than financial problems as their reason. In lower socio-economic groups, however, boys indicated lack of finances more frequently than lack of interest.

Bowman (ASCD, 1960, p. 43) cites Liddle's study of the high school records of graduates from two elementary schools, one serving predominantly a lower class neighborhood, the other a middle class population. In the high school no student from the lower class school made an "A" in an academic subject over a three-year period, but 45 per cent of the students coming from the middle class school made "A's". On the other hand, no graduate of the middle class school made an "F" in the three year period, but 44 per cent of the lower class school graduates drew "F's". These differences exceeded the variation found by Rosen (1959) among children representing different ethnic groups. Edwards and Wilson (1961) found similar differences in contrasting eight elementary schools in Berkeley. In upper occupational households, 90 per cent of the children were reading at grade level. Only one-third of the children of semi- or unskilled manual laborers were doing as well. The teachers' judgment of students' achievement, when related to occupational status, was parallel to scores they earned on standardized tests.

In sum, there is no question that economics plays a role in determining college attendance. Academic achievement is no doubt related to socio-economic standing. However, the father's occupational classification apparently makes a greater impact than does his bank balance. And more important than financial ability, socio-economic, or occupational status is motivation—perceiving college as a goal.

ETHNIC INFLUENCES

Studies of differing achievement levels and variations in college attendance among individual ethnic groups confirm the significance of value patterns in motivation. Contrasts among groups are very much reduced when individuals with the same values are found in the groups being compared. Strodtbeck (*in* McClelland, 1958) has provided a valuable insight in his analysis of differences in achievement among second generation Jewish and second generation Italian families in New Haven. When members of each group adhered to the group's typical scheme of values, differences were marked. The greatest differences in values between the two groups were found in respect to individual endeavor, family behavior patterns, and belief in the reign of order rather than luck. But achievement in both groups was equally high when individual families held the same values. If Strodtbeck's studies are valid, there is no reason to accept a biological determinism in estimating the level of ability to be expected from any ethnic group. Achievement is seen as culturally rather than biologically determined. The school, the family, and other community institutions may be effective in stimulating greater achievement if they find productive ways of influencing the values children hold.

In human affairs, of course, it is never fully possible to disentangle the twisting threads of multiple causation. Edwards and Wilson (1961) surveyed patterns of achievement in eight elementary school zones in Berkeley against a background of social and psychological influences. They found high socio-economic status, high occupational classification, membership in an ethnic minority, high ability, high aspirations, and high achievement all associated. Conversely, low ratings in all these categories went together. Which is cause, which effect? They noted with interest, however, that regardless of socio-economic and occupational status, the tendency was to regress to the norm of a particular school. The low status child in the school in the "good" neighborhood did better than his compeer in a "poor" neighborhood. Similarly, the child of the professional worker in a "poor" neighborhood did more poorly than his compeer in a "good" one. Membership in an ethnic minority appeared to yield different results. Negro children in a heavily Negro school did better than in a more heterogenous situation. Edwards and Wilson hazard the guess that minority status in a heterogeneous group can be discouraging. Perhaps "a socially segregated minority can generate and maintain higher hopes than when integrated." The authors make the guess that in a group where they are dominant, the minority is "not demoralized by continuous tokens of imposed inferiority" (*Ibid.,* p. 51).

THE SCHOOL'S EFFECT

The fact that aspirations and achievement of children regress toward the norm of their school suggests the importance of the school itself—as an environment—apart from its personnel and curriculum. This item would seem to negate Edwards and Wilson's effort to explain higher achievement in the kind of segregated school situation existing in Berkeley.

Teachers apparently adapt their expectations to a particular school population. Because they attempt to deal with the class as a group, teachers "contribute to the strata differences in achievement, and may also affect the students' aspirations" (*Ibid.*, p. 58). But fellow students as well as teachers have a profound effect upon the pupil. "The ubiquitous quest for popularity and respect among one's associates leads to a homogenization of values" (*Ibid.*). Considerations like the preceding contributed to the Supreme Court orders for racial desegregation in the schools. "Separate but equal" was regarded judicially to be anomalous.

SEX DIFFERENCES AND ACADEMIC MOTIVATION

The individual's sex is found to have bearing upon achievement just as socio-economic status, the parents' occupational status and ethnic derivation do. A study in Indiana in 1959 of almost two thousand high school graduates highlights the failure of our culture to attract capable girls into the professions. Of girls in the top decile 36 per cent do not enter college. Nor do girls who enter have a high record for persistence. Women earn only one-third of the bachelor's and master's degrees, only one-tenth of the doctorates. Doctorates tend to be concentrated in "women's fields"—education, fine and applied arts, English, journalism, and foreign languages. Relatively few women earn degrees in the natural sciences, mathematics, law, or medicine (Shertzer, 1960, p. 211).

Once again, the culture and its values seem to be at the bottom of differences in this case as in the others. The small proportion of American women in dentistry, medicine, and the physical sciences is in sharp contrast to larger proportions of European women in these fields. Not differences in native ability, but differences in cultural expectations, may be found to underlie differing achievement of the two sexes in these and other fields. Despite the sharp rise in careers for women outside the home, girls in secondary schools and colleges follow a course of aspiration, thought, and action which center upon marriage and homemaking as an exclusive concern. In studies where boys indicate basic interest in achievement, girls put their interest in social accommodations that they believe pave the way to successful marriage. "It's dreadful to be taller than a boy but fatal to be smarter" is the archetypical remark of the very bright girl. The critical element in differential motivation toward achievement between the two sexes is, as in other cases, not native ability but the values through which each sex sees the world.

New research by Lesser and French is directed at determining patterns of academic motivation among girls and women in a variety of college situations. A study by Lesser, Krawitz, and Packard (1961) at Hunter College High School revolved around efforts to increase achievement motivation. High achievers and low achievers responded differently to these efforts but related probably to different perceptions of their sex role. The girls were asked to respond to pictures showing men and women in poses of achievement. The high-achieving girls responded favorably to pictures of women as achievers; the low achievers responded favorably to pictures of men as achievers. One is led to presume that girls may be induced to strive for success only if they regard such a pattern as consistent with their concept of the female role.

A general consensus prevails among researchers on motivation. They do not deny the obstacles that economics, ethnic derivation, and sex may place in the way of the superior student. However, they cite the much greater impact of value systems of the sub-culture and the force of individual motivation.

MOTIVATION FROM A PERCEPTUAL POINT OF VIEW

The importance of motivation has not been overlooked in massive efforts under way to improve the output of underachieving bright students. Counseling, curriculum adaptations, improving the cultural climate of the community are all coming into their own as ways of stimulating greater interest in intellectual achievement. To the extent that they transform the way in which the student looks at himself and his world, these mechanisms may be effective.

To a large extent, however, proposed solutions represent manipulation of the environment. There is good reason to identify motivation as an aspect of personality rather than the environment—as existing within rather than outside the individual. We may find ourselves on the threshold of a hopeful approach to problems of motivation in the perceptual psychology of Maslow (1954), Rogers (1962), Moustakas (1956), Combs (1959), and others. These writers start from the premise that the key to behavior is in the individual's immediate perception of the situation and his current self-concept. They take an ancient philosophic viewpoint that we do not see things directly but through a system of perception which includes psychological as well as sensory perceptors. The important thing in motivation, then, is not to manipulate the environment but to help the individual to see himself and his world more positively.

In this process we are aided by the view of human nature which this group of psychologists advocates. They posit a will to health as characteristic of the normal human being. We are born with potential abilities and with a will to use them. We are not born to the idle life (to shirking assignments, to seeking the easy way out, to satisfaction with C's if easier to come by than A's); we find joy in achievement. Since man is both a social and an intelligent creature, he does not express these tendencies directly. Social interaction and intelligence serve as mediators. The individual's evaluation of the total situation and of his place in it determine whether or not he will follow a healthy path toward achievement and self-expression.

George Herbert Mead spoke of a "self-other" process to explain the way in which an individual learns his own identity. He sees himself only through the reactions of others to him. In like manner the phenomenologists describe development of the self-concept (Combs, 1959). The individual meets himself only as he perceives the reaction of others. If he is encouraged to think positively of himself he finds more encouragement in the reaction of others; if he has been led to downgrade himself he meets the reactions of others with suspicion. If teachers help Johnny to appraise his efforts as generally, though not always, successful, he views himself as an achiever and may seek ever higher standards for himself. If teachers are perpetually critical, Johnny loses faith in himself and gives up easily in the face of difficulty.

An interesting example of this hypothesis may be found in the Horace Mann-Lincoln Institute of School Experimentation research in New York City at DeWitt Clinton High School (Goldberg, 1959). Working with a group of underachievers the Institute found some effectiveness after long exposure of the group to a warm, supportive, sympathetic teacher who combined the roles of homeroom and social studies teacher. When the same boys were assigned in a subsequent semester to a teacher who placed greater emphasis on meeting academic standards than on emotional support, the boys drifted back to patterns of poor achievement. The habitual pattern of self-abasement was apparently open to some modification, but in the face of opposition, and with support removed, the boys returned to their previously established self-concept.

From this point of view, then, motivation is not a matter of external stimulation, not a matter of the carrot *or* the stick. Motivation is simply a characteristic of the person who is self-actualizing, of recognizing one's powers and putting them to use. Combs, Rogers, and their colleagues describe the self-actualizing person as one who is open to experience. Such a person trusts himself and trusts life. He goes out to meet life joyously and unafraid. He is not fearful of himself and, therefore, forever on the defensive protecting himself against life and new experience. The self-actualizing person is also described as one who identifies with his fellows. His positive self-concept leads to constructive relationship with others. In Combs' words, "The feeling of oneness with one's fellows produces in the truly adequate person a high degree of responsible, trustworthy behavior" and "a deep sensitivity to the feelings and attitudes of others" (ASCD, 1962, pp. 54, 55). Because human beings live in a culture, the truly adequate person also has "a field of perceptions, rich and extensive enough to provide understanding of the events in which he is enmeshed and available when he needs them" (*Ibid.*, p. 59). If motivation is to be regarded as a characteristic of a fully functioning personality, those who seek to build a desirable level of motivation must look to the components of the self-actualizing person: a positive view of self, openness to experience, identification with others, and possession of a rich perceptual field. The perceptualists regard all these qualities as learned. The school is one arena in which such learning can take place.

While the school is interested in all of the external factors that affect motivation, it may find more fruitful results in working within its own realm to help pupils fulfill themselves. The school can do little to influence patterns of family interaction or basic value patterns in the home. It can work mightily, however, in the directions suggested by the perceptualists. The 1962 Yearbook of the Association for Supervision and Curriculum Development devotes itself to ways in which the school can help students develop a positive self-concept, explore new experiences hopefully, relate more freely to other people, and build a rich background of meaningful information and understanding.

THE UNDERACHIEVING PERSONALITY

Many studies have been made of the opposite of the self-actualizing person. The person who does not fulfill himself is called the underachiever. In academic terms he is generally defined as the student whose achievement is markedly inferior to his tested intellectual ability. If one is willing to use the intelligence quotient as the criterion, the underachiever may be regarded as any student whose achievement record in a particular area is more than one standard deviation below the point which might be expected on the basis of his IQ.

Beasley (1957) has brought together the findings of a considerable number of studies of underachievement. From a number of studies she reports a positive relationship between personality difficulty and low academic performance. Findings of inferiority feelings are somewhat more frequent among underachievers. "Maladjustment and/or radicalism" show a negative effect on achievement. She is not, however, impressed by the evidence cited in the reports:

The evidence from the above findings, though indicative of slight group differences on various measures of adjustment, is insufficient to conclude that differences in adjustment are a major factor in scholastic achievement, especially since other studies fail to differentiate the underachiever group from the normal or overachieving population on personal adjustment scores . . . . the heterogeneity which apparently exists within and among groups of various achievement levels would seem to negate the adjustment factor as the sole basis for differences in scholastic functioning. (Beasley, 1957, p. 5) *

Beasley substantiates her conclusion that personal adjustment is not related to achievement by citing studies showing little difference in personal adjustment scores between (1) college men on academic probation and those of superior achievement, (2) men in the highest and lowest deciles of college ability, (3) gifted high school students failing two or more subjects and those with good academic records. She presents studies by Griffith, Morgan, Owens and Johnson, Ryan, Leibman, Pearlman, Monroe, Montalto, and Conklin which yield results showing striking similarity in personality adjustment scores. Many of the recognized tests available were used: the Bell Adjustment Inventory, the Minnesota Multiphasic Personality Inventory, the Darly and McNamara Personality Scale, the Rorschach, and detailed clinical studies. Beasley's conclusion:

> The inconclusive and somewhat contradictory evidence on the relationship of total adjustment to achievement may be due to the problems inherent in assessing personality functioning, the types of instruments and inventories available as well as the varying definitions of underachievement. Or it may be a spurious notion, indeed, that adequate school performance necessarily correlates with the commonly accepted standards of good adjustment. . . . Stanger suggests in view of the lack of linear relationship between objective measures of personality and either academic aptitude or academic achievement that personality influences achievement in an *indirect way* by affecting the degree to which use is made of the individual's potentialities. (*Ibid.*, p. 7)

Numerous efforts have been made to describe characteristic personality traits of underachievers. Beasley, following these in detail, reports considerable disagreement, contradiction, or failure to find significant differences between high and low achievers. The careful study by the Quincy Youth Development Project, coming since the publication of

---

* From "Underachievement: Review of Literature," by J. Beasley. Horace Mann-Lincoln Institute of School Experimentation, Teachers College, Columbia University, 1957. Reprinted with permission of J. Beasley.

Beasley's review, may have some promise however. Pierce and Bowman (1960) report the effort to assess motivation of high school students in the tenth and twelfth grades by using the following instruments:

(1) Unconscious need for achievement (McClelland's n-Achievement test)

(2) Conscious value placed on success (Strodtbeck's V-scale)

(3) Overt emphasis placed on achievement behavior (deCharms' V-scale)

(4) Strength of educational motivation (interview with student).

Personal and social adjustment were measured through the California Psychological Inventory, a sociometric test, and a behavior rating by teachers. Other comparisons included measures of value orientation, socio-economic status, religious activity, family background, parental value orientation, and attitudes toward children and the teacher's value orientation. High-achieving boys and girls at the two grade levels were compared with low-achieving students of the same sex at each level.

The following distinctions were found to characterize the high as compared with the low achievers:

Parents were better educated.

Parents of boys placed early emphasis on responsibility and independence training.

Both boys and girls showed more responsibility and independence.

Parents placed value on the child and his intellectual achievement; parents held higher educational and occupational aspirations for their child.

Children came from smaller families; were more often first-born children.

Children identified more with parents, had similar values.

High achievers were more involved in more activities in and outside of school, had somewhat more friends and more leadership positions.

Achievers were more strongly motivated toward education; more of them went to college.

Boys had stronger unconscious needs for achievement.

Both boys and girls were better adjusted socially.

Achievers valued school-related concepts more highly.

Girls in particular placed high value on achievement.

Some important sex differences were noted:

High-achieving boys had mothers who held democratic attitudes; mothers of low-achieving boys showed attitudes of interfering, controlling or fostering dependency. On the other hand, high-achieving girls had mothers who were authoritarian, controlling and strict, but who believed in equalitarianism. Low-achieving boys were aggressively more maladjusted than low-achieving girls. Their sex role adjustment was also poorer. (Pierce and Bowman, 1960)

In the development of a school program, the time when underachievement begins to manifest itself would seem of prime importance. Shaw and McCuen (1960a), studying "The Onset of Academic Underachievement in Bright Children," in two large city high schools, compared male and female achievers and underachievers. They discovered significant differences in achievement for boys starting in the third grade. For girls, differences did not become significant until the ninth grade. Shaw and others (1960b) also reported that achieving boys see themselves as stable, realistic, and intelligent, while underachieving boys are more negative in their self-concept. Achieving girls were more ambitious and responsible; underachieving girls showed ambivalence in feelings toward themselves.

STRENGTHS OF HIGH ACHIEVERS

As already indicated in studies reported above, one method of investigating the characteristics of underachievers is to note the countervailing strengths of their achieving classmates. Nason, in a study of 237 superior high school students in Long Beach, California, pointed to a pattern of circumstances accompanying high performance. These included:

1. Satisfactory social and personal adjustment
2. A plan for college in the future
3. A fairly specific vocational goal
4. Expectation by their parents that the students would go to college
5. A sense of inspiration, a source of inspiration, or encouragement to succeed. (Cited in Pierce and Bowman, 1960, p. 31)

Gowan (1957) also uses a contrast between high and low achievers to describe the student who does not seem to be performing up to his potential. He notes "the underachiever lacks all of the personality traits essential to succeed":

1. Clearness and definiteness of academic and occupational choices
2. Strong ego controls
3. Social interaction (as compared with withdrawal)
4. Good use of time and money
5. Reading and arithmetic ability

6. Positive character integration as compared with psychotic and neurotic tendencies
7. Permissiveness, intraception and creativity as compared with authoritarianism in the parental home environment or in the student himself
8. Parents who provide motivation as compared with autocratic or laissez-faire parents
9. Goals which are clear and possible to attain
10. Maturity, responsibility and seriousness of interests
11. Awareness and concern for others
12. Dominance, persuasiveness and self-confidence
13. Enthusiastic socialized activity; an oriented view of life as compared with apathetic withdrawal (Gowan, 1957, p. 100) *

Bowman (ASCD, 1960, pp. 45-52) posits five elements as factors in motivation. First is Murray's concept of an unconscious need for achievement which apparently varies greatly from individual to individual. It is the need which McClelland and his associates have attempted to measure through projective use of pictures in their *n Ach* test. A second factor is the "need to know," a value set on learning for its own sake. This value was one of the common characteristics noted by Anne Roe in her study of fifty-nine outstanding scientists. Third are the social values of the family and neighborhood. Strodtbeck's studies already discussed shed light upon the importance of this factor. The fourth factor is "the way we perceive other people." Bowman cites studies including his own research in Quincy which show that students who achieve well are those who feel the approval of their parents and teachers. Also, the teachers selected as most inspiring by pupils perceived themselves and their students very much more favorably than did other teachers. Finally, self-perception plays apparently a highly significant role. High achievers have a much more positive view of self than do underachievers.

Bowman summarizes:

> There are surprisingly few contradictions in the picture of the underachiever as painted by the various studies. The characteristics that distinguish the underachiever are not superficial ones; they involve the deepest roots of personality. One could generalize that most of the characteristics of the underachiever can be accounted for by either an intellectually sterile background in the home and early grades or an emotionally frustrating background arising from interpersonal tensions at home and at school. (ASCD, 1960, p. 52)

---

* From "Dynamics of the Underachievement of Gifted Students," by J. C. Gowan. Reprinted with permission from *Exceptional Children*, November, 1957, and J. C. Gowan.

Bennett (1961) suggests there are two types of variables—internal and external which may account for differences in motivation and achievement. Internal factors include "an intrinsic love for learning which cannot be precisely defined," and a personal need for achievement such as Murray has set forth. This need for achievement is believed to be related to the age of beginning training, to severity of training, to training in the home for independence, and to the home's cultural values.

External factors include family, society, peers, and adult models. The influence of family, society, and peer attitudes toward intellectual achievement have already been discussed. A number of studies agree on the absence of adequate father relationships for many underachievers. Gowan indicates little identification with adult models in general. Gough and Gowan, in studies of underachievers, are investigating the assumption that underachievement may be interpreted as failure of the child to adjust to prevailing cultural demands. The achiever, on the other hand, has learned what is expected of him and adapts readily to producing what is required.

Davidson, Greenberg, and Gerver (1962), studying achievers from a severely deprived environment, support Gough and Gowan's thesis. They found the school achievers to be "relatively controlled, cautious, but with a degree of originality and creativity." They generally conformed to adult demands and had a positive view of authority and self-confidence. They showed superiority in analytic and organizing abilities and processes requiring convergent thinking. Poor achievers showed opposite performance and contrasting attitudes toward authority, adult demands, and self-confidence.

RESEARCH ON MOTIVATION

Influence of Teachers and Peers. A considerable body of research is growing on factors influencing educational motivation. Zander, Curtis and Rosenfeld (1961) have reported a study on the influence of teachers and peers on the aspirations of youth. They discovered that teachers had greater impact on aspirations of their students when students identified with them (when students wanted to be like them) than when they tried to coerce students with threats of punishment. Students were more susceptible to the teacher's efforts to raise their aspirations when they felt that the teacher was fair in his treatment of them. They also responded to perceived expertness on the part of the teacher. Students were more willing to work hard if they regarded the goal as within their reach, i.e., if their level of aspiration was within hailing distance of their percept of their own ability. Indiscriminate rewards and punishment correlated negatively with aspiration (Zander, 1961, pp. 7-26). This research supports long-held beliefs that the most effective teachers impress their students as being expert and equitable in their treatment of students. The importance of the teacher as a model is also underlined.

A second part of this research inquired into the effect of peer influences. By and large, peer relationships reflect the same principles as teacher influences. When students identified with their peers, they were more highly motivated than when they were coerced by their peers. Also, they found peers in the friendly situation more attractive than peers who might hold coercive power over them (*Ibid.*, pp. 27-51).

Standards. Third, the researchers inquired into the results of reported failure on a test and the influence of standards in evaluating one's own behavior. Students who were given a set of standards evaluated their performance more rigorously and were motivated to greater effort than did students who had no standards to apply. A control group who were given high scores on the test were more favorable to all aspects of the situation and to themselves than were low scorers. This research corroborates other studies on the effects of success on aspiration. It also supports the establishment of standards to assist students in self-evaluation (*Ibid.*, pp. 52-79).

Barwick and Arbuckle (1962) throw further light on the relationship between parental acceptance and academic achievement in a study of eighth grade adolescents in a suburban junior high in Massachusetts. High-achieving boys perceived their fathers as more accepting than did their low-achieving peers. The former believed their fathers and mothers to be equally accepting. Average- and low-achieving boys regarded their mothers as more accepting than their fathers. Among girls there was a correlation between perception of acceptance and achievement.

Non-intellective Factors in Motivation. Since the achievement of all students scoring high on intelligence measures is not consistent with their apparent potential, two explanations are possible: that the intelligence measures are inaccurate or that non-intellective factors play a major part in achievement. Efforts to improve identification instruments have been discussed in Chapter 4. A considerable amount of research activity currently centers around efforts to discover non-intellective factors and to determine their effect. McClelland (1958) and a research group at Yale University have been proceeding in this direction for some years. Their volume, *Talent and Society*, reports several studies they have undertaken.

McClelland starts with H. A. Murray's assumption of the existence of an unconscious need for achievement (*n-Ach*), and he has developed projective tests to measure this need. In an earlier volume, *The Achievement Motive*, McClelland (1953) reported on his research with his new instrument. He provides the following definition in relation to the response of subjects confronting stimulus pictures in a projective test:

> By achievement goal is meant success in competition with some standard of excellence. That is, the goal of some individual in the story is to be successful in terms of competition with some standard of excellence. The individual may fail to achieve this goal, but the concern over competition with a standard of excellence still enables one to identify the goal sought as an achievement goal. This, then, is our generic definition of n-Achievement. (McClelland, 1953, pp. 110-11)°

In general, McClelland found a significant relationship between projective technique protocols and various indexes of achievement and vocational interest. The researchers then looked to the home background of persons with high and low *n-Ach* scores. Achievement motivation apparently developed most strongly where there was "emphasis on the independent development of the individual. In contrast, low achievement is associated with families in which the child is more dependent on his parents and subordinate in importance to them" (*Ibid.*, p. 328). The parents whose children develop strong achievement motives may be either autocratic or democratic, but in either case "they still act as if the child exists as an individual worth developing in his own right" (p. 329). The low scorers are more likely to come from homes where they must subordinate their interests for the sake of the family.

Sex differences in motivation scores are apparently closely related to social expectations. "Women have achievement drives which are tied up with getting along successfully with other people, whereas men have achievement drives associated with 'getting ahead' (i.e., getting a good job, being cleverer than other men, leading others, and so on)" (p. 331). It is not suprising, then, that men's achievement motivation falls off with age. More of them have "arrived," and now they temper further achievement more and more to reality.

Other writers also reflect the widespread belief that motivation is more a matter of personality than intellect. Marshall R. Jones (1962), summarizing a symposium on cognitive factors in motivation, concedes that "cognitive change has no corresponding effect on non-cognitive motivational components," but notes that "*some* non-cognitive components

---

° From: *The Achievement Motive*, by David C. McClelland, John W. Atkinson, Russell A. Clark, and Edgar L. Lowell. Copyright © 1953, Appleton-Century-Crofts, Inc. Reprinted by permission of Appleton-Century-Crofts.

will be affected" (p. 76). Since the primary mission of the school, as assigned by society, is cognitive, one may expect a certain inevitable amount of frustration as efforts are made with intellective tools to root out non-rational bases of underachievement.

THE LARGER CULTURE

Motivation is not solely an individual and family matter. Perhaps more pervasive is the culture's attitude toward achievement. Riesman's provocative speculations (1950) on the development of personality types as a function of the total social structure provide some clues. Nineteenth century America with its desperate needs to produce developed a type which Riesman calls "inner directed." It adopted standards, internalized them and clung fiercely, rigidly, perhaps neurotically, to them. Twentieth century America has by and large solved the bread-and-butter problems of production. Now we find ourselves with leisure on our hands to contemplate each other and to set consumption rather than production as the criterion of success. In this kind of culture we compulsively keep up with our neighbor's standard of consumption. We are "other directed." Stress is not on what we can make and what we can do, but on what we can use up and how we can manage with a minimum of effort. In place of these two types, Riesman idealizes a third, the "autonomous" personality which is driven neither by tyrannical inner standards nor dictatorship of the Joneses. Instead, he finds his *raison d'etre* in what Maslow calls "growth motivation." This is the "will to health," the drive to employ powers, and competences which clamor to be used —Veblen's "instinct of workmanship," Murray's "need for achievement."

As part of the larger culture, adolescent society is a powerful influence on the motivational drives of young people. The detailed study by Coleman (1961) and the values patterns reported by Tannenbaum (1962) are important sources of information, albeit discouraging in their general findings of low academic aspirations among adolescents. The reader is referred to discussion of these two studies in Chapter 1.

At this time there are signs that our culture may be awakening from the doldrums of the post-depression, post-war period. The strenuous struggle against "fear itself" in the 1930's was followed by the all-out mobilization of World War II. A longing for "normalcy" was to be expected, but Russia's gains in the fifties have apparently galvanized a new will to move onward, to broach "new frontiers" in the sixties. Apart from the stern and grim realities of the Cold War, the national mood may be one which is more conducive to achievement, especially by the gifted. "To strive, to seek, to find, and not to yield" may replace "playing it cool." The style of the Kennedy administration was expressed in an inaugural address which placed a premium on what America, as a people had to *give*, rather than on the blessings it had already received. The proposal of an idealistic youth Peace Corps found ready acceptance throughout the country and a multitude of responses from young people.

PRODUCTIVITY, COMMITMENT, AND INDEPENDENCE

This shift of emphasis may signify the passing of the baton from the "cool" to a productive type described by Hobbs. Hobbs (1959) cites two intriguing differences between young persons he regards as productive and those he describes as non-productive. First is the intensity of commitment. Not the sheer number of activities, but the "concentration of effort and intensity of purpose," distinguishes the two groups. Second is the extent to which the productive group "regard themselves as relatively autonomous, goal directed people." The nonproductive subjects tended to depend on others, mostly parents and teachers for rewards, admonitions and guidance. "By adolescence, the high productive youngsters have their own built in system of reinforcement" (p. 18). New national goals, new values appear to make this productive type the model for emulation. If so, the gifted are likely to find sources of stimulation in the whole national mood.

By teachers and parents two cues may be found in this concern with the gifted. One is the need to develop challenging goals and a sense of deep commitment to these goals for their own sake. Another is the admonition to wean the young from their parents and teachers—and, in return, the adult preceptors from their students and children! Tasks requiring independent action, and goals set by the student himself leading to self-imposed tasks—these would seem to have more meaning than additional scholastic burdens imposed by the teacher.

COMPETITION AND MOTIVATION

One of the frequent attacks laymen make upon schools to explain underachievement centers about the alleged failure of current programs to stimulate competition. Vaughan and Diserens (1938), in a summary of the literature on competition, find little support for a doctrine of competitive activity to enhance education of the gifted. Most studies of competition have involved very simple learning tasks. The simpler the task, the greater the effect of competition. The less the threat of failure, the greater the impact of competition. And most important, the less gifted the learner, the more effective are competitive activities. Precisely for the group in question, the gifted, is competition less promising, and precisely with the kind of learning that is most important—judgment, reasoning, interpretation.

Freehill states effectively the case against undue reliance on competitiveness:

> . . . some children have little need to compete, others are fearful to compete, and not all who compete truly make progress. Students may neglect appropriate subjects or participate in less useful activities in order to secure prizes . . . . They may concentrate on trivial but popular aspects of a particular course. The student involved in a science competition may bend all his efforts toward making an attractive display and pay little attention to genuine scientific thought or ingenuity. Such pupils become competitors intent on prize-getting and are devoid of social responsibility or self-criticism.
>
> The intentional use of vigorous competition is most frequently rejected because there are negative by-products. Losers withdraw from the very activity which competition is supposed to promote. Planned competition may also interfere with the development of social morality. (Freehill, 1961, p. 169) *

Of vital concern, too, is the effect of competition on creative endeavor. Creative activity depends upon absorption in a problem because of its intrinsic interest. It demands total commitment. It involves a willingness to experiment, an openness to experience. To these qualities the prospect of failure must make no difference. Competition normally is viewed in relation to others. The seeker of the prize cannot afford to experiment with the unknown. He is constrained to stick with the tried and the true.

Our culture places high value on competition in certain situations. Certainly gifted students should be prepared to cope with this emphasis. They can apparently complete some simple learnings more effectively when competition is part of the picture, but different persons respond differently to competition as a stimulus. Where complex learning and creative work are sought, the weight of evidence is against competition.

PRESSURE FROM ADULTS

The studies by the McClelland (1953) group at Yale support other research on the positive influence of families which set firm standards for their children. Inquiring further into the effects of parental pressure on children at the University of Chicago Laboratory School, Haggard discovered that "one can have too much of a good thing." Haggard (1957)

---

investigated the relationships among socialization, personality and academic achievement in a longitudinal study of forty-five children from grades 3 to 9. Included in his definition of "socialization" was parental pressure upon children to achieve academically.

Haggard found striking differences among the high general achievers as they matured. In grade 3 they were "sensitive and responsive to socialization pressures." They accepted adult values, got along better with teachers and parents than with peers. They were "more tense, competitive, aggressive." By grade 7 the high general achievers were "still responding to the socialization pressures of adults, but had developed strong antagonistic attitudes toward adults, a marked increase in anxiety and a corresponding decrease in intellectual originality and creativity." They were also "more aggressive, persistent, hard driving, competitive, willing to be aggressive and destructive to defeat and win over other persons" than were the lower-achieving peers. Haggard notes that the values of parents act as strong pressure even without any overt activity on their part (Haggard, 1957, p. 396). He concludes, "One can have too much of a good thing and, if carried to excess, socialization pressures may serve to cripple the child, both emotionally and intellectually. . . . Our findings indicate that the best way to produce 'clear thinkers' is to help children develop into anxiety-free, emotionally healthy individuals who are also trained to master a variety of intellectual tasks" (*Ibid.*, p. 409).

Bronfenbrenner (1961) arrives at parallel conclusions in a discussion of "the changing American parent," and his new techniques in disciplining his child. The basic tactic in the contemporary middle class home appears to be withdrawal of love—a technique which seems to be more lenient but is actually more compelling. Children from these homes tend to excel lower class children in self-control, achievement, responsibility, leadership, and adjustment in general. However, Bronfenbrenner warns that achievement is not all, that the prospect of a society organized to maximize achievement drive "is not altogether a pleasant one. . . . True, children from achievement-oriented homes excel in planfulness and performance, but they are also more aggressive, tense, domineering and cruel. . . . It would appear that education for excellence if pursued single-mindedly may entail some sobering social cost" (Bronfenbrenner, 1961, pp. 16-17).

RESEARCH ON CORRECTING UNDERACHIEVEMENT

Recognition of prevailing patterns of underachievement has led to considerable research on solutions to the problem through guidance, grouping, and curriculum adjustment. No definitive findings can be enunciated but some clues may be found in recent reports.

A research team from the University of Illinois worked with Evanston Township High School in the late 1950's to determine the effect of group counseling on academic and personal adjustment of underachievers. An eight-week period of group sessions was undertaken. Within the treatment period no startling improvement could be identified. Nor at the time of an eighteen-month follow-up did the subjects improve their grades significantly. However, the research group reported:

> With varying degrees of depth each client discovered: (1) that expressing his own real feelings about people, things, and ideas helped him to understand himself and the forces that disturbed him; (2) that at least one adult could accept him and that this adult, the counselor, wanted to understand him; (3) that his peers had problems too; (4) that, in spite of his faults, which his peers wanted to help him correct, his peers could accept him; (5) that he was capable of understanding, accepting, and helping others; and (6) that he could learn to trust others. When a client discovered that others accepted him, he found that he could better accept others, and eventually, that he could better accept himself. After he began to accept himself, then, and only then, could he accept the fact that he was gifted, and make plans which required him to use his great potentialities. All of this takes time (and more than eight weeks). (Ohlsen and Proff, 1960, p. 18) *

The investigators at Evanston saw the underachiever as one who "tends to feel rejected by the important others in his life." He does things which deserve rebuke since this is the only way he knows how to get attention. Rebuke lowers the self-concept and, in a cycle, causes more negative behavior. The remedy, we are told, lies in a cooperative effort of counselor and teachers to understand the gifted underachiever and help him build a more realistic, more positive self concept. Three of the four groups "made significant growth," but the team agreed with other investigators "that underachievement is not a surface phenomenon which can be easily changed" (*Ibid.*, pp. 19, 13).

Another investigation of group counseling for remediation of underachievement was conducted by Sister Mary Viterbo McCarthy (1957) in the greater Boston area in 1956 and 1957. Twenty-four boys were selected from seventeen high schools on the basis of high IQ (125 and

---

* From *The Extent to Which Group Counseling Improves the Academic and Personal Adjustment of Underachieving Gifted Adolescents,* by Merle M. Ohlsen and Fred C. Proff. Urbana, University of Illinois, 1960. Reprinted with permission of Merle M. Ohlsen and Fred C. Proff.

over) and low achievement (school average under 75 per cent). An experimental group was exposed to six one-hour counseling sessions revolving about discussion of twelve case studies highlighting problems of underachievement and the outstanding traits of the group members. The counselor maintained as non-directive a role as possible in the group situation "affording the experimental members maximum opportunity to ferret out the problems in each disguised case, to diagnose the failures, and to plan remedial measures."

Members of the experimental group were compared with members of a control group through pre- and post-counseling test results. Unfortunately, significantly greater changes did not occur in the experimental group. Sister Mary Viterbo suggests two hypotheses to explain the failure to make significant growth. One is the short time available to produce a change in a relatively deep-seated condition. The other hinges on the non-directive nature of the counseling. The students revealed in the group sessions a need for information about the self. Had the counselor been permitted to provide desired information concerning ability, aptitudes, interests, and goals, Sister Mary Viterbo hypothesizes better results.

From Sister Mary Viterbo's study two points stand out. One is the old refrain of "too little and too late." Underachievement has to be caught early. Whenever caught, it is likely to respond only to a sustained program of some length and depth. A second provocative suggestion is the need for more directive counseling where underachievement is involved. In this counseling, information about the self may be a primary need.

GUIDANCE PLUS TEACHING METHOD

The Talented Youth Project of Teachers College (Columbia University), working cooperatively with De Witt Clinton High School, an all-boys high school in New York City, undertook a study with two objectives: (1) to determine social and personal factors related to underachievement, and (2) to experiment with school procedures which might improve the performance record of gifted underachievers (Goldberg, 1959). Underachievers were divided into experimental and control groups of thirty-five each and they in turn were compared with a group of high-achieving boys. The experimental group were placed with a home room teacher who was warm and outgoing, interested in the problem and able to combine flexibility with the maintenance of high standards. The study aimed to discover whether substantial improvements in school attitude and performance would result if these students were grouped together, if they shared each other's problems, and if they identified with and received support from this teacher.

Pre-tests of the high and low achievers yielded highly comparable IQ, reading, and arithmetic scores. The major academic difference lay in the wide difference in ninth year grades. There were also large differences in sociometric ratings in favor of the high achievers. Of the low group one-third had been enrolled in special progress classes in junior high school, of the high group about 45 per cent.* Goldberg (*op. cit.*, pp. 10-11) remarks in her report, "These findings (supported by similar findings from the junior high school records of subsequent groups) suggest that during the elementary and junior high school years most bright youngsters, regardless of classroom performance as reflected by school grades, acquire considerable mastery of basic skills and knowledge."

The study of personal characteristics indicated closely similar patterns for high and low achievers—with respect to appraisal of their own abilities and characteristics, their occupational aspirations and their family background. However, one noticeable exception supports findings from other studies. Broken homes were far more frequent among the underachievers. As a result, Goldberg expresses the theory that underachievement among boys, twice as great as among girls, "may be related to inadequate identification with a father figure" (*Ibid.*, p. 12). High achievers were more satisfied with their school performance and stated higher expectations than did the lows.

In the first year of the study the homeroom teacher worked with the experimental group in the twenty-minute homeroom period and for a full class period as their social studies teacher. No gain was shown over the control group in the first semester, but by the end of the year, the experimental group outdistanced the control group in most respects. Goldberg credits no single incident such as praise or complimentary remarks to a parent. "It was rather the entire range of experiences, interactions and every-day relationships which the teacher saw as responsible for bringing about improvement in many of the boys. A carefully planned social studies program, an expression of interest and concern with problems of both a personal and academic nature, a friendly, and in general, more supportive and flexible teacher role combined with the support that students in the special group seemed to give to one another, all contributed to help many of the students gain the maturity and confidence necessary for successful school work" (p. 21).

In the following year (eleventh grade), the experimental group remained with their homeroom teacher but were assigned for the first semester to an honors course in social studies with a woman teacher who

---

* Classes specially selected for completion of three year program in two years. See chapter on secondary school programs.

was accustomed to demanding high standards of her honor students. The loss of a male figure with which to identify combined with rigid application of standards resulted in poorer academic performance and misbehavior in class. The initial improvement was thus not sustained when the group was returned to a more conventional situation and held to "uniformly high standards, both of conduct and achievement." Being grouped together was not enough. "The important element is, apparently, the performance of the teacher in utilizing the group spirit constructively" (p. 25). In the second half of the year, the group was placed with another man teacher who utilized the experience of the two previous teachers and did not maintain his usual honors class standards. He attempted to create a warm and accepting climate, allowed leeway in performance standards, and showed interest in students' individual problems. He also concentrated on teaching much needed study skills. Once again the average performance of the experimental group improved.

In both the experimental and control groups "improvers" and "nonimprovers" were identified. Those who were able to make strides during the two years when compared with the others showed higher scores on the Iowa Composite and Correctness of Writing tests. Other differences did not reach the level of statistical significance. These included for nonimprovers a greater gap between perceived and wished-for abilities, more divorces in the family, fewer decisions reached as to vocational goals, and fewer siblings in college who might act as models (*Ibid.*, p. 27).

Goldberg concludes with the conviction "that academic underachievement is a symptom of a wide variety of more basic personal and social problems." By the time they have entered high school some students have passed the point where any help can be given profitably by the school. Unfortunately, criteria for earlier prognosis are not available. For students who can profit, Goldberg points to two crucial factors:

(1) Identification with a teacher who is constantly interested and supportive
(2) Assistance in mastering skills of learning which may not have been developed at the usual time (*Ibid.*, p. 33)

Havighurst ties together guidance and curriculum revision in underachievement. He bases his approach on the assumption of four factors in motivation:

(1) Need for achievement
(2) Identification with persons who have gone to college
(3) Social pressure coming from parents, teacher and friends
(4) Intrinsic pleasure in learning.

Having posited these factors, Havighurst suggests the following procedures to increase motivation:

For boys:
Counseling to identify able boys not well motivated for college
Giving awards, extra-curricular and community recognition; build-
   ing social prestige of scholastic attainment
Making school work more interesting

For girls:
Parent-counselor conferences to encourage academic aspirations of
   girls
Contacts with professional women as intellectual models
Assistance by counselors to girls in understanding how a career and
   homemaking role may both be pursued. (*In* Shertzer, 1960, pp.
   230-37) *

BASIC SKILLS AND UNDERACHIEVEMENT

While underachievement is often rooted in broad family, community,
and national values, the school cannot evade responsibility for functions
within its realm. The NEA invitational conference on identification of
the gifted (Conant, 1958) underlined a number of school-connected factors in poor academic attainment. Some of the more important problem
areas follow:

In some cases the desire to think and to know is not fully stimulated.
Often the pupil sees no meaning or purpose in subjects he is required to study.
Sometimes the student is keenly interested in one field to the exclusion of others. Below the graduate university level, schools are
   not prepared to permit such specialization of interest and generalization of ignorance.
At times the student overestimates his own knowledge and is not
   helped by the school to look beyond his limitations.
Inefficient reading and study methods are a frequent handicap.
The influence of the peer group may be antagonistic to school
   achievement.
Poor relationships with teachers may discourage interest (Conant,
   1958)

To these, Edwards (1961) adds his observation that low expectations on
the part of faculty coincide with low aspiration levels on the part of stu-

---

* Bruce Shertzer, editor. *Working with Superior Students.* (Chicago: Science
Research Associates, Inc., 1960). Reprinted by permission of Science Research
Associates, Inc.

dents. Schools can make positive efforts to correct such conditions. Where causes are more deep-seated, these efforts will not always succeed. It is the school's responsibility, however, to make sure that school-related causes of low motivation are kept to a minimum.

A common characteristic of underachievers is inadequate performance in the basic study skills—reading, writing, listening, arithmetical computation, problem solving, and independent study. Most frequently these failures are symptoms of low motivation, emotional problems, or deprivation of some kind. In addition, they almost always induce failure to make progress at higher school levels. School personnel recognize that these failings are often symptoms, not causes. They justifiably do what they can to help identify the causes. However, the expected role of the teacher is to work in these basic areas, not on the causes underlying failure in them. The teacher may therefore *refer* the underachiever for assistance at a psychologically deeper level, but he must *work* with the student at the academic level. Of course, he must avoid aggravating emotional problems and reinforcing psychological blocks. However, he may be able to reduce underachievement if he can alleviate to some extent even the symptom.

Because the school's expected role is in the academic realm, schools give major attention in approaching problems of underachievement to remedial work in the foundation areas. The Demonstration Guidance Project in New York City, for example, put its major in-school emphasis on small remedial classes in language arts and mathematics. To this were added the counseling services of psychologists and social workers and the stimulation of attendance at cultural activities in the community. While one may protest the weight of attention given to a symptom rather than a cause, no amount of psychological and social service workup can substitute for remedial learning that is generally necessary. The teacher who works alone without such services, however, should have no illusions about the difficulty and probable futility of his efforts.

NCA PROJECT ON GUIDANCE AND MOTIVATION

In 1958 the North Central Association of Colleges and Secondary Schools established its Project on Guidance and Motivation of Superior and Talented Students primarily to investigate causes of, and to correct, the situation in those schools where fewer than half of the high school graduates were entering college. One hundred such high schools were identified and participated in the program, studying their students and inaugurating practices that might, hopefully, result in increased academic motivation. In a bulletin to participating schools, the Project defined three problem areas:

Problems dealing with goals, aspirations and self-concepts
Problems dealing with peer group, family and community attitudes
Problems dealing with studying, reading, listening, and self-appraisal skills

In the first area, the following problems were identified:

Influence of immediate, rather than long-range goals
Helping students realize they have special abilities
Preparing students for realistic thinking about educational goals and plans
Assisting students to plan for an appropriate occupational choice
Lack of interest or desire to achieve; lack of understanding of the personality qualities that are "musts" in maximum development of talent

Peer group, family and community attitudes included these problems:

Competing for grades rather than developing an interest in the material for its own sake
Reluctance of students to enter a new program or special classes
Evaluating work of students in special classes
Parents who do not wish children to attend college
Increasing the school's power to hold capable students who are potential drop-outs
Financial need preventing college attendance
Negative attitude of students toward high achievement or scholarship

Study, reading, listening and self-appraisal problems include improvement of these four skills. In addition, the lack of supplementary materials in the school and a dislike for writing represent academic obstacles (North Central Association, 1959, pp. 1-4).*

To attack these problems the Project makes a series of recommendations in a booklet, *Guiding Superior and Talented High School Students.* A number of suggestions are made for these purposes:

Promoting community understanding
Early identification of superior students
Special provision for counseling

---

* From *Problems in Motivation*, 1959. Reprinted with permission of Superior and Talented Students Project, North Central Association of Colleges and Secondary Schools, Chicago, Illinois.

Special provision for challenging and stimulating activities through
the curriculum
Recognizing and honoring academic achievement
Special cooperation by business and professional leaders
Special cooperation by colleges and college students
Securing understanding and cooperation by parents (Endicott,
1961, pp. 40-45)

SUMMARY

The burst of research activity in the late 1950's on motivation and
underachievement has a dual significance: (1) It developed an awareness of the magnitude and importance of the problem. (2) It disclosed
a recognition that we do not yet know why individuals react differently
to environmental stimuli, personal handicaps and native ability. Financial limitations, low socio-economic status, minority group membership,
being born female—all of these interfere seriously with college entrance,
but more powerful than all of these is motivation to succeed. Lack of
such motivation outweighs favorable circumstances of birth, economics,
or neighborhood.

Investigators continue to work assiduously on factors in motivation
since the will to achieve appears to overshadow all external conditions.
Unfortunately, research has thus far yielded contradictory findings with
respect to the personality of underachievers and their emotional and
social adjustment. Certain conditions may characterize underachievers
taken as a group, but they may also describe a significant proportion of
high achievers as well. Competition is not viewed as a great spur to
motivation, nor is strong pressure from parents. Instead, motivation is
seen as a normal facet of a healthy personality. A healthy self-concept is
viewed as leading to positive relations with others, openness to experience, and the development of a store of accurate perceptions. This perceptual field—information, understandings, concepts, generalizations—
serves the individual well in facing immediate problems. It also begets
further growth. The more one knows in a particular area the more one
wants to know, the more one needs to know. In this view, motivation is
not imposed from without; it is instead an expression of a healthy personality seeking wholesome experience with other people and with objects
in its environment.

There is some agreement that strongly motivated persons have an
unconscious need to achieve; that their families value training for independence; that they define their career objectives at an early age; that
they are encouraged by their parents in plans to go to college; that they

have an adult figure with whom they can identify; that they have mastered basic learning skills; that they take pleasure in learning for its own sake. They come infrequently from broken homes.

Many children who show signs of high ability do not have these favorable factors in their background. Some become "underachievers." Even their "ability" or "aptitude" scores begin to decline. The school has to do more than point regretfully at the circumstances surrounding failure. It has a responsibility to circumvent the obstacles that keep potential Miltons mute and inglorious. A few large-scale efforts have been made; more are in process. One approach is to assume the need for greater personal guidance. A number of projects have centered on increased personal, academic, and vocational counseling. A second approach is to adapt the curriculum. These efforts have included modernization of subject matter and utilizing practical applications of theoretical studies and intensive programs to bring the underachiever "up to grade level" in fundamental learning skills. Exposure of students from culturally impoverished environs to the many faces of metropolitan culture represents still another curricular approach. Some efforts have been made to combine guidance and curriculum emphases. Unfortunately, the phrase "no significant differences" pops up with disappointing frequency in these researches. The investigators in their conclusions underline the stubbornness of underachievement, its deep-seated and long-term character. The school is often working alone on a problem which is steeped in community and sub-culture influences.

Repeated investigations into the nature and etiology of underachievement put stress on the same theme: the complexity of the phenomenon and its resistance to remedial efforts. Academic underachievement and low motivation for scholastic performance seem to be closely related. Efforts to raise the student's academic aspirations may, hopefully, produce higher achievement. The following means find support in raising motivation levels:

1. How the student sees himself is of primary importance. The school can help able students build positive self-concepts. The student who shows academic promise should be helped to see himself as a collegian. Negative criticism should be avoided; instead, parents and teachers should help the young person build a feeling of personal worth.

2. Community, neighborhood, and peer-group attitudes toward intellectual performance have a powerful influence on motivation and school achievement. The school must know what these attitudes are, help develop these in desirable directions, and assist the student to identify with constructively directed groups. School authorities, other youth agencies, the local press, service clubs in the community and local businessmen

should be invited to examine their programs for signs of attitudes that encourage, overlook, or actually discourage intellectual distinction.

3. General policies of the school affect motivation. Are students given opportunity for independent academic work? Do they develop a sense of commitment, a feeling of excitement, in their school work? Are sufficiently high standards maintained? Are competition and pressure from adults serving as stimulants or depressants? Current tendencies to look to the past for educational solutions deny the importance of independence and commitment in learning.

4. High achievers generally have clearer vocational goals than low achievers. The school should examine its curriculum and guidance to determine whether individual students are securing early and realistic help in planning for careers.

5. The underachiever is obviously not adapting to the standard program. Curriculum adaptation is apparently needed. The school program must present a challenge. It must be flexible enough to avoid penalties for students with blind spots in particular areas. It should be adaptable to the non-conformist, providing opportunity for free effort, for undirected, and creative work. Free use of laboratories, workshops, studios, and practice rooms is called for. Contests, games, papers, plays, teams, and clubs represent devices that are helpful in stimulating interest. The curriculum has to be geared for gifted students who do not fit the "able and amibitious" standard.

6. The most effective and direct efforts that the school can make lie in its traditional realm. No bright student should remain handicapped by early failure to learn fundamental tools. Small classes and personal attention appear necessary for effective remedial teaching in reading, mathematics, speech and social studies skills.

7. Curriculum and cocurriculum should aim at widening the students' cultural perspective. Frequently, the unmotivated student is also culturally underprivileged. Attendance at concerts, plays, museums, libraries, and college functions often helps the student begin to see himself in a new light.

8. Guidance services are potentially a strong arm in redirecting the underachiever. Individual and group efforts should be directed at helping the student assess his potential and then to exercise it. Personal, educational and vocational guidance are all needed. Counseling parents with respect to their children's abilities and needs seems especially necessary for the underachiever.

9. While no environment guarantees high achievement or consigns the student irrevocably to low achievement, greater problems will be found in certain economic sectors, ethnic groups, social classes, and

geographic areas than others. The school should be close enough to its own community to recognize such factors which predispose to success or failure. As unobtrusively as possible, it should make particular efforts to prevent underachievement among children in disadvantaged groups.

10. The feminine gender presents a special problem. The average superiority of girls in the lower grades gradually declines, and fewer girls of high ability go on to college. Far fewer go on to graduate work. Girls of superior ability should find help in recognizing the possibility of combining a professional career with a feminine role in life.

11. Of considerable importance is the identification of the gifted child with adults who serve as appropriate models. Children often set their aspirations after beloved or admired members of their family. Teachers often cast a longer influence through example than instruction. The teacher's own professional activity, his interest in students, and the warmth of his personality combine to invite emulation by students. The school provides still another source of inspiration by introducing students to other adults with whom they may identify readily. Similarity with the student's background, relative youthfulness, reputation, or a particular career choice are factors in such identification.

12. Underachievers apparently perform more successfully with teachers who are supportive than with teachers who are simply demanding of high achievement. The choice of teachers is especially important for the able student who is not fulfilling his potential.

13. While underachievement is not primarily economic in its source, financial assistance is necessary for some students. Knowledge by the family that such help is available may avoid early rejection on financial grounds of dreams of higher education for their children. Scholarships may include not only tuition costs but supplementary items while the student is still in tuition-free schools. These items include various instructional materials and cultural opportunities outside the school. Sometimes, the symbol of interest by others in the child is more important to the young person and his family than the financial aid itself.

14. No finding is more ubiquitous in research on underachievement than the need to start early. Underachievement, like envy, seems to feed on itself. A poor start snowballs into chronic failure, possibly because of immediate influence on the child's academic self-concept. For this reason early identification of giftedness and early discovery of failure to achieve as expected are essential. Concerted efforts to relieve underachievement have generally failed of their purpose when delayed of inception till the senior high school. A continuous program of guidance, diagnosis and identification needs its beginning apparently in the primary grades.

Chapter 17

Teachers for Gifted Children

> *A teacher affects eternity; he can never tell where his influence stops.*
>
> —Henry Adams

Of all the variables in the teaching-learning process, none is more significant for the pupil than the teacher. Researchers in education are frequently humbled by the fact that variation attributable to individual teachers often exceeds variation due to the experimental factor chosen for investigation. A case in point is the New York City study of grouping in elementary school where the individual teacher and his influence were considered to affect student growth far more than the pattern of grouping (Passow and Goldberg, 1961).

Whatever the significance of the teacher to students in general, the influence of the teacher of gifted students is magnified by several factors. The teacher's most obvious role is direct instruction, and in this role he may confidently expect to secure unusual results with unusually able pupils. The teacher is also a primary pole for students in an interactive process that is basic to learning. Again, superior intelligence will function best in interaction with a stimulating teacher. Third, the teacher is inevitably a model. Because of the potential of intellectually gifted students, the teacher's role as a professional and scholarly worker is most significant.

What does one seek, then, in the teacher of the unusually apt learner? Are there particular traits of personality especially desirable in such a teacher? Is special training necessary; if so, are definably different components of academic knowledge and professional skill needed? Should

412

such training be part of the total pattern of a teacher's preparation or should it be a specialty added onto the basic structure established for all teachers? What should school systems do to prepare teachers for special assignments with gifted students?

CURRENT PATTERNS OF PREPARATION

It is instructive as a point of departure to examine existing patterns in preparation and assignment of teachers for the gifted. Over a series of years Wilson (1953; 1955; 1957; NSSE, 1957, Chapter 15) surveyed programs of pre-service, graduate and in-service education for teachers of intellectually superior students. Since then more recent but limited surveys have been reported by French (1961), Hawes (1961) and James (1960), among others.

In general, undergraduate work in teacher education makes little specific provision for the prospective teacher of the gifted. Excellence in the liberal component and academic specialization of a college curriculum is crucial in the basic equipment of the teacher of the gifted. Built upon these is the program of professional development which normally places primary emphasis on general competence of the beginning teacher prior to specialization for teaching the gifted, the retarded, or other specific groups. Extremely few undergraduate courses in curriculum, methods, or materials for the gifted appear as part of the professional sequence in education. Units are studied in some colleges that relate to variability in learning capacity and ways of dealing with the extremes in the range of ability. A small handful of institutions provide observation or student teaching with academically talented children and youth.

On the graduate level, an increasing number of universities are offering at least one course in education of the gifted. Fewer than a dozen were offering more than one course as late as 1960. French (1961) reports the following composite of graduate courses in thirty institutions:

    I. Introduction
        A. Work with the gifted child (present emphases, issues, philosophy, history)
        B. Definition of gifted and talented youth
        C. Characteristics of the gifted child
    II. Identification of the gifted child
   III. Educational provisions for the gifted
        A. Aims and goals of democratic education
        B. Culture and community involved
        C. Survey of specialized programs

        D. Provisions for enriching the curriculum
        E. Acceleration
        F. Administrative aspects of curricular patterns
        G. Development of curricular materials
    IV. Adjustment of the gifted child
     V. Problems of the underachiever
    VI. Motivation of the gifted child
   VII. Teacher and the gifted child
  VIII. Parents and the gifted child
    IX. Community and the gifted child
     X. Research and evaluation

                         (French, 1961, pp. 69-72) °

With the relative scarcity of specialized work offered, only a small fraction of teachers in special classes report any particularized preparation to teach gifted classes. Hawes (1961) secured responses to a questionnaire from 173 communities, population 5,000-24,999, known to have special classes for the gifted. "Fewer than half" of the 219 teachers so employed had had either undergraduate or graduate courses devoted to education of the gifted. Only 8.1 per cent had supervisors employed full-time to service these courses. The same percentage (8.1) of school administrators thought that specific educational preparation was the most important single qualification for teachers of the gifted. Teaching experience (26.6 per cent) and personality (23.7 per cent) secured more support as the single criterion of most importance. However, Cole and Fliegler reported that in their sample 79 per cent of the teachers of gifted children regarded special preparation as essential (Fliegler and Bish, 1959).

To compensate for the dearth of college course work for teaching the gifted, some school systems offer workshops of limited duration, consultant assistance, in-service courses in cooperation with university graduate schools, conferences, curriculum development projects, visitation to other schools, and publications. Through a combination of pre-service, graduate, and in-service programs, a pattern for preparing teachers for the gifted has developed. Currently, however, these activities are so limited in number and extent that they should be regarded more as pilot programs than as a universally available pattern of preparation.

QUALIFICATIONS OF TEACHER OF THE GIFTED

Since the good teacher in general must be a paragon of pedagogic virtues, the teacher prescribed for the gifted by various authorities,

---

° From "The Preparation of Teachers of the Gifted," by Joseph L. French. Reprinted with permission from *Journal of Teacher Education,* March, 1961.

pupils, and parents, turns out to be a paragon of paragons. Relevant questions to be asked in describing a teacher for the gifted are these:

What qualities of a good teacher are especially needed in teaching the gifted?

Are any qualities needed for gifted classes that are not generally essential?

Can one distinguish between "the best teachers" and "the best teacher for the gifted?"

Does a teacher of the gifted have to be exceptionally able himself in the same dimensions as his pupils?

These questions will be considered after summarizing qualities frequently mentioned as characterizing the teacher for gifted students.

PERSONAL CHARACTERISTICS[*]

There is general consensus that the intellectually gifted child needs a teacher who is intellectually superior. "Intellectual stature," "intellectual acumen," "love of learning," "inquiring mind," "independence of thought," "a range of skills and accomplishments," and "versatility of interests" are terms used to identify cognitive qualities sought for the special teacher. This ability is to be reflected first in general cultural attainments—"a rich fund of information and cultural background," "well rounded to help students see the interrelationships of life," "a philosophy of life," "informed in areas other than his own specialty." Second, his intellectual excellence is notable in his field of specialization —"knowledge of his own and related fields," "special aptitudes and interests," "scholarship in academic areas."

Not only is the desired teacher intellectual; he is also creative. Expressions such as the following appear: "flexible and creative persons," "creativeness, originality, inventiveness," "productivity in a creative area," "creative thinking ability."

Good health, *mens sana in corpore sano*, is also prescribed, including physical superiority and athletic interests and activity.

The good teacher is not only intellectual, creative, and healthy. He exemplifies the best of human qualities—"modesty, kindliness and concern for others," "psychological maturity," "responsibility in emotional and social development," "respect for the importance of individual personality," "fairness, tolerance, good will, alertness, attractive personality"

---

[*] The following sections sample representative lists of qualifications for teachers of the gifted taken from the following sources: Abraham (1958), De Haan and Havighurst (1957), Educational Policies Commission (1950), Freehill (1961), French (1959), James (1960), NSSE (1957), Passow (1951), Torrance (1960b), Ward (1961) and Worcester (1956).

and, a substantial sense of values. He participates as a member of the community.

As a teacher, he shows special characteristics, too. He is supportive, being alert and sensitive to pupil needs. He is liked and respected by children. He is willing to take extra time to listen to children's ideas, go places with them, and do things in which they are interested. This interest in his students is also enlarged to a sense of social and professional responsibility. The desirable teacher is able to stimulate and inspire his students. He is not jealous of superior potential apparent in some of his students, and he is able to take occasional correction from students, just as he is able to accept criticism from adults and make necessary changes in his pattern of action. Similarly, he has a capacity for self-criticism. He knows how to let others assume responsibility, and he challenges students to enrich their learning on their own initiative. Children with strong ideas of their own and highly developed initiative do not trouble him. Most important, he has an urge to do something over and above what is normally expected of him as a teacher. He *wants* to teach gifted children.

The good teacher also puts to effective use what he has learned from psychology. He understands children and accepts them, and he has a special sympathy for children with exceptional ability. Learning theory is applied in differentiating activities for the intellectually able. The teacher knows how to develop a classroom atmosphere conducive to good mental health. He has a knowledge and understanding of social and emotional problems that may be created for the gifted due to their accelerated mental development. The teacher displays skill in human relationships and sensitivity to children's problems in dealing with each other. Identification of special ability is a meaningful concern to him, and he has some competence in discovering talents of various kinds.

The teacher of the gifted is also a master of educational methodology. Of superior professional competence, he takes pains to modify curriculum and activities so as to release the creative energy of gifted children. He provides a rich environment for independent efforts in such fields as science, art, and music. Opportunities are found for students to work in groups in order to learn group-working skills. The best pupils are stimulated and challenged; they know that they are expected to achieve at their top level of ability. Standards are kept appropriately flexible. The teacher knows how to use laboratory and workshop methods. He is able to teach a problem-solving approach to learning, to apply this to independent study and research, and to teach children to evaluate their own progress. He is able to develop a flexible, individualized, enriching curriculum suited to individual needs and avoiding identical, stereotyped demands. Emphasis is placed in his teaching on social responsibility, a desire to serve society, and recognizing the work of others. In short, he is resourceful in developing teaching techniques. Finally, he knows how to work well with parents and others who are vital parts of the child's learning environment.

Surveys have been taken in a number of cases to determine students' reactions to their teachers. Representative of these is N. Davis' list (1954) compiled from responses of gifted students who were graduates of the Cleveland Major Work Program:

Sense of humor
Encouragement of responsibility
Knowledge of subject
Firmness and fairness
Understanding of children
Enjoyment of teaching

While there is no unanimity, student responses cluster around the items in Davis' listing. Dressel and Grabow (1958) expand and reinforce Davis' items with the following criteria elicited from gifted students in Michigan high schools:

1) Arousal of students' curiosity
2) Insistence that work be redone until it is of high caliber
3) Insistence that students engage in activities requiring initiative and self-reliance.

Most of the items in the list of personal characteristics and list of teaching qualities might well be demanded for teachers of all children. One might argue strongly that some of these qualities are more essential for the average, slow, or handicapped child than for the gifted. It is difficult to maintain the viewpoint that the *best* teachers should all be assigned to the gifted, but it seems logical to ask that teachers who *work best* with the gifted be assigned to do so.

In an effort to determine which teachers are most successful with this special group, Brandwein studied the background and personal characteristics of teachers whose students had won awards in the Westinghouse Science Talent Search. Of the twenty-two whom Brandwein knew personally, he classified eight as inspiring master teachers, "ten as superior teachers, and four as average." He observed that teachers of the gifted exhibit some of the same characteristics as do the students themselves: high intelligence, persistence, and "questing"—a restless searching for better explanations than presently exist of the natural universe. These teachers were well trained in their subject matter and active in professional pursuits such as curriculum development projects and professional organizations. They demonstrated a liking for children, particularly adolescents. All of them were experiencing enough satisfaction with teaching to indicate their intention to continue in the profession. They presented a father or mother image to their students, appearing to be people who were sympathetic to their problems and meriting their trust. In addition, however, these teachers held firm and high standards of achievement (Brandwein, 1955, pp. 63-70).

From the distinctive characteristics of intellectually gifted children, a number of qualities seem to be more needed for teachers of such children than for others. Respect for intellectual ability is essential in working with young gifted children. With adolescents, unusual intellectual acumen itself is essential. Second, scholarly attainment must have grown out of the teacher's superior ability. Not only must the teacher of the gifted be able to keep up with his students; he must also serve as a model of academic achievement. This should be notable both in general cultural background and in specialized study in a field or discipline. The teacher should be doing some creative work, preferably in his own field. He must be mature and secure psychologically so that students of high potential are a source of gratification rather than a threat. He must be "free" psychologically so that he can accept originality on the part of students and challenges to his own academic authority.

The teacher of the gifted must also be a master of the art of teaching. He must promote opportunities for students to assume responsibility and initiative in their own learning. The teacher must be able to relate to students both as a model of scholarly performance and as a supportive figure in Brandwein's sense of a father-mother image. He must be committed to a philosophy of individual differences in his appraisal of the teaching task. He must recognize the uniqueness of individuals and be able to adapt his teaching program to provide adequate challenge and assistance to each learner. Part of this recognition is a firm understanding of the nature of giftedness, the potentials residing therein, and the problems that individuals in our culture face because of intellectual uniqueness. The gifted child's pedagogue must be a master of teaching techniques, drawing upon old and new methods to secure maximum results for each child's hours in school. Fundamentally, he must like working with gifted children, rejoicing in their accomplishments, recognizing them as children with both usual and unusual emotional needs, and refusing to exploit their exceptionality.

A teacher who meets these requirements may not be the best teacher in the school system. He will probably not be the best teacher for slow, average, or handicapped students. What is needed is not the best teacher but the teacher who is best for working with a particular group of children; every child deserves such a teacher.

PREPARING TEACHERS TO WORK WITH GIFTED STUDENTS

The preceding paragraphs set forth the proposition that the teacher of academically gifted students should have some competences which are different in kind or degree from those needed by all teachers. What experiences in college, graduate school, and on the job should contribute to these special abilities? A thoughtful discussion of a program of teacher education for the gifted is presented in the National Society Yearbook (NSSE, 1958) by Frank Wilson out of his long years of experience in preparing such teachers at Hunter College. James (1960), Ward (1961), Abraham (1957), and French (1959) also contribute important insights with respect to the various components of undergraduate and graduate preparation of the teacher who is to work with high-ability students.

Proper screening and selection of candidates is important in the preparation of all teachers. At the point of initial selection it is too early to predict whether a candidate will become a teacher of the gifted. Screening of all prospects should therefore be accomplished in terms of motivation to teach, a professional commitment, academic promise, social values, interest in working with young people, psychological maturity, personality characteristics and health standards. At a later stage, Torrance (1962) suggests that the student with an interest in teaching the gifted should demonstrate creative thinking ability. His range of interests, personality characteristics, and previous experiences should reflect creative motivation. Ward (1961) asserts that "the personality characteristics of the teacher of the gifted should be adapted to the particular types of stress and demand which arise in dealing with children who have marked initiative, strong and sometimes distinctive interests, and exceptional rational capacity" (Ward, 1961, p. 115).

There is general agreement that the teacher of the gifted has first to be prepared as a good teacher in general. At the undergraduate level the candidate needs a solid background of general education in order to ensure the breadth of preparation that truly gifted students should be able to draw upon. The candidate ought to develop a philosophy, values, and professional ideals which will equip him as a guide for the gifted students who should in turn set high store upon social service and concern for others. While such an outcome is not guaranteed by the required pattern of courses that go under the name of general education or liberal arts in most colleges, the faculty as a whole and the teacher education department in particular should be directing attention to the ends and not just the means of college education. Jacob (1957) has called attention to the general lack of success colleges have had in affecting student values, but he has also indicated the effectiveness of a few institutions in this regard and the worthwhileness of the effort. Training for independence in learning is another important facet in preparing teachers of the gifted. Teachers who themselves have simply followed their professors' directions and bibliographies are not likely to know how to guide their students in independent work. Certainly, a student who wants to teach gifted children should have himself completed some independent study and honors type courses. A college endorsing a graduate for work with exceptionally able pupils should be able to point to scholastic independence reflected in the prospective teacher's academic experience.

Not only should the candidate's scholastic exposure be broad, but his immersion should be relatively deep. The current move by state education departments to require more concentrated specialization of both elementary and secondary school teachers should help to accomplish this aim. The specialization of the teacher for the gifted should be qualitatively, and perhaps quantitatively, deeper. A serious problem arises, however, in the differences between organization of disciplines in universities and subjects in the common schools. Teaching needs should take precedence over a narrow preparation for advanced graduate work. The English teacher with a field in literature limited to a single century is not well equipped to deal with reading skills, composition, mass media, reading materials for students, and linguistics and speech problems which are everyday realities in elementary and secondary schools. Botany and political science are too limited as major fields for the high school teacher of science or social studies, let alone the elementary school teacher in the "self-contained" classroom. For the sake of the teacher candidate it is desirable to redefine the discipline in terms of probable teaching assignments. Finally, the student needs a broad view of his field which is philosophic and historical as well as factual. He should have some idea of structure in his discipline (*the* structure, if agreement exists; *a* structure which gives meaning to his work, if there are multiple viewpoints). He should be able to explain to laymen and children the methods of his field. The science teacher should have some grounding in philosophy and history of science, and other majors should be similarly oriented to their fields.

The professional education of the teacher should be divided among undergraduate, graduate, and in-service phases. Most authorities agree on deferring specialization (as in teaching the gifted) to the graduate level. If appropriate time is to be given to general education and to development of major fields, the professional component in undergraduate programs is limited to the general preparation of the teacher. This is all to the good since more advanced work depends upon substantial teaching experience if it is to be meaningful. However, the laboratory experiences that characterize most strong programs of teacher education afford opportunities for young people to explore teaching the gifted. School visits that are often part of introductory courses should include visits to special classes for the gifted where such classes exist; otherwise discussion of some visits should focus upon the children of superior ability in classes observed. Tutorial work, big-brother arrangements, and work in community agencies are sometimes employed as adjuncts to courses in educational psychology. Here again, work with gifted students can be included for candidates who are so oriented. "September experiences," observation, and student-teaching also provide opportunities to study or work with bright children while first establishing general principles of operation for the teacher of all children. Certainly, educational psychology and methods courses should give strong emphasis to the doctrine of individual differences, to the identification of different levels of ability, to the respect of each individual as a person of dignity, and to the adaptation of teaching methods and curriculum in keeping with individual ability.

Maturity is an important quality of the teacher. Vocational and avocational experiences can make a strong contribution to development of psychological maturity. Teacher education students should be encouraged to seek out part-time and summer jobs or to participate in cooperative work-study programs. It is indeed desirable for students to have had some contact with the business world as well as with summer camps, day camps, after-school centers, community agencies, and other youth-serving groups.

GRADUATE WORK

Professional specialization for the teacher of the gifted begins at the graduate level. Some organized study of education of the gifted should be undertaken by every teacher planning to work with special classes. A composite course outline, developed from thirty institutions by French, has already been presented in this chapter. Problems of identification, curriculum adaptation, grouping, acceleration, enrichment, evaluation, guidance, underachievement, and motivation are highlighted, as are more general concerns with administrative provisions for educating the gifted, social issues, and the characteristics of exceptionally able children. Such a course should be built upon previous work on curriculum planning in general, on intensifying understanding of child development, on understanding the dynamics of human personality, and on measurement of ability and achievement. Where possible, a practicum in working with gifted children should be provided. This should involve opportunities to appraise ability, to develop special programs of study for individual children or small groups, and to carry out limited research projects with small groups of bright children. Some observation and demonstration teaching may also be included.

Few, if any, universities offer such programs at this time, particularly of the graduate type described. Wilson (NSSE, 1958) cites the following primary needs where practical action is immediately possible regardless of course and program structures:

> Correcting "misconceptions about gifted and talented children"
> Developing "more realistically an awareness of the great range of exceptionalities and of the broad sweep of different capabilities"
> Providing "firsthand experiences with very capable children to enable teachers to understand them"
> Acquainting "students with basic resource materials which they can use constructively"
> Developing "familiarity with and practice in using community resources"
> Acquainting "students with classroom procedures particularly suitable for the full development of the children"
> Studying "administrative plans and instructional procedures in regard to the gifted." (NSSE, 1958, pp. 374-75)

The development of improved programs in colleges for teachers of the gifted depends upon a number of factors. First, there is need for a strong teacher education program in general which provides both a theoretical and experiential framework for understanding learners as individuals. Such a framework depends both upon the normal academic resources and upon the existence of teaching-learning laboratories in campus schools and affiliated public school systems. Second, there has to be a philosophical commitment to the development of the learner's full potential, including goals of academic excellence. Third, opportunities for cooperative relationships with other institutions and provisions for wide communication are essential to avoid a narrow provincialism in the development of pioneer programs. Finally, there is need for continuous experimentation and research "lest one good custom should corrupt the world." To do so, the institution must have ready access to school situations in its own laboratory school or in associated school systems. It also needs a staff with sophisticated research techniques to ensure rigorous evaluation of experimental projects.

IN-SERVICE PROGRAMS

While there may be great value in graduate courses in education of the gifted, direct action to improve actual programs for gifted children is more likely to come from work and study projects conducted within a particular school or school district. The university course offers academic resources and a scholastic regimen that facilitate concerted study of gifted children and their education. The university makes its contribution by enriching the insight of persons who attend. Actual development of programs, however, is more likely to ensue when teachers from a common background work within an administrative framework where action is possible. A single teacher returning from a summer workshop at State University may be enthusiastic to develop a meaningful program in his school or community, but he finds it difficult to convey the enthusiasm he feels to persons who have developed other interests which are equally legitimate. As a result, he is most often limited to improvement of the program for his own classes alone. In-service projects have the advantage of bringing together persons who normally work with each other, who recognize the problems of a particular school environment, and who can often join with each other to secure changes in desired directions. The most effective program may be a combination of university study, utilizing the resources and the perspective of such an institution, and in-service projects which capitalize upon factors which must be considered on the scene.

A number of channels are open for on-the-job training of teachers for the gifted. Some large school systems operate in-service courses. Ideally these courses combine the systematic approach of a university program with attention to a specific school system and its needs. Teachers preparing to work with the gifted in a school system currently operating programs for the bright children can derive benefit from such courses. Some systems provide for interchange of ideas among teachers with particular specialties. A newsletter on education for the gifted can serve such a purpose. Periodic meetings are held in some cities for teachers assigned to special classes or interested in the program because of bright children in the heterogeneous classes they teach. In the New York City area the Metropolitan Association for Study of the Gifted provides a forum five times a year for teachers, administrators, college personnel, and lay people with an interest in the gifted.

Consultant service also proves an effective method of improving instruction of the gifted. The consultant may be a member of the central school staff or a visitor from a university or other school agency. He may work individually with teachers in developing plans, studying particular children, reviewing teaching techniques, locating materials for children, or finding resources in the community and outside. He may work instead with committees of teachers concerned about educating the most able youngsters, or he may combine the two approaches. The effective consultant provides in this way both professional and psychological support to the teacher who is trying his wings in a new element.

Another productive means for teacher education in any area is participation in curriculum development projects A genuine reappraisal of programs for the gifted or planning to develop new programs for bright children provides a dynamic center of interest for teachers who simultaneously improve their own competence and work on school-wide or system-wide problems. Such programs, of course, have to involve responsible administrative personnel if there is to be a good prospect for adoption of recommendations made by the study group. It is desirable, too, that provision be made for utilization of consultants from other schools, agencies or unversities, in order to avoid dangers of insularity and ignorance. An essential resource is a library of curriculum materials and major publications concerned with the gifted and their education. In addition, finances should be available for visiting of other schools where programs of interest are underway.

The opportunity to see actual programs in operation can be most meaningful to teachers who are seeking new ideas and some direction as they plan programs for the gifted. Some districts are able to provide time and travel costs for a few teachers and administrators to visit other school systems, near and far. Some districts have tried to establish demonstration centers of their own. With assistance from the Illinois State Education Department, the Chicago Public Schools (1964) have provided such centers in one high school and four elementary schools. The main purpose of these centers is to facilitate observation and personal evaluation of instructional practices organized for gifted students in these schools.

Many school systems provide workshops of short duration or "institutes" before the opening of the school year in which teachers are given a brief exposure to problems in education of the gifted. If such programs are to be more than a momentary spiritual uplift, there is serious need for sustained attention to the problem over a long period of time. Some work and study structure has to be developed which outlives the institute. Workshops are useful if conducted long enough to yield serious study of a problem and working plans that teachers may put to work in the ensuing school year. Provision should be made for careful follow-up activities of workshops as well as other activities of shorter duration. In education of the gifted it is especially apparent that the schools provide only part of the environment for learning. Widening use is being made of community personnel resources. In South Orangeburg, New York, for example, foundation support provided finances for employment on Saturday mornings of artists, architects, scientists, mathematicians, and other specialists living in the community, and the school district furnished compensation for school personnel who served as coordinating agents in particular areas. While providing an unusual service for interested high school youth, teachers were able to find fresh insights into certain fields of endeavor and to learn new ways of enlivening their classrooms during the week.

Finally, teachers and administrators can learn themselves while trying to add to knowledge available generally on teaching the gifted. Part of the in-service growth effort of the school system should be research which it sponsors in various fields. School personnel should be encouraged to participate in research on characteristics of gifted learners, identification procedures and instruments, development of creativity, teaching techniques in working with exceptionally able children, motivation, non-intellective factors in achievement, and the host of other problems in educating the gifted which remain to be studied. Some programs should be initiated by the school systems themselves. In other cases affiliation with university, state, or federal research projects may be possible. The teacher who is also a scholar not only builds his own background; he also serves as a model for emulation by intellectually superior students.

SPECIALIZED PERSONNEL FOR GIFTED PROGRAMS

Most advocates of strong programs for the gifted advocate separate budgets and special departments for the gifted in state and district school systems. Obviously, personnel organization is a function of particular situations, and what may work in one place may be unsuccessful elsewhere. The author, however, does not believe that such separatism is helpful except, possibly, in mammoth organizations where special programs may be overlooked unless specific provision is made.

Gifted students are not a breed apart. Whether special classes are provided or not, a significant proportion of high ability students will continue to be found in the "regular" classroom. Teachers and supervisors should not be misled by the establishment of separate organizations into a belief that the gifted are no concern of theirs. Supervisors with broad responsibilities can help prevent this compartmentalized point of view.

Education for the gifted cannot be set up as an elite program to com-

Within this framework, such officers should earmark a substantial part
pensate for a poor school program in general. It can be only as strong
as the rest of the organization. It should enrich the whole program and
in turn be enhanced by the larger part. This kind of operation calls for
planning for the gifted as an integral part of the school system's total
curriculum development, staff recruitment, supervision and budgeting.

Rather than look to separate organization, the school district should
give serious consideration to assignment of staff and educational responsibilities. Supervisory personnel should have considerable freedom in
assigning teachers as needs and interests change. No individual should
be pegged irrevocably as a teacher of the gifted or non-gifted. Better
than appointment of one firebrand director of gifted programs would be
coordinated responsibility and action where the curriculum director,
chief guidance officer, subject supervisors, and principals affirm education of the gifted as an identified and important part of their jobs.
of their time, activity, and resources to planning and supervising programs for the exceptionally able. The top administration should require
of these persons an annual accounting of their stewardship of the gifted
as well as other programs.

SUMMARY

The teacher of the gifted is essentially a good teacher but with some
special attributes and qualitative differences. He is interested in intellectual achievement in young people with superior scholastic potential. He
is excited about learning and is able to communicate this excitement to
students. He is a warm human being and serves to some extent as a
father or mother image, but he also demands that students attain high
standards consistent with their individual promise. He recognizes the
extremes of individual difference and has the professional competence
to arrange the educational milieu to provide for these variations. He is
psychologically mature and not troubled by the possibility that some of
his students may ultimately exceed his own academic attainments.

Few teacher education institutions currently offer specialized work
for the aspiring teacher of the gifted. Advocates urge that undergraduates learn to work effectively with individual differences but concede
that specialized study is the function of graduate rather than undergraduate programs. A growing number of institutions are offering such work
at the graduate level.

While formal course work has the advantage of providing more organized background for individual teachers, in-service activities in school
districts give greater promise of developing planned programs for the

gifted. Course work in the school district, curriculum development activities, workshops, conferences, and the use of consultants are major channels available for on-the-job study. A combination of graduate course work to provide organized background material and curriculum development activities in a school building or for the school system as a whole offer the best potential for special preparation of the teacher of gifted children.

Chapter 18

Research: Endeavors and Opportunities

To strive, to seek, to find and not to yield ...

—Tennyson

Because of the inherent fascination of the subject, education of the gifted has stimulated considerable research in the past and continues to offer a challenge to research workers. Research on the gifted has reflected the modes of inquiry that have prevailed at a given time, and the range of procedures has included biography, literary studies, the development and testing of measurement instruments, the comparison of segments of the population, long-term longitudinal studies, controlled group comparisons in schools, and action research to test proposals for program development in actual school situations.

EARLY RESEARCH ON THE GIFTED

Toward the close of the nineteenth century the influence of Darwin and the new sciences of biology and genetics aroused an interest in the hereditary nature of genius. Genius was defined in terms of notable performance in various fields. A number of researchers employed biographical and literary methods to inquire into the hypothesized hereditary quality of exceptional talent. These inquiries were limited, of course, by the absence of objective measures, by the inability to distinguish between ability and achievement, by the necessity to trace backwards from performance to heredity and education, and by the consequent lack of experimental controls. The data were also limited to highly subjective and often fragmentary biographical and autobiographical accounts.

Development of objective instruments for measuring intelligence at the turn of the twentieth century ushered in an era of frenetic testing activity. Tests were administered and then related to a host of factors in attempts to describe the characteristics of the population to be found at a particular segment of the ability curve as measured in the new tests. Of these, the most significant have been the longitudinal studies initiated by Terman and his colleagues in California. Terman combined a pioneer's interest in psychological measurement with an abiding interest in the gifted. The research he directed yielded the largest scale longitudinal study of a population that education and psychology have yet encountered. The classic study of more than one thousand men and women started with a group of subjects who were then in elementary school and who earned scores of 140 or higher in Terman's revision of the Binet intelligence scales. Detailed testing, interviews, and questionnaires have produced over a period of thirty-five years a mass of data covering family background, physical development, economic position, ethnic origin, class membership, career and recreational interests, special abilities, vocational preparation and achievement, social and marital adjustment, psychological characteristics and mental health, personality and character traits, patterns of motivation and achievement.

Terman's work also stimulated similar studies in other sections of the country, and the work continues with different perspectives on identifying the gifted and describing their characteristics. Fascination with the new instruments for measuring intelligence stimulated hundreds of studies which sought to describe the characteristics of persons of high intelligence, i.e., those who scored high on one intelligence measure or another. These included the types of description and analysis utilized by Terman and moved forward with new psychological discoveries to employ projective techniques, to study self-concepts, and to relate each new dimension of personality to longer established intellectual factors.*
Many of these studies are excellently summarized in Miles' chapter on the gifted in the *Manual of Child Psychology* (Miles, 1954).

PROBLEMS IN RESEARCH PROCESSES;
NEEDS FOR RESEARCH

Inevitably questions arise as to the adequacy of research methods. Research techniques in these early studies was reasonably straightfor-

---

* Reference to a number of these studies may be found in Chapters 2 and 3.

ward. A gifted population was selected via a specified test of intellectual ability. Then, a selected variable was measured and related to ability-test scores. Unfortunately, the results have not always been meaningful even though they may have been statistically significant. For one thing, new research on creativity and social leadership places in doubt the comfortable assumption that high scores on intelligence tests and high intelligence are necessarily the same thing. Second, in many fields, such as character and personality traits, subjective rating by observers raises serious questions concerning the scientific nature of the measurement employed. Third, the variability of the human species is such as to cloud the meaning of results. Gifted children, for example, tend to be somewhat superior physical specimens. Yet many gifted children reinforce the stereotype of the intellectual as a physical weakling. Again, somewhat more gifted children come from well-to-do families than from families representing an economic average. Yet many gifted children come from poor families, and many average and subnormal children come from economically favored homes. The averages and correlations produced by this kind of research often have little applicability in planning the education of particular gifted children.

If defining the characteristics of gifted youngsters is difficult, evaluation of education programs for the gifted is even more complex. Research problems are much magnified when agreement is hard to achieve on the purposes of educational programs. Aims and objectives often remain vague even in the minds of the investigators. Evaluation obviously must be geared to objectives. In the absence of clearly defined objectives, instruments for evaluation are necessarily undirected, vague, or simply geared to measure traditional goals.

Even if a clear statement of goals were to be made available, the shortage of sophisticated measurement techniques in the behavioral sciences in general makes proper evaluation most difficult. What does an intelligence test measure? Where should emphases in standardized achievement tests lie? As efforts are made to include some of the more amorphous goals of education—attitudes, social adaptation, self-expression, mental health, for example—the inadequacy of existing instruments is underlined. In lieu of this difficult type of evaluation, investigators settle too frequently for measurement of traditional goals rather than the exciting objectives to which their experimental programs have been directed. Small wonder, then, that results are frequently "statistically not significant." Results may indeed be of major importance, but failure to delineate goals carefully and absence of adequate measures lead to findings of statistical insignificance. Behavioral studies will continue to be a step removed from scientific status until measurement techniques are developed to compare in their precision with instruments used in the natural sciences.

Improvements in research processes are making an impact, however. On the statistical end, research studies in the behavioral sciences are developing increasing relevance and accuracy with the development of techniques in sampling, testing for significance, factor analysis, and analysis of co-variance. To the extent that the host of factors influencing human behavior at any one time may be identified, statistical techniques are being developed to take such factors into consideration and to separate out the effects of irrelevant factors. On the substantive side, important advances are being made as attention is being focussed on a number of important subjects, such as the statement of educational aims, factorial descriptions of intelligence, non-intellective factors that relate to academic achievement, the influence of particular sub-cultures, and the nature of creativeness and its nurture.

Of particular significance is the growing effort to describe objectives in behavioral, measurable terms. An excellent example is to be found in Bloom's *Taxonomy of Educational Objectives* (Bloom, 1956). As the first step in an effort to classify all the objectives of education, Bloom reports a classification of goals in the "cognitive domain." These goals make an excellent point of departure for teachers and invesigators working with intellectually gifted students. The suggestions of Bloom's committee for evaluation of the achievement of these goals make the volume especially valuable to teachers and research workers.

Nature of Intelligence. Continuing efforts to come to grips with the nature of talent and intelligence also bear substantial promise for investigators of education for the gifted. Emphasis on many different intellectual factors supports the search for highly special talents in addition to focus on the "well-rounded" individual of "general" intelligence. The more specific these factors become, the more susceptible they become to development through educational programs. As they become more firmly established, they also yield clues for more accurate identification of potential ability. New interest is seen in identifying the dimensions of intelligence and other talents as well.

Related to research on intelligence is a burgeoning interest in thinking and in concept formation. Piaget's work (1950) on children's concept formation has been followed up by studies of different cognitive styles (Kagan, 1960; Bruner, 1958), of intellectual patterns of gifted children (Gallagher and Lucito, 1961), of different methods of approaching problems (Bloom, 1950), of training in the use of inquiry (Suchman, 1961), and of educational programs to foster intellectual development at very early ages (Wann, 1962). Thomson (1959) indicates that the whole area of concept development is just beginning to be explored. None could be more significant to education of the intellectually gifted.

Non-intellective Factors. Research on non-intellective factors in talent and achievement promises to widen the concepts of intelligence and education for achievement which currently prevail. McClelland (1958) has offered a model for study of the nature and origin of talent which may serve as a much needed paradigm for interested researchers. In addition, however, the efforts of his group have added new insight into factors that affect motivation and achievement.

The need for increased attention to sociological and psychological influences is indicated. Elsewhere in this volume research by Strodtbeck and others on relationships between ethnic backgrounds, cultural values, and achievement is reported. Additional research will no doubt be forthcoming as a result of the strenuous efforts toward racial integration of schools and the provision of greater opportunity for culturally submerged minorities. Finally, the dynamics of groups themselves influence achievement, regardless of social origin of the group. Research is also under way on the influence of the group itself on an individual's performance (McClelland, 1958).

From still another perspective comes concern with the effects of personality structure on the realization of intellectual potential. This interest led to the efforts by Terman, Hollingworth, and other early investigators to relate "character traits" to intellectual giftedness. The early subjective ratings suffered from a species of halo effect, with an apparent tendency to ascribe all things good to the elite being studied. Development of new measures, including projective techniques, holds out promise of more objective research. Sarason's work (1960) on the effects of anxiety on elementary school children has been productive. The concern of the perceptualist school of psychology with "self-actualization" and "mental wellness" (Maslow, 1954; ASCD, 1962) contributes a positive view of personality structure in relation to a life pattern, including achievement.

Creativity. A field of inquiry which has blossomed in the late 1950's and early 1960's is the study of creativity. It is almost impossible in the midst of this period to keep up with the variety of efforts (1) to define creativity in behavioral, tangible, objective terms, (2) to describe the creative process, (3) to factor out elements in the creative personality, (4) to trace the genesis and development of creativity, (5) to identify and evaluate factors in creativeness, (6) to institute and evaluate school programs that seek to encourage and nurture creative thought and performance. Yet, these efforts have already established notable findings. They have indicated the shortcoming of intelligence tests that do not include a creativity factor. They have established common factors to be found in creativeness in a variety of unrelated fields. They demonstrate the non-identity of such creativeness factors with the factors now included in most intelligence tests. They indicate the possibility of success in developing creativity as schools address themselves to the promotion of certain of these factors. Of extreme interest to school personnel is emphasis of investigators in this area on time for individual effort, or room for individual maneuvering, in place of the emphasis of traditionalists on increasing the academic load of the gifted as a major approach to education of the most able.

Social Leadership. Even more amorphous than creativity is the constellation of characteristics and skills referred to as social leadership. Gibb (1954) in the *Handbook of Social Psychology*, and Hare (1962) in the *Handbook of Small Group Research* refer to a variety of research efforts on identification and development of leadership. Attempts to come to grips on a research level with this field in school programs are not common. DeHaan (NSSE, 1958) has prepared a chapter in the National Society for the Study of Education Yearbook on *Education for the Gifted* which provides more of a theoretical framework than a description of school-related programs. Zander and Van Egmond (1958), and Cassel and Haddox (1959) report on efforts to relate social leadership to academic ability. As yet, more usable definitions of leadership, workable measures to identify social leaders, and research on programs for education of leaders are all needed. Results of these studies point to no clear relationship between intellectual ability as measured by the usual tests and social leadership. They suggest the possible existence of a moderately high intellectual threshold for social leadership rather than any direct relationship beyond that level. In this case, as in creativity studies, two presumptions are warranted and will bear further analysis: that leadership represents an ability factor which is part of intelligence and should therefore be included in intelligence tests which are otherwise invalid; or, that leadership represents a set of abilities quite apart from intellectual factors except that it finds its origin only above a specifiable intellectual plateau.

Motivation. In school settings as well as in university research centers, motivation, achievement, and underachievement have been foci for concern and study. Why many students do not fulfill the promise of their aptitude test scores or of early performance remains a perplexing problem. Studies continue to be made, and more information is still needed on a variety of fronts. We do not know yet whether underachievement is always a failure to live up to ability or whether it is actually an artifact produced by shortcomings in intelligence tests. If intelligence tests in reality do not measure all the factors that are important in intelligence, it should not be surprising that some students will score high on such tests and still perform poorly in school. Further study of test instruments therefore represents one front on which an attack must continue. Second, research at this point has not been able to establish definitively a relationship between specified personality factors and underachievement. Many studies have been made, but a new perspective or more carefully designed endeavors are needed. Third, new evidence points to the effect of environment on motivation. More information is needed on actual effects of the immediate neighborhood, class, ethnic, and cultural values, and attitudes of the total culture on one hand. On the other hand, action research with attendant evaluation is needed to probe methods of overcoming negative effects of the environment where they exist.

Guidance. In efforts to counteract underachievement, guidance has represented the major experimental method employed. Chapter 16 on Motivation and Underachievement cites studies by Ohlsen and Proff (1960), McCarthy (1957), Fair (1959) and Goldberg (1959) of efforts to solve such problems through group or individual guidance. These studies do not adduce the positive results one might hope for. They underline, however, the need for long-term longitudinal studies. Whether guidance or some other mechanism is the key, deep-seated problems of long duration are not likely to be amenable to short-term treatment.

Research on other guidance activities might also be helpful. To what extent should independent study under guidance replace part of the usual curriculum for bright students? What are the most likely contributions that guidance workers can make in dealing with parents of the gifted? How may the guidance counselor best help students who are facing personal and social problems? What is the most effective kind of group guidance program, if any, for classes of selected students of high ability? Despite the assumptions of current educational practice, is it conceivable that a highly gifted population needs the enforcement of a single demanding standard more than it does the adjustment of standards implicit in the "guidance approach"? The author himself has strong doubts as to the validity of such an hypothesis, but there is no clear evidence for its adoption or rejection.

Curriculum. Guidance versus enforcement of standards is, however, only one phase of the larger issue of the appropriate school program for the gifted child. A very considerable amount of exploration has taken place in developing special programs. The reasons for inconclusive findings, contradictory results or poorly established evidence have been treated elsewhere in this volume. Accordingly, the need is great for tighter research designs and more objective evaluation of proposed and existing programs. There is also great need to devise more imaginative and more effective programs rather than relying upon outdated programs whose main claim for support is their rigor or distastefulness.

There is a wide variety of program adaptations which invite research. Some studies support liberalized, individualized programming as compared with a single rigorous curriculum (Aiken, 1942; Katterle, 1955). Replication of such efforts should focus more explicitly on a highly gifted population in contrast with the research cited which included the broader spectrum of all students attending college. Considerable attention has been directed to the rapidly expanding Advanced Placement classes leading to a national standardized examination and college credit for special work in high school. Studies indicate success in college for students who perform well on these examinations. There is no yardstick, however, to compare the Advanced Placement program with locally developed honors classes or even special work in conventional classes. Comparisons should be made between equated groups of superior students who follow one procedure or the other. Advocates of honors classes in college put much emphasis on independent study with the implication that some junior version should be profitable on the high school level. Little evidence is available on independent work or "tutorials" in high schools. Here again is the need to study performance of high ability students in contrasted programs—conventional, tutorial, independent.

Comparisons among different kinds of curriculum should also be profitable. One of the questionable assumptions underlying many programs is that the best preparation for academic work in college is academic work in high school. This assumption is rejected in Katterle's study (1955) noted above. Little experimentation has been carried on, however, substituting work in art, music, creative writing, industrial arts, or vocational areas for the more conventional fifth or sixth major in an academic area such as mathematics, science, social studies, or foreign languages. Even more fundamental would be exploration of the effectiveness of these areas in lieu of so-called basic areas in the curriculum. The hypothesis here is not that whatever is is wrong. It is conceivable that there might be more useful studies than advanced subject matter in high school, much of which has to be re-taught in college anyway. Is it possible that a more generous diet of individually expressive, creative activities in high school might result in greater emotional maturity leading to more effective academic study in college? The writer has neither evidence with which to answer the question nor an axe to grind. The hypothesis is suggested simply as another way of looking at the high school curriculum when most attention is being given to college-type studies at an earlier stage for gifted students.

Grouping. No area in education is so marked with contradictory "evidence" as ability grouping. The inconclusive studies of grouping in the past are being followed by large-scale studies like the New York City study of grouping in the intermediate elementary school grades (Goldberg, 1958) and a series of inquiries into "streaming" in England (Daniels, 1961). That grouping may affect different social classes in different ways is suggested by the study of such effects in Stockholm (Husen and Svensson, 1960). Some tentative efforts have been made to identify social effects of grouping (Mann, 1957, e.g.) but the area remains largely unexplored. While the effectiveness of ability grouping seems to "stand to reason" for most laymen and teachers, no substantial body of research evidence supports this stand. Considerable research is still needed on the effect of grouping on academic achievement, social values, and general interests. Also wanting are studies relating grouping to social class, to variations in curriculum, to guidance procedures and to instructional methods and media.

Acceleration. Studies on acceleration seem to point overwhelmingly to the effectiveness of procedures which enable exceptional students to complete their formal education at an early age. These studies generally contrast students of given ability who are making normal vs. accelerated progress. In all cases a certain amount of immaturity is constant. Grundtvik made a contrary assumption in organizing the prototype of the Danish Folk School (Davies, 1931). From fourteen to sixteen, he said, a boy was better at work than in school. With some added experience and maturity, the boy would do better on his return to school after sixteen. The American economy and culture make experimentation of this type practically impossible. Research with gifted youngsters in other cultures may add light of a new kind on both the curriculum and acceleration issues. One possibility in the United States, however, is exploration of work experience programs during high school years for gifted students as well as for potential drop-outs and students in non-academic curricula. Another is the expansion of "junior year abroad" plans in college, extended cooperative work-study programs in college, and Peace Corps or Armed Services membership coming as an interlude in the total college experience. Time and experience might have the effects Grundtvik sought for youth in Denmark, or, on the other hand, research might prove the superiority of acceleration proposals of Pressey (1949), Keys (1938), Worcester (1956), Terman (1947) and others.

Despite the endorsement given to acceleration in most existing studies, American social trends are not likely to support any large scale reduction in the years spent in formal education below the collegiate level. An example of this tendency is found in the enthusiastic reception accorded to Advanced Placement Programs as contrasted with the failure to implement the favorable findings of the Early Admissions Program. As a result it seems more meaningful to emphasize research which centers on accelerating the level of studies undertaken rather than studies of the effects of early school completion.

Advanced Placement should not be a term limited to lower level college work offered to capable students still in high school. The "educational lockstep" affects college students, too. More upper-classmen might be given the opportunity to take graduate work leading to graduate degrees before they are twenty-two years old. The kind of independent study which eventuates in Ph.D. dissertations might also be embarked upon at an earlier stage. While society is not ready to accept high school graduation at age fifteen or sixteen, certainly industry and research seem eager to accept Ph.D.'s in their very early twenties. Universities offering such alternatives would be in the position to evaluate the effectiveness of such programs. Follow-up studies ten and twenty years thereafter could determine the differences in total productiveness of Ph.D.'s with conventional and accelerated programs.

The Teacher and Teaching. The general shortage of scientifically acceptable research on teaching methods and teaching personality applies to teaching of the gifted as well. Brandwein's study (1955) of the teachers of Westinghouse Talent Search Winners is perhaps the only systematic study of teachers of successful pupils. The generalizations Brandwein adduces are interesting, but the study covers a very limited sample numerically, is restricted to a single teaching field, and is in many ways highly subjective. Replication of this study in science and the many other subjects at various school levels might prove valuable. Reasoning back from successful students to the teacher and his methods appears to be a tenuous approach because of the many uncontrolled variables in the life of the student, his performance, and recognition. However, other approaches as well have inherent procedural deficiencies. Problems of invidious comparisons arise in attempting to assign equally gifted pupils to teachers representing contrasting personality types (to the extent that these can be measured). In efforts to compare methods of teaching, it is difficult to characterize one teacher as employing one approach and another teacher as the advocate of a second approach, when most teachers vary their procedures considerably. At any rate, a very large and sophisticated project is needed to account with statistical reliability for the many personality and pedagogical variables inherent in a given classroom for a whole semester or the full year.

Despite these difficulties there are many questions about teaching practice whose answers might be productive in improving educational opportunity for the gifted. What particular procedure is most effective in teaching bright students, and at what levels is each procedure most productive: lecture, discussion, the developmental lesson, the socialized recitation, committee work, project and activity methods, the unit approach? At what levels and in what areas can independent study be employed for superior results? Is the teacher's major contribution made from his own scholarly resources or from his ability to inspire student learning? Is the most effective teacher a giver of information, an enforcer of standards, a maintainer of constructive classroom climate, an emotional bulwark, a catalyst of group activity, or a combination of these? Is it possible that the student's reaction to teachers is so individual that no generalization of this kind can be maintained? Our present state of knowledge seems to support only the simple statement that the classroom should be a constructively exciting arena for learning and stimulus for further study. Certainly, there is need to pin down more specific, helpful guides to good teaching practice.

Learning Media. Research should also be directed toward differential effects on gifted students of various media of instruction. Current emphasis on programmed instruction, teaching machines, and "reinforcement" as a primary mechanism in learning, calls for study of possible uses of these learning programs with very able young people. Comparisons should be made between conventional instruction at a high level of competence with programmed material of high quality. Findings of importance would cover the depth of learning achieved, the time factor, attitudes toward the material learned, and subsequent learning in the same field. Of equivalent significance would be evidence as to the effect of programmed material on creativeness and independence, since existing programs give major emphasis to extremely small steps in learning and little attention to intuitive jumps that are being stressed at this time in mathematics and science. Evidence in favor of programmed material might pave the way for more effective enrichment in the classroom through improved individualization of instruction. It might solve the problem of providing adequate challenge for the very fast learner. If such evidence is forthcoming, the next step, however, would be determination of the appropriate balance between programmed instruction of a highly individual nature and group learning activities.

Television as a mode of instruction also represents an area where research is needed. Commercial and educational channels provide some programs presented as "courses" and some material which is intended to be generally cultural and informational. If any students can profit from these programs, it should be the brightest. Research might help establish the usefulness, if any, of both types of presentation. Do students learn enough from these programs to make viewing desirable? How does learning in this way compare with results from similar instruction given in school, or from time spent in directed reading outside of school? Is the additional learning paid for in emotional tension when leisure time is used in this way rather than in freer kinds of recreaton? What are qualitative differences between the TV "course" and the TV "cultural" presentation in learning results and emotional impact?

Summer Programs. Summer programs of various types are being offered to able high school students. Evaluations in general are in the form of subjective reactions given by students, teachers, and parents. Such testimony should be reinforced by objective evidence that compares different kinds of summer experiences, that recognizes non-scholastic values as well as academic achievement, and that measures each experience against desirable summer objectives. These criteria include learning advances made during the summer; physical vigor and emotional readiness for the new academic year; relative academic achievement five and ten months after the summer adventure; reading ability and interest at the end of the summer and in mid-year; social maturation; physical skills developed; the universe of information acquired; and experience, if any, with the work-world. Not all of these values are comparable, nor can they all be placed in the same hierarchy. To weigh all summer experiences in only one or two of these scales, however, is to arrive at a distorted evaluation.

ORGANIZED RESEARCH PROGRAMS

In the face of all the studies that need to be done on education of the gifted, considerable research is in process and valuable leads come from some studies already reported. Some large scale and cooperative programs suggest relatively "massive" attacks upon a number of problems.

Project Talent, directed by John C. Flanagan at the University of Pittsburgh with sizable support from United States governmental agencies, is gathering more data than have ever been available before on the abilities of children now in school. About 440,000 students in 1,353 high schools in all parts of the country, took a two-day battery of tests to serve as the "first national inventory of human resources" (National Inventory of Aptitudes and Abilities, December, 1960). Aptitude, achievement, and information tests were administered, and information secured on personal characteristics, background and interests of the students. The measures employed are described in some detail by Dailey and Shaycroft (1961) in *Types of Tests in Project Talent*. These devices have yielded thirty-seven "Talent" scores for each student which are intended for educational and vocational advising. In addition, all these data are being processed through high speed electronic computers in order to yield findings on:

1. What aptitude youth has
2. What youth knows
3. What youth wants to do.

The variety of test scores, the large scale of the sample and the modern statistical and computational procedures available promise an exceptionally rich source for information about youth and their gifts for research in the future. Follow-up studies will relate experience in adult life to the data secured from these young people as high school students. Because the project makes a sampling of the total population, all of the high scoring young people in the sample will be found and not only those noted by teachers or observers. Because of more advanced sampling techniques and statistical processes, comparisons of the high ability students in the sample with norms for the group will provide more accurate data than were available to Terman, Hollingworth, and others. The result should be a large-scale updating of earlier studies of characteristics of gifted children.

Of related interest is the Conservation of Human Resources Project sponsored by the Carnegie Foundation since 1957 (Ginzberg, 1962). This project is studying the influence of the first ten years of work experience on the performance of a selected group of seven hundred talented young people. Emphasis is being placed on the effect of intellectual ability, crises in life experiences, external disruptions, occupational and employment trends, family, faulty occupational choice and work versus other values. Important light may be shed on achievement as a function of these variables.

Project Talent is representative of a host of projects supported under the Cooperative Research Program of the United States Office of Education. Since the 1950's, a number of studies on various aspects of education of the gifted have been sponsored under this program, and some of them have been reported in the Cooperative Research Monographs series published by the Office. Such topics as motivation, identification, and creativity have been included. Several of these studies are cited in various chapters of this volume.

The National Education Association organized its Project on the Academically Talented Student in 1958. An important result has been a series of pamphlets developed by various professional organizations at the request of the NEA. Most of the pamphlets are addressed to secondary education, and these are in subject fields such as English, Social Studies, Foreign Languages, Art, Music, Business Education, Mathematics, and Science. One pamphlet is devoted to elementary schools, and a number of general publications include a summary in 1961 of research on the gifted, bulletins on administration of programs for the gifted, guidance of the gifted, and an excellent annotated bibliography.*

Two study programs have involved professional groups which include large regions in the United States. One of these is the Superior and Talented Student Project (STS) of the North Central Association of Colleges and Secondary Schools. The Association was given a large grant by the Carnegie Corporation of New York in 1958 for a two-year study of the motivation of superior high school students. Fifty participating schools were selected "to carry on action programs of identifying, motivating, and guiding superior and talented students." These schools were chosen on a number of criteria including the following:

Matriculation by no more than 35 per cent of the graduates in a three-year period in a two- or four-year college.

Failure of at least 20 per cent of the graduates of above average ability to enter college.

Commitment by school authorities to send the principal and a counselor or teacher to special five-day summer workshops in 1958 and 1959; to allocate necessary resources for a pilot program, and to conduct a pilot program for two years, sharing information with other schools.

Fifty additional schools were designated as associated schools. Because they did not meet all criteria established they did not receive the same services as participating schools. The project has extended its services to more than one hundred schools in nineteen states under the aegis of the North Central Association since the expiration of the Carnegie grant which had been extended through 1961. The project has operated under the hypothesis that proper identification, adequate guidance and

---

* The project also reprinted earlier in the same series the 1959 summary of research on the gifted in the *Review of Educational Research* (Fliegler and Bish, 1959).

special provisions for motivating superior and talented students should increase the motivation of such students to continue their education beyond high school, make more appropriate career plans and attain achievement levels appropriate to their ability. This large scale program under the direction of J. Ned Bryan and Bruce Shertzer and assisted by the staff members of Science Research Associates has reached many schools through its publications as well as the schools affiliated officially with the program. The action program included the summer workshops already noted, regional conferences during the year, and consultant services to help schools implement plans developed at the workshops or at home. A newsletter (*News, Notes and Nuggets*) has contained articles of considerable interest. A useful pamphlet, *Problems in Motivation* (North Central Association, 1959) was published. Among other publications, a large booklet by Endicott (1961) on guidance of superior students, and a book by Shertzer, *Working with Superior Students* (1960) combine the experience of the project with relevant research findings.

A second regional project of significance is the Southern Regional Project for Education of the Gifted. This project has enlisted the participation of consultants on gifted programs working in state departments of education and has entailed sessions on a university campus and visits to a number of schools operating special programs for the gifted. One outcome of the project is a booklet entitled *The Gifted Student: A Manual for Program Development* (Southern Regional Project, 1962). Virgil S. Ward of the University of Virginia has been a leading figure in conduct of this project.

A number of states have officially established programs to support research on, and development of, programs for the gifted. New York State is one such example, having appropriated resources for administration through the State Education Department for research by school districts on a matching-funds basis. The State Department in this case performed a useful function in insisting upon a research design and not simply an action proposal without appropriate evaluation. A problem arising in this type of funding is frequent failure of school districts to make adequate provision for research as required in the matching grants arrangement. Other state-wide programs of interest have included the Study Project on Programs for Gifted Children in California (Martinson, 1961) which involved one thousand students in addition to controls in several different grades, and the work of the Connecticut Committee for the Gifted.

The Fund for the Advancement of Education (Ford Foundation) provided the initial support for two significant research and action efforts—the Early Admissions to College program and the Advanced Placement program. Both of these are treated elsewhere in this volume. Individual systems, like Portland and Quincy, also enjoyed assistance from the Fund in experimental programs. In addition, many persons were given individual grants to study first-hand programs for the gifted in various parts of the country. The Carnegie Corporation has supported some individual programs and has made a major contribution through support of large scale projects like the North Central Superior and Talented Student Project, the NEA project on the Academically Talented Student, and the Inter-University Committee on the Superior Student program which centers its efforts on extension of honors programs (*The Superior Student*, 1958 *et seq.*).

Two of the large test publishers are also making an important contribution to research on the gifted. The Educational Testing Service in cooperation with the College Entrance Examinations Board has been a major factor in support of curriculum project in mathematics, sciences, foreign languages, and recently English. All of these projects have had a basic orientation toward curriculum for the gifted. Science Research Associates, as noted above, has participated in the North Central project.

Some important research projects have been university centered. The Talented Youth Project under the direction of Passow and Goldberg, at Teachers College, Columbia, has served as part of the Horace Mann-Lincoln Institute of School Experimentation. As such, it has carried on research in school systems cooperating with the institute, such as Norfolk, Evanston, Denver, and New York City. Attention has been focussed on action and research with respect to motivation, underachievement, grouping, and curriculum projects in such fields as mathematics (Passow and Goldberg, 1961). Guilford's interest in structure of intelligence and creativity has attracted support for research at the University of Southern California in these areas. Torrance and his associates at the University of Minnesota have carried on research on creativity in elementary school children. Getzels and Jackson have conducted parallel studies in secondary education at the University of Chicago. The Committee on Human Development at the University of Chicago, also, gave leadership assistance through Havighurst and Bowman to the Quincy Youth Development Commission activities (Bowman, 1956). The studies under Eells (1951), Davis (1948) and others of cultural influences on intelligence testing and learning have been sponsored as well by the University. Hunter College of the City University of New York, with unique laboratory schools for education of the gifted only, has concentrated in recent years on measures for identification of talent, but has also given attention to exploration in curriculum areas. At Michigan State University, Drews has directed study of various aspects of education for the gifted with some particular attention to social and economic backgrounds. DeHaan at Hope College has led research on social leadership.

Of particular interest are the research programs conducted by the New York City Public Schools which have had a long tradition of interest in special programs for the gifted. Studies have been reported on acceleration (Justman 1952, 1953), grouping (Greenberg, 1941; Abramson, 1959; Goldberg and Passow, 1962), underachievement (Goldberg, 1959), and efforts to compensate for cultural deprivation (Hillson and Myers, 1961; Schreiber, 1958). Both the problems and the resources of the city are likely to lead to additional research on education of the gifted.

Other large scale programs have been conducted in and around other cities. The Gifted Child Project in Portland, Oregon, and the Quincy Youth Development Commission are two programs which received substantial support from the Ford Foundation and developed early in the 1950's to stimulate many attempts which followed. Excellent descriptions have been written of the Portland program by Williams (NSSE, 1958, pp. 395-414; Williams, 1959), and of the Quincy program by Havighurst (1952) and Bowman (1953, 1956). Both programs placed heavy emphasis on improving the identification of superior and talented students. Concerted attention has been given to social leadership, its discovery and development. Provision of special academic and artistic opportunities for especially capable students has featured programs developed in these cities.

THE SHAPE OF RESEARCH TO COME

Because major problems in education of the gifted remain unsolved, continuing research efforts may be expected in the major areas involved:

Identification of the components of exceptional ability
Identification of special abilities in individuals
Further inquiries into the nature and structure of intelligence
Concept development and critical thinking
Environmental (physical and cultural) influences on ability
Motivation, achievement, and underachievement
Creativity, the creative process, and the creative individual
Modes of accelerating educational development
Potentials of individual and group guidance in educating the gifted
School program variations, such as:
    Independent study

Programmed instruction
Use of new media
Grouping alternatives
Curriculum alternatives (variations in content and structure),
including reorganization within many subject areas
Social leadership

In many cases, shifts in emphasis have been foreshadowed which will at times place research on the gifted in other perspectives. Current concern with creativity, for example, does not center around intellectual giftedness. However, research on identification and development of creative gifts is bound to have important implications for education of the intellectually superior child. It is hoped that social psychologists will mount a similar attack on the mysteries of social leadership. Anxiety in official quarters over problems of the big cities must eventually transcend concern with educating the culturally deprived alone, and come to grips with superior educational opportunity for young people in the culture-rich metropolis. Part of the problem of the big city has been the relatively higher standards imposed upon urban applicants for college attendance and scholarships when compared with students from small-town and rural areas. A genuine interest in utilizing all the nation's talents cannot continue to discriminate against the big city. At any rate, a spate of research on urban education that may be expected in the next decade cannot fail to give some attention to problems of educating the gifted in large cities. Finally, research on programmed instruction and new media is also bound to throw some light, albeit tangentially, on education of the gifted.

Research on the gifted is therefore likely to benefit from a two-pronged attack. On the one hand we may look for expanding research on the problems in educating the gifted per se. On the other hand, further insight is likely to grow in planning programs for the gifted as more light is shed upon larger educational problems of which developing the potential of extremely able students is but one part. Education of the gifted must continue, therefore, to serve as an inseparable facet of the total pattern of education in a community.

Bibliography

References

Abraham, Willard. "A Hundred Gifted Children." *Understanding the Child*. 6:116-20, October, 1957.
———. *Common Sense about Gifted Children*. New York, Harper & Row, 1958.
Abramson, David A. "The Effectiveness of Grouping for Students of High Ability." *Educational Research Bulletin*, 38:169-82, October 14, 1959.
Aikin, Wilford M. *The Story of the Eight-Year Study*. New York, Harper & Row, 1942.
Allison, Harold. "California Principals Study a Curriculum for the Gifted." *Bulletin* of National Association of Secondary-Schools Principals, 43:102-106, February, 1959.
Altus, Grace T. "Some Correlates of the Davis-Eells Tests." *Journal of Consulting Psychology*, 20:227-32, June, 1956.
American Association for Gifted Children. *The Gifted Child*. Edited by Paul Witty. Boston, D. C. Heath, 1951.
American Council of Learned Societies. "Report of the Art Panel." *ACLS Newsletter*, 9:9:12-15, November, 1958.
Anderson, C. Arnold. "The Dilemma of Talent-Centered Programmes: U.S.A." *The Gifted Child*: 1962 Yearbook of Education. New York, Harcourt, Brace & World, 1962, pp. 445-57.
Anderson, Harold H., ed. *Creativity and Its Cultivation*. New York, Harper & Row, 1959.
Anderson, John E. "The Nature of Abilities." In *Talent and Education*, edited by E. Paul Torrance. Minneapolis, University of Minnesota Press, 1960, pp. 9-31.
Anderson, William. "An Attempt through the Use of Experimental Techniques to Determine the Effect of Home Assignments upon Scholastic Success." *Journal of Educational Research*, 40:141-43, October, 1946.
Applbaum, Morris J. "A Survey of Special Provisions for the Education of Academically Superior Students." *Bulletin* of National Association of Secondary-Schools Principals, 43:26-43, October, 1959.
Arnold, John E. "The Generalist versus the Specialist in Research and Development." In *The Creative Person*. Berkeley, Institute of Personality Assessment and Research, University of California, 1961.
Aschner, Mary Jane. "The Analysis of Verbal Interaction in the Classroom." In *Theory and Research in Teaching*, edited by Arno A. Bellack. New York, Teachers College, Columbia University, 1963, pp. 53-78.
Association for Supervision and Curriculum Development. *Freeing Capacity to Learn*. Washington, D.C., The Association, 1960.
———. *Perceiving, Behaving, Becoming: a New Focus for Education;* 1962 Yearbook. Washington, D.C., The Association, 1962.

Ausubel, David P. "Prestige Motivation of Gifted Children." *Genetic Psychology Monographs*, 43:53-117, 1951.

Baldauf, Robert J. "A Comparison of the Extent of Educational Growth of Mentally Advanced Pupils in the Cedar Rapids Experiment." *Journal of Educational Research*, 52:181-83, January, 1959.

Barbe, Walter B., and Frierson, Edward C. "Teaching the Gifted—a New Frame of Reference." *Education*, 82:465-67, April, 1962.

Barber, Leroy E. "Why Some Able High School Graduates Do Not Want to Go to College." *School Review*, 59:93-96, February, 1951.

Barkan, Manuel. *A Foundation for Art Education*. New York, Ronald Press, 1955.

Barron, Frank. "Creative Vision and Expression in Writing and Painting." In *The Creative Person*. Berkeley, Institute of Personality Assessment and Research, University of California, 1961.

————. "The Disposition toward Originality." *Journal of Abnormal and Social Psychology*, 51:478-85, November, 1955.

————. "The Psychology of Imagination." *Scientific American*, 199:3:150-66, September, 1958.

Barwick, Janice M., and Arbuckle, Dugald S. "A Study of the Relationship between Parental Acceptance and the Academic Achievement of Adolescents." *Journal of Educational Research*, 56:148-51, November, 1962.

Bayley, Nancy. "On the Growth of Intelligence." *American Psychologist*, 10:805-18, December, 1955.

————, and Oden, Melita H. "The Maintenance of Intellectual Ability in Gifted Adults." *Journal of Gerontology*, 10:91-107, January, 1955.

Beasley, J. *Underachievement: Review of Literature*. New York, Horace-Mann-Lincoln Institute of School Experimentation, Teachers College, Columbia University, 1957, Processed.

Bello, Francis. "The World's Greatest Industrial Laboratory." *Fortune*, 58:151-57+, November, 1958.

Benne, Kenneth D., and Sheats, Paul. "Functional Roles of Group Members." *Journal of Social Issues*, 4:2:42-47, Spring, 1948.

————, and Muntyan, Bozidar. *Human Relations in Curriculum Change*. New York, McGraw-Hill, 1951.

Bennett, Clayton L. "Motivating the Underachiever." *News and Nuggets* (North Central Association of Colleges and Secondary Schools, Chicago), 3:5:21-28, June, 1961.

Berger, Max. "A School Art Project." *High Points*, 41:7:25-33, October, 1959.

Berman, Abraham B., and Klein, Abraham. "Personality Study of Maladjusted Pupils of Superior Mentality." *High Points*, 24:2:57-63, February, 1942.

Bienenstok, Theodore. "Why Many Fail to Go to College." University of the State of New York *Bulletin to Schools*, 43:161-62, January, 1957.

Bloom, Benjamin S. *Taxonomy of Educational Objectives*. New York, David McKay, 1956.

————, and Broder, Lois J. "Problem-solving Processes of College Students." *Supplementary Educational Monographs*, No. 73. Chicago, University of Chicago Press, July, 1950.

Bloom, Samuel W. "The Early Identification of Potential Scientists." *School Science and Mathematics*, 55:287-95, April, 1955.

Blumenthal, Frances. "A Study of the Correlation of Pupil Ability with Chronological Age." *Educational Administration and Supervision*, 35:279-94, May, 1949.

Boehm, Leonore. "The Development of Conscience: A Comparison of American Children of Different Mental and Socioeconomic Levels." *Child Development*, 33:575-90, September, 1962.

Bonthius, Robert H., and others. *Independent Study Programs in the United States*. New York, Columbia University Press, 1957.

Bowman, Paul H., and others. *Mobilizing Community Resources for Youth*. Supple-

mentary Educational Monographs, No. 85. Chicago, University of Chicago
      Press, 1956.
————. *Studying Children and Training Counselors in a Community Program.*
      Supplementary Educational Monographs, No. 78. Chicago, University of Chi-
      cago Press, 1953.
Bragdon, Henry W. "Advanced Placement: Rising Tide with Breakers Ahead."
      College Board Review, No. 42, 18-20, Fall, 1960.
Brandwein, Paul. *The Gifted Student as Future Scientist.* New York, Harcourt,
      Brace & World, 1955.
Bratton, Patrick J., and others. "Status and Student Leadership in the Secondary
      School." *Educational Leadership*, 13:209-14, January, 1956.
Bray, Douglas W. *Issues in the Study of Talent.* New York, King's Crown Press,
      1954.
British Journal of Educational Psychology. "Contributions to Intelligence Testing
      and the Theory of Intelligence." The *Journal*, 27, Part III, November, 1957.
Bronfenbrenner, Urie. "On the American Child." *Journal of Social Issues*, 17:1:6-18,
      1961.
Brownell, William A., and others. *Arithmetic in Grades I and II: A Critical Summary
      of New and Previously Reported Research.* Durham, N.C., Duke University
      Press, 1941.
Brumbaugh, Florence. "What Is an IQ?" *Journal of Experimental Education*,
      23:359-63, June, 1955.
————, and Roscho, Bernard. *Your Gifted Child: A Guide for Parents.* New York,
      Holt, Rinehart & Winston, 1959.
Bruner, Jerome S. *The Process of Education.* Cambridge, Mass., Harvard University
      Press, 1960.
————; Goodnow, Jacqueline J., and Austin, George A. *A Study of Thinking.* New
      York, John Wiley, 1958.
"Building an Honors Program." *Superior Student*, 1:1:11, April, 1958.
Buros, Oscar, ed. *Tests in Print.* Highland Park, N. J., Gryphon Press, 1961.
Burt, Cyril. "The Evidence for the Concept of Intelligence." *British Journal of
      Educational Psychology*, 25:158-77, November, 1955.
————. "The Inheritance of Mental Ability." *American Psychologist*, 13:1-15,
      January, 1958.
Burton, William H.; Kimball, Roland B., and Wing, Richard L. *Education for
      Effective Thinking.* New York, Appleton-Century-Crofts, 1960.
Burton, William H. *The Guidance of Learning Activities.* Second Edition. New
      York, Appleton-Century-Crofts, 1952.
Carlson, Edith F. "Project for Gifted Children: A Psychological Evaluation." *Ameri-
      can Journal of Orthopsychiatry*, 4:648-61, October, 1945.
Carlson, Ruth K. "Emergence of Creative Personality." *Childhood Education*,
      36:402-4, May, 1960.
Carnegie Corporation. *1962 Annual Report.* New York, The Corporation, 1962.
Carr, Edwin R.; Wesley, Edgar B., and Murra, Wilbur T. "Social Studies." *Encyclo-
      pedia of Educational Research.* Revised Edition, edited by Walter S. Monroe.
      New York, Macmillan, 1938, pp. 1213-38.
Cassel, R. N., and Haddox, Genevieve. "Comparative Study of Leadership Test
      Scores for Gifted and Typical High School Students." *Psychological Reports*,
      5:713-17, 1959.
Caswell, Hollis L., and Foshay, A. Wellesley. *Education in the Elementary School.*
      Second Edition. New York, American Book Co., 1950.
Cattell, R. B., and Cattell, A. K. S. *The IPAT Culture-Free Intelligence Test: a
      Measure of "g".* Champaign, Illinois, Institute of Personality and Ability
      Testing, 1958.
Cheyney, Arnold B. "Parents View their Intellectually Gifted Children." *Peabody
      Journal of Education*, 40:98-101, September, 1962.

Chicago Public Schools. *Program of Education for the Gifted*. Study Report No. 12. Chicago, The Schools, 1964.

Citizenship Education Project. *Laboratory Practices in Citizenship*. New York, The Project, Teachers College, Columbia University, 1958; also, *Building Programs in Citizenship*. The Project, 1958.

Clark, Willis W. "Sex Differences in Mental Abilities among Students of High Intelligence." *Ninth Yearbook*, National Council on Measurements Used in Education. Fairmont, W. Va., The Council, 1951.

Coelho, George V. "Personal Growth and Educational Development through Working and Studying Abroad." *Journal of Social Issues*, 18:1:55-67, 1962.

Cohen, Helen L., and Coryell, Nancy, eds. *Educating Superior Students*. New York, American Book Co., 1935.

Cohen, J. W. "On Honors Programs." *Superior Student*, 1:5:2-8, November, 1958.

Cohler, Milton J. "Scholastic Status of Achievers and Non-achievers of Superior Intelligence." *Journal of Educational Psychology*, 32:603-10, November, 1941.

Cole, Charles C., Jr. *Encouraging Scientific Talent*. New York, College Entrance Examination Board, 1956.

———. "Current Loss of Talent from High School to College." *Higher Education*, 12:35-38, November, 1955.

———. "Varying Curricular Patterns for Able College Students." *College Board Review*, No. 36, 23-25, Fall, 1958.

Coleman, James S. *The Adolescent Society*. New York, Free Press of Glencoe, 1962.

Coleman, William, and Ward, A. W. "A Comparison of Davis-Eells and Kuhlmann-Finch Scores of Children from High and Low Socio-economic Status." *Journal of Educational Psychology*, 46:465-69, December, 1955.

College Entrance Examination Board. *Advanced Placement Program Syllabus*. New York, the Board, 1958.

———. *Appendices to the Report of the Commission on Mathematics*. New York, The Board, 1959 (a).

———. *Program for College Preparatory Mathematics*. New York, The Board, 1959.

———. *A Guide to the Advanced Placement Program*, 1960-61. New York, The Board, 1960.

Combs, Arthur W., and Snygg, Donald. *Individual Behavior*. Second Edition. New York, Harper & Row, 1959.

Conant, James B. *The American High School*. New York, McGraw-Hill, 1959.

———, ed. *The Identification and Education of the Academically Talented Student in the American Secondary School*. Washington, D.C., National Education Association, 1958.

Cox, Catherine M., and others. *The Early Mental Traits of Three Hundred Geniuses*. Vol. II, Genetic Studies of Genius. Stanford, Cal., Stanford University Press, 1926.

Crutchfield Richard S. "The Creative Process." In *The Creative Person*. Proceedings of Conference, October 13-17, 1961. Berkeley, Cal., Institute of Personality Assessment and Research, University of California, 1961.

Cunningham, Ruth, and Associates. *Understanding the Group Behavior of Boys and Girls*. New York, Teachers College, Columbia University, 1951.

Curry, Robert L. "Effect of Socio-economic Status on the Scholastic Achievement of Sixth Grade Children." *British Journal of Educational Psychology*, 32:46-49, February, 1962.

Dailey, John T., and Shaycroft, Marion F. *Types of Tests in Project Talent*. U.S. Office of Education, Cooperative Research Monograph No. 9. Washington, D.C., U.S. Government Printing Office, 1961.

Daniels, John C. "Effects of Streaming in the Primary School: II. A Comparison of Streamed and Unstreamed Schools." *British Journal of Educational Psychology*, 31:119-27, June, 1961.

Davids, Anthony. "Generality and Consistency of Relations between the Alienation

Syndrome and Cognitive Processes." *Journal of Abnormal and Social Psychology*, 51:61-67, July, 1955.

Davidson, Helen H.; Greenberg, Judith W., and Gerver, Joan M. *Characteristics of Successful School Achievers from a Severely Deprived Environment.* New York, The City College of the City University of New York, 1962 (mimeo).

Davies, Hugh Sykes. *Grammar without Tears.* New York, John Day, 1953.

Davies, Noelle. *Education for Life: a Danish Pioneer.* London, Williams and Norgate, 1931.

Davis, Allison. *Social-Class Influences upon Learning.* Cambridge, Mass., Harvard University Press, 1948.

Davis, Allison, and Eells, Kenneth. *Davis-Eells Test of General Intelligence or Problem-Solving Ability, Primary (grades 1-2), Intermediate (grades 3-6).* New York, Harcourt, Brace & World, 1953.

Davis, Frederick B., and Lesser, Gerald S. *The Identification and Classroom Behavior of Elementary-School Children Gifted in Five Different Mental Characteristics.* New York, Educational Clinic, Hunter College, 1959 (mimeo).

Davis, Nelda. "Teachers for the Gifted." *Journal of Teacher Education*, 5:221-24, September, 1954.

Davis, Olive B. *An Integrated Arts Program for the Gifted.* Final Report, 1961-62. New York, Hunter College High School, 1962 (mimeo).

DeHaan, Robert F. *Guidelines for Parents of Capable Youth.* Chicago, Science Research Associates, 1961.

————, and Havighurst, Robert J. *Educating Gifted Children.* Chicago, University of Chicago Press, 1957.

————, and Kough, Jack. *Teacher's Guidance Handbook.* Vol. I, Identifying Students with Special Needs; Vol. II, Helping Students with Special Needs. Secondary Edition. Chicago, Science Research Associates, 1956.

Doll, Edgar A. "The Four IQ's." *Exceptional Children*, 24:56-57+, October, 1957.

Dressel, P. L., and Grabow, J. M. "The Gifted Evaluate their High School Experience." *Exceptional Children*, 24:394-96, May, 1958.

Drevdahl, John E. "Factors of Importance for Creativity." *Journal of Clinical Psychology*, 12:21-26, January, 1956.

————, and Cattell, R. B. "Personality and Creativity in Artists and Writers." *Journal of Clinical Psychology*, 14:107-111, April, 1958.

Drews, Elizabeth M. *Effectiveness of Homogeneous and Heterogeneous Ability Grouping in Ninth-Grade English Classes with Slow, Average, and Superior Students.* U.S. Office of Education, Cooperative Research Program, Project No. 608. Washington, D.C., U.S. Government Printing Office, 1959.

————. "A Four-Year Study of 150 Gifted Adolescents." Paper read at convention of American Psychological Association, December 26, 1957. Lansing, Michigan State University, 1957 (mimeo).

————. "Realization of Talent among Children and Young People." In *The Gifted Child*. 1962 Yearbook of Education. New York, Harcourt, Brace & World, 1962, pp. 366-87.

Dunn, Halbert L. *High-Level Wellness.* Arlington, Va., R. W. Beatty, 1961.

————. "High-Level Wellness for Man and Society." Appendix to *Report on the Possibility of Measuring Positive Health.* Washington, D.C., Public Health Service Doc. NC 261, May 16, 1958.

Durkin, Delores. "An Early Start in Reading." *Elementary School Journal*, 63:147-51, December, 1962.

Eash, Maurice J. "Grouping, What Have We Learned?" *Educational Leadership*, 18:429-34, April, 1961.

Edelston, Harry. "Educational Failure with High Intelligence Quotient." *Journal of Genetic Psychology*, 77:85-116, September, 1950.

Edmiston, R. W., and Benfer, J. G. "The Relationship between Group Achievement and Range of Ability within the Groups." *Journal of Educational Research*, 42:547-48, March, 1949.

Educational Policies Commission. *Education of the Gifted*. Washington, D.C., National Education Association, 1950.

Educational Testing Service. *Annual Report, 1960-61*. Princeton, The Service, 1961.

Edwards, T. Bentley, and Wilson, Alan B. *A Study of Some Social and Psychological Factors Influencing Educational Achievement*. Berkeley, University of California, 1961, (mimeo).

Eells, Kenneth, and others. *Intelligence and Cultural Differences*. Chicago, University of Chicago Press, 1951.

Ekstrom, Ruth B. "Experimental Studies of Homogeneous Grouping: a Critical Review." *School Review*, 69:216-26, Summer, 1961.

"Emphasis on Excellence." Carnegie Corporation of New York *Quarterly*, 7:3:1-5.

Endicott, Frank S. *Guiding Superior and Talented High School Students*. Chicago, North Central Association of Colleges and Secondary Schools, 1961.

Engle, Thelburn L. "A Study of the Effects of School Acceleration upon the Personality and Social Adjustments of High School and University Students." *Journal of Educational Psychology*, 29:523-40, October, 1938.

Ennis, Robert H. "Needed: Research in Critical Thinking." *Educational Leadership*, 21:17-20+, October, 1963.

ETS Developments. "Differences in Problem-Solving Styles Affect the Essential Nature of a Test." *ETS Developments*, 11:3:2. Princeton, Education Testing Service, November, 1963.

Everett, Samuel, ed. *Programs for the Gifted: A Case Book in Secondary Education*. Fifteenth Yearbook of the John Dewey Society. New York, Harper & Row, 1961.

Fair, Jean. "A Comprehensive High School Studies Learning." *Educational Leadership*, 16:351-54, March, 1959.

Fay, Leo; Horn, Thomas, and McCullough, Constance. *Improving Reading in the Elementary Social Studies*. Bulletin No. 33. Washington, D.C., National Council for the Social Studies, 1961.

Featherstone, W. B. "Special Schools for Honors Pupils." *1939 Yearbook*, New York Society for the Experimental Study of Education. Brooklyn, The Society, 1939.

Feldhusen, John F., and Klausmeier, Herbert J. "Anxiety, Intelligence and Achievement in Children of Low, Average, and High Intelligence." *Child Development*, 33:403-9, June, 1962.

Flagg, Elinor B. "Mathematics for Gifted Children." *Educational Leadership*, 19:379-82, March, 1962.

Flesher, Marie A., and Pressey, S. L. "War-Time Accelerates Ten Years After." *Journal of Educational Psychology*, 46, 228-38, April, 1955.

Fliegler, Louis A. *Curriculum Planning for the Gifted*. Englewood Cliffs, N.J., Prentice-Hall, 1961.

————, and Bish, Charles E. "Gifted and Talented." *Review of Educational Research*, 29:408-50, December, 1959.

Frankel, Edward. "A Comparative Study of Achieving and Underachieving High School Boys of High Intellectual Ability." *Journal of Educational Research*, 53:172-80, January, 1960.

Freehill, Maurice F. *Gifted Children*. New York, Macmillan, 1961.

Freeman, Frank S. *Theory and Practice of Psychological Testing*. Revised Edition. New York, Holt, Rinehart & Winston, 1955.

French, Joseph L., ed. *Educating the Gifted: A Book of Readings*. New York, Holt, Rinehart & Winston, 1959.

————. "The Preparation of Teachers of the Gifted." *Journal of Teacher Education*, 12:69-72, March, 1961.

Fund for the Advancement of Education. *They Went to College Early.* New York, The Fund, 1957.

Galbraith, John K. *The Affluent Society.* Boston, Houghton Mifflin, 1958.

Gallagher, James J. *The Gifted Child in the Elementary School.* What Research Says to the Teacher, No. 17. Washington, D.C., National Education Association, 1959.

———, and Crowder, Thora. "The Adjustment of Gifted Children in the Regular Cla_sroom." *Exceptional Children,* 23:306-12+, April, 1957.

———, and Lucito, Leonard J. "Intellectual Patterns of Gifted Compared with Average and Retarded." *Exceptional Children,* 27:479-82, April, 1961.

Galton, Francis. *Hereditary Genius: An Inquiry into Its Law and Consequences.* Third Edition. London, MacMillan, 1914 (First Edition, 1869).

Gardner, Eric F., and Thompson, George G. *Social Relations and Morale in Small Groups.* New York, Appleton-Century-Crofts, 1956.

Gardner, John W. "Renewal in Societies and Men." *Annual Report.* New York, Carnegie Corporation of New York, 1962.

Getzels, J. W., and Jackson, P. W. "Occupational Choice and Cognitive Functioning: Career Aspirations of Highly Intelligent and Highly Creative Adolescents." *Journal of Abnormal and Social Psychology,* 61:119-23, January 1960 (b).

———, and ———. *Creativity and Intelligence.* New York, John Wiley, 1962.

———. "Distinctive Characteristics of Able Learners." In *Promoting Maximal Reading Growth among Able Learners.* Supplementary Educational Monographs, No. 81. Chicago, University of Chicago Press, 1954, pp. 16-21.

———. "Social Values and Individual Motives." *School Review,* 65:60-63, Spring, 1957.

———, and Jackson, P. W. "The Highly Intelligent and the Highly Creative Adolescent." In *University of Utah Research Conference on Identification of Creative Scientific Talent.* Salt Lake City, The University, 1959, pp. 46-57.

———, and ———. "Meaning of Giftedness." *Phi Delta Kappan,* 40:75-77, November, 1958.

———, and ———. "The Study of Giftedness: A Multidimensional Approach." In *The Gifted Student.* Cooperative Research Monograph, No. 2. U.S. Office of Education. Washington, D.C., U.S. Government Printing Office, 1960 (a).

Ghiselin, Brewster, ed. *The Creative Process.* Berkeley, University of California Press, 1952.

Gibb, Cecil A. "Leadership." In *Handbook of Social Psychology,* edited by Gardner Lindzey. Cambridge, Mass., Addison-Wesley, 1954. Vol. II, Chapter 24.

Gibbs, E. G., and Matala, D. M. "A Study of the Use of Special Teachers in Science and Mathematics in Grades 5 and 6." *School Science and Mathematics,* 61:569-72, November, 1961.

Ginzberg, Eli. "Talent and Performance: A Report from Columbia University." *The Gifted Child.* 1962 Yearbook of Education. New York, Harcourt, Brace & World, 1962, pp. 438-44.

Glaser, E. M. *An Experiment in the Development of Critical Thinking.* Contributions to Education, No. 843. New York, Teachers College, Columbia University, 1941.

Glennon, Vincent J., and Hunnicutt, C. W. *What Does Research Say about Arithmetic?* Washington, D.C., Association for Supervision and Curriculum Development, 1952.

Goldberg, Miriam L. "A Report on Recent Research in the Field of the Academically Talented." *Teachers College Record,* 60:150-63, December, 1958.

———, and Passow, A. Harry. "The Effects of Ability Grouping." *Education,* 82:482-87, April, 1962.

———, and Associates. "A Three-Year Experimental Program at DeWitt Clinton High School to Help Bright Underachievers." *High Points,* 41:5-35, January, 1959.

Goslin, David A. *The Search for Ability.* New York, Russell Sage Foundation, 1963.

Gough, Harrison. "Techniques for Identifying the Creative Research Scientist." In *The Creative Person.* Proceedings of Conference, October 13-17, 1961. Berkeley, Institute of Personality Assessment and Research, University of California, 1961.

"The Governor's School." Carnegie Corporation of New York *Quarterly,* 12:1:1-4, January, 1964.

Gowan, J. C. "Dynamics of the Underachievement of Gifted Students." *Exceptional Children,* 24:98-101, November, 1957.

Greenberg, Benjamin, and Bruner, Herbert B. *Final Report on the Speyer School Experiment.* Publication No. 12. New York, Board of Education, 1941.

Griffin, Dorothy Park. "Movement Responses and Creativity." *Journal of Consulting Psychology,* 22:134-36, April, 1958.

Grotberg, Edith H. "Adjustment Problems of the Gifted." *Education,* 82:472-76, April, 1962.

Guilford, J. P. "Creativity." *American Psychologist,* 5:444-54, September, 1950.

———. "Factors that Aid and Hinder Creativity." *Teachers College Record,* 63:380-92, February, 1962.

———. "The Structure of the Intellect." *Psychological Bulletin,* 53:267-93, July, 1956.

———, and others. "Development and Application of Tests of Intellectual and Special Aptitudes." *Review of Educational Research,* 29:26-41, February, 1959.

———, and others. *A Factor-Analytic Study of Creative Thinking.*

"I. Hypotheses and Description of Tests." Reports from the Psychological Laboratory, No. 4, April, 1951.

"II. Administration of Tests and Analysis of Results." Reports from the Psychological Laboratory, No. 8, July, 1952.

Los Angeles, University of Southern California.

———, and others. *A Revised Structure of Intellect.* Reports from the Psychological Laboratory, No. 19. Los Angeles, University of Southern California, April, 1957.

Hage, Gerald. "Two Studies on the Gifted." *Minutes,* Metropolitan Association for Study of the Gifted, January 21, 1960. New York, The Association, 1960 (mimeo).

Haggard, Ernest A. "Socialization, Personality and Academic Achievement in Gifted Children." *School Review,* 65:388-414, Winter, 1957.

Hall, Theodore. *The Cleveland Story.* New York, World Publishing Co., 1956.

Haller, A. D., and Miller, I. W. *The Occupational Aspiration Scale: Theory, Structure and Correlates.* Lansing, Michigan State University, 1961 (mimeo).

Hampton, Nellie D. *Effects of Special Training on the Achievement and Adjustment of Gifted Children.* Third Report. Cedar Falls, State College of Iowa, 1962.

Hanna, Geneva R., and McAllister, Mariana K. *Books, Young People, and Reading Guidance.* New York, Harper & Row, 1960.

Hardin, Garrett. *Nature and Man's Fate.* New York, Holt, Rinehart & Winston, 1959.

Hare, A. Paul. *Handbook of Small Group Research.* New York, Free Press of Glencoe, 1962.

Havighurst, Robert J. "Conditions Favorable and Detrimental to the Development of Talent." *School Review,* 65:20-26, March, 1957.

———. *Human Development and Education.* New York, David McKay, 1953.

———, and Rodgers, Robert R. "The Role of Motivation in Attendance at Post-High School Educational Institutions." In *Who Should Go to College?* by Byron S. Hollinshead. New York, Columbia University Press, 1952 (b).

———, and others. "*A Community Youth Development Program.*" Supplementary Educational Monographs, No. 75. Chicago, University of Chicago Press, 1952 (a).

————, and others. *A Survey of the Education of Gifted Children.* Chicago, University of Chicago Press, 1955.

Hawes, Vincent L. *A Survey of Selected Teacher Preparation Programs and Personnel Practices for Teachers of Gifted Children in Elementary Schools.* Unpublished Doctoral dissertation. Chestnut Hill, Mass., Boston College, 1961.

Henry, Jules. "Working Paper on Creativity." *Harvard Educational Review,* 27:148-55, Spring, 1957.

Hersey, John. *Intelligence, Choice and Consent.* New York, Woodrow Wilson Foundation, 1959.

Hildreth, Gertrude. "Characteristics of Young Gifted Children." *Journal of Genetic Psychology,* 53:287-311, December, 1938.

————. "Three Gifted Children: A Developmental Study." *Journal of Genetic Psychology,* 85:239-62, December, 1954.

————, and others. *Educating Gifted Children at Hunter College Elementary School.* New York, Harper & Row, 1952.

Hilgard, Ernest R. "Creativity and Problem Solving." In *Creativity and Its Cultivation,* edited by Harold H. Anderson. New York, Harper & Row, 1959, pp. 162-80.

Hillson, Henry T., and Myers, Florence C. *The Demonstration Guidance Project, 1957-62: Pilot Program for Higher Horizons.* New York, New York City Board of Education, 1963.

————, and ————. "Demonstration Guidance Project." *High Points,* 43:5:5-20, May, 1961.

Hirshberg, Al. "Prodigy at Harvard." *Saturday Evening Post,* 230, 38-39+, September 14, 1957.

Hobbs, Nicholas. "Motivation to High Achievement." Address delivered to Annual Conference of Association for Supervision and Curriculum Development, March, 1959. Washington, D.C., The Association, mimeographed.

Holland, John L. "Creative and Academic Performance among Talented Adolescents." *Journal of Educational Psychology,* 52:136-47, June, 1961.

————. "The National Merit Research Program." *Education,* 82:477-81, April, 1962.

————, and Stalnaker, Ruth. "A Descriptive Study of Talented High School Seniors: National Merit Scholars." *Bulletin* of National Association of Secondary-School Principals, 42:236:9-21. March, 1958.

Hollingshead, August B. *Elmtown's Youth.* New York, John Wiley, 1949.

Hollingworth, Leta S. *Gifted Children: Their Nature and Nurture.* New York, Macmillan, 1926.

————. *Children above 180 IQ.* New York, Harcourt, Brace & World, 1942.

Hollinshead, Byron S. *Who Should Go to College?* New York, Columbia University Press, 1952.

Holmes, Darrell, and Harvey, Lois. "An Evaluation of Two Methods of Grouping." *Educational Research Bulletin,* 35:213-22, November 14, 1956.

Hopkins, L. Thomas. "Classroom Climate Can Promote Creativeness." *Educational Leadership,* 13:279-82, February, 1956.

Hoppock, Anne S. *All Children Have Gifts.* Bulletin No. 100. Washington, D.C., Association for Childhood Education, International, 1958.

Horn, Ernest. *A Basic Writing Vocabulary.* University of Iowa Monographs in Education, First Series, No. 4. Iowa City, University of Iowa Press, 1926.

————. "Spelling." *Encyclopedia of Educational Research,* edited by W. S. Monroe. Revised Edition. New York, Macmillan, 1950, pp. 1247-64.

Horrocks, John E. *Assessment of Behavior.* Columbus, Ohio, Charles E. Merrill, 1964.

Hullfish, H. Gordon, and Smith, Philip G. *Reflective Thinking: the Method of Education.* New York, Dodd, Mead, 1961.

Hummell, William, and Huntress, S. Keith. *The Analysis of Propaganda*. New York, William Sloane, 1949.

Hunt, Earl B. *Concept Learning: an Information Processing Problem*. New York, John Wiley, 1962.

Hunter College Elementary School Faculty. *Gifted Children: As We See Them*. New York, Hunter College Elementary School, [1958].

Husen, Torsten, and Svensson, Nils-Eric. "Pedagogic Milieu and Development of Intellectual Skills." *School Review*, 68:35-61, Spring, 1960.

Inhelder, Barbel. "Some Aspects of Piaget's Genetic Approach to Cognition." In *Thought and the Young Child*, edited by William Kessen and Clementina Kuhlman. Monographs of the Society for Research in Child Development, Serial No. 83, 1962. Vol. 27, No. 2, 19-34.

Institute of Personality Assessment and Research. *The Creative Person*. Proceedings of Conference, October 13-17, 1961. Berkeley, The Institute, University of California, 1961 (mimeo).

Jacob, Philip E. *Changing Values in College*. New York, Harper & Row, 1957.

James, Katherine G. *A Report of the Study in the Preparation of Teachers for the Gifted in the Elementary School*. New Haven, Southern Connecticut State College, 1960 (mimeo).

Jenkins, Martin D. "The Upper Limit of Ability among American Negroes." *Scientific Monthly*, 66:399-401, May, 1948.

Jenkyns, F. C., and others. "Comparative Study for the Improvement of Education." *Southern Association Quarterly*, 10:9-132, and 10:372-488, February and August, 1946.

Joe Berg Foundation, 1712 South Michigan Avenue, Chicago 16, Ill.

Jones, Daisy M. "An Experiment in Adaptation to Individual Differences." *Journal of Educational Psychology*, 39:257-72, May, 1948.

Jones, Marshall R., ed. *Nebraska Symposium on Motivation*. Lincoln, University of Nebraska Press, 1962.

Junge, Charlotte W. "The Gifted Ones—How Shall We Know Them?" *Arithmetic Teacher*, 4:141-46, October, 1957.

Justman, Joseph. *A Comparison of the Functioning of Intellectually Gifted Pupils Enrolled in Special Progress and Normal Progress Classes in Junior High School*. New York, Board of Education, May, 1952 (mimeo).

————. *Intellectually Gifted Accelerants and Non-accelerants at the Bronx High School of Science. I. Achievement in the Tenth Year*. New York, Board of Education, January, 1953 (mimeo).

Kagan, Jerome, and others. "Conceptual Style and Use of Affect Labels." *Merrill-Palmer Quarterly*, 6:261-76, July, 1960.

Kallen, Horace M. "Dewey's Individualism." Dewey Centennial Lecture, Hunter College, New York, October 10, 1959.

Katterle, Zeno B., and Craig, Robert. "Exposing an Academic Fallacy." *Washington Education*, 34:5:10-11+, February, 1955.

Keys, Noel. "Should We Accelerate the Bright?" *Journal of Exceptional Children*, 8:248-54+, May, 1942.

————. *The Underage Student in High School and College*. Berkeley, University of California Press, 1938.

Knapp, R. H., and Goodrich, H. B. *Origins of American Scientists*. Chicago, University of Chicago Press, 1952.

Kough, Jack. *Practical Programs for the Gifted*. Chicago, Science Research Associates, 1960.

Kreuter, Gretchen. "The Vanishing Genius: Terman and the Stanford Study." *History of Education Quarterly*, 2:6-18, March, 1962.

Larrick, Nancy. *A Teacher's Guide to Children's Books*. Abridged edition. Columbus, Ohio, Charles E. Merrill, 1963.

Laycock, Samuel R. "Counseling Parents of Gifted Children." *Exceptional Children,* 23:108-110+, December, 1956.

Leese, Joseph. "Underachievement among Gifted Is Worth Some Faculty Time." *New York State Education,* 46:661-63+, June, 1959.

Lehman, Harvey C. *Age and Achievement.* Princeton, Princeton University Press, 1953.

———, and Witty, Paul A. "The Play Behavior of Fifty Gifted Children." *Journal of Educational Psychology,* 18:259-65, April, 1927.

Lesser, Gerald S., and Davis, Frederick B. *Identification of Gifted Elementary School Children with Exceptional Science Talent.* New York, Hunter College, 1960 (mimeo).

———, and others. "Experimental Arousal of Achievement Motivation in Adolescent Girls." Paper read at American Psychological Association, 1961. New York, Hunter College, 1961 (processed).

———, and others. "Identification of Gifted Elementary School Children with Scientific Talent." *Educational and Psychological Measurement,* 22:349-64, Summer, 1962.

Lessinger, Leon M., and Martinson, Ruth A. "The Use of the California Psychological Inventory with Gifted Pupils." *Personnel and Guidance Journal,* 39:572-75, March, 1961.

Leuba, Clarence. "A New Look at Curiosity and Creativity." *Journal of Higher Education,* 29:132-40, March, 1958.

Lewis, W. Drayton. "Some Characteristics of Very Superior Children." *Journal of Genetic Psychology,* 62:301-309, June, 1943.

———. "Relative Intellectual Achievement of Mentally Gifted and Retarded Children." *Journal of Experimental Education,* 13:98-109, December, 1944.

Little, James K. "The Persistence of Academically Talented Youth in University Studies." *Educational Record,* 40:237-41, July, 1959.

Lombroso, Cesare. *The Man of Genius.* London, Robert Scott, 1891.

Longnecker, Don D., and others. "An Experimental Summer High-School Program. *Educational Research Bulletin,* 38:113-19+, May 13, 1959.

Lorge, Irving. "Social Gains in the Special Education of the Gifted." *School and Society,* 79:2024:4-7, January 9, 1954.

———. "Superior Intellectual Ability." *Journal of Heredity,* 32:205-8, June, 1941.

Lowenfeld, Viktor. "The Case of the Gifted Child." *School Arts,* 55:13-18, April, 1956.

———. *Creative and Mental Growth.* Third Edition. New York, Macmillan, 1957.

———. "Creativity and Art." *ACEI Branch Exchange,* May, 1959, p. 12.

———. "Current Research on Creativity." National Education Association Journal, 47:538-540, November, 1958.

Luchins, Abraham S., and Edith H. "Children's Attitudes toward Homogeneous Grouping." *Journal of Genetic Psychology,* 72:3-9, March, 1948.

Ludlow, Herbert G. "Some Recent Research on the Davis-Eells Games." *School and Society,* 84:146-48, October 27, 1956.

MacKinnon, Donald W. "Characteristics of the Creative Person: Implications for the Teaching-Learning Process." *Current Issues in Higher Education, 1961.* Washington, D.C., Association for Higher Education (NEA), 1961 (a), pp. 89-92.

———. "The Highly Effective Individual." *Teachers College Record,* 61:367-78, April, 1960.

———. "The Study of Creativity." In *The Creative Person.* Berkeley, Institute of Personality Assessment and Research, University of California, 1961 (b).

MacLean, Malcolm S. "Should the Gifted Be Segregated?" *Educational Leadership,* 13:215-20, January, 1956.

McCarthy, Sister Mary Viterbo. *The Effectiveness of a Modified Counseling Pro-*

cedure in Promoting Learning among Bright Under-achieving Adolescents. Final Summary. Weston, Mass., Regis College, 1957 (mimeo).

McClelland, David C., and others. *The Achievement Motive.* New York, Appleton-Century-Crofts, 1953.

————, and others. *Talent and Society.* Princeton, D. Van Nostrand, 1958.

McCracken, Robert A. "Accelerating the Reading Speed of Sixth Grade Gifted Children." *Exceptional Children,* 27:27-28, September, 1960.

McFee, June King. *Preparation for Art.* San Francisco, Wadsworth Publishing Co., 1961.

McGuire, Carson. *Creativity and Emotionality.* Report No. 12, Laboratory of Human Behavior. Austin, University of Texas, 1962 (mimeo).

Maddox, H. "Nature-Nurture Balance Sheets." *British Journal of Educational Psychology,* 27:166-75, November, 1957.

Mann, Horace. "How Real Are Friendships of Gifted and Typical Children in a Program of Partial Segregation?" *Exceptional Children,* 23:199-201, February, 1957.

Mann, Maxine. "What Does Ability Grouping Do to the Self-Concept?" *Childhood Education,* 36:357-60, April, 1960.

Marksberry, Mary Lee. *Foundations of Creativity.* New York, Harper & Row, 1963.

Martens, Elise H. *Teachers' Problems with Exceptional Children, II. Gifted Children.* Washington, D.C., U.S. Office of Education, Pamphlet No. 41, 1940.

Martinson, Ruth. *Educational Programs for Gifted Pupils.* Sacramento, California State Department of Education, 1961. (See also summary of preliminary report in *Exceptional Children,* 26:339-45, March, 1960).

Maslow, Abraham H. *Motivation and Personality.* New York, Harper & Row, 1954.

Mead, Margaret. "The Gifted Child in the American Culture of Today." *Journal of Teacher Education,* 5:211-14, September, 1954.

Meer, Bernard, and Stein, Morris I. "Measures of Intelligence and Creativity." *Journal of Psychology,* 39:117-26, January, 1955.

Mendelowitz, Daniel M. *Children Are Artists.* Stanford, Cal., Stanford University Press, 1953.

Mensh, Ivan N. "Rorschach Study of the Gifted Child." *Journal of Exceptional Children,* 7:14, October, 1950.

Meyers, C. E., and others. *Primary Abilities at Mental Age Six.* Monographs of the Society for Research in Child Development, Serial No. 82. Vol. 27, No. 1, 1962.

Miami University. *The University Study Program for Superior High School Students, July 1, 1958 to June 30, 1961.* Oxford, Ohio, Miami University, 1961.

Miles, Catherine C. "Gifted Children." In *Manual of Child Psychology,* edited by Leonard Carmichael. Second Edition. New York, John Wiley, 1954, pp. 984-1063.

Miller, Leonard M., ed. *Guidance for the Underachiever with Superior Ability.* U.S. Office of Education, Bulletin 1961, No. 25. Washington, D.C., U.S. Government Printing Office, 1961.

Miller, Vera V. "Creativity and Intelligence in the Arts." *Education,* 82:488-95, April, 1962.

Millett, John D. *Financing Higher Education in the United States.* New York, Columbia University Press, 1952.

Mooney, Ross L. "Cultural Blocks and Creative Possibilities." *Educational Leadership,* 13:273-78, February, 1956.

————. "Groundwork for Creative Research." *American Psychologist,* 9:545-46, September, 1954.

————. *A Preliminary Listing of Indices of Creative Behavior.* Columbus, Bureau of Educational Research, Ohio State University, 1953 (mimeo).

————. Classification of Items in "A Preliminary Listing . . ." Columbus, Bureau of Educational Research, Ohio State University, 1953 (mimeo).

————. *A Conceptual Model for Integrating Four Approaches to the Identification of Creative Talent.* Columbus, Bureau of Educational Research, Ohio State University, 1957 (mimeo).

Moreno, John L. "Psychodrama and Problems of Releasing Creativity in Children and Adolescents." *The Gifted Child.* 1962 Yearbook of Education. New York, Harcourt, Brace & World, 1962, pp. 388-98.

Moser, Harold E. "Levels of Learning." *The Arithmetic Teacher,* 3:221-25, December, 1956.

Moustakas, Clark E., ed. *The Self: Explorations in Personal Growth.* New York, Harper & Row, 1956.

Muller, Karl. *Success of Elementary Students Admitted to Public School under the Requirements of the Nebraska Program of Early Attendance.* Unpublished doctoral dissertation. Lincoln, University of Nebraska, 1955.

Mulligan, Raymond A. "Socioeconomic Background and College Enrollment." *American Sociological Review,* 16:188-96, April, 1951.

Murphy, Gardner. *Human Potentialities.* New York, Basic Books, 1958.

————. *Personality.* New York, Harper & Row, 1947.

Murphy, Lois Barclay, and collaborators. *The Widening World of Childhood: Paths toward Mastery.* New York, Basic Books, 1962.

Mursell, James L. *Music Education: Principles and Programs.* Morristown, N.J., Silver Burdett, 1956.

Myers, Sheldon S. "A New Approach to Evaluation of Competence." *Bulletin* of National Association of Secondary-School Principals, 43:247:150-54, May, 1959.

National Council for the Social Studies. *A Guide to Content in the Social Studies.* Washington, D.C., The Council [1958].

————. *Skills in Social Studies.* Twenty-fourth Yearbook. Washington, D.C., The Council, 1953.

————. *Skill Development in the Social Studies.* Thirty-third Yearbook. Washington, D.C., The Council, 1963.

National Council of Teachers of English. *The English Language Arts.* New York, Appleton-Century-Crofts, 1952.

————. *The English Language Arts in the Secondary School.* New York, Appleton-Century-Crofts, 1956.

————. *Language Arts for Today's Children.* New York, Appleton-Century-Crofts, 1954.

National Education Association. Project on the Academically Talented Student. Washington, D.C.:
Administration for the Academically Talented Student. 1960 (a).
An Annotated Bibliography on the Academically Talented Student. 1961 (a).
Art for the Academically Talented Student. 1961 (b).
Business and Economic Education for the Academically Talented Student. 1961 (c).
Elementary Education and the Academically Talented Pupil. 1961 (d).
English for the Academically Talented Student. 1960 (b).
Finding and Educating the Academically Talented Student. 1958.
Guidance for the Academically Talented Student. 1961 (e).
Mathematics for the Academically Talented Student. 1959 (a).
Modern Foreign Languages and the Academically Talented Student. 1960 (c).
Music for the Academically Talented Student. 1960 (d).
Research on the Academically Talented Student. 1961 (f).
Science for the Academically Talented Student. 1959 (b).
Social Studies for the Academically Talented Student. 1960 (e).

National Education Association. Research Division. "Teacher-Opinion Poll." *National Education Association Journal,* 50:4:62, April, 1961 (g).

National Inventory of Aptitudes and Abilities. *Bulletin.* Pittsburgh, University of Pittsburgh, Project Talent Office, 1959 *et seq.*

National Society for the Study of Education. *Education for the Gifted.* Fifty-seventh Yearbook, Part II. Chicago, University of Chicago Press, 1958.

———. *The Grouping of Pupils.* Thirty-fifth Yearbook, Part I. Bloomington, Ill., Public School Publishing Co., 1936.

———. *Intelligence: Its Nature and Nurture.* Thirty-ninth Yearbook, Parts I and II. Bloomington, Ill., Public School Publishing Co., 1940.

———. *Rethinking Science Education.* Fifty-ninth Yearbook, Part I. Chicago, University of Chicago Press, 1960.

———. *Theories of Learning and Instruction.* Sixty-third Yearbook, Part I. Chicago, University of Chicago Press, 1964.

Newland, T. Ernest. "Implications of Research in the Area of the Gifted." *Exceptional Children,* 25:195-98, January, 1959.

New York City Board of Education. "Creativity and the Curriculum." *Curriculum and Materials,* 13:No. 4. New York, The Board, March-April, 1959 (c).

———. *Demonstration Guidance Project. Third Annual Progress Report, 1958-1959.* New York, The Board, 1959 (b).

———. *The Gifted Student in the New York City Schools.* New York, The Board, 1959 (a).

———. *Report and Recommendations of the Committee on Junior High Schools.* New York, The Board, 1939.

———. *Specialized High Schools in New York City.* New York, The Board, 1946.

———. *A Three-Year Program for S. P. Classes, First Year.* New York, The Board, 1960 (mimeo).

New York State Education Department. *Advanced Placement Program in American History.* (Also: Chemistry, English, French, Mathematics). Albany, The Department, 1960 (mimeo).

———. Bureau of Elementary Curriculum Development. *Curriculum Adaptations for the Gifted.* Albany, The Department, 1958.

———. *56 Practices for the Gifted from Secondary Schools of New York State.* Albany, The Department, 1958.

———. Bureau of Guidance. *High Potential.* Albany, The Department, 1959, *et seq.*

New York *Times.* "Negro Curb Cited by Psychiatrists." The *Times,* February 28, 1960, p. 47.

———. "Soviet Is Testing New Curriculum." The *Times,* October 27, 1963, p. 18.

Nisbet, John D. "Intelligence and Age: Retesting with Twenty-four Years Interval." *British Journal of Educational Psychology,* 27:190-98, November, 1957.

Nisbet, J. F. *The Insanity of Genius.* London, Kegal Paul, Trench, Trubner and Co., 1891.

North Central Association of Colleges and Secondary Schools. Superior and Talented Student Project. *Identification.* Chicago, The Association, 1958.

———. *Problems in Motivation.* Chicago, The Association, 1959.

Ohlsen, Merle M., and Proff, Fred C. *The Extent to Which Group Counseling Improves the Academic and Personal Adjustment of Underachieving Gifted Adolescents.* Urbana, University of Illinois, 1960 (mimeo).

Osborn, A. F. *Applied Imagination: Principles and Procedures of Creative Thinking.* Revised Edition. New York, Scribner's 1957.

Passow, A. Harry. "The Comprehensive High School and Gifted Youth." *Teachers College Record,* 58:144-52, December, 1956.

———. "Identifying and Counseling the Gifted College Student." *Journal of Higher Education,* 28:21-29, January, 1957.

———. "The Maze of Research on Ability Grouping." *Educational Forum,* 26:281-88, March, 1962.

———, and Goldberg, Miriam L. *The Talented Youth Project: A Progress Report,*

1961. Horace Mann-Lincoln Institute of School Experimentation. New York, Teachers College, Columbia University, 1961.

———, and Brooks, Deton J. *A Guide for Rating Provisions for the Gifted*. New York, Teachers College, Columbia University, 1960.

———, and others. *Planning for Talented Youth*. New York, Bureau of Publications, Teachers College, Columbia University, 1951.

Pegnato, C. W., and Birch, J. W. "Locating Gifted Children in Junior High Schools." *Exceptional Children*, 26:300-304, March, 1959.

Philadelphia Suburban Schools Study Council, *Programs for the Gifted*. Philadelphia, Educational Service Bureau, University of Pennsylvania, 1950.

———. *Guiding Your Gifted*. Philadelphia, Educational Service Bureau, University of Pennsylvania, 1954.

Piaget, Jean. *Logic and Psychology*. Manchester, University of Manchester Press, 1953.

———. *The Origins of Intelligence in Children*. Translated by M. Cook. New York, International Universities Press, 1952.

———. *Psychology of Intelligence*. London, Routledge and Kegan Paul, 1950.

Pidgeon, D. A. "National Survey of the Ability and Attainment of Children at Their Age Levels." *British Journal of Educational Psychology*, 30:124-33, June, 1960.

Pierce, James V. and Bowman, Paul H. "The Educational Motivation Patterns of Superior Students Who Do and Who Do Not Achieve in High School." *News, Notes and Nuggets* (Chicago, North Central Association of Colleges and Secondary Schools) 2:3:13-16, April, 1960.

Pitts, Lilla Belle. *The Music Curriculum in a Changing World*. New York, Silver Burdett, 1944.

Pooley, Robert C. *Teaching English Usage*. New York, Appleton-Century-Crofts, 1946.

Portland Public Schools. *Gifted Child Project*. Progress Report No. II of the Cooperative Program for Students with Exceptional Endowment. Portland, Ore., The Schools, 1954 (mimeo).

Pregler, Hedwig. "The Colfax Plan." *Exceptional Children*, 20:198-201+, February, 1954.

Prentice, W. C. H. "The Honors Program at Swarthmore College." *Superior Student*, 2:3:13-14, April, 1959.

Pressey, Sidney L. *Educational Acceleration*. Bureau of Educational Research Monographs, No. 31. Columbus, Ohio State University, 1949.

———. "Educational Acceleration: Occasional Procedure or Major Issue?" *Personnel and Guidance Journal*, 41:12-17, September, 1962.

Preston, Ralph C., and others. *Guiding the Social Studies Reading of High School Students*. Bulletin No. 34. Washington, D.C., National Council for the Social Studies, 1963.

Rasey, Marie I. "Creativity and Its Psychological Implications." *Educational Leadership*, 13:283-88, February, 1956.

Resnick, William C., and Heller, David H. *On Your Own in College*. Columbus, Ohio, Charles E. Merrill, 1963.

Riesman, David. *The Lonely Crowd*. New Haven, Yale University Press, 1950.

Riley, Susan B. "Finding and Launching the Superior Student." *Superior Student*, 1:7:9-11, January, 1959.

Robinson, Helen M. ed. *Promoting Maximal Reading Growth among Able Learners*. Supplementary Educational Monographs, No. 81. Chicago, University of Chicago Press, 1954.

Rockefeller Brothers Fund. *The Pursuit of Excellence: Education and the Future of America*. Garden City, N. Y., Doubleday, 1958.

Roe, Ann. *The Making of a Scientist*. New York, Dodd, Mead, 1953.

Rogers, Carl R. "Toward Becoming a Fully Functioning Person." In *Perceiving, Behaving, Becoming*. 1962 Yearbook of Association for Supervision and Curriculum Development. Washington, D.C., 1962, The Association, pp. 21-33.

Rosen, Bernard C. "Race, Ethnicity, and Achievement." *American Sociological Review*, 24:47-60, February, 1959.

Rosenblum, Sidney, and others. "Davis-Eells (Culture-fair) Test Performance of Lower-Class Retarded Children." *Journal of Consulting Psychology*, 19:51-54, February, 1955.

Rothman, Esther, and Levine, Madeline. "From Little League to Ivy League." *Educational Forum*, 28:29-34, November, 1963.

Rudd, W. G. A. "The Psychological Effects of Streaming by Attainment." *British Journal of Educational Psychology*, 28:47-60, February, 1958.

Russell, David. *Children's Thinking*. Boston, Ginn, 1956.

Sanford, Nevitt. "Creativity and Conformity." In *The Creative Person*. Proceedings of Conference, October 13-17, 1961. Berkeley, Institute of Personality Assessment and Research, University of California, 1961.

Sarason, Seymour B., and others. *Anxiety in Elementary School Children*. New York, John Wiley, 1960.

―――. "What Research Says about Test Anxiety in Elementary School Children." *National Education Association Journal*, 48:26-27, November, 1959.

Sattlee, Helen R. "Reading Guidance for the Gifted Child." *The Brooklyn Teacher*, 1+, October, 1960.

Scheifele, Marian. *The Gifted Child in the Regular Classroom*. New York, Bureau of Publications, Teachers College, Columbia University, 1953.

Schmieder, Fred J. *Fostering and Developing Science Talent*. Bulletin No. 1. Columbus, Center for School Experimentation, Ohio State University, 1959 (mimeo).

Schreiber, Daniel. *The Higher Horizons Program*. First Annual Progress Report, 1959-60. New York, Board of Education, 1961.

―――. "Identifying and Developing Able Students from Less Privileged Groups." *High Points*, 40:5-23, December, 1958.

Schwab, Joseph J. "The Teaching of Science as Enquiry." In *The Teaching of Science*, by Joseph J. Schwab and Paul F. Brandwein. Cambridge, Harvard University Press, 1962.

Segel, David, and others. *An Approach to Individual Analysis: Educational and Vocational Guidance*. U.S. Office of Education, Bulletin 1959, No. 1. Washington, D.C. Government Printing Office, 1958.

Service Center for Teachers of History. Pamphlet Series. Washington, D.C. American Historical Association, 1957 *et seq.*

Shaftel, Fannie R. "Cultural Understanding in a World Community." *Educational Leadership*, 19:535-42, May, 1962.

Shane, Harold G., and McSwain, E. T. *Evaluation and the Elementary Curriculum*. Revised Edition. New York, Holt, Rinehart & Winston, 1958.

Shaw, Merville C., and McCuen, John T. "The Onset of Academic Underachievement in Bright Children." *Journal of Educational Psychology*, 51:103-8, June, 1960 (a).

―――, and others. "The Self-Concept of Bright Underachieving High School Students as Revealed by an Adjective Check List." *Personnel and Guidance Journal*, 37:193-96, November, 1960 (b).

Sheldon, Paul M. "Isolation as a Characteristic of Highly Gifted Children." *Journal of Educational Sociology*, 32:215-21, January, 1959.

Shertzer, Bruce, ed. *Working with Superior Students*. Chicago, Science Research Associates, 1960.

Shotka, Josephine. "Critical Thinking in the First Grade." *Childhood Education*, 36:405-9, May, 1960.

Shotwell, Anna M. "Fallibility of the IQ." *National Elementary School Principal*, 25:34-37, February, 1946.

Simmons, Rachel M. *A Study of a Group of Children of Exceptionally High Intellectual Quotients in Situations Partaking of the Nature of Suggestion.* Teachers College Contributions to Education, No. 788. New York, Bureau of Publications, Teachers College, Columbia University, 1940.

Simpson, Roy E., and Martinson, Ruth A. *Educational Programs for Gifted Pupils.* Sacramento, California State Department of Education, 1961.

Slobodkin, Lawrence B. "A New Honors Approach in Science." *Superior Student,* 1:5:11-12, November, 1958.

Smith, Donald C. *Personal and Social Adjustment of Gifted Adolescents.* Council for Exceptional Children Research Monograph No. 4. Washington, D.C., The Council, 1962.

Smith, Joseph A. "Teaching Creative Thinking." In *Frontiers of Elementary Education,* Vol. IV. Syracuse, Syracuse University Press, 1957, pp. 74-82.

Soutar, Alexander F. "Saturday Seminar: A Route to Excellence Via a Community-School Project." *New York State Education,* 51:4:20-22, January, 1964.

Southern Regional Project for the Education of the Gifted. *The Gifted Student: A Manual for Program Development.* Atlanta, Southern Regional Education Board, 1962.

Spearman, C. *The Abilities of Man.* New York, Macmillan, 1927.

Stein, Morris I. "Creativity and Culture." *Journal of Psychology,* 36:311-22, October, 1953.

Stiassni, Christine. "Experimental Language Program for Intellectually Gifted Children." *The Public and the Schools.* Bulletin of Public Education Association, No. 503, June, 1959.

Stoddard, George D. *The Meaning of Intelligence.* New York, Macmillan, 1943.

Strang, Ruth. "The Psychology of Gifted Children." *Journal of Teacher Education,* 5:215-17, September, 1954.

————. *Helping Your Gifted Child.* New York, E. P. Dutton, 1960.

Stratemeyer, Florence B., and others. *Developing a Curriculum for Modern Living.* Second edition. New York, Bureau of Publications, Teachers College, Columbia University, 1957.

STS News, Notes and Nuggets. Chicago, North Central Association of Colleges and Secondary Schools, 3:2:35, November, 1960.

Subarsky, Z. "What Is Science Talent?" *Scientific Monthly,* 66:377-82, May, 1948.

Suchman, J. Richard. "Inquiry Training: Building Skills for Autonomous Discovery." *Merrill-Palmer Quarterly,* 7:147-69, July, 1961.

————. "Inquiry Training in the Elementary School," *Science Teacher,* 27:42-43+, November, 1960.

————. "Learner Autonomy and Individualized Education." Paper delivered at Annual Conference of Association for Supervision and Curriculum Development. St. Louis, 1963.

Sumption, Merle R. *Three Hundred Gifted Children.* New York, Harcourt, Brace & World, 1941.

Super, D. E., and Bachrach, P. B. *Scientific Careers and Vocational Development Theory.* New York, Teachers College, Columbia University, 1957.

Superior Student. Newsletter of the Inter-university Committee on the Superior Student. Boulder, Col.

Sur, William R., and Schuller, Charles F. *Music Education for Teen-Agers.* New York, Harper & Row, 1958.

Tannenbaum, Abraham J. *Adolescent Attitudes toward Academic Brilliance.* New York, Bureau of Publications, Teachers College, Columbia University, 1962.

Tate, Merle W., and Voss, Charlotte E. "A Study of the Davis-Eells Tests of Intelligence." *Harvard Educational Review,* 26:374-87, Fall, 1956.

Taylor, Calvin W. "Effects of Instructional Media on Creativity." *Educational Leadership,* 19:453-58, April, 1962.

————. "A Tentative Description of the Creative Individual." *Research Conference on Creativity.* Salt Lake City, University of Utah, 1959 (mimeo).

Taylor, Donald W. "Environment and Creativity." In *The Creative Person.* Proceedings of Conference, October 13-17, 1961. Berkeley, Institute of Personality Assessment and Research, University of California, 1961.

Terman, Lewis M. "The Discovery and Encouragement of Exceptional Talent." *American Psychologist,* 9:221-30, June, 1954 (a).

————. *Mental and Physical Traits of a Thousand Gifted Children.* Vol. I, Genetic Studies of Genius. Stanford, Cal., Stanford University Press, 1925.

————, and Oden, Melita H. *The Gifted Child Grows Up.* Vol. IV, Genetic Studies of Genius. Stanford, Cal., Stanford University Press, 1947.

————, and ————. *The Gifted Group at Mid-Life.* Vol. V, Genetic Studies of Genius. Stanford, Cal., Stanford University Press, 1959.

————, and ————. "Major Issues in Education of Gifted Children." *Journal of Teacher Education,* 5:230-32, September, 1954 (b).

Thomson, Robert. *The Psychology of Thinking.* Baltimore, Penguin Books, 1959.

Thorndike, Edward L., and others. *The Measurement of Intelligence.* New York, Bureau of Publications, Teachers College, Columbia University, 1926.

Thurston, L. L. "The Perceptual Factor." *Psychometrika,* 3:1-17, March, 1938.

Torrance, E. Paul. "Current Research on the Nature of Creative Talent." *Journal of Counseling Psychology,* 6:309-16, Winter, 1959.

————. *Education and the Creative Potential.* Minneapolis, University of Minnesota Press, 1963.

————. *Guiding Creative Talent.* Englewood Cliffs, N. J., Prentice-Hall, 1962.

————. "Priming Creative Thinking in the Primary Grades." Elementary School Journal, 62:34-41, October, 1961.

————. "Recent Research in Gifted Children." Paper read at Annual Meeting of American Association of Colleges for Teacher Education. St. Paul, Bureau of Educational Research, University of Minnesota, 1960 (a) (mimeo).

————, ed. *Talent and Education.* Minneapolis, University of Minnesota Press, 1960 (b).

————, and others. *The Minnesota Studies of Creative Thinking in Early School Years.* St. Paul. Bureau of Educational Research, University of Minnesota, 1960 (c) (mimeo).

Tyerman, Maurice J. "England's Special Schools for the Gifted." *School and Society,* 87:168-69, April 11, 1959.

Vaughan, James, and Diserens, Charles M. "The Experimental Psychology of Competition." *Journal of Experimental Psychology,* 7:76-97, September, 1938.

Verburg, Wallace A. "Reflections on Educating the Gifted." *Educational Leadership,* 13:206-8, January, 1956.

Waetjen, Walter. "Sex Differences in Learning." Paper read at Annual Conference of Association for Supervision and Curriculum Development. St. Louis, 1963.

Wallin, Norman E., and others. "The Outcomes of Curriculum Modifications Designed to Foster Critical Thinking." *Journal of Educational Research,* 56:529-34, July-August, 1963.

Wann, Kenneth; Dorn, Miriam S., and Liddle, Elizabeth A. *Fostering Intellectual Development in Young Children.* New York, Bureau of Publications, Teachers College, Columbia University, 1962.

Ward, Virgil S. *Educating the Gifted: An Axiomatic Approach.* Columbus, Ohio, Charles E. Merrill, 1961.

Warner, W. Lloyd; Havighurst, R. J., and Loeb, M. B. *Who Shall Be Educated?* New York, Harper & Row, 1944.

Warren, Jonathan R., and Heist, Paul A. "Personality Attributes of Gifted College Students." *Science,* 132:330-37, August 5, 1960.

Warrington, Willard G., and Saupe, Joe L. "Development and Applications of

Tests of General Mental Ability." *Review of Educational Research,* 29:15-25, February, 1959.

Wechsler, David. *The Measurement of Adult Intelligence.* Second edition. Baltimore, William and Wilkins, 1941; Fourth edition, 1958.

――――. *The Range of Human Capacities.* Second edition. Baltimore, Williams and Wilkins, 1952.

Wilhelms, Fred R. "The Nature of Classroom Grouping for Learning." Paper read at Annual Conference of Association for Supervision and Curriculum Development. San Francisco, San Francisco State College, 1958 (mimeo).

Williams, Clifford W. *The Gifted Child in Portland.* Portland, Portland Public Schools, 1959.

Williams, Meta. "Acceptance and Performance among Gifted Elementary-School Children." *Educational Research Bulletin,* 37:216-20+, November, 1958.

Wilson, Frank T. "Early Achievement in Reading." *Elementary School Journal,* 42:609-15, April, 1942.

――――. "Educators' Opinions about Acceleration of Gifted Students." *School and Society,* 80:120-22, October 16, 1954.

――――. "In-service and Undergraduate Preparation of Teachers of the Gifted." *Educational Administration and Supervision,* 43:295-301, May, 1957.

――――. "Preparation of Teachers for Gifted Children." *Exceptional Children,* 20:78-80, November, 1953 (a).

――――. "Some Special Ability Test Scores of Gifted Children." *Journal of Genetic Psychology,* 82:59-68, March, 1953.

――――. "Teacher Education and the Gifted." *Journal of Teacher Education,* 6:263-67, December, 1955.

――――. "Working with the Motives of Gifted Children." *Elementary School Journal,* 57:247-52, February, 1957.

Wilson, Robert C., and others. "A Factor-analytic Study of Creative Thinking Abilities." *Psychometrika,* 19:297-311, December, 1954.

Witty, Paul. "Educational Programs for the Gifted." *School and Society,* 87:165-67, April 11, 1959.

――――. "Evaluation of the Nature-Nurture Controversy." *School and Society,* 54:151-57, September 6, 1941.

――――. *A Study of One Hundred Gifted Children.* Lawrence, Kansas, University of Kansas Bulletin of Education, Vol. 2, No. 7, 1930.

――――. "Improving the Reading of Gifted Children and Youth." *The Packet* (D. C. Heath) 6:1:3-17, 1956.

――――; Conant, James B., and Strang, Ruth. *Creativity of Gifted and Talented Children.* New York, Bureau of Publications, Teachers College, Columbia University, 1959.

――――, and Lehman, Harvey C. "A Study of the Reading and Reading Interests of Gifted Negroes." *Journal of Educational Psychology,* 34:35-45, January, 1943.

――――, and Theman, Viola. "A Follow-up Study of Exceptional Attainment of Gifted Negroes." *Journal of Educational Psychology,* 34:35-45, January, 1943.

Wolfle, Dael. *America's Resources of Specialized Talent.* New York, Harper, 1954.

――――. "Diversity of Talent." *American Psychologist,* 15:535-45, August, 1960.

Woolever, John. "Is Homework One Answer?" *School Science and Mathematics,* 55:704-6, December, 1955.

Worcester, D. A. *The Education of Children of Above-average Mentality.* Lincoln, University of Nebraska Press, 1956.

Wright, John C., and Kagan, Jerome. *Basic Cognitive Processes in Children.* Monographs of the Society for Research in Child Development, Serial No. 86, Vol. 28, No. 2, 1963.

Wrightstone, J. Wayne. *Class Organization for Instruction.* What Research Says to the Teacher, No. 13. Washington, D.C., National Education Association, 1957.

Wyatt, Nita M. "Research in Creative Writing." *Educational Leadership,* 19:307-10, February, 1962.

Young, Clarence W. *Freedom for Vitality.* Yorktown, N. Y., First Supervisory District of Oneida County, 1959.

Zander, Alvin, and others. *The Influence of Teachers and Peers on Aspirations of Youth.* Ann Arbor, Research Center for Group Dynamics, University of Michigan, 1961 (mimeo).

————, and Van Egmond, E. "Relationship of Intelligence and Social Power to the Interpersonal Behavior of Children. *Journal of Educational Psychology,* 49:257-68, October, 1958.

Index

Ability grouping, see Grouping
Ability roster, 78, 79
Abraham, Willard, 43, 44, 415, 419
Abramson, David A., 310, 444
Academic achievement of gifted children, 42-44
Acceleration, 328-351; social policy, 328-29; practices, 152, 157, 167, 330, 335-38; case for, 330-33; case against, 350; historical precedents, 334; criteria, 338-39; research, 339-45, 436; social adjustment, 338-41, 345-48
Activity program, 139-40
Administrative structures, 138
Adult pressure, 400
Advanced Placement Program, 18, 168-69, 224, 267-69, 337, 348-50, 435, 437
Age and achievement, 330-32
Aikin, Wilford M., 284, 435
Alberty, Harold, 317
Algebra, teaching thinking in, 191
Allison, Harold, 163-64
Anderson, John E., 90, 100
Anderson, William, 170
Anxiety, 35-36, 72
Applbaum, Morris J., 162-63
Aptitude tests, 82
Arbuckle, Dugald S., 395
Army General Classification Tests, 301
Arnold, John E., 116
Art, 287-92
Artists and creativity, 110, 116
Aschner, Mary J., 195
Association for Supervision and Curriculum Development, 389
Associative thinking, 198
Ausubel, David, 40
Autonomous interests, 358
Autonomy, 116-17

Balance in education, 146-47
Baltimore, 158, 303, 334
Barkan, Manuel, 298
Barron, Frank, 104, 113-14, 116, 118
Barwick, Janice M., 395
Basic skills, 143-44, 404-6
Batavia, N.Y., 301
Bayley, Nancy, 66-67
Beasley, Jane, 389-90
Begle, E. C., 276
Behavioral characteristics, 80
Behavioral Description Chart, 94
Benne, Kenneth D., 245
Bennett, Clayton L., 394
Berger, Max, 291
Berkeley, Cal., 385
Berks Co., Pa., 335
Bienenstok, Theodore, 384
Binet, A., 25, 50, 57, 63, 103
Biological Sciences Curriculum Study, 267

Biology, teaching thinking in, 190
Birch, J. W., 93
Blackwood, Paul, 260
Bloom, Benjamin S., 188, 201, 431-32
Bloom, Samuel W., 257
Blough, Glenn O., 260
Boehm, Leonore, 41-42
Bonthius, Robert H., 178
Bowman, Paul H., 27, 349, 384, 391-93, 443
Bragdon, Henry W., 349
"Brainstorming," 19
Brandwein, Paul, 88, 91, 255, 257, 265, 417-18, 437
Bray, Douglas W., 8, 11, 30, 65
Brim, D. G., 317
Broder, Lois J., 188, 201
Bronfenbrenner, Urie, 324, 400
Bronx High School of Science, 344
Brookline, Mass., 335
Brooks, Deton J., 148
Brownell, William A., 274
Brumbaugh, Florence N., 83-84, 373
Bruner, Jerome S., 188, 431
Budget for education of gifted, 139-40
Buffalo, University of, 174
Burk, Frederic, 301
Burt, Sir Cyril, 53, 54, 69
Burton, William H., 106, 185, 186, 189, 190-91, 197, 200-4, 242-44

Calhoun, S. R., 79
California, 104, 163, 308; State Department of Education, 442
Cambridge, Mass., 301
Careers, 46, 363-67
Carnegie Foundation, 440, 443
Carr, Edwin R., 243
Carlson, Ruth K., 127, 129
Cassel, R. N., 433
Cattell, R. B., 116
CAVD test, 54
Characteristics of gifted children, 25-49
Chemistry, 267-68; teaching thinking in, 190
Chemical Bond Approach, 267
Chemical Education Material Study, 267
Cheyney, Arnold B., 357
Chicago Public Schools, 86 fn, 303, 333, 337, 424
Chicago, University of, 168, 188, 443; Laboratory School, 399-400
Citizenship, education for, 237-53, 318
Clark, Willis W., 32
Class differences, 41
Cleveland Major Works Program, 26, 153-56, 232, 302, 307, 417
Club period (elementary), 155
Coaching on intelligence tests, 59
Coelho, George V., 323

466